FREUD AS WE KNEW HIM

Bust of Freud by Oscar Nemon
(Harry Diaz, Photographer)

FREUD
as we knew him

edited and introduced
by Hendrik M. Ruitenbeek

Wayne State University Press
Detroit 1973

Published simultaneously in Canada
by the Copp Clark Publishing Company
517 Wellington Street, West
Toronto 2B, Canada.

Library of Congress Cataloging in Publication Data
Ruitenbeek, Hendrik Marinus, 1928–   comp.
  Freud as we knew him.
  Includes bibliographies.
  1. Freud, Sigmund, 1856–1939.   2. Psychoanalysis.
I. Title.
BF173.F85R84   150'.19'52   [B]   72–6471
ISBN 0–8143–1488–0

for Richard McConchie who wanted this book

—het leven maakt mij geweldig opgewonden
—Hans Lodeizen

Sigmund Freud war es gegeben, ein neues Universum zu entdecken.
—Ministerpräsident Dr. Phil. Georg August Zinn

Contents

Acknowledgments

I would like to single out a few friends and colleagues who were helpful in the preparation of this book. Dr. Richard McConchie, besides translating some of the French essays, assisted me in Europe to trace various sources of recorded interviews with Freud. Dr. Helene Zahler of Brooklyn College counseled me on my own essay and some of the translations. Finally, Masud Khan of London aided in what he calls "my peripatetic chase after Freudiana." I owe him particular gratitude for drawing my attention to the Breton interview in *Les Pas Perdus*.

Permissions and Credits

With the exception of my own contribution, the essays and sketches in the book have been previously published elsewhere. Those not in the public domain appear by permission, which I gratefully acknowledge.

Albrecht, Adelbert, "Professor Sigmund Freud," *Boston Transcript*, 11 September 1909.

Alexander, Franz, "Recollections of Berggasse 19," *The Psychoanalytic Quarterly* 9 (1940): 195–204.

Auden, W. H., "In Memory of Sigmund Freud," from *Collected Shorter Poems, 1927–1957* (London, Faber & Faber, 1966). With the permission of the publishers.

Bernays, Anna Freud, "My Brother, Sigmund Freud," *The American Mercury* 51 (1940): 335–42.

Bernfeld, Siegfried, "Freud's Scientific Beginnings," *American Imago* 6 (1949): 163–96. Copyright by Siegfried Bernfeld, 1949.

Bernfeld, Siegfried, and Suzanne Cassirer Bernfeld, "Freud's Early Childhood," *The Bulletin of the Menninger Clinic* 8 (1944): 105–15. Copyright 1944 by the Menninger Foundation.

Bernfeld, Siegfried, and Suzanne Cassirer Bernfeld, "Freud's First Year in Practice, 1886–1887," *The Bulletin of the Menninger Clinic* 16 (1952): 37–48. Copyright 1952 by the Menninger Foundation.

Binswanger, Ludwig, "My First Three Visits with Freud in Vienna," from *Sigmund Freud: Reminiscences of a Friendship* (New York, Grune & Stratton, 1957). Excerpts with the permission of the publisher.

Blum, Ernst, "The Human Image of Sigmund Freud," *Schweizerische Zeitschrift für Psychologie und ihre Anwendungen* 15 (1956): 141–47. Excerpts translated by Dr. Hendrik M. Ruitenbeek.

Bonaparte, Marie, "Letter to Freud," from *Drives, Affects, Behavior* (New York, International Universities Press, 1965). Excerpts reprinted with the permission of the publisher.

Breton, André, "Interview with Professor Freud," from *Les Pas Perdus*, Editions Gallimard, 1969, with their permission. Translation copyright by Dr. Richard McConchie, 1972.

Brill, Abraham Arden, "Reflections, Reminiscences of Sigmund Freud," *Medical Leaves* 3 (1940): 18–29.

Brill, Abraham Arden, "Reminiscences of Freud," *The Psychoanalytic Quarterly*, 9 (1940): 177–83.

Brody, Benjamin, "Freud's Case-Load," from *Psychotherapy* 7 (Spring 1970): 8–12. With the permission of *Psychotherapy*.

Choisy, Maryse, "Memories of my Visits with Freud," *Psyche* 10 (Paris 1955): 471–76. Original title, "Qu'est-ce qu'ils en feront? Souvenirs de mes visites de Freud." Translation by Dr. Hendrik M. Ruitenbeek.

Deutsch, Felix, "Reflections on Freud's One Hundredth Birthday," *Psychosomatic Medicine* 18 (1956): 279–83.

Deutsch, Helene, "Freud and His Pupils: A Footnote to the History of the Psychoanalytic Movement," *The Psychoanalytic Quarterly* 9 (1940): 184–94.

Doolittle, Hilda, "Analysand of Freud," excerpts from *Tribute to Freud* by H. D. (New York, Pantheon, 1956). Reprinted by permission of Norman Holmes Pearson, owner of the copyright.

Ellis, Havelock, "Freud's Influence on the Changed Attitude toward Sex," *The American Journal of Sociology* 45 (November 1939): 309–17. With the permission of the Journal.

Federn, Paul, "Freud Amongst Us," *Psychiatric Quarterly* 22 (1948): 1–6. With the permission of the Quarterly.

Ferenczi, Sandor, "Ferenczi to Freud," excerpts from "Ten Letters to Freud," trans. Joan Riviere, *International Journal of Psycho-Analysis* 30 (1949): 243–50.

Freud, Harry, "My Uncle Sigmund," from *Aufbau* (New York), 11 May 1956. Excerpts reprinted by permission of the publisher.

Freud, Martin, "Freud: My Father," from *Sigmund Freud: Man and Father* (New York, Vanguard Press, 1958). Excerpt with the permission of the publisher.

Goetz, Bruno, "Some Memories of Sigmund Freud," excerpts from "Erinnerungen an Sigmund Freud" *Neue Schweizer Rundschau* 20 (May 1952): 3–11. Translation by Dr. Hendrik M. Ruitenbeek.

Grinker, Roy R., "Reminiscences of a Personal Contact with Freud," *American Journal of Orthopsychiatry* 10 (1940): 850–55. With the permission of the Journal.

Grotjahn, Martin, "A Letter by Sigmund Freud with Recollections of his Adolescence," *Journal of the American Psychoanalytic Association* 4 (1956): 644–52. With the permission of the Journal.

Grotjahn, Martin, "Sigmund Freud and the Art of Letter Writing," *Journal of the American Medical Association* 200 (3 April 1967): 13–18. With the permission of the Journal.

Hacker, Frederick J., "The Living Image of Freud," *The Bulletin of the Menninger Clinic* 20 (1956): 103–11. Copyright 1956 by the Menninger Foundation.

Heller, Judith Bernays, "Freud's Mother and Father," *Commentary* 21 (1956): 418–21. Reprinted from *Commentary* by permission; copyright © 1956 by the American Jewish Committee.

Holland, Norman N., "Freud and H. D.," *The International Journal of Psycho-Analysis* 50 (1969). Copyright Norman N. Holland, 1969. With the permission of the author.

Holland, Norman N., "H. D. and the 'Blameless Physician'," *Contemporary Literature* 10 (Autumn 1969): 474–506. Copyright 1969 by the Regents of the University of Wisconsin.

Hyman, Stanley Edgar, "Freud and Boas: Secular Rabbis?", *Commentary* 17 (1954): 264–67. Reprinted from *Commentary* by permission; copyright © 1954 by the American Jewish Committee.

Jones, Ernest, "Freud's Early Travels," *The International Journal of Psycho-Analysis* 35 (1954): 81–84.

Knight, Robert P., "A Visit with Freud," *The Bulletin of the Menninger Clinic* 1 (1937): 144–47. Copyright 1937 by the Menninger Foundation.

Kupper, Herbert I. and Hilda S. Rollman-Branch, "Freud and Schnitzler—(Doppelgänger)," *Journal of the American Psychoanalytic Association* 7 (1959): 109–26. With the permission of the Journal.

Laforgue, René, "Personal Memories of Freud," from *Action Pensée*, Geneva, 1956. Excerpts translated by Dr. Richard McConchie.

Lehmann, Herbert, "Sigmund Freud and Thomas Mann," *The Psychoanalytic Quarterly* 37 (1970): 198–214. With the permission of the author.

Lenormand, H. R., "An Impression of Freud," excerpts from *Confessions d'un auteur dramatique* (Paris, Albin Michel, 1949). Translation by Dr. Richard McConchie.

Ludwig, Emil, "A Visit," from *Der entzauberte Freud* (Zurich, Carl Posen Verlag, 1946). Excerpts translated by Dr. Hendrik M. Ruitenbeek.

Mann, Thomas, "Freud's Position in the History of Modern Culture," *Criterion*, London, 1933. Translated by H. T. Lowe-Porter.

Marcuse, Ludwig, "Freud's Aesthetics," *The Journal of Aesthetics and Art Criticism* 17 (September 1958) no. 1. With the permission of the Journal.

Meng, Heinrich, "Freud and the Sculptor," *Schweizerische Zeitschrift für Psychologie und ihre Anwendungen* 15 (1956): 149–51. Excerpts translated by Dr. Hendrik M. Ruitenbeek.

Nemon, Oscar, "How I Made the Bust of Freud," *Psyche* 10 (Paris 1955): 483. Original title, "Comment j'ai fait le buste de Freud." Translation by Dr. Hendrik M. Ruitenbeek.

Pannetier, Odette, "Appointment in Vienna," *The Living Age*, October 1936.

Papini, Giovanni, "A Visit to Freud," *Colosseum*, 1934.

Peck, Martin W., "A Brief Visit with Freud," *The Psychoanalytic Quarterly* 9 (1940): 205–206.

Putnam, James, "Personal Impressions of Sigmund Freud and His Work," *Journal of Abnormal Psychology* (December 1909): 1–30.

Racker, Heinrich, "Some Notes on Freud's Personality," *Samiksa* 11 (1957): 147–56.

Recouly, Raymond, "A Visit to Freud," *Outlook* 5 (September 1923).

Reich, Wilhelm, "Reich on Freud," from *Reich Speaks of Freud* (New York, Farrar, Straus & Giroux, 1967). Excerpts with the permission of the publisher.

Riviere, Joan, "A Character Trait of Freud's," from *Psychoanalysis and Contemporary Thought*, ed. J. D. Sutherland (London, Hogarth Press, 1958). With the permission of the publisher.

Riviere, Joan, "An Intimate Impression," *The Lancet* (30 September 1939). With the permission of *The Lancet*.

Sachs, Hanns, "Freud: Master and Friend," from *Freud: Master and Friend* (London, Imago Publishing Co., 1945).

Saussure, Raymond de, "Sigmund Freud," *Schweizerische Zeitschrift für Psychologie und ihre Anwendungen* 15 (1956): 136–39. Translated by Dr. Richard McConchie.

Schneck, Jerome M., "A Note on Freud's Neighbor," *The American Journal of Psychotherapy* 13 (1959): 139–41. With the permission of the Journal.

11

ACKNOWLEDGMENTS

Stern, Adolph, "Some Personal Psychoanalytical Experiences with Professor Freud," *New York State Journal of Medicine* 22 (1922): 21–25.

Weiss, Edoardo, "An Impression of Freud," from *Sigmund Freud as a Consultant* (New York, Intercontinental Medical Book Corp., 1970). Excerpts reprinted with the permission of the publisher.

Wortis, Joseph, "Fragments of an Analysis," excerpts from *Fragments of an Analysis with Freud* (New York, Simon & Schuster, 1954). With the permission of the author.

Zweig, Stefan, "Likeness," from *Mental Healers* by Stefan Zweig, trans. Eden and Cedar Paul. Copyright 1932, © 1960 by The Viking Press, Inc. Reprinted by permission of The Viking Press, Inc.

H.M.R.

Introduction

The main purpose of this book is to put the *man* Freud in perspective. It certainly is not a book about his theories, although references to his work are abundant in the personal recollections. Much of the material was not included in the biography of Freud by Ernest Jones, simply because it had not yet appeared or in some instances, such as the small book by H.D., Jones was unaware of its existence.

While compiling this book I became more than ever convinced that Freud's letters should be collected, as were his other works. They are a testimonial not only to his work, but also to the kind of man he was, his rich interests, and his concern for humanity. It seems a shame that his letters are now being published piecemeal—or some not at all, being held back or suppressed by anxious literary heirs or relatives of those who corresponded with Freud. In a sense this book is a first attempt to collect the manifold impressions of his friends, pupils, and colleagues.

In determining what to include and what to leave out our standard was primarily how these pieces illustrated Freud's lifestyle. Some do an admirable job. Others, unfortunately, are poor substitutes for what I really would have liked to include. To cite an example, Marie Bonaparte is represented with a letter to Freud, but we know she kept a personal diary about her relationship with him, which again is being held back by the literary heirs. I also would have liked to include a personal impression by Freud's daughter Anna, but knowing the reticence of the Freud family on such matters, I did not even attempt it. This is a pity, for Freud deserves better. Moreover, there is nothing to

13

hide. Although Freud was a reserved and orderly man, there were no dark secrets in his life, and the almost pathological secretiveness of some of his followers does not serve Freud's memory well.

In many ways working on this book proved to be a joy, especially in discovering the small jewels of Freud's wit and concern, his humaneness and his warmth. I hope these small revelations will dispel once and for all the myth of Freud's coldness and detachment.

I would like to have had more recollections from his early and very close followers, such as Ferenczi, Abraham, and Rank. I know how fond he was of all three of them. We have only the published correspondence with Abraham. We are still awaiting the correspondence with Ferenczi, some 2,000 letters. Rank left no record of his early years with Freud.

Of course we know there is more. We continue to discover new letters, and there are all those letters we do not know about! We have few recollections of his private patients; many are still alive but are reluctant to share their intimate and private memories.

In putting the manuscript together we were faced with various problems. Not all of the contributors knew Freud personally but their stories are relevant enough to include in this book. Others relate or interpret an incident in Freud's life, justifying their inclusion. The papers are in chronological order. We could have put all the analysands together, but that posed problems in that many of them were also his friends. Putting colleagues under one heading presented us with the same problem. Some of them were analyzed by Freud, others were not. Some of the papers included irrelevant material which I felt need not be published in a book of this kind. I am solely responsible for this kind of editing.

The omissions are obvious to the insider. The New York generation of second generation analysts is hardly represented here. Their insistence upon being the representatives of true Freudianism in this country does not coincide with a strange absence of personal memories of the Professor. For example, the Heinz Hartmann and Rudolph Loewenstein interviews recorded for the Oral History Collection at Columbia University are so thin that one is almost embarrassed in reading them.

The interviews on the whole confirm a picture of Freud as a relaxed and easy man. Curious and even adventurous, Freud was willing to listen and explore. There is a popular notion that he was rigid and defensive about his discovery (of psychoanalysis) and that he was intolerant vis-à-vis those who disagreed with him on its fundamental aspects. But one would expect Freud *would* defend his own concepts and not yield to the first dissenter. His discussions with Binswanger bear this out, that indeed he was capable of seeing another side of psychoanalysis, a side he perhaps was not able to embrace at that time but was perfectly willing to look at.

And even to his last days he *was* unorthodox. He had an uncanny ability to pick up a patient's lifestyle and tune in on it. His activity in the psychoanalytic situation, which De Saussure blames on Freud's not being analyzed himself, was an asset rather than a disadvantage to the patient. Perhaps at times he was impatient, but he had the courage to show his impatience rather than to hide behind a neutral screen.

And he was tolerant of his patients' lifestyles. One only has to read the moving interview by Bruno Goetz to have this confirmed. Above all he was loyal to his friends, patients and colleagues. If he was loyal, should he not expect the same from them? The experience of Ernst Blum is relevant here. Coming back to Freud after twelve years, Freud asked him, "And why didn't you write me?" Blum replied that he did not want to burden him, knowing how busy he was. And again there is this amazing down-to-earth human quality in Freud when he answered Blum, "But I might have enjoyed your letters."

There are a few personal recollections of some of Freud's relatives in this book. His son Martin wrote a perfectly charming book about his father, from which there are excerpts. Freud's sister Anna, a niece, and a nephew complete the picture of the Freud family. But these memories are just glimpses of Freud's relationship to his family. The book, a real personal biography, on his relationships to his immediate family has yet to be written.

As one who is interested in the history of the psychoanalytic movement, I hope the present collection of documents of encounters with and impressions of Freud will stimulate organized efforts to place the man Freud into a more objective perspective. He deserves it.

The Professor

HENDRIK M. RUITENBEEK

It was a snowy December day some years ago when I arrived in
Vienna to find out more about Freud, the places he lived in, the streets
he walked, the cafes he visited, the university which treated him so
shabbily. I had been in Vienna before, but not for the specific purpose
of finding out what Freud meant to Vienna and what memories of him,
if any, were left in the city.

As it turned out, I probably was as disappointed as many visitors
before me. Freud was and still is unknown in Vienna. When I drove to
Berggasse 19 to visit Freud's apartment and told the driver why I was
going there, the first thing he said, "Ah, Freud, er wahr ein Jude, nicht
wahr?" (Oh, Freud—he was a Jew, wasn't he?), scarcely encouraged
me to continue the conversation. Many have gone to Berggasse 19
and, like me, have wondered why there is hardly any trace of Freud,
except the plaque placed there in 1953 by the World Federation of
Mental Health. The city (and apparently Austria as a nation) does not
care to commemorate one of its greatest sons and citizens.[1]

Other visitors who have gone to Vienna in search of Freud have
had similar experiences. Natalie Davis Spingarn tells how, on visiting
one of Vienna's major psychiatric clinics, the Psychiatrisch-Neurolo-
gische Universitats Klinik at Lazarettgasse 14, she noticed that Freud's
picture did not hang among those of many famous psychiatrists on the
walls.

"How about Freud?" she asked one of her psychiatrist-hosts,
"After all, he started a good deal of this." "Well," he replied, "he was
only an *assistant* professor here." When she seemed taken aback, her
host added that there was a bust of Freud in the university, "but not in
the main lobby—around the corner a bit." [2]

If Vienna and Austria forgot about Freud, many friends, colleagues, and patients certainly did not. They have left many accounts
of their relationships with the Professor, as he was affectionately called
by his close followers. From these accounts there emerges a picture of

17

Freud as a human being, a picture which shows a man of considerable warmth, real concern, and a never-ending interest in the world around him.

Of course the Professor was bourgeois, but what could be expected of a man who grew up and worked most of his adult life in the most bourgeois surroundings one can possibly imagine? His family life was indeed rather dull and routine. He certainly did not marry an imaginative and intellectual woman. On the contrary, Frau Freud was the typical example of a devoted *Hausfrau*, whose world consisted of her husband and children, and who had no ambitions of her own. She realized this very much herself when in writing to Ludwig Binswanger after Freud's death she states her position. "It is small comfort for me to know that in the fifty-three years of our married life not one angry word fell between us, and that I always sought as much as possible to remove from his path the *misere* of everyday life. Now my life has lost all content and meaning." [3]

That Freud's relationship with his wife had none of the intellectual stimulus of which he was so fond is no dark secret. He obviously found that kind of intellectual companionship with his witty and sharp sister-in-law Minna Bernays, who lived with the Freuds for a major part of her life, with Princess Marie Bonaparte, with Lou Andreas-Salome, and perhaps with some of his more challenging female analysands, such as the poet Hilda Doolittle (H.D.), Alix Strachey, and Joan Riviere.[4] Nor can we forget the character of his relationship with his daughter Anna, who ranks so high among the creative figures in the discipline he founded.

Freud's energy was astounding. He carried on a full-time practice; the sheer bulk of his writing is astonishing. The volume of his letter writing is almost beyond comprehension, especially when one realizes that he had no secretary and did not use a typewriter. Then there was the endless stream of visitors: friends, colleagues, famous men and women who traveled to Vienna to meet Freud, if only for an hour or less. And he met them all and was always interested, sometimes a bit sarcastic or ironic when they tried his patience, of which (we know now) he did not have much!

They came and were welcomed in the waiting room by either Aunt Minna (Minna Bernays) or Anna Freud. Then they were ushered by the Professor himself into his study or consulting room. More privileged visitors were often invited to stay for tea, or Freud received them in his living quarters and talked to them there. Often visitors were struck by the simplicity of his surroundings. No elaborate furnishings or luxurious quarters for him. The only valuable item in the house was his cherished collection of Greek antiquities. There were animals around. Marie Bonaparte had introduced him to chows, of which he became extremely fond. His favorite chow stayed quietly in the consultation room when he saw patients, sitting soberly through their analytic sessions. It is probably little known that Freud and his daughter Anna translated Marie Bonaparte's book *Topsy, the Story of a Golden-Haired Chow.*[5]

Today it is fashionable to talk about the *engaged* analyst, someone who is truly concerned about his patients and feels a strong commitment to them. I believe that Freud was such a man. His engagement with and commitment to life is shown in his immense correspondence, which illustrates and serves as a monument to the depths of his interests and concerns.

His dedication to work, patients, and family was phenomenal. Only a completely prescribed routine of work and leisure could enable him to do so much. Freud's average day ran as follows: up at about 6 in the morning, breakfast with the whole family at 7. From 8 to 12 work with patients. Then Freud took a walk around the Ring and was back at the apartment at one o'clock to have lunch with the family, including his married daughter Mathilde, who lived in Vienna. Often these lunches were shared by good friends, such as Hans Lampl, who used to come almost every day.[6] Then from 2 until 7, more patients. At 7 the family gathered for dinner. From 8 until 10 Freud often played cards with his sister-in-law Minna. At 10 he returned to his study, where he usually wrote until 12 or later. He went to bed rather late.

In analytic sessions Freud was certainly not passive. Some of his patients have repeatedly assured me that Freud was an active analyst, who ignored what has become the orthodox pattern of non-interference.[7] On the contrary, he was chatty, sometimes even gossipy in analytic sessions. His interest in his patients went beyond the material they presented in treatment; he often spent social hours with them. Although this was understandable, as many of them saw analysis as a start for their own careers as analysts, still the presence of some analysands at Sunday afternoon teas at the Freuds' indicates the easy atmosphere surrounding his practice of psychoanalysis. We must look at the situation in the context of time and place, of course. Few analysands at that time (say in the 1910s and 1920s) had come to Vienna; by and large the training and practice of psychoanalysis was still on a small scale. Many of the students and teachers knew each other, often very well. They came from the same social and cultural background; they often shared friends and interests. They were gossipy, and frequently envious of one another's position, vis-à-vis the Professor. Although the Professor tried to stay out of the various intramural quarrels, he could not help becoming involved at times. Organizing psychoanalysis as a profession was no simple matter. Although Freud received considerable support from the Committee (Ernest Jones, Karl Abraham, Sandor Ferenczi, Otto Rank, Max Eitington, Hanns Sachs) he often felt alone; more than once he felt he was tired of it all. His constant awareness that he was aging and must soon die made him feel somewhat helpless in the face of the many difficulties confronting the growing psychoanalytic movement.

Fortunately, the Professor never got trapped in the structure of orthodox psychoanalysis. He felt that he could step out of that structure at any time, and he did! He had his favorite patients; he spent time with them outside the analytic situation; he loaned them money or even gave them money. He was interested in the totality of their lives, not just in what they told him at their analytic sessions.

Freud was a man of extraordinary erudition; his interests were not restricted to psychoanalysis. His writings are full of quotations from the great works of world literature. He enjoyed the company and acquaintance of many literary men, such as Stefan Zweig and Rilke. Thomas Mann was a devoted follower with whom he corresponded for many years. In fact, he grew up with one of the greatest Viennese playwrights, Arthur Schnitzler, and cherished his friendship for a long time.

And he was a kind man. He never failed to answer any request for an interview; no question brought to him would fail to get an answer. His letter to an American mother in response to her question about her son's homosexuality is but one of the many examples that he cared, that he was concerned.[8]

He was not arrogant or ostentatious. And his patients took note of that. The Wolf Man, who was one of Freud's most famous cases, reports on Freud's lifestyle:

> From the beginning, I had the impression that Freud had a special gift for finding a happy balance in everything he undertook. This characteristic expressed itself also in the appearance of his home in the Berggasse. I can remember, as though I saw them

today, his two adjoining studies, with the door open between them and with their windows opening on a little courtyard. There was always a feeling of sacred peace and quiet here. The rooms themselves must have been a surprise to any patient, for they in no way reminded one of a doctor's office but rather of an archeologist's study. Here were all kinds of statuettes and other unusual objects, which even the layman recognized as archeological finds from ancient Egypt. Here and there on the walls were stone plaques representing various scenes of long-vanished epochs. A few potted plants added life to the rooms, and the warm carpet and curtains gave them a homelike note. Everything here contributed to one's feeling of leaving the haste of modern life behind, of being sheltered from one's daily cares.[9]

And so we are left with the image of an astonishingly simple but great man. He never allowed anything to disturb the order of his life. That in effect might be the secret of his tremendous achievements.

Notes

1. Apparently the International Psychoanalytical Association, together with the newly founded Freud Society, has taken the initiative in making Freud's apartment into a museum.

2. "Nobody Ever Heard Of Freud In Vienna," *Mental Hospital* 11 (1960) (2): 52.

3. Letter, 7 Nov. 1939.

4. See my forthcoming book *Freud and Women.*

5. Amsterdam, Allert de Lange, 1939; English translation by Marie Bonaparte's daughter Princess Eugenie, London, Pushkin Press, 1940.

6. Lampl was one of Freud's early analysands, as was his wife Jeannette Lampl-de Groot, who lives in Amsterdam.

7. Mrs. Alix Strachey and Mrs. Eva Rosenfeld were especially helpful in giving me a picture of Freud as an analyst.

8. See "Letter to an American Mother" in *The Problem of Homosexuality in Modern Society* (New York, E. P. Dutton, 1963), ed. Hendrik M. Ruitenbeek.

9. *The Wolf-Man* (New York, Basic Books, 1971), p. 139.

Professor Sigmund Freud

(1909)

ADELBERT ALBRECHT

When Freud visited America in 1909 to receive his only honorary doctorate (Clark University) he was interviewed by Adelbert Albrecht for the Boston Transcript *(11 September, 1909).*

It was certainly an excellent idea of President Stanley Hall's to invite Professor Sigmund Freud of Vienna to the twenty years' jubilee of Clark University as guest of honor. Professor Freud needs no further introduction to physicians and psychologists, but for the lay public it may be said that Dr. Freud is not only one of the most eminent neurologists of Europe, but also that he is recognized especially by the most serious young scholars of the present generation as one of the greatest, if not the very greatest, of psychotherapeutists. Of his many books and writings, his contributions to the treatment of neurotic diseases, his extremely interesting book on "Psychopathologie des Alltagslebens" (Psychopathology of Every-Day Life), which is also easily understood by the layman, and his "Studien ueber Hysterie" (Studies of Hysteria) may be particularly mentioned. His book on "Traumdeutung" (The Significance of Dreams) was a considerable step forward on a way along which we have wandered for centuries in darkness in the fullest sense of the word, and his studies on the sick soul-life of children are nothing short of epoch-making. The "Story of Little Hans" will probably remain a unique and model study of a child's soul.

After long acquaintance with his writings I had the pleasure of meeting him personally in President Hall's house. One sees at a glance that he is a man of great refinement, of intellect and of many-sided education. His sharp, yet kind, clear eyes suggest at once the doctor. His high forehead with the large bumps of observation and his beautiful, energetic hands are very striking. He speaks clearly, weighing his words carefully, but unfortunately never of himself. Again and again he emphasizes the merits of his colleagues, particularly of his friend, Dr. Jung of Zurich, who is staying with him at President Hall's. It is with great difficulty that he can be persuaded to talk about his method of psychotherapy, which he calls the analytical, but this is a fair summary of his conversation:

Emmanuel Movement Will Die

This Emmanuel Movement, which, however, I have not had time to study carefully, will die down as have so many other movements. When I think that there are many physicians who have been studying modern methods of psychotherapy for decades and who yet practise it only with the greatest caution, this undertaking of a few men without medical, or with superficial medical training, seems to me at the very least of questionable good. I can easily understand that this combination of church and psychotherapy appeals to the public, for the public has always had a certain weakness for everything that savors of mysteries and the mysterious, and these it probably suspects behind psychotherapy, which in reality has nothing, absolutely nothing, mysterious about it. What may appear so is perhaps its great age, for it is in no sense a modern method of healing. It is the oldest therapy that medicine uses. Richard Löwenfeld has written a book on psychotherapy in which you can trace its history back to the ancients and, even farther, to primitive times. You must know how it has always been a custom to get patients into a state of "faithful expectation," which is as much in vogue today as ever, with the same results.

Yes, indeed, psychotherapy is as old as illness, and we doctors could not give it up if we wanted to, because the other party to our methods of healing—namely the patient—has not the slightest intention of doing without it. The modern history of psychotherapy, however, begins with the school of Nancy, with Liebault, Bernheim, etc., and with Moebius, who unfortunately died early, though not until his studies on suggestion had borne much fruit.

We all practise psychotherapy, often even without knowing or intending it. Certain diseases, particularly nearly all those of neurotic nature, are, as is well known, far more susceptible to psychic influences than to any other treatment. These patients are not healed by the drug but by the physician.

As you ask me about my own method of psychotherapy I must

first mention that there are of course many sorts and ways of psychotherapy. All are good if they accomplish their object, that is, effect a cure. Our words of comfort, used so freely, "Don't worry, you will soon be all right again," are an example of one therapeutic method. But a deeper insight into neurotic diseases shows such comfort to be insufficient. Then we have the technique of hypnotic suggestion, of psychotherapy by means of diversion, by exercise, developed to bring about the desired emotions. I despise none. If in reality I have limited myself to practice of one, which my friend, Professor Breuer, calls "cathartic," though I myself would rather call it analytic, personal motives more than anything else have led me to this course. I may nevertheless affirm that it is the analytical method that is most thorough in its effect, that brings about the greatest change in the patient. But it is also the most interesting because it teaches us the most about the origin and connection of the symptoms of the disease. The insight that it affords us into the mechanism of the sick soul might even enable it to lead out beyond itself and to show us other ways of psychotherapeutic influence.

His Analytical Method

The treatment according to the psychoanalytical method rests on the recognition that unconscious imaginings—better, the unconsciousness of certain psychic processes is the first cause of diseased symptoms. This unconsciousness, however, is not that of the philosophers; do not be alarmed. Look at it from my standpoint. You must see that the translation of this unconsciousness in the mind of the patient into consciousness must have the result of showing the patient that he departs from the normal. As soon as he recognizes this the compulsion under which his soul life stands is raised, for the conscious will reaches as far as the conscious psychic processes and every psychic compulsion is caused by unconsciousness.

The finding out and translation of the unconsciousness is of course accomplished in the fact of the constant resistance (so well known to physicians) of the patient. The attempt to help the patient to uncover the unconsciousness himself is almost always painful for him, or at least extremely tedious. The patient must therefore be trained by the physician. Much inner resistance must be overcome, particularly in cases where the sexual life plays a part. It is difficult enough to bring patients to a complete confession of these things when they are entirely conscious, how much more difficult then if they are unconscious of them! Such resistance can, in my opinion, be overcome only through the psychoanalytical method, which may be practiced only by a physician who is himself a serious, broadminded character with nothing of that mixture of lasciviousness and prudery which unfortunately marks some confessors in some churches.

When I asked Professor Freud whether he had heard that several psychotherapeutists in America claim to have cured hundreds of cases of alcoholism and its consequences by hypnotism, he made the following highly interesting reply:

Hypnotism and Suggestion Fail

Years ago I gave up the use of hypnotism in my treatment of patients. I found it useless. Altogether I must repeat that the analytical method of psychotherapy has nothing to do with hypnotic suggestive treatment. There is the greatest contrast between the suggestive and the analytical technique. The suggestive technique does not concern itself with the origin, extent and significance of the symptoms of the disease, but simply applies a plaster—suggestion—which it expects to be strong enough to prevent the expression of the diseased idea. The analytical therapy, on the contrary, does not wish to apply a plaster, does not wish to inject anything, but to take away, to get rid of, and for this purpose it concerns itself with the origin and progress of the symptoms of the disease, with the psychic connection of the diseased idea which it aims to destroy. I have given up the suggestive technique and with it hypnotism because I despaired of making the suggestion strong and durable enough to effect a permanent cure. In all severe cases I saw the suggestion crumble away, and the disease again made its appearance.

Further, there is another important point for my method. Particularly in the most complicated cases suggestion and particularly hypnotism do not help at all, because, as Bernheim has pointed out long ago, most people cannot be hypnotized. Do not believe the wonder-doctors who try to tell you that every human being is subject to their hypnotic art. That is not so. From its medical side hypnotism has been much overestimated. And still another thing. This

25

desire to hypnotize at all costs has its moral side too. The morality of it is doubtful—even if you should succeed—if you give a patient honey under the suggestion that he is receiving a dreadful poison in scientific doses, that will certainly destroy certain germs of disease. In time this fraud cannot fail to be discovered by an intelligent patient and its effect on people about the patient who see through it from the beginning is simply demoralizing. Such tricks often remind one unpleasantly of the dances and pills of feather-decorated, painted medicine men. Finally, such a course of action has a bad influence on the status of physicians themselves among whom unfortunately there are black sheep enough. How much is sinned with electricity for instance!

Hamlet as a Neurotic

In what my technique consists I cannot explain so easily. The instrument of the soul is not so easy to play and my technique is very painstaking and tedious. Any amateur attempt may have the most evil consequences. I am reminded of the burst of fury of a world-famous neurotic who, indeed, was not in the hands of a doctor, but only in the fantasy of a poet's brain. I mean Prince Hamlet of Denmark. The King has sent Rosencrantz and Guildenstern to him to find out the secrets of his ill-humor. He defends himself against them. Flutes are brought onto the stage. Hamlet takes up a flute and asks one of his tormentors to play on it, it is as easy as lying. The courtier refuses for he has never even had a flute in his hand. Then Hamlet bursts forth, "Why, look you now, how unworthy a thing you make of me, You would play upon me; you would seem to know my stops; you would pluck out the heart of my mystery; you would sound me from my lowest note to the top of my compass; and there is much music, excellent voice, in this little organ, yet cannot you make it speak. Sblood, do you think, I am easier to be played on than a pipe? Call me what instrument you will, though you can fret me, you cannot play upon me."

The psycho-analytical cure, as I have implied, makes difficult demands on the patient and on the physician. Also, it is not yet complete. Of the patient it requires absolute frankness, occupies a great deal of time, and is therefore expensive. It takes also a large amount of the physician's time and because of the difficult technique, is most tedious, but—and that is the most important thing—

it is radical. I have been able to apply my method only to cases which were severe cases. By that I do not mean that analytical psychotherapy is simply a means of treating neuropathic degeneration. I do not believe that a sufferer from neurotic disease is stamped as a degenerate, but one often accompanies the other. The method is also not suited to those who do not want to be cured, but are sent to the physician by their relatives. Everything depends on whether the patient can be trained to subject himself to the method. Even if that has been done with success, the number of cases where it can be employed is limited. If it is necessary to dispel threatening symptoms quickly it is difficult to use it because of its tediousness, and then, too, in cases of long standing it will seldom prove suitable. But for all forms of hysteria and in the wide field of delusions it is, in my opinion, indispensable.

I should like to have asked Dr. Freud some questions about his latest investigations of the significance of dreams, a subject which would certainly have been of general interest, but his time was limited. He is much occupied by the celebrations at the university, where he, too, will give several lectures on the "Psychopathology of Everyday Life," which should be heard by everyone who is interested in psychology.

Personal Impressions of Sigmund Freud and His Work
(1909)

JAMES PUTNAM

James Putnam (1846–1918) was one of the first distinguished American psychiatrists to take a serious interest in Freud and psychoanalysis. He met Freud in 1909 at Clark University and remained for the rest of his life an ardent and loyal supporter of psychoanalysis. This selection was first published in The Journal of Abnormal Psychology (*December 1909): 1–30. Putnam noted that he wrote with special reference to Freud's lectures at Clark University.*

I wish to call the attention of the readers of this journal to a recent occurrence of which perhaps few persons save a handful of psychologists, neurologists, and social workers took definite cognizance, yet which might well attract the notice of a far wider circle.[1]

Within a few years we have had two visits and two sets of lectures from the well-known Pierre Janet of Paris,[2] one of the great pioneer leaders of the generation that is now passing, in the investigation of a series of phenomena of the highest importance alike for medicine and psychology. This summer we have had a similar visit from another great leader, Professor Sigmund Freud, of Vienna, of whose work the same statement can, with warmth, be made. Though little known among us, Freud is no longer a young man, and indeed he outlined his life work and "laid his course" so many years ago that it is a reflection on our energy and intelligence that we have not gained a closer knowledge of the claims and merits of his doctrines.

With Freud came two younger friends and colleagues, who are devoting themselves with vigor to the same cause with him, Dr. C. G. Jung of Zürich and Dr. Sandor Ferenczi of Budapest.

Dr. Jung's observations, full of personality, fire, and life, have already excited much comment and—like the work of Freud—much criticism from the neurologists of Europe. Dr. Ferenczi has written a number of admirable papers, partly in Hungarian, which are bound soon to bring him prominently into notice.

We owe their visit, and the gathering of the intelligent audience who came to hear them, to the energy of the officers of Clark University in Worcester, which recently celebrated, with intellectual sumptuousness, the twentieth anniversary of its founding. Some of your readers will recall that on the occasion of the tenth anniversary of this institution, two other eminent students of the nervous system and its disorders, Professor August Forel, formerly of Zürich, and the distinguished Spaniard, Ramon-y-Cajal, came over and lectured as its guests.

The doctrines of Freud and his colleagues have been made known to us here more through the gossip of prejudice and misconception (on account of their insistence on the importance of the sexual life in the etiology of the psycho-neuroses) than by the testimony of those who have really tested them, and this, in itself, is an interesting fact. For these doctrines involve at every point the belief that the hidden motives which help to rule our lives, and which frequently show themselves as prejudices, are made up of "attraction," "desire," "acceptance," on the one hand, and, on the other hand, of "repulsion," "repression," "denial," mixed in equal parts. A strong prejudice often means a strong, instinctive attempt to set aside as false an influence which we feel that, if differently presented, we might be forced to accept, at least in part, as true, and the strength of the prejudice usually measures the importance of the half-felt but perhaps wholly suppressed truth. To say the least, our prejudices express feelings that at the moment we cannot or will not put to the test of reason.

Let me now attempt the task of modifying this prejudice—shared formerly by myself.

In brief, the history of Freud's investigations and opinions is the following: In 1881, an older colleague, Dr. J. Breuer, of Vienna, had occasion to treat an intelligent young woman suffering from hysteria in a serious form for which he tried the usual means in vain. At length, after long and tireless searching, he found that the facts offered by the patient in explanation of her illness, although they were freely furnished and represented her entire history so far as she consciously could furnish it, constituted only a tithe of the story which, in the end, her memory succeeded in drawing from its depths. Under the influence of a special method of inquiry, many hidden facts, representing painful experiences long ago forgotten, came one by one to light

29

and were as if lived over, attended by the emotions that originally formed a part of them. And just in proportion as this happened, in proportion as the dense barriers were overcome that separated this hidden portion of the patient's past from that of which she had remained consciously aware, one and another of her distressing symptoms dropped away and disappeared forever. The details of the long and significant history of this case cannot be given here. Let it suffice to say that although no further investigations based on it were undertaken for ten years, yet the facts observed had made a deep impression upon Dr. Freud and were meditated on by him during this decade, a part of which he passed as a student of Charcot's in Paris, and that on his return he begged Breuer to take the matter up again. After this, for a considerable length of time, they worked together; later, Freud alone. It became gradually more and more clear to them that the childhood of this patient had been in an unsuspected degree and sense the parent of her later years.[3]

For not only had it been found that many of the events which counted for so much in the production of her illness dated back to days of early youth, but the later experiences which had come upon her, one after another, and which were the ostensible and apparently sufficient causes of her illness, were discovered to owe a large portion of their power for harm to the fact that they reproduced in a new shape old emotions of childish form and substance, of which, before her treatment, she would truthfully have professed herself to be entirely unaware. Only when these emotions were reached and the experiences corresponding to them lived over, in memory and in speech, was the recovery complete.

There is little in the bare outlines of this proposition that a psychologist need count as wholly novel. Everyone has heard the claim that no experience is ever wholly lost, that our present acts are the outcome of all our antecedent acts; that our perceptions, even when apparently new, are in reality nine parts memory,[4] and that disclosing and talking over old troubles clears the mind and relieves the feelings of distress. But this dictum of the psychologists has now received a practical confirmation of an unexpected sort. The number and character of the revelations eventually made; the demonstration that memories apparently so wholly lost could with sufficient effort be recovered; the discovery that symptoms of illness and old forgotten emotional states were not only connected by a certain bond, but by a bond so subtle and yet so strong that this patient, through living her experiences over again in words, could succeed in freeing herself from the signs—physical as well as mental—of her present illness; the discovery, finally, that the nature of some of these experiences was what it proved to be; these were the surprising facts.[5]

The physical signs of the hysteria in this case consisted partly in a paralysis and contracture of the arm and a peculiar affection of the speech. Such signs are of very common occurrence, and the fact of their mental origin had been clearly pointed out by Janet. But the study of their specific relationship to this patient's mental experiences was utilized by Breuer and Freud as the basis of an elaborate theory of "conversion," or substitution, which has proved to be of wide bearing. It would be an instance of such conversion if a person wishing to exclude from his mind an unpleasant thought or memory should strive instinctively to aid himself by closure of the eyes and then should find that an actual and uncontrollable closure of the eyes had remained as a persistent memorial of the misjudged attempt at self-concealment. We can "convert" or we can neutralize the effect of our experiences, but we cannot kill them. Every experience retains the right and need to express its influence in our later history. We can accept it, work it out, assimilate it to the remainder of our conscious lives, or we can repress it. If we adopt (instinctively or consciously) the repressive policy, we may give birth to a sort of evil genius, who keeps himself concealed only on condition that we yield up to him some physical or mental evidence of the hold that, until exorcised, he will have on us. The physical symptoms of hysteria are thus analogous, to use Freud's simile, to the monuments which people set up to commemorate important events in history. It became clear to Breuer and Freud, further, and in harmony with the principle just expressed, that this patient's painful memories of the past, which at first had seemed as dead to her as if the experiences which they stood for had never occurred, represented in reality living and acting forces.[6] And not only this but that the very barriers which had to be overcome in reproducing them represented living and active forces too, all vibrating with significance for the present moment and for the details of the illness. In other words, the term "barrier" as used for the "forgetting" of the hysterical patient was shown to be a misnomer. Indeed, the forgetting of persons in normal health is largely repression, an active process of lending oneself to the task of learning how *not* to dwell upon a subject now painful but which perhaps had once a powerful interest. It has often been remarked that the conscious memory picks out the pleasant items of life

31

and rejects the rest. We remember the charms and novelty of an ocean trip, of foreign travel, and conveniently "forget"—in reality turn away from—the seasickness, the dirty inns, the sleepless nights. It was the significance of this species of forgetting and its relation to sickness and to health that Freud was led to study, and to which he has devoted all the powers of a keen and well-trained mind for twenty years. In the course of these investigations Freud and Jung and their followers have dived more deeply than any one before into the mysteries of the unconscious life. These investigations were inspired primarily, not by theory but by the recitals of patients who had been helped to search out their memories and their motives to a degree that never before had been made possible. New evidence has thus been brought to show that this hidden life, if technically "unconscious," is anything but inactive.[7] On the contrary, it is the living supplement of our conscious and willed existences, the dwelling-place and working-place of emotions which we could not utilize in the construction of the personality that we had shaped and rounded and that we longed to think of as standing completely for "ourselves." It is the study of this portion of our lives, repressed yet active, and not the attempt to push forward the sexual element in our experiences, that has constituted the main feature of Freud's work, looked at broadly and as a whole. The sexual element has indeed been pushed forward, but this has been due to two causes. In the first place, Freud's patients themselves, one after another, when urged to analyze the motives and influences that had prompted them to this or that act of repression or self-reproach, uniformly referred to one or another manifestation of this great passion as the ultimate source from which these motives sprang; and no wonder, for it is the basis of most of what we care for in this world. In the next place, the frequent references to the sexual life have been seized upon by Freud's critics as the basis for attack against the remarkable and truth-seeking observations of a remarkable man. I shall try, in the second instalment of this paper, to explain in more detail just what influences it is that, in Freud's view, the sexual life does introduce into the composition of our characters. What I wish to do here is to make a plea for open-mindedness in this matter. There are many subjects intensely disagreeable for discussion, from the social standpoint, which nevertheless the trained man of science studies eagerly and without a trace of unpleasant feeling. This is true, for example, of the bodily excretions. The study of sexual problems in all their manifold bearings is being taken up in this same spirit by an increasing number of persons of fine feeling and scientific instinct and a desire to work for the remedy of great practical evils. Each one of these persons has had to overcome an intense sense of aversion to this task of dwelling on details, of odious social connotation, but he has overcome it, at least to the extent of setting his intelligence moderately free to act. Most physicians are still in the grasp of this aversion and strive to justify themselves by denying the importance of the inquiry and the significance of the facts adduced. Meantime, the aversion means something more than it seems at first sight to mean. It indicates that the topic has or has had a sort of hold on us or a right to demand our interest and attention, and that we fain would persuade ourselves that this was not the case. This hold on our attention which we instinctively feel this subject has the right to claim even when we repudiate this right, constitutes one instance of the "desire," which is made to play such a large part in Freud's doctrines. What once was an instinctive desire, the expression of a perfectly natural craving, the basis of the natural curiosity, of an infant or young child, becomes, next, something to be repressed, as incompatible with the social life which the child grown older plans to lead. Either one of several consequences is liable to flow from this repression. First, it may be adequate and successful. The craving, the curiosity, the desire may find some sufficient outlet, may be assimilated or neutralized, and disappear permanently from view. Next, instead of this, the process of repression may go too far, may become too manifest, may impress the character too strongly with its own features. Then the "desire" utterly disappears from memory, but the eventual outcome is an individual of so-called over-sensitiveness and refinement, over-watchful of himself. Or, again, the "desire" or "craving" element may be too strong, or the mechanism whereby it should have been assimilated or neutralized may have been inadequate. Then the patient—for such we may now call him—becomes conscious of a lack of harmony with himself. He is one person who wishes and strives, consciously, to lead a certain life, but is also another person with an unsatisfied craving. As the result of this tendency he becomes predisposed to undergo a still more complete and definite cleavage, and this may, through "conversion," on the occasion of some new mental strain or trauma, earn for him the title of "hysteric" (a portion of the symptoms becoming *physical*) or may cause him to adopt some "phobia" (through a process of substitution) in accordance with a principle to be described later. Thus fear and repressed desire are shown to have an intimate kinship.

33

The cravings based on the sexual instincts of infancy and childhood take their place, in this scheme, along with those of adolescence and adult life, and along, too, with a great number of other cravings and ambitions, emotional interests and desires, of manifold character and force. It should be recognized that the doctrines and methods of Freud are full of interest as throwing light upon the mode in which the mind works, independently of the particular nature of the emotions that are involved. The life of every one, even the most commonplace person, even the most harmonious and best balanced, is complex enough to furnish the material for many a romance, for many a study of the conflicting tides of feeling. Every one acts from motives, many of which he does not clearly grasp; if it were not so no novels would be written, wars would have been few, and the great tragedians and mythmakers would never have existed. And yet, although we do not clearly grasp our motives, either as regards their nature or their origin; and although, if set to the task of describing ourselves and the history of our development we should leave out much that was important, yet the very fact that we understand novels and tragedies and character studies, and find them so entrancing, is an indication that we have felt, in some measure, the sentiments they are based on, and that we have passed through something corresponding in type with all the situations pictured. It may not be necessary that every one should become intimately acquainted with all these crooked byways and obscure corners of himself, or that each person should force himself to recognize his kinship with others whose qualities he deplores or whose acts he regards as criminal. But there are times when such knowledge becomes necessary for the preservation of the mental health, and the physician should fit himself to be the guide to its attainment.

I propose, in the rest of this communication, to consider a little further some of these psychological principles which Freud's observations have brought out in a new light, and to show their bearing on his therapeutic methods. The principles which I select as examples are embodied in the following propositions:

A. Desire, or craving, furnishes the motive for many thoughts and acts that seem actuated by sentiments of a different and even of an opposite character.

B. The principle of "conversion" in accordance with which the physical symptoms of hysteria are produced, is one manifestation of the wider principle of "substitution." Other manifestations of the same general tendency are: (1) the attributing to other persons, without adequate reason, qualities whose interest for us lies in the fact that we ourselves possess or have possessed and have, likewise, sought instinctively to repress them; (2) the harboring of prejudices for or against certain persons, on similar grounds; (3) the identification of ourselves with others, as in the assumption of ailments similar to theirs; (4) the transference to one person of interest originally centered on another; (5) the substitution of fear or of some morbid impulsion, for desires which cannot be adequately gratified.

C. The "forgetting" considered typical of hysteria and kindred forms of mental disharmony and disturbance is a feature of every one's mental growth.

D. Dreams are closely related, psychologically, to psychoses, and, like them, are classifiable, from certain points of view, as "compromises." Dreams likewise furnish valuable information of the unconscious life and are analyzable to a hitherto unsuspected degree, in the interests of therapeutics.

E. Finally, I wish to add a few more words on the principles involved in Freud's treatment.

A. Desire and craving are generally admitted to be powerful if only partial motives to conduct. One need not accept the doctrine of "hedonism" as alone binding in order to admit that we all have instincts and passions which press for gratification, and that ungratified or imperfectly gratified desires remain as unwelcome comrades to our thoughts. The point which mainly calls for comment is that even concealed and partial desires and cravings play an immensely important part in health and in disease. A few illustrations may take the place of argument. The partial wishes or cravings of young children are familiar to every one. Accustomed to deal with fairy tales, living in a world of fancy, and subjected to but slight censorship in his fancies, the child gives his desires free rein. It is often felt as a fine thing by a child to be in the eye of friends and comrades, even when the cause for distinction is really a cause for grief. A partial hostility towards a parent is entirely compatible with warm affection, but it is not recognized that when the child in question is of hysterical tendency, that is, when he is a person whose unconscious life plays too large a part in controlling his acts and thoughts, making him fitful, moody, and capricious, the affection may stand for an infantile passion, and the hostility which develops out of it may reach a high grade. The fable of the sour grapes hints at such a mixture of half-hidden and half-felt sentiments. The mental operations of older children and adults are not exempt from the working of these principles. The craving for recognition and sympathy flames in the eye and thrills in the voice of many a person who would deny that he was subject to these motives; disappointed hopes, the necessity for sacrifice and renunciation tinge a sincere grief with unwelcome and perhaps scarcely recognized longings. In these and in kindred ways mental conflicts arise, although the actual battle may be concealed from view.

The curiosity and emulation of children, as also of adolescents and adults, are other species of desire. They may be of manifold sorts, and in certain of their forms they represent cravings that are instinctively concealed. Out of such materials as these, in the manner thus indicated, and in the same ratio as we build the conscious personality, we form and feed and organize the unconscious life.

B. It will be recognized by every close observer that in entertaining a series of conflicting emotions, such as that typified by the sourgrapes illustration, for example, the instinctive effort is to escape from one distressing situation by grasping at another, which if in some respects worse is in some respects also better. This process is characteristic of the nervous invalid's mental life and, unsatisfactory as it is, it is often justified by the fact that it leads to the substitution of a definite evil for an indefinite. The operation of the principle under the form of "conversion" has been alluded to, but there are many other kinds of substitution, of analogous sort, and one of these is the substitution of a specific fear for a sense of humiliation or self-reproach. It is sometimes possible for a patient to witness the actual occurrence of this process of substitution. Certain forms of stage fright are of this order. In analogous fashion the personal relationship between two individuals, as a pupil and a teacher, may be felt to have in it an element of excess or wrong, and this feeling may tinge the next friendship, not in itself objectionable, with a sense of fear which may spread by unconscious paths to a general sense of apprehension, but finally concentrate itself in some one direction. Similarly, the strong ambition to gain a social success and the dread of failure are said by Freud to account for some of the fears of appearing in public places (as in agoraphobia), or where people must be met, or even of travelling in trains. In other words, this fear is the accepted substitute for an exaggerated form of self-consciousness attended by a sense of shame or guilt. Thus "self-consciousness" means the consciousness of oneself as seen by others in an unfavorable light.

Of course I indicate here only the bare outlines of a transformation which might be accepted only when delineated in detail. Usually, the process of transformation is hidden, even from the patient. He finds himself with a fear—the fear of open windows, or of the railroad train, or with one or another of the morbid impulses enumerated by Janet or by Loewenfeld—but it may be only with difficulty and after overcoming reluctance that he can be led to see the full force of the desires which he represses or the fact that it was to escape from them that he grasped the fear, to justify, as it were, the perturbation of his mind, as a drowning man catches at a straw. Janet has indicated, in an interesting paper published in this journal, other modes of unsatisfactory substitution through which psychopathic patients instinctively seek relief.[8]

C. It has been strongly urged by Freud that in the amnesia of hysteria, which every close student of the subject, since Janet, would admit to be a sort of active process, a contrivance for the obliteration of the memories of the unhappy and the disagreeable, we have an exaggerated form, a type of much of the forgetting of ordinary life. This principle is indeed admitted and widely acted on, but, as in the other cases, it is in the detail, in the fulness of illustration and in pointing out that the principle applies when we feel unwilling to apply it, that Freud's main service lies.

Every one agrees that "hell is paved with good intentions," which means that we sooth our consciences with words, satisfy ourselves by calling ourselves bad names, and then proceed to actively forget our duties and to close our eyes to the real images of ourselves. But it takes a truly scientific conscience, or the conscience of a person who is sick and sees a real chance of getting well, to recognize the complexity, the elaborate exactness of the machinery which, through this forgetting, we construct for the torment of our lives.

D. The laying down of the theory and mode of analysis of dreams is one of the most remarkable, and in principle the most original of Freud's contributions.

Accustomed as we are to see in dreams only phantasmagorias of the fancy, sparks leaping to and fro on burnt-out paper, to use William

James' simile, it is hard for us to believe the explanations and constructions of this analyst, who shows, as one or two others have done in part, that they occupy a definite and useful place in the economy of life.

In our dreams as in our illnesses our unconscious and repressed thoughts and emotions find expression. But, as in our illnesses, again, the revelations are not straightforward, the instinct for compromise and concealment makes itself everywhere apparent. In the night dream as in the day dream, wishes are fulfilled, but they are often partial wishes, and such as in our waking moments we do not admit even to ourselves. Symbolisms and innuendoes take the place of direct statement, and the possession of a treasury of dramatic power is revealed by the sleeper, of which his waking moments may indicate no trace, so deadening, even though useful, is the repression of education and convention. The volume devoted to the interpretation of dreams indicates the method of analysis which underlies all Freud's work, and it must be studied carefully by any one who would be either a critic or an investigator working on his lines. Let it be, if one will, that there is exaggeration, too much ingeniousness of interpolation and explanation. That criticism is nothing. No student need accept, in his own interpretations, more than he believes true. The fact remains that—in my view at least—Freud has offered us a master-key to many of the mysteries of life, and we need not reject this because we find ourselves inclined contemptuously to deny the reports brought back by this or that explorer of the dark realms of the unconscious.

E. Freud's therapeutic method is his method of analysis into the structure and working of the whole mind, the whole man, carried out with a searching and merciless vigor that is in the end fully justified by the fact that it brings at least a sense of freedom and of manhood.

A critical or rather a hostile feeling invariably raises itself in the mind of each new listener to these and kindred statements, and it is one that every earnest student of the subject, including the pioneers themselves, has had to deal with in himself before he could proceed. This critical sentiment favors the view that such inquiries as those here sketched out are unwholesome, unhealthy, morbid. The pretended cure is worse, it is said, than the disease. Introspection is of the devil. Why show us that we once were little animals, having no touch with the things that now make life so sacred and showing propensities our riper interests have no use for? Let us rather press constantly forward into the free air and more abundant light, and let those who have had a dark history forget it. Look forward and not back.

This is a fine cry, but unfortunately it has served the cause of ignorance, narrowness, and prejudice as well as that of progress. It was the cry of the church against Darwin, when he sought to "introspect" the history of life, and its echoes have drowned the voices of those who have sought to talk about the problems of sex, no matter with what earnestness. The cause of formal modesty and reticence has indeed had many noble martyrs, both before the days of Paul and Virginia and since. But there is such a thing as paying too dear for this niceness, especially when, through the opposite course, we can have all that we should gain by this, and more besides. Strikingly enough, this outcry against one or another sort of investigation is never raised except with regard to our neighbors' efforts to find the truth; the purity of our own motives, the value of our own inquiries, provided they are genuine, rarely come in question. We may kill animals for food and put them to pain for our convenience, but may not inflict any pain on them as physiologists, even for the sake of preventing infinitely more. The detective novel is welcome at every fireside, but the scientific student of human acts and motives is considered a disseminator of morbid tendencies. We are ready enough to say "why worry" when the answer is only to show that it is unphilosophical to anticipate trouble, but we may not ask "why *do we* worry" if there is danger of finding out that we worry because we are unwilling to see ourselves as we are, or to recognize that we are what we are partly because we were what we were.

All this is wrong. A fool's paradise is a poor paradise. If our spiritual life is good for anything it can afford to see the truth. No investigation is wrong if it is earnest. Knowledge knows nothing as essentially and invariably dirty. It is a piece of narrow intolerance, cruel in its outcome, to raise the cry of "introspection" in order to prevent an unfortunate invalid, whose every moment is already spent in introspection of the worst sort, forced on him by the bigotry, however well meant, of social conventions, from searching, even to the death, the causes of his misery, and learning to substitute the freedom, liberality, tolerance, and purity that comes from knowledge for the tyranny of ignorance and prejudice.

This outcry against intolerance may seem overdone and out of place, but it is not so, and one evidence of the fact is that these remarkable researches of Freud and Jung, and their small band of followers, have met with such bitter opposition, even among physicians.

It is a delightful task to lead our invalids to the mountain top and urge them to look out over the splendid fields around them, waiting for them to till. But it is cruel to attempt this when they must drag thither a heavy burden under which they are forced to stagger, pale and panting, to find themselves, at the summit, unable to proceed further. The real mountain top is always within the mind, and outward activity, which is so much prized, is of little value unless it is the symbol of an inward harmony and peace. At every feast Truth should have the first place.

To sum up the essential facts, let me say that Freud's main thesis, as I apprehend it, may be stated somewhat as follows: (1) Whereas, hitherto, the most important cause of the functional psycho-neuroses has usually been considered to be a constitutional and in general an inherited taint, and the influence of environment and education has been rated as of secondary significance, the facts point to a different conclusion. Our inheritance varies indeed within wide limits, but that which makes us sick or well (so far as the symptoms of these psycho-neuroses are concerned) is the influences to which we are subjected after birth. This is not to depreciate the importance of what we bring with us to the world, but to exalt the significance of education taken in a wide sense. (2) But if the influence of education, whether for good or ill, is to be exalted, it must be shown that these influences are to be given a broader meaning than that usually accorded to them; and (3) in so far as it is held that adult invalids are susceptible of cure through re-education, to a greater extent than others have believed, it must be proved that there are educational influences hitherto unrecognized or insufficiently recognized, which can be called to aid in this work.

In support of both these propositions Freud brings forward a remarkable array of evidence, based on the actual recitals of his patients. Some of these have been published by him or by his colleagues, while many others, for obvious reasons, have been withheld. These recitals are held to justify a number of subpropositions, such as those which follow, and as the result of my reading of the published communications, from personal conversations with Freud, and with his colleagues, and from my personal observations, I believe these claims to be well founded.

(*a*) From birth onward our lives are builded on a double principle.

We have ostensible personalities and concealed personalities, and though the two may harmonize fairly well they are never fully in accord. Society and our own choice and effort make us what *ostensibly* we are—artists, merchants, honorable citizens, persons following an aim. But in order to fit ourselves to moulds of such a sort we must, of course, at every moment discard temptations and repress emotions out of harmony with this or that set purpose.

(b) These emotions and temptations, in spite of being discarded and repressed, not only were but continue to be important portions of ourselves. They may never come to light again individually and in their own form, but at the least they contribute something, if only a note of seriousness, to our perceptions and our thoughts. When they do not help us to remember they may be forcing us to forget, and in reality these two results are often one. Even our discarded, repressed, forgotten childhood lives actively in our adult years, helping to form that variously named portion of our mental lives, of which we are not consciously aware, and *cannot make ourselves entirely aware except with special aid;* never, perhaps, completely.

(c) These repressed emotions and thoughts organize themselves more or less definitely into groups,[9] and there is a constant interplay between them and the thoughts and emotions of our conscious lives. Thus, the repression of a desire gives rise to a vague sense of disquiet; and this feeling attaching itself to a definite object may be felt as a morbid impulse or a defined fear. The desire and repression may never, at best, have been more than half-conscious processes, and finally become wholly forgotten, in the sense above described.

The vague distress (*flottierende Angst*) is consciously felt as something unendurable, and is at once attached to a special object, as in obedience to an impulse which counts as "protective," although the relief afforded may be anything but complete. The fears of water, of the dark, of certain animals, of meeting people, of crowds, of church and theatre, and so on through all their multitudinous forms, are made up in part, according to this view, of *fears of ourselves, i.e.,* fears engendered in the course of the effort to set aside a situation felt to be unbearable. Sometimes the whole process can be witnessed, as when a morbid fear of meeting people, or even a so-called misanthropy, arises out of the half-awareness that one has been living under conditions that were socially compromising. Often, however, the links of this chain pass wholly out of sight, and a person finds himself fearing or

41

hating a person or set of persons without knowing why, when in fact it is because these persons stand as representing certain aspects of our past selves.

It is a little harder to explain the common fears of open windows, bridges, and the like, than fears of less external sorts, but there can be little doubt that these also are at least partly due to a similar substitution. We would shine, we would be virtuous and recognized as such, consequently we fear to fall. "Natural" fear and symbolism do the rest.

In the foregoing pages I have given, in broad outlines, some of the main principles of the doctrine of mental analysis introduced by Breuer and Freud, and the conclusions to which they led.[10] In what follows I propose to call attention to certain points in more detail.

It is an interesting fact that the unfavorable criticisms which these researchers have called forth, whether directed against their validity or against their value, have been of strikingly contradictory sorts. Most of these criticisms have centered really, whether the fact was admitted or concealed, on the prominence given by Freud to the sexual element in the causation of the psychoneuroses. This was considered as a disagreeable topic on which we had closed our eyes so long that we thought we might permit ourselves to regard it as legitimately outlawed. Its vast literature—well known to be of great importance—was repulsive, and should not be seen upon our shelves. It counted for but little that this immense subject was daily and hourly thrusting itself upon our notice, whether as the cause of terrible sufferings, of terrible crimes, of terrible misunderstandings and misjudgments, and that it has played a huge part in the history of religion and of civic progress; those who have ventured to study it scientifically have been, nevertheless, regarded widely as disturbers of the peace. There can be no doubt that prejudices of these sorts have warped the reasoning of students, otherwise of fair judgment, and have led to contradictory kinds of depreciation of Freud's work. Some able men claim to have thoroughly tested his opinions by methods which they regard as entirely equivalent to his, and declare his conclusions to be unverifiable and absurd. They believe that Freud mischievously introduces sexual notions into his patients' minds, and a mistaken conception of their importance into a medical doctrine. Other men believe, on the contrary, that just because sexual influences, even morbid influences, are so widely prevalent, so much more so than the more serious forms of the psychoneuroses, they cannot play the important part in pathology which Freud assigns to them.

Without undertaking to discuss these conflicting differences of opinions it is clear that they suggest the prevalence, not only of serious prejudices, but also of real misunderstandings. Meantime, one good reason for hesitating to take up afresh the study of the sexual aspects of psychopathology has been for many persons the instinctive feeling that nothing practically satisfactory could come of it, either because of their belief that the wall of social repugnance is too strong, or because of doubt whether any new arguments could be more convincing than the old. Neither of these reasons seems to me applicable in the present case. There is an audience, small, perhaps, but constantly increasing, to which the researches of a band of workers, of whom Freud is one, strikingly appeal. Freud's particular contribution is of unquestionable importance, and yet there are so many investigators working on lines parallel with his that the conclusions of each one are sure to be both supplemented and controlled.

One other point needs special emphasis which, if understood, should place this whole matter, for intelligent students, on a better footing. The principal objection to the discussion of sex questions, or the prejudice against it, rests on the assumption that "sexual" means "sensual," and that to speak of sexual influences as of fundamental importance for psychopathology is equivalent to imputing immorality to the fine, intelligent men and women whose experiences might be at stake. But this hasty prejudice needs correction. In the first place, Freud's whole doctrine is permeated with the belief that much of the later neuropathic history of the adult patient was practically determined in his infancy, *i.e.*, at a period which indeed needs watching, but when "sensuality" is not in question. In the second place, it is an essential feature of his thesis that "repression" is one of the main agencies in the production of nervous symptoms, and also that much of what goes on lies for the most part outside the patient's conscious knowledge. The possession of the finest, the noblest qualities of thought and sentiment is thus not incompatible with nervous invalidisms of every sort, and certain types of invalidism are the outgrowths of both early and late repression of sexual instincts under personal effort or parental discipline: *Die Tugend ist der vollendete Kampf.* Every one has sexual instincts, if the word be correctly understood. Their possession is one of the universal properties and glories of all living things, and to assume that this is not so would be a piece of false and narrow pride. Here, again, it is the "sensuality" connotations that confuse the issue. As a corollary to this proposition it should be recognized that with regard to this, as with regard to many other matters, no line is to be sharply drawn between disease and health. Stronger efforts to attain our own ideal of virtue always are in place, but so, too, is a deep recognition of the old sentiment, *nil humanum a me alienum puto*, and a consequent willingness to arrest judgment, except when some practical decision is at stake. In place of moral judgments the physician may well substitute a wider knowledge. Morbid sexual tendencies are, indeed, extremely common, but the physician may and should study them with these sentiments in mind.

So true is this, that the argument ought to be recognized as properly applying to the medical estimate even of persons and acts classifiable as "abnormal," "criminal," or "perverted." For it is true, however those who have not looked into the matter may think otherwise, that, in the eye of science, perverted instincts—such, for example, as an excessive passion for a person of the same sex, carried from the realm of thought into that of act—finds its analogue in many overdone or even quasi-normal relationships of daily life. It is a question of degree that is at stake, and although for purposes of punishment, prevention, public self-protection and social standards, we must draw sharp lines, yet knowledge should make us prudent in passing scientific judgments. Furthermore, it is one of the propositions of the writer whom we are here reviewing, that from certain points of view, as, for example, in the production of symptoms and of dreams, thoughts count as acts, and if this dictum is accepted society would have to recast its estimates of the criminal and the abnormal. Let it not be imagined that it is in the annals of criminology alone that we should look for these analogies. The literature of the great myths and great tragedies call to mind the existence of tendencies in human nature which prove that conventional morals, important as they are, as indicating standards towards which every one should, for certain reasons, strive, are often, in a wider view, extremely narrow.

The course followed by Freud in classifying as "sexual" many common emotions, as of affection, and their opposites,[11] as well as a great variety of apparently indifferent sentiments, longings, and "physiological" habits, having no obvious connection with the reproductive functions is, from the medical and scientific standpoints, useful and indeed essential. He and his colleagues have sought conscientiously for some

44

wider term which might include the idea "sexual" yet without making that word so prominent, but they have come to the conclusion that the attempt was useless and, perhaps, not worth making. Dr. Jung discusses this point in a footnote to his valuable paper on the influence of the father on the evolution of the child (*Die Bedeutung des Vaters für das Schicksal des Einzelnen. Jahrbuch für Psychoanalytische und Psychopathologische Forschungen. I. Hälfte, p. 155*), saying, in reference to the word "libido," which they widely use, that this term corresponds to the "longing and striving" (*Wollen und Streben*) of the older psychiatrists, but, as employed by Freud, is a *denominatio a potiori*.

The English word "craving" seems to me perhaps the most significant for general uses; but the main thing is that we should strive to comprehend the truth and not miss the important analogies, inferences, and symbolisms which are here at stake. The burden of proof lies with those who are willing to let their ignorance of the facts obscure their judgment.

Freud's position as to this question of sexuality, or of unsatisfied craving for which equally unsatisfactory outlets are instinctively being sought, and their significance for social evolution, is expressed in many places, but nowhere in a more significant and comprehensive form than in an article entitled, *Die "kulturelle" Sexualmoral und die moderne Nervosität*, published in his *Sammlung Kleiner Schriften zur Neurosenlehre: Zweite Folge, 1909*. (In this paper the evolution, normal and morbid, of the individual is traced out in relation to the evolution of society.)

Without trying literally to summarize this article, I shall strive to give in my own words some of the principles there laid down, together with certain others brought forward in his earlier papers. The task which the human race finds itself called upon to meet is one of twofold character. We must seek to build up a civilization corresponding to our higher needs, yet are forced to recall that we are under sacred obligation to see that our species is perpetuated, and that, too, under the best conditions. These two sets of obligations often come, broadly speaking and narrowly speaking, into striking conflict. The pressure which all of us are under to make individual interests subservient to community interests finds its strongest, its most fundamental expression at the point where the problem is in question, how to raise to what may be called a higher level, the intense and varied emotions and tendencies that cluster round the great instinct and function of reproduction. This process of transforming our instincts into what may be

45

called by courtesy nobler forms is designated by Freud as one of "sublimation," and he is surely right in saying that in it, that is, in the repression of our instincts in the interests of other sorts of gain, the march of culture towards a higher culture virtually consists. But the special form of instinct repression which is here in question and which is the most fundamental one of all, is not accomplished without a corresponding sacrifice, a sacrifice which falls partly on the individual and partly on the community as well.

It is true that this sacrifice is often unattended by a marked sense of personal loss, but this is because of the immense power of the influences which social imitation and convention, religion, and the obligations under which we instinctively place ourselves in the interest of common happiness and stability, exert upon our emotions, our habits, and our thoughts. Every watchful observer, nevertheless, can trace, from infancy onwards, the working and the conflict of these two great influences, natural instinct and the repression of this instinct for the sake of society as a whole. This conflict complicates and underlies all the great movements by which the emotions, the hopes, the fears of men are stirred, and those investigators who claim not to trace its influence in psychopathology are either blind or do not know of what they speak. The greatest problem for the psychopathology of the future is to learn how to detect the subtle working of this conflict and the principles which it implies.

When the symptoms and history described by an adult nervous invalid are scrutinized it may be that we obtain at first no obvious trace of the sexual emotions and tendencies which played so important a part in the conflict from which his symptoms sprang. Least of all is he himself able to recognize these tendencies. He appears to himself a puzzle and a problem, and his symptoms seem as irrational as if he were possessed by some parasitic demon. Like the balking horse, who through repeated vain attempts to draw his load has learned to expect failure, he often stands as if paralyzed before the problems of his life, or he may have learned to exchange his uncertainty for fear; or, as if in cramplike attempts to gain relief, he may have constrained himself to convert his fears into some impulsive act of useless outcome. Or, again, if he would make a strong fight against his troubles, he is likely to feel himself, like Braddock's army in the Virginia Wilderness, helpless against an unseen foe. It is only after a long and patient analysis of motives, instincts, and desires, that the real enemy from whose attacks he suffers is found to consist in the above described discarded elements that went to make up the secondary and hidden stream of life, described in the earlier portion of this paper. It is needless to refer here to these elements in so far as they form a portion of his adult experiences alone, because these are reasonably well known to all. I would only repeat that, as I have said elsewhere, if the process of gaining the knowledge of them is to be compared in any sense, as it has been compared, to the confessional of the Catholic Church, it should be understood that the real analysis begins where the confessional leaves off.[12]

The remarkable fact, however, is that the nervous invalid is always discovered at least to be still partially under the sway of the influences of childhood. Few persons remember much of their infantile existence, but the researches of able men have made it clear that the sexual life of infancy and the conflicts involved in childish forms of "sublimation" are of remarkable complexity and force. The child has many desires, complex sensations, and interests besides those which might be classed as intellectual or emotional in a higher sense. One series of his deeper feelings are related, of course, to hunger, but it has become certain that others form a large connected group, of which the most important members are those which later go to subserve the functions of reproduction. In the period of infancy he does not by any means distinguish clearly between the different members of this latter group—which comprise, amongst others, the various sensations referable to all the orifices of the body, the nose and mouth, as well as the vagina, the urethra, and the anus—but only knows that through them all he can obtain analogous sorts of gratification. Thus equipped, the child is launched upon the task of evolution and repression. He is expected to follow a stated pathway, to retain and nourish the great function of transmitting his inheritance, but to do so under conventional and often highly artificial limitations. What wonder if, in the attempt to accomplish this, he so often goes at least partly wrong even when seeming to go most right. Why is it that sensitive, refined children are so prone to grow timid, shy, self-conscious, over-conscientious, morbidly dependent on a parent or a teacher? These questions and others which they suggest have been variously answered and there are doubtless various influences at work; but it is certain that every answer must be false which denies the action of the subconscious and unconscious mental repressions and conflicts of the sexual period of infancy and childhood; and that every answer must be inadequate that is not based on an intimate knowledge of the real contents of the child life from which we emerge, and which, in the sense in which forgetting has been above

47

described, we so soon forgot. It is, of course, true that we know as yet little of the exact part played by hereditary influences in the production of the neuropathic invalid. What we do, however, know, is that we can inherit what may be called a predisposition only. The tuberculous adult was not tuberculous as a newborn infant, and there are many who through care and prudence escape the destiny to which many another less careful falls a victim. The same thing is true of nervous invalidism, and of some, at least, of the severer forms of mental illness. These new researches open a distinctly new door for hope. I find myself believing more strongly in the reasonableness of this hope; in this opportunity—furnished by a better self-knowledge—to work out our possibilities and to escape from our temptations. I cannot pretend to have verified as yet all the many inferences and conclusions of Freud and his companions, reaching as they do infinitely further than I have here been able even to suggest. But I have learned to believe fully in the theory and in the value of their methods of analysis and of treatment, and I am the more ready to accept their views for having made the personal acquaintance of the three men mentioned at the beginning of this paper, and for having found them so kindly, unassuming, tolerant, earnest, and sincere. I believe there is still a good deal to be said on the psychological side of the discussion, and believe also that the intimate knowledge of ourselves, which is so essential, needs to be supplemented by more or less distinct study of motives of a social and ideal sort. But these considerations do not detract from the importance of the ideas here referred to. However strongly we may believe in the importance of character and its relationship to social, philosophical, and religious training, it is not to be forgotten that one deep root of character lies in the influences brought to bear during the remote period and by the remote conflicts of infancy and childhood.

Notes

1. The essential principles of Freud's treatment have been admirably described in an article by Dr. Ernest Jones of Toronto, a pupil and friend of Freud, and a thorough student of his writings. This article was published as part of a symposium on Psychotherapy in the *Journal of Abnormal Psychology* for June 1909. The whole series has been reprinted in book form by Richard G. Badger under the title *Psychotherapeutics*. A number of Freud's papers have been translated into English by Dr. Brill of New York and published in a volume entitled "Selected Papers on Hysteria and other Psychoneuroses," as No. 4 in the Monograph Series of the *Journal of Nervous and Mental Disease*. Ed. Jour. Ab. Psych.

2. Freud has never claimed and no one of his adherents need claim for him more than is his due. Janet has been working from the first on lines more or less parallel with his, and if I do not attempt here to adjust the claims of these two observers and of the others who have followed them, it is because to do this lies outside my present aim. In general terms, Janet's work has been *descriptive* of the mental "dissociation" which takes place in hysteria and the "reassociation" through which the mind seeks to establish a new equilibrium. Freud's observations have gone further in the line of pointing out the *causative influences* here at work and have proved themselves to be of great practical value in indicating, with remarkable sharpness, the immense part played by *education*, taken in both general and special senses, in producing the results.

3. I make no attempt in this hasty sketch either to separate the principles developed through the study of this first case from those of subsequent development, or to state these principles in the historical order of their discovery. Neither does this communication claim to furnish an authorized or systematic record of the Worcester lectures. My purpose is solely to reproduce the more prominent of my own impressions obtained through reading, private conversations and the lectures, and reinforced through personal observation in my own practice.

4. Cf. especially Bergson, *Matière et Mémoire*.

5. At first, the aid of hypnotism, later of "hypnoid" states, was invoked to secure this enlargement of the memory. Later it was found that quiet and relaxation, with the encouragement of the physician and the opportunity of talking and reminiscing, rather in his presence than under his scrutiny, were sufficient. This is in accordance with the observations of Bernheim that the amnesia of the hypnotic state, profound as it at first sight seems, may be invaded and overcome by the power of the subject's memory, if sufficiently urged thereto.

6. Cf. Bergson, *Matière et Mémoire*; also Janet, *État Mental des Hystériques, etc.*, and the works of other writers.

7. Eminent psychologists sometimes deny the propriety of using the term "consciousness" for a mental state of which we are not at the moment given consciously aware. This criticism has been expressed and met in a discussion on the Subconscious, published in the *Journal of Abnormal Psychology* for June-July 1907. It is there satisfactorily shown, as I think, by Dr. Prince, that "awareness" is not necessary for "consciousness," and that the suppressed mental states of hypnotized and hysterical patients, for example, are properly designated as conscious states.

8. Fits of anger and the commoner forms of depression, as I have elsewhere pointed out, are species of substitution whereby a person seeks to escape from the necessity of showing courage and clear thought. Unpleasant as those states are they really represent a sort of self-indulgence.

9. The organization of hell, as figured by Milton, may fairly be taken as representing a part, though only a part, of this unconscious realm of suppressed thoughts.

10. An excellent account of Freud's doctrine of dreams and their analysis was read by Dr. Ernest Jones at the recent meeting of the American Psychological Association, and will be published in the *American Journal of Psychology*. A valuable paper on the subject of dreams was also read by Dr. Morton Prince. In view of these publications I feel myself absolved from the obligation of saying anything further on this important topic. Cf. the sexual significance of violence inflicted or received.

11. Cf. the sexual significance of violence inflicted or received.

12. This comparison and contrast are introduced for the sake of calling attention again to the fact that the thoughts, memories and emotions which the physician seeks to set free are not simply with regard to matters which are "on the mind" of the patient. They form, indeed, a supplementary complex of vast amount and one which is unified by one thread, running from infancy to later years and reappearing again and again in moments of abstraction and in dream-life; but neither thread nor complex are to be discovered except by long and patient searching.

Some Personal Psychoanalytical Experiences with Professor Freud

(1922)

ADOLPH STERN

Adolph Stern was a charter member of the New York Psychoanalytic Institute (1931) and served twice as president of the New York Psychoanalytic Society (1922–23; 1940–42). He knew Freud for over thirty years. This selection was originally delivered as a lecture at the annual meeting of the Medical Society of the State of New York, Brooklyn, 5 May 1921, and published in the New York State Journal of Medicine 22 (1922): 21–25.

As an indication of the interest taken in psychoanalysis in Europe, it may be mentioned that the sixth International Congress of Psychoanalysts held at The Hague in the early part of September 1920 was the first international congress of the medical profession held since the war, at which the members attending were nationals of nearly all the principal warring and neutral nations. Great interest and activity were displayed by those present, who came from England, Holland, Switzerland, America, Germany, Austria and Russia. At some of the sessions fully 100 individuals, mostly members in good standing, were present. All the members were of the Freudian school. Many papers of great value on technical and applied psychoanalysis were read. All in all, attendance at the meeting was stimulating, and gave one an inkling of the progress of psychoanalysis in Europe. Reports by the various members of the different countries were, in general, encouraging as to the advance of psychoanalysis, both in a special and applied sense. Especially noted was the advance in England during and since the war. The status of analysis in Austria, as evidenced in Vienna, is very satisfactory. It is to be noted that in Vienna there is no attempt, as far as I know, to found a psychoanalytical society by any of those who seceded from the Freudian school. I have reference to Wilhelm Stekel and Alfred Adler. On the contrary, the followers of Freud have a very active membership in the Vienna Psychoanalyst Society, to the number of about twenty-five. The members are actively and keenly interested in the work. Meetings are held every two weeks, and are well attended. The impression I took away with me, both from the International Psychoanalytic Congress at The Hague and from my associations with the members of the Vienna group of analysts, is a very favorable one, and leads one to expect greater progress in the near future.

So much for a very brief summary of the situation in general. In presenting to you some of my personal experiences with Prof. Freud, I shall give in detail, not so technical as to make it uninteresting to the non-analyist or the general neurologist, the technique of analysis as I noted its employment by him in his analysis of me.

It is a generally accepted fact among analysts, and a point frequently emphasized by Freud, that a psychoanalyst must have been himself analyzed before he can hope to master the technique. Freud has also stated that in persons exceptionally free from conflicts and psychic inhibitions, a self analysis of his own dreams may be sufficient to enable such an individual to practice psychoanalysis. Such individuals must, however, be few in number. However, as the technique grew in complexity, owing to the fact that continued work with the neuroses demonstrated the existence of more numerous factors concerned in their formation than were previously evident, it gradually became clear that reading of psychoanalytical literature, analysis of one's own dreams, and the attempt to apply practically knowledge thus gained, fell far short of being the ideal method of becoming proficient in the practice of psychoanalysis; a thorough analysis by a competent analyst is a *sine qua non* for the individual who wishes to do satisfactory work in this field.

In nowise does the analysis of one who intends to practice psychoanalysis differ from that to which one suffering from a neurosis submits himself at the hands of an analyst. The student must submit himself to the same technique as does a patient. It is only in this way that the student can master the technique. In this respect instruction in other branches of medicine differs radically from that in psychoanalysis. This is due to the fact that as far as unconscious mental processes are constituted, they differ in the normal from those in the neurotic in degree only, and perhaps also in their more ready demonstration in the latter. The difference does not lie in kind. He who wishes to become an analyst must realize in himself the existence of such unconscious mental functioning, its nature, its mode of acting, its mechanism in evidencing

51

itself, and also its ability to conceal its activities. It is essential for one practicing analysis to know himself in a very literal sense before he is able successfully and in a competent manner to treat a patient. Knowing one's self is preliminary to knowing the mental processes that govern human conduct in general, and in particular to knowing the psychic nature of the neurotic disturbances. If the analyst himself be not free from psychic conflicts and inhibitions, he will be unable to help the patient recognize such impediments to a cure.

Prof. Freud, then, analyzes the future analyst under the same conditions, with the same technique as obtains in the case of a patient. He sees all patients, certainly until well along in the treatment, every day, except Sundays and holidays. Each session lasts one hour. With few exceptions the analysts in this country are in the habit of seeing their patients three times a week. Before my experience with Freud, like the other analysts, I, too, saw my patients three times a week. I have, therefore, some means of comparison, and feel that seeing a patient daily has at least two distinct advantages. Firstly, it cuts the total duration of the treatment in months at least in half. I mean that the treatment extends over a period of fewer months. Secondly, and this is the more important of the two, the rate of progress is more steady and satisfactory, on account of the fewer interruptions. More of the material produced by the patient, as, for instance, in the dreams, is available for the analysis.

All analysts on the Continent, and in England also, have their patient recline on a couch, with the head towards the analyst, who sits at the head of the patient, just out of range of the latter's line of vision. The reclining posture has the advantage of producing relaxation, and enables the analyst to note even minor movements of an involuntary or unconscious nature on the part of the patient, who at the same time cannot be occupied with watching the analyst. We in this country, with few exceptions, had been in the habit of having the patient sit in a chair facing the analyst. I feel that this has the disadvantage of the patient paying too much attention to the person of the analyst, especially to his facial expression, attempting to interpret looks, gestures, etc. In other words, the patients analyze the analyst.

With the patient (future analyst) in the reclining position, the next step is to proceed with free associations. He is told to give whatever comes into his mind, without any reservations whatsoever; to omit nothing, however trivial or irrelevant or unimportant the thought may appear. The patient is to lay aside all critique. No questions of a nature meant to lead on the patient are put to him by the analyst.

The next point of interest which I wish to take up is that of the resistance, indicated frequently early in the treatment by silence; the patient says that no thoughts occur to him. The management of this phenomenon requires great technical skill. The resistance originates from two sources: firstly, from the repressed material in the patient, and, secondly, from repressed thoughts the patient has in reference to the analyst. The phenomenon illustrates the point previously mentioned, that there is no qualitative difference between the unconscious mental processes of normal and neurotic, and perhaps lends emphasis to a statement made by Ernest Jones that a wholly normal person is an anomaly, and that a so-called normal person is more likely to be abnormal than a neurotic.

The resistance originating from the attitude of the patient to the analyst embraces the phenomena of the transference. To one like myself, Freud holds the position of the father of psychoanalysis, and he very readily becomes a father substitute, and brings out nicely the situation of child and parent. As in the case of patients in general, so in this instance the phenomena of the transference were very interesting and very important for the progress of the analysis. The phenomena of the transference constituted a very important phase of the psychoanalytic experience. They demonstrated that the bringing to the conscious and the correct interpretation of these phenomena constitute the steps necessary to verify the statement so frequently made that the neurotic lives through with the analyst (brings to the analyst) in the course of treatment, in a wholly unconscious manner, experiences in his early life, and tends to identify the analyst with individuals in his early childhood with whom the patient was intimately associated; that the latter manifests feelings for the analyst identical with those felt for individuals in the past, in instances where the points of resemblance (identification) are of the most superficial or minor nature. These phenomena also demonstrated that their analysis is very vital for a convincing understanding and acceptance of the existence of infantile or unconscious mental processes, in so far as they still activate not only neurotic symptoms, but also general personal characteristics, dreams, slips of the tongue, etc. As I mentioned before, this phase of the treatment demands the best of the analyst, for the success of the treatment depends on the handling of the transference.

The resistances originating from the repressed material of the individual analyzed offer less difficulty after the resistances originating from the transference are dealt with adequately.

In handling the free associations given, for instance, to a dream, the values of the different elements in the chain of associations must be determined by the analyst. Free associations to some part of a dream may be unlimited in number; it is the duty of the analyst to recognize the value and pertinence of the different elements in the free associations in their bearing on the emotional life of the patient. To do this accurately requires, naturally on the part of the analyst, a most intimate knowledge of the life history of the patient, and of his deep-seated or unconscious impulses. This phase of the treatment requires further on the part of the analyst a very retentive memory for details. For though the history of the patient, with great detail may have been recorded by the analyst in writing, yet this cannot be used during the analysis proper; for the entire attention of the analyst is required for the patient at the moment. A great mass of detail is carried in the memory of the analyst, and such parts thereof as have a bearing on what the patient is saying at the moment becomes conscious to the analyst.

As I just mentioned, to evaluate the different elements in the free associations requires on the part of the analyst a most intimate knowledge of the history of the patient, a knowledge of the deep-seated impulses, the instinctive impulses, the partial sexual impulses, the ego instincts, etc. Not that they are ever absent, or that their presence as such are to be demonstrated. Their early manifestation and their present-day activities are sought for. While no elements in the free associations are overlooked, yet after some progress in the treatment has been made, such associations are emphasized and called to the attention of the patient as appear to Freud to evidence the activity of infantile unconscious impulses or wishes. He seeks the significance of the deeper associations, but by no means overlooks the superficial.

In respect to dream interpretation, I might say that Freud does not vary from the generally accepted method. Namely, if not spontaneously indicated by the patient for the elucidation of the dream in question, the attention of the patient is directed to the rule that a dream originates in some thoughts or experience of the day preceding the dream, and he is requested, if possible, to find the origin of the dream, or more properly the dream incitor. From the free associations to the various dream elements, an attempt is made to seek the unconscious repressed wish or wishes, which have made use of the day remnants (thoughts) as a means of finding a disguised expression in the dream. Wherever inference from the free associations permits, deep-seated wishes are sought to be made conscious to the patient. An attempt is made to make evident the repressed wishes in as concise a form as possible.

The question has frequently arisen as to what factors in the treatment are the important ones in bringing about a cure in psychoanalysis. Is it the bringing to the conscious knowledge of the individual, of the repressed, unconscious wishes that produces the benefit? Or does the resolution of the conflicts have the curative effect? Is it the ability to sublimate impulses previously inhibited from obtaining satisfactory outlet? It is difficult, if not impossible, to evaluate the rôle played by these different factors. They are all concerned, perhaps, to a varying degree. There is, however, one factor not enumerated above which I believe plays the most important rôle. It is this factor which brings a feeling of conviction as to the correctness of the interpretations, and as to the existence of unconscious mental processes. I refer to the living over by the patient in the course of the analysis, of situations, experiences, or phantasies, long past or even forgotten and recalled during the analysis. Freud has repeatedly mentioned that an intellectual acceptance of phenomena psychoanalytically demonstrated brings about no curative effect or deep-seated conviction. For this purpose they must be emotionally accepted. In the treatment the patient usually with lasting effect after the phenomena of the transference have been made conscious to him re-lives in a conscious way, experiences, actual or phantasied, with all the emotions present at the time, even though years may have elapsed. Anger, joy, envy, hate, love, etc., once more are experienced in connection with situations or persons in regard to whom they originally existed. All analysts have repeatedly observed this in patients. I have also. It was, however, a novel and convincing experience to be the subject myself.

A few words as to the rate of progress of the analysis. It is not at all steady, but quite irregular. A week or more may go by, with little or no profit, apparently. Then valuable data appear, and valuable deductions are made. There is then again a period of slack, and then some loose ends are gathered and united. Things touched upon perhaps some weeks before, not very clear at the time, now become more clear. Very little, usually no direct effort can be made to proceed along definite lines. As a rule the immediate work in hand depends on the material produced by the patient at the moment. Though recently what has been called by the analysts in Europe "active therapy" has been employed, yet I find that this addition is a minor detail, and of itself gives no hope that more direct means are at hand for obviating the great difficulty brought about by the almost complete reliance for the rate of progress and of material handled on the productions given by the patient. No short cut to a cure has been found as yet.

I wish to mention briefly that in the employment of dream symbolism, Freud relies almost exclusively on the free associations of the patient for its interpretation. Only in very few instances does he lay any stress on the so-called generally accepted symbols, and in such cases also seeks corroboration for their interpretation on their close connection with and relation to the free associations given by the patient. While Freud recognizes that some symbols are universally interpreted in the same way, yet such symbols serve their purpose better for descriptive than for therapeutic purposes, except as I mentioned before when the patient's associations warrant a generally accepted interpretation. Freud at no time insists on the absolute correctness of his interpretation, but leaves it to the repeated recurrence of the material for confirmation or denial of the correctness of the interpretation. For in the therapeutic application of the psychoanalytic technique, only the truth or accuracy of the interpretation in relation to the individual is of value, and not the general applicability of the symbolism. The therapeutic aim in this sense is direct and immediate.

I will close by giving in brief the duty of the analyst in the course of a psychoanalytic treatment. Firstly, he must exercise great patience, a quality that Prof. Freud possesses in a great measure. He must not be hurried by the demands of the patient. He must feel a genuine interest in the work. To the emotional outbursts of the patients; to their exhibition of the various attitudes that become evident in the phenomena of the transference; to their immoralities and perversions, the analyst must take a strictly scientific attitude, if I may call it that. There must be a complete absence of the attitude of judge or moralist. Only one who has been well analyzed can take the proper attitude.

The active part of the duty of the analyst consists in what he has to tell to the patient. He must know what to tell the latter, and more important still, when to tell it. As a rule the analyst speaks little, and Freud is no exception to the rule. However, that which he has to say is clearly and concisely put, and properly timed. By the latter statement I mean that the analyst, after he has become well acquainted with many details of the patient's history, usually can see a little further ahead, than the patient, while the latter is giving free associations. That is that the analyst knows more about the patient than the latter knows of himself. The analyst then tells the patient what he thinks the latter can comprehend or appreciate at its true value. Care is taken not to interpret too far in advance of the patient's progress. Freud makes it a rule to encourage the patient to make his own interpretations, to work out his own difficulties, wherever possible, especially after the patient has made some progress.

The main points of interest have, I believe, been covered, though very briefly. I trust I have made myself understood, for I realize the difficulties under which I am laboring in reading such a technical paper before a non-psychoanalytical audience. I do hope that you will see the absolute necessity of an individual being analyzed by a competent analyst before he undertakes to treat the psychoneuroses by means of the psychoanalytic technique.

A Visit to Freud

(1923)

RAYMOND RECOULY

Raymond Recouly was a French journalist in the 1920s when Freud was quite accessible to interviews. Although it is not very favorable, this interview is included as an example of what Freud was up against in terms of popular opinion! This selection was published in The Outlook *(5 September 1923). I was unable to trace the translator.*

One of the best-known professors of the University of Vienna, Mr. X, who bears the formerly much envied title of *Hofrat* (Aulic Councilor), has courteously offered to take me to see Freud, his intimate friend. I accept this invitation joyfully, for I had very much desired to meet the celebrated inventor of psychoanalysis during my stay in Austria.

A telephone call. An appointment is made for the next day but one, after lunch.

When one meets a statesman, even the head of a state, no matter how illustrious he may be (this has happened to me in almost every country in the world), he can be accosted freely, on an easy footing, and without any initiation.

It is not the same with philosophers. I devote the two remaining days to re-reading some of Freud's books, especially the "Introduction to Psychoanalysis," which contains a summary of his doctrine. It is the extreme ingenuity of his theories that strikes the layman. Of this obscure and up to now hardly explored domain of the "unconscious self" which feeds, if it does not even dominate, our intellectual and emotive activity Freud has become the explorer who is as subtle as he is adventurous. He takes us by the hand, lights his lantern, and shows us all our innermost recesses. We follow him—very much interested, sometimes very much astonished, quite often shocked. He throws a blinding light on everything we have in our minds; and the contents of our minds are appalling.

He finds a meaning in our dreams when we did not think they had any. He guides us, like Ariadne, through our hallucinations and our nightmares. Our errors and our "lapses," those of tongue as those of wit, are what he calls "repressed urges;" the thousand ideas of our child life, of our slumbering existence—thanks to him, all that which to us appeared so confused, so vague, so inexplicable—are explained, classified, labeled.

Freud would willingly revive, in his own way, the celebrated saying of La Rochefoucauld, and affirm that all passions, all the sentiments of men, lose themselves in sensuality, or rather in sexuality, as rivers flow into the sea. Even when we have just been born, sexual instinct controls everything in us. We have the impression that Freud always takes us back there with excessive and in more than one case arbitrary complacency. It is the *leit-motif*, the *pièce de résistance*, of his doctrine. As it is, however, with all its exaggeration this doctrine remains extremely interesting.

So it is with much curiosity, in the company of my amiable introducer, the Aulic Councilor, that I wend my way towards Freud's house in the Berggasse.

A rather vast apartment, containing a large number of works of art, chiefly Egyptian and Greek busts, casts, photographic reproductions. This is the atmosphere, recalling a museum rather than a library, in which Freud receives us.

We see an extremely accentuated Jewish type, the air of an old rabbi just arrived from Palestine, the thin and emaciated face of a man who has passed days and nights discussing with his initiated followers the subtleties of the Law, in whom one feels a very intense brain life and the power of playing with ideas as an Oriental plays with the amber beads of his chaplet.

When he speaks of his doctrine, of his disciples, he does so with a mixture of pride and detachment. However, it is pride that dominates. He is proud of his school, of his numerous disciples, scattered throughout the universe, certain of whom, upon the whole, are not without creating embarrassment for the master by the over-independent manner in which they interpret his ideas.

We speak of his theories, of the road he follows to bring them into the daylight and spread them. "The starting-point," he says to me, "is found in Charcot's lessons at the Salpêtrière."

Thereupon Freud shows me the celebrated engraving of Charcot, "The Lesson at the Hospital," on the walls of his study, occupying the place of honor. At the beginning of his career he studied under Charcot at Paris, commencing to study the mechanism of hysteria with him from a purely medical standpoint.

In him—and this is an essential point—the philosopher is combined with the doctor; or rather, he is first of all a doctor, and a philosopher afterwards. He is not content with understanding and explaining, but his first aim is to cure. It is by studying sick persons that he is able to understand people who are healthy. The abnormal sheds light on the normal. Starting from disease, Freud always has a tendency to return to it.

Thus the germ of his theories is found in the lessons of Charcot and of Bernheim, a professor at Nancy.

According to the definition of Freud himself, psychoanalysis is essentially a method of treating certain nervous diseases. One of his colleagues in Vienna had the idea of hypnotizing a hysterical person by making him go back, from association to association, up to the source of apparently incoherent words which he had pronounced during his attacks. From that experiment the considerable part played by the unconscious mind was revealed to the young doctor.

However, he separated himself at an early hour from his masters, to found his own doctrine. He reproached them for not attacking the root of the evil, but only its effects. He was thus brought to state precisely and co-ordinate his theories more and more. One of the essential points of it was always the famous "psychical regression," the "talking cure," which consists in forcing the sick person to relate his story and cure himself.

"It is by that," says Freud to me, "that I have been led to my theory of the unconscious mind. The more I followed up my observations, the more was I convinced of their richness, of the full extent of that unconscious mind. It is a vase filled to overflowing, in which it is proper to seek and find the source of our emotive life, not only in disease, but also in a state of health. All our 'repressed urges,' our lapses, our errors, our distractions, our dreams, are connected with more or less repressed sentiments, sometimes innocent, sometimes of a rather improper nature."

"No one," I say to the doctor-philosopher, "excels more than you do in following them on the trail, in tracking them like the most skillful of detectives, and going back, from step to step, to their origin. This origin is hardly ever very pure. But it is surely not your fault!"

And I thought to myself, without daring to speak of it to my interlocutor, of the well-known French line which nine times out of ten would apply rather well to his theories, or rather to those who are the object of them: *"Tout homme a dans son cœur un cochon qui sommeille!"*

Afterwards Freud speaks to us of his pupils, who are scattered all over the vast world, in the New Continent as well as in the Old, of their works, of the Congress which reunites them periodically, of the "Review of Psychoanalysis," which they have founded.

"It is in France that I have the least number of followers," Freud remarks. "My theories have been least studied and made public in France."

"How do you explain this?" I ask.

"I do not really know. I believe that there are many reasons for it. Perhaps politics have something to do with it."

"I can assure you that this is not the case," I say, energetically. "There is no country in the world where people are so ready as in France to welcome ideas from outside, no matter from where they come. Besides, your doctrines have been much talked of lately. A certain number of books and studies and articles have been devoted to them."

"I foresee another explanation," he adds. "As my theories, at least at the commencement, were connected with those of your great Charcot, the French have been less anxious to follow their development on foreign ground, in a foreign spirit and language. They were content with the development that these ideas had taken in your country."

Freud found this explanation forthwith, as if he were playing with it. I have the impression that he found it chiefly to please me; if he had only sought elsewhere, he would have found another—and very different, if not an opposite—explanation.

The extreme facility with which explanations and nascent hypotheses abound in him is most significant. It is even a mark of his nature. If it be a question of interpreting a lapse, above all, a dream, then his ingenuity has really no limits. The explanation of some dreams must be read in the "Introduction to Psychoanalysis." It is impossible to push subtlety further, and also, it must be said, fantasy.

"A young woman crosses the drawing-room of her flat and knocks her head against the chandelier suspended from the ceiling; a bleeding wound is the result." Here is apparently a most simple dream. You cannot imagine all the developments that Freud draws from it at once, the analogies and comparisons to which he connects it. Moreover,

61

these comparisons are all of an extremely concrete order. They all go back to some very simple acts. Although the starting-points may be of the most varied kind, the point of arrival is always identical, and always depends as directly as possible on our sexual life.

In short, that is the point to which everything leads. This insistence to bring us back to it appears excessive and even, more than once, irritating. For sexual life, even if it does hold an important place, is certainly not everything in man. There are also other things, many other things. Freud persists fearlessly in saying, No. According to him, they are simple, external aspects, under which he claims he can always show us the same eternal reality.

But nothing forces us, fortunately, to believe him. Nothing forces us to see in each one of our fellow-men the lascivious and lustful animal to which he wishes, by force, to prove our relationship.

Interview with Professor Freud

(1924)

ANDRÉ BRETON

André Breton (1896–1966), a founder of surrealism and the Dada movement in France, is not very sympathetic towards Freud in this interview, which he must have conducted in the early twenties in Vienna, since the book (Les Pas Perdus) was published in 1924. Les Pas Perdus was reprinted in 1969 by Gallimard in Paris. The translation was done by Richard McConchie especially for this book.

Young people and romantic souls who, because there is a fad this winter for psychoanalysis, must imagine for themselves one of the most prosperous sanctums of modern charlatanry, the office of Professor Freud, with its apparatus for pulling rabbits from hats and transforming all blotting paper blue. I am not angered to learn that the greatest psychologist of this age lives in a commonplace house in an out-of-the-way quarter of Vienna. "Dear Sir," he had written me, "Since I have very little free time these days, I beg of you to come to see me this Monday (tomorrow, the 10th) at 3 o'clock in the afternoon in my office. Very truly yours, Freud."

A modest plaque at the entrance, "Pr. Freud, 2-4," a not especially pretty maid, a waiting room decorated with four feebly allegorical engravings—Water, Fire, Earth, and Air—and a photograph representing the master with his collaborators—ten or so consultants of the most common sort. Once, when the doorbell rang, some cries in the wings, but nothing to nourish even the meanest reportage. This until the famous padded door opens for me. I find myself in the presence of a not very attractive little old man, who receives one in the somewhat shabby office of a general practitioner.

Ah! He does not like France very much, as she alone has remained indifferent to his work. However, he shows me with pride a brochure which has just appeared in Geneva and is nothing more than the first French translation of five of his lectures. I try to get him to talk by alluding to Charcot and Babinski, but either because I referred to too distant memories or because he is conversing with a stranger, he chooses to fall back upon a prudent reticence. I can draw from him only generalities such as, "Your letter was the most touching one I have received in my life," or "Happily, we are counting a great deal on young people."

Freud's Position in the History of Modern Culture

(1929)

THOMAS MANN

Thomas Mann (1875–1955) was a literary giant of the early 20th century. Freud was fond of maintaining close touch with the literary figures of his time and Mann certainly was one of them. They kept up a busy correspondence. This essay was originally published as "Die Stellung Freuds in der modernen Geistesgeschichte" in Psychoanalytische Bewegung.[1] *(1929): 3-32 and was subsequently translated by Clara Willard and Smith Ely Jelliffe (an American psychiatrist who became very much interested in Freud's work as early as the 1910s). Parts of this paper also appeared in the lecture Mann delivered for the* Wiener Akademischen Verein fur medizinische Psychologie *on the occasion of Freud's 80th birthday, 6 May 1936.*

Freud wrote to Mann on his 60th birthday, "Please accept a heartfelt message of affection on your sixtieth birthday. I am one of your 'oldest' readers and admirers; I could wish you a very long and happy life, as is the custom on such occasions. But I shall refrain from doing so; the bestowal of wishes is trivial and seems to me a regression into the era when mankind believed in the magic omnipotence of thought."

If I should be asked which one of Freud's courageous and revolutionary contributions has made the strongest impression on me, and which of his literary works first occurs to me when his name is mentioned, I should answer without hesitation "Totem and Taboo," the great essay in four parts in the tenth volume of his "Collected Papers." It is not likely that I am alone in this preference. It is an evidence of almost touching scientific modesty, in view of the world-wide appreciation today accorded to all of his writings, both in relative and positive sense, that Freud feels called upon to draw a line of distinction between this and others of his writings, ascribing to it, as an exception, a claim on the interest of a larger circle of cultured persons. Indeed in purpose and insight this essay goes far beyond the medical sphere into that of general science and opens up for the reader interested in the questions confronting mankind, a boundless perspective and throws light into the spiritual past, the early historical and prehistorical moral, social, and mystical depths of human development.

Its extraordinary fascination may be explained in various ways: first of all it is without doubt the one of Freud's productions which has the greatest artistic merit; both in conception and literary form, it is a literary masterpiece allied to, and comparable with, the greatest examples of literary essays. This is not surprising and yet there is something mysterious about it, for the great readability of just this work, rising above the clinical sphere to that of general human interest, the nature of the law of form is revealed, the metaphysical relationship between human nature and form which pervades and dominates in the sphere of poetry and belles lettres. This is the world of things which defy expression—but which are nevertheless well expressed, the world of the poet and the novelist. This is the world to which this work undoubtedly belongs. It is not ordinary scientific hack-work, but a piece of world-literature.

Freud calls it "an attempt to apply the results of psychoanalysis to unexplained problems of racial psychology." The clinical point of view is therefore preserved and it must be said, preserved in masterly fashion. From Nietzsche we have the idea of the value of disease for a knowledge of the development of life generally. The psychologist of the neuroses, in these studies, reveals to us, in exact detail, how close are these relations and how deep goes the connection between neurosis and human nature. If, on the one hand, making use of the neuroses, he lends meaning to reflected glimmerings from primitive life, from prehistorical and early historical traces of human progress and explains the deepest foundations of cultural life, on the other, he presents the neurotic type as archaic in the sense of the subtitle of this essay, which modestly reads, "Some resemblances between the psychic lives of savages and neurotics." By "psychic life of savages" he doubtless means life of primitives in paleontological and prehistorical connotation. This "application of the results of psychoanalysis to the history of mankind" doubtless signifies transference of the celebrated "deep psychology" beyond the individual clinical sphere and its projection in time and immeasurable space, which further explains the special charm of this genial rhapsodical work. It is an astonishing example of expansion and contraction, in so far as it contains *in nuce* the entire theoretical system of psychoanalysis with all its elements: dream psychology, oedipus-complex concept, concept of ambivalence, theory of repression, of transformation of instincts and what not besides, and at the same time

66

it is the most far-reaching psychological literary undertaking that has ever been attempted from the point of view of medical science.

It would be idle, and I have not space here, to recapitulate even in general outline, the trains of thought which are brought together in this great endeavor. But to the honor of Freud and in recognition of his position in cultural history, especially in German cultural history, I beg leave to add certain remarks and comments suggested by a re-reading of this work.

In a critical aphorism under the heading "The enmity of the Germans to enlightenment," Nietzsche discusses the contribution which the Germans, their philosophers, historians, and natural scientists, made to general culture in the first half of the nineteenth century, and calls attention to the fact that "the main general tendency was directed against enlightenment and against those social revolutions which by a gross misunderstanding were mistaken for consequences of enlightenment." The piety towards everything that existed, he says, tried to become piety towards everything that had ever existed "only in order that the heart and mind might be permitted to fill themselves and gush forth again, thus leaving no space for future and novel aims." He speaks of the rise of the cult of feeling in place of the cult of reason, and of the sublime share which German musicians, more successful than all the other artists in word and thought, took in building up the temple. Taking into account that many good things were said and investigated, he does not wish it to be forgotten that in all this there was "a general danger and one by no means small" of setting "knowledge altogether below feeling under the appearance of an entire and definitive acquaintance with the past" and, to use an expression of Kant, of making "way again for belief by giving the limits of knowledge." "The hour of this danger is past," writes Nietzsche (1880!). "We breathe freely again." The very spirits which these Germans conjured up with such eloquence at length became the most dangerous for the intentions of those who did conjure them up. "History, the comprehension of origin and development, sympathy with the past, the new passion for feeling, after they had been for a long time in the service of this obscure, ecstatic, retrograde spirit, have once more assumed another nature and are now soaring with outstretched wings over the heads of those who once upon a time conjured them forth, as new and stronger genii of that very enlightenment to combat which they had been resuscitated. It is this enlightenment which we now have to carry forward—caring nothing for the fact that there has been and still is a 'great revolution' and again a great 'reaction' against it; these are but playful crests of foam when compared with the truly great current upon which we float and want to float!"

The vital force of these words, their immediate and invigorating applicability today will be felt by everyone who reads them again, nearly half a century after they were written. Those who do not wish the clear vision of the future of mankind to be distorted by the "ephemeral play of the waves," do not wish to be confused by the self-applause of those who interpret the present and serve the hour, will hear them again with all honor to the genius and greatness of Nietzsche, at whose feet lay the problems of our own age, whether we are conscious of it or not, all its thoughts, endeavors, opinions and strivings, so that its struggles and convulsions seem like contortions of satyrs and are petty scurrilous repetitions of his spiritual experiences, the problems over which it quarrels having all been solved by him on a larger scale. What are our political controversies but debased imitations of his epochal conflict with Wagner, a symbolic combat representing the conquest of romanticism in him and through him?

We of today have good reason to reflect on romanticism and enlightenment, reaction, and progress, and have learned caution in the use of these terms when the question is not one of mere combat and victory, but of knowledge itself; we have learned that caution which Nietzsche counsels in a superscription to be found in "Human; all too Human," namely the phrase "Reaction as Progress." He speaks there of great and forceful natures who are survivals of the past and invoke again a by-gone epoch of mankind, as evidence that a new direction is not yet strong enough to oppose this past. As an example of a triumphant retrogressive genius of this sort he offers Schopenhauer; in Schopenhauer's teachings the entire prescientific cosmic view belonging to the Christian concept and the human outlook of the middle ages finds resurrection, notwithstanding the fact that dogmatic Christianity had been successfully abandoned. With exemplary insight Nietzsche points out the advantages to be gained from the influences of such retrogressive natures by at times forcing us back to powerful older ways of regarding the world and mankind, to which the backward-leading path could otherwise hardly be found. These natures bring inestimable benefits to history and truth. Nietzsche explains that the enlightenment with its historical method of envisaging the subject, was unable to do justice to Christendom and its kindred Asiatic religions. Schopenhauer's metaphysics corrected the errors from a general retrogressive point of view and only after this great triumph of justice could the banner of enlightenment be carried forward, "the banner bearing the three names, Petrarch, Erasmus, Voltaire." From reaction, he says, came progress.

In these reflections may be seen a foreshadowing of the aphorism from "The Dawn of Day," which I called to mind in the foregoing, and here equally instructive pronouncements are given as to the complexity and many-sidedness of all that pertains to the spiritual and as to the caution necessary in the use of concepts relating to it. Reaction as progress, progress as reaction—this interlacing is a phenomenon constantly recurring in history. Luther's Reformation as result of conviction—what can be learned from it in relation to reaction and progress? It is revolution and liberation, the German form of revolution and precursor of the French revolution; it is also a retrogression to the middle ages, a past falling dead-ripe in the springtime of the Renaissance. It is an interlacing of the two elements, a mixture of life and deed and personality, which could never have been arrived at through purely mental avenues.

Christianity itself, whatever inestimable significance it may have had for mankind, for his spiritual and social elevation, and whatever forces it may have set in motion in the direction of progress—who can fail to see in Christianity with its invocation and revival of older religious rites of civilized antiquity, its belief in souls, in the communal feast of the blood and flesh of a divine sacrifice, a modified reversion to earlier atrocities, an atavism, in which literally the lowest has become the highest.

To what extent the Christendom which Luther "reformed" was itself a reformation, namely a reversion to a more primitive cult and a spiritual repetition of it, and how little reformations in their real nature have to do in general with progress, restoring as they do in altered form the old or the very oldest, at a time when the new has already taken place—all this became clearer as I reread certain pages of "Totem and Taboo," which treat of the totem feast and of the very realistic notion at its foundation, the notion of community of blood as identity of substance—this the first ceremonial feast of mankind, a celebration in commemoration of the original sin of slaying the father, "with which so many things began, social organization, moral restrictions and religion." The genial manner in which Freud follows through the ages the "identity of the totem feast with the animal sacrifice, the theanthromorphic human sacrifice, and the Christian eucharist" and explores with the pitiless probe of the physician the world of disease as throwing light on the terrible but culturally productive phenomena of incest fear, feeling of guilt for murder, and need for expiation and redemption, lead to thoughts unconnected with religious origins and the deeply conservative nature of revolution, above all to thoughts about the author himself, as to his relation to others in the scientific world and as to his position in cultural development—thoughts which bring us back to Nietzsche's discussion of reaction as progress and of Germany's relation to the enlightenment.

Freud, as the explorer of the psychic depths, ranges himself in the series of writers of the nineteenth and twentieth centuries who, be they historians, philosophers, critics of culture or archeologists, oppose the rationalism, intellectualism, classicism, in a word the spiritual faiths of the eighteenth century and emphasize, cultivate, elevate scientifically, and defend the primacy of the lower, earth-derived psychic forms, "will," passion, the unconscious, or, as Nietzsche says, place "feeling" above "reason." Here the word "revolutionary" has a meaning paradoxical to its logical usage, for while elsewhere we are accustomed to associate the concept of revolution with the powers of light and the emancipation of reason, with the idea of the future, in this movement its message and appeal are the opposite, in the sense, namely, of a great backward movement into darkness, into the original, the pregnant preconscious, the mythical, the historical, the romantic womb of the mother. This is reaction, but now with revolutionary emphasis. In every sphere in which this movement is manifest—in history, where Arndt, Goerres, Grim opposed the idea of folk-origins to that of humanity as a whole; in tracing the creation of the world, where Carus celebrates a blind unconscious life-force at the cost of spirit, and Schopenhauer degrades intellect far below will, before calling on intellect for moral conversion and self-elevation; in archeology, where from Zoega, Creuzer, Muller, down to Bachofen, the defender of mother right, recognition and sympathy are turned, in purposeful opposition, from the aesthetics of reason belonging to classicism and to the chthonic darkness, to death and the demonic, in short to the pre-Olympian primitive earth-derived divinities—always the will is evident to force back our ways of looking at world and mankind to older and more powerful positions, as though this were a new word, the word of life; always, in revolutionary fashion, a sacred past and fruitful death is opposed to the idealism and optimism of the cult of the future and Apollonian light. By this movement the powerlessness of the spirit is contrasted with the strength of lower psychic forms, with the dynamism of passion, of the irrational, of the unconscious, and these are defended with militant devotion. This series continues to Klages, the rediscoverer of Bachofen and to Spengler's pessimism in history, on down to the present attitudes and forms of thought, which promise to afford opportunity of studying the strange psychological coexistence of unbelief and hatred of belief. A realization of the weakness of spirit and reason and of their inability to determine life did not give rise to pity and the wish to protect and extend succor; on the contrary this school proceeds as though there were danger that these elements might become too strong, as though they were too much of spirit on earth; the feebleness of the spirit became a further reason for despising it and hating it, as digging the grave of life.

It cannot be ignored that in all this there is that "enmity against enlightenment" which Nietzsche characterizes as especially German, and describes in his aphorism with a complacency of which consciousness of a danger past renders him capable. This danger consisted in the tendency to favor romantic antipolitical trends directed against social revolution and "future and novel aims" and "under the appearance of entire and definitive acquaintance with knowledge of placing knowledge below feeling and then of turning speculatively to a cult of "feeling in place of a cult of reason," thus furnishing scientific support to the "obscure ecstatic retrogressive forces." This danger was, Heaven be praised, past, Nietzsche believes. At length these forces had proved themselves adjuvants of that enlightenment against which they were first evoked; the first phase was merely a play of waves in comparison with the really great current which is sweeping mankind along. Is this in keeping with our experience and with our convictions today? Can we also regard as past that danger for humanity of which Nietzsche speaks? Yes, if we can rise to his exalted point of view and call to our aid a wider knowledge of the great currents of life—of the great world trends as a whole. Decidedly no, if we accept the impressions forced on us by the present day and hour.

The great nineteenth century, to belittle and disparage which is one of the most insipid habits of modern literature, was "romantic," and indeed not only in the first half. Through the decades of its second half, those really bourgeois, liberal, constructive, materialistic decades with their monistic trends, are scattered fragments and remains of romanticism. It is this circumstance which causes romanticism to be regarded as an integral part of bourgeois life, and it must be remembered also that this was the time of the triumph of the art of Richard Wagner, that art which filled his entire century, bore the stamp of all its qualities, and was overcharged with its instincts, that art which was worthy to serve as the symbolic adversary in the heroic combat waged by Nietzsche, the conqueror and dragon-slayer of that age, the initiator of all that is new and better which has survived from the anarchistic confusion and descended to us. An attempt is made today to preserve a fiction, an attempt which finds extraordinary favor, as if the cultural position of the moment is the same as at the beginning of the nineteenth century; as if in the enmity to spirit in the form it has assumed today, following Bachofen and the romanticists, that is in the form of the cult of natural dynamics, and of the instinctive, could be discerned a movement of genuine revolutionary character against intellectualism and the rationalistic belief in progress belonging to a past decade; as if now as then nationalism in romantic trappings, the racial doctrines stand in full revolutionary force, as new youthful and in keeping with the spirit of the times against a "retrogressive humanity," against a senile cosmopolitanism. But this attempt is untenable and must be characterized for what it is—a fiction full of the tendencies of the day—at the point where spirit ceases and politics begins. This fiction deserves further discussion. Where now could be found any optimistic beatitude of reason and insipid defense of humanity as a whole conquest of which we might witness by a revolutionary movement today? The world war, that mighty explosion of unreason, in which the positive-cosmopolitan forces of the time, the church as well as socialism, and the negative-cosmopolitan forces, imperialistic capital, succumbed to international-nationalism, would be a strange climax to such an epoch. Be it said again, the nineteenth was "romantic," not only in the first half. Throughout all its decades its scientific pride, which, apart from a certain number of narrow-minded monistically inclined, was hard and gloomy, was balanced for, indeed outweighed by its pessimism and its music colored with shadings of death and darkness, on account of which we love it and defend it against the detractions of the present. Through Nietzsche onward, whose combat against the opposition of Socrates to instinct endears him to our prophets, while they explain that because that, because of his psychological method of investigation, he was incapable of understanding mythology or find his way about in it—through Nietzsche onward the antirational tendencies of the nineteenth century continued down to the present, in extreme cases less through him than quite above and beyond him. Did it not actually happen that a bemused editor of "Mutterrecht" compared Nietzsche with Bachofen? This is an example of the absurd attempt to find equality between the very much greater and the undeniably great, but comparatively immeasurably smaller, which leads me to reflections on a presumptuous sort of comparison which is blind to proportion.

Aware of the complexity of spiritual things and of all life, we have imposed on ourselves the intellectual duty of using the words "progress" and "reaction" with the greatest caution. Through the occurrence of that historical phenomenon which Nietzsche designated "reaction as progress" arises the problem of that revolution of today, which, with its vague meanings, schisms and ambiguities so confuses the minds of the present—especially the mind of youth, and poses the question of how the old and dead can take on the guise of the most wonderfully new and youthful.

To guard against misunderstanding a clarification of the concept of revolution becomes extremely urgent. This concept is determined by relations to the past and to the future. The revolutionary principle is simply the will turned toward the future and toward that which Novalis has called "the essentially better world." There is involved a pressure of the will to destroy, by bringing their falseness to consciousness, certain things in life, which are wrongly regarded as perfect and harmonious, but which are really based on insecure and morally useless unconscious elements. Through phases of dissolution, which, from the angle of cultural unity, might be characterized as anarchic, phases in which there is no possibility of standing still or returning to the past, no "restauration," no lasting rebuilding, this pressure of the will, gaining by means of analysis or "psychology" realization of a more secure and freer unity of life, leads on to culture and to the complete self-consciousness of fully developed human beings. This alone is revolution. Only this will oriented toward the future and leading to the process of making conscious through analytical separation into elements deserves the name of revolutionary will. This is a fact which must be impressed on the youth of today. There is no preaching of a great past, no compulsion to return to the past, no fervor for the past, which does not make use of the name of the past for the obvious purpose of causing confusion. By this is not meant that the revolutionary will ignores the past. It must know a great deal about, wishes to be acquainted with it, and be at home in it. Only this obscure world must not exert a lure for its own sake, so that it is embraced because of a false appearance of religion and value, in short because of reactionary qualities. Only with full consciousness of freedom should the revolutionary will penetrate to those dungeons in the dark regions of the past where are hidden both horrors and treasures.

This definition of the reactionary and revolutionary worlds, as determined by their different orientation toward the past and toward the future accepted (I know no other), it would be a downright error in history to see in German romanticism a reactionary movement, a movement really opposed to spirit. This would be at least a one-sided judgment. Within romanticism, doubtless there is a historical school which might be designated "reactionary" in the sense of the word which we have adopted. In this school is found a passionate devotion to darkness, that Joseph Goerres complex with content of earth, race, nature, past, death—a world of feeling almost irresistibly enticing but which, in spite of Nietzsche, it would be difficult to regard as exclusively German in view of the fact that a French naturalist, Maurice Barrès, had attracted attention to all these chthonic experiences with great charm. Besides the historical attitude is, in its very nature a conservative attitude, an attitude oriented toward the past; it would be difficult to find a historian with revolutionary sympathies. The historian, with attention directed backwards by both inclination and calling, does not love history in so far as it is taking place, but only in so far as it has already taken place and he will nearly always hate contemporary changes because they seem to him without law, incoherent and venturesome, in a word "not historical"; his heart belongs to the coherent, tranquil historical past; the past possesses the harmony of the timeless, of the eternal and this soothes the nerves of the historian as the audacities of the present and future cannot. The past has become eternal, that is it is dead and death is the state of tranquility and exalted peace. How could a historian entertain revolutionary sympathies. But nevertheless, though it may seem to do violence to traditional prejudice, the German romantic is not essentially historically inclined. His orientation is toward the future, and this to such a degree that romanticism may be regarded as the most revolutionary and most radical of German cultural movements. Novalis' words describing the future as "the essentially better world" confirm this view, but in other isolated examples hundreds of traits, theories and enthusiastic paradoxes of this school conform, word for word, with our explanation given in the foregoing, of the real nature of revolution. Thoughts and poetical expressions of the romanticists are directed toward extension of consciousness and so keen was their sensibility to detect the irreligion and inhumanity of torpid conservatism that Wackenroder, the friar, a devotee of music, gave voice to his discontent with "the futile innocence, and oracle-like ambiguous obscurity of music." This sensitiveness to, and aversion from, ineffectiveness is romantic. In art it is romanticism to see not only nature but its opposite. In the duality of nature and spirit, to unite which in a third romanticism sees as the aim of humanity, art ranges itself always on the side of spirit, in full realization that art is meaning, consciousness, purpose, unity. This was Novalis' view when he characterized Wilhelm Meister as "wholly a work of art, a work of the understanding." The romanticists have never understood the concept of art other than as the contrary of that which is material, instinctive, unconscious. They ran the risk at times of going too far in this direction and of losing sight of the dual nature of art which, in reality, like Proserpina, belongs at the same time to the chthonic powers and to those of light. Art conceded that the flesh must be born of the flesh and it knew much of dreams and premonition, and of a poesy which exists before thought; the "better" poesy, however, the poesy more worthy of mankind's present level of development they called that which "accords with clear thought, associates itself with the aims of thought and follows in its service," and this spiritual inclination for what is modern, of today and of the future, in a word for what is revolutionary, that is romanticism.

Therefore, though there is a romantic history and a romanticism of history, it would be a gross misunderstanding to regard the romanticist and the historian as identical. Furthermore that the romanticist is revolutionary is most clearly revealed by his relation to health and disease. The romanticist saw in so-called health just that which in our definition of "revolutionary" we characterized as false perfection and false harmony in life. In his opinion health is there to be destroyed. In what way? Through consciousness. Consciousness, as the romanticist saw it, is disease in comparison with that preconscious condition of an earlier and more primitive harmony of life which conservatism strove to preserve or restore; in disease he saw the expression of a transition to a higher level. Novalis spoke the words of courage, "All diseases resemble sins in that they are transcendent." These words might have been spoken by one of those Russian religionists and moralists who arrived at the position of regarding sin as an indispensable means of salvation and who were seriously religious in so regarding it. To the romanticist, the Catholic middle ages seemed spiritual in comparison with innocent, preconscious antiquity. In the Reformation he saw a necessary schism in the Catholic cultural unity, that element of anarchy which Friedrich Schlegel called "the creative element of religion," an analytical transitional epoch where there is no restoration for comfort's sake, and which, such was the hope of religious humanity, would lead to a new Catholicism, returning on a higher level, and to a fuller conscious unity of life rendered secure by emancipation. This is the "Europe of Christendom" of Novalis—not a reactionary work, showing enmity to mind and thought, but a revolutionary work in the noblest sense of the word, a work expressing courageous and sincere faith in spirit.

Misconception as to the "revolutionary" character of German romanticism could arise only from one circumstance, namely, that no social revolutionary interests were manifested or were only obscurely reflected, and that, occupied with spiritual qualities, it seemed to neglect political aims. But political interest is latent in every mental attitude, and to what extent the "French revolution" is reflected in the spiritual radicalism of Novalis, for example, and what subtle spiritual understanding may pass from one people to another is most happily recognized and set forth by George Brandes in his work on the romantic school in Germany. It is hardly probable that Nietzsche did not recognize this and that he seriously regarded German romanticism as a reactionary movement with enmity toward spirit and opposed to a future—especially as, in wider sense, he must have regarded himself as a disciple of this school. He even avoided using the name romanticism when speaking of the enmity to enlightenment and those trends toward the past, toward origins and feeling which for a time served the "obscure, ecstatic and reactionary powers," but which at length showed themselves to be the very instruments to bring about that enlightenment against which they were at first evoked, the first movement being but the foam of the waves in the great current. While he says of these trends that they were directed against social revolution, against future aims, he admits by the title of his aphorism "Reaction as Progress," that at length they worked in revolutionary constructive direction for the general progress of mankind. He thus concedes that the revolutionary need not always manifest itself on earth as the cult of reason and as intellectual enlightenment. He further indicates that enlightenment in narrower historical sense may signify only one technical spiritual measure for renewing and promoting life, and by measures just the opposite the great and general enlightenment may be favored and is favored, through interchange of spiritual attitudes and convictions.

One must try to accept this broader and more tolerant and hopeful attitude in contemplating the antagonism to spirit today, that pervading and dominating anti-idealistic and anti-intellectualistic tendency to do away with the primacy of mind and reason, to despise mind and reason as the most fruitless of illusions, and to elevate in triumph, as the original authorities over life, the powers of night and darkness, the instinctive and irrational. To call this tendency which today predominates nearly everywhere, particularly in Germany, romantic, would be a grave critical error. Love of mind, passionate utopianism, orientation toward the future, conscious revolutionary trends are such decisive elements and characteristics of romanticism that this name could find no application here. Further just as romanticism, whose relation to the French revolution we called to mind cannot be understood as a pure reaction to the eighteenth century and its classicism, so the veneration for the irrational of today cannot be regarded as a simple movement against the nineteenth with its alleged lack of understanding of life. An epoch which in its second half was dominated by such geniuses as Schopenhauer, Wagner, Bismarck, and finally Nietzsche can scarcely be regarded as so asthenically rational and shallow, with life force so attenuated as to have provoked a return to myths and a cult of the underworld, as the only possible response. The relationship of our times to that epoch, occupied as it was with great problems and grave issues, is more complex than is the problem of the relationship of romanticism to the eighteenth century. The movement against enlightenment which we are witnessing today and which consists in enmity to thought and disparagement of reason is traversed and supplemented by other tendencies, recent faith in thought and inclination to universal rational humanitarianism, in short by a new idealism. This establishes a relationship between the twentieth and the eighteenth century and this new idealism can more suitably claim to stand in revolutionary opposition to the pessimism, nationalism and human antagonism of the nineteenth century than any deification of instinct. We are little inclined to recognize certain shameful failures of the nineteenth century as definitively physiognomic of this epoch. We deny that the philistinism of the monistic conceptions constitute the real foundations. Those of its elements which were properly corrected by modern irrationalism are known to us and for these corrections gratitude is due.

The narrowness of the professional views which prevailed in the nineteenth century, without original ideas, alien to the high and profound questions confronting humanity has now given rise to fruitful longing for community of vision and the wish for higher aims of knowledge; the rigidity of its concepts, its criticalness, its strictness and futile methods of research have been modified or balanced by new, immediate modes of approach, by ways in studying life which recognize the rights of feeling, intuition and spiritual factors; art has been recognized as the true means of understanding so that it has become possible to speak of an infusion of genius into science and of new possibilities of uniting its concepts with real wisdom. All these are accomplishments promising so much happiness to mankind that no intermingling of antagonism to reason or disparagement of mind could determine us to associate this movement with the concept of reaction. When such a book as "Urwelt, Saga and Menscheit" by Dacqué is today rejected by a "strict" and "correct" science with self-assumed authority, to the ruin of the author's academic career, there can be no doubt as to which side we take—that of the book which is truly revolutionary, or that of the "rejection," by which nothing is really accomplished. I do not insist on this single example. Nothing is more certain than that the "inestimable gain" of which Nietzsche speaks and ascribes to certain antirational, retrogressive ways of regarding the world and mankind may come to us through this new form of science. Its way of envisaging things does not follow the concepts and technique of rational enlightenment, but nevertheless it is oriented toward the future in revolutionary manner and therefore serves enlightenment in the broader sense.

If we can here speak of a danger, namely the one which Nietzsche saw connected with those movements that tend to place knowledge under feeling and thus serve the retrogressive powers, this danger lies in the new science only in so far as these powers, without asking permission of the new science, enter into a bold and deceitful bond with it. That is a danger only for the day and the hour: it is no danger when regarded from a broader point of view and in the long run, but there is danger of temporary confusion and of diverting for a time valuable forces from the purposes of life and of the future.

A modern abuse may be here mentioned; everyone will at once see that it arises from the oscillations in the concept of revolution. This uncertainty of concept has permitted reaction to usurp the place and take on the guise of revolution in such way that to the straightforward mind of youth, little accustomed to such artful tricks that which is oldest and longest dead assume the appearance of most enticing novelty in life. In so far as the phenomenon and the trick itself are concerned, they may be regarded as novelties. It is not likely that a similar situation ever occurred before, at least ever took place in the same manner, as though by arrangement and at command. There has always existed those bent on preserving the present or restoring the past, turning from progressive life with pious and reflective melancholy and defiantly oriented backward and in sympathy with death. These may possess even more mental ability than others who are going joyously forward. They do not deceive themselves but accept their doom, all the time feeling or believing that they are superior to life and finding ironical satisfaction in an attitude of proud and persistent hopelessness. This behavior and attitude is to to be found at the present time— characters and works whose self-conscious conservatism deserves admiration. I once described such a work in detail with appreciation, "Palestrina" by Hans Pfitzner which, as a work of talent, towers head and shoulder above the operas of his contemporaries and is a striking and most representative psychological expression of this attitude. It would be philistinism to moralize in the name of life and values over this earnest mode of existence, this endurance of life which consists in disregarding time and living the past in the present. There is no danger here. This is only melancholy and can be estimated only from an aesthetic point of view. Impatience and abhorrence first awakens when what is destructive to life tries to steal the features of what is young and hopeful and assumes the disguise of youth in order to accomplish dark purposes. This abhorrence grows when it begins to seem possible that the revolutionary hocus-pocus of such legerdemain might succeed in luring innocence to follow to the mountain of death.

I believe that the time has come to protest and to give a critical explanation of this proceeding. Again be it said that this ambition on the part of what is old is itself new. At other times the old wishes to remain old and contends with unmistakable directness against the new. Today the old wishes to become new; it decorates itself in the colors of life and in the twilight of uncertain day the deception is favored to a certain degree. Success of the artifice of establishing as revolution what the spirit hates becomes possible because there is a real revolution against spirit. Modern science, favoring just those views which, to use Nietzsche's words, strive to place knowledge under spirit and work in the service of the lowest in the soul, the unconscious, the instincts, sensuality, or whatever be the name given to the demonic-natural, appears before the throne of life to accuse and disparage spirit. How flattering these accusations and disparagements sound to evil ears whose enmity to spirit is of quite another and much more "genuine" sort! How easily the pessimism of modern views, those conceptions of mankind and the world which are based on the lower psychic elements degenerate to a defeatism of humanity, without faith in the heart in "future and novel aims" and despising such faith as a stupid and outmoded "enlightenment" of yesterday! In this the opponents of the higher forms may see no reason for disquiet and may wish to see none. But we are forced to see the encouraging effect which these new theories have on certain reactionary movements and have reason to speak of a "general danger and one by no means small."

In reality there is today no falsely pious conservatism, no antagonism to a future, no fear of a future, no hypocrisy, no fidelity to silly deceptions, no brutal regression, no yearning for inaction and restoration, no turning aside from the path of understanding and richer consciousness—I say there is nothing of this sort which does not borrow strength from the irrational sympathies of the newer modes of investigation of life, which does not seek to make contacts with them, does not draw support from them, does not seek to change places with them and, above all, does not aim to introduce them into politics and apply them in antirevolutionary sense and thus present crude reaction in the guise of revolution. This interchange is simple. If spirit is the powerless enemy of life, if nature, impulse, darkness, instinct are the all-in-all in the world pattern and if this discovery is the newest and latest, then all that is old is in verity new and modern and all that was before reason and below reason is the true and lifesaving; so that whoever speaks of ideas, of freedom, perhaps, or justice, does not understand the spirit of the times and belongs to "retrogressing humanity." Then every attempt to place reason above instinct—and indeed above evil instinct is a crime against life, for there are no evil instincts, if instinct itself possesses chthonic divinity. It is barren and retrogressive intellectualism to wish to make reality conform to the position of understanding to which spirit had attained, to seek to lessen the painful tension which exists between the two, today more dangerous than ever. In keeping with these views social benevolence, participation in the search for new and more wholesome forms is the Marxian materialism of yesterday; effort to meet human needs, sympathy with the universal, yearning for spiritual unity, political synthesis, community of peoples—all this is shallow internationalism, pacifistic nonsense, and against this outmoded idealogical rubbish the dynamic principle stands in youthful strength, nature freed from spirit, the soul of the tribe, hate, war.

This is the great reaction in the form of revolution, the great retrogression, adorned and bedizened as storming toward the future. How shall this vanity be understood? For it is vanity, a need for the approval of the spirit, the wish to feel in contact with it (if only in reverse sense), at no cost to feel forsaken of the gods. In last analysis this is a great compliment to the concept of revolution, a proof of the power of this concept as dominating all time. Even the decadent feels that without this concept it cannot attract attention, so it calls itself revolutionary—as in the year 18 feudal conservatism hoisted the flag of the people's party.

And youth—will it fall victim to this crude distortion of the deep meaning of modern knowledge of life? It would seem so, or at times it seems so. The depressing spectacle of young bodies carrying the weight of senile ideas is no longer strange to us; they carry them forward—the youths—marching in quick step, songs of joy on their lips, the arm raised in Roman salute, the beautiful buoyancy of youth withering in these ideas. This all becomes still more confusing when youth lends its biological charm to age and to the sins of age. But this charm is due to a visual deception, an illusion. The sins of age do not become good, because youth commits them; they do not become fitting or charming even though youth tragically dies for them. Errors and misunderstandings of this sort do not endure and are destined to be set in order and discarded. For the purpose of acceleration the process of restoring order, occupation with a new form of modern study of life might be recommended to youth, a form which more effectively than any other resists efforts to misuse it to the end of obscuring the concept of revolution. I refer to psychoanalysis and by this long and roundabout way I finally come back to my original purpose of doing justice, in the most exact words I can find, to the special position of the founder of psychoanalysis in modern cultural history.

Naturally one no longer today regards this theory as merely a therapeutic measure—recognized or still subject of controversy. Though certainly its founder did not dream of this in the beginning, it has gone far beyond the strictly medical sphere and has become a world movement embracing all fields of mind and science: research in literature, mythology, anthropology, paedagogy and so on. Through

81

their constructive and practical zeal its adepts have thrown about this psychiatric medical nucleus an aura of effectiveness, comparable to that which surrounded the personal work of Stefan George. With this, psychoanalysis, in origin a curative measure, has preserved its therapeutic character, its humane and ethical tendency to relieve man in sorrow and disease and rescue him from destruction in general. In psychoanalysis the force impelling to a study of the deep significance of disease is not in the last analysis interest in the depth and the disease for its own sake, and therefore is not enmity to spirit. On the contrary the interest is centered on the advantages to be gained from a broader understanding of life and from better acquaintance with what is dark and obscure in it; it never loses sight of its main purposes, redemption, cure and enlightenment in the most humanitarian sense of the word. This, in my opinion is what determines the special place of psychoanalysis within the scientific movement of the present day.

That psychoanalysis belongs to this movement is clear. It receives a part of its strength from the spirit of this movement—which it may be said does not wish to hear very much about spirit. With its emphasis on the demonic in nature, its passion for searching in the dark regions of the soul, it is as antirational as any brand of the new spirit which wages victorious war against the mechanistic and materialistic elements of the nineteenth century. It is revolutionary wholly in the sense of this spirit. "As psychoanalyst," Freud explained in a short autobiographical sketch, "I have more interest for the affective than for the intellectual processes, for the unconscious psychic life of the soul than for the conscious." A most straightforward sentence which says much. The most striking thing about it is the matter-of-course way in which "unconscious life of soul" is mentioned. One has no conception today of the affront offered to academic psychology and to philosophical usage by the conjunction of these two words in psychoanalysis. Freud himself speaks of it in his essay on "Resistances to Psychoanalysis" and very pertinently compares the "psychological insult" offered to human self-love by his theory to the "biological insult" offered by Darwin's theory of the descent of man and the earlier cosmological insult offered by the discoveries of Corpernicus. "Unconscious life of the soul"—this seemed an unpardonable innovation, a contradiction *in adjecto* or, in case it was not a contradiction, a revolt against all psychologies. Psychic and conscious had always been regarded as synonymous; conscious phenomena were regarded as the entire content of the soul. This "unconscious psychic" it was hoped was a foolish oversight. Hope deceived. Freud proved that the soul in itself is unconscious and that consciousness is only a quality which may be added to it, but which changes nothing in the soul, if it be absent. His theory of neurosis rests on this fact for it asserts and proves the phenomenon of repression, that is the exclusion of instincts from consciousness and their conversion into neurotic symptoms, a proof the wide significance of which in fields beyond medicine and for man's knowledge generally, was not suspected by him who established it, but is now grasped by the entire world. This proof was revolutionary wholly in the sense of the antirationalistic and anti-intellectualistic movement and in consonance with it from cultural-historical point of view. An equally revolutionary and striking effect was produced by what has been called Freud's "pansexualism," his theory of sexual desire and its neurotic satisfaction by substitutions, a theory which received this opprobrious vulgar designation, first because it was not realized that the character of this element was erotic rather than merely sexual, and secondly, because the fact was overlooked that, in the theory of repression, the censor, a psychic instance, constituted an element opposed to the libidinous.

Culturally and historically regarded, then Freud's discoveries in the unconscious, his explorations in the dark regions of the soul with the relentlessness of the physician and his deep psychology belong to the general retrogressive movement of our day, directed against the mechanistic and materialistic tendencies of the previous century. That which distinguishes these discoveries from the general modern movement is the decidedly more retrogressive character of those features which are to be regarded as revolutionary. The unpretentious expression which I have cited, testifying to Freud's greater interest in affective processes than in intellectual, suggests reflections on the psychology of interest, a psychology which is not without its own dangers and pitfalls. An interest easily enters into a relationship of solidarity and final sympathy with its object; it tends to affirm that which it starts out to investigate. An interest is itself interesting. Where it exists a question arises as to why it exists, for what purpose. For example the question whether a predominant interest for affect is itself of affective nature or of intellectual. In the first case it signifies an overestimation —something which should not enter into scientific interest. Freud's interest for affect, however, does not have the quality of overestimation of its object at the cost of intellectual clearness. He is antirational in insisting on insight into the really powerful ascendancy which instinct possesses over spirit, but this does not imply an awe-stricken and abject adoration of this ascendancy and rejection of spirit. In this theory there is no possibility of mistaking one thing for another. Nothing is more usual than to misidentify the character of a theory with the idea favored by the theory. For example a theory, the central concept of which is intuition, is an intuitionistic theory, but it need by no means originate from intuition, even when it may regard itself as so originating. It is far from Freud to offer nourishment to deceptions of this sort. Unmistakably, and with no opportunity for misidentification, his "interest" in instinct is not negation of spirit and a nature-conserving sycophancy in regard to instinct; he stands in the service of a revolutionary victory for reason and spirit, for a future and for enlightenment; this despised word has here its broader significance as independent of the "ephemeral play of waves." "We should like to emphasize again," Freud says, "that the human intellect is weak in comparison with the human instinctive life; but there is nevertheless something peculiar in this weakness; the voice of the intellect is soft, but it is never silent until it has made itself heard. At last after countless warnings it finds hearing." These are his words and it would be difficult to make any reactionary use of a theory in which the primacy of reason is expressly called "the psychological ideal."

Freud's theory is revolutionary not only in scientific sense and in relation to earlier epistemologies. It is unmistakably, unpervertably revolutionary in the sense which the word took on in application to the German romanticists. It is touching that Freud was obliged to pursue the difficult path to his discoveries wholly alone, without the consolation and encouragement which acquaintance with literature might have given to him and without that feeling of partisanship which would have arisen from personal contacts. Perhaps it was best so, however. The impact of his discoveries was doubtless increased by these unfavorable conditions. He was not acquainted with Nietzsche in whose works everywhere appear lightning-like gleams of insight anticipatory of Freud's later views. That he did not know Novalis directly would be still more regrettable, if it be granted that one could wish things had been made easier for him. In this connection where the concept of the unconscious plays so decisive a rôle psychologically, it may be in place to speak of unconscious transference of thought and of super-personal relations. The concept of influence is mysterious; what one calls influence is often so subtle, so mediate, of such mental or atmospheric nature that the word influence gives only a crass indication of the process. When I wrote my novel "The Magic Mountain," in which indeed psychoanalysis is introduced in humorous light, I was not acquainted with Freud's works except in a most general way; I had read none of them carefully. In this book in a chapter under the heading "Research" I make my young adventurer in the realm of thought, this searcher enamored of biology, speculate as to the origin of life and consider the assumption of a first creation and of the origin of the living from what is not living. I make him understand this process as one midway between two others, an earlier and a later, between the genesis of the material out of the immaterial and the arising of consciousness in living matter. "The first step toward evil, toward desire and death, was taken precisely then, when there took place that first increase in the density of the spiritual, that pathologically luxurious morbid growth, produced by the irritant of some unknown infiltration; this, in part pleasurable, in part a motion of self-defense, was the primeval stage of matter, the transition from the unsubstantial to substance. This was the Fall. The second creation, the birth of the organic out of the inorganic, was only another fatal stage in the progress of the corporeal toward consciousness, just as disease in the organism was an intoxication, a heightening and unlicensed accumulation of its physical state; and life, life was nothing but the next step on the reckless path of the spirit dishonored; nothing but the automatic blush of matter roused to sensation and become receptive for that which awakened it." These are the words of the novel. One acquainted with Freud would have recognized them as strikingly Freudian. Much later, in the remarkable essay "Beyond the Pleasure Principle," which gives a new direction to the Freudian theory by introducing the opposition of the life and death drives, I read the following: "At one time or another, by some operation of force which still completely baffles conjecture, the properties of life were awakened in lifeless matter. Perhaps the process was a prototype resembling that other one which later in a certain stratum of living matter gave rise to consciousness. The tension then aroused in the previously inanimate matter strove to attain an equilibrium; the first instinct was present, that to return to lifelessness."

I give these two citations as examples of sympathetic relations which can be only roughly indicated by such words as support or dependence. Of this sort are Freud's obvious and most remarkable relations to German romanticism, relations, the signs of which are more striking than are those of his unconscious derivation from Nietzsche, and which have hitherto received little critical attention. When Freud considers the first instinct to be that to return to the lifeless, when he attempts the further solution of the problem of instincts by subsuming self-preservation and preservation of the species under the concept of Eros, the force "working silently in opposition to the death instinct as the instinct of destruction" and understands instinct in general as "pressure to restore a situation which had once existed and had been destroyed by a factor from without"; when he speaks of the essentially conservative nature of instinct, and defines life as the action in concert and in opposition of Eros and the death drive, this all sounds like a paraphrase of the aphorism of Novalis, "The drive of our elements is toward deoxydization; life is forced oxydization." Novalis sees in an all-preserving Eros the principle which forced the organism to combination in unities of ever increasing size, and the erotic radicalism of his social psychology is a mystical voice announcing Freud's speculations and discoveries in natural science. It is Amor which binds us in groups —this is Novalis. And when Freud speaks of a narcissistic libido of the ego and derives it from fragments of the libido which join the soma-cells, one to another, this is so completely in accord with the biological dreams of romanticism that one may regard it as a thought which only by a mere chance did not find explicit expression in romanticism. That which has been falsely called Freud's "pansexualism," his libido theory, is in short only romanticism disrobed of mysticism, romanticism become scientific. It is this which makes him a depth-psychologist and explorer of the unconscious, permits him to understand life through disease and places him in the general antirationalistic scientific movement of today, and yet elevates him above it. But there is in his theory an element of spirituality which prevents it from being misused in any reactionary sense opposed to the spiritual; which limits its anti-intellectualism to the understanding, without allowing it to encroach on the will; and this spiritual element is just bound up with the idea which has awakened the strongest resistance, for the reason that Catholic prejudice has accustomed us to regard it as impure and sinful, that is with the idea of sex. Freud describes the death drive and the destructive drive as the striving of that which is living to return to the tensionless state of that which is not living. This drive back is traversed by sex as the "real life drive" and with sex are connected all the inner tendencies toward higher development, union and perfection. This lends to sexuality a character of revolutionary spirituality which Christendom was far from ascribing to it.

To what degree Freud's entire cultural psychology is founded on the fate of the instincts, is well known, and what rôle sublimation and repression play in it. An analysis of healthy persons renders clear that these "sexual components turned from their immediate aim and diverted to other aims, represent the most important contributions to the cultural performances of individuals and of the community." Under repression psychoanalysis understands the exclusion from consciousness of archaic and social impossible instincts by the censorship and their fettering in the unconscious; a process which is less culturally creative than culturally conditioning, for civilization is only possible under the pressure of certain prohibitions supported by definite moral and physical force. As a real and true internalizing of these prohibitions, which would mean emancipation, cannot be attained by the majority of mankind, even in the form of religious redemption, the result is a state of cultural hypocrisy to which society gives sanction through an antianalytic command of silence concerning cultural purposes. "Human culture," Freud says, "rests on two supports, one is the mastery of natural force, the other, the limitation of the instincts. Fettered slaves bear the throne of the victress. Among the instinctive components which have become so useful those belonging to the sexual instinct—in the narrower sense—stand forth by their strength and fury. And if these should be set free the throne would topple; the victress would be trampled under foot. Society knows this and imposes silence." Why this silence? Freud answers because society has an uneasy conscience in more than one direction: "First it has set up a high ideal of morality. Morality is limitation of instinct, which society demands of all its members without taking into account how difficult this obedience may be for the separate members. Society, too, is neither so rich nor so well organized that it can recompense the separate members in proportion to their renunciation. Therefore it is left to the individual to find in what way he can obtain compensation for the sacrifices demanded of him sufficient to preserve his spiritual equilibrium. In general he is forced to live psychologically above his level, while cultural demands make him feel the constant pressure of his unsatisfied instinctive demands." Here then, in Freud's opinion, is the source of "that hypocrisy which society supports and which is accompanied by so much uncertainty and the need to protect this lability by prohibition of criticism and discussion." To this resistance, he believes no continued duration can be assured. "No human institution can escape for long the effect of just critical insight."

A benevolent, sympathetic, and, above all, demonstrably true thesis—a thesis of real enlightenment and undeniably revolutionary timbre. That it is meant in revolutionary sense and as having reference to life in community with social, even social implications, is shown with sufficient clearness in more than one place in Freud's writings. This socialism and revolutionism is not the politics of catastrophe, however; it is the opposite. Freud wishes to avoid catastrophe and ward it off in a spiritual way; he has cure in mind and thinks as a physician. In reality analysis is the physician's form of revolution.

We are acquainted with the theory of the neuroses of this physician: for him the neurotic symptom is a result, not a necessary result, but the pathological result, of repression. If one looks more closely, it becomes clear that he sees the entire cultural condition of today in the symptoms and picture of the repression neuroses. But these cultural conditions are more than replicas and resemblances; they are literally and actually the same thing, the resemblance, however exceeding the literal identity. Freud sees in our culture a thoroughly labile pseudo-perfection and pseudo-harmony, resembling (and more than resembling) the condition of a neurotic without will to recovery who reconciles himself to his symptoms, a form of life "which has neither the prospect of enduring nor deserves to endure." Here begins that surprising relationship of his theory with the philosophy of consciousness of romanticism, as presented by Novalis, which is so significant from cultural historical point of view. His theory has the same conscientious sensibility as romanticism to inhumanity and apathetic conservatism, to that cant and hypocrisy which strives to preserve early morally unworthy social forms resting insecurely on unconscious foundations. This theory enjoins the necessity of separating unstable forms into their factors and of analyzing them with critical insight. It does not, like romanticism, believe in a transcendent chaos. The remedy Freud prescribes is to bring to consciousness and analyze the conditions, a proceeding in which there is no standing still, no going backward, no restoration of the "good old past." The goal he points to is a new order of life, deserved and rendered secure by consciousness, and resting on emancipation and sincerity. This theory might, in view of its method and goal, be called enlightenment, but the concept of enlightenment has undergone so many vicissitudes, that it might even be taken as implying the reproach of serene stupidity. The theory may be called antirational as the interest of its researches centers on the obscure, dreams, instincts, states below consciousness. At its very origin is the concept of the unconscious, but Freud is very far from placing this in the service of the "obscure, ecstatic reactionary powers." This theory is that phenomenal form of modern irrationalism which is unambiguously opposed to every reactionary misuse. We wish to express our conviction that it is one of the most important stones which have been brought for the foundation of the future and for the construction of a dwelling for free and wise mankind. Its message is the same as that of the benevolent utterance of Marcus Aurelius in reference to the Christian's "Let Madness vanish! Then the 'Woe is me!' vanishes, and with the 'Woe is me!' the woe itself."

Portrait of Freud
(1932)

STEFAN ZWEIG

Stefan Zweig (1881–1942) was a poet, novelist, short story writer, and biographer. He and his brother Arnold knew Freud well when he was still a young poet around 1908. Both remained in close touch with Freud for the rest of his life. The following selection has been taken from Zweig's Mental Healers, *translated by Eden and Cedar Paul (New York, Viking Press, 1932). The editor selected the excerpts and the title of this selection.*

For nearly half a century Sigmund Freud has lived a retired life behind the sombre portal of quarters rented in Vienna. This personal existence of his has been so modest, so inconspicuous, that he scarcely seems to have existed at all. Seventy years in the one town and more than forty of them in the same house, carrying on his activities in the same rooms, sitting in the same chair to read or at the same desk to write. The father of six children, a man of few wants, whose only passions would appear to have been those of his occupation and calling. Of this time, allotted at once thriftily and lavishly to his work, not an hour has ever been squandered upon posing before the public, upon offices and dignities. Never has the creative individual thrust himself into the limelight in front of the created achievement. The rhythms of his daily life have been ceaselessly subordinated to the unceasing and equable rhythm of his labours. During every week for thousands of weeks he has pursued the same round of circumscribed activities, each day exactly like another. When still attached to the university, he lectured there once a week; on Wednesday evening there was always a gathering of disciples, an intellectual symposium after the Socratic model; on Saturday afternoon, in earlier years, a card-party. Apart from these little interruptions, from morning till evening (or, rather, till long past midnight) every minute was devoted to analyses, the treatment of patients, study, and original writing. There was never a blank page in the inexorable timetable, never a vacant hour during the interminable succession of fifty years.

To this indefatigable brain, persistent directed thought is as natural as uninterrupted pulsing is to the heart. For Freud, work is not something to which he must constrain himself, but an agreeable, a functional, a physiological necessity. All the same, his unresting alertness is one of the most amazing among the manifestations of his mentality, one in which normality has become phenomenal. For forty years he has been accustomed to undertake eight, nine, ten, eleven analyses every day, this meaning that for a corresponding number of hours his attention has been concentrated upon another's mental life, upon listening to and weighing that other's every word, while at the same time his memory has been engaged in comparing the data of this particular sitting with those of all previous ones. Thus he was actively entering into an alien personality while simultaneously contemplating it from without with the dispassionate gaze of the psychological diagnostician. At the close of the hour he had abruptly to switch his interest into a new circle, that of the mind and the ailments of the new patient, and must do this again and again, eight or ten times a day—keeping distinct in his own mental storehouse, without notes or other technical aids, the details relating to hundreds upon hundreds of such analyses in their finest ramifications. Obviously all this put an exceptional strain upon the nervous energies, and those of most people would begin to flag after two or three hours of it. But Freud is one of those rare beings endowed with superabundant vitality to whom mental fatigue seems unknown. After nine or ten hours of analysis, he could sit down at his desk and proceed to elaborate the results, could engage upon the literary labours which have brought him worldwide fame. For decade after decade he has toiled unremittingly in ways that have influenced many millions of his fellows, and has done all without a secretary or other assistants. He has written every letter with his own hand, completed every investigation unaided, shaping the upshot in splendid isolation. It is the magnificent regularity of his creative production amid an existence outwardly so trivial which betrays the man's fundamental daimonism. Freud's uniqueness, his incomparability, shines forth in his creative achievement.

Such an instrument of precision, capable of unfailing and sustained mental labour for so long a series of years, is only conceivable if its material groundwork be of premier quality. As with Handel, Rubens, Dickens, and Balzac—likewise men whose creative work flowed forth in a steady stream—Freud's intellectual profusion has been the expression of a thoroughly healthy constitution. Until he was approaching

91

seventy, this great physician was never seriously ill; this shrewd observer of nervous workings was entirely free from nervous disorder; this clear-sighted student of mental abnormalities, this much-vilified pansexualist, remained almost uncannily hale and single-hearted in the manifestations of his personal life. As far as his own experience is concerned, he has known nothing of the everyday lesser maladies which, for most of us, again and again interfere with the smooth course of thought and action, and he has hardly ever suffered from headache or fatigue. Throughout the greater part of his working life, he found no occasion to consult a colleague, and was never compelled by illness to break an appointment. Not until he was nearing the patriarchal span did an ailment come to mar a health record worthy of Polycrates. There were then fears that the trouble was exceedingly grave but an operation was successful, and so soon as the wound had healed Freud resumed his labours with the old grit, the familiar zest. For him, indeed, health is synonymous with breathing, to be awake means the same thing as to work, creation is identical with life. Moreover, just as he tenses every nerve upon his tasks in his working hours, so does his iron frame enjoy the benefit of perfect relaxation during sleep. A brief period of repose suffices him. When he sleeps he sleeps more soundly, when he wakes he wakes more thoroughly, than most of us.

His bodily aspect conforms to his mental characteristics. Here, too, all the details are harmoniously proportioned. He is neither too tall nor too short, neither too stout nor too thin. His lineaments are, indeed, so average that his face has long been the despair of caricaturists. In that well-shaped oval they can find no feature that lends itself to the pencil's specious exaggeration. Not even when you compare photographs taken at long intervals, the portraits of the youth with those of the man of middle age, can you detect an outstanding trait, or one of characterological importance. At thirty, at forty, at fifty, he is the same: a goodlooking man, virile, one whose aspect is regular to a fault. His dark and searching eyes no doubt suggest the thinker, but with the best will in the world we cannot discern in these fading sun-pictures anything beyond the bearded, strong face of a typical physician—such a man as Lenbach or Makart loved to paint—somewhat unfathomable, gentle, perhaps overserious, and nowise bearing witness to powers that have exerted so far-reaching an influence. We are inclined at this stage to fancy that we must abandon any attempt to find characterological lights in a countenance so unrevealing in its harmony.

But when we come to the more recent likenesses, they suddenly

begin to speak. With most men age tends to blur the individual dif-
ferentiae and to accentuate the generic type of undistinguished senility, but in Freud's case it is advancing years and illness that seem to
have chiselled a physiognomy out of that which previously had been
nothing more than a face. Now that his hair has grizzled, now that his
beard has thinned until it no longer covers the firm chin completely
nor conceals so effectually the sharp outlines of the lips, now that the
bony structure of the visage has become more conspicuous, there has
been revealed something harsh and unconditionally militant—the expression of an indomitable, almost mordant will. In the earlier portraits the glance was simply contemplative, but now it is piercing and
gloomy; the brow is deeply furrowed, as if with bitterness and suspicion. The lips are narrowed, tensed, as though he were uttering an emphatic "No," or coldly saying "That is false." For the first time we are
aware that a mightly impetus, the severity of a formidable nature, are
manifest in the face, and we murmur to ourselves: "No, this is not a
good, grey old man, mellowed by the years, but an inexorable scruti-
neer, a rigorous examiner, who will neither try to deceive nor allow
himself to be deceived." We should be afraid of telling a lie to such a
man, feeling him to be one whose insight would enable him to detect
every prevarication and to flash a revealing glare that frightens rather
than one that liberates and charms, but nonetheless transfigured by
the intensity of the profound thinker; the face, not of a merely superficial observer, but of one who sees pitilessly into the depths.

This dash of Old Testament grimness, this unconciliatory spirit
that speaks so plainly in the fierce eyes of the veteran, must not be ignored, must not be omitted from the picture under stress of a desire to
make it pleasing. Had Freud lacked the ruthlessness and decisiveness
that are among his most salient characteristics, his achievement would
also have been devoid of its best and most decisive features. If Nietzsche philosophized with a hammer, Freud has philosophized with a
scalpel; and neither of these implements would be of any value in
hands too gentle, too considerate, to make good use of them. Cour-
teousness, sympathy, and considerateness would have been wholly incompatible with the revolutionary thought-trend of Freud's creative
temperament, his essential mission being to make extremes manifest,
not to reconcile them. His combativeness and forthrightness have always made him want a for or an against, a plain yes or a plain no,
rather than a betwixt and between, or an admission that there is perhaps about as much to be said on one side as on the other. He has ever

been a man unwilling to make reservations and provisos, to come to terms with or forgive an adversary. Like Jehovah, he is less likely to pardon a lukewarm supporter or a tepid doubter than an outspoken renegade. Fair probabilities seem worthless to him; he wants absolute, hundred-per-cent truth. Vagueness of any kind, whether it be in personal relationships or takes the form of that sublime obscurity of thought and feeling which passes by the name of illusion, arouses in him an impetuous desire to analyse, delimit, and arrange, for to him the first of all requirements are clarity and sharpness of definition. This does not mean that he has to exert himself, to direct his will in an effort to secure them. The urge to analyse, the renouncement of chiaroscuro in favour of a cruelly bright illumination—these are with him instinctive and inborn trends which nothing can restrain. Unless Freud understands a thing promptly and unconditionally, it remains unacceptable to him; and no one can explain anything to him unless, of his own self, he can grasp it without reserve. He is thus unfailingly autocratic and intransigent; and it is above all when he is at war, fighting alone against a multitude, that there develops the unqualified pugnacity of a nature ready to face overwhelming odds.

But if he is inexorable to others, Freud is no less harsh and mistrustful in his dealings with himself. Trained to follow a man's most skilfully masked inveracities into the darkest recesses of the unconscious, to delve beneath what had seemed the lowest stratum and lay bare a lower yet, to extract from behind an open confession another confession more open still, to find at the core of every truth a truth having even greater validity—he analyses himself as keenly as he analyses others, ever awake to the necessity for analytical self-control. That is why I think that those who are fond of describing Freud as a "bold thinker" have chosen an inapt term. Freud's ideas are not improvisations at all, and they smack very little of intuition. Being neither easy-going nor hasty in the matter of formulation, he often waits for years before he proclaims as an opinion what has in the interim been only a supposition. To a constructive genius of his calibre, sudden leaps of thought or premature generalizations are out of the question. Unblinded by enthusiasm, advancing warily step by step, Freud is the first to see where the footing is treacherous. Again and again we encounter in his writings such cautionary phrases as "This should be regarded as nothing more than a hypothesis" or "I know that in this matter I have little fresh light to shed." Where Freud shows his mettle is at a later stage, when he has convinced himself. A pitiless disillusionist, he has first to fight down his own suspicion that he may be going to do no more than add a new wish-fantasy to the mass of illusions with which the world is plagued. Only then will he utter an opinion. But once he has recognized an idea and publicly acknowledged it, it becomes part of his flesh and blood, grows into the framework of his existence, and no Shylock may cut a fibre of it out of his living body. Certainty comes slowly to Freud; but when he has acquired it, nothing can rob him of it.

The tenacity with which he clings to his own opinions has made Freud's opponents accuse him of dogmatism, and even some of those who fight on his side have voiced the charge with varying emphasis. But Freud's absoluteness is a necessary part of his character; it is not the outcome of mulishness, but a natural expression of the peculiar way in which he looks at things. What he sees creatively, he sees as if no one had ever contemplated it before. When he thinks, he forgets everything that previous thinkers have thought about the matter. He sees things as he must see them, solves his problems after the manner prescribed for him by his own nature: wherever he opens the sibylline book of the human mind, for him the page is a new one; and before his critical thought has begun to deal with its contents, his seer's vision has initiated its creative work. Now one who holds an opinion can be convinced of error, whereas the seer's creative vision is infallible—for the seer. His vision lies outside the range of influence, and the creative is independent of his will. What do we mean when we speak of the "creative," if not this: the contemplation of abysmally old and inalterable things as if the human eye had never before shone on them; the utterance of that which has been said a thousand times already, but with so virgin a freshness that we seem to hear it for the first time. Since it cannot be learned, this magic of the intuitive vision of the seer cannot be taught, so that the persistence with which a genius abides by his first and unique flash of insight is not a mark of obstinacy. He cannot do otherwise.

Freud, therefore, has never tried to persuade his readers or his hearers to accept his views, has never tried to talk them over or to convince them. He has simply laid his opinions before them. His perfect sincerity forbids him to couch even the most vital of his ideas in a metaphorical form which might give them a wider appeal, or to make certain morsels that are hard and bitter more palatable to sensitive persons by using conciliatory forms of expression. Compared with the intoxicating prose of Nietzsche, full of artistry, scintillating with rhetorical fireworks, Freud's writing seems jejune, cold, and colourless. It does not stir the reader; it does not woo him; it has no background of poesy, nor any musical rhythm. He himself tells us that he has no taste for music; and he obviously shares the opinion of Plato, who said that music tends to interfere with the purity of thought. It is purity or clarity of thought which is Freud's sole aim. He might be said to model himself on Stendhal's dictum: "Pour être bon philosophe, il faut être sec, clair, sans illusion." In all human manifestations, linguistic expression included, clarity is for him the first thing, the last, and the best. Artistry he considers of no moment as compared with lucidity and perspicacity, and it is to a diamantine sharpness of style that he owes the incomparable plastic energy of what he writes. Unadorned, severely to the point in accordance with the best Latin models, his prose is free from all flourishes, saying what has to be said boldly and pithily. Naturally, then, he is sparing of images; but when he has occasion for a simile it will crack like a well-handled whip and drive the meaning home. Such metaphors as he does use have the sparkle of gems, shining forth from a sober setting, and they cannot be forgotten. But never in his philosophical argumentation does he leave the straight path. Circumlocution is as distasteful to him as errancy of thought, and within all the pages of his numerous books you will not find a single sentence which could seem ambiguous even to the most uninstructed of readers. The result is a style that looks homely, but is really luminous to an extreme, and no other could so well serve his passion for a quasi-geometrical exactitude.

Every genius, says Nietzsche, wears a mask. Freud has chosen one of the most opaque, the mask of inconspicuousness. When we look at him we see at first a commonplace, almost philistine figure, that of Mr. Everyman; but behind the mask an untiring creative genius, a daimon, is at work. The very achievement of this famulus, though audacious beyond compare, and world-shaking in its effects, has quite a modest aspect, and masquerades as the commonplace production of any university dryasdust. His language tricks us by it sobriety into overlooking its crystalline perfection as an instrument most aptly suited to the purposes of one whose life-work has been to destroy in order to rebuild. This genius is one who does not wish to shine as such, but to appear a moderate of the moderates. So the moderate is what we see to begin with, until immoderacy looms up from the depths. Always there is more in Freud than he allows to transpire, and yet in every form of self-expression he is unambiguously the same. For whenever in a human being the law of a higher unity holds creative sway, that unity reveals itself plainly and victoriously in every element of his nature: in his speech, his work, his looks, and his life.

A Visit to Freud

(8 May 1934)

GIOVANNI PAPINI

Giovanni Papini (1881–1956) was an Italian writer of poetry, fiction and criticism, as well as of pamphlets covering a wide range from politics to religion. He is not considered a major Italian writer and many find him mediocre and shallow. The present selection appeared first in Colosseum (1934), a British quarterly, in an article entitled "Two Visits" (the other was to H. G. Wells). This paper is virtually unknown in psychoanalytic literature. Jones does not mention it and its veracity has been questioned; nevertheless, it is an interesting glimpse into Freud's own feelings about friends, pupils, and colleagues.

Two months ago I bought a lovely marble statue, Greek, of the Hellenistic period; according to the archeologists, it represented Narcissus. Knowing that Freud had just finished his seventy-seventh year—he was born 6 May 1856—I sent him the statue as a present with a letter written in homage to the "discoverer of Narcissism."

This well chosen offering brought me an invitation from the patriarch of psychoanalysis. I have just come back from his house and want to jot down the essential parts of our conversation.

He struck me as being rather tired out and melancholy. Birthday parties, he told me, are too much like commemorations and recall the idea of death.

The shape of his mouth made a deep impression of me: a full, sensual mouth, with a touch of the satyr, which visibly explains the theory of the *libido*. He was glad to see me, however, and thanked me warmly for the Narcissus.

"Your visit is a great consolation. You're neither a patient, nor colleague, nor a disciple, nor a relative! I live all year long surrounded by either hysterical or obsessed people who confide their turpitudes to me—nearly always the same ones; by doctors who despise me if they're not jealous of me, and by disciples who can be classed either as chronic parrots or ambitious schismatics. But at last I can speak freely to you. I taught others the virtue of confession and have never been able to lay bare my own soul. I wrote a short biography, but more for purposes of propaganda than anything else, and if ever I did make a fragmentary confession, it was in *Traumdeutung*—'the Divining of Dreams.' Nobody knows or has ever guessed the real secret of my work. Do you know anything about psychoanalysis?"

I answered that I had read several of his books in English translation, and that I had stayed over in Vienna merely to see him.

"Everybody thinks," he went on, "that I stand by the scientific character of my work and that my principal scope lies in curing mental maladies. This is a terrible error that has prevailed for years and that I have been unable to set right. I am a scientist by necessity, and not by vocation. I am really by nature an artist. Ever since childhood, my secret hero has been Goethe. I would have liked to have become a poet, and my whole life long I've wanted to write novels. All my gifts —my school teachers, too, admitted it—were of a kind to lead me towards literature. But when you realize under what conditions Austrian literature in the last quarter of the nineteenth century had to exist, you will understand my dilemma. My family was poor, and poetry, on the testimony of the most celebrated contemporaries, brought in little or was remunerative too late. Moreover I was a Jew which obviously put me in a condition of inferiority under an anti-semite monarchy. Heine's exile and wretched end discouraged me. Always under Goethe's influence, I chose Natural Science. My temperament, however, remained romantic. In 1884, in my haste to join my fiancée a day or two earlier—she was a long way from Vienna—I botched a work on the coca and had others steal from me the honor and profit of the discovery of cocaine as an anaesthetic.

"In 1885 and 1886 I lived in Paris and in 1889 I spent some time at Nancy. This stay in France had a decisive influence over me. It was not so much what I learned from Charcot, Bernheim, but the fact that the French literary life in those days was rich, prosperous and active. As a good romantic I passed hours on the towers of Notre Dame, but in the evenings I frequented the cafés of the Latin quarter and read the books most discussed in those years. The literary struggle was at its height. Symbolism raised its banner against Naturalism. Mallarmé and Verlaine were gaining influence over the young generation at the expense of Flaubert and Zola. Soon after my arrival Huysman's *A Rebours* appeared—and the disciple of Zola went over to the Decadents. And I was in France when Verlaine's *Jadis et Naguère* was published as well as the collected poems of Mallarmé and the *Illuminations* of

99

Rimbaud. I don't provide you with this information to give a fine impression of my culture, but because these three literary schools—Romanticism, but recently deceased; Naturalism, which was already threatened; and Symbolism, still on the up-grade—were the inspiration of all my later work.

"A man of letters by instinct, though a doctor by necessity, I conceived the idea of changing over a branch of medicine—psychiatry—into literature. Though I have the appearance of a scientist I was and am a poet and novelist. Psychoanalysis is no more than the interpretation of a literary vocation in terms of psychology and pathology.

"As was natural the first impulse which led to the discovery of my method came to me from my beloved Goethe. As you must know, he wrote *Werther* to free himself from the morbid oppression of a sorrow: for him literature meant a *catharsis*. And in what consists my method of curing hysteria save in making the patient tell *everything* to free him from the obsession? I did no more than force my patients to act like Goethe. Confession is liberation and that is cure. The Catholics knew it for centuries, but Victor Hugo had taught me that the poet too is a priest; and thus I boldly substituted myself for the confessor. The first step was taken.

"I very soon realized that the confessions of my patients formed a precious selection of 'human documents.' That is to say I carried out the very same plan as Zola. He turned these documents into novels—I was constrained to keep them to myself. Then my attention was attracted to the similarity between dreams and works of art and the importance of the language of symbols by the poetry of the Decadents. Psychoanalysis was born—not as they say through the suggestions of Breuer or the sharp sayings of Nietzsche or Schopenhauer, but as a result of the scientific transposition of the literary schools I like best.

"I will explain myself more clearly. Romanticism took up once more the traditions of medieval poetry, proclaimed the primacy of passion and reduced every passion to love; and this suggested to me the concept of sexuality as center of human life. Under the influence of the naturalistic Romantics, of course, I gave a less sentimental and mystical interpretation to love, but the principle remained the same.

"Naturalism, and especially Zola, had made me used to the most repugnant but common and well-known sides of human life: sensuality and lust under the hypocrisy of fine manners, in fact, the bestial man. And my discovery of the shameful secrets of the unconscious are nothing more than one more proof of Zola's unprejudiced act of accusation.

"Symbolism, therefore, taught me two things. The value of dreams as assimilated by poetry and the place occupied by symbols and allusions in art—that is to say in the dream made manifest. It was then that I undertook my great book on the interpretation of dreams, which uncover the subconscious—that very subconscious which is the fount of inspiration. I learned from the symbolists that every poet must create his own language, and so I have created the symbolical vocabulary of dreams, the idiom of shame.

"To complete the picture of my literary source I will add that the study of the classics—in which I was first in my class—suggested to me the myths of Oedipus and Narcissus. I learnt with Plato that genius, which is a gushing forth of the unconscious, is the foundation of spiritual life and finally, with Artemedorus, that every nocturnal fantasy has some hidden significance.

"That my culture is essentially literary is proved abundantly by my repeated quotations from Goethe, Grillparzer, Heine and other poets. My soul, by its constitution, leans towards the essay, the paradox, the dramatic, and has nothing of the pedantic technical stiffness which belongs to the true man of science. And of this there lies an irrefutable proof: which is that in all countries into which psychoanalysis has penetrated it has been better understood and applied by writers and artists than by doctors. My books, in fact, more resemble works of imagination than treatises on pathology. My studies on Daily Life and on Wit are really and truly literature and in "Totems and Taboos" I have tried my hand at the historical novel. My oldest and strongest desire would be to write real novels, and I possess a mine of first-hand materials which would make the fortune of a hundred novelists. But I am afraid now it would be too late.

"Nevertheless, I have been able to win my destiny in an indirect way, and have attained my dream: to remain a man of letters, though still in appearance a doctor. In all great men of science there is a leaven of fantasy, but no one proposes like me to translate the inspirations offered by the currents of modern literature into scientific theories. In psychoanalysis you may find fused together, though changed into scientific jargon, the three greatest literary schools of the nineteenth century: Heine, Zola and Mallarmé are united in me under the patronage of my old master, Goethe. Nobody has noticed this open secret and I would have revealed it to no one if you had not had the splendid idea of presenting me with a statue of Narcissus."

At this point the conversation changed and we spoke of America, Keyserling and the habits of the ladies of Vienna. But the only things worth noting are what I have already written. As he ushered me out Freud asked me to be silent about his confession:

"Luckily you are not a writer or a journalist, and I am sure you will not spread my secret."

I reassured him—and sincerely; these notes are not destined for the Press.

Appointment in Vienna

(1936)

ODETTE PANNETIER

Odette Pannetier was a French journalist who went to Vienna to get an appointment with Freud under false pretenses. What is true or false in this account is difficult to evaluate. It seems to me that she took advantage of Freud's kindness in receiving her. This essay was first published in Candide, *a Paris conservative weekly, and was translated and published in* The Living Age *(October 1936). The name of the translator could not be traced.*

I shall be frank. When I fly 1,214 kilometers in a straight line to get to Vienna, it is not merely to be able to say that the Viennese women have thick-set figures, or that the *Heurigen* are full of mosquitoes and serve suspicious looking *petits vins:* it is to see Freud.

As a matter of fact, I had wanted to meet the illustrious sage for a long time. It seemed an impossible thing; Freud had given categorical orders: he did not want to receive any journalists, any patients, any visitors. Under these circumstances, to see him, to speak to him, became especially tempting. It was no longer a mere interview, it was sport. And what sport! To meet at last the "founder" of psychoanalysis, of introversion, of the explanation of insanity through dreams! To find out at last why it is that when one dreams of dead eiderducks it means that one has a libidinous desire for one's maternal grandmother —what joy! what intoxication!

Here, alas, I must make a confession. I ask your pardon, dear Doctor Logre, dear great psychiatrist! The lady whom you interviewed in your Paris office two weeks ago was *not* called Madame Dubois. She was *not* the victim of an *idée fixe.* She had never dreamed of committing suicide, and not for anything in the world would she have broken one of your knick-knacks. You have cured the only illness from which she was suffering, and that was a desire for the precious letter you gave her urging the illustrious Professor Freud to make an exception in the case of poor Madame Dubois and see her. Soon thereafter you could have seen from your window that same Madame Dubois, in the middle of the Avénue Montaigne, breaking into an Indian war dance which, at any other time, would have landed her in the prison hospital in ten minutes. Luckily at that moment the police were busy lynching French citizens near the Étoile. For that reason Madame Dubois could board her airplane for Vienna unhindered.

In Vienna a dear friend of mine telephoned to Freud's daughter, who helps her father in his work. The results were disappointing. The Professor stubbornly refused to receive any visitors.

"What shall I do with Madame Dubois?" the dear friend moaned. "She is terribly overwrought. She will break everything in my house if she doesn't see Professor Freud."

"I have nothing more to say to you. Get in touch with Doctor Paul Ferden, who is my father's virtual successor."

The "virtual successor" confirmed Miss Freud's words by phone. "By the way," he added, "has Madame Dubois got any money?"

"Has she money!" exclaimed my friend in a flash of inspiration. "She is disgustingly rich!"

"Well then, send her to see me tomorrow morning at eleven o'clock. At a pinch I could even see her this evening; but I usually see the lunatics in the morning."

The "virtual successor" lived in a market section of Vienna, in an apartment where the shutters were all closed and an enormous bunch of lilies emitted a warm, heavy perfume conducive to headaches and nervous attacks. The "virtual successor" had a jovial manner, a patriarchal beard combed hair by hair, and a rabbinical nose such as one sees only in anti-Semitic caricatures. Just in case, I had adopted a frightened air, an awkward manner and a fixed stare. An interne friend had gladly furnished me with a wealth of details about my own particular kind of madness: fear of dogs, and, if necessary, other characteristic phobias.

"I want to see Freud," I said dully. "I want to see Freud because he is the only one who can stop the dogs from biting me."

"Really, Madame Dubois?" asked Doctor Ferden, who speaks French like a member of the Académie Française.

"Yes, I don't know why, but all the dogs bite me. They have bitten me—oh, I don't know—more than two hundred times."

"Just imagine! Are you sure, Madame Dubois, that you really have been bitten over two hundred times?"

"Well, look for yourself. This is where I was bitten only the day before yesterday."

The black-and-blue mark received from an involuntary contact between my knee and a table leg was obviously not of canine origin. Nevertheless the Doctor preserved his impassive air, his assumed naïveté.

"I can well understand that under these conditions you are afraid of dogs. But there aren't any here, you see. And besides, in Vienna all the dogs are muzzled. You have no reason to be afraid."

"Muzzled!" I cried bitterly. "I know just what they do. They take their muzzles off and then they rush at me. They grab me with their paws and then they bite me."

I abandoned my crushed air and became suddenly violent. "But I am not crazy, you know; I am not crazy! I want to see Freud because he is the only man who can cure me; but I am not crazy!"

"Nobody says you are," said the doctor, becoming somewhat anxious. "Now when you say 'I want to see Freud,' you are being reasonable; but when you say 'He is the only one who can cure me,' you are *not* being reasonable, because, although he is a great scientist, there are others."

He twisted on his chair, smiled, and seemed about to chuck me under the chin in an effort to pacify me and persuade me to let him cure me.

I jerked my head and looked straight in front of me as if it were too tiring to look anywhere else. I was as single purposed as the warrior of Marathon.

"And of what else are you afraid?" asked the virtual successor.

"I am afraid of dying. One day I was out walking in my bathrobe when I looked into a mirror and saw a death's head! I have a horror of food, particularly meat. Pah! How disgusting! It's dirty; it's unwholesome. But then everything is dirty, everything! One must keep on washing oneself, and that is so tiring."

"Aha!" said the doctor, jubilantly. "So you wash often?"

"About a hundred times a day. The trouble is that the minute one is through, one must begin all over again, because one is always dirty: it's so tiring."

I was on the point of repeating "I want to see Freud" when this good, this excellent, this adorable Doctor Ferden interrupted me.

"I think that you might interest Professor Freud very much. Only

105

there are conditions which perhaps will seem too . . . how would you say it in French? excessive, extravagant, perhaps? I can take you to see Doctor Freud tomorrow, but he charges three hundred schillings for a consultation, which is nine hundred francs, isn't it? As for me, you owe me fifty schillings for today and fifty schillings for tomorrow."

He picked up the telephone in my presence. I know very little German, but enough to understand that the conversation was about me and the dogs. Let me be fair and admit that there was no talk of money. The result of the telephone call was magnificent, unhoped-for, miraculous. The next morning, at ten o'clock, we were to be received by Doctor Freud.

It was agreed that the next day I should call for Doctor Ferden at his house at half-past-nine. Why was he not surprised that a poor mad woman like me should come to Vienna all by herself, or that she should not be accompanied by some hired guardian angel? He just did not think of these things, which was all the better for me and all the worse for the real lunatics in his care.

Well, there were the two of us in a taxi driving far out of Vienna to the suburb where Freud lives. The weather was beautiful. Life itself would have been beautiful had I not been obliged to stay mad. Every time I caught sight of some wretched mongrel taking his morning promenade looking important with his ridiculous steel muzzle, I had to bound upon Doctor Ferden, clutch his arm, pinch it, and howl. All this with the awful fear that I might have a lapse and in an absent-minded moment look some pooch in the face with complete composure—which would immediately have demolished my superb edifice of lies and dissimulation.

"In short," Doctor Ferden recapitulated conscientiously, "the dogs bite you; you have a horror of eating because it is dirty; you are afraid to die; and—have you any other fear? Of horses, for example?"

I very much wanted to answer: "Don't you think those are enough?" But perhaps that would not have been very clever.

At last we arrived at our destination, a beautiful house, freshly painted, with chestnut-colored shutters gleaming in the sunshine. This was where Freud lived, and this vast garden, all full of sunlight, trees and birds—it was here, walking up and down these paths, that Freud used to meditate on psychoanalysis. On tables and alongside gravel walks there was a profusion of luxurious potted plants, cacti and dwarf aloes.

106

"The Professor has two dogs who are always with him," remarked Doctor Ferden. "But don't be afraid; they are locked up."

My display of terror was only half assumed, because I really was in a funk. That I had deceived Doctor Logre and Doctor Ferden seemed amazing but possible. But Freud! I foresaw myself being unmasked by him, driven forth covered with blushes—and no longer afraid of dogs. We mounted some stairs, passed through a porch full of wicker couches with pretentiously hideous cushions; we entered an office; and in the office was Freud.

He is eighty years old, but looks only sixty. He has beautiful white hair, well combed and well brushed, a short beard, and spectacles behind which his eyes have retreated so far under the arch of his eyebrows that you feel they are looking at you hard without your being able to see what color they are.

He stood up, slender and elegant. He was wearing a natty gray suit like a gigolo's, but it did not seem ridiculous because there was still so much youth in his way of walking and moving about. His hands also were strangely young, a little red and heavy, but without wrinkles, without those spots which usually cover the hands of old men. Under his chin, on the left side, a great lump moved and oscillated ceaselessly. He had had a grave infection of the larynx, and was operated on and saved by a miracle. This painful experience had left him with an impediment in his speech reminiscent of paralytics or of deaf-mutes.

He gave me his hand in the German manner, the elbow held at a right angle, the hand turned in. His look weighed upon me and seemed so pointed and powerful that I felt as though I were melting and dissolving. "Let the Last Judgment come," I thought. "I know just how it will feel." Regardless of me and of my heart, which was galloping madly, Doctor Ferden indulged in bows, scrapings and flowery smiles as he presented me as the Madame Dubois of whom he had spoken to the Herr Professor over the telephone. He handed him some loose papers upon which he had jotted down some notes about me. Freud ran through them with an attentive eye.

Suddenly he turned around. He was seated directly opposite me, at a small, modest desk whose green felt must have nourished generations of moths. Freud put his elbows on it, perhaps to make himself more comfortable, perhaps to reprove the moths. He seemed plunged in meditation, which neither his virtual successor nor I dared interrupt. The pounding of my heart filled the whole room. Suddenly, with the decisiveness of a railway semaphore, Freud straightened out his arm and pointed it at me. I thought: "This is the end of my lies and pretences. I am unmasked without having stammered out one little fib!"

But no; Freud, the great, illustrious Freud did not for one moment psychoanalyze the false introversion and the real anxiety in my lost look. He emitted a sort of cackle, rather hard and sardonic, and lined with gold. He looked like an old cannibal fresh from the hands of an American dentist.

"Madame Dubois, do you speak German? No? Well, then, how do you expect me to practise psychoanalysis? Doubtless you speak only French. I knew that too, but a long time ago. I am old. I shall soon be eighty-one years old. I have forgotten everything!"

"I speak English too," I offered timidly. "Not well, of course, but rather I think to . . ." Freud cackled again, pivoted, and faced Doctor Ferden.

"What is she saying? I understand she is speaking English, but if she does not speak louder, there is not the slightest use beginning any treatment. I am a little bit deaf—it is my age. I cannot understand a word. Ask her if she can't raise her voice."

I could do that, of course. There is not a telephone operator who does not call me Monsieur when I telephone without giving my name. But to raise my voice, to speak a strange language almost fluently—is this compatible with a fear of dogs, with aversion to meat and other nourishment? It is easy to assume a stricken air when one speaks low. But let the voice be raised and instantly the eyes clear, the brow smooths, an animated color comes into your cheeks, and there is nothing of depression and distress left.

"I will try," I shrieked, in English, at the top of my lungs.

Freud cast a triumphant glance at Doctor Ferden. "What did I tell you? These patients insist on talking in a low voice when actually they can express themselves as distinctly as anybody else."

He appeared to have lost all interest in me; but I felt that he was looking at me obliquely. The other doctor did likewise, and I felt so weak, so menaced, that the terrors of a lamb in the claws of a wolf seemed nothing compared with mine. For I had two wolves upon me.

"Why do you insist on my treating you?" Freud asked in English. "A treatment by psychoanalysis is very long. It will take at least a year, probably more, and meanwhile I may die. Then what are you going to do? Eh? Kill yourself? Don't you ever want to kill yourself? You do, don't you?"

Doctor Ferden writhed distractedly, like a man trying to seize a windmill.

"No, no, Herr Professor. I have asked her that already. She does not want to kill herself. On the contrary, she is afraid of dying."

Freud shrugged his shoulders. "My dear fellow, the two always go together."

"Certainly, Herr Professor, but not at the same time. Madame Dubois has told me specifically that . . ."

In our conversation there was something grotesque, something improbable, something reminiscent of the Ballet Russe, clowns and madmen, and the writers of tall tales. I heard an impossible mixture of German and French words and English phrases: as if the pages of three tattered dictionaries had been pasted together at random. And this old man, who did not look like an old man, but rather like a flattering and youthful statue of an old man; who spoke in a grating voice; with a lump that rose and fell like the counterweight of an elevator.

It was warm. The sky seemed bursting with health. Oh, to be a blade of grass, or a bird! But there were the three of us playing a new version of *Dr. Knock.*

I was given a few moments respite while they discussed some point. What? Me? Dogs? Fees? Oh, Molière, that you should have missed Freud, and psychoanalysis, and psychoanalysts! Again the Master plunged into meditation reminiscent of the trances of the Pythian priestess upon her tripod. He straightened up. His arm shot out like a snake whose charmer has stopped playing the flute.

"I have a confession to make," he said, this time in grinding, lugubrious French, which seemed to stick in his poor, sick throat. "I am afraid that you will not be able to come to me for an analysis. I have two dogs. I love dogs. Eh? Shall you dare come even so?"

My eyes became haggard, and I wrung my hands like a bashful virgin to whom a lecherous gentleman has just proposed a gallant *rendez-vous.* "I—I don't know. Perhaps—if I were sure that I should never encounter them . . ."

I shook. I felt that if I could only see myself, I should feel sorry for myself.

"They are very well-behaved, you know. Don't you want to see them? *I* love them."

"Yes, but they don't bite *you.* I, too, used to like them, before—but now that they all bite me . . ."

109

Doctor Ferden shook his head. "Poor young woman, to be in such a state at her age! What a pity."

"I believe you said *before*. Before what?"

"I don't know . . . before . . ."

Freud glanced at Ferden's notes. "Before your marriage, perhaps?"

"Perhaps . . . I don't know any more . . . Yes, I think so."

The two prophets exchanged a look pregnant with the modest triumph of men who are never wrong.

"What did I tell you?" Freud rejoiced.

"Absolutely, Herr Professor."

"It is a classic case."

"I thought as much, Herr Professor."

"I am going to show you something else."

Once more I felt that magic, dictatorial look which weighed upon me, crushed me, robbing me of all will except to see and hear.

"Why don't you smile?" said Freud, setting me an example. In the light his teeth sparkled like gold nuggets. I tried to smile in return, and achieved the distant and dolorous smirk of Lillian Gish in *Broken Blossoms*. After only three short minutes, I succeeded in smiling.

"Ah," cried Freud, become wheedling and paternal, "You are charming now. Why don't you always want to smile?"

"Because the dogs bite me," I replied with oppressive stubbornness.

"All this is very significant," Freud murmured. "I can begin my treatment next week, but before that it is imperative for me to see your husband. Can he come and join you? Besides, you cannot stay here alone. You must have a woman companion to whom I can give instructions for your treatment. A friend of yours, perhaps."

I agreed.

"It is very curious," muttered Freud, in an aside to Doctor Ferden. "I am sure that she is afraid not only of dogs but also of pictures of dogs." He raised his voice to include me in the conversation. "Shall I show you a photo of my little dogs?"

I made such a gesture of aversion that he burst into laughter. "What would she say if I let her see the little statuette of a Pekinese I have here?"

"Shall I show it to her?" asked Doctor Ferden.

"No, no. Why? If she threw a fit after that, it would help a lot,

110

wouldn't it! No, I think we have talked enough for today. Now about the fee."

"I told her it would be three hundred schillings, which she brought, Herr Professor."

"Yes, but the treatment?"

"Ah, that's so." Another consultation, this time in *really* low voices.

"Professor Freud wants me to tell you that the treatment will cost a hundred schillings a day," Doctor Ferden explained to me, in French.

"Oh, that's nothing. That is understood."

"I can also show you the sanatorium, where you and your companion would be very comfortable," Ferden proposed. "It is the best sanatorium in Vienna. It *is*, to be sure, somewhat expensive. It would cost you sixty schillings a day for yourself and thirty for your companion if she sleeps in the same room with you."

In short, I might hope that after spending a thousand francs a day for at least one year, perhaps two, I should lose all fear of dogs!

Freud rose. He extended a hand; I extended an envelope. His gesture seemed friendly rather than professional. But he took the envelope.

"One must live," Doctor Ferden explained to me in the taxi that took us back to Vienna. "There is nothing shameful about accepting money when you have earned it. Now I shan't ask you any more questions. I am going to leave you to the analysis."

Back in Paris, I have done a good deal of thinking. I am going to give up the idea of being psychoanalyzed by Freud. But I *am* going to buy Fido a muzzle.

A Visit with Freud

(1937)

ROBERT P. KNIGHT

Robert P. Knight (1902–1970), who was an active member of the American Psychoanalytic Association and the International Psychoanalytical Association, might now be termed a second-generation analyst. This selection first appeared in the Bulletin of the Menninger Clinic *1 (1937): 144–47. Note the rather sharp sarcasm of Freud at the end of the interview.*

During ten years of interest in psychoanalysis I had cherished the ambition some day to visit Freud in Vienna, but the ambition had always been tempered by the realization that I probably could never achieve it. However, through a combination of fortunate circumstances, I was able to gain an audience with him last summer when I was in Europe to attend the Fourteenth Congress of the International Psychoanalytic Association in Marienbad, Czechoslovakia. I shall relate the incidents leading to the visit to explain why I was so fortunate as to be received by the illustrious father of psychoanalysis.

I had been told by several close acquaintances of Freud in America that it was practically impossible to see him since his advanced age (he was 80 in May 1936) had forced him to adopt the policy of seeing only old friends. One of these old friends, Dr. Ernst Simmel, formerly of Berlin, now in Los Angeles, had offered to write a letter for me. Dr. Simmel had visited the Menninger Clinic some months before and had been pleased to find our work so similar to that of his Tegel Clinic in Berlin, in which Freud also had been interested. I learned later that it was due to Dr. Simmel's account of the Menninger Clinic that my request for permission to pay a visit was granted by Freud. I had also been advised to write a letter from London to Freud's daughter Anna, who in addition to assisting her father has achieved a high place in psychoanalysis through her own work. I did so and requested her to write me in Paris. However, I had to leave Paris before her reply arrived, and when I finally reached Vienna I was quite in the dark as to the prospect of my being able to arrange a visit.

On Saturday, 1 August, I called on Professor Dr. Marburg, the noted neurologist, under whose tutelage so many American neurologists have studied in Vienna, to convey greetings from Dr. N. L. Blitzsten of Chicago. In the course of the conversation I asked him if he were friendly with Freud. "Oh, yes," he said, "I spoke about his contributions to neurology at the celebration in Vienna of his eightieth birthday." I told him about my apparently frustrated plans to call on Freud, and asked him to suggest how I might proceed. "But Freud sees no one," he told me. "And now, especially, he is ill. Last week he had another minor operation on his throat. I am sure it is impossible to see him, but I will telephone him if you wish." I seized upon this offer, and he went into the next room to telephone. In a few moments he returned. "He will see you," he exclaimed. "Tomorrow at eleven o'clock." And so through Dr. Simmel and Dr. Marburg the visit was arranged.

That afternoon, I went out to the Vienna Psychoanalytic Institute on the Berggasse, a street made famous by the fact that Freud's office has been there for so many years. While arranging my registration fee for the Congress, I saw some new photographs of Freud, taken a few months before, and purchased three. Later I conceived the idea of asking Freud to autograph them.

It was about a twenty minute taxi ride from the Grand Hotel in Vienna to Freud's summer residence in Grinsing, a suburb of Vienna. As I alighted from the cab that Sunday morning, I looked up at the house and saw him standing at the window, his hands in his back pockets. He turned from the window as I rang the bell at the wall gate. As I entered, the housekeeper appeared in the yard and, evidently perceiving me to be an American who would know no German, silently motioned me to accompany her to the entrance. I was ushered into a large room which seemed to serve as living room and office for the professor during the summer, when he closes his office in the Berggasse.

Freud is a slightly built, somewhat stooped man of about five feet seven or eight inches. His hair and beard are white, but his skin is unwrinkled, his gait is unfaltering, his expression is alert, and his faculties are unimpaired. In spite of his advanced years, he has four hours of appointments daily, and is still an active contributor to psychoanalytic literature. He greeted me cordially in English. In a husky voice, the words spoken with obvious effort, he excused himself for his difficulty in speaking and explained that he had had a minor throat operation a few days before. He then asked me what he could do for me. I told him that I had long wished to pay him a visit, and that I was pleased to have the privilege granted. I said that I only wished to chat with him briefly and did not want to impose upon him. He spoke perfect English, and we conversed for some minutes. He expressed interest in our work at the Menninger Clinic and asked about Dr. Karl Menninger, who had visited him at the time of the Congress in Lucerne in 1934. He told me that Anna Freud had written giving me an appointment at 4 o'clock the preceding Thursday, and that they had expected me then, having had no word until Dr. Marburg called. I explained about my not having received her letter, and expressed my regret at not being able to see her before she left for the Congress.

He asked me if I had seen his Chow dogs, of which he is very fond. I replied that I had seen one of them running about the grounds as I entered. He wished to show me the grounds, and as we walked to the door opening onto the stone porch he exclaimed, "My, but you're a big fellow," and crouched down roguishly to accentuate the disparity of almost a foot in our statures. He was very proud of the grounds, which covered some ten acres enclosed by a wall. When we had returned to the house and had seated ourselves, he asked me what I had brought in the package. Feeling rather foolish, since I am not an autograph seeker and do not know the proper approach, I unwrapped the photographs, explaining that I had purchased them at the Institute and that I hoped he would sign them for me. To my surprise, he demurred. He did not see how his signing them would make any difference. I told him that I wished to keep one and give two away to analytic colleagues who would prize the photographs much more if they were autographed.

"I will sign yours," he said, "but why should I sign two for persons whom I do not know?" But I persisted, telling him that he did know both of the analysts I had in mind, and I told him who they were. Still a little reluctant to comply with such an American request, he took his pen and began signing the pictures with a firm hand. "This is what you Americans call 'large scale production,' is it not?" he remarked, smiling.

I spoke about an article I had seen in a French newspaper by a French woman journalist telling of her posing as a neurotic patient with a dog phobia in order to get an interview with him. He took from his desk a letter in French from the Parisian psychiatrist who had referred her, and showed it to me. "If you," he said, "should come to me telling me you were Mr. Jones and wished help from me, I should accept you in good faith—especially if a physician whom I knew had written me about you." I remarked that it was regrettable that such impositions should occur. "It was nothing," he said, with a gesture which seemed to say that a man learns to accept all things philosophically.

He showed me his collection of *objets d'art* which were scattered about his desk and some shelves and tables in the room. These included many small Egyptian figurines and other treasured objects, collected over many years. He handled them lovingly and spoke about certain specimens in detail. Being entirely ignorant regarding such matters, I nevertheless expressed interest, but apparently unconvincingly, for he remarked, "You do not have much appreciation for such things, do you?" I confessed my ignorance.

After a very delightful visit of thirty minutes, he dismissed me cordially. "When next you come to Vienna," he said, "if I still exist, I hope you will come to see me again."

In Memory of Sigmund Freud

(d. Sept. 1939)

W. H. AUDEN

W. H. Auden is probably one of the greatest poets of this time. He wrote In Memory of Sigmund Freud *on the occasion of Freud's death in 1939. It appears in his* Collected Shorter Poems, 1927–1957 *(London, Faber & Faber, 1966).*

When there are so many we shall have to mourn,
when grief has been made so public, and exposed
    to the critique of a whole epoch
    the frailty of our conscience and anguish,

of whom shall we speak? For every day they die
among us, those who were doing us some good,
    who knew it was never enough but
    hoped to improve a little by living.

Such was this doctor: still at eighty he wished
to think of our life from whose unruliness
    so many plausible young futures
    with threats or flattery ask obedience,

but his wish was denied him: he closed his eyes
upon that last picture, common to us all,
    of problems like relatives gathered
    puzzled and jealous about our dying.

For about him till the very end were still
those he had studied, the fauna of the night,
    and shades that still waited to enter
    the bright circle of his recognition

turned elsewhere with their disappointment as he
was taken away from his life interest
    to go back to the earth in London,
    an important Jew who died in exile.

Only Hate was happy, hoping to augment
his practice now, and his dingy clientele
    who think they can be cured by killing
    and covering the gardens with ashes.

They are still alive, but in a world he changed
simply by looking back with no false regrets;
    all he did was to remember
    like the old and be honest like children.

He wasn't clever at all: he merely told
the unhappy Present to recite the Past
    like a poetry lesson till sooner
    or later it faltered at the line where

long ago the accusations had begun,
and suddenly knew by whom it had been judged,
    how rich life had been and how silly,
    and was life-forgiven and more humble,

able to approach the Future as a friend
without a wardrobe of excuses, without
    a set mask of rectitude or an
    embarrassing over-familiar gesture.

No wonder the ancient cultures of conceit
in his technique of unsettlement foresaw
    the fall of princes, the collapse of
    their lucrative patterns of frustration:

if he succeeded, why, the Generalised Life
would become impossible, the monolith
    of State be broken and prevented
    the co-operation of avengers.

Of course they called on God, but he went his way
down among the lost people like Dante, down
    to the stinking fosse where the injured
    led the ugly life of the rejected,

and showed us what evil is, not, as we thought,
deeds that must be punished, but our lack of faith,
    our dishonest mood of denial,
    the concupiscence of the oppressor.

117

If some traces of the autocratic pose,
the paternal strictness he distrusted, still
    clung to his utterance and features
  it was a protective coloration

for one who'd lived among enemies so long:
if often he was wrong and, at times, absurd,
    to us he is no more a person
  now but a whole climate of opinion

under whom we conduct our different lives:
Like weather he can only hinder or help,
    the proud can still be proud but find it
  a little harder, the tyrant tries to

make do with him but doesn't care for him much:
he quietly surrounds all our habits of growth
    and extends, till the tired in even
  the remotest miserable duchy

have felt the change in their bones and are cheered,
till the child, unlucky in his little State,
    some hearth where freedom is excluded,
  a hive whose honey is fear and worry,

feels calmer now and somehow assured of escape,
while, as they lie in the grass of our neglect,
    so many long-forgotten objects
  revealed by his undiscouraged shining

are returned to us and made precious again;
games we had thought we must drop as we grew up,
    little noises we dared not laugh at,
  faces we made when no one was looking.

But he wishes us more than this. To be free
is often to be lonely. He would unite
    the unequal moieties fractured
  by our own well-meaning sense of justice,

would restore to the larger the wit and will
the smaller possesses but can only use
    for arid disputes, would give back to
  the son the mother's richness of feeling:

118

but he would have us remember most of all
to be enthusiastic over the night,
    not only for the sense of wonder
   it alone has to offer, but also

because it needs our love. With large sad eyes
its delectable creatures look up and beg
    us dumbly to ask them to follow:
   they are exiles who long for the future

that lies in our power, they too would rejoice
if allowed to serve enlightenment like him,
    even to bear our cry of 'Judas',
   as he did and all must bear who serve it.

One rational voice is dumb. Over his grave
the household of Impulse mourns one dearly loved:
    sad is Eros, builder of cities,
   and weeping anarchic Aphrodite.

Freud's Influence on the Changed Attitude Toward Sex

(1939)

HAVELOCK ELLIS

Havelock Ellis was the famous English sexologist whose works pioneered the sexual atti-tudes of the early twenties. He corresponded with Freud and respected his work. This se-lection was published in The American Journal of Sociology 45 *(November 1939): 309–17.*

No pioneer in science or art has aroused such fiercely opposed reac-tions, enthusiastic and hostile, as Sigmund Freud. The first reaction to every pioneer is indeed opposition. One such, Lombroso—like Freud a Jew—considered this an instinctive and invariable impulse and named it "misoneism," the hatred of novelty.

Whatever we may think of this view, there were special reasons why in the case of Freud a double reaction of enthusiastic acceptance and indignant rejection should be emphatically marked and long per-sistent.

In the first place, there is no subject, save only religion, which has been so long and so firmly intrenched by tradition and so passionately guarded as sex. In the field of religion opposition has grown milder during the past century, except in so far as we may regard the modern racialism as a religious myth. But the traditional attitude toward sex had remained almost untouched and, indeed, in some respects even stronger both as regards its sanctity and as regards its obscenity. For this attitude became concerned quite as much with expression as with action, a matter of speech fully as much as of morality. Freud cannot be said even to have attacked conventional sexual morality. He pointed out some of the evils which it involves, but he can scarcely be said ever to have advocated definitely any revolutionary moral change. In that respect he preserved the correct attitude of the conventional

120

physician. But in the matter of expression and speech his attitude was completely revolutionary. In this way he shocked alike those who viewed sex as very sacred and those who viewed it as very indecent. In a simple, precise, and detailed manner he described the sex phenomena presented by his patients, without attenuation or apology, but as a matter of course. This had never been done before in medical literature. Even in the outspoken days of the seventeenth century anatomists would ask to be excused if they referred to the sexual organs. Freud never seemed to be aware that even the professional public he was addressing still expected some sort of similar apology from those who thus ventured to offend its modesty. More even than this, Freud attached a new and fateful significance to sex in fields where such significance seemed to most of the professional public an alarming novelty. This was notably the case in his insistence on infantile sexuality and his introduction, first clearly made in 1905, of such terms as "incest" and the "Oedipus complex" which have no meaning for children who are simply likely to manifest affection to those persons who happen to be nearest.

Various medical authorities before Freud had recognized the importance of sex as well as its aptitude to appear in childhood. But they had been careful to make their statements with moderation and to express them temperately, so that they might be accepted without arousing either enthusiasm or hostility. Freud's outspoken and even extravagant presentation of the subject, fortified by a literary skill which has not always been recognized, was on the one hand warmly welcomed by those who had never dared to reveal a secret sense of the importance of sexual phenomena, and on the other hand indignantly rejected by those who cherished all the ancient traditions of the mingled sacredness and obscenity of sex.

The frank appeal of Freud's doctrines carried away several men of ability who became his close disciples but later drew back, unable in the end to accept his more extreme views. Freud himself, whose mind has ever been receptive, flexible, and versatile, was constantly modifying even what seemed his most essential principles. It is a characteristic of his genius, but it is largely responsible for the contradictory impressions which that genius has made upon psychologists and sometimes even upon the same psychologist. If, for instance, we take as distinguished and influential a psychologist as the late Professor McDougall we find even him extravagant alike in praise and dispraise of Freud.

My own rather difficult position in regard to Freud may be said to exhibit something of the same kind of opposition. I have from the first recognized his importance, with a resulting friendly personal relationship by correspondence, while at the same time I have been constantly critical of special doctrines and special tendencies. By a curious coincidence his first book (in conjunction with Breuer) appeared in the year 1895 when the first published volume of my *Studies* was already in the press, and both—by another curious coincidence—were in German and both were published at Leipzig. I was slightly younger than Freud, but he was newer to the study of sex, having only recently been brought to it by his association with Breuer, while I had been preparing myself through many years, even from youth. It was natural, therefore, that I should have obtained the Freud and Breuer volume on publication and found it of great interest. I was preparing my study of auto-erotism for what was later to be the first volume of my *Studies in the Psychology of Sex*. (My study of *Sexual Inversion*, which was the first volume of the *Studies* to be published, appeared in German in the same year as the Breuer and Freud volume.) I was impressed by Breuer's and Freud's method of presentation even apart from its ingenious skill in detecting sexual origins at the source of hysteria, which I was not inclined altogether to reject. Hysteria had been originally associated with the womb, and in more recent days some eminent psychiatrists, like Clouston, had emphasized the part played by the sexual impulse in setting up hysterical states. I had myself in *Man and Woman*, published a few years earlier, ventured to express the opinion that the part played by the sexual emotions in the causation of hysteria had been underestimated. But there had in general been a reaction against that view, perhaps notably due to the influence—indirect rather than direct—of Charcot, but largely furthered and supported by the puritanic discredit into which sexual phenomena had fallen in the nineteenth century, so that there was a tendency to avoid ascribing a disordered nervous condition to a source of this kind. I had myself, of course, no sympathy whatever with this attitude, so that I took pleasure in meeting what might even be an extreme insistence on the importance of the sexual impulse. In dealing with the study of auto-erotism, which I had then in hand, I devoted half a dozen pages to an exposition of the doctrine of Breuer and Freud, the volume being published in 1899 in London and shortly afterward in Philadelphia. It has always been a satisfaction to me that this was the first book in the English language in which Freud's name was introduced and his work (i.e., in its immature first stage) expounded. It was evidently also a satisfaction to Freud himself to receive this early recognition. He entered into correspondence with me and sent me his books as they appeared; the friendly relations thus set up continued unbroken, although my attitude was always somewhat critical and Freud never regarded me as a disciple. But he gained suggestions from my work, as well as one or two new terms, notably "auto-erotism," although he used it somewhat differently.

It is a proof—though it may seem an ambiguous proof—of Freud's profound and fruitful genius that some of the most brilliant and gifted of his early disciples have branched off along various lines of their own, usually with considerable vexation to the master himself. We have to remember, however, that, as Dr. Hans von Hattingberg has remarked in his *Technique of Psycho-analysis* (1932), "At the first approach psycho-analysis is an almost impenetrable chaos." It was inevitable that the more penetrating minds among those who sought to find their way in this chaos should fix on special lines of advance to which they happened to be individually drawn. So it was that Adler and Jung and Stekel found their own paths, sufficiently definite and individual to separate them from Freud, yet each clearly revealing the Freudian starting-point. They may not always be entitled to term their methods "psycho-analysis" but these methods are all essential outcomes of the Freudian movement. Significant is the attitude of Otto Rank, who was for long years closely associated with Freud and the development of his most typical doctrines, being indeed his most scholarly associate. Rank, however, finally left him to become an acute critic of Freudianism, yet still upholding an attitude that is definitely Freudian. At an early stage Freud himself declared that his doctrine (he later found that there had been a suggestion of it by Schopenhauer) of sexual suppression with transference and resistance was "the foundation stone on which the edifice of psycho-analysis rests," and that every investigation which starts from these points, whatever results it leads to, is psycho-analysis. It is more usual now to confine the term to strictly Freudian methods and to refer to others simply as "analysis." The doctrine of infantile sexuality came later; that, too, already existed, not indeed as a doctrine but simply as an occasional fact; but Freud sought to generalize it. The emphasis on dream interpretation developed gradually (very considerably by Freud's self-analysis), with its two aspects of the symbolism of dream imagery and the reduction of dream representation to inner conflict, together with the distinction between

123

the manifest and the latent. Freud's book on the interpretation of dreams is the most elaborate of his works and that to which he attaches most importance.

But to return for a moment to his first book, the studies of hysteria written with Breuer, we already see the typical Freud. It contains the germs of many of his later doctrines and that flexibility of mind that made possible those developments. We may perhaps also detect that looseness in definition which has always marked Freud and while in one respect a weakness, especially by leading to misapprehensions, also a valuable quality because it lends itself to new developments and enlargements; in this way, for instance, the fundamental term "libido" has so enlarged in Freud's hands as completely to change its meaning and to be perhaps better expressed by the term "conation." We may at the same time find here that charm of personal style to which I should attach importance as a factor in securing Freud's immense influence. Immature as this first book may be, it always seems to me—as I myself chanced to find it—one of the best portals to the elaborate Freudian edifice of later data.

At one vital point indeed Freud soon outgrew it. That was the hypnotic method which with Breuer he was inclined to rely on at this first period. But he quickly rejected hypnotism as an unsatisfactory method. Indeed, even in this first book he was moving with Breuer toward his own later method which was the opposite of hypnotism, being a method not of putting in but of drawing out, a method of bringing to the surface a repressed and corroding element. Breuer termed this method "cathartic," but Freud a little later preferred to term it "analytic," probably because he could not accept Breuer's conception of "a foreign body in consciousness." Freud's method is indeed, as in hypnotism, not that of putting something in but that of taking something out—as Freud has himself expressed it, after a manner analogous to the sculptor's art.

When he had fully developed his own method, Freud began to see in it far-spread possibilities much beyond its original scope, as a new process of diagnosing and treating nervous troubles. Even so, this method was not in itself quite so new as Freud supposed. Many years ago I pointed out that in 1857 Dr. Garth Wilkinson, a noted Swedenborgian and mystic of his day, set forth what he considered a "new method" and termed "Impression." It consisted in listening to the deepest unconscious expressions from within, the first of which follow the writing-down of a theme, for thus we catch the response to the man's desire for the unfolding of the subject. Garth Wilkinson, however, though a physician, confined this method to literary and religious aims, while Freud directed it into medical and scientific channels. The adoption of such a method has confirmed my view that Freud is a great deal of an artist, though he himself vigorously repels that attribution, declaring that he is nothing but a man of science.

In any case, as his use of his method developed he came to see in it the widest possibilities. These he enumerated in an article in *Scientia* in 1913. The various sciences to which he held that psycho-analysis had become applicable included (1) language; (2) the hypotheses of philosophy; (3) biology, by doing justice to the impulse of sex and mediating between biology and psychology; (4) it recreated the conception of evolution and showed how even in the psychic sphere the individual repeats the experience of the race; (5) it contributed to the history of civilization, and helped to explain myths and legends and social institutions; (6) similarly in the fine arts it revealed the artist's hidden motives; (7) it likewise concerned sociology and the repression of the individual to social demands; (8) it was important for methods of education by revealing the nature of childhood and the significance of sublimation, for, as Freud views it, "our highest virtues have arisen as reactive sublimations from the foundation of our worst predispositions."

To survey the vast field in which he has desired to move is indeed to raise the question whether Freud is properly regarded as a man of science. To raise that question, as I have long since done, is not to belittle Freud, for it is possible to maintain that the greatest men of science really belong to the sphere of art. While Freud himself, as I have found in correspondence with him, at once protests that he is a man of science and nothing else, one may ask: "What science?" The obvious answer should be: "Psychology." But many are the psychologists who cannot regard the investigation of an unknown "Unconscious" as the legitimate field for any would-be scientific psychology. And the varied fields of unquestioned scientific study which Freud has entered, he has entered as an amateur, deliberately disregarding any other method of approach and, when he seeks support, not always selecting that which carries most weight. This attitude of mind suggests that of the artist rather than that of the scientist. It seems in itself enough to account for the mixed enthusiasm and hostility which Freud even still arouses among men of science. When Garth Wilkinson initiated that method of "Impression" by which he became in a small way a precursor of

Freud he had no idea—though he was a physician—of giving it any scientific validity. But it left open the field for the largest display of artistic genius. Freud's art is the poetry of psychic processes which lie in the deepest and most mysterious recesses of the organism. He has even at times allowed himself a free hand which to the most casual observer is that of the artist. I need only mention the essay on Leonardo da Vinci or that on Jensen's novel, *Gradiva*. It would be fantastic to find any trace of science in either of these delightful essays, and yet they are typically Freudian.

To emphasize the artist in Freud is not, I would hasten to add, by any means to diminish his significance even for science. At the highest points of human genius science and art become indistinguishable. To admit that Freud may be viewed at such a point is clearly to recognize the wide significance of his work, even if we cannot define that significance with precision.

To me it seems that we are still too near to achieve that precise definition. I accept as still reasonable, even if a little extravagant, the ambivalent attitude of Freud's distinguished contemporary in the same field, W. McDougall: the recognition of Freud as one of the greatest masters in thought together with a radical criticism of most of the results he has reached.

To sum up: In what way has Freud most specifically affected the changed attitude toward sex alike in the scientific and in the popular mind?

It must be plainly stated that there can be no doubt whatever that the frank and open recognition of sex would have been reached even if Freud had never been born. As we look back it would be easy to enumerate the various paths, theoretical and practical, along which sex was slowly moving to that place in human economy which it now occupies. The immense importance of sex is indeed implicit in the biological conception of life as it began to take shape in the middle of the last century and the ancient dictum that hunger and love are the pillars of life became developed in all the human sciences. Claims for the scientific, medical, hygienic, and social recognition of sex were being independently put forward, while at the same time on quite different ethical lines the assertion of the "sacredness" of sex was being remade by pioneers in morals. But nearly all those approaching this alarming and dangerous subject were careful to do so with discretion and consideration and full allowance for the still flourishing traditions and conventions.

Freud made no such allowance. He was thus fully justified in claiming that his approach was strictly and exclusively scientific. Whether or not he was justified in seeing the place of sex as so large, he was simply stating what he saw. That the expression of his statements often seemed unnecessarily extravagant and offensive cannot be denied. There was no occasion for Freud to be surprised or hurt at the world's response to his new revelations.

There is thus really no doubt about Freud's specific contribution to the changed attitude to sex which marks our time. Whatever we may ultimately come to think of psycho-analysis as a technical method, it supplied an immense emphasis to the general recognition and acceptance of the place of sex in life.

The emphasis was primarily confined, as was natural, to the psycho-pathological field. Freud's incursions into other fields of science and art may be said to belong to a different order. They are more definitely those of an amateur. It is true that Freud might be termed an amateur throughout, since he has always almost ostentatiously ignored the results of previous workers, except when he chanced to find that they supported his own. But in all these other fields he was obviously an outsider, and his views were often novel. It may be claimed that such novelty exerted by a thinker of distinction from outside is of high value even when far from carrying conviction, because it stimulates new inquiry and research. The results, as estimated by recognized authorities, may be sometimes positive, sometimes negative, but in either case are of unquestionable value in their stimulating and challenging quality. As I have elsewhere sought to make clear, Freud has in these fields revealed the possibility of new depths, new subtleties, new complexities, and new possible mechanisms.

An Intimate Impression
(1939)

JOAN RIVIERE

Joan Riviere belonged to that remarkable generation of British female analysts, including Sylvia Payne and Melanie Klein, who made significant contributions to the theory and practice of psychoanalysis. Joan Riviere met Freud in 1920 and started her analysis with him in 1922. She subsequently practiced in London and also translated some of Freud's works. This selection appeared first in The Lancet *(30 September 1939).*

When I knew Professor Freud in Vienna in 1922, he was aged 65 and more or less at the height of his career. Soon after 1910 the solitary obscurity which had surrounded him and his work for something like 20 years had begun to lessen, while the war neuroses in Europe had generated, both in the medical profession and in the general public, an interest in the psychological approach to such disorders. This had brought his work into the foreground and made his name known. In 1922 he and his followers in Vienna, Berlin, and Budapest were fully occupied with teaching and training (first and foremost by analysing them personally) the group of English, American and Swiss physicians, and others, who were taking up the new study of psycho-analysis. A few years later, in 1924, the serious but successful operation on his jaw caused him ill health at times, though it affected only slightly his capacity for work and his speech. He afterwards went about even less than formerly, and the future will probably judge his later work as falling short in various ways of his earlier achievement.

I had met Professor Freud at The Hague in 1920, at the first International Congress of Psycho-Analysis held after the war. He impressed one as an exceptional personality. His appearance was not typically that of a medical man, nor was it particularly Jewish. The long pale face with grey beard and stooping shoulders were those of an intellectual and might have suggested a learned professor, but for two other essential characteristics. There was his lean but broad and sturdy figure, the rather stern expression and firm jaw, which bespoke a great reserve of dignity and hidden strength—an indomitable tenacity. He appeared somewhat aloof; in fact he could easily be bored by crowds and gatherings. His most striking feature, however, was the forward thrust of his head and critical exploring gaze of his keenly piercing eyes. Finally, this rather awe-inspiring appearance was lightened by the glow of an enchanting humour, always latent and constantly irradiating his whole person as he spoke, which reassured one that the Olympian was indeed a mortal too. I knew already from his writings of his astonishing knowledge of literature; of his memory, especially for Shakespeare; and of his other tastes, his love of all antiquities, of Greece and Rome and the art of earlier cultures. But on this occasion I first realised his amazing command of the English language. Although he had not been in England for over 40 years, his contribution to the scientific work of the small Congress was an extempore lecture given with absolute mastery in the simplest and most perfect English without any notes.

These impressions were confirmed during 1922 when I studied with him and got to know him. Like his psychology, his personality was really one to concern itself with individuals. The aloofness, which was never indeed coldness or hauteur, but rather indifference to superficialities, vanished and one met a vivid, eager mind seizing on every detail with astonishing interest and attention. The vitality, the current of his great energy was felt. How he disliked preambles and polite nothings! My first analytic hour with him he opened—contrary to rule and inadvisably—saying, "Well, I know something about you already; you had a father and a mother!" meaning of course, "Quick, I can't wait for you and your inhibitions, I want something to start with; give me an outline to get hold of!" He would allow himself liberties with his medium, like any master, until he recognised a new problem and bent himself as a student to that.

But whether in analysis or not, his interest, with all its intolerance of preliminaries and imperativeness, was curiously impersonal. One had always the impression of a certain reserve behind the eagerness, as though it were not for himself that he so peremptorily demanded to understand things, but for some purpose outside himself. There was a simplicity in this impersonal eagerness that was perhaps the most significant thing about him. He was so concentrated on the inquiry he

129

was pursuing that his self functioned only as an instrument. His penetrating attentive eyes had not only the simplicity and innocent clearsightedness of a child—one for whom nothing is too small, and nothing either common or unclean—there was also in them a mature patience and caution, and a detached inquiry. The half-peering and half-piercing gaze beneath the heavy brows showed a power to see beneath the surface and beyond the boundaries of ordinary perceptions. But it also expressed a capacity for patient, careful scrutiny and for suspended judgment so rare as to be unrecognisable by many; his cool scepticism has even been misread as cynicism or pessimism. There was in him a conjunction of the hunter on an endless trail and the persistent, immovable watcher who checks and revises; it was from this conjunction that his power of discovering and understanding the sources of the feelings and behaviour of men and women sprang. Indomitable courage and tenacity, coupled with an unswerving honesty, were the characteristics supporting his gifts of observation, his "intrepid imagination" and insight, which led to his great achievements. Both these capacities, the power to see new facts and to check his observations, diminished considerably in him after his operation in 1924.

Along with these qualities, to which essentially we owe his great work, his personality had many very human features which endeared him to his friends. The inimitable dry humour of his writings became in ordinary intercourse a charming gaiety and capacity for finding amusement in most situations; and though he could be tolerant and philosophical, he was apt to be both impatient and intolerant. His humour was often witty and barbed, and he could be choleric, resentful and unforgiving. Nor would I claim that he suffered fools gladly. He was compelled by destiny to be a great man in his work; but he lived his private life as an ordinary man, and he believed in that kind of life. He disliked pathological types and extremes of any kind. From this attitude of mind his intolerance of religion in my view largely derived; for religion tends to see life in black or white and cannot accept the compromises and complexities in it which are the subject matter of scientific psychology. Once when a heated discussion on political topics arose, he was accused of being neither black nor red, Fascist nor Socialist; his amused reply was, "No, one should be flesh colour"—the colour of ordinary men. And again, apropos of a young scientist interested in psycho-analysis who might have proved of service to the new science, Freud said to me mournfully, "But I can't regard it as normal, you know, that he has married a woman old enough to be his mother"!

130

I could but laugh at the discoverer of the Oedipus complex; and he met the laugh with a twinkle, but he was seriously disappointed.

In later life a certain reserve, dislike of publicity and a concentration of interest on his work was characteristic of him; one surmises that this trait had developed as a result of the hostile reception for so long accorded to his discoveries. But he was no captious hermit; numerous eminent contemporaries, especially in the literary world, sought his acquaintance and met or corresponded with him; among these were notably Romain Rolland, Thomas Mann, Arnold and Stefan Zweig. But any genuinely inquiring visitor, too, could always see him, and met with a frank and friendly reception. Whatever the outcome of the interview, those who preferred fair dealing to favours found nothing in him to alienate them. Above all, Freud was entirely without pose. He could be mistaken; but deception or disingenuousness were not to be found in his nature, and this essential honesty was the hallmark of his mind. He wrote: "I can say I have made many beginnings and thrown out many suggestions. Something will come of them in the future, though I myself cannot tell whether it will be much or little." These words sum up and express the fearlessness, the acceptance of truth and love of it which characterised him and inspired his work.

Recollections of Berggasse 19
(1940)

FRANZ ALEXANDER

Franz Alexander (1891–1964), one of the most prominent psychoanalysts in this country, knew Freud well. He studied at the Berlin Psychoanalytic Institute when Sachs and Abraham were still active there. For many years he was associated with the Chicago Institute for Psychoanalysis. In his last years he lived in California, where he taught at the University of Southern California, Los Angeles. This selection appeared first in The Psychoanalytic Quarterly 9 (1940): 195–204.

Sigmund Freud was unquestionably one of the most controversial figures of our time. Attempts to evaluate his contributions to psychiatry, to medical philosophy and to the social sciences already fill volumes. Now, after his death, the process of assimilation of his teachings continues and the final judgment rests with the future.

The intention here is not to evaluate his work but rather to recall a few impressions of him which may give a more vivid picture of this great man.

It was my good fortune to have known Freud and to have been in close contact with him from the time I became a psychoanalyst until I left Europe ten years ago. Since then I have seen him only on three occasions, the last time in the summer of 1935.

In 1920 when I became the first student to register at the Psychoanalytic Institute in Berlin, teaching of psychoanalysis was not organized and standardized as it is today. In fact, the founding of the Berlin Institute was the first step toward organized teaching. Up to that time teaching of psychoanalysis was like medieval medicine when students gathered around famous teachers. Teaching was a highly personal matter between students and teachers who knew each of their students well and took personal interest in their progress. A well organized curriculum and teaching staff, credits given for attendance, a number of obligatory and elective courses were unknown. To some degree in our small psychoanalytic institutes this personal relationship between teacher and student still obtains. In those earlier days Freud himself was the center of all psychoanalytic teaching. He knew almost all the promising young analysts in Europe and took great personal interest in them. To go to Berggasse 19 in Vienna to have a talk with Freud was a common procedure both for teachers and students of psychoanalysis. It was not only natural to do this but it was more or less expected. I remember Freud once talking to me with some indignation about a European analyst who had made valuable contributions to psychoanalysis: "Imagine, he has never once paid me a visit to make my personal acquaintance." He shook his head and muttered something about 'ambivalence.' He proved to be right: this follower later gave ample evidence of his hostility to Freud.

During my first visit with him I was fully aware of the fact that I was facing one of the greatest minds of all times. A great man is a lucky combination of hereditary qualities and later experiences. How one recognizes this quality of genius is indefinable, but it is unmistakable. Certainly the aura surrounding a great man is not based on his intellectual capacity alone. A combination of genuineness and courage contributes to this impression, as well as other intangibles which cannot be stated precisely.

Freud's whole personality emanated this combination of fundamental genuineness, directness and courage, in the person of a jovial Viennese physician with all the charm, urbanity and worldliness that was characteristic of the burghers of that ancient residence of the Hapsburgs. In fact, this latter appearance was so pronounced that it might have been deceptive in making Freud appear merely a well settled, cultured and conservative physician, a home-loving husband and father. However, it required only a brief contact with him to discern the towering figure of a great man, devoted to one great cause. The shadow of centuries fell over his study and one felt that one was facing an intellectual mountain peak of which only a few in each age are connected with each other by invisible ranges. The story is told—perhaps it is an invention—that even the Nazi Storm Troopers who brutally invaded his home soon began to treat him respectfully with the awe which great men instil even in the most primitive people.

Freud's speech, even during the most informal conversation, was like his style of writing—clear, to the point, and devoid of redundance. There was no tenseness in his manner, no attempt to impress. He propounded the most significant ideas in a light conversational, casual tone. He liked to illustrate a point with anecdotes and jokes, was an

133

excellent raconteur, and even serious topics were robbed of the artificial austerity with which they are so frequently invested.

Freud had strong convictions but he never became dogmatic and when uncertain he always admitted it. This made conversation with him delightful, especially the discussion of problems which puzzled him. To a suggestion he would respond with a question or with a 'perhaps,' spinning the idea further and waiting for the other to take up the thread again and offer some new suggestion. One had the feeling that one and Freud were working out something together.

One unforgettable visit with him was an occasion on which his daughter Anna was also present. We talked almost two hours and this conversation provided me with a lasting stimulation. At that time I had just read Maeterlinck's book on termites and was very much intrigued by the weird facts of the termite society which validly can be considered to be a transition between a more loosely constructed society like the human (in which the social members are still more or less individuals), and a biological organism in which the cells could not continue their individual existence alone without coexisting with each other. While talking with Freud about the relation of psychoanalysis to sociology and biology I mentioned the termite state as an example of an organization where the members of the unit have abandoned their freedom to a degree unknown in human societies, and asked him whether he thought human society would develop gradually towards such a highly planned and organized system. This conversation took place before Hitlerism, at a time when in Europe only Russia and Italy had totalitarian organizations. Freud's answer was one of those quick, lightening replies which put the problem in its broadest perspectives. In my opinion this faculty showed his genius more than anything else.

He said, and I remember his words almost verbatim:

Well Doctor, the human organism consists of cells which gave up their individual freedom and selfishness to such a degree that the human being as a whole can afford to retain its individuality. After all [he continued,] why do cells organize themselves into higher units? Only in order to survive, to become more effective in defending themselves against external dangers. Termites are the weakest creatures of the earth; they have not even a protecting hard shell like ants; no wonder they seek to survive by cooperation, and sacrifice their freedom for the sake of sheer existence. But man, the crown of creation, the master who dominates the world, why should he give up his freedom to such an extent as the weak help-less termites do? Who is man's enemy against whom he must organize himself in such a rigid fashion?

To which I replied:

Nobody except other men. We see that in war, countries organize themselves more rigidly and approach a termite state.

Freud shrugged his shoulders:

Well, that is true, but still I do not think that for man it will ever become necessary to give up his individuality so completely as the pitiful termites do.

It is obvious that in my reasoning I had followed the current concept of evolution, that smaller units gradually merge into higher systems. According to this principle, man, a cell-state, sometime in the future should form a superstate, a social superorganism. Freud immediately introduced into this argument the salient dynamic issue, namely that organization is not an aim in itself but takes place only under pressure as a necessary measure for the sake of survival. The question is whether or not for men this necessity will ever arise. Certainly it is thinkable that if man could settle the problems of his existence rationally and peacefully with his fellow men, he could save his individuality and freedom at least as long as no new type of a powerful biological creature appears on the scene and forces him in self-defense to organize and degrade himself to the status of a termite.

It may appear a contradiction that Freud, who developed such daring abstractions as that of the life and death instincts and the theory of the primal horde, was fundamentally a very realistic and practical thinker. He had an unusual sense for essentials and when he indulged in deductions, he never disregarded those immovable corner stones of experience which must always be taken into account. In other words, he was not only original, brilliant and penetrating, but wise. He used his wisdom frequently to bring his pupils down to earth from esoteric heights or premature theories.

For many years once every month, Freud invited a selected number of his pupils to an evening discussion. On one of these evenings I was asked to present the case of a delinquent young man whom I had studied in a prison. It was the case of an obsessed automobilist, a young waiter who, under the pressure of a compulsion, took long taxicab rides although he knew in advance that he would not be able to pay for them. I had neatly worked out the unconscious motivations of this peculiar but self-destructive hobby and used it for the demonstration of an instinct ridden personality so common among criminals.

Freud listened attentively and at the end made some quite complimentary remarks about the analytic interpretation of the case, but then he added:

> Only I do not see how this case can throw light upon the essential problem of criminality. If your patient had been the son of a millionaire, he might have become a record-breaker and as such a national hero. Only because of his social position and because he was a poor waiter, he could not give expression to his compulsion or hobby in a legal way.

This simple statement more than anything else demonstrated to me the fact that criminal psychology alone can solve the problem of crime just as little as the knowledge of human aggressiveness alone can ever explain war. Whenever I read smart criticisms of Freud accusing him of neglecting sociological factors, I have to smile remembering this evening in Freud's home.

The history of the psychoanalytic movement shows several occasions when Freud seemed to have been harsh and unforgiving. I saw him become impatient and intolerant only when intellectual integrity was at stake. The search for truth had the sanctity for him that it has for every real scientist. He could not tolerate it when people for personal advantages or even only for comfort's sake changed their intellectual convictions or abused their reasoning power for ulterior motives. He could not stand the twisting around of an argument only to defend an untenable position. On such occasions he became harsh and sarcastic and knew no mercy. Once I told him about hearing in a medical group one of the usual pseudo rational arguments attacking his teachings and saw the shade of anger flash across his face, followed by a contemptuous waving of his hands. Lack of intellectual integrity was the one human weakness to which he could not reconcile himself. The other was the competitive jealousy of his pupils. The discoverer of the œdipus complex was extremely sensitive towards the œdipus tendencies of his sons. I heard from one of the older Viennese psychoanalysts that Freud on one occasion, referring to one of the younger members of the Viennese group, said: "I cannot stand the parricidal look in his eyes."

136

It is often said that Freud was inaccessible to the suggestions and innovations of his pupils when they touched on the fundamental principles of his teachings. My own impression is that he was not intolerant about original ideas if they were genuine. What he could not tolerate was the kind of pseudo originality which serves only the desperate, competitive urge to excel. On the other hand, it seems that he had to follow the pathway of his own intellectual development and instinctively defended himself against outside influences. In one place he writes that he did not want to be hurried in his thinking by other people and had to follow the immanent course of his own ideas. Adler undoubtedly recognized earlier than Freud the significance of hostile impulses, but when Freud—much later—understood their role in neurosis and personality structure, he drew a much deeper and more adequate picture.

I never felt that Freud was inaccessible to suggestions which did not correspond exactly to his ideas. However I must say that whatever I contributed to psychoanalysis was along lines which he had initiated. After I had worked out the psychology of conscience and its role in neurosis and dream, Freud after some hesitation accepted my formulations. When I stated to him the differences of our views concerning nightmares, to my surprise he told me that there was no difference between our conceptions. I am afraid he may have overlooked the differences.

Psychoanalysis is in a state of rapid development and some of our present conceptions have come gradually to depart considerably from the original formulations of Freud. I consider it entirely out of place to try to point out the significance of this progress by emphasizing the defects of earlier freudian concepts. Our work is based on those solid foundations which Freud laid down.

Some of the modern purifiers of psychoanalysis, no matter how sound some of their ideas may be, fail to see in proper light the relation of their contributions to Freud's ideas. They are inclined to describe the development of their concepts as a revolution against orthodox freudism. What they do not see is that this progress is nothing but the natural evolution of their ideas from those of Freud's. Every type of science goes through the same type of evolution, yet no modern physicist would describe the development of physics from Newton's mechanics through the electromagnetic field theory of Maxwell to the modern theory of relativity by trying to minimize the achievements of previous periods. It is a disheartening view that in our field some of the

137

workers cannot take the same constructive attitude toward past accomplishment which is universal in all other fields of natural science.
Obviously these followers of Freud are blinded by their emotions, not
so much in the conceiving of their ideas but in the proper evaluation
of their significance.

In this respect they could learn much from Freud, who (another
sign of his wisdom) never overvalued the significance of his own work.
This is best seen in his attitude toward psychoanalytic therapy. He was
keenly aware of the limitations of therapy which are due to the rigidity
and weakness of human nature. Therefore he never expected too
much and was conscious that whatever slight but real and permanent
change psychoanalysis may bring about in an adult personality must
be considered a real victory of the therapeutic technique, an entirely
novel accomplishment of man, a step towards the much advocated but
never really achieved mastery of self. These therapeutic changes in the
personality although less spectacular than the accomplishments of
physics in the technical mastery of nature really are more miraculous.

I often witnessed his wisdom in regard to therapy. He was apt to
be sceptical about real changes and did not believe in the naive idea of
anyone being completely analyzed. As a young analyst I often heard in
our Psychoanalytic Society of the necessity of making the patient entirely independent of his analyst at the end of the treatment. The ideal
goal of the psychoanalytic treatment is, of course, that the patient,
who during the treatment necessarily becomes emotionally dependent
upon his physician, should become able after his treatment is completed to dispense with the analyst's help and give up entirely the infantile dependent attitude he felt toward his physician during the
treatment. Since I never could believe in complete things in connection with human endeavors I once consulted Freud about this matter.
I was not surprised to hear from him that according to his experience
in the majority of successful cases the success is based to a considerable degree on the continued faithful attitude of the patient to his analyst even though he may never see his physician again. The ego of most
severely neurotic people is too weak to endure the complete abandon-
ment of this dependence upon the physician he said; if it were not
weak, the patient would not have become a neurotic. The patient
carries around in his fantasy the image of the analyst and continues to
have towards this fantasied person a similar trusting and dependent attitude as he had had towards the analyst.

Therefore I was quite surprised that in his book, *The Future of an*

Illusion, he took a much more optimistic attitude towards mankind as a whole, demanding that it give up its faithful dependence on God. Obviously Freud was emotionally involved in the problem of religion. The greatest rationalist of the nineteenth century, he had just as little use for it as his great eighteenth century predecessor, Voltaire. I wonder whether Freud changed his views on this question, witnessing the appalling events of recent years which show that if you try to rob man of his heavenly God he will turn to worship human gods of much smaller caliber.

In his therapeutic technique Freud was less rigid and orthodox than most of his pupils. Although he was aware of the danger of the technique becoming ritualistic in the hands of the average man, he nevertheless did not encourage laxity, knowing that the majority needs rigid rules. A highly individual handling of cases requires a degree of independent judgment which is beyond the capacity of most physicians.

Although there is no precise evidence for it, I believe that times produce the type of great man and the type of knowledge which is needed at the moment. The greatness of a man consists in this faculty to anticipate these needs earlier than others. He is like a sensitive instrument which registers what is invisible to others. Freud's rôle in medicine has been described as a reaction against a too mechanistic trend which pervaded medicine with the introduction of laboratory methods. But his real significance is that in a time when man's whole interest was directed toward an increased mastery of the external world, he tried to understand man and man's relation to man. We are witnessing today the alarming fact that without this understanding, technical advancement becomes mainly a tool of mutual destruction. Psychoanalysis by its deeper knowledge of man's destructive impulses may be the antidote against the one-sided technical development which threatens to destroy civilization. It may lead to a more constructive social life in which man, by recognizing it, will control his unconscious destructiveness and use his scientific mastery of nature more for mutual help than destruction.

My Brother, Sigmund Freud
(1940)

ANNA FREUD BERNAYS

Freud's sister Anna married Ely Bernays, the brother of his wife. She and her husband emigrated to America at the end of the 19th century. This selection appeared in The American Mercury *51 (1940): 335–42.*

On the evening of 23 September 1939 I learned from a radio news report in New York that my brother Sigmund Freud had died in London, an exile. He had never been seriously ill during the greater part of his long and active life, not until sixteen years ago, when he was stricken by the affliction which finally caused his death.

My memories of my brother go back to the year 1864, when he was a boy of eight. I was his junior by not quite three years, but my mother told me many stories about his earlier childhood. Sigi and I were born in Freiberg, a small town in Moravia, where our father owned a textile factory. Many decades later our birthplace was marked by the Czechoslovakian government with a memorial tablet, which has probably been removed since March 1939. When Sigi was three the family moved to Vienna and we occupied a large apartment in Glockengasse.

My mother, as was natural, hoped great things of her first born and treasured early incidents which gave body to her hopes. She recalled, for instance, that the four-year-old Sigmund, having spoiled a chair by spotting it with soiled hands, consoled her: "Don't worry, mother. When I grow up I shall be a great man and then I'll buy you another chair." One afternoon a total stranger, in a pastry shop, looked at the boy and exclaimed, "You're a lucky mother! Some day the whole world will talk about this little fellow." At the time she told no one of this prophecy, but she believed it in her heart, and returned to the story often in later years when its import had been fulfilled. There were other incidents and premonitions. Perhaps my mother's trust in Sigmund's future destiny played a definite part in the trend given his

140

whole life. Though I am a Freud, I am not enough of a Freudian to analyze that trend in detail.

Our quarters on the Glockengasse seemed spacious when we first
moved in, but as more and more children arrived they became too
small and we moved once more. When my parents married, my father
was thirty-six, twice my mother's age. After fourteen years of marriage
they had seven children, two sons and five daughters. By an earlier
marriage father had two sons, but by the time that we of the second
family were born, these boys were grown up and lived in Manchester,
England, where father had business interests.

No matter how crowded our quarters, Sigmund always had a room
to himself. There were a parlor, a dining room, three bedrooms which
the rest of us shared, and a so-called cabinet, a single room separated
from the rest of the apartment. This cabinet, long and narrow, with a
window looking on the street was allotted to Sigmund. Here he lived
and worked until he became an interne in the General City Hospital.
All through the years of his school and university life, the only thing
that changed in this room was the increasing number of crowded
bookcases added to the writing desk, bed, chairs and shelf which furnished it.

Normally children in old Austria attended a primary or public
school for four years, beginning at the age of six, before entering high
school. But Sigmund never went to such a school. My father taught
him privately until he entered high school, where he headed his class
through all the eight years' course. He did his lessons in his cabinet,
going there, alone or with his friends, immediately after school hours.
During his 'teens he did not join us at our evening meals, but took
them alone in the room where he pored endlessly over his books. Indeed, his friends were not play- but study-mates. There were no such
things as "sports" then, either in or out of school. Sigmund, however,
was an enthusiastic walker and nature lover, and would roam the forest and woods near Vienna with his friends, bringing back rare plant
and flower specimens.

The household became familiar with the fact that Sigi constantly
won prizes for excellent school work. When he was eleven, at the close
of his first year in high school, he was awarded a famous *History of Animal Life*. I still remember how Sigmund bowed modestly while the
book was handed to him by the principal. It may well be that the gift
of this book had its part in arousing his interest in natural science.

Our father was a truly liberal man, so much so that the democratic

141

ideas absorbed by his children were far removed from the more conventional opinions of our relatives. Consequently, we saw very little of them. At that period, about the middle of the last century, the father was all-powerful in a European family and everyone obeyed him unquestioningly. With us, however, a much more modern spirit prevailed. My father, a self-taught scholar, was really brilliant. He would discuss with us children, especially Sigmund, all manner of questions and problems. We called these sessions "the family council." When the youngest son was born, father took Sigmund aside to consult him on the name to be given to the boy. I remember how Sigmund enthusiastically chose Alexander, basing his selection on Alexander's generosity and prowess as a general, and how he recited the whole story of the Macedonian's triumph in support of his choice. His choice of name was accepted.

In spite of his youth, Sigmund's word and wish were respected by everyone in the family. When I was eight years old, my mother, who was very musical, wanted me to study the piano, and I began practising by the hour. Though Sigmund's room was not near the piano, the sound disturbed him. He appealed to my mother to remove the piano if she did not wish him to leave the house altogether. The piano disappeared and with it all opportunities for his sisters to become musicians. Nor did any of my brother's children ever receive musical instructions where he would have to hear it. This wish for peace and quiet while he was working dominated his whole life, though he was not spoiled or demanding in other respects, being content with the simplest of clothing, food, and entertainment.

Not only did he read a great deal himself, but he exercised definite control over my reading. If I had a book that seemed to him improper for a girl of my age, he would say, "Anna, it is too early to read that book now." When I was fifteen, I remember, he felt that I should not read Balzac and Dumas. I read them, of course, notwithstanding, hiding the forbidden volumes among the linens. On the other hand, he was generously helpful in connection with our lessons. The wish to come to the aid of others, strongly implanted in Sigmund's character, later induced him to drop his original intention to devote himself to natural science. Though he could not bear the sight of blood, he overcame this aversion and entered the field of medicine.

In 1866, when my brother was ten years old, there was war between Prussia and Austria. At the North Station in Vienna long trains arrived bringing wounded soldiers to the city hospitals and my father would go there, taking Sigmund with him, to see them taken from the trains to hay-filled carts which bore them to the hospitals. Sigi was greatly impressed by the plight of the wounded. He begged my mother to let him have all her old linen so that from it he could make "Charpie," which was then used instead of medicated cotton. We girls made "Charpie" in our schools and Sigmund begged his teachers to organize "Charpie" groups in his boys' high school as well.

When Sigi was twelve my father commissioned a painter to do a portrait of the seven children. The painter came to our house and arranged a group in the parlor, with Sigmund, the eldest, at the head and two-year-old Alexander at the foot, between them the five little girls, all ages and sizes. I can image that he had no little trouble keeping such a diversified group quiet and interested. Sigmund, I recall vividly, started conversations on art with the painter. One day he said to the man, "Art and Nature go together; painting and music show the thoughts and emotions of human beings. If a man loves too much, it is a poem, and if he mourns too much it is a tragedy." When the art work was finished, my father examined the canvas carefully and discovered that there were only thirteen, instead of fourteen, feet for the seven of us. In the interests of realism that leg was added somewhere, almost at random. The masterpiece is still extant in some Vienna storehouse, with the household goods of my younger brother, now released by the Nazis.

During the Franco-Prussian war of 1870 the fourteen-year-old Sigmund had a large map on his writing desk and followed the campaigns by means of small flags. While he did this, he lectured to me and my sister Rose about the war in general and the importance of the various moves of the combatants. I remember how affected I was by the news of Louis Napoleon's imprisonment and my wild fit of tears on hearing of it, while Sigmund explained to us the meaning of the Paris Commune.

Another episode that remains clear in memory is our visit to the American Pavilion at the Vienna World's Fair in 1873. I was especially impressed by a model of an American school, with a separate desk for every pupil, instead of the long benches in front of long desks in our Austrian classrooms. Sigmund, however, was fascinated by an exhibit of President Lincoln's letters in facsimile, and the Gettysburg Address. We were living in a country with few liberties or free ideas, and these documents, as well as the American Constitution, naturally stirred the imagination of a boy from a liberal household. Sigmund already read and spoke English at the time, having learned it partly in school and partly through correspondence with his Manchester half-brothers. He obtained copies of those American documents and soon knew them all by heart. I remember him declaiming and explaining the Gettysburg Address to his sisters.

Sigmund knew a great deal about America and its culture. He was particularly enamored of Mark Twain, whose books he read as they came out. Naturally he kept abreast of all our native literature. He well appreciated also the humor and gaiety of Viennese folk-songs, and he would hum them while working though he could not keep a tune.

A by-product of the Fair was the modernization of our dining room light; the old stationary oil lamp gave way to a petroleum lamp that could be raised and lowered on chains above the table—a great luxury and one of the first lamps of its kind in Vienna. In our bedrooms we used candles, though Sigmund had an oil lamp. We had many rooms and were fairly prosperous, but there was no bathroom or even bathtub in our home. Once a fortnight, when we were small, a great wooden tub, with several kegs of hot and cold water, was brought into the house by a pair of strong carriers from a public bathing establishment. All this was put into the kitchen on the stone flags, and we were put into the tub, after being well soaped, one after the other. The next day the men returned and took the tub and kegs away again. As we grew older, however, our mother took us into a bathing house, of which there were several in Vienna, and to our great pride would hire a cabin with two tubs and an extra stove in the corner. While we scrubbed and bathed, the little stove roared and the apples we had brought along roasted and spluttered on its top.

At eighteen, Sigi passed all his examinations at the Gymnasium *summa cum laude.* Successful graduates were usually given a treat by their families before entering the university or business, and my father sent Sigmund to Manchester to visit our two half-brothers. During his stay the elder, Emanuel, wrote enthusiastic letters about him in a funny mixture of English and German which delighted us sisters at the family council.

You have given us great pleasure by sending us Sigmund. He is a splendid specimen of a fine human being, and if I had the pen of a

Dickens, I could well make a hero of him. . . . All your descriptions of him have been worthless; only now, since he is with us, do we see him as he really is.

It was in England that Sigmund resolved to study medicine on his return to Vienna, and so informed my father. Not satisfied with this decision, father stated his objections, claiming that Sigmund was much too soft-hearted for the task. But Sigmund's mind was made up, though at first he planned to do only research. "I want to help people who suffer," was his reply. He won the day and registered as a student at the University of Vienna in the Faculty of Medicine.

In the spring of 1878 my brother was given a fellowship by the University which enabled him to go to Trieste during the summer vacation to continue his studies at the Biological Institute. Trieste, the only harbor of the former Austrian Empire, had a research station noted for its collection of marine plant and animal life. Sigmund, who had been interested in biological research since childhood, buried himself in biological studies all that summer. It seemed almost as though he would decide to remain in this theoretical field of natural science. But when he returned to Vienna and received his degree of Doctor of Medicine, he became an interne at the Vienna General Hospital, attached to the staff of Professor Ernst Brücke. From that time on he did not leave the field of applied medicine.

He now lived at the hospital and returned to us only on week ends, staying in his little hall-room. Many of his friends came to see him there. One would have imagined that the presence in the house of five young women would have had some attraction for these young men, but they seemed less interested in entertainment than in scientific discussion with our learned brother, and disappeared into his room with scarcely a glance for any of us! We were too shy and diffident to break through their reserve. Many of these young men became famous in later years in the fields of medicine, pure science, and law. Among them was Dr. Breuer, with whom my brother published his first book and whose studies of a case of hysteria first gave impetus to Sigmund's growing distrust of the methods then used to cure mental ailments.

Compulsory military service forced my brother to interrupt his work at the hospital in 1879 to spend one year as a so-called volunteer —the name given to educated young men whose military rank was between that of a noncommissioned and a commissioned officer. There was little of the voluntary in this service as far as Sigmund was concerned; he was genuinely happy to return to his hospital work.

During the winter of 1881 both Sigmund and I became engaged; my future husband and Sigmund's bride were brother and sister—Ely and Martha Bernays. We planned a double celebration of our unions in my parents' home. A few weeks before this took place, on 8 December 1881 a terrible catastrophe shook the hearts of the Viennese. That evening we two engaged couples had tickets for the performance of *The Tales of Hoffman* at the State Theater; but we had accepted another invitation. Returning late at night from our party, we saw a red glare lighting up the sky and heard that the theater had been in flames all evening. Hurrying towards the site, we joined the thousands of people standing on the Ring watching the flaming theater. Finally the roof fell in with a crash. Though we were told at first that all the audience had been saved, the truth came out on the following day. More than 600 people had lost their lives in the overcrowded theater, and there was great mourning throughout the city. From all over the world came money and gifts for the survivors. Public funds were set aside for relief work headed by Emperor Franz Joseph himself. He decided that a large apartment house, the House of Atonement, should be built on the site of the fire, the revenues to be used for the needy.

Five years passed. During this time Sigmund went to Paris to do research work under the great Charcot, and I married. My brother married in 1886, after his return from France. It was hard to get tenants for the apartment house where so many people had lost their lives. My brother, far from sharing the general superstition, did not hesitate to establish himself there with his young wife, and his example quickly encouraged others. When Sigmund's eldest child was born there in 1887, the Emperor honored this first-born of the *Suehnhaus* by presenting him a handsome vase from the Royal Porcelain Workshops.

My brother's life as a private individual soon passed into another phase, that of the founder of the new psychoanalytical theory of mental life which was to place him among the immortals of science. The child of the *Suehnhaus* was followed by five others, three sons and two more daughters, of whom all are alive except one young daughter who succumbed in the influenza epidemic following the World War. Though I came to America with my family in 1892, I have seen and visited my brother often during these long years. The last memento that I have of him is a letter, dated 14 May 1939, from his English home in reply to my greetings on his eighty-third birthday:

My dear Sister:

By mutual consent we have ceased to send one another birthday wishes, since we have come to know that to grow old is not unmixed with happiness, but rather a part of the fate which must be borne with patience like everything else life brings.

Yet I am glad to know that you like your task of being a great-grandmother, and I hope that you will live to have much happiness through your children and their children. As ever,

Your faithful

Sigmund.

The deep feeling shown in this letter is understandable in the light of the fate which sent him into exile at an advanced age. His happiness would have been far greater if he had come to America as I did half a century ago. Here in my adopted, beloved fatherland, I have lived and brought up my children—four daughters and one son, Edward L. Bernays. My brother, too, would have seen his descendants, as I see my children and grandchildren and great-grand-children, build up free and happy lives. America saw my brother's greatness, while Europe's politics have blinded it. His discoveries owe a debt to America, one that my descendants will help to repay.

Reminiscences of Freud
(1940)

ABRAHAM ARDEN BRILL

A. A. Brill (1874–1948), a pioneer analyst in America, knew Freud over a period of almost thirty years. He was Freud's New York host and guide when he visited the United States in 1909. This selection was in The Psychoanalytic Quarterly 9 (1940): 177–83.

Although he had been ill for over fifteen years, the death of Sigmund Freud in September 1939 was a great shock when the sad news came. Once, on my parting from him, he said, "This is the last time I shall see you." I replied saying, "No, you will live as long as your mother did." She lived ninety-five years. Despite his chronic illness and his age—he was eighty-three years old—I could not believe his death was imminent.

Through his death the world has lost one of its foremost figures, science has lost one of its most earnest workers, and his pupils are bereft of a great teacher, a spiritual father. Our only consolation is that he has left us a great heritage: his *Gesammelte Schriften*, his great work, through which we can still commune with him.

To attempt an evaluation of Freud's life and personality is no simple task for one who was in close contact with him for thirty-two years. His life was beset with many trials but with no small measure of satisfaction. It was certainly a very busy and full life. Most of his years were punctuated with hardships and annoyances; but being a realist, he learned to adapt himself to all circumstances. He never complained in adversity, he accepted his lot with fortitude. Nor was he overjoyed when finally he achieved recognition. I was with him on a few occasions when he was sorely troubled. I was deeply moved, but when I looked at him his face mirrored the unclouded clearness and the exalted serenity of the true sage. One must not however picture him as imperturbably placid. He was not always calm. He had often to contend with great difficulties and annoyances, and he reacted appropriately. He once said to me, "I can scold and fight as well as anyone." But even in his most trying disappointments he never lost his temper.

I cannot help recalling that he was deeply disappointed in some of his pupils, and in the treatment accorded him by the academic world which failed to understand him. There was, however, one bright spot which shone resplendently throughout his life. He was an ideal husband and father. Those who had the pleasure of being admitted to his family circle were deeply impressed by the placid and genial home environment. His relation to his children was ideal. I happened to be present when his daughter, then a very young girl, asked him whether she might read his book, Leonardo da Vinci, which had appeared only a few days before. He looked at her benignly and said, "Certainly you may read it." I was somewhat taken aback by his unequivocal response. I had just finished reading the book and wondered whether such a young girl should become engrossed in the problems treated in it. That was in 1910, after I had been a psychoanalyst only about two-and-a-half years and had not yet assimilated the meaning of the 'family romance.'

Those who know his works and have followed the vicissitudes of the development of psychoanalysis are familiar with his later struggles and disappointments. The anti-Semitic problem was vividly impressed upon him at a very early age and recurred throughout his life. He refers to it often in his *Traumdeutung* and *Selbstdarstellung*, but he reacted to it always in the same manner. When he was forced to leave his beloved Vienna where he had lived for seventy-eight years and go into exile, he was calm and stoical.

The New York Psychoanalytic Society was founded in 1911 for the study and promulgation of psychoanalysis, and the Institute, the first of its kind in this country, was founded in 1931 on the same principles, namely, to disseminate and promote Freud's teachings. We could always turn to him for instruction and advice; he was always ready to help any of his pupils. With many of us he was in close touch until he died, and we particularly shall miss him.

During thirty-two years of my psychoanalytic life he was always ready to advise and encourage me. He was reluctant to sympathize if one were not ready to carry his own burden. In the beginning of my leadership here I complained to him that the burden of it was quite heavy. I naturally expected him to sympathize with me. He looked at me and said: "Well, you are young; you should not complain, but act."

Thereafter we frequently discussed personally and by correspondence every difficult and important situation, but I never again asked him for sympathy. In his relations with his pupils he did not hesitate to speak with psychoanalytic frankness when the occasion demanded, but he was a dear and true friend with whom it was a joy to spend an evening. It is perhaps trite to mention that the author of Wit and its Relation to the Unconscious was a very witty man, and one of the most pleasant impressions that he left with me was his incomparable sense of humor.

Let me mention some of his scientific accomplishments. He began as a researcher in physiology and neurology, or rather in biology. (Nowadays very few neurologists or psychiatrists begin their histological investigations on the spinal cord of the *Ammocoetes-Petromyzon*.) He had a long and thorough preparation in neurology. He was proud to report that he was the first in Vienna to diagnose a case of acute polyneuritis which was later confirmed by autopsy. His neurological works (Cerebral Diplegia in Childhood; Aphasia and Infantile Cerebral Paralysis) were very highly regarded when they appeared, and are still considered classics. It is interesting to note that in his Infantile Cerebral Paralysis (Volume III of Nothnagel's *Spezielle Pathologie und Therapie*) he quotes the works of two American neurologists, James J. Putnam and Bernard Sachs, who later played some part in the psychoanalytic movement of this country—one, I might say, on the positive side. I had the pleasure of introducing Dr. Putnam and Professor William James to Professor Freud at the Clark University celebration. We are all acquainted with Dr. Putnam's psychoanalytic works and have fully appreciated his active and sincere support. On the other hand, Dr. Sachs, who was a fellow student of Freud in Vienna, became the most influential opponent of psychoanalysis soon after I introduced it here. Yet, it was Bernard Sachs who proposed Freud for honorary membership in the New York Neurological Society on the occasion of his eightieth birthday.

Freud continued his interest in neurology for a number of years after he and Breuer published their Preliminary Communications on the Psychic Mechanisms of Hysterical Phenomena. Thus his contribution to the Nothnagel textbook appeared in 1897, after he had written his paper, On the Etiology of Hysteria (1896). It was only natural that the more absorbed he became in psychoanalytic mechanisms the less attention he paid to neurology, but despite the fact that he later espoused the cause of lay-analysis, he never lost sight of the patient's organic make-up. In 1910 Dr. F. Peterson referred a patient to me for analysis. His diagnosis was "neurasthenia" and the patient informed me that he had been treated by other neurologists without getting any help. His main symptom was headaches which appeared on physical or mental exertion. He had other symptoms characteristic of neurasthenia which he claimed were alleviated by medication, but the only temporary relief for his headaches was obtained through the application of copper plates which had been recommended by Dr. Charles L. Dana. After seeing me a few times he informed me that he had to go abroad for a few weeks on pressing business, and when I heard that he was to visit Vienna, I suggested that he consult Professor Freud. A few weeks later I received a letter in which Professor Freud told me that the patient was not a case for analytic therapy; that he suffered from "chronic internal hydrocephalus." I was very much impressed by this diagnosis because no one here had thought there was anything organic to account for the patient's complaints.

In his autobiography Freud tells us how he happened to go to Paris, to Charcot's clinic in 1885. He stayed there about a year. Anyone who knows something of Charcot's works and has followed Freud's scientific career can readily see the profound influence that Charcot exerted on him. Freud often quotes him, especially in his early works, and we know the part that hypnotism played in the cathartic method. Breuer himself was influenced by Charcot's popularization of hypnotism. It was really hypnotism, and, I might say, accident that resulted in the famous Anna O. case which Breuer related to Freud before he went to Charcot. Freud became one of Charcot's favorite pupils as well as his German translator.

What he learned in Charcot's clinic interested him immensely. He became impressed by the facts that through hypnosis Charcot could remove and produce hysterical symptoms, that hysteria was a real disease which was not confined to the female sex, that there were also male hysterics. He tells us that Charcot called hysteria the most enigmatic of all nervous diseases which he wished to solve; for before Charcot came on the scene, hysterics were called "liars" and "deceivers" whom no one would take seriously.

Freud tells us that he was fascinated by a picture which hung in the lecture hall at the Salpetrière. It is the famous painting which shows citizen Pinel causing the removal of the chains from the insane. Freud goes on to say that Charcot continued this liberation of the mentally afflicted in the case of hysteria. He made respectable patients

151

out of putative swindlers. If you read the literature of those times, you will find that this was no easy task since the old timers, the conservatives, sneered not only at the patients but at the doctors who treated them by hypnotism.

Freud continued the liberation started by Pinel and followed by his master, Charcot. Freud went further than his predecessors. He outdid his master by removing from hysteria the stigma of the *famille nevropathique* imposed on it by Charcot. According to Charcot heredity is the only cause of hysteria; *ergo*, hysteria is a form of *dégénéré* that cannot be eradicated. I need hardly mention that the concept of *dégénéré* has no place in Freud's psychoanalysis. He began with the individual and showed us that there is logic and reason in the most peculiar mental manifestations. Aches, paralyses, obsessions, hallucinations, delusions, that had hitherto baffled physicians and mankind became perfectly clear through analysis. The dualism of soma and psyche vanishes as soon as we know the whole being. It was inevitable that Freud should have gone from the adult individual to his childhood, and thence to the childhood of the race. Dream interpretation led directly to the meaning of myths, fairy tales and primeval history. There is a psychic unity, a sort of monism, which courses through his works and which culminates in his Moses and Monotheism. Freud here takes his place with Darwin, Lamarck, Hering, Butler, Haeckel, Semon, Bleuler and others. He states for the first time that acquired characteristics in the form of memory remnants are inherited: "I have no qualms in saying that men have always known—in this particular way—that once upon a time they had a primeval father and killed him."

On the happy occasion when we celebrated his seventy-fifth birthday, I said that I was so readily attracted to Freud because his thoughts or, if I may say so, his system reminded me of Spinoza to whom I became attached by a very strong bond long before I heard of Freud. After reading Moses and Monotheism, I was again reminded of Spinoza and impressed by the fact that throughout all his works Freud consistently and clearly follows almost the same mode of thought as Spinoza. I cannot avoid comparing Spinoza's *substantia* with Freud's *libido*. One might say that *mutatis mutandis* there is a marked resemblance between them which can be seen if one recalls Freud's definition of instinct as given in Beyond the Pleasure Principle, and then follows the course of libido development as presented in his subsequent works ending with Moses and Monotheism. Taking Moses as his starting point, he shows paleo-psychologically not only some of the rem-

152

nants of primeval history that have become incorporated into our modern life, but also the course of the libido as it manifests itself phylo- and onto-genetically from the beginning of organic existence. It is quite obvious why he illustrates his views through the Jews and their religion. To Freud, as to Spinoza, who looks at everything *sub specie aeternitatis,* his coreligionaries, the Jews, merely represent a *mode* of the *substantia.* It so happens that the Jews not only furnish records of what took place five or six thousand years ago, but their religion and traditions contain much material from primeval times, preserved by them in pristine form. Through monotheistic religion, which seems to have developed on the scheme of a traumatic neurosis, one can best follow the course of libido through the ages. The trials and tribulations which Freud had to endure as a Jew kept the fate of his people vividly before his eyes.

Freud has left us a great patrimony which we must and shall guard. I have no doubt that in the course of time some of Freud's views may be modified, but I am sure that the luster of the man, the glory of his great achievements, will remain permanently a scientific mile post no matter what the future may bring.

Reflections, Reminiscences of Sigmund Freud

(1940)

ABRAHAM ARDEN BRILL

This selection appeared in Medical Leaves 3 (1940): 18–29.

It is very difficult for me to tell in the space at my disposal what courses through my mind about Sigmund Freud, the man and the scientist. Such a task would have been simpler for one who was perhaps less familiar with all phases of his life. I have been attached to him by very strong ties for thirty-two years. I was his first English translator and I introduced him to this country. When I informed him in January 1936 that I had now definitely retired from my official psychoanalytic activities, he wrote me a very warm letter, in which he expressed his gratitude for all that I had done for the analytic cause during such a long period and said, *Sie haben sie nicht nur in Amerika eingeführt und vertreten.* Modesty keeps me from quoting further. There was nothing of any moment that happened to Sigmund Freud, or to psychoanalysis, that we did not discuss personally or by correspondence. I can say with no fear of contradiction that for all these years we mutually shared our pleasures, triumphs, trials and tribulations.

As his translator and expositor, I was naturally the ready target for all the criticisms that his new and provocative views aroused in this country. But I also shared his triumphs. For after having encountered here enormous opposition, psychoanalysis is now firmly established in mental medicine and in the allied sciences. No work on psychiatry, psychology, anthropology, or sociology can be considered up-to-date or complete, which does not take due account of Freud's theories.

Freud tells us that we pay insufficient attention to the accidental factors of life. My meeting him was seemingly purely accidental. Like many other young psychiatrists in the beginning of this century I became surfeited with the descriptive psychiatry of the German School, which did nothing but describe and classify. Freud was then hardly known outside of a small circle of pupils in his own home. I visited the Vienna clinics in 1905, but I never heard of him. On my way back to New York, I stopped at the Exposition in Liège, Belgium; there I met a young man who happened to be placed near me at the small table where I was dining. We introduced ourselves. He had just been through his military training in the Austrian army and was commissioned a lieutenant. Like me, he was alone on vacation visiting the fair. We soon became friendly and traveled together for the next week. On parting we hoped to meet again in 1907, when I expected to pay another visit to some European clinic. I doubted, however, whether I would go to Vienna, his home, for I had already decided to spend most of my time in some clinic in Paris. In his effort to change my mind my traveling companion casually said: "Why don't you come to Vienna and take courses with Freud?" As I had never heard of Freud, I expressed my opinion that he could not be famous enough to go to for courses. "Oh," he said, "he must be somebody; else he would not have so many opponents!" For some reason I was impressed by this rejoinder.

That happened in September 1905. In the spring of 1907 I was working in the *Hospice de Bicêtre* in Paris, in Pierre Marie's service, and felt convinced that my quest for more knowledge on borderline cases of mental diseases would not be gratified in this hospital. My former friend and mentor, Dr. Frederick Peterson of New York, then suggested that I might visit the Clinic of Psychiatry in Burghölzli, Zurich. He said, "They are experimenting there with the Freud theories, which I think will interest you." The name, "Freud," immediately recalled the remark of my erstwhile traveling companion, that Freud had many opponents, and this decided me to go to Zurich on the following day.

When Jung, whom I first met at that clinic, asked, "Did you read Freud's *Traumdeutung?*" I was somewhat puzzled by the title, but I acted as if I knew Freud quite well. I cannot enter into my work at the psychiatric clinic in Zurich. I merely wish to repeat what I have already said, that I soon became impressed and fascinated by the psychiatry as it was practiced at the Zurich school. Everything was so interesting because the patients were studied by Freud's psychoanalytic methods. Every case assumed life and interest, which I had never seen before. After a few weeks of observation and study I decided to make

Freud's works accessible to our readers, and until 1918 I gave most of my leisure time to the translation of Freud's works. In addition to my work as translator, I have taught, read and discussed his theories until this very day. No wonder that I have remained in close contact with him throughout all these years.

On my first visit to him I became much impressed by his very genial and alert personality. Theoretically he was no longer a stranger to me, for I had witnessed for months the application of his theories in the Zurich clinic, and I, myself, had diligently applied them to patients. Yet, I was in a mixed state of mind on my first visit to him—I might call it a state of anxiety. That feeling was dispelled on our first encounter. To be sure, I felt that he looked right through me, and this seemed confirmed by some casual remarks which he expressed every once in a while during our conversation, but I soon realized that the old saying, *Tout savoir, c'est tout pardonner*, was embodied in his whole being. He was a very benign and understanding scrutinizer, and soon made you feel at ease. I was particularly impressed by his ready sense of humor. Whenever we conversed, he was sure to illustrate his statement by some witticism. My last visit to him was in 1936, while he was sick in bed following one of those many operations to which he had been subjected for the control of the cancerous growth. My heart was full of sorrow at the sight of his emaciated physiognomic expression, but this feeling soon vanished because as the conversation continued, he resorted to his wonted witty mode of illustration.

Professor Freud led a very full and a very satisfactory life. When I say a "full life," I mean that he was a most indefatigable worker, who labored incessantly throughout the day with patients and at night on his writings. In the early part of his psychoanalytic life he gave from 10 to 12 hours daily to patients, and until shortly before his death, he gave 5 hours daily to his patients. His literary productions are prodigious. His *Collected Papers* comprise twelve large volumes and he left enough material for two more volumes. The last two published volumes, XI and XII, consist of works which he produced during the 16 years of his illness. But even long before 1923, when his malady was first diagnosed as carcinoma of the upper maxillary, he practiced and wrote in the face of the greatest discouragements that were ever meted out to any man. From 1892 until he began to gain recognition about 1910, he was severely criticized and reviled by most of his psychiatric contemporaries whenever any of his theories were published. Any unknown nobody could gain recognition by hurling mud at

Freud. In a letter of 2 May 1909, he wrote with some gratification that there seemed to be an upswing in favor of psychoanalysis, judging by the increasing demand for his works as reported by his publisher. He ends the paragraph with the following prophetic words: "I often fear that when the triumph will come, I will be at the end of my vigor and health, but I immediately repel these dark thoughts. To die in harness is my resolution."

He did finally achieve fame after many years of hardships and disappointment. Freud never forgot these dark days of his life. In his answer to Dr. Alfonso Paquet, who informed him in 1930 that he was selected as the recipient of the Goethe Prize, he said: "*Ich bin durch öffentliche Ehrungen nicht verwöhnt worden und habe mich darum so eingerichtet dass ich solche entbehren konnte.*" (I have not been spoiled by public honors and I have, therefore, adjusted myself that I could dispense with the same.) And shortly before these remarks to Dr. Paquet, he expressed himself similarly to Georg Fuchs, the author of *Wir Zuchthäusler*, a book on prison reform. Herr Fuchs, while asking Professor Freud to write an introduction to the above book, referred to him as the standard bearer of cultural Germany, to which Professor Freud answered, "But it seems to me that I am *persona ingrata*, if not *ingratissima* to the German nation—not only to the educated, but also to the uneducated classes." For up to this time he had not only received no honors, but for many years he had been the subject of the most malicious, or rather the most ridiculous misrepresentations. No wonder he became used and hardened to his lot.

On his 80th birthday he received a great many honors from all parts of the civilized world when he was a very sick man. Shortly before his birthday he wrote: "You may think of me on my 80th birthday, but do me the favor not to have any festivities." And in another letter he states that despite his wishes preparations are made in Vienna in honor of his 80th birthday and remarks: "That I am looking forward with some dismay to most of the festivities will not surprise you" (26 April 1936). He added that the only bright spot in all these arrangements was a lecture to be given by Thomas Mann, who would speak "about me and the future." And in a letter of 16 May 1936 he writes, "The noise about my birthday is now fortunately at an end," and adds, "*Der Höhepunkt war ein öffentlicher Vortrag von Thomas Mann, betitelt, 'Freud und die Zukunft.'*" Thomas Mann's essay on *Freud and the Future* is not only a great tribute to Freud, but a masterpiece of literature and thought. When I visited the master about two months later, he was quite proud to show me clippings, telegrams and cables telling of the honors that were showered on him on this memorable occasion. To one who, as it were, empathized himself with everything that befell the master since 1907, this was a very touching scene. It was on this occasion that I again urged him to leave Vienna as the political situation was growing more ominous. He gave me the same answer that he had given me before in a letter, namely: "I shall leave Vienna only if the Nazis come here."

Throughout all his trials there was one bright spot, his home life. Those of us who were fortunate enough to be admitted to his home were especially impressed by his placid, nay, ideal family life. A spirit of congeniality and freedom pervaded the atmosphere of his home. It may be trite to state that the master who traced all our good and evil qualities back to early childhood knew how to bring up his children properly. This is not always the case even in the best psychoanalytic families, but in Freud's home one sensed a certain relationship, a sort of subdued freedom, between parents and children, which I have seen nowhere else. Despite the fact that his opponents continually harped on the fact that Freud saw sex in everything, none ever expressed anything against his moral standards. No breath of scandal was ever connected with his name. He brought up three sons and three daughters, of whom five are now living (let us hope) in London. Only one of his children, his youngest daughter, Anna, has followed in her father's footsteps. Anna is a chip off the old block. She has published numerous valuable works on human behavior, some of which have been translated into English.

Long before the First World War, Freud expressed to me considerable concern about the future of the children in Austria, and that was at a time when Austria was still a great nation and seemed to offer many opportunities for young people. When I expressed these last views to him, he said prophetically that everything might look nice on the surface, but the storm might come at any time. He had in mind the Jewish problem, which had haunted him throughout his life, and struck him so hard towards the end of his days.

In his *Interpretation of Dreams* and in his autobiography he relates numerous anti-Semitic episodes from his early and later life, which apparently affected him profoundly; he describes how he came face to face with the problem in his early boyhood and when he entered the university in 1873. He states that it struck him as unreasonable that he was supposed to feel inferior and extra-national because he was a Jew.

He rejected the first with all the resoluteness he could muster; he said that he could not grasp why he should be ashamed of his origin, or as they began to say, of his race. It also struck him as unreasonable that he was supposed to feel inferior and extra-national because he was a Jew. This denial to him of nationality, he states he gave up without much regret. He felt that there would surely always be a bit of room for a zealous fellow worker within the sphere of mankind without the necessity of any enrollment. He adds significantly: "But these first university impressions produced one very important result for the future. I became familiar with my destiny—to belong to the opposition, and to be proscribed from the compact majority. A certain independence of judgment was in this way developed."

In his *Wit and Its Relation to the Unconscious* the master tells us that: "A particularly favorable case for tendency-wit results if the intended criticism of the inner resistance is directed against one's own person, or more carefully expressed, against a person in whom one takes an interest, that is, a composite personality such as one's own people." He goes on to say that this explains why a number of excellent jokes which he has quoted as illustrative specimens should deal with the Jewish national life. The stories which he gives in his book were invented by Jews and were directed against Jewish peculiarities. He states that the Jewish jokes which originate with Jews admit the Jewish shortcomings, but also expose the Jewish merits. "Incidentally," he says, "I do not know whether one often finds a people that makes merry so unreservedly over its own shortcomings."

If one reads this very profound work, one finds that many of the witticisms which Freud selected as illustrations for his theories are of Jewish origin, and some, if divested of the theoretical material for which they are façades, are far from creditable to the race. This has been noticed by some observers who criticized Freud for having selected these examples. It occurred to me that the author has unconsciously utilized these Jewish jokes to disburden himself of the tension which was accumulated in him since his early childhood by some anti-Semitic experiences.

In his autobiography Freud states: "My parents were Jews and I remained a Jew." And in a letter dated 26 February 1925, which he had written to the editor of the *Jüdische Presszentrale* in Zurich, he states: "*Ich kann sagen dass ich der jüdischen Religion so ferne stehe wie allen anderen Religionen, d.h. sie sind mir alle als Gegenstand wissenschaftliche Interesse hochbedeutsam, gefühlmässig bin ich an ihnen nicht beteiligt. Dagegen habe ich immer ein starkes Gefühl von Zusammengehörigkeit mit meinem Volke und es auch bei meinen Kindern genährt. Wir sind alle der Jüdischen Konfession geblieben."* (I can say that I am as little an adherent of the Jewish religion as of any other religion, *i.e.*, I consider them all most important as objects of scientific interest, but I do not share the emotional feeling that goes with them. On the other hand, I have always felt a strong feeling of kinship with my race and have also nurtured the same in my children. We have all adhered to the Jewish religion.)

In short, Freud, like many scientists—Jewish or non-Jewish—was not orthodox in religion, but was fundamentally as good a Jew as Spinoza, Einstein, and many others. I recall *e.g.* that while he was here during September of 1909, when he participated in the Clark University celebration, he sent a *Rosh Hashana* good wishes cable to his wife and family in Vienna. In the letter just mentioned he also explains in a way why he was not orthodox. He says: *"Meine Jugend fiel in einer Zeit da unsere freisinnige Religionslehrer keinen Wert auf die Erwärbung von Kenntnissen in der Hebraischen Sprache und Literatur bei ihren Schülern legten. Meine Bildung ist daher auf diesem Gebiete recht Zurückgeblieben, das ich später oftmal bedauert hatte."* (My youth happened in a period when our free-minded teachers of religion placed no value on their pupils' acquisition of knowledge in the Hebrew language and literature. This part of my education was therefore quite neglected, which I often regretted later.)

Judging by what I know of the Austrian Jews, I can say that any Jewish boy whose Hebrew education was not stressed could not have been brought up very religiously.

Concerning his origin, Freud stated that he had reason to believe that his father's family was settled for a long time on the Rhine (at Cologne), that as a result of a persecution of the Jews during the 14th or 15th century they fled eastwards, and in the course of the 19th century they migrated back from Lithuania through Galicia into German-Austria.

It may also be of interest to mention that soon after the advent of Hitler one of Freud's former followers, C. G. Jung of Zurich, called Freud's psychology "Jewish." A number of Aryans took strong exception to this statement. As Dr. Mauerhofer expressed it, "To speak of Freud's work as 'Jewish psychology' is crypto-anti-Semitic. One may as well speak of a Jewish physics, a Jewish mathematics, or a Jewish

160

chemistry, expressions which are indefensible in science." Jung, himself, thereupon emphatically disavowed any anti-Semitic implications in his peculiar term. Freud's works also formed part of Hitler's sacred pyre, but as the bulk of this pyre consisted of works of non-Jewish thinkers, it is quite evident that at least in this instance Hitler was bent more on the destruction of science in general rather than specific Jewish sciences.

Nevertheless, I feel that Freud's Jewish descent—constitution—and his later experiences—environment—played a great part in the moulding of his character, and in directing his future interests. Without going into an analysis of his character one can mention a few of his outstanding qualities. He had an inordinate curiosity for knowledge and a stubborn perseverance in the pursuance of the same. Only those thoroughly versed in his works, who at the same time possess a thorough knowledge of the status of psychiatry before he came on the scene, can fully appreciate the magnitude of his achievements. To be sure, a strong desire for knowledge is no Jewish monopoly, but he did come from a race who even long before the diaspora were wont to drum into their male children's heads that "Knowledge is better than pearls." And through the thousands of years of persecution when the Jew served as the scapegoat for so-called civilized Europe, he held on to learning with grim determination. It is my feeling that the Jew was the first to recognize the great value of "knowledge for knowledge's sake." Moreover, Freud tells us that despite his father's meagre finances, he was free to follow whatever vocation he himself selected. Unlike many a father who, as it were, stunts his son's curiosity for learning by directing, nay, often forcing him into a career which he thinks is best for the son, Freud's father gave him free rein. In other words, the shock he received at the university enrollment, which caused him to conclude that he was proscribed from the compact majority and that he was, therefore, independent, was really not a first or a new impression; it was merely an emergence from the unconscious of a well developed path of reaction. May we not assume that this feeling of not being bound by enrollments was also later responsible for his bold venture into hitherto undiscovered fields?

In his *Interpretation of Dreams* Professor Freud tells us that at an early age while walking once with his father, the latter was trying to acquaint him with his views of life, and to show him how times had improved since his own youth he related the following episode: He walked along the street of his home town one Saturday, dressed up in

161

his best clothes, a new fur cap on his head. Along came a Christian who knocked off his cap into the gutter and shouted to him, "Off the sidewalk, Jew!" "And what did you do?" "I went off the sidewalk and picked up my cap," was the calm answer.

Professor Freud states that this did not seem very heroic on the part of the tall, strong man who now was leading a little boy by the hand, and dilates at some length on this episode. It evidently impressed him very deeply. Yet, despite his conscious rejection of his father's behavior, this episode seemed to have served as a symbol for a large part of his own attitude towards the trials and vicissitudes of life. For many a hooligan tried to push him into the gutter, but he calmly ignored it and always reacted to it with calm composure. He never complained in adversity and accepted his lot with fortitude. It was this quality of his mind which so often reminded me of Spinoza, the great sage, who anticipated so many of Freud's views. Indeed, the essence of Spinoza's philosophy, which was expressed in his dictum *"Humanas actiones non ridere, nec lugere, nec detestare sed intelligere"* (Human actions should not be mocked, should not be lamented, nor execrated, but should be understood), could be taken as the *fons et origo* of Freud's whole system.

For about 16 years before his death, Professor Freud had been suffering from carcinoma, which although more or less controlled by surgery and x-rays, nevertheless, caused him much annoyance and pain. During all these years he rarely, if ever, uttered any complaints. Only on a very few occasions did he express his real feelings. Thus, in a letter dated 22 May 1931, in which he expressed his appreciation for the celebration of his 75th birthday in New York City, he told me that he had recently undergone an operation which left him in a very depleted state of health, and expressed the fear that another one like it would probably end his life. The American press reported from time to time that he was seriously ill, and on two occasions stated that he had died. Following one of these reports, he wrote (28 December 1933): "That the press should be so very impatient to report my obituary is surely not pleasant and must be denied on each occasion; yet, some day it will be true and that will not be so far off. Don't you think that 77–78 years is enough for a person, especially when he can no longer do what he likes and can enjoy so little? That would be something that one could wish me for the new year."

Like Spinoza who turned away from Jewish orthodoxy, yet became the "God intoxicated man," as Novalis called him because he could not stop occupying himself with religion, Freud, too, seemed to be fascinated by religion. In a letter of 4 December 1911, he wrote: *"Ich bin von meinen Studien über Religionspsychologie ausserordentlich in Angriff genommen."* (I am extraordinarily absorbed in the study of the psychology of religion.) And about a month later (28 January 1912) he stated: *"Meine nächste Arbeiten werden sich mit der Psychologie der Wilden beschäftigen als Einleitung zur Religionspsychologie."* (My next work will deal with the psychology of savages as an introduction to the psychology of religion.) At that time—that is, in the beginning of 1912—he had already finished most of his papers on the neuroses, except his metapsychological papers. In brief, he had demonstrated that the neurotic symptom has a definite and logical meaning (psychogenesis), that it results from a repression of a disagreeable and painful past occurrence to which the patient could not at the time react adequately, that this repressed material—the idea with its concomitant affects—remains unconscious but dynamic, and that in due time there is a failure in the repression and the old episode works its way to the surface by some devious path in the form of pains, obsessions, anxieties, delusions, or hallucinations. He also established the fact that sex, or as he called it *libido*, follows a definite course with various fluctuations in both the normal and neurotic person from childhood to adult life.

What is most important to note is that in studying patients by the method of free association and interpretation (psychoanalysis) he soon wiped out the putative line of demarcation between the so-called normal and abnormal mental processes. He removed the stigma of *dégénéré* from the neurotic and showed that the only difference between him and the so-called normal is one of degree.

In the course of years he revolutionized the theories relating to normal and abnormal psychic life by showing how one readily merges into the other, that the reactions in both are the same and that their various manifestations depend altogether on constitutional and environmental factors. All this he demonstrated in a novel and provocative literature. *The Psychopathology of Everyday Life, The Interpretation of Dreams,* and *Wit and Its Relation to the Unconscious* deal with problems and mechanisms which are applicable to normal as well as to abnormal mental processes. They vividly show that the normal civilized individual cannot always express himself in ordinary speech and actions, but must often resort to devious ways. The neurotic symptom is a symbolization or dramatization of the conflicts between the primitive self, what Freud calls the *Id*, and the ethical self, the *Ego*. The same is true of the lapses in talking, writing, or handling, which are so frequently seen in the actions of normal people. Wit, which is a specific creation of civilization, uses the same distortions as the neurotic symptom and the everyday mistakes, to express those thoughts which are forbidden by culture. Wit permits us to obtain pleasure from forbidden sources. The dream serves the same purpose insofar as it permits the individual to get rid of that tension which accumulates during the day because of unattainable and prohibited desires. To accomplish this purpose the dream again makes use of symbolization and dramatization. For our ego or rather our ideal or superego tends to guide the average person in the straight and narrow paths laid out for him by the *mores* of his environment.

In giving this very superficial outline of Freud's achievements it is not only intended to show the difference between his views and those of his predecessors, but it is desired to point out that Freud considered the total personality of the patient while his forerunners considered only isolated phenomena in the same way as the early physicians treated cough or fever. But it is quite plain that Freud's mode of approach brought in its wake many issues and implications, of which his predecessors were unaware. Freud's investigations not only led to the childhood of the individual, but to the childhood of the race; it involved not only ontogeny, but phylogeny. For in solving the meaning of dreams, which Freud called the *via regia* to the unconscious, he also found the meaning of myths, fairytales and folk-lore. Thus, the oedipus complex, which represents the first struggle between the son and his father, which he found in the analysis of person's dreams, led directly to primitive history. Every neurotic symptom was based on some early trauma, but the study of the reaction to such traumas often enough showed that they did not strictly refer to the individual's own experiences, but fitted far better into some phyletic model and could generally be explained only on the basis of such an influence. This is especially noticeable in tracing the reactions to the oedipus and castration complexes, in the study of animal phobias, and in the phobia of being eaten by the father. After noticing this state of affairs for many years, Freud finally made the effort to bridge the behavior reactions of modern man to those of prehistory.

The best approach to this nebulous period was by way of religion and naturally by way of primitive religion. This soon led to the study of the psychic life of primitive man. Following the announcement as quoted from his letter of January 1912, there appeared three substantial papers, which were later published in book form under the title of *Totem and Taboo*. In this work he leans heavily on the works of Darwin, Atkinson, Robertson Smith, and others, to demonstrate that there is a remarkable resemblance between the psychic lives of neurotics and savages. He also shows there that the oedipus complex, or the struggle between the father and son, came to a different issue in prehistoric society. In our society it often shows itself in death wishes against the father, which are manifested in dreams of the father's death, whereas in prehistoric society this wish was actually effectuated through the slaying and devouring of the primeval father by his rebellious sons. Indeed, Freud traces religion and other moral and social institutions to that earliest of all dramas.

But let us confine ourselves to the part of the book which deals with religion, for as I have shown above, that was the theme which impelled the author to take up the investigation of the psychic life of savages. As early as in 1907 he published a paper on *Obsessive Acts and Religious Practices*, in which he demonstrated that the obsessive behavior and ceremonials observed in neurotic symptoms showed a marked resemblance to religious ceremonials. These views were dilated upon and amplified in his *Totem and Taboo*. In 1927 there appeared *The Future of an Illusion*, in which he goes into the deeper relations between religion and culture, and in his work on *Civilization and its Discontents*, which appeared in 1930, he again devotes considerable space to religion and its relations to the individual and the future of civilization. His last work, *Moses and Monotheism*, treats exclusively of the religious history of Judaism and Christianity from historical and prehistorical times.

In *Moses and Monotheism* he describes the psychological basis of monotheism on the scheme of a traumatic neurosis in the individual. We cannot here enter into a full discussion of this great and ingenious work, which must be read and studied to be appreciated, but the sum and substance of it is that like in a traumatic neurosis one can recognize in religion the same historical and emotional background. In his own words: "Mankind, as a whole, also passed through *conflicts of a sexual, aggressive nature, which left permanent traces,* but which were for the most part *warded off and forgotten;* later, after a long *period of latency,* they *came to life again* and created religious phenomena similar in structure and tendency to neurotic symptoms." Professor Freud freely admits that this prehistorical survey leaves many gaps, but he

165

maintains that there is considerable evidence for his assumptions, that some are historically proven and that "others have survived in remarkable replicas." As an example, he gives the rite of the Christian communion, wherein the devout symbolically incorporate the blood and flesh of their God, and thus reproduce the inner meaning of the totem feast. He mentions numerous other survivals of our forgotten early history found in the legends and fairy tales of people and in the analysis of children, of which some were mentioned above.

Having demonstrated the analogy between the stages of development of monotheism and traumatic neurosis, Professor Freud encountered some difficulties when he attempted to translate individual into mass psychology. For in the traumatic neurosis one can say that memory traces of the traumatic event continue to exist in the individual's unconscious and can be brought to life again, but how does an active tradition exist in the life of a people? Professor Freud answers this question by saying that the masses, too, retain impressions in the form of unconscious memory traces—that is to say, that the psyche of man probably consists of not only personal experiences, but also of what he brought with him at birth. In other words, the mind contains also fragments of phyletic origin, i.e. an *archaic inheritance*, which is made up of certain dispositions which are common to all living beings. And as experience shows that men differ in their mode of reaction to stimuli and impressions, we can say that the archaic inheritance contains these differences, which may be recognized as the *constitutional* elements in the individual. The archaic heritage thus consists of not only dispositions, but also ideational contents, or unconscious memory traces of the experiences of former generations. Professor Freud thus affirms his belief in the transmitability of acquired characteristics; indeed, he states that he cannot imagine biological development without the consideration of this factor. "After these considerations," he states, "I have no qualms in saying that men have always known that once upon a time they had a primeval father and killed him."

This conclusion, which forms a direct path from ontogeny to phylogeny, epitomizes everything Professor Freud expressed from the beginning of the development of the cathartic method to the present. The individual begins with the lawless *id-psyche* which, as a result of struggles with the outer world, gradually becomes moulded into a conscious *ego* and later into a *super-ego*. The race which constitutes an aggregate of individual beings is subjected to the same trials and vicissitudes and reacts to stimuli in the same manner, and with the same results as the individual. The *super-ego*, the highest evolution of man, plays the same part in both. In the individual it is the precipitate, or the representative of the earthly father, while in the race it represents the heavenly father, or the ideals and traditions of the race. Conflicts between these psychic forces produce neuroses or psychoses in the individual, and psychic upheavals in the race.

No reader should dismiss these conclusions, nor need he accept them on the basis of the fragmentary statements presented here. Only after a thorough study of the original can one judge Professor Freud's paleo-psychological reconstructions. He himself was fully aware of the wide gaps that must perforce exist in any work which deals with prehistory. In the preface to his first detailed analysis, the Dora Case (published in 1905), in which he for the first time traces everything to the earliest period of childhood, he states: "In the face of the incompleteness of my analytic results, I had no choice but to follow the example of those discoverers whose good fortune it is to bring to the light of day after their long burial the priceless, though mutilated, relics of antiquity. I have restored what is missing, taking the best models known to me from other analyses; but like the conscientious archeologist I have not omitted to mention in each case where the authentic parts end and my construction begins."

But as he continued his psychic explorations in the manner described in this case, he came to the realization that the dictum of science that ontogeny is a repetition of phylogeny is equally true in the psychic realms. Briefly, every civilized boy goes through today the same struggle with his father as his prehistoric brother did in the dimmest past. In prehistory the struggle was unabated and inexorable until the father was slain, while in the modern boy, because of his long cultural heritage, everything must be hidden. Unless he be a defective, he simply dreams that his father died. As Plato puts it—the virtuous man contents himself with dreaming of that which the wicked man does in actual life. By a virtuous man we mean of course one who is influenced by his mores, especially by religion, and by a wicked man one who is incapable of assuming such restraints. Be that as it may, the continued existence of such dreams definitely points to the link between the present and the past, between the individual and the race.

That Professor Freud selected monotheism or the Mosaic religion as the medium for his demonstration is not determined solely by his own religion or by his special interest in Moses. There is no better road to the remote past and to cultural evolution than by way of the Bible or the Jewish religion. For whether one considers religion in the theological sense, or merely as a code which came into being through force of necessity and later became invested with mystery and ceremonials, the fundamental nucleus of it is the same. Religion depicts the efforts of the wise and strong father to curb and control the impulsive aggression of the young sons. It is for this reason that religion is the greatest asset of civilization. If mankind is to survive at all, regardless of whether it inherits the kingdom of heaven, it will be on the basis of controlling its aggression and entertaining a wholesome regard for the neighbor. And that is precisely what all great religions have preached from the very beginning of their existence. The Golden Rule which Jesus bequeathed to the Christian world he took directly from Judaism, but its basic principles formed the foundation of all the religions which have existed before Judaism and Christianity.

To summarize, we can say that Professor Freud followed the same code of identification when he attempted to bridge the present with prehistory as he did in tracing his patients' present life and behavior to their earliest childhood. To one versed in psychoanalytic technique his method is as rational as, let us say, that of the paleontologists who reconstructed whole species of prehistoric beasts *ex ossiculo Dinosauria* long before Roy Chapman Andrews discovered their eggs and embryos.

Professor Freud related that in his childhood he often heard the story that his mother's delight at his arrival was enhanced by the prophecy of an old peasant woman, who declared that a great man had come into the world. He goes on to say that such prophecies must be quite common. "There are so many hopeful mothers, and so many old women whose influence on this earth is a matter of the past, and who have, therefore, turned to the future." He concludes this narrative with this sentence: "Perhaps this story is the source of my longing to become great."

The fact that Freud remembered this story and even had the desire to report it, would show that it made a deep impression on him. Such episodes often play an important part in one's later life, but to be effective such prophecy must fall on fertile soil, on a good constitution. Whatever the determining factors might have been, Sigmund Freud was an outstanding genius who influenced the world in a most fateful manner. Like another great genius, his kinsman, Spinoza, he learned early in life to look at everything *sub specie aeternitatis,* and after over half a century of incessant toil in the face of the greatest difficulties, he transvaluated all values in his field of endeavor as well as in all of its collateral branches. His influence on the world of thought and letters can hardly be estimated at the present time. In the speech mentioned above, Thomas Mann summed up the feeling of many a modern *literateur* when he called him the greatest living man of letters, whose discoveries pointed the way to an art which might be bolder, freer, blither, than any possible in our neurotic, fear-ridden, hate-ridden world. Psychoanalysis, the instrument which he had discovered and bequeathed to us, enables us not only to realize the hitherto almost impossible task of knowing oneself, but it has also opened the path which leads directly from the historical present to the primordial past.

Freud and His Pupils:
A Footnote to the History of the
Psychoanalytic Movement

(1940)

HELENE DEUTSCH

Helene Deutsch (1884–) was probably one of Freud's favorite pupils. He analyzed her during the years 1918–1919 and terminated the analysis because he needed the time to take the "Wolfman" back into analysis. Helene Deutsch certainly was among the women to whom Freud was attracted. In Brother Animal (New York, Knopf, 1969) Paul Roazen says Freud "had a penchant for a narcissistic type of woman who is very attractive to men." Helene Deutsch's "emotional transference to him was immense," Roazen writes. "Like other patients she became temporarily convinced that her analyst was in love with her. She remembers standing before a shop window after an analytic hour and musing: 'But what will poor Frau Professor do?' " With her husband Felix Deutsch she came to America in 1933 and settled in Boston. Her The Psychology of Women is still a classic in psychoanalytic literature. This selection appeared first in The Psychoanalytic Quarterly (1940): 184–94, translated by H. A. Bunker.

People like Freud have difficulty in preserving an incognito. To keep distinct the work and the personality of its creator seems impossible. In its instinctive desire to keep alive the former, the world strives through the medium of the personal to obtain a better grasp of the magnificence of Freud's achievements and thus, as it were, to bring them down to its level. Such an attempt turns in part upon the testimony of witnesses, in part—particularly in the case of the biographers of the future—upon a process of reconstruction. Most biographers—as is the habit of the majority of them—will be swayed by some more or less unconscious bias of their own: through an effort at popularization, some will falsify both work and master by superficiality; with others, fear of the truth will produce a hostile interpretation; still others—and these are the most dangerous—will be moved by an excess of adoration to present a cult in place of keeping to reality.

170

In his *Autobiography*, Freud himself has set barriers to further efforts at biography and to the analytic interpretation of his actions, in saying: "Here I may permit myself to bring my autobiographical remarks to a close. Of such other matters as my personal relations, my struggles, my disappointments and successes, the general public is not entitled to know more. In any event, I have been more candid and more sincere in certain of my writings than those who describe their lives for contemporaries and posterity are wont to be."

This brief account is in no way a contravention of Freud's wish. It is, rather, a small contribution to the history of the psychoanalytic movement, a backward glance towards a bit of the past of the Vienna group which, closest to Freud, had its own changes and chances.

My membership in this group through a period of more than twenty years will not impair, I trust, the objectivity of my account. This testimony of an eye-witness, refracted as it must be through that witness's own affects, naturally cannot plead complete freedom from the subjective limitation of 'as I saw it.' The freshness of an experience always clouds its objective clarity; distance in time, on the other hand, has the disadvantage of fading of the material from memory; in either case one must subject the 'historical facts' to the test of scrutiny. In the remarks that follow, a modest attempt will be made to apply this scrutiny to Freud's relationship to his first pupils as a group rather than as individuals, and to their relationship to him.

To this circle Freud was not alone the great teacher; he was the luminous star on the dark road of a new science, a dominating force that brought order into a milieu of struggle. For at that time the battle waged was both an outward and an inner one: externally it was fought with and for Freud against the scientific and professional milieu from which one had sprung; internally it was fought over Freud himself, for his favor and recognition. It is the latter which makes understandable many of Freud's later difficulties with his pupils.

Let us review for a moment the earliest beginnings of this group, the psychological conditions that gave it birth. Freud's *History of the Psychoanalytic Movement* and *Autobiography* furnish a graphic description of this period of his activity. There he stood alone in his heroic fight for truth! In his first attempts to acquaint the scientific world with his findings he met with 'only incredulity and contradiction.' "For more than a decade after my separation from Breuer I had no followers. I stood completely isolated."

To this first heroic period of his creative activity one may well give the title, "The Birth of a Genius." Until that time Freud had been a supremely gifted man with a great future and doubtless too with certain difficulties within himself. Now, with his inspired psychological discoveries, he was to endure the tragedy of one who, a scientific pioneer and a discoverer of new truths, is condemned to be an alien completely misunderstood by his contemporaries.

This period of splendid isolation seems to me the truest and most impressive epoch of Freud's career. He says in his *Autobiography*: "I understood that henceforth I belonged among those 'who have disturbed the sleep of the world' (Hebbel), and that I must not count on objectivity or consideration." And further: "It was a beautiful, heroic period; the splendid isolation was not devoid of advantages and charm."

Again and again in the course of the years, we who knew directly or from tradition Freud's fight for his ideas were reminded of Ibsen's *An Enemy of the People*, wherein the hero who fights for the purity of the water supply finds himself despised and forsaken by the representatives of officialdom, and culminates his fight with the discovery that 'the strongest man in the world is he who stands most alone.'

Freud once made the remark in a small circle of his pupils that absolute happiness falls to the lot only of an absolute Narcissus, free from all dependences. Without this narcissism not even the strongest can bear isolation in the long run. Ibsen's hero asks for a man who, "free and high-minded, would dare take over my task when I am dead"; then surrendering the imposing castle of splendid isolation, he says: "To begin with, I must have at least twelve lads; don't you know a couple of street urchins—any regular ragamuffins? Bring me a few of them; I shall experiment with the street curs for once in a way; sometimes there are excellent heads amongst them."

When Freud gathered his first few adherents about him, he must certainly have put the question to his scientific destiny, "Where is the man who, free and high-minded, would dare . . . ?" And he took the lads as they came, not so much for experimentation as out of sheer necessity, to break through the splendid isolation which in all likelihood had become a prison house to him.

This development of analysis is in keeping with its profoundest nature: it is *de facto* the achievement of an inspired seer and discoverer, no matter how much Freud himself hid this fact behind the empiricism of his findings. What he saw empirically remained invisible to others, not demonstrable and consequently nonexistent. But Freud was above all a scientist, and the great artist and seer Freud put his discoveries to the test of empiricism. All who could observe Freud at his work knew with what conscientiousness he pursued this empiricism, how he insisted upon finding proof again and ever again before being willing to give expression to a new discovery. "I learned to restrain speculative tendencies, and, following the never-forgotten advice of Charcot, I looked at the same things over and over again until they began to give their own testimony."

It was particularly from this empirical attitude that there arose the need of followers and collaborators. But there were also other motives. The genius in Freud had to suffer solitariness and renounce recognition. He gives up his struggle for an orthodox career, renounces—probably in great bitterness—the recognition of universities; but Freud the man can bear the splendid isolation no longer. This conflict between the solitariness of genius and the human need of recognition, while still alive, from a receptive public, is like the reflection of the double nature of psychoanalysis spoken of above: on the one hand, the creation of an artist, on the other, the empirical data of a scientist. Freud himself discredits the former in a facetious remark—to which, however, he lends seriousness by his attitude—when he says of his lecture tour in America: "The short sojourn in the New World flattered my vanity. In Europe I felt myself rather outlawed; there I found myself received as an equal by the best of them. It was like the realization of an incredible daydream when I stepped up to the lecturer's chair in Worcester to give my five lectures on psychoanalysis. So then! Psychoanalysis was no longer a phantasm; it had become a valuable piece of reality." One notes here, in his indirect likening of it to illusion, Freud's rejection of isolation and the strong need he felt to give to his ideas the full value of reality through their recognition and acceptance by the world at large. It was out of this need that the psychoanalytic group had to come into being. But it goes without saying that this did not settle the matter of Freud's solitariness; it only changed it, as it were, into a spatially enlarged, socialized solitariness, the value of which, however, was to become for Freud threefold: above all, the appeasement of the social conscience, which in the long run does not permit isolation; second, it subserved the illusion that the world at large had sent out the first harbingers of acceptance of his teachings; and finally, the powerful and substantial motive that psychoanalysis, being from its very beginning an empirical science, needed with its expansion collectors, assemblers and sifters of its empirical material.

173

On contemporary observers certain human weaknesses of Freud made a particularly strong impression because he displayed them openly yet without ever making concessions to them in his scientific work. Despite his disdain for official position, Freud was very happy whenever he received recognition from such a source, or when a successful colleague of acknowledged scientific rank found his way to analysis. Here again his unwillingness to make concessions expressed itself—so strongly indeed, that in such cases he was tempted to make it a condition that the person in question should give up his official position for the sake of collaboration with the psychoanalytic group. One sometimes felt inclined to interpret this as an act of affective vengeance on the part of Freud against officialdom. Its actual basis, however, lay in his own personal experience, in that during those early days of analysis there was no possibility whatever of reconciling a career with the burden of Freud's teachings while, *per contra*, one could not be a trustworthy collaborator under the restrictions inherent in official position.

Freud's need for an assentient echo from the outer world expresses itself particularly in his relationship to his first small group of pupils. In the fervor of his work, in the overcoming of his own doubts which he expresses so often and with such humility in his writings, he had to have peace in his scientific house. His pupils were to be above all passive understanding listeners; no 'yes men' but projection objects through whom he reviewed—sometimes to correct or to retract them —his own ideas.

Freud has often been reproached for this very obvious demand on the part of a creative man. What is accorded as a matter of course to every mediocrity who is an officially appointed chief of a clinic or of any scientific field of activity was to be subjected in Freud's case to a particularly devastating criticism. The conditions, it is true, under which Freud formed his circle were exceptional and difficult: on the one hand, his overwhelming intellectual superiority; on the other, the lack of recognition which necessitated a special selection of pupils from a group possessing very special and definite ideas of what to expect. For he who attached himself to Freud at that time knew that he was going into exile, that he would have to renounce his career and the usual gratification of professional ambition. One might therefore expect these first pupils to have been revolutionists of the spirit who stood out from that average to which Freud remained unintelligible— a select and courageous advance guard. Such an expectation could be realized only in individual instances. Surveying in retrospect the original Vienna circle which gathered about Freud, and seeking the motives which induced its members to approach psychoanalysis, it should particularly be borne in mind that it was only the few who could do so out of purely scientific interest or out of a clinical experience which corroborated Freud's findings. Many came out of an intuitive inner urge; others were impelled by their own neurosis, or were driven by contrariety or by an identification of their own lack of recognition with Freud's lot. To achieve such an identification was very uplifting for it created in the person concerned the illusion of feeling himself to be something he was not: a misunderstood genius.

All, however, created the same atmosphere about the master, an atmosphere of absolute and infallible authority on his part. It was never any fault of Freud's that they cast him in this rôle and that they —so rumor has it—became mere 'yes men.' Quite the contrary; Freud had no love for 'yes men' and so it fell out that the very ones who proved to be the most loyal and the most reliable adherents were not the recipients of a warmer sympathy on his part. He loved those who were critical, who were independent, who were of interest for their brilliance, who were original.

Gradually it came about that to many in this group the objective truth of Freud's researches was of less importance than the gratification of the emotional need to be esteemed and appreciated by him. This emotional factor of subordinating one's intellectual freedom to the personal element became the source of the severest conflicts within the confines of this affect-laden circle. Each wished to be the favorite, and each demanded love and preference as compensation for having made the sacrifice of isolation.

The rigid scientific criticism and objectivity to which Freud subjected his own work and that of the others preserved the group from sectarianism. But under the affective conditions just mentioned, he could not prevent the occurrence of emotional tensions and discharges which also had their influence on the development of the psychoanalytic movement. To the weaker personalities their identification with the great man was of considerable advantage. The attention an insignificant person attracts to himself through his connection with a genius contributes to the increase of his own narcissism. Narcissistic conceit, however, exaggerates into grandiosity and caricature, and thereby devaluates the true worth of the cause it represents. Freud with the impressive modesty of a great savant has often emphasized the weaknesses and defects of analysis: "Psychoanalysis has never pretended to be a panacea, or claimed to perform miracles." Never does he set forth his theses dogmatically but always with the skepticism of the genuine seeker after truth: "If I am not mistaken," "if the future confirms it," etc. Those pupils have not trodden in Freud's footsteps who presumptuously claim that analysis is capable of curing all neuroses, remolding character, and revolutionizing the age-old laws of nature and of the cosmic order.

Freud has suffered many disappointments in his pupils. The attempt has been made to explain this fact analytically as a 'tragic' inevitability. It is indeed striking that experiencing disappointments should be displaced from the beloved teachers of Freud (as related in his *Autobiography*) to his beloved pupils. Analytic interpretations would be platitudinous here and would besides contribute little to psychological understanding. Direct observation seems to admit of a less profound but likewise a more illuminating explanation. Everybody around Freud wanted to be loved by him, but his intellectual accomplishment meant infinitely more to him than the people around him. As an inspired pathfinder he felt justified in regarding his co-workers as a means towards his own impersonal objective accomplishment; and with this end in mind, probably every impulse towards originality, when it subserved other than *objective* purposes, annoyed him and made him impatient. Freud was too far ahead of his time to leave much room for anything really new in his own generation. It seems to be characteristic of every discoverer of genius that his influence on contemporary thought is not only fructifying but inhibitory as well.

The striving for independence was of course particularly strong in those pupils who felt disappointed in their personal emotional relationship to Freud or threatened by their own ambivalence. While the less gifted expressed their ambivalence in a reactively increased dependence and in the overvaluation of the practical value of analysis mentioned above, the more gifted denied this dependence in a more direct but still scientific form and separated themselves from the group in either a noisy and hostile or in a more veiled and passive manner. This conjoining of the affective and personal with the rational and scientific, this more or less unconscious process of displacement, was the provocation for Freud's often emphasized intolerance. Anyone in a position to observe Freud directly can testify to the tolerance, the patience and the respect which he showed for the opinions of others if they were of a purely factual character, even when they did not coincide with his own ideas. But towards affective motivations concealed behind intellectual and scientific claims, especially when these motives involved his own personality, he was particularly severe and relentless.

It must be admitted—or to put it more mildly, it may be supposed —that in Freud as well, back of the factual criticism of the factual, affective motivations and displacements played a part and lent to this intolerance a peculiar intensity. At all events, upon the discovery of such unconscious attitudes towards himself on the part of his pupils, his clearsightedness often failed him.

One often hears it said that Freud was afraid of plagiarism, especially on the part of his pupils, and his autobiographical writings seem to bear this out. Of this fact I may offer the following explanation based on personal observation: in his method of working Freud was always scrupulously intent upon having an empirical control set up. His gift of observation made him see and grasp things quickly. He was wont to subject his findings to strict proof and empirical confirmation before he gave them out in either written or spoken form. Manuscripts lay in his desk for months, even years, and only after long and repeatedly confirmed observation did he publish them in the cautious, modest form characteristic of him. In his contacts with his pupils it might easily happen that the allusion to some surprising finding, to some new idea, had an immediately stimulating effect before it could attain the ripeness which Freud himself would have wished to give it. This frequently gave rise to the danger of unconscious plagiarism on the part of the others, and induced Freud to be cautious and self-protective in this regard.

The small circle around Freud grew with the years, and those who entered it later could now lay claim to professional and scientific motives. Furthermore, the aims of the group changed with its growth. Its program became broader and more social; it was no longer an atmosphere of absolute isolation and of conflictual attachment to the spiritual leader which dominated it. The founding of the teaching Institute and the Polyclinic, the training of pedagogues, the intensified interest in child analysis, the influx of foreign students, all changed completely the character of the group at whose head Freud had fought his first battles.

One thing remained, however, which gave to the Vienna group up to its final days a wholly personal stamp: tradition. This tradition continued to be preserved for several years—perhaps the pleasantest and most serene ones—through the personal contact with Freud in those

177

monthly meetings in which Freud communicated to the small select group his new ideas or amplified and corrected his older ones. He did not succeed in creating in us the illusion that it was we who gave and he who received, although he made the effort to do so, opening every meeting with the words: "Now let me hear what you have to tell me." And we brought him our big problems and our little findings, always to see the real purpose of our coming wonderfully fulfilled when Freud took up the discussion. It is to be hoped that these *Gespräche mit Freud*, eagerly committed to writing by a few, will one day be published. Here I want to say but one thing: again and again, despite his greater tendency towards speculation in those years of his creativeness, Freud directed us back to empiricism and cautioned us against speculation. "For a short while," he said, "I allowed myself to leave the sheltered bay of direct experience for speculation. I regret it greatly, for the consequences of so doing do not seem of the best."

History repeats itself. And so did the history of the Vienna group, with its ever active tradition, repeat itself. Out from a large circle with new problems there crystallized again a small group of younger pupils in active contact with Freud—exactly as thirty years before—who experienced directly in their devotion the uniqueness of this great mind, formulated his ideas into principles, and set themselves the task of preserving the heritage of Freud's teaching in its purest and most dignified formulation and of continuing it by ever enlarging it.

History repeats itself; and sometimes, although seldom enough, it draws upon earlier experiences and corrects the old mistakes. But a tragic fate, unfortunately, has prevented us actually from realizing this expectation. Freud said: "The interests of the various members emanate from the common source and tend in different directions. Some place principal emphasis upon the clarification and extension of psychological knowledge, others are interested in furthering its connections with internal medicine and psychiatry." Freud was aware that in its practical application analysis must undergo dilution. This is but the natural fate of every great ideology: it loses its noblest characteristic, its splendid isolation, and acquires practical value only in its dilution, alteration, adaptation. This is necessarily the destiny too of analysis because as an empirical science it serves practical ends wherein the immediate result must be of permanent value. Thus of the genius-given gift of Freud humanity will acquire its fullest social value only when it becomes by this dilution a common property, even indeed divorced from the name of its creator.

The loyal band of the chosen few of two generations has undertaken the noble task of preserving the original kernel of Freud's teaching in its best and truly freudian sense. Sometimes his pupils' adhesion to the orthodoxy of his teaching seems like stubbornness and folly. How the two tendencies will become interwoven and be reconciled with each other only the future will show. Even if the more conservative and loyal followers seem at times to be out of touch with reality, they nevertheless discharged by their piety the debt we owe for our common spiritual existence. Not for a long time will theirs be a merely antiquarian task, even though it may seem so amid the vexations of the present time.

In defense of those who have disclaimed this immediate task, let it be said that it makes a great difference whether one has grown out of the intimacy with Freud into independence as a loving heir, or whether one owes his independence to an emotional conflict.

Reminiscences of a Personal Contact with Freud

(1940)

ROY R. GRINKER

Roy R. Grinker is a well-known psychoanalyst in Chicago. He met Freud in 1933 and entered analysis with him. This selection appeared first in the American Journal of Orthopsychiatry *10 (1940): 850–55.*

My impressions of Freud, the person, do not come from those contacts an *upright* man makes with a colleague, as has been the privilege of others, or with a teacher in the usual sense, but they were gained from the position of an analysand. All know that in this position one is somewhat handicapped physically and emotionally in making an objective evaluation of the personality of his analyst. Bearing this in mind I shall give you a few candid camera shots of Freud the man. If they seem out of focus or lacking in perspective, remember the position from which they were taken.

My reasons for going to Freud for analysis did not include any special appreciation of his analytic contributions but rather a conscious respect for his neurological researches. I was vaguely aware of Freud's comparative anatomical studies on the medulla oblongata, and knew and prized his classical works on infantile cerebral palsies and on aphasia. I found that his interest in neurology was still alive and his questions concerning modern concepts were indicative of an excellent knowledge. A secretary at the Verlag died suddenly of a Landry's type of paralysis and he discussed it thoroughly and with great interest in the modern ideas of the syndrome. In fact, when my book appeared he pointed out the omission of several references to important classical research in neurology. Freud's biological and neurological orientation attracted me, but he several times pointed out that no knowledge of neurology could help in any understanding of practical psychoanalysis.

180

As part of biological science psychoanalytic knowledge is, of course, intimately to be integrated with neurology as well as other fields.

I met Freud for the first time in the late summer of 1933 at his villa. He impressed me as extremely energetic, with long fingers and hands, constantly moving about. He appeared much younger than his actual age. His hair was white and sparse, beard short and well trimmed. Behind rather thick spectacles were eyes that were magnetic and gave a reassuring feeling of great kindliness. Freud's manners were charming and immediately gave one a feeling of ease and security, yet his questions were direct and searching. One such meeting was sufficient to evoke a strong positive transference.

This Freud I never saw again. After two interviews and my first hour he developed an acute heart failure, pulmonary infarct and pneumonia. At his advanced age, and with this serious illness, Freud resumed analytic work in only a few weeks, but physical liveliness was gone. He walked very slowly and the abounding energy in his movements had disappeared. The next summer he moved only around the porch of his villa. Later, in discussing illness and age, he showed quite a fatalistic attitude. He indicated his hereditary longevity and sadly stated that he would have to bear the burden of living for quite a time yet. I felt that he was really tired of living and would gladly have given up. He stated that he felt analytic progress would increase after his death and not be at all deterred. He also knew his name would be more revered after death and the psychoanalytic movement furthered, for the figure of his person as the originator of psychoanalysis would be unavailable for attack.

In Vienna, at 19 Berggasse, one saw on the ground floor a butcher shop, on the street wall of which was a simple sign "Prof. Dr. Freud." He lived on the first floor of this building for over forty years. One rarely saw his family, except Fräulein Anna who shared the same waiting room for her patients. After ringing the bell and waiting for a long time while dogs barked and growled, a polite maid ushered the analysand into a bare hallway and removed his wraps. A small waiting room, fitted with furniture apparently from the last century, was never well heated and the best of associations could be frozen in only a few minutes. On the table were ancient magazines replenished only by occasional gifts, while a small bookcase held gift volumes which the Professor found unsuitable for his own library.

Suddenly the door of the sanctum would open and Freud appeared. He first looked at his analysand and that of his daughter and then waved his hand in friendly greeting. He invariably grasped the outstretched hand only by the fingers and swept or pulled his analysand into the analytic chamber. This room always smelled musty, was well lighted by a modern indirect lamp and heated with a coal oven. On the wall were many Egyptian figures of priests. Directly through a wide opening without doors was the Professor's own study. The central attraction was the desk covered with ivory figures and relics. The walls were lined with shelves filled with reference books and sets of the Professor's works translated into numerous languages. The Professor sat in a comfortable armchair, with a footstool for his slippered feet.

His throat disease had resulted in the loss of part of his tongue so that his speech was very low. To emphasize his points in analysis he pounded the arms of his chair and often the head of the couch. When most intent and excited in an explanation he would lean forward, almost directly over the head of his patient, to whom his excitement was thus transmitted. He had a great zest for details in associations and dreams. When names of places were mentioned he would go into the library and ask to be shown the place on the map, which he would then study. He had to understand thoroughly locations and relationships of houses and rooms, frequently asking that diagrams be drawn. He opened and closed each hour with a few remarks such that the analytic situation blended imperceptibly into real life.

Into this household access by strangers was seldom obtained. No one could see the Professor without an appointment made through Fräulein Anna, after consultation with the Professor. John Gunther told me that he was unable to see Freud, although Mrs. Freud gave him an interview which he reported in *Cosmopolitan*. She reminded him of "old lace and lavender." The Professor's wife was rarely visible except with her companion.

There was no legitimate excuse for absence from hours even on the coldest days. During the socialistic uprising, when Vienna streets were barricaded with barbed wire and patrolled by armed soldiers, some way had to be found to get to Freud's house. Vacations were infrequent, just the legal holidays and a few days at Christmas. Freud worked constantly from September to August and rarely took more than one day away from work.

The Professor was greatly concerned about the caliber of analysands, hoping that the oncoming generation of students would be interested not because of their own needs but because of the work itself

That wish has certainly been realized in this country. He believed that personal analysis was necessary as preparation for analytic work but indicated that rare, very normal individuals, like Abraham, could do without. He strongly urged, not fractional analysis, but a return for a renewed analysis after five year intervals.

So far as the caliber of analysts was concerned, Freud at least believed they were better than at the beginning of the movement. For Adler he had absolutely no use, explaining that he had to make the best of those co-workers available at the time. He had nothing but good to say about Rank—his imagination and brilliance—but simply stated "he was a naughty boy." Bitterness regarding Jung was always apparent and extended from the person to his people. The details of Jung's defection are well known, but perhaps less well known is the fact that Freud remembers Jung telling him of a personal dream six months before his overt antagonism came to the surface. The Professor stated that he should have known from this dream what was to happen.

Freud did not forget or forgive easily. His attitude to Americans dated from his visit to this country with Putnam in 1909. He was successful in explaining analysis and convincing people of its importance, but was unhappy and sick here. "That's too bad" still rang in his ears twenty-five years later, for this expression and nothing more was all he received while suffering from intestinal cramps at Putnam's Adirondack camp. Probably Jung's letters from America to him several years later helped, for then Jung found that soft-pedaling sexuality helped him in disseminating interest in analysis. Freud could not tolerate this disguise, which Americans apparently needed then.

The black days of the socialist massacre were filled with uncertainty. Dolfuss at the behest of the Church had removed his only bulwark against the Nazis and no one could know what would happen to analysis. The Professor did not want to leave his home. A more jittery time was experienced when Dolfuss was assassinated. Freud then stated that if the Nazis came in he would go to Verona, Italy. He felt that the only liberal European countries were England, France and Italy. Italy, of course, he loved because there he went for many vacations. But nothing came of it and Freud stayed too long.

Freud's pleasures were numerous and his hobbies entrancing. His life was, as most of ours, pretty well laid down in pattern and custom. Saturday night card games with three old cronies who had played with him for decades were the rule. In fact, when Königstein, the ophthalmologist to whom Freud first suggested the use of cocaine for ocular anesthesia, died, his place in the card game was taken by another Königstein. The hours I have spent at bridge didn't seem so wasted after hearing this. Freud believed the card game saved his life. For months he suffered from intractable headaches for which no cause could be found. Suddenly he discovered that the headaches were milder on Sunday than on any other day. Each night he worked in his study but Saturday night the card game was in session elsewhere. Freud surmised that the headaches came from the study. Subsequent investigation disclosed a small leak in a gas pipe in the study which had been giving him a chronic carbon monoxide poisoning.

Another technical device which the Professor used was the telling of stories so sharply pointed that they accentuated the value of his interpretations. I shall give you one example. Speaking of using substitute gratifications Freud told the following story. "A man took his little boy to hear a most marvelous instrument played, something he had never heard before. The most beautiful sounds would come out of this air blown instrument. The little boy went to hear the performance with his father, who exclaimed after the first notes: 'There, doesn't it sound just as if he were playing a violin?' The little boy said, 'But Papa, why don't we go and hear a real violin played?' " These stories seemed to be endless and stored each for a specific occasion.

The problem of lay analysis was brought into discussion by my reading his book. I was forced to admit that nothing I had known medically or neurologically had helped me in understanding at least the Vienna point of view. I think it has been pointed out adequately elsewhere that in this country such a statement would not hold. The swing of analysis is to fields of medicine and biology so certainly that lay analysts, with the exception of those working with children, would be left far behind.

The Professor commented on the problem of part-time analysts—those who can do only two or three cases at a time. His opinion was that such people can never really become analysts—that one must be constantly attuned to the unconscious and not have to focus back and forward, like a presbyopic person, from purely conscious problems to those of the unconscious.

He would never accept the belated half recognition in Viennese medical circles that Freud himself was a genius but that his followers went too far. He interpreted this only as a displaced resistance against analysis. I found it true that lay Viennese were much more Adlerian minded and knew less about psychoanalysis than individual psychology. To criticisms leveled at him for the death instinct theory, he pointed out it was definitely labeled as speculative and one that he was least pleased with. Yet he used it in his language.

My impressions of Freud are, of course, of the man in his life's last decade. They may not hold for his younger days. I was struck by his warm, gentle and kindly manner in personal contact, but as a contrast was his extreme intolerance for intellectual mediocrity.

Freud never overcame the trauma which antisemitism brought upon him. In reading "Moses and Monotheism," after hearing his personal views, I am convinced that he unconsciously felt he was a new Moses come to lead the people out of another bondage. The actual realization of failure in Vienna and the world at large for this generation must have been a great disappointment to him.

His living presence among analysts resulted in a continued recapitulation of an attitude based on Freud's own experiences during the development of psychoanalysis, like a religious ritual the meaning of which has long been forgotten and the necessity for it long passed. The isolationistic tendencies of the Viennese analysts, while not entirely directed by Freud, was evidence of an inbred group about him. The supposed danger to analysis from opening its borders has been shown to be nonexistent. In fact, a free traffic in this country, especially in Chicago, has benefited psychoanalysis as well as medicine and biology.

One day after an analytic society meeting I described with great surprise how one of the distinguished members entered into a heated, quite emotional, argument. Freud answered, "Why be surprised? Analysts are still human and possess emotions." So I have tried to point out to you examples of Freud, the man, in life, and indicate certain facets of his personality which I believe detracted not one whit from him but serve only to bring him out of the range of the ambivalent awe of unapproachable genius into the place of a human, possessing one of the greatest minds and insight the world has ever known. Psychoanalytic science will be much more progressive and productive in the way Freud himself would have wished if we do not deify him and deny him the human privilege of error.

A Brief Visit with Freud

(1940)

MARTIN W. PECK

Martin W. Peck was a Boston psychoanalyst who visited Freud briefly in 1937. Even at this time, when he was old and feeble, Freud was always prepared to receive visitors. This short piece is especially interesting vis-à-vis the remarks of Freud on America and the Americans! This selection appeared first in The Psychoanalytic Quarterly 9 *(1940): 205–206.*

While in Europe during the summer of 1937 my wife and I were happily able to make an arrangement to visit Professor Freud. At the time he was convalescing from a mild intercurrent illness and, although not well enough to take up his usual work, he was somewhat restless at his confinement and eager for any diversion. The family was then living in the pleasant suburb of Grinzing.

Professor Freud was resting on the porch when we arrived. He looked, as he was, an old man and ill, but there was nothing in his manner or mental activity to justify this impression. He was cordial and alert; his steady and keen eye seemed to miss nothing; he spoke rapidly in excellent English. He found pleasure in the fact that his dog Luni, formerly owned by Helene Deutsch, paid friendly attention to Mrs. Peck, and professed to see in this a contribution to international good feeling. He listened with complete attention to what he considered of interest, dismissing other matters somewhat brusquely.

The conversation, more or less guided by Anna Freud, became a discussion of psychoanalysis. His own position of authority and leadership Freud brushed aside as inconsequential. The essence of his comment was that in America medical application of psychoanalysis was the rule, and contributions to its structure were the exception. He used the term 'medical fixation' for the American scene, and regretted the alliance between psychiatry and psychoanalysis. He made frequent reference to the 'core of psychoanalysis' and expressed his belief that this core should be kept separate from other disciplines for a long time to come. He stated with deep conviction that "psychoanalysis is a part of psychology and for its proper development, it should be kept free from biology, philosophy—and also psychiatry."

I expressed the opinion that everyone was in agreement concerning the value of the earlier isolation policy, but that now—in America at least—it seemed the time had come for closer cooperation with medicine; that legal considerations and other indigenous conditions made the situation at home rather different from that of Europe. Freud replied that there was implicit in this argument a false assumption that the validity of psychoanalytic findings and theories was definitely established, while actually they were still in their beginning, and needed a great deal of development and repeated verification and confirmation. He suggested that in its attitude toward Europe, America was still fighting the Revolutionary War.

Before departing, I told Freud that our Boston group would welcome some word from him which I could deliver in person. At first he was inclined to take my request lightly and proffered his felicitations and good wishes, but he soon became serious and said very earnestly that I could inform the Boston group that in his opinion it would be to their advantage "to add to the American self-sufficiency a few drops of the European spirit." When I replied that it would be my added pleasure to present to my colleagues as well as I could the substance of our talk, Freud said most amiably that it would be a very nice thing to do, but that it would accomplish no good whatever.

Freud's Early Childhood

(1944)

SIEGFRIED and SUZANNE CASSIRER BERNFELD

It has been noted already that both Bernfelds have contributed a number of significant papers on various aspects of Freud's life and career. This selection appeared first in The Bulletin of the Menninger Clinic 8 *(1944): 105–15.*

1. Introduction

In his *Autobiography* Freud covers his early childhood with one sentence: "I was born on May 6, 1856, at Freiberg in Moravia, a small town in what is now Czecho-Slovakia. . . . When I was a child of four I came to Vienna." However references to this first period of his life occur in several of his writings. Collected and assembled in their proper order they, unexpectedly, form quite a coherent record of his first three years. When, at the age of forty-two, Freud turned his attention to the recollections of his childhood, he was not satisfied with their manifest content. He analyzed his memories, and even published some of the results. Though he did not intend to write the psychoanalysis of his childhood, and uses the material in various contexts and for various purposes—now, as an example of a certain mechanism, again, as the starting point for a general discussion, always casually and with restraint—it so happens that the broad lines of the development of the child and the essential traits of his personality do emerge.

The authors feel that this addition to Freud's *Autobiography* deserves to be brought together in one piece rather than being dispersed through numerous German volumes, some of the material not even having been translated. To the psychoanalyst these autobiographical fragments suggest two kinds of elaborations. First, implications by definition. If, for instance, Freud speaks of the rivalry with his father, in the Oedipus situation, the sexual wishes toward the mother are implied—though not specifically mentioned—since they are a factor in the Oedipus rivalry, as Freud defines the term. He expected to have psychoanalytical readers, thus these implications must be considered as parts of his written autobiography.

Second, interpretations, some of which may force themselves upon the mind of the psychoanalyst as being beyond doubt. Still, they are hypothetical, since they are based only on that selection of facts which Freud communicated incidentally, without attempting a "case history."

We have kept our elaborations strictly within the first group. We are presenting Freud's own analysis of his early childhood; we are not attempting to psychoanalyse him.

We have, however (in sections 2, 3, and 5), augmented the childhood story by facts from the environment in which they occurred. Our presentation approaches a narrative. The necessary philology is confined to the appendix.

2. Freud's Birth—Facts and Legends

At birth, the baby Sigmund Freud had such an abundance of pitch-black ruffled hair that his young mother nicknamed him her "Little Moor." An old peasant woman prophesied to her that she had brought a great man into the world. The proud and happy mother, herself a descendant of a one-time famous scholar (Nathan Halevy Charmatz of Brody, Poland), firmly believed in this prediction. It became one of the constantly repeated family stories, a part of the atmosphere in which the child grew up.

Thus, the hero's garb was in the weaving, right at the cradle. But Freud, the great debunker, was not willing to wear it. "Such prophesies," he wrote when he was over forty, "must be made very frequently; since there are so many happy mothers full of expectations, and so many old peasant women, who, their mundane powers having deserted them, turn their eyes toward the future. Also, no prophetess expects to be unrewarded for her prophesies."

When, in 1931, a committee of citizens of Freiberg (Pribor)° set out to install a memorial tablet on the house in which Freud was born, it was discovered that contrary to all the "Who's Whos" and to Freud's own statement, the city register lists Sigmund Freud's birth on the day of March 6, 1856. All these birthday wishes, then, addressed to Freud for seventy-five years, first by his family and then by his friends,

° Freiberg became a part of the Czecho-Slovakian Republic in 1918. At that time the old Czech name of Pribor (Przibor) meaning "Near the ruins" became official.

189

and later by practically the whole world—did they all go wrong, missing by two months the right day?

Freud was not interested in this possibility. He only resented that somebody had tried to make him two months older. He had the date from his mother, "who ought to know best." The Committee accepted his view and engraved, as the memorable date in the history of the town: "May 6, 1856." So, although in cold Moravia the mother of a first-born boy might well have wished to celebrate his birthday in real spring; and, although we know the power of such wishes over reason and facts, we too, accept the traditional date.

The president of the committee, Mr. Benes—Director of the Worker's Health Insurance Institute in Pribor—explains the discrepancy as an error by the Czech clerk, who had to make the entry in the register in the German language, which the clerk neither knew too well nor liked too much. It so happens that the only name of a month with a similar spelling in German and Czech, is "May." This makes Mr. Benes' explanation not convincing.

Thus, upon entering into this world, the "Little Moor" caused one of those odd slips, which as Professor Freud forty years later he was destined to explain.

3. The Setting

In March or May 1856, Freiberg was a town of 4,800 Germans and Czechs, belonging to the Austrian Empire, or more precisely to the Margravate Moravia, in the district of Neutitschein, 150 miles northeast from Vienna. It was situated in the rolling foothills of the Carpathian mountains—then a peaceful pastoral countryside—half a mile from a dense forest, on a steep bank over the Lubina—a little trickle in summer, but broad and tearing in spring. On a hill, inside the town, the steeple of St. Mary's Birth Church rose almost 210 feet high, and had the best chimes in the province. In the center of the town was an unusually large market square, surrounded by arcades of well-built houses. One of these houses conspicuously displayed a memorial of the Thirty Years' War. In those glorious days, the bellicose shrewdness and tough endurance of the citizens had become proverbial: "Brieg, Freiberg und Bruenn make Swedish armies thin." The coat of arms, granted the town "for valor," shows on a field of gold and red two big, vicious-looking pruning knives.

Somewhat off the market place and close to fields and pastures, at

117 Schlossergasse, Jacob Freud (1815–1896) lived comfortably with his family. The home, built around 1800, was extremely simple—a detached, rather small, two-story house, without ornamentation, constructed of plastered bricks, with a slate roof. In 1855 Jacob, then over forty years of age, married a second time. He married Amalia Nathansohn (1835–1930), who was not yet twenty. The following year Sigmund was born.

At that time Jacob Freud was already a grandfather. Emanuel, the eldest of the two sons of his first marriage—then in his twenties—had a son, John, one year of age, and a newborn daughter, Pauline. Both of these families lived in Freiberg as a closely knit unit.

From the very beginning, then, the position of Sigmund was full of complications and of paradoxes. He was the eldest son of this marriage, yet at the same time he was the youngest child in his family group. He was an only child, but for all practical purposes he had an older brother and a twin sister; and to confuse matters all the more, these sibling equivalents were his nephew, one year older than he, and his niece, of approximately his own age. Thus his privileges as eldest son and his benefits as only child and youngest boy became uncertain. He had to fight for them. Even his authority as an uncle was in question.

Sigmund's young mother, half-brothers and sister-in-law were approximately the same age; his father was old enough to be his maternal grandfather. In fact, Jacob was the grandfather of Sigmund's closest brother-like friend and rival, John. In relation to his father, Sigmund was rather "in the third generation," as Philip, the younger of his half-brothers, put it twenty years later to the student Freud, who felt the expression to be very illuminating. Sigmund's relations to his mother were natural and simple. She was his. She was proud of her son. She was affectionate, and she nursed him. There was a Nanny to help with the housework and the care of the child.

In this setting, then, the "Little Moor" lived his first three years "as the happy child of Freiberg, the first-born son of a youthful mother," as Freud summarized his earliest childhood in the letter which was read at the unveiling of the tablet at the house of his birth.

4. The First Three Years

In Freud's story of his childhood, as he refers to it at various times in his writings, one of the *personae dramatis* is not mentioned; his sis-

191

ter-in-law, the mother of John and Pauline. In fact very little is said about his own mother, but we are made to feel that there was a mutual, deep attachment between mother and child.

We learn a good deal about the Nanny, "that prehistoric old woman." She was ugly but very clever and efficient, and she often treated him less than pleasantly. She scolded him bitterly and most likely even spanked him when he did not show sufficient appreciation for her standards of cleanliness. Yet he gave her his love and all of his pennies. He missed her a lot when she later disappeared.

We also get a vivid picture of the alternately friendly and hostile relations between the young uncle and his older and stronger nephew John. They were inseparable. They loved each other and fought each other. Occasionally John was a tyrant who mistreated the younger playmate. But the little uncle had courage and knew how to stave off permanent submission. He hit back. For years the family remembered the speech of exculpation with which the two-year-old retorted when his father called him to account: "Why did you hit John?" "I hit him 'cause he hit me!"

Freud relates only one incident in which Pauline appears. It all happened on a gently sloping green meadow, covered with "beautiful yellow flowers." On top of this slope was a farmhouse in front of which a peasant woman, wearing a kerchief, and Nanny, chatted busily with each other. On the slope the children were playing peacefully, picking the yellow flowers. Pauline had collected the prettiest bouquet, when suddenly uncle and nephew, as if by premeditated agreement, jumped at her and grabbed the flowers out of her hand. Crying, Pauline ran up the slope, where the peasant woman, as consolation, gave her a large piece of dark bread. As soon as the boys saw this, they threw their booty away and they, too, hurried up to the house and demanded their share of the bread. And they got it. The peasant woman cut the pieces of bread for them from the loaf with a long kitchen knife. "Never has bread tasted better."

Freud tells us a few significant things about his relations with his father. They would go into the "beautiful forest" together and as soon as the little boy could walk, he would try to toddle off on his own. He grew to admire his father as the wisest, wealthiest, and most powerful man he knew. In fact, Father Freud was the ultimate judge at the top of the hierarchy of authorities: Father, Emanuel, Nanny, Mother, John. He exercised his patriarchial powers in a gentle and kind way. Still, he appears as the frustrating and censoring force, as for instance

192

when he interfered in the bickerings between grandson and son, or again, in a very early incident when the Little Moor, impelled by sexual curiosity, intruded into his parents' bedroom and was driven out by his father's emphatic command.

The reaction to this authority was neither submissive nor hostile. One wants to say that the boy displayed a manly attitude towards his father, as in the exculpation speech, or in that scene, at the age of two, when he occasionally still wet his bed, and when reproved for doing so, consoled his father by the promise to buy him, in Neutitschein, the district capital, a beautiful new red bed.

In the Little Moor's life there were, of course, the usual tragedies of childhood; a soiled bed and an occasional nightmare. Also the following highly moralistic accident: alone in the pantry, the little boy climbed up on a footstool to get from the table or chest, something good and forbidden, all for his very own. The footstool tumbled over, and its edge struck the child behind the lower jaw. It might well have knocked out all his teeth. The wound bled profusely, but the one-eyed family doctor sewed it all together again. A scar persisted as if to remind the culprit that he had been served right.

Freud's half-brother, Emanuel, twenty years his senior, was one of the most important persons in the boy's mental and emotional development. He appears as the leading figure in the decisive last six months in Freiberg, as Freud was becoming three years of age. Of this period Freud recalled only one episode—a scene that was singularly vivid in his mind; "I see myself in front of a chest," he wrote when he was forty-two, "the door of which was held open by my half-brother. I stood there demanding something and screaming. My mother, pretty and slender, then suddenly entered the room, as if returning from the street. I am tempted to explain this picture as the memory of a hoax by my elder brother, which was interrupted by my mother." But his self-analysis reveals that the memory was a screen, covering the two following traumatic events.

The Little Moor was just two and a half years old when his mother gave birth to another child—a girl, Anna. (Between Sigmund and Anna was a boy, Julius, who died when eight months old. Freud does not mention him in his writings.) He was not at all agreeable to this addition to his family. He did not know the why's and how's and wherefore's of it all, and he worried distrustfully lest more little sisters might appear.

Immediately thereafter, and without forewarning, Nanny disappeared. She had been caught at extensive stealing and put into jail by the resolute Emanuel. The Little Moor was doubly distraught, for added to his grief at losing Nanny was worry about the other sudden change. He knew nothing for certain but he sensed that his brother had played some sinister part in Nanny's disappearance. He asked him where she was. Evasive and witty as he was, Emanuel said: "She is cased in," and that was final. Of course, this remark could not pass as an answer. It simply added another riddle.

Thus the child was left to his own observations, imagination and powers of deduction. He reached a firm and definite, though incomplete, conviction—a theory, as Freud would say: Sister came out of mother's womb; he who had made Nanny disappear, Emanuel, had cleverly slipped the baby into mother.

The screen memory expresses this theory in the language of dreams and of the symbolic thinking of early childhood. The chest symbolizes the mother's womb; the slender figure of the returning mother alludes by contrast to the deformation of pregnancy. What the child had demanded so urgently was to look into the chest; and he screams at finding it empty. It is the brother, the knowing culprit, who knows all too well how to handle chests, to whom the child addresses his wish.

In the German original, Nanny's disappearance is neatly condensed with the episode of mother's baby. Emanuel evaded a direct answer to the child's question by using the ambiguous German expression, "Sie ist eingekastelt," which to any adult, would have meant, "She's in prison." The child understood it more literally, "She is in a chest," or as we said, "She is encased."

The "theory" of course did not aim primarily at intellectual satisfaction. It sought a solution to the perplexing libidinal conflicts created by the changes. From now on the child had to live with an intruder and he had to learn to love her, or to say the least, not to hate her; he had to go along without the give and take of Nanny and had to remain within the standards of civilization free from her supervision.

But, as evidenced by the "theory," it seems that the boy's most urgent need was to live in peace with his father. In the "theory," the brother occupys the father place. Emanuel, not Jacob, is the powerful, all-knowing, all-tricking man, closest to mother and the creator of her child. Thus father is removed from the center of envy and jealousy. It may be that the boy loved his father more than he did Emanuel, or

194

that he felt more threatened by him; in either case, stress was relieved by this shift of passions from father to brother.

Soon, it seems, the Little Moor learned to bear the existence of a sister. He discovered that the little Anna did not usurp his mother for very long. And as she came back "slender as ever," so she remained "the young mother of her first-born boy." Secure in this position, his grief about Nanny might have quickly vanished. After all, without her he could keep all his pennies and taste freedom.

The boy hardly had time to get accustomed to the new shape of things, when, at the age of three, he started on the long journey to a big, foreign city—to Leipzig. After a long trip by horse-drawn conveyance, he got his first sight of a railway; and, after a ride of many hours, he found himself divorced for good from the beloved home, the pastures, hill and forests of Freiberg, and from Emanuel, John and Pauline.

With this railroad journey, the recollections of childhood come to an end. At forty-two, Freud hardly recalled a single episode from the year spent in Leipzig and the following two or three years in Vienna. "Those were hard times, not worthy to be recalled."

5. The Background of the Migration

The Little Moor did not realize that the sudden and disrupting change in his and his family's life was but one of the countless incidents in the steady industrialisation of Central Europe.

The peaceful little town with the beautiful name Freiberg (Free Mountain) now contained much of fight, despair and constraint. Cloth manufacture, which was its main source of income, had been on the downgrade since 1835—and Jacob Freud was a wool merchant. Everywhere in Central Europe the introduction of machines threatened handwork increasingly. In the Forties the new Northern Railway, from Vienna to Germany and to Galicia, had bypassed Freiberg. This dislocated trade there and put increasing numbers of artisans out of business. Jacob Freud's business was directly affected. Furthermore, a serious inflation from 1852 on increased the poverty of the town, which, by the year 1859, was pretty well ruined. The Austro-Italian War in 1859 added its bit to make the future still more dark. For the Freuds, these facts made it seem advisable, if not imperative, to move away from Freiberg.

195

Very likely there were other equally good reasons. Since 1851, Austria had been under the political reaction of the Restoration, which even a Prussian general admiringly described as "completely Russian." This evil did not directly touch people who kept away from politics, as the Freud family likely did, even though Jacob and Emanuel were deeply impressed by the short awakening of freedom from 1848 to 1851. However, the shortlived revolution had produced another effect from which it was less easy to withdraw. The revolution had definitely established Czech nationalism as a power in Austrian politics and consequently had fanned the Czech hate against the Germans, the ruling class in Bohemia and Moravia. Now the Jews, who in language and education were German, became the objects of Czech anti-Semitism.

In his youth in Freiberg, Jacob had experienced German anti-Semitism. He had taken it stoically as an inevitable heritage of Jewish birth, a small matter compared with the relative freedom which the Jews enjoyed in Moravia. Later, the revolution of 1848 in Bohemia, neighbor of Moravia, started with Czech riots in Prague against Jewish textile manufacturers. Hostility from both Germans and Czechs threatened the Jews, and right in Freiberg the grumbling cloth-makers got used to holding the Jewish textile merchants responsible for their plight. These rumblings did not actually threaten the life and property of the few Jewish families in Freiberg, but they were more ominous in this small and backward community than they would have been in one of the great capitals.

Finally, Freiberg did not promise educational opportunities suitable for a bright boy. It is true that in 1858 the citizens had enjoyed a partial re-opening of the high school (gymnasium) which had been closed since 1827. This poor beginning was made possible by a fund which over a period of thirty years finally had grown sufficiently to permit the establishment of the lowest grades. Slim, indeed, were the facilities for developing greatness in Freiberg.

Want of bread, of education and of freedom from persecution are the motors of emigration at all times and everywhere. Following a pogrom in Cologne, in the 14th century, these forces had moved the ancestors of Jacob from the Rhineland east to Lithuania and from there to Poland, and then west to Moravia. So, in 1859 the Freud migration was resumed. Emanuel, with John and Pauline, went to Manchester in England. Jacob with wife, son and daughter, went to Leipzig, and from there to Vienna. There Freud lived until 1938 when the final migration to London occurred.

196

Freud: Master and Friend
(1945)

HANS SACHS

Hans Sachs (1881–1947) was one of Freud's most devoted and loyal followers. He made his acquaintance in 1904, when he attended one of Freud's lectures in Vienna. Trained as a lawyer, he soon became involved in the psychoanalytic movement, finally becoming a psychoanalyst himself. The six members of the committee which assisted Freud in the early and often stormy days of psychoanalysis received rings as a token of his appreciation for their loyalty and assistance from Freud (Ernest Jones, Karl Abraham, Sandor Ferenczi, Otto Rank, Max Eitington, and Hanns Sachs). In 1920 Sachs became a training analyst at the Berlin Psychoanalytic Institute and subsequently trained many of the first generation analysts. Early in 1932 he settled in Boston where for many years he was active in training, analysis, and writing. The following selections were taken from Freud: Master and Friend *(London, Imago, 1945), which Sachs wrote as a tribute to Freud.*

First Acquaintance

On a dark winter evening in 1904 I walked through the long courts and narrow doorways of the Allgemeine Krankenkaus (general hospital) toward the auditorium of the Psychiatric Clinic cluster of buildings. It was near the Narrenturm (fools' tower), a circular building which still formed a part of the Psychiatric Clinic, and in which until the beginning of the nineteenth century the insane were kept chained to the wall.

This beginning is a bit like the trick by which a novelist tries to captivate the imagination of his readers and although this incident tells nothing but the plain truth, I have to pay the novelist's penalty and to mention a few things that preceded this evening.

By this time I had finished my studies at the law school and passed, by hook or by crook, the prescribed examinations. The law did not interest me and I did not feel especially attracted toward medicine. My interests were centered in literature, almost to the exclusion of everything else. It seems queer that my love for literature should land me at the Psychiatric Clinic, yet this was the perfectly logical, although indi-

197

rect, outcome. The connecting link was formed by my boundless admiration of Dostoevski. I wanted to find, led by the hand of science, the secrets of the soul which he had almost succeeded in revealing in their nakedness; I hoped to tread in broad daylight the obscure and labyrinthine paths of passion which he had traced. I turned first to psychology, at that time under the influence of Wundt, and found it disappointing. It seemed to consist mainly of a long-winded terminology, which did not lead anywhere in particular, certainly not nearer to the mysterious springs of human emotions. I began to read about epilepsy, which played so conspicuous a part of Dostoevski's life and work, and from there my interest glided over to the neighbouring fields of psychiatry and psychopathology. What I found looked promising and so I became extremely interested in them. Besides, these sciences held the somber charm of gruesomeness, something like the "occult sciences," which satisfied my youthful longings for the sensational and exotic. All this appealed much more to me than the pedestrian textbooks of "Normal Psychology." At least the facts were stirring, even when the explanations seemed often not sufficiently illuminating and sometimes disappointingly shallow. In the course of these desultory studies a book fell into my hands with the fascinating, but bewildering title *Traumdeutung*. From the first I felt strongly aroused by its outstanding originality and I was excited by the entirely new angle under which many trivial, long known facts assumed a startling significance. No other scientific book had told me about problems that I, like everyone else, always had before my eyes and yet had never seen or tried to understand. No other book made life seem so strange and no other book had explained its riddles and self-contradictions so fully. I said to myself that these stupendous revelations needed and merited the most complete scrutiny; even if it should in the end turn out that every theory advanced in its pages was wrong, I would not regret the loss of time. I was resolved to spend months or even years if the task should require it.

I knew that the author of this electrifying book lived in the same city with me, not far from my home. I heard his name mentioned now and then by people who were acquainted with him and his family. I also knew that he and his science were rejected by the official academic circles but that he had been given the title of professor-extraordinary in recognition of his earlier work in neurology. I found in the catalogue of the university that Professor Freud lectured at the auditorium of the Psychiatric Clinic on Saturday evenings for two hours—an unusual time and not likely to attract a big audience. And now we are back at the starting point.

I knew the lecture hall well because I had been there to listen to the lectures on psychiatry given by the regular professor, Wagner von Jauregg. (He later won the Nobel Prize for his work on the fever-therapy of general paresis; his mind was not open to psychologic subtleties, least of all to psychoanalysis. Freud and he had been medical students together and maintained a tenuous relation which was entirely lacking in warmth, but not in mutual respect.) When I had seen the hall before, it was in plain daylight and all the benches had been crowded with students. Now the windows were dark and the only light came from a few bulbs suspended above the table and chair of the lecturer; the ascending rows of empty benches in the dusk gave the room a somewhat sepulchral aspect. Being well aware of my shyness and timidity in the face of any new adventure, even such a modest one, I had persuaded a cousin of mine, a medical student, to come with me; I hoped his presence would give me support. In these unusual and gloomy surroundings I felt more panicky every moment and as a middle-aged gentleman, evidently the professor, entered, I started toward the door, whispering to my cousin a hurried explanation that we were at the wrong place.

What would have happened if my attempt to escape had succeeded? Certainly, my initiation into analysis would have been delayed for a year or more, but it is not impossible that my whole life might have taken another course. Luckily, I did not succeed. The middle-aged gentleman, who wore a short, dark brown beard, was slender and of medium size. He had deep-set and piercing eyes, and a finely shaped forehead, remarkably high at the temples. Pointing to a row of eight or ten chairs, which stood in a semicircle in front of the benches, close to the table of the lecturer, where a few people were already sitting, he said in the politest way: "Won't you come nearer and be seated, gentlemen?"

We followed his invitation and when he had started his lecture I soon lost every trace of shyness and inhibition. All of it was dissolved in my zealous interest aroused by what he had to say, and in my admiration of the way he said it. This effect widened and deepened the more I listened and learned. My shyness, which he had waved aside at our first meeting, disappeared and with it went bit by bit many other inhibitions and inner obstacles that had been standing in my way. Of course I attended faithfully every one of the successive lectures.

199

The chairs had been placed in front of the empty benches because Freud disliked to strain his voice, which was singularly lacking in what is called "metal." A dozen years later when his growing fame attracted big audiences, he lectured in another larger, but not amphitheatrical auditorium, and was able to make himself distinctly heard in every part of it. But it meant a great exertion, which he disliked, and since in these new audiences serious scientific interest was adulterated by large doses of snobbism and ordinary curiosity, soon afterwards he gave up his academic lectures altogether. After the war he spoke, with rare exceptions, only at the meetings of the Psychoanalytic Society and at its conventions. His faultless elocution and careful accentuation made him always perfectly audible, although his voice had none of the full, rich tones which roll forth and lend a suggestive force to the words. I never heard him raise his voice in anger or excitement.

On these Saturday evenings, which soon became the pivot around which my private universe revolved, the atmosphere was imtimate and informal. The number of aficionados was six or seven at first and never amounted to more than fifteen. Nearly all of them belonged to the circle which had begun to form around Freud and became the nucleus of the first Psychoanalytic Society. All the topics and problems of psychoanalysis which existed then or were just in the process of development were discussed. Dream interpretation, the unconscious and repression, and the structure of neurosis were, of course, the favourite subjects. But the many new vistas opening before our eyes, the unexhausted possibilities for new fields, and new methods of exploration in almost every branch of science added a great deal to the absorbing interest of these hours. We learned something about the nature of transference and began to understand the unconscious as the presence of an inner destiny which decrees that the same pattern must be re-lived since the wheel of life turns around a fixed center, and that the oldest experiences repeat themselves over and over again under various disguises (repetition-compulsion). We got the first glimpse of "applied analysis" —of using the knowledge of the unconscious and of the analytic technique for interpreting works of art and literature, for the investigation of social problems as well as of those of neurosis and dreams. All this was not preached in a pretentious manner, no great words proclaimed the grandeur of the new discoveries. Freud did not assume the role of the prophet who tells of the mysteries that were revealed to him. The prevailing tone was a simple conversational one, often interspersed with witty or ironical remarks; his conviction of the far reaching consequences of the new truth was too deep to stand in need of emphatic asseveration.

Freud did not always lecture on these evenings. We had some seminar periods when members of the audience were scheduled to give reviews and criticisms of books or articles, followed by a general discussion. One occasion I remember particularly well. A newcomer I did not know had to give a review on the Association Experiment. He started by explaining that the experimenter pronounces a series of words and expects the subject to utter the word that comes first to his mind after each one. "For instance," he continued, "the experimenter says 'horse' and the subject reacts with 'library' (*Pferd—Bibliothek*)." Here Freud interrupted him: "If I am not mistaken, you are a former cavalry officer and have written a book on the psychology of the horse?" "Yes." "Then you have unintentionally given the best proof of the strict determination of associations. With the example you chose at random you have presented yourself and your field of interest to the audience."

At another time we had a series of discussions on the right method for interpretation of literary art. Should and could the same technique be used as for the reconstruction of the unconscious content of a dream? The "radical wing," the supporters of the "mother-womb" fantasy, maintained this opinion and tried to exemplify it in Hamlet.

I remember one occasion when Freud illustrated a scientific principle by an anecdote from his personal experience which is too characteristic to be omitted. The problem he treated was that of "over-determination," that is, of the multiple causality which exists everywhere but is especially important for the products of the unconscious. He warned us not to be easily satisfied even when the known causes seemed perfectly sufficient to produce the effect: "Many years ago," he told us, "an old professor of medicine died who had ordered in his will that his body should be dissected. The autopsy was performed by a renowned pathological anatomist and I functioned as his assistant. 'Look here,' the anatomist said to me, 'these arteries! They are as hard and thick as ropes. Of course, the man couldn't live with them.' I answered, 'All right. But it is a fact that the man did live till yesterday with these blood vessels.'"

When he discussed with us the psychoanalytic therapy of neurosis, he used a picture postcard of the most ordinary kind for making his point. The picture showed a yokel—we would say a hill-billy—in a hotel bedroom trying to blow out the electric light like a candle. "If you attack the symptom directly, you act in the same way as this man. You must look for the switch."

Freud told us about the past as well as about the future of psychoanalysis and especially of the initial stages of his work, which had led him step by step towards psychoanalysis. He spoke with warmth and gratitude of Charcot as a truly great man and teacher who had encouraged the unknown stranger by admitting him to the circle of his intimate disciples. He loved to quote Charcot's answer when anyone tried to contradict an experience by an appeal to an authority. "Cela n'empeche pas d'exister" (That does not keep it from existing). His favorite was evidently Liebault, the simple provincial doctor who, without personal ambition and unaided by the trained staff of a clinic, had the courage to help his patients by hypnosis, a method that hitherto had been considered highly unscientific and undignified. I remember now, not without a note of sadness, that Freud, who had no trace of any "racial" predilection one way or the other, in showing us Liebault's photograph, pointed out how un-Latin (today the word would be "Nordic") his face was and how well this was suited to his name, which evidently was a variant of the Germanic *Luitpold*.

In later years Freud spoke to me more than once of his student days in Paris, of which he kept a tender reminiscence. Once he told me: "I remember how, on a spring-day on the boulevard Michel, a group of young men and girls walked in front of me. Every now and then they stopped walking and fell spontaneously into a few dance steps without any apparent cause or motive, just because they were young and in Paris, and it was springtime."

While I was listening eagerly to Freud's lectures, I assiduously studied his technique of exposition (with a view of modelling my own after him). I wondered how he succeeded in producing something unexpected and stupendous while his talk moved in simple terms, dispensing with the fireworks of baffling profundity or glittering paradoxes. I found that he made use of Schopenhauer's recipe for a good style: "Say extraordinary things by using ordinary words." He followed this advice intuitively without being acquainted with it. (I know positively that he read Schopenhauer for the first time many years later when he borrowed my handy pocket-edition for the summer.) The startling effect of his lectures was based on a peculiar contrast. He gave all the necessary facts, dissected all the basic principles, even those one would have taken for granted, with the greatest accuracy. He then introduced his conclusions cautiously, on a firm foundation;

before he undertook the next step forward, he surveyed all possible objections, formulated them clearly and answered them fully, so that when he moved on in an unexpected direction, it seemed the most natural thing to do. When he had to leave an argument unfinished or incomplete, he pointed it out and went back to it at the right moment. In this way he led his hearers insensibly on, never giving them the impression that they were participating in a difficult and quite original investigation. They were surprised when they arrived in the end, without mental gymnastics or contortions, at results that contrasted strangely with some of their previously most cherished opinions or prejudices.

During this time the first threads of our personal relations were fixed on more than one point. I became friendly with several persons who attended the lectures and also participated in the informal meetings in Freud's house. A friendship started with Otto Rank, who was then and remained for a long time Freud's "right-hand man." A review I had to give of Ferenczi's article, "Projection and Introjection," brought me in correspondence with the author. And then came the day when I entered Freud's house and for the first time had a long and familiar conversation with him.

My translation of Kipling's *Barrack-Room Ballads* had just been published (it was the farewell, or rather the tombstone, for my purely literary interests) and I went one afternoon, not without some heart beating, to present a copy to Freud.

Freud had lived then for many years, and continued to live until he left Vienna, in the same house, Berggasse 19. The street deserved its name (Hill Street), since a part of it was, even for the uneven ground of Vienna, exceptionally steep. As often happens in old cities, the two ends of the street belonged to different worlds. It started at the Tandelmarket, Vienna's historic flea market, and ended at the Votivkirche, a modern Gothic cathedral, which dominated one of the most notable ornamental squares of Vienna, flanked by the university and other public buildings. No. 19 was in the comparatively level part of the street, nearer the Tandelmarket, but in a quiet and respectable, if not exactly distinguished neighbourhood. Originally Freud's office had been on the ground floor and his home on the second. At the time of my visit the office had been moved to the second floor of which he had become in this way the sole occupant. Home and office communicated internally, but each had a door on the opposite sides of the landing (and, of course, at whatever side one chose to ring the bell, the other door was opened). Freud told me some years later that the apartment had been inhabited before him by his former fellow student, Dr. Victor Adler, who was, as I have mentioned, the leader of the Social-Democratic Party and who became secretary of state for a short time after the war. The room that was Freud's study had been the nursery of Adler's son, a famous figure of the First World War. He killed the prime minister, Count Sturgkh, as a protest against his despotic rule. His death sentence was commuted and after the armistice he was set free.

The office consisted of a dark little anteroom and three chambers —waiting room, consultation room, and a library study behind. Each room had but one window opening upon a courtyard, in the middle of which stood a beautiful tall tree. None of the rooms got much light or sunshine; they were comfortably furnished in the taste and style of middle-class homes in the eighties, much the same as the one in which I had grown up. There was nothing modern or strikingly personal about them, nor about the living rooms, which I saw later. Only the study had a strong individual note, not due to the style of the furniture, but to the full bookshelves, covering the walls almost to the ceiling, and to the glass cases containing Freud's collection of antiques. Although the latter was then still in its initial stage, some of the objects at once attracted the visitor's eye. I shall say more about this later.

I have forgotten exactly what we talked about on this visit. I only know that Freud received me with his characteristic urbanity. Literature was the general topic of the conversation, because of my book, and I have a vague memory that we joined in the praise of Conrad Ferdinand Meyer, the great Swiss poet and novelist. I was at that time his enthusiastic admirer, being especially fond of his *Versuchung des Pescara* (I am still enthusiastic, but not so ardently), and from quotations and other little hints in Freud's lectures, I had concluded that he, too, knew and loved the same author.

This visit occurred in the spring of 1909. In the following winter I learned that the hitherto informal group had formed a Psychoanalytical Society. I asked for admission as a member in a letter to Dr. Alfred Adler, then president, giving Professor Freud as a reference. I was admitted and came to the next meeting with two or three other new members who like myself had all assiduously attended Freud's lectures. The meeting place was a big room belonging to the Medizinische Doktoren-Kollegium (College of Physicians) which the group had rented for one evening—Wednesday—each week. We new members were naturally somewhat diffident at the beginning and did not take part in the discussion until Freud said, "We won't be divided into an upper house that does all the talking and a lower house that plays the part of a passive listener." This broke the ice and loosened our tongues. The subject, if I remember aright, was some instructive examples of dream interpretation by Freud.

At this meeting, and at others, Dr. Adler presided, but soon his new theories and divergent views resulted in a conflict. His opinions were fully explained and defended by one faction and equally thoroughly discussed and criticized by the other. Freud took a prominent part in the discussions; he did not spare his opponent and was not afraid of using sharp words and cutting remarks, but never descended to personalities. Whoever has taken part in discussions of this type knows that they have a tendency to lose themselves in a tangle of minor details, instead of clarifying principles. Thanks to Freud's insistence, this did not happen. The net result was that Adler's theories, after he had eliminated the importance of infantile sexuality, repression, and the unconscious, had very little in common with psychoanalysis. The logical consequence was that he left the Psychoanalytic Society. Some other members went with him, including the new ones who had joined the group with me. Most of these men did not share Adler's views; their decisions were influenced by their beliefs that the whole proceeding violated the "freedom of science." It may well be that Freud's incisive and harsh criticism had hurt their tender sensibilities and made them willing to think that Adler's complaint of intolerance was justified. Adler's new group, therefore, at first called itself the Society for Free Psychoanalysis. This name was abandoned when Adler, in the further development of his new attitude, dropped the term "Psychoanalysis" altogether and substituted for it "Individual Psychology."

A word about "freedom of science" will be in place here, since this slogan has been widely used from this first occasion to the present day, and in extreme cases even with the pretension of defending the "democratic principle." It will probably be used no less in the future whenever a psychoanalytic housecleaning occurs. What I have to say about it is Freud's view—and incidentally my own too—which I have heard him express variously on so many different occasions that I cannot give his exact words, but can warrant his sense.

Freedom of science means that anyone who so desires may arrive at his own opinion on every question imaginable without being restricted in his choice of sources of information or forms of research; it also means that anyone may formulate and publish his opinion and try to convince others who are willing to listen to him, by communicating to them his data and his arguments. The danger against which this freedom must be protected comes from those who have the power to interfere with it by force and suppression, whether it is a government, a political party, a church, or any pressure group which succeeds in influencing public opinion. Scientific bodies, if they do not use the name of science as a cover for political or religious propaganda, are not interested in power politics. Psychoanalysis is in this respect quite safe, since it has been mistrusted and still is suspect to the compact majority.

The question of who shall belong or not belong to a certain scientific group has nothing to do with the freedom of science. It is a question of expediency in the highest sense of this word. Cooperation among scientists in the form of research or discussion can only be fruitful if all participants agree about fundamental principles. The more specialized the problems under investigation are, the wider becomes the range of concepts for which a complete accord is necessary. If a group of economists organizes to study the intricacies of the theory of marginal value, the organization cannot be blamed if it does not want to be joined by orthodox Marxists who maintain that economic value is not subjective at all, but depends on the amount of expected labor. The foundation of scientific convictions is not exempt from further scrutiny and investigation, but this reinvestigation cannot be carried on by the same group while it is busy constructing the fifth and sixth stories of the edifice. Consequently, when one or several members of such a scientific group abandon part of the common basis which was the reason for their coming together, the only reasonable thing left for them to do is to break away. If they hesitate too long, those members whose work is constantly hampered by useless discussions may justifiably point to the door. This action is neither an infringement of freedom of thought and conscience nor an obstacle put in the way of the search for truth, least of all a ban pronounced against schismatics. A discussion on the broad basis of general principles, conducted indiscriminately with everyone who is interested in the argument, may now and then be useful. It is hardly an advantage for those who are brought together by their endeavour to reap new fruits from the tree of knowledge if they have not agreed beforehand about the place where the tree stands. Consequently, when the defenders of liberty have founded a school of their own, they will regularly see to it that their group consists of homogeneous elements; there is simply nothing else left that they could do. No "orthodox" psychoanalyst has ever complained about not being admitted to Adler's or Jung's organizations. Why should he want to be?

Once when we spoke about a German professor who pleaded in an obstreperous and excessive manner for the suppression of unnecessary noises, advocating rigorous police enforcement, formation of an antinoise league, and so on, Freud said with a smile, "He wants to make all the noise himself."

There is, of course, the risk of narrowmindedness. Disagreement on minor points may become a dangerous instrument in the hands of personal antagonists, fanatics, or shortsighted individuals fixing their attention on minor details. Such things may happen among scientists as well as elsewhere, but an open break is always better than growing sterility. These conflicts are now so far removed that they can be viewed dispassionately. Personally—although it befits me as well as Master Silence in Henry IV, that I should "be of the peace"—I am convinced that as soon as discussions and arguments show tendencies to move constantly in circles and to come back to the same points, a break-up is decidedly indicated.

After Adler and his followers left, Freud had no choice but to resume the official leadership of the Viennese group. Although he would have greatly preferred to leave all formal functions to others, he kept this leadership from then until the advanced age when illness necessitated his retirement. Filling an official post, being the figurehead, standing personally in a prominent position—these were things that went strongly against his grain. He wanted to surround himself with people who shared his ideas and devoted themselves to psychoanalysis for its own sake, and he wanted to keep at a distance those who followed him blindly, "hypnotized" by his personality (or "led on by their positive transference," as we analysts would say). For this reason he had made Adler his successor in the presidential chair, a mistake he repeated very soon afterwards on a larger scale by insisting on the installation of Jung as president of the newly founded International Association.

This continuous series of errors in judging those around him seems out of keeping with Freud's reputation as one of the great psychologists for whom the mind should hold no secrets. He himself always insisted that he was not a *Menschenkenner* (mind reader). I was first surprised, even shocked, when I heard him say that. It contradicted not only my own notion of the sweet uses of psychology, but also my actual experiences with him. Once or twice the force of circumstances had compelled me to disclose to him a part of my life which hitherto I had strictly kept secret. I found regularly to my surprise, and sometimes to my consternation, that he had known my secret all the time. He had drawn his conclusions from the observation of the smallest signs, in the spirit of his "Psychopathology of Everyday Life." In spite of all that, he was not quite wrong in accusing himself of lacking mind reading ability. He saw every single trait and hidden factor correctly, but elevated the whole personality to a higher plane than that on which ordinary minds usually move. He saw passionate zeal, strength, endurance, and high minded motives where only a trace of these fine things existed.

Besides his dislike of being in the limelight, there was another reason why he would have preferred to have nothing to do with the direction and management of the group. This was the tension, sometimes breaking out in open hostility, between individual members of the society or between small groups. The reason it never came to the formation of two opposing camps was solely due to the criss-crossing of the various personal antipathies, which were so complicated and variable that they never solidified. Two men, hating a third in common, may at times dislike each other so much that even their joint aversion is not strong enough to form a bond between them. It would have been reasonable to expect that the members of a small group, all of them sincerely and deeply interested in the same thing—which they really were—and kept under constant pressure by the enmity of the outside world, would be closely knit together by a feeling of comradeship. But it was not so. Jealousies, contending claims for priority, and offensive criticisms stirred smouldering fires. To meddle with these petty disputes and petulant remonstrances would have been an endless and unprofitable task, and an especially hard one for Freud because, much against his will, rivalry for his acclaim and approbation was the mainspring of these wranglings.

This situation may have contributed to his proposing me as a member of the executive or steering committee when, after Adler's and his friends' secession, a reconstruction had become necessary. In the meantime, my friendship with Otto Rank had come as near to mutual intimacy as is possible with a person of such extreme reticence in all personal matters as he was. Freud probably thought it would be a good thing to have at least two men near him who were willing to team together without jealousies and animosities. Our friendship lasted until Rank turned his back on Freud and psychoanalysis, and during all those years our good relations were of great help to Freud in his task of building up the Psychoanalytic Association and editing *Zeitschrift* and *Imago*. Rank and I became joint authors of a book on applied psychoanalysis, a serviceable compendium of the first efforts to use psychoanalysis in many new fields; repeatedly after that we were partners in writing, and what was still more fertile, we exchanged all our plans and ideas, so that every product of this period bears some marks of our discussions. All this came to a full stop with Rank's book on birth-trauma. He did not say a word about his new ideas to me until he presented me with a printed copy, although we had stayed at the same summer resort and had seen each other almost daily while he was writing the book.

During our friendship we not only worked well and smoothly together, but also had a great deal of fun; we were eager to help one another whenever the opportunity offered itself. It seemed perfectly mutual, except to such a keen observer as Freud, who possessed what Socrates called his "gift from the gods" (in Plato's *Lysis*): "The faculty to distinguish in each pair the lover and the loved one." He never gave the slightest hint of his insight into the real state of our relations, till the time of the rupture. When he heard me deplore the loss of my best friend and noticed how strongly I felt about it, he said musingly, "Yes, I knew that your friendship has always been somewhat one-sided."

The end of our friendship was, at the time of which I am speaking, still a part of the invisible and unimaginable future. Whatever his reason, Freud proposed me for election to a seat in the *Vorstand* which, after less than a year of membership, was a definite mark of confidence. Not that I had any important function whatever. Freud recognized the value of organization, but he disliked here, as everywhere, the "pomp and circumstance"—the empty formalities—here perhaps more than anywhere else, because he probably foresaw that the superficial distinction by title, office, and social position would influence many weaker minds to the prejudice of scientific progress. Once a year we had a business meeting which Freud opened by saying, "Today we must play high school fraternity" (*Heute mussen wir Verein spielen*), or words to that effect. Then the treasurer would read some figures and state the society was not in debt. After that someone would move a vote of approbation and propose the reelection of the *Vorstand*, which was duly done, whereupon the scientific work was resumed. I think I was first appointed librarian. The library consisted then of two or three shelves of books and the little work connected with it was performed by Rank, the secretary, who was "Lord Everything Else," with the exception of presiding at the meetings and keeping the accounts.

The actual change in my position was marked by my sitting from then on at the upper end of the table ("above the salt," so to speak) beside Rank, who as secretary sat at Freud's left, and—this was of real importance—by the fact that Rank and I habitually accompanied Freud home. In spite of his sedentary life, Freud was an indefatigable walker, and the way home was extended to long promenades through the silent streets. (Vienna, except for a few nightspots, went to bed before eleven.) On these promenades the subjects that had been debated at the meetings, and many others, were discussed and reexamined. Freud communicated to us his new ideas and theories; of these, some have been incorporated in his books, but many others were abandoned when they did not stand up well under further scrutiny. Behind every discovery he showed us a long row of new question marks. We learned how it happened that he was progressing restlessly, never coming to a standstill. The element of self-satisfaction was not present in his nature.

In these discussions Freud often regretted that interest in the technique and theory of dream interpretation, instead of being kept in the fore of research where it belonged, was often bypassed by those who preferred their psychoanalysis easy and shallow. He used to say that he could judge the ability and psychological insight of an analyst best by seeing how he handled the interpretation of a dream. He resented the efforts to simplify the structure of dreams by stressing the importance of the anagogic function, of the manifest dream-content or of the dream-material. I learned in these nightly hours many things about the "via regia to the understanding of the Unconscious," as Freud called it, which I had not been able to get out of his book.

In the relaxed mood of these nightly promenades Freud indulged more freely than at other times in his habit of illustrating a difficult point with a story. When he found in his rich treasure of anecdotes one that answered exactly his purpose, he did not care if it was not "quite nice." Once he discussed with us the curious phenomenon that some people can contemplate a great amount of their moral deficiencies and misdeeds with unruffled consciences, whereas something comparatively insignificant that "hits the spot" may upset them entirely. He quoted Anatole France's *Histoire Comique* (later he discussed and explained the same point in his article on "character-types" by the analysis of Rebecca West in Ibsen's *Rosmersholm*). He wound up his exposition with this story: In the Magnaten Club in Budapest (at the time its most exclusive club, open only to the high aristocracy) one member made a bet with another that he could eat a goodly portion of fecal matter (Freud's term was monosyllabic). It was served, of course, on a golden platter, and he fell to with a will. Suddenly he paused, spluttered, and could not go on eating. He had found a hair in it.

During the first winter of these ambulating colloquies I made a further step toward closer contact with Freud by my proposal to found a periodical for applied psychoanalysis (*Anwendung der Psychoanalyse auf die Geisteswissenschaften*). I explained the use and value of such a periodical in a paper to which I gave the superscription "Treugehorsamstes Promemoria" (Faithfully most obedient Promemoria), using by way of a joke the title of the document in which Goethe—who seems to have been fond of these baroque forms of eighteenth century court formalities—recommended to the Grand Duke Karl August the appointment of Schiller as a professor of history at the University of Jena (of course, without a salary). Freud acknowledged his favorable reception of my proposal in a characteristic manner. At the next meeting he used a passage from it in his remarks about the subject under discussion. He took my project up and pursued it with his usual energy. His first move was an attempt to secure the collaboration of the publisher of his books. We—Rank and myself—met the publisher and his manager in Freud's study and discussed our plans; at first he seemed favourably inclined, but later decided our project was too much of a financial risk. This cautious old German businessman learned some years later that his timidity had made him turn down one of the best business propositions he ever came across, since as the publisher of the periodical, he would have acquired the rights for "Totem und Tabu" and a number of other articles which first appeared in it. Freud found a younger and more enterprising man who was willing to start our journal. The title of the new publication gave us some headaches. Freud used to say that a title ought not to be a condensed summary of the contents, but a designation by way of easy association of ideas. Nor was he in favor of high sounding pseudo-poetic names. Finally my suggestion prevailed and it was called *Imago* after Carl Spitteler's novel in which the tricks and masks of the unconscious, its inroads into consciousness, and its stimulation of the creative powers are presented with consummate mastership. Carl Spitteler, whom I visited several times when I went to Lucerne, was duly flattered by becoming godfather of a scientific journal, but not at all interested in a systematic disquisition about the nature of the unconscious. He shrank instinctively from anything that could disrupt his artistic intuition.

Already I had been introduced to Freud's family and invited several times to his house, but after the founding of *Imago* and the beginning of my constant collaboration, I became a regular guest on certain evenings—nearly always together with Otto Rank—and a permanent fixture of the "inner circle." It was then that I had the best opportunity to observe Freud, to see how he did his work and his way of living.

A Visit

(1946)

EMIL LUDWIG

The famous biographer Emil Ludwig visited Freud in 1927. As the interview shows, he is somewhat skeptical about psychoanalysis and Freud's persistent questioning about the psychological dimensions of Goethe, Napoleon, and Leonardo da Vinci. The encounter with Freud was first published in Ludwig's Der entzauberte Freud *(Zurich, Carl Posen Verlag, 1946), pp. 177–80. The editor translated this excerpt.*

I visited Freud only once. I was always intrigued, when looking at his picture, by his dark, penetrating eyes, and wished for a long time to meet this strange man. I had, of course, met many of his students and adversaries.

When I stopped off in Vienna in 1927 for a visit I got in touch with Freud and he invited me in a personal note (written in his clear handwriting) to visit him the next evening. I was impressed with the simplicity of his surroundings. He lived on the second floor of an apartment building which had a great many shops on the ground floor.

I was struck by his general simplicity, and above all, by the seriousness of his look, which I found more brooding than penetrating. He was already seventy then, and had suffered much; as a result he received very few visitors. I admired his calm appearance, knowing that he endured considerable pain from his mouth cancer. With his old fashioned tie, his watch chain and cuffs, he reminded me of my own father, there in that dark office. Although my father was about 25 years younger, nevertheless he resembled Dr. Freud in his dress and the professional surroundings where he received his patients. I was careful however not to disclose my feelings about identifying Freud with my father, for that would have complicated matters.

With the utmost seriousness, which did not leave him during the two hours that I visited him, he started without preliminaries a philosophical conversation. I was surprised that he knew a few of my books, since he started to question me about three of them. This all took place in a witty and at the same time polite manner, so that I had the opportunity to study his physiogonomy. That was one of the reasons why I had come to see him. Some feeling of coldness did not leave me during the whole time; nor did it leave him.

"You wander freely among many individuals," said Freud, "somewhat anarchistic and completely to your liking; but here we concern ourselves to discover the laws and their consequences."

With that statement he touched the point which separated us. I was glad he conducted the conversation, and answered only, "You are a scientist and I am an artist." He did not seem satisfied and asked why I had not dealt with the psychological aspects of Goethe's childhood in my book on Goethe.

"Because there are no documents," I said.

"But there is one," he said, "and moreover in a very prominent place, just at the beginning of Goethe's memoirs." And he cited the anecdote in which the three-year-old Goethe, to his great delight, throws some dishes out of the window. When I asked him the meaning of this incident, he proceeded to explain it in great detail—I did not comprehend his explanation. At that time I was not aware of the fuss which had been made about Goethe in Freudian circles.° I just took in what he said and recorded it for my own use and played the role of listener and watcher.

After that Freud started to talk about my biography of Napoleon and made the same objection. "Why did I not take any clues from the childhood of Napoleon?" In the course of discussing this he proposed an explanation, which has never been printed and which I report here briefly.

"Who," asked Freud in his didactic manner, "was Napoleon's closest brother?"

"Lucien," I said.

"No, Joseph."

As I noticed that he did not know Napoleon's relationship to his brothers, and yet used Joseph, I simply said:

"What do you mean with Joseph?"

"Joseph," answered Freud, "the oldest brother, had replaced his father in Napoleon's feeling. He saw him as his father." Continuing, he presented a long monologue on the suggestive influence which Joseph as a father surrogate would have had on Napoleon, and concluded:

° In the original text Ludwig uses the term *Zirkus*. I am sure he did not mean Freudian circus, but rather, the great-to-do about Goethe in Freudian circles.

214

"While he discovered his father in *Joseph*, Napoleon married a woman named *Josephine*. And in tribute to Joseph he went to *Egypt*."

I thought I was dreaming. But as that was rather dangerous in Freud's presence, I collected myself and dismissed this second fantasy with a polite nod.

Somewhat later he rose, led me to a door, and pointed to two pictures, attached to the door without frames, I believe. He then proceeded again to talk about another of my subjects, Leonardo da Vinci, and felt compelled to demonstrate that again I had ignored a childhood memory. The pictures were two versions depicting Saint Anne with two other figures. One was after the painting in Paris, the other after the well-known sketch [in London].

Freud then explained that this was a kind of two-headed Madonna, corresponding with Freud's thesis that Leonardo had two mothers.

"Which one do you think," asked Freud, "is the oldest of these pictures?" "This one," I said, pointing to the sketch.

"Exactly," he said. "How did you know?"

"Because most of the time sketches are made before paintings."

There was a short pause and I decided that in that room a simple question seldom got a simple answer.

Freud Amongst Us

(1947)

PAUL FEDERN

Paul Federn (1871–1950) was one of the first medical practitioners in Vienna to embrace psychoanalysis. He was introduced to Freud in 1902 and soon became a member of his inner circle. Until his departure for New York in 1938 he was a leading figure in the Viennese Psychoanalytic Society. Freud trusted him as a close follower whose loyalty was unquestionable. He was among the first psychoanalysts who believed that psychotherapy could be used to treat psychotics. A forerunner of the ego-psychologists, he practiced in New York until he took his own life because of an incurable cancer.

This selection, delivered as a tribute at the dedication of the statue of Freud by Oscar Nemon at the New York Psychoanalytic Institute on 12 November 1947, appeared in Psychiatric Quarterly 22 (1948): 1–6.

Any dedication of a statue or other memorial satisfies the personal feeling of love for, and gratitude to, the dead person. Usually the dead are really pitiable—they are soon forgotten, and are rarely mentioned by friends or opponents. We all constantly use and enjoy the fruits of their labors without thinking of the geniuses who have devoted their lives to gain them. Many of these men while living were despised or ignored, or even persecuted because of their works. Our forefathers reacted against them as we try not to react. Posterity should bestow even more honor to the dead, but also be ashamed of the futility of such honor after the death of the great. This dedication of Freud's statue should remind us all to render justice to the living who do original work.

The German-Austrian scientists, and, particularly, the faculty of the University of Vienna refused to recognize Freud; he never obtained the clinical position he needed and deserved. If Freud had died young, as did other great discoverers, he would have suffered the tragic experience of the rejected genius. Because Freud lived over 80 years, he himself experienced the satisfaction of the spread of his work and fame over the world.

At his seventieth birthday when we—Ferenczi, Jones, Sachs, Storffer, Eitingon, K. Pichler and myself—gave him the two volumes dedicated to his septuagenary, he was still very uncertain of the permanence of his work. He warned us not to deceive ourselves. He remarked that psychiatrists were becoming accustomed to give recognition to his name while they combatted psychoanalysis. Ten years later, at his eightieth birthday, the victory of his work could not be doubted. Yet, enormous patience and consistent application were necessary in order to resist the long period of opposition and stupid criticism, neglect and slander.

For us who knew the young and healthy Freud, this statue is sad and pathetic. The statue represents Freud as an old man, with the impress of constant strain and striving. Humor, charm and affability were strained by the fight against age, disease and pain. Yet his face retained the expression of strength, of kindness, clarity and truthfulness. We see him resting but undefeated; there was no fatigue or defeat in his whole personality.

Freud is the representative of all heroic fighters who advanced a truth which contemporaries were unable to accept and even to understand. This very opposition became another objective of his studies. Every great man must overcome three kinds of difficulties: first, the resistances in himself; second, the friction and fight with his contemporaries; and third, the difficulties arising from his work itself.

Freud was not only the first psychoanalyst, but he was also the first person to be psychoanalyzed. He analyzed himself. His book, *The Interpretation of Dreams*, contains a good deal of his self-analysis. This procedure gave him the knowledge of his own resistances and also the method of overcoming them. His self-analysis convinced him of the validity of his discoveries. During such studies he himself made all possible objections; they were the same resistances which he later met in his patients and pupils.

Quite a few of his followers deserted him. Once I was indignant about the ingratitude of one of these deserters. Freud explained it with psychological argument. He was immunized against being deeply grieved by any betrayal—through his early experience with Breuer, which itself was no betrayal, of course. The discoverer of "repression" and the initiator of the therapy of the neuroses, Breuer deserted his own work. Breuer could not tolerate the results of the method he himself had promoted.

The United States was the first country to acknowledge Freud as

217

the outstanding discoverer and innovator in psychiatry. Stanley Hall and James Putnam were his first sponsors when Freud came to this country to receive the honorary degree of Doctor of Law at Clark University. Since then, Americans have accepted Freud's work with increasing interest. Books and papers are still filled with Freudian problems, findings and advices. Much of this is superficial, much is well understood and clearly written. Americans have become interested in psychoanalysis. It appears to me that this success was due to the ingrained American willingness to give everyone a fair hearing. The principle of free speech and press has exerted its educating influence. And when psychoanalysis received the opportunity to prove itself, the merits of a daring scientific discovery and the fascinating style of a modest and sincere writer won general recognition.

Three times in my life, I have had the same experience: While in New York in 1914, I gave lectures on psychoanalysis at the Liberal Club. I expected a small audience; however to my great astonishment some hundred persons were present. There was no room in the auditorium; I saw them standing before the windows and doors on Washington Square. I could not see the end of the crowd, and felt that Freud was transmitted by me to an unlimited number of people—to mankind itself. The same thing happened when Freud's medallion was unveiled at the house of his birth. On the four or five streets which joined before the house the crowd was endless. Again it happened when I spoke concerning Freud to Viennese students on his seventy-fifth birthday.

Since then, more and more, Freud's scientific work has become the common knowledge of the whole of literate mankind. The consequence is that more and more people are not satisfied with the surface appearance of pathological, of abnormal, and even of normal mental life, individually and socially. They know that there are concealed meanings, unconscious tendencies and complicated genetic developments—things deeper and more powerful than the manifest.

The common quality of all of the works of Freud lies in this:

The symptom is the disease and is only the surface—the conflict and repressed drives are behind. These must be found and deciphered.

Errors, forgetting, slips of the tongue, of the pen, etc., are the manifest surfaces; the unconscious etiology is the interesting objective.

Psychosis and neurosis; character and resistances; social and political relations are the surface; in them, unconscious forces have to be revealed and checked.

However, such is the work of every originator in science—he is not satisfied with appearances and "standarized," accepted explanations. Freud has extended the natural science method over the whole of civilization. His influence has become enormous. Nobody today is satisfied by conscious knowledge of conscious motives. Whosoever seeks, or merely questions, repressed, hidden tendencies, motives and causes is co-worker with, and follower of Freud.

Freud was the strongest character I ever met. One must think of Galileo, Cromwell, Zola, Jefferson, Lincoln, to find his equal. He was convinced that any knowledge of the truth enables us to fulfill better any task of civilization—be it medical, psychiatric, educational, individual or sociological. However painful it is first to accept the truth, illusions and rationalizations must be recognized and given up. Then only can we become able to use the truth and to cope with realities. The discovery of the unconscious and of unconscious mechanisms is a painful step, but one aimed to *protect* civilization, not to destroy it. When Freud found that neurosis is the disease of our civilization, he never wanted to sacrifice civilization in order to avoid the neurosis, but he sought to find new methods to free civilization from the neurosis which endangers its existence.

For this reason, Freud is still with us, not only as an honored guest, but as leader and teacher. He recommends that we study his truth and understand it, not only to practice psychoanalytical therapy, but to teach and spread the conviction that the dreadful concomitants of civilization, neurosis and psychosis, criminality and psychopathy can be overcome, can be prevented. Psychoanalysis found that the adult suffers from the residue of unfavorable childhood circumstances. Psychoanalysis of the adult neurotic, or psychotic, or criminal, takes much time, and is hard work; belated because the injury took place long ago, and the consequences are strongly established.

But today the prevention of neurosis, psychosis, psychopathy and criminality, and of lesser degrees of maladjustment, through the mental and social hygiene of the infant, the child and the adolescent, are made possible through, and still need, the method initiated by Freud. The truth is a relief for the scientist whose doubt and anguish drive him forth to seek the answer. For everyone who wants to better conditions it is necessary to know the truth. On the other hand, it is pleasanter to ignore the truth, if one does *not* want to better conditions. Therefore Freud's revealing science of the human mind and of the causation of mental disease is a challenge to us all. Not only are those of the relatively small group of psychoanalysts and psychiatrists his fol-

219

lowers—all are. Civilized mankind remains his patient, until we have all learned to use his truth to establish mental health in civilized man.

Therefore when Freud's statue is erected here, may it be a symbol that he and his spirit are welcome and accepted in this country, not merely in this institute.

In this institute itself Freud's presence reminds us of the aims and motives and purpose of the psychoanalytic association. He foresaw that many shades and deviations and derivations necessarily would develop. In the international society, those may work together who want to continue and to complete the *whole* psychoanalytic concept. Only in this respect, are we "orthodox"; but we are open to every change which is progress—without abandoning the established truth and the principles confirmed by our scientific method.

That Freud's statue is here, proves that history fulfilled what in his lifetime was not accomplished. He was exiled from his home-land, and with him his European followers. They owe to the prestige of his name and his psychoanalysis the fact that they were received in the Anglo-Saxon countries and especially in the United States by their American colleagues. In our new country, our work continues. Therefore Freud and psychoanalysis are greatly indebted to American hospitality.

Freud came once as a "visitor" to New York. It is well known that, however thankful he was for acknowledgment, invitation and for much kindness he received here, he had the impression that there was not enough libido actually to be found and felt by him. When I myself enjoyed much hospitality in New York in 1914, I did not have this feeling. But I also formulated my parallel impression in the statement that the United States had developed the reality-principle to the highest degree, frequently *at the expense* of the pain-pleasure-principle. The Italian steward on the boat on which I returned to Europe said the same: *"America é soltanto per lavore niente per gioia."* (American is only for work; nothing for joy.)

I think that all this has changed to a remarkable extent. Today, libido is not deficient in the United States. We have seen a remarkable example during the Second World War. While one understands that military organization is built on the reality-principle, psychiatric treatment was based on the use of libido, of transference, of understanding. In this war every soldier who became mentally ill was certain to meet kind understanding and to meet psychoanalytically-minded physicians and nurses. The organization of military psychiatry by Gen. William Menninger, M. C., was a major step forward, thanks to the acceptance of psychoanalysis by American psychiatry, and thanks to the acceptance of American psychiatry by the United States War Department.

The same is becoming more and more true in dealing with illness and social work, in general. Therefore the increase of active libido itself in this country is due, in some measure, to the influence of Freud.

I hope that his statue, too, will become a "resident" amongst us. His, Freud's, spirit is thankful to the United States which accepted his work, but it is also receiving the gratitude of the American people for the contributions of psychoanalysis to American science and culture.

Freud's Scientific Beginnings
(1949)

SIEGFRIED BERNFELD

Bernfeld's research papers on Freud constitute a major contribution to the history of the psychoanalytic movement and of psychoanalysis in general. This paper was originally published in American Imago *6 (1949): 163–96.*

The childhood phantasies and the adolescent day dreams of Freud, as far as we know them, do not foretell the future originator of psychoanalysis. They fit a general, a reformer or a business executive rather than the patient, fulltime listener to petty complaints, humdrum stories and the recounting of irrational sufferings. It was a long way from the child who devoured Thier's story of Napoleon's power; who identified himself with the Marshal Massena, Duke of Tivoli and Prince of Essling, to the psychoanalyst who cheerfully admits that he has, in fact, very little control even over those symptoms and disturbances which he has learned to understand so well. Twelve years old, he still thinks of himself as a candidate for cabinet rank and, as an adolescent, he plans to become a lawyer, and to go into politics. Then, at seventeen, shortly after his graduation from high school, Freud suddenly retreats from his search for power over men. "The urge to understand something about the mysteries of the world and maybe contribute somewhat to their solution became overwhelming." [1] He turns to the more sublime power over nature, through science, and he decides to study "natural history"—biology to us today. Power, prestige and wealth should come to him only contingent to his being a great scientist.

Great he had to be. "I fear mediocrity," he says in a remarkable letter to a friend, in the days of the final examination.[2] This friend had recently tried to console him: "He who only fears mediocrity is quite secure." "But," answers Freud, "at night—June 16, 1873 . . . with a somewhat somnolent philosophy. . . . Secure from what, I must ask;

certainly not secure and assured that one is not mediocre? What does it matter whether you fear something or not? Isn't it most important that what we fear is true? Quite true that even stronger minds are gripped by doubts of themselves; is therefore anyone who doubts his own merits a strong mind? He may be a weakling in intellect, but an honest man withal—because of education, habit, or even self-torture. I don't want to ask you to mercilessly dissect your reactions whenever you find yourself in some doubtful situation, but if you do it, you will see how little certainty there is within you. The magnificence of the world is founded on this multitude of possibilities, only that is unfortunately no strong basis for knowing ourselves."

In the fall of 1873, with high ambitions and vague ideas and plans, he registered at the University of Vienna. He chose the medical department (*Medizinische Fakultät*) which combined what we call here the pre-medical curriculum and the medical school proper. It was the place of training for physicians as well as for future research men in biology—the field in which Freud's hopes lay. In sharp contrast to the closely supervized and rigidly regimented life and learning at the gymnasium (high-school), the university offered an almost complete freedom from disciplinary rules. Students, who like Freud, craved for knowledge could satiate their thirst freely, without concern for grades and credits, in any one of the many lectures, seminars and labs. Few rigid requirements were laid down, and between the Matura (graduation from high-school) and the first conprehensive examination for the M.D. the student could enjoy several years of unmitigated "freedom of thought," a condition of which Freud took good advantage, in his first three years. He indulged in varied and chaotic studies and, as he has repeatedly confessed, turned out to be a dismal failure, particularly in chemistry and zoology. In his third year he settled down in Brücke's Institute of Psychology and, with few interruptions, staid there six years. He passed, in 1881, with great delay, but in one stretch, the examinations required for the M.D. diploma. In 1882, when he was twenty-seven, he left Brücke's Institute for economic reasons and prepared himself for private practice in neurology. During these nine university years Freud published five scientific papers and the translation—from English—of a volume of essays.

These scientific beginnings Freud has treated summarily with a few lines in his autobiographical writings. Brun and Gray have carefully listed them and Brun, Dorer and Jeliffe have given a brief evaluation of some of them.[3] In the following pages I will give a more thorough report on them together with information I have been able to gather on the scientific situations in which they were planned and written and on Freud's teachers and their institutes.[4] I have tried to evaluate the merits of the papers in their time and their place in Freud's scientific evolution. I will not limit myself strictly to the 1873 to 1882 period but will include in this study four papers which were written and published during the years 1883 and 1884, for they belong to Freud's beginnings as elaborations or continuations. I will further discuss his physiological efforts in 1878 and 1883 which have not resulted in papers and are unknown to Brun, Jeliffe, Gray and Dorer.

I. Zoology.

Freud's efforts in zoology resulted in a paper on the testes of the eel.[5] This first scientific study by Freud, though his second publication, provides the opportunity to confront Freud's deprecatory judgment about himself as a zoologist with an opinion independently arrived at.

The sex life of the common eel had been a puzzling problem since the days of Aristotle; in 1876 it still seemed unsolved. "No one ever has found a mature male eel—no one has yet seen the testes of the eel, in spite of innumerable efforts through the centuries." [5] In 1874 Dr. Syrski had announced the most recent solution. He had discovered a small lobed organ and described it as the testes of the eel. Carl Friedrich Claus, chief of the Institute for Comparative Anatomy in Vienna, assigned to his student Freud the task of checking Syrski's observations. (Though Claus' main interest was in coelenterta and crustaceae, the problem of the eels was closely linked to his own earlier studies on hermaphroditism in animals.)[6] Freud dissected 400 eels, finding the Syrski organ in many of them. On microscopic examination he found the histological structure of the organ such that it could well be an immature form of the testes, though he found no definite evidence that this was the case.

This study is inconclusive. Although it is written in a precise and animated style, always self-assured—at places, even cocky—its content is neither exciting nor brilliant. Still it is by no means proof as Freud asserts "that the peculiarities and limitations of my gifts denied me all success in many of the departments of science into which my youthful eagerness had plunged me. Thus I learned the truth of Mephistopheles' warning: 'It is in vain that you range around from sci-

ence to science; each man learns only what he can learn.'—*Faust*, Part
I."[7]

Claus obviously thought well of the young scientist. In the fall of
1873 Claus had come from Göttingen to Vienna with the intent and
assignment to modernize the zoological department. One of his pet
projects was a marine laboratory, and in 1875 he succeeded in founding the Zoological Experiment Station in Trieste, according to the patriotic official *History of Zoology and Botany* in Austria, "one of the
first institutions of its kind in the world." Claus had sufficient funds at
his disposal to send a number of students to Trieste for several weeks
of study and research twice a year. Among an early group, in March
1876, was Freud. Such a trip to the shores of the Adriatic, at the department's expense, was certainly much sought after and the assignment was valued as a reward or a distinction. In fact, Anna Freud Bernays remembers, more than a half a century later, this grant as an
important episode in the life of her brother Sigmund.[8]

In September of the same year Claus renewed Freud's assignment.
He procured for Freud the needed eels of the larger size which appear
only late in the season from October through January. On March 15,
1877, Claus had already presented Freud's paper to the Academy of
Sciences and had it published in the April issue of the Bulletin of the
Academy. Of course he would have enjoyed announcing that his institute had solved the old problem of the reproduction of eels for good.
Yet he knew too well how progress in science inches ahead in a long
succession of just such indecisive, unexciting little papers. Nothing
shows that he was disappointed in his student's work.

In fact, Syrski's claim soon was confirmed. The lobed organ which
he had discovered is the testes of the eel. Freud's paper was the first of
a series which accumulated the evidence.[9] But this did not change
Freud's hostile attitude toward his first scientific study. Twenty years
later Freud had privately printed the list of his thirty-eight scientfic
writings in order to set forth his scientific merits in the hope of furthering his promotion to the position of professor extraordinarius. Though
the abstracts were brief, never exaggerated, sometimes even under-
stated, they did put forward the results, the new findings or new aspects of each of the items. Regarding the first paper on this list he says:
"Dr. Syrski had recognized a lobed . . . organ as the long searched-for
testes of the eel. On the suggestion of Professor Carl Claus I have, in
the Zoological Station in Trieste, investigated the occurrence and the
histological structure of this lobed organ."[10]

This is not merely a modest understatement. Were this a review by a colleague, the author would be justified in complaining of malicious falsification. In the meantime Freud had obviously learned that Syrski's discovery had been recognized by the zoologists, due to his own investigation, among others. His abstract, however, leads one to believe that Syrski's recognition occurred prior to Freud's study; and under this assumption, of course, his paper appears to be utterly futile, aimless, and pointless, for which, in revenge, Claus bears the responsibility. (This abstract, it should be noted, is the only one in which the suggesting teacher is mentioned!)

This condemnation of his own zoological efforts, which the student felt so intensely and the old man never corrected, seems even stranger when we consider that in method, general scientific goals and spirit, the institutes of Claus and Brücke were alike. The studies in the comparative anatomy of the nervous system which Freud conducted to his own satisfaction under Brücke differed in topic only from his research in zoology.

Was the topic so repulsive to him that he felt devoid of the ability to deal with it? The eighteen-seventies were prudish and hypocritical and the moral standards of Freud's family were strictly Victorian; Freud shared them with conviction. In her old age, his sister still complains that he had not permitted her to read the improper writers, Balzac and Dumas. Or is it just one of those strange coincidences that the discoverer of the castration complex wrote his very first paper on the missing testes of the eel, and let almost twenty years go by before he gave sexuality another scientific thought?

Or was, perhaps, the teacher and the atmosphere in Claus' Institute the source of his discontent? Of Brücke's Institute Freud says: "Here I found the teachers whom I could take as my models," intimating clearly that the conditions for finding himself and his talents had been lacking in the preceding years.[7] Claus was a scientist of great reputation; "his works in zoology . . . take the first place amongst the zoological text books of the present day," says Adam Sedgwick in the English translation of Claus' Zoology. He was a very stimulating teacher—ambitious, intent and able to create emulation in his students. He was, like Brücke, a Darwinist, a conscientious worker and an ardent physicalist; narrower and of smaller scientific stature than Brücke, but not narrow and not small. Of course, the ways of admiration and affection are mysterious, at least, as long as we cannot enlist the cooperation of the subject for a psychoanalytical investigation of his preferences. However, we might guess at one factor in the complex picture though we cannot estimate its relative weight. Brücke was Freud's senior by forty years, while Claus held his powerful position as a comparatively young man only twenty years older than Freud. Brücke was the contemporary of Freud's father. Claus was the same age as Freud's half-brother. These are irrelevant data which ought not to influence one's success or failure in any given field. They ought not —quite true—but they do, in the average student as well as in the singularly gifted one. From Freud's self-analysis we know that in his early childhood in Freiberg he concentrated all his love, admiration and trust on his father, and had shifted his distrust and rebellious and hostile attitudes to the brother, yet without ceasing to love him." [11] The young man accepted guidance and criticism from the old Brücke— "the greatest authority I ever met"—as he had admiringly and with awe looked up to his father in those early childhood years in Freiberg. Toward the younger Claus he may have felt that same mixture of love and hostility, of admiration and distrust, which had colored his relationship to his half-brother. Tempted to rebellion and competition, inhibited by the wish to learn and by genuine appreciation for the teacher's ideas and achievements, he lived in an irritating atmosphere full of frustration, doubts and comparisons. This was sharply contrasted by the inner peace in which he could learn and grow to self-esteem under an authority which was unchallenged and unsuspect. How to grow away to full independence from such an authority in later years then becomes a problem which has destroyed and distorted many a talent; but not Freud's. In 1876, when he exchanged zoology for physiology, this test was still six years away.

II. Histology of the Nerve Cell.

The Viennese medical student of the Seventies was requested to attend the classes of Ernst Brücke on "physiology and higher anatomy," and was expected to work at least one short term in Brücke's Institute of Physiology. Freud was little concerned about requirements, but in search of a teacher and a field for his ambitions he tried Brücke and stayed on for six years. "I was stuck there," as he puts it. In this institute he not only worked to his own and Brücke's complete satisfaction, but what he experienced there was of such singular importance to him that in his autobiographical comments this period of his life is the one of which he speaks in unrestrained superlatives as

227

"the happiest years." What the reasons for this gratitude were we do not know. But we can say with certainty, that it was during these six years that Freud acquired or developed to maturity those qualities which were to become characteristic of him as a scientist.

It has been shown that in fundamentals as well as in many details the Freudian concepts and theories have their roots in the Brücke Institute; that, to a certain degree, they are transformations of the ideas and methods Freud had learned there.[12] This justifies my giving in extenso on the following pages, the background in which Freud worked during these years although the papers published in this period might, in themselves, not deserve so much space.

The Physiological Institute was miserably housed in the second story and basement of a dark and smelly old gun factory.[13] It consisted of a large auditorium and of two rooms—one of them being Brücke's office—with two windows each. The microscopes for the freshmen students had their place in the auditorium. Further, there were a few small cubicles, some without any light, serving as electro-physiological, chemical and optical laboratories. Of those, some adjoined the auditorium and Brücke's office in the second story. Others were in the basement. The animals were kept in a shed in the yard. There was no gas and no water. All heating had to be done over a spirit lamp and the water was brought up from a well in the yard. This was the job of the janitor who carried one bucketful up the two stories every morning and deposited it in the large room in which he doubled as the mechanic and which he shared with Brücke's two assistants, the professors Fleischl and Exner, and with their famuli. Yet, this institute was the pride of the medical school due to the number and distinction of its foreign visitors and students.

In fact, Brücke's Institute was an important part indeed of that far-reaching scientific movement best known as Helmholtz' School of Medicine. The amazing story of this scientific school started in the early forties with the friendship of Emil Du Bois-Reymond (1818–1896) and Ernst Brücke (1819–1892) soon joined by Hermann Helmholtz (1821–1894) and Carl Ludwig (1816–1895). From its very beginning this group was driven forward by a veritable crusading spirit. In 1842 Du Bois wrote: "Brücke and I pledged a solemn oath to put in power this truth: 'No other forces than the common physical chemical ones are active within the organism. In those cases which cannot at the time be explained by these forces one has either to find the specific way or form of their action by means of the physical mathematical method or to assume new forces equal in dignity to the chemical physical forces inherent in matter, reducible to the force of attraction and repulsion.' " [14]

These men formed a small private club which in 1845 they enlarged to the *Berliner Physikalische Gesellschaft*. Most of its members were young students of Johannes Müller—physicists and physiologists, banded together to destroy, once and for all, vitalism, the fundamental belief of their admired master. Strangely enough, Johannes Müller did not mind. On July 23, 1847, at the meeting of this society, Helmholtz read a paper on the principle of the conservation of energy—with the modest purpose of giving a sound foundation to the new physiology. Thus, casually, started the career of one of the leading physicists of the century. Du Bois, Brücke, Helmholtz and Ludwig remained lifelong friends. Within twenty-five or thirty years they achieved complete domination over the thinking of the German physiologists and medical teachers, gave intensive stimulus to science everywhere, and solved some of the old puzzles forever. As for vitalism—they lived long enough to see it rise again in 1890. However, in the seventies they and their physiology were a power not yet seriously challenged.

Brücke, whom in Berlin they called "Our Ambassador to the Far East," kept, in his Viennese classes, very close to his elaborate notes. These, in 1874, he published as Lectures in Physiology. The first forty pages contain, in substance, the general ideas of the physicalistic physiology which captivated the student Freud.

Very briefly they are: Physiology is the science of organisms as such. Organisms differ from dead material wholes in action—machines—in possessing the faculty of assimilation but they are all the phenomena of the physical world; systems of atoms, moved by forces, according to the principle of conservation of energy formulated by Helmholtz; the sum of forces (motive forces and potential forces) remains constant in every isolated system. The real causes are symbolized in science by the word "force." The less we know about them, the more kinds of forces do we distinguish; mechanical, electrical, magnetic forces, light, heat. Progress in knowledge reduces them to two—attraction and repulsion. This applies as well to the organism man. Contrary to Descartes, one cannot believe that the perpetual changes which we experience and which happen to our ego are not the effect of external causes. Brücke then turns to an elaborate presentation in two volumes of what was then known about the transformation and interplay of physical forces in the living organism. I do not know how

229

better to describe the spirit and content of Brücke's lectures than with the words which Freud used in 1929 to characterize phychoanalysis from its dynamic standpoint: "The forces assist or inhibit one another, combine with one another, enter into compromises with one another, etc."

Very closely connected with this dynamic aspect of Brücke's physiology was its evolutionistic orientation. The organism is not only a part of the physical universe, but the organismic world itself is one family. Its apparent diversity is the result of divergent developments which started with the microscopic unicellular "elementary organisms." It includes plants, lower and highest animals, as well as man, from the hordes of the anthropoids to the peak of his contemporary western civilization. In this evolution of life, no spirits, essences, or entelechias, no superior plans or ultimate purposes are at work. But the physical energies alone cause effects—somehow. Darwin had shown that there was hope of achieving in a near future some concrete insight into this "How" of evolution. The enthusiasts were convinced that Darwin had shown more than that—in fact had already told the full story. While the sceptics and the enthusiasts fought with each other, the active researchers were busy and happy to put together the family trees of the organisms, closing gaps, rearranging the taxanomic systems of plants and animals according to genetic relationships, discovering transformation series, finding behind the manifest diversities the homologous identities.

This physiology was a part of the general trend of western civilization. Slowly, continuously, it had risen and grown everywhere through the preceding two or three hundred years, steadily gaining momentum from the end of the eighteenth century and increasing rapidly in velocity and expansion after the eighteen thirties. This trend, weaker in Germany than in England and France, was interrupted there from about 1794 to 1830 (from the great to the little French revolution) by the period of *Naturphilosophie* (philosophy of nature).[15]

Naturphilosophie is the name of the pantheistic monism, close to mysticism, which, professed by Schelling—repeated, developed and varied by a host of writers—was eagerly accepted by the average educated man and literary lady. The Universe, Nature, is one vast organism, ultimately consisting of forces, of activities, of creations, of emergencies—all these—organized in eternal basic conflicts, in polarity; reason, conscious life, mind, being only the reflection, the emanation, of this unconscious turmoil. These ideas have been expressed before and since and contain the seeds of some of the scientific theories of the nineteenth century and of our time. But it is not the ideas which are characteristic of the movement nor the romantic temper which envelopes them. This was a general European trend. What characterizes the *German Naturphilosophie* is the aspiration expressed in the name "speculative physics" (which Schelling himself gave to his endeavors) and the unbalanced, megalomanic emotionalism of the fantasy and of the style of these writers. Fechner praised "the gigantic audacity" of Oken, a prominent representative, while a sober English historian puts it thus: "They exhibit tendencies that seem foreign to the course of European thought; they recall the vague spaciousness of the East and its reflection in the semi-oriental Alexandria."

Physicalistic physiology—although not by itself—overthrew philosophy and took its place. As has happened before, the conqueror introjected the emotionalism of his victim. "Unity of science," "science," "physical forces" were not merely directing ideas or hypotheses of scientific endeavor; they became almost objects of worship. They were more than methods of research—they became a *Weltanschauung*. The intensity of this temper varied with scientist to scientist; from place to place. In Berlin with Du Bois-Reymond it was at the maximum, strangely mixed with Prussian nationalism. In Austria, *Naturphilosophie* never had much power, therefore the physiology-fanaticism was at a minimum in Vienna and with Brücke. Yet it was there.

Brücke's writings cover a long span of time and a wide variety of topics. They begin in 1841 with the physiology of stereoscopic phenomena and end in 1892 with a pamphlet on how to protect life and health of one's children. Among them are classical pieces of research on the movements of mimosa pudica, the color change of chameleons, the structure of the "elementary organism," the biochemistry of urine, while the bulk—well over one hundred and twenty books and papers —were of more or less transitory importance only. He himself used to say: "A scientific truth lasts five years at most." Amongst these papers are many which, in terms of physicalistic physiology, deal with problems of psychology and social psychology: seeing, hearing, language, poetry and art. The following list of his publications during the six years in question gives only a faint impression of this variety:

1. The Sources of Ammonia in Distilled Water (1876)
2. Suggestions Concerning Improvement of Drinking Water Through Heating (1876)

3. The Absorption Spectra of Potassium Permanganate and its Uses in Quantative Analysis (1876)
4. A Contribution to Thermo-dynamics (1877)
5. Fragments of a Theory of the Formative Arts (1877)
6. Voluntary Movements and Cramps (1877)
7. The Schistoskop (1877)
8. Some Sensations Belonging in the Field of the Optical Nerves (1878)
9. The Relationship between the Formation of Spontaneous Oil Emulsions and of the So-called Myelin Sheath (1879)
10. Some Consequences of the Young-Helmholtz Theory (1879)
11. Training in the Classical Languages is Necessary for Physicians (1879)
12. The Metric Accentuation in Verses (1879)
13. Nitrogen and Sulpha-containing Non-cristalizable Acid Obtained by Treatment of Chicken Protein with Potassium Permanganate (1881)
14. Action in Painting and Sculpture (1887)
15. The Determination of Urea with Oxalic Acid (1881)

Brücke preferred that the student presented his own plans and projects but he was quite ready to formulate a problem for those beginners who were too timid or too vague in their interests. Freud belonged in the latter group when he entered the Institute as famulus (which is about the equivalent of a postgraduate research fellow) in 1876—probably in the fall, on his second return from Trieste. Brücke set him behind the microscope on work concerned with the histology of the nerve cells. This topic obviously was part of Brücke's great interest in "psychology."

Freud formulated, a few years later, the general situation as he found it in this field in the following words: "Very soon after the recognition of the nerve cells and of the nerve fibres as the fundamental parts of the nervous system began the efforts to clarify the finer structure of these two elements, motivated by the hope of using the knowledge of their structure for the understanding of their function. As is well known, up to now neither sufficient insight nor agreement has been reached in either of these two directions. One author thinks of the nerve cell as granulated, the other as fibrilose; one thinks of the nerve fibre as a bunch of fibriles but another as a liquid column. Consequently while one elevates the nerve cell to the basic source of nervous activity another degrades it to a mere nucleus of the Schwann sheaths." [16]

Together with the problem of the structure of the nervous elements goes the interesting question of whether the nervous system of the higher animals, at least of the vertebratae, is composed of elements different from the nervous system of the lower animals; or whether the simple and the complicated systems alike are built of the same units. This topic was highly controversial at that time. The philosophical and religious implications seemed to be very disturbing. Are the differences in the mind of higher and lower animals only a matter of degree of complication? Does the human mind differ from that of some mollusce—not basically but correlative to the number of the nerve cells in both and the complication of their respective fibres? Scientists were searching for the answers to such questions in the hope of gaining definite decisions—in one way or another—on the nature of man, the existence of God and the aim of life.

Into this vast and exciting field of research belonged the very modest problem which Brücke put before Freud. In the spinal cord of the Amoccetes (Petromyzon), a genus of fish belonging to the primitive Cyclostomatae, Reissner had discovered a peculiar kind of large cell. The nature of these cells and their connection with the spinal system elicited a number of unsuccessful investigations. Brücke wished to see the histology of these cells clarified. After a few weeks Freud came up with the quite unexpected discovery that the roots of the posterior nerves originated in some of these Reissner cells. Although this find did not explain the nature of the cells, it did promise a simple solution and eliminated the various hypotheses current in the literature. Brücke, it seems, thought that this was good enough for a beginner, and pressed for publication. Freud obliged by hurriedly putting together a report. His dissatisfaction with the unfinished work, however, is noticeable in many places in the paper. In style and organization it is far below the paper on the eels and of the succeeding publications of his student years. Brücke filed the study with the Academy of Science at its meeting of January 4, 1877. It appeared in the January bulletin of the Academy.[17]

Freud continued on his thorough investigation of the Reissner cells, and published a second report on Petromyzon in July of the following year.[18] Here he assembled an amazingly complete bibliography—eighteen pages of his report deal with the literature. This historical conscientiousness was not quite favorable to the young scientist's ambitions: "I must accuse myself of having falsely thought that I was the first one to describe—based on direct and certain observations—the origin of the posterior nerve roots in certain cells of the petromyzon. Only shortly after the publication of my paper did I find in Stieda's abstracts of the Russian literature an abstract of a paper by Kutschin which contains important information on the origin of the posterior root. Due to the friendliness of Professor Stieda in Dorpat, who had sent me the Russian paper, I could examine the pictures by Kutschin and satisfy myself that Kutschin had seen, already in 1863 in his preparations, convincing proof of the origin of the posterior roots in the posterior cells. By way of apology I can only say that Kutschin's statements—perhaps because his pictures were not available to the German histologists—were quite generally overlooked." Thus was not Brücke wrong after all, to insist on the publication of the preliminary paper?

Aided by an improvement in the technique of the preparation, Freud established definitely that the Reissner cells "are nothing else than spinal ganglion cells which, in these low vertebratae, where the migration of the embryonic neural tube to the periphery is not yet completed, remain within the spinal cord." [18] "These scattered cells mark the way which the spinal ganglion cells have made throughout their evolution." [10] This solution of the problem of these cells is a triumph of precise observation and genetic interpretation—one of the thousands of such small achievements which have finally established among scientists the conviction of the evolutionary unity of all organisms.

But Freud made even a major discovery on Petromyzon: "The spinal ganglion cells of the fish were known for a long time to be bipolar (possessing two processes) while those of the higher vertebratae are unipolar." This gap between higher and lower animals Freud has closed. "The nerve cells of Petromyzon show all transitions from uni- to bipolarity including bipolars with T-branching." This paper, in content, presentation, and implication is without any doubt well above the beginner's level. Brücke filed it with the Academy on July 18, 1878, and it appeared in its Bulletin, eighty-six pages long, the next month.

The same general problem is the aim of Freud's next investigation which he conducted by his own choice in the summer months of 1879 and 1881. This time the objects are the nerve cells of the crayfish. Here he examines the live tissues microscopically—a technique which, at that time, was as yet very little used, undeveloped and difficult—and he reaches the definite conclusion that the nerve fibres have without exception fibrillose structure. He recognizes that the ganglion consists of two substances, of which one is net-like, and the origin of the nerve processi. This study, which Freud himself filed with the Academy of Sciences at the meeting of December 15, 1881, and which appeared in the Bulletin of the Academy in January 1882, excells in the choice of its method, the exacting care given to its development, the caution shown in the argumentation, the direct approach to the key problem as well as in its precise, definite and significant results.[19]

With this paper and the two preceding ones Freud has done his share to pave the way for the neuron theory. One might safely go even a little further and claim, as did Brun and Jeliffe, that Freud had early and clearly conceived the nerve cells and the fibrils to be one morphological and physiological unit—the later neurones. In his research papers he confined himself strictly to the anatomical viewpoint, although he makes it clear that his investigations were conducted with the hope of gaining insight into the mystery of nerve action. Only once, in a lecture on "the structure of the elements of the nervous system" which summarizes his work, does he venture into this land beyond histology with the one paragraph: "If we assume that the fibrils of the nerve fibre have the function of isolated conductive pathways, then we may assume that the pathways which are separated in the nerve fibre are confluent in the nerve cell; then the nerve cell becomes the beginning of all those nerve fibres which are anatomically connected to it. I would transgress the limitations which I have imposed on this paper were I to assemble the facts which are in favor of that assumption; I know that the existing material is not sufficient for a decision on this important physiological problem; yet if that assumption could be proved we would take a great step in the physiology of the elements of the nerve system. Then we could consider the possibility that the nerve as a unit conducts the excitation." [20]

This lecture Freud delivered at the psychiatric society—within a year after he left the Brücke Institute—in 1882 or 1883. It was published in the *Jahrbücher für Psychiatrie* early in 1884. Here he gives to a broad audience of physicians—not to specialists in nerve histology—an account of the general problem situation in which his highly specialized investigation originated. He details his methods and his findings and in a few sentences he intimates the far reaching vistas opened by his results. We find here the same caution and boldness, the

235

same style of argumentation which characterizes the many accounts of his findings in psychoanalysis which Freud later gave to audiences unfamiliar with the goals, methods and experiences of the specialist. The first lecture of this kind shares with its successors the condensation of complex nets of facts and of complicated chains of thought in a few simple and lucid sentences. But in contrast to them this lecture contains sharp criticism of opponents. Although in controlled language, they are quite out of keeping with his previous and later characteristic aloofness.

Amongst his victims is Fleischl, his friend and teacher in the Brücke Institute. He dissects and rejects a study of Fleischl's on the structure of the fibres, though in gentle words, but thoroughly, resorting even to the method of the agonistic use of psychological interpretation; pointing out what the psychological motives of the observer might be, which lead him to an erroneous foundation for his findings. One wonders whether the dissatisfaction and frustration caused by his leaving the institute did not break through his usual contained literary attitude.

Should this be true or not—the polemic against Fleischl serves us as a reminder that the anticipation of the neuron theory with which we credit Freud was not implied in the teaching of Brücke and his staff. Although this theory is in the spirit of their teaching, neither Brücke nor Fleischl nor probably Exner and Paneth had at that time directed their thoughts in this direction. It seems they were Freud's own. Still it ought to be stressed that Freud had no part in the actual development of the neuron theory. His histological papers were noticed and occasionally quoted by some neuro-anatomist. They certainly served to create for him the reputation of a coming young man but they had hardly any influence on the course of research and theory. His physiological ideas condensed into one little paragraph hidden away in a popular lecture to phychiatrists most certainly was not even noticed. It had to wait for a friendly biographer to be discovered.

III. New Methods.

Freud's success in the histology of the nerve cells was greatly facilitated, if not made possible, by an improvement in technique on which he hit in 1877, soon after he entered the Institute of Physiology. He writes in a brief "Note on a Method for the Anatomical Preparation of the Central Nervous System," dated May 26, 1879: "I use Reichert's mixture as I have modified it for the purpose of preparing in a guaranteed and easy way, the central and peripheral nervous system of the higher vertebratae (mice, rabbits, cattle) . . . I have tried the method with the cerebral nerves of infants—Professor Dr. E. Zukerkandl kindly participating. We have found that it considerably facilitates the preparation of nerves situated in the bone channels and in the preparation and disentanglement of anastomoses and nerve nets . . . Furthermore, I used it successfully for the preparation of phlegm and perspiration glands, pacini bodies, hair-roots, etc." [21]

This is evidence of the scope of Freud's studies which surpassed the problem on which, on Brücke's suggestion, he worked at that time. The new technique, moreover, helped him in his days as a "demonstrator" at the Institute of Physiology. The equivalent of a teaching assistant, this position required him to prepare the anatomical specimens and histological slides for the classes of Brücke and his assistants.

Freud's modification of the Reichert formula prescribes the mixture of one part of concentrated nitric acid, three parts of water and one part of concentrated glycerine. It seems that nobody outside the institute gave any attention whatsoever to this invention. In fact to call it an invention—although logically correct—may sound like idolatry, a weakness quite common to biographers of great men. However, to Freud this modest achievement was the first realization of a high ambition. Six years later he returns with a second effort to this field.

"Innumerable methods were devised by histologists which proved themselves useful in the hands of their inventors only—this is why I have decided to publish even the pettiest directions" of a "new histological method for the study of nerve tracts in the brain and spinal cord." [22] This method Freud had developed in the fall of 1883. At that time he had left the institute of Brücke, prepared himself for private practice and took time out for research in Meynert's Institute of Brain Anatomy.

Freud was convinced of the usefulness of this new method. He praises the "wonderfully clear and precise picture" which one receives if one carefully follows his way of dyeing the brain preparation with gold chloride. The results achieved were far superior to any other dye technique known at that time and he was satisfied with its complete reliability. No longer does he speak modestly of having "hit on it."

237

This method he had laboriously and successfully developed in many experiments following a hint which Flechsig had published in 1876 but had not, himself, followed through.

This time, so it appears, Freud was determined to carry the day. He published a brief sketch,[23] as histologists usually do, but in order to escape "the fate of other inventors," as he says and of his own first trial six years previously—as one may assume—he followed up this publication with the detailed seven-page presentation which contains the lines quoted above. Not satisfied with this he writes a third version— this time in English—and published it in *Brain*.[24] These efforts brought him some success. This invention was not completely overlooked. Some students, off and on, have used it and at least one of them, in one American journal, still remembered the method in 1888.[25] However, it was not the gold chloride preparation of nerve tracts which became known as the Freudian method.

These two new methods and their fate would be of no importance were it not that they complete the picture of the young scientist Freud. It is a picture that has a striking likeness to that of the inventor of the psychoanalytic method. For Freud, as he has many times emphasized, psychoanalysis is first of all a new technique by which a whole realm of facts, inaccessible before, can be brought to light. It is a new instrument of observation, a new tool of research. In the second place only is it a body of new knowledge gained by the use of the new instrument. The Freudian discoveries are the almost incidental results of the Freudian invention. From his early scientific days on, his central aspiration was, so it appears, to do more than to collect and to marshal facts already known; more than to add a few units to the army against the dark and the unknown. He longed to provide it with a new type of weapon—an achievement which, with one magic stroke might multiply its fighting power.

Whether or not these metaphors which try to establish some continuity from Freud's early day dreams to his life work have any validity or are just a matter of style I do not know. Yet I want to stress emphatically that Freud's persistent interest in the invention of methods, though due to the individual trend of his mind, coincides with the basic ideas of the Brücke Institute and with the logical structure of science. Scientific progress runs from a new instrument to a new body of facts. The invention of the microscope, for instance, preceded histology. And in the history of any limited scientific field only new instruments and techniques can, in the long run, bring new facts. From there science proceeds to a new theory: the organization of the new and the old knowledge into one body of facts; and from the theory it finally runs to "speculation"—that is to the guessing at questions and answers beyond existing means of observation. It is very rare when one and the same man is productive in several of these phases, and almost never does it happen that he is equally effective in all. Psychoanalysis is an example of this rarest case: Freud invented the instrument, used it for a great number of discoveries, provided the organizing theory and the speculation beyond the known. The remarkable fact is, that he had already reached out for such encyclopedic achievement in his twenties. Freud's lecture on "The Structure of the Elements of the Nervous System," delivered at the Psychiatric Society in 1882, presents the new technique, the new findings due to it, the theory adequate to them and some glances beyond.[20] Every Freudian essential is there—in nucleo—but already sharply defined.

IV. Physiology.

Commenting on his professional education, Freud remarked that the physiology of his student years "was far too much concerned with histology." [1] This mild reproach stands out sharply against the background of the superlative praise with which Freud usually spoke of Brücke and his school. Moreover, among all the possible objections to Brücke's teaching this one is the least justified. True, in Brücke's Institute the microscopic and experimental approaches were still not separated in the seventies. Physiological experimentation, including the biophysics and biochemistry of today, became at that time increasingly the via regia, and some physiologists indulged in contempt of the microscopists. Not so Brücke. He continued to announce his classes in the lingo of the Vienna University as "Physiology and Higher Anatomy." To him the knowledge of the spatial organismic structure seemed as necessary as the knowledge of the forces playing on this apparatus, changing or reproducing it. The structure can be revealed by the microscope only. In Brücke's mind there was no opposition between anatomy and physiology; between microscope and experiment. This was the attitude which had already made famous his first major work in 1847. Yet in Freud's time the work done by Brücke and his assistants Fleischl and Exner was, in fact, almost completely physiological in the narrow sense of the word, dealing with organismic function and using animal experiment as one, though not as the only method.

There were few institutes in Europe where one could learn physiology equally well.

We have no indication that Freud made use of this opportunity. Considering the full freedom which existed in Brücke's Institute it is quite unlikely that any kind of external pressure kept him behind the microscope after he had finished his first histological assignment on the Reissner cell in 1878. In 1883, shortly after Freud left the Institute to prepare for medical practice, he again took up research. Yet even then—although undoubtedly free to choose topic and method—he returned to anatomical investigations. Only when clinical neurology took more and more of his increasingly fewer spare hours he discontinued all anatomical-histological research. His work in neurology Freud did not consider to be scientific research at all, in spite of its impressive quantity and the unanimous recognition which it found. Only in the middle nineties, when, as a cathartic psychoanalyst he again found himself behind an observation object, studying the structure of the mind, hoping for insight into the workings of the brain, did he feel that he had returned to science and enjoy this fact "as the triumph of his life." Thus it might be concluded that his heart simply was in histology, and that physiology did not appeal to him. However he stressed too frequently and too seriously the subordinate character of the study of forms, for the understanding of the function—guessing the drama from the stage setting, one might say. From the beginning of his scientific career, the knowledge of the acting forces certainly was a cherished goal, but for many years, like Moses, he stood before the forbidden promised land with only a guess of what it might look like.

A fact not mentioned in Freud's autobiography and overlooked by his biographers puts this conflict into sharp relief. Freud did make several efforts in the field of physiology proper during his student years, but not in Brücke's Institute. At that time a great deal of physiological research was done under the guidance of Stricker. Solomon Stricker, a contemporary of Claus (born 1834), trained by Brücke, had been Professor Ordinarius and chief of the Pathological Institute since 1873.[26] His early reputation was derived from embryological studies. His later work was concerned with the physiology of the vascular system and with the theory of consciousness, speech and thought. He is credited with transforming pathology from an anatomical into an experimental physiological discipline. In his institute a large amount of meritorious work was accomplished in various fields of physiology. His assistants were good men, but very few great talents developed in his school. His vanity, quarrelsomeness, righteousness, and some personal and scientific eccentricities were at fault—so it was gossiped in Vienna at that time. Freud worked in this institute at least twice; once in 1878 and again in 1883 to 1884.

At the meeting of the Medical Society in Vienna on October 17, 1879 Stricker introduced his paper on *Azinous Glands* with the statement that his student Freud had, at his suggestion, conducted experiments on this topic for a period of half a year, but had accomplished nothing. After Freud's failure Stricker collaborated with Spina and obtained interesting results.[27] Allowing half a year for these new experiments, Freud's efforts must have started sometime in the second half of '78, at the latest.

Thus Freud had tried his hand in experimental physiology soon after he had completed the histology of the Reissner cells in Petromyzon. He failed. Immediately afterwards he returned, by his own choice, to Brücke's Physiological Institute. Here he did not take up physiology but he went back to the microscope and started work on the *Nerve Cells of the Crayfish*, using the live-tissue method of which Stricker and not Brücke was the protagonist in Vienna.

In 1883, after he had left Brücke, we find him again in Stricker's Institute.[28] There he participated, together with Wagner-Jauregg, Gaertner, Spina and Koller, in animal experiments as part of a research project on the function of glands and of the circulatory system. Again Freud accomplished nothing. Simultaneously he had started research in brain anatomy and worked on his second invention—the gold-chloride method. The resumption of physiological research, it seems, was only half hearted but it indicates that his urge to go into physiology proper was still alive. Unlike Moses, he tried to penetrate the promised land but was forced back on every attempt. Not the lack of facilities, of opportunities, of teachers or of stimulation frustrated him. And certainly there was no lack of interest. Instead the ability for physiological work was missing. This can be said on the negative evidence that no physiological achievements of his are extant. There is even one positive clue: Freud has published, in 1885, a single piece of experimental work—the effect of cocaine, measured by the dynamometer.[29] It is a very poor effort indeed. In concept and technique it is oversimplified, uncertain and uncritical—the work of a beginner with little promise; quite different from the qualities of his initial histological work. Not, as he said, zoology, but physiology was really the field in which "the peculiarities and limitations of his gifts denied him all success."

Thanks to Freud, such "gifts" are no longer the last entities to psychological understanding. Beyond them exist determinants, of "peculiarities and limitations." As in the case of Freud's alleged failure in zoology, we might guess at one or the other reason for his suppressed failure in physiology. Stricker was, even less than Claus, a teacher whom Freud "could respect." One can see very well why he had not succeeded with Stricker. But why had he not grasped the opportunities at the Brücke Institute? Why had he accepted Brücke as authority and model only in the investigation of the setting and not of the drama? Brücke had started him on the dissection of the dead body. Had Freud unconsciously taken this advice to mean that Brücke had exiled him to the preliminary lowlier study of the structure and had reserved for himself and the older members of the Institute the higher wisdom about the workings of the living organism? Had he thus reaffirmed Freud's father's angry scolding of the child "when he, driven by early sexual curiosity, had intruded into the parental bedroom"? [12] And had he therefore tabooed physiology? Perhaps.

One feels on safe ground in pointing to a more superficial but probably concomitant factor. The animal experiment is a far more brutal exercise of power over the rights and life of the creature than the investigation of the corpse. And life cells of the crayfish?—but are they not "dead" compared with living guinea pigs, rabbits and dogs? As an adolescent Freud retreated from the power over man into the science of nature. The same basic design will reappear when Freud in his middle-thirties gives up hypnosis in search for "a less coarsely interfering" method. These were the two turning points in Freud's relation to science; at the first, he became a scientist; at the second, he invented psychoanalysis. And in between these two marks he stayed away from experimental physiological activity or, after brief excursions, returned to the more subtle exercise of power, to the role of observer of mere structure.

V. Translations.

To Freud's university years belongs the only work ever published by him which has no connection with his scientific or therapeutic interests. In 1879 Freud did a German translation of some essays of John

Stuart Mill. The editor of Mill's collected writings in German was Theodore Gomperz, a philosopher and historian of high standing in the university and in the society of Vienna. Freud substituted for Eduard Wessel, the young translator who had died suddenly during the preparation of the twelfth volume. He started the work in the fall of 1879 and completed it in December of that year.[30]

Why Freud accepted this commission is not known. He was at that time on involuntary leave from science, serving his one-year term in the army, which was compulsory for all physically able students. He was no model soldier it seems; he recalls gleefully how he spent his twenty-first birthday, May 6, 1880, under arrest. I can imagine that he seized the opportunity to kill the boredom of the barracks and to forget the discomforts of garrison life, by mental exertion—a kind of relaxation which has a touch of bravado indeed, considering the physical, psychological and moral strain of the service. Furthermore, even a modest translator's fee must have been quite welcome, in this year especially.

However, the task may have interested Freud beyond such secondary motivations. When Freud decided to take his place among the scientists and not with the politicians, he had by no means abandoned interest in and curiosity for social questions. Three of the four essays by Mill which he translated deal with the labor question, the enfranchisement of women, and socialism. Freud, in his later years, heartily abhorred philosophy and it is not likely that he ever had much interest in it. But Mill's philosophical work is in distinct contrast to the metaphysical systems which were specifically called "philosophy." Mill's work was very close to the empirical physicalistic spirit of the Brücke Institute. It is quite possible that Freud was attracted by the topics of the essays and by the writer as well. And it is certain that he liked to translate. Freud loved languages and writing. He read Greek and Latin for pleasure in his high-school years. He had an early command of English and French and later wrote several papers in these languages. He did a considerable amount of translating during his life—two volumes of Bernheim and two of Charcot, though on these occasions, even more than with Mill, secondary determinations existed. Freud as a translator was so careful, so brilliant and so rapid that translating, as such, must have appealed to him as a challenging pastime.

When Theodore Gomperz' son Heinrich, himself a philosopher and historian, prepared the biography of his father he asked Freud how he became the translator of the twelfth volume. Freud replied, in a letter dated June 9, 1932 (in translation): "I know that I was recommended to your father by Franz Brentano. Your father at a party . . . mentioned that he was looking for a translator and Brentano, whose student I then was or had been at a still earlier time, named my name." [31] That he had personally known Brentano; that he once had been his student and was well remembered by him, seems strange. Franz Brentano has not published much, and his teaching in philosophy and psychology did not create a great stir during his lifetime.[32] But Husserl's phenomenology and the various shades of logic and psychology ("Gegenstands-theorie") of Meinong, Marty and others, trace their origins to him. Several newer trends in psychology like the schools of Stumpf and more recently that of the Gestalt psychology, acknowledged him as one of their distinguished forerunners. In fact he had, in 1870, turned from metaphysics and physiological physicalism alike and developed psychology as a science based on empirical observation of the consciously "given." One is inclined to think of Brentano and Freud as almost diametrical opposites.

Heinrich Gomperz comments on the relation between Freud and Brentano which he feels is "not quite insignificant: We ought to remember that Freud had always opposed the more or less materialistic medicine of his time, stressing the relative independence of the 'psychic apparatus' from the physical, and in this connection maintained that it is possible to influence psychical maladies psychically. May we speak, perhaps, of a certain after-effect of the influence of a psychologist, who, more than any other, distinguished between 'physical' and 'psychic' phenomena and erected his whole doctrine on the basis of this distinction?"

That Gomperz misinterprets Freud's position follows clearly, if there were any doubt, from the preceding chapters of the present paper.

It is impossible that Freud at that time, or at any time for that matter, was a follower of Brentano. One even wonders whether he would have cared to understand the finer points of his arguments. This does not exclude the possibility that Freud was impressed by some of Brentano's polemics and statements, that he preserved them in his preconscious and that they influenced his thoughts twenty years later when he, disappointed in the existing psychological theories, ventured into this broad field on his own. Brentano's classification of the mental phenomena (perception, judgment and love-hate); his ideas concerning genius; his determinism, and—in some complex way—his emphasis on

244

the fact that all psychological phenomena refer to an object (intentionalism)—to put it crudely—all these thoughts could have had a belated influence on Freud in the nineties. So could have, as T. H. Merlan points out, Brentano's thorough historical presentation and most serious consideration of the doctrine "of the unconscious" in spite of Brentano's rejection of the concept of unconscious psychic activity. All these could have—if Freud had ever been a student of Brentano. In his letter to Gomperz Freud states that he had been a "Hoerer" of Brentano which means that he had "attended his lectures"; literally that he was one of Brentano's "listeners" rather than one of his pupils. Brentano was a very famous personality in the academic Vienna of his time and his lectures were crowded not only by students but by visitors and academic notables as well. Yet very few of his "Hoerer" came to study his philosophy and psychology.

Brentano held the attention of all Vienna from the moment he arrived from Würzburg as a professor of philosophy in 1874. His very name made him interesting. A nephew of the famous romantic poet Clemence Brentano, a grandson of Sophie La Roche, the friend of Goethe's youth, a nephew of Bettina, the famous addressee of Goethe's "Correspondence with a Child"—he was welcomed in the literary circles and salons. But more exciting than the history of his family was his own. A doctor of philosophy at the age of twenty-four, he decided to study theology and was ordained two years later as a Catholic priest. At thirty-two he courageously led the fight against the Pope's intention to set up the dogma of infallibility. Failing in his efforts, he defrocked himself and resigned his professorship in Würzburg. The Viennese liberal scientists acclaimed his appointment and soon found out that his personality, in sincerity, courage and charm, matched his pedigree and his spectacular action. Just at the time when Gomperz was looking for a translator, Brentano offered Vienna another exciting spectacle. He wanted to marry Ida Lieben, "one of the most noble daughters of Vienna," but the reactionary interpretation of an old Austrian law made such a marriage illegal for a former priest. Brentano resigned his position, acquired Saxon citizenship and finally married in Leipzig on September 16, 1880. He returned to Vienna to resume his lectures at the university—this time a simple lecturer (*Privat-dozent*).

That Freud was interested in Brentano and respected him as a man and a fighter there can be no doubt. Yet I have no clue to the understanding of Brentano's interest in Freud. However, the recommendation of a young student as a translator for some rather unphilosophical

245

essays by Mill does not necessarily indicate a high esteem for him. The assignment certainly did not require adherence to Brentano's teachings. It was more important to find someone who knew English. That Freud excelled in Brentano's seminar with his linguistic knowledge is possible. But it is equally possible that Brentano might not have been impressed by Freud at all—might hardly have remembered him personally—but was following the suggestion of one of their mutual friends. Fleischl, Exner, and Freud's close friend, Paneth, were personally and through their families, well acquainted with Brentano; Joseph Breuer was his family physician. At any rate, since we do not know how close Freud's acquaintance with Breuer and Paneth was in 1879, the reconstruction presented is hypothetical.

Horace Gray, in his list of Freud's 65 pre-analytic writings, makes a subjective comment on only one, the Stuart Mill translation. "In a footnote to the German version the editor Gomperz tells us (1) that the author inserted in the reprint of the essay a short preface, in which he explains that by far the greatest part of it is the work of his wife, since dead in 1858, highly valued by him for her preeminent qualities of mind and character; and (2) that he publishes no translation of Mill's later related work *The Subjection of Women*, 1869, which had been translated as *Die Hoerigkeit der Frauen*. The above facts are interesting in connection with Freud's later comment: 'That hostile embitterment displayed by women against men, never entirely absent in the relation between the sexes, the clearest indications of which are to be found in the writings and ambitions of emancipated women.'—In passing we note the high quality of the German translation of the *Enfranchisement* in its close adherence to the original without sacrificing smoothness. A curious point is the spelling of the translator's name as Siegmund, both on the title page and in the editor's epilogue."[3]

The influence of English philosophy, literature and political thought on Freud is an interesting topic which deserves a separate study. As everyone who mentions Freud's translation feels provoked to comment on it, I also want to make a remark. In a conversation about Plato, Freud admitted in 1933 that his knowledge of Plato's philosophy was very fragmentary but that he had been greatly impressed by his theory of anamnesis and that he had, at one time, given it a great deal of thought.[33] Amongst the essays in the twelfth volume, Stuart Mill's paper on "Grote's Plato" takes a conspicuous place. Mill's presentation treats the theory of reminiscence with sympathy and in general is a forceful debunking of the views on Plato's philosophy which high-school teachers were accustomed to preach at that time. Mill's common sense must have appealed to Freud very much and this essay could well be the main source of Freud's "fragmentary knowledge."

Notes

1. "Concluding Remarks on the Question of Lay-analysis." *Intern. Journal of Psychoanalysis* 8 (1927): 392–98.
2. "Ein Jugendbrief von Sigm. Freud." *Intern. Zeitschr. f. Psychoanalyse u. Imago* 26 (1941): 5–8.
3. Brun, R. "Sigmund Freud's Leistungen auf dem Gebiete der organischen Neurologie." *Schw. Arch. f. Neurologie u. Psychiatrie* 37 (1936): 200–7.
Gray, Horace, "Bibliography of Freud's Preanalytic Period." *Psychoanalytic Review* 35 (1948): 403–10.
Dorer, M. *Historische Grundlagen der Psychoanalyse.* Felix Meiner. Leipzig, 1932.
Jeliffe, S. E. "Sigmund Freud as a Neurologist. Some Notes on His Earlier Neuro-biological and Clinical Studies." *J. Nerv. and Ment. Dis.* 85 (1937): 696–711.
4. Some information on Freud's teachers is to be found in *Dorer* and in Bernfeld, S. "Freud's Earliest Theories and the School of Helmholtz." *Psychoanalytic Quarterly* 13 (1944): 341–62.
5. "Beobachtungen über Gestaltung und feineren Bau der als Hoden beschriebenen Lappenorgane des Aals." Arbeiten aus dem Zoologisch-Vergleichendanatomischen Institute der Universitaet Wien. *Sitzungsberichte der K. Adademie der Wissenschaften Wien* 75 (April 1877): 419–31.
6. Information on Claus from *Botanik u. Zoologie in Österreich in den Jahren 1850 bis 1900,* Wien, 1901., Eisenberg, L. *Das Geistige Wien,* 1893; and from his writings.
7. "An Autobiographical Study." *Int. Psychoanalytical Library No. 26* (1936): 15.
8. "My Brother Sigmund." *Am. Mercury* (Nov. 1940). [Sel. 16]
9. *Dean's Bibliography of Fishes* (1923) 3: 639. Personal communication from Earl S. Herald, Curator, California Academy of Sciences.
10. *Inhaltsangabe der wissenschaftlichen Arbeiten des Privatdocenten Dr. Sigmund Freud (1877–1897).* Wien, 1897. *Intern. Zeitschrift. f. Psychoanalyse* 25 (1940): 68–100.
11. Bernfeld, Siegfried and Suzanne C. "Freud's Early Childhood." *Bull. of the Menninger Clinic* 8 (1944): 107–15.
12. Bernfeld in *Psychoanalytic Quarterly* [n. 4].
13. Information on Brücke and the Physiological Institute from Brücke's writings and from sources listed by Bernfeld [n. 4].
14. This paragraph and the two following are reprinted—with slight changes—from Bernfeld [n. 4]: 348–50.
15. This paragraph and the two following are reprinted—with slight changes—from Bernfeld [n. 4]: 353–54.
16. *Struktur der Elemente d Nervensystems:* 221 [n. 20].
17. "Über den Ursprung der hinteren Nervenwurzeln im Rückenmark von Ammocoetes (Petromyzon Planeri) (Tafel: Freud del.)" *Sitzungsber. Kais. Akademie d. Wiss. Wien* 3, pt. 75 (1877): 15–27.
18. "Über Spinalganglion und Rückenmark des Petromyzon." *Sitzber. Kais. Akademie d. Wiss. Wien* 3, pt. 78 (1878): 81–167.
19. "Über den Bau der Nervenfasern und Nervenzellen beim Flusskrebs." *Sitzber. d. Kais. Akademie d. Wiss. Wien* 3, pt. 85 (1882): 9–46.
20. "Die Struktur der Elemente des Nervensystems." *Jahrbücher f. Psychiatrie* 5, no. 3 (1884): 221–29.—Freud [n. 10: 73] does not list this publication, but gives the title

with the addition: "(Vortrag im psychiatrischen Verein. 1882)" Brun [n. 3] has: "Wiener akad. Sitzb. Bd. 85. 1882." I was not able to find a journal with this title. It is not in Sitzber. der Kais. Akad. Wiss.—Gray [n. 3] has erroneously: "Jahrbücher . . . 1885."

21. "Notiz über eine Methode zur anatomischen Praeparation des Nervensystems." *Centralbl. f. d. Med. Wiss.* 17, No. 28 (Berlin 1879): 468–69.

22. "Eine neue Methode zum Studium des Faserverlaufs im Centralnervensystem." *Archiv f. Anat. u. Physiol. Anatomische Abth.* (Leipzig 1884): 453–60.

23. "Eine neue Methode zum Studium des Faserverlaufs im Central-Nervensystem." *Centralbl. f. d. med. Wiss.* 22, No. 11 (Berlin, 1884): 161–63.

24. "A new histological method for the study of nerve-tracts in the brain and spinal chord." *Brain* 7 (London 1884): 86–89.

25. Upson, H. S. "On Gold as a Staining Agent for Nerve Tissues." *Journ. of Nerv. and Ment. Dis.* (1888): 685.

26. Information on Stricker from: Eisenberg, L. *Das geistige Wien*, 1893; *30 Jahre experimentelle Pathologie*, Wien, 1898; and from Stricker's writings.

27. *Wiener Medizinische Presse*, No. 44 (2. Nov. 1879): 1403–06.

28. Koller, Carl. *Wiener Medizinische Wochenschr* (1935): 7–8.

29. "Beitrag zur Kenntnis der Cocawirkung." *Wiener Md. Wo.* 35, No. 5 (1885): 129–33 (report on experiments conducted in 1884).

30. "Über Frauenemancipation. Plato. Arbeiterfrage. Sozialismus." John Stuart Mill's Gesammelte Werke. Leipzig 1880.

31. Philip Merlan. "Brentano and Freud." *Journ. f. History of Ideas* 6 (1945): 375–77.

32. Information on Brentano from his writings; and from Oskar Kraus, "Franz Brentano (1838–1917)." *Neue Öster. Biographie* 1 (1926); Kraus, Stumpf, Husserl, *Franz Brentano. Zur Kenntnis seines Lebens u. seiner Lehre.* München 1919.

33. Personal communication from Mrs. Suzanne Bernfeld.

Ferenczi to Freud
(1949)

SANDOR FERENCZI

The story of Freud and Ferenczi still has to be written. It probably will prove one of the most interesting documents in the history of psychoanalysis. Ferenczi knew Freud since the very early days of psychoanalysis. With Rank he was one of Freud's most trusted friends and followers. Freud had a close emotional attachment to Ferenczi and addressed him at various times in letters as "my son." Ferenczi belonged to the committee which supported and counseled Freud in the difficult days of establishing the organization of psychoanalysis. He traveled with Freud to America and made trips with him to Italy. Dr. M. Balint has mentioned that a diary which Ferenczi kept during the last years of his life will eventually be published, but so far nothing has materialized. Nor are we allowed to look at the approximately 2,000 letters exchanged between Freud and Ferenczi.

The following excerpts are from ten letters Ferenczi wrote to Freud, the only letters so far published. They appeared in International Journal of Psycho-Analysis 30 (1949): *243–250. The translation is by Joan Riviere. These excerpts illustrate, contrary to other opinions, how close Ferenczi remained to Freud, even in his last days.*

Capri, Hotel Quisisana, 10.10.1931

Lieber Herr Professor,

. . . It is the first time for years that I am on holiday without patients; both body and soul were vehemently crying for absolute rest. Capri offers one everything one hopes for in Italy—sun, sea, people. We are very contented here. When you are able to travel again, you must not miss a long stay here. . . . I will certainly not deny that subjective factors do influence, often very considerably, both the form and the content of what I produce. In the past this has at times led to exaggerations. Eventually, however, I believe I succeeded in understanding how much and where I had gone too far. . . . I must suppose that something of the kind applies to your diagnosis of a 'third puberty.' Assuming that the diagnosis is correct, the value of what is produced in these conditions must above all be assessed objectively. Besides, I can also fall back on a quotation from Schiller (which you yourself told me) in which he says that the novel and unexpected should be met with

249

encouraging interest, even if it appears to some degree false or fantastic. My latest views are only in process of formulation. My ideas always originate in the variations of response to treatment shown by my cases and I confirm or reject my hypotheses by reference to this material. . . .

Budapest, 1.5.1932

Lieber Herr Professor,
The tone of gentle reproach in your letter is, I am sure, deserved. To be quite frank, I was prepared for much worse. . . . Of later years, it is true, I have been very much, perhaps far too much, absorbed and preoccupied in my work, trying to understand my patients. But whatever the motives leading to this kind of isolation, it is not necessarily a bad or worthless thing in itself. . . . Deeper self-analysis shows me indubitably that from earliest childhood I have had a tendency to become involved in situations which I can only master with great difficulty and excessive strain. I suppose that mentally I have never allowed myself any real holidays. . . .

Budapest, 3.5.1933

Lieber Herr Professor,
Only a few short lines to tell you that the date of your birthday is continually in our mind. Let us hope that this next year will not bring forth such unpleasant events as the last has. . . .

An Impression of Freud
(1949)

H. R. LENORMAND

The visit of the French playwright Lenormand to Freud's office was a short one, but nevertheless, it captures in a few sentences his essential impression. This incident was first published in Confessions d'un auteur dramatique 1 *(Paris, Albin Michel, 1949): 270–71. The translation, made especially for this book, is by Dr. Richard McConchie. The title was selected by the editor. The exact date of the visit could not be traced.*

Freud was not mistaken about the meaning of *Mangeur de Rêves.* When one of my plays was being given in Vienna, I took him a box of chocolates from one of his Zurich disciples. It was the first time I found myself face to face with him and I felt some uneasiness as I entered his office on Gotthard Strasse, which resembled the typical consultation room of a university professor. By then Freud had been stricken with cancer of the tongue and spoke only with difficulty. (This incident occurred several years after I wrote *Mangeur de Rêves.*) He said simply: "It's a play . . . hmm. Oh, very witty!"

We both laughed and the ice was broken. His superiority to his disciples was immediately evident by the absence of any apparent dogmatism. Although Freud's illness painfully impeded him in conversation, it was clear that even at the height of his glory, and in spite of the narrow fanaticism of his followers, he retained the liberty of judgment, the open-mindedness, the essential agnosticism characteristic of genius. As he led me into his library where Shakespeare stood among the Greek tragedians, Freud said: "Here are my masters. Here are my respondants."

I was struck by the significant modesty of this statement. Reduced to the dimensions of a poetic intuition, of an artistic interpretation of the soul, assuaged by its therapeutic claims, stripped of the metaphysical superstructures with which it had been embellished by disciples of a religious turn, like Jung, psychoanalysis remains the most audacious of the pathways beaten by man in quest of the mystery of his origins.

251

Freud's First Year
in Practice, 1886–1887
(1952)

SIEGFRIED and SUZANNE CASSIRER BERNFELD

When asked to write a recommendation for Bernfeld, Freud replied:

January 22, 1931
Wien IX Berggasse 19

Dear Sir:
You want my judgment about Dr. Siegfried Bernfeld? This is easy to render, since he is an unambiguous personality. He is an outstanding expert of psychoanalysis. I consider him perhaps the strongest head among my students and followers. In addition, he is of superior knowledge, an overwhelming speaker, and an extremely powerful teacher. . . .

Sincerely yours,
Freud

Bernfeld, who knew Freud since the early twenties, was also perhaps the first to establish a link between psychoanalysis and education. His contributions to the history of the psychoanalytic movement are unsurpassed. He and his wife wrote a series of papers on Freud that are still fundamental sources for any Freud scholar. After practicing in Berlin and Vienna, the Bernfelds came to America in 1936 and settled in California. This selection appeared first in the Bulletin of the Menninger Clinic 16 *(March 1952): 37–48.*

"*Sigmund Freud, M.D.*, Lecturer in Neuropathology at the University of Vienna, has returned from a six months' trip to Paris, and now resides at Rathausstrasse 7."

This, and similar notices, appeared in the Viennese medical journals in the beginning of May 1886. After Freud left Paris at the end of February, he spent several weeks in Berlin, refreshing his pediatric knowledge with Baginsky, then in April he opened his office in Vienna. He was ready to see patients on Easter Sunday. In a letter of April 12, 1936, he wrote: "Easter Sunday signifies to me the fiftieth anniversary of taking up my medical practice." This was an unusual opening date, as Easter Sunday was elaborately celebrated in Vienna; all businesses and offices were closed, and even emergency services were not readily available. The calendar shows that Easter Sunday of that year fell on April 25.

Although Freud's circle of friends was large, including such influential men as Nothnagel, Breuer, and Chrobak, it seems likely that during the first months of his practice he had fewer patients than he would have wished. However he was not idle. Shortly after settling in the Rathausstrasse, he completed the translation of Charcot's lectures that he had begun in Paris. In his introduction, dated July 18, 1886, Freud expressed his satisfaction that a German version of Charcot's important work was published even before the French original. In July, Freud also reported on studies he had made of the *nervus acusticus* in Meynert's laboratory the year before. Furthermore, sometime between May and July he took up his duties as chief of the newly organized Neurological Outpatient Clinic at the Children's Hospital (Oeffentliches Kinder Kranken Institut), which was under the energetic and ambitious direction of Kassowitz.

In September he travelled seven hundred miles to Wandsbeck near Hamburg to marry Martha Bernays, his fiancee for more than four years, who lived there with her mother and sister. On September 16, 1886, the wedding took place in the City Hall. Sixty-four years later, Frau Professor Freud still vividly recalled how the official at the ceremony teased her for signing her new name readily and without the least hesitation in the marriage register. She was twenty-five at that time, and Freud was past thirty.

Before leaving Vienna to fetch his bride, Freud had leased a four room apartment for his future home and office. It was located in the Kaiserliches Stiftungshaus (Imperial Memorial Building) overlooking the Schottenring, in a district near the new university, which since the sixties had become one of the most fashionable residential areas of the city. The house was dignified, the rooms large and beautiful.

The Stiftungshaus was better known by the somber name of House of Atonement. On December 8, 1881, a fire had destroyed the Vienna Ring-Theater, a few minutes before the scheduled Viennese première of the *Tales of Hoffman*. Over four hundred and fifty people met a terrible death, and it became known that but for the unbelievable negligence of the authorities most of them would have been saved. With his own funds Emperor Franz Joseph subsequently erected a large apartment building on the site of the catastrophe: the rents were to go forever to Viennese charities. "It was hard to get tenants for the apartment house where so many people had lost their lives," says Anna Freud-Bernays in her recollections. "My brother, far from sharing the general superstition, did not hesitate to establish himself there with his young wife, and his example quickly encouraged others. When Sigmund's eldest child was born there in 1887, the Emperor honored this first baby born in the House of Atonement by presenting him with a handsome vase from the Royal Porcelain Workshops." The contemporary Viennese newspapers do not mention such a presentation, and as they scarcely would have missed this moving story of a personal action by the Emperor, we accept the more modest version that the Imperial Chancery sent a congratulatory letter.

We have no precise information on the beginning of Freud's practice other than that contained in the following two anecdotes. The first Freud related in a conversation. One day while he was alone in his office, he heard the doorbell ring, and then the voices of his maid and a lady, talking together in the hall. Impatient because the visitor was not immediately led in, he went into the hallway, interrupted the conversation, and himself ushered the visitor to a chair beside his desk. She glanced around, but remained silent. "Don't you like it here?" he asked. "On the contrary," she said, "I like it very much." "Then what seems to be the trouble?" continued Freud. "Nothing much, doctor, but I am late already, and I'm supposed to pick up the headache pills for Mme. X"—a distant relative of Freud's, whose maid he now recognized.

The second anecdote concerns a cure, and was told to us by the owner of one of the many secondhand book stores in Vienna's Wollzeille. When he noticed our interest in old neurological books by Freud, he asked whether the famous Professor might not be the same Dr. Freud who in the fall of 1886 had operated a faradization machine in the House of Atonement. He explained that at that time, as a boy of fourteen, he had been run down by a taxicab on the Ringstrasse and developed hysterical fits from the shock. One of the bystanders suggested calling the new doctor in the near-by apartment house. This Doctor Freud had cured him after several weeks of faradic treatment, and he had always remembered his kindness and his wonderful eyes.

While Freud's practice started in a slow and commonplace fashion, an event of far-reaching influence on his future occurred in the meeting of the Viennese Physicians' Society of October 15, 1886—less than a month after his marriage. To this body Freud felt obliged to report on his Parisian trip, which had been sponsored by a grant from the University. The Society was not a compulsory, semi-official organization, comparable to the American Medical Association; but among the various independent medical societies, it enjoyed the greatest scientific and professional prestige. The numerous medical weeklies in Vienna—and in all other German-speaking academic centers for that matter—covered its meetings with special correspondents and usually reported the proceedings in great detail. This has made it possible to reconstruct Freud's paper and the discussion that followed more completely than he himself has done in his brief account in his *Autobiography*.

The meeting was the first after the summer vacation. The chairman, the internist Prof. von Bamberger opened the session with a formal speech of welcome. "Unfortunately," he said, "a bitter drop of vermouth is mixed with the happiness of reunion, because of the severe illness of Dr. von Arlt, the Honorary President of the Society, and the death of one of our most meritorious members, Dr. Theodor von Jurié." After the audience stood for a brief period in honor of the deceased, Dr. Grossman presented a case of lupus of the gums.

Then Freud spoke on male hysteria. While in Paris, he began, he had had the opportunity to familiarize himself with the recent work of Charcot, who at that time was almost exclusively occupied with the study of hysteria. Freud said at the outset that he would present only a small part of Charcot's findings and ideas, which in his opinion were as important as they were new. He then continued by expressing the hope that nobody would object to his statement that physicians, in general, did not connect a definite scientific concept with the word hysteria but commonly used the term as a loose equivalent to the word "nervous." The diagnosis in most cases, he pointed out, was based on the age and sex of the patient, on the course of the ailment, on the instability of the symptoms, but primarily on a negative relation: namely, on the impossibility of fitting this complex of symptoms into any other nosological entity known at the time. It was further the general opinion that hysteria was exclusively a disease of the female sex.

In contrast, Freud told them, the great merits of Charcot were, first, that he had—as in the case of many other diseases—arrived at a type, the *grande hysterie*, which was characterized by a number of positive diagnostic features: (1) the specific four-stage seizures; (2) the disturbances of the sensory system, frequently in the form of cerebral hemianaesthesia; (3) visual disturbances; (4) motor disturbances; (5) the hysterogenic regions. Not every case fully represented the type, but the diagnosis could be based on the degree of approximation to the type. Though Charcot had established the type after the term "hystero-epilepsy" was coined, he had come to recognize such cases as hysteria. Charcot's second merit, Freud said, was that he had proved the existence of a clearly defined order in hysterical symptoms, and that he had destroyed the prejudice that classed hysterics as malingerers. Finally, Charcot had shown that there was no necessary connection between hysteria and the sex organs. Hysteria in males, which up to Charcot's time was considered a curiosity or even an etymological contradiction, was a fact—and not a rare one, at that. Charcot had found no symptomatic difference between male and female hysterics. On the contrary, the grand type appeared frequently in men. Even the region that in men corresponds to the ovaries was hysterogenic, Charcot believed. He also thought that in men, hysteria followed after insignificant traumata, probably due to psychic shock, whether or not the individuals were hereditarily conditioned. This Freud illustrated with a detailed presentation of Charcot's first case of male hysteria, which Freud himself still had the opportunity of seeing at the Salpêtriére.

In concluding, Freud touched on a consequence of Charcot's theory, which possessed practical importance. Charcot tended to recognize as hysteria most of the pathological states that appeared after railway accidents—the so-called "railway spine" or "railway brain." On this point Charcot was in agreement with several Americans, while German physicians strongly contradicted him. Although this question had not been definitely answered—since Charcot had not yet investigated such cases—Freud thought it deserved the attention of the physicians.

The discussion was opened by Rosenthal, who remarked that it was well known that hysteria occurred in men, although much more rarely than in women, and described at length two such cases that had come to his attention in the eighteen-sixties. It was equally well known, he said, that psychic shock caused by quite insignificant trauma might bring on hysteria. Here, he said, the excitation usually originated in the cortex.

Meynert, who followed Rosenthal, commented that in his clinic he had for ten years observed cases of psychological alterations combined with epileptic seizures and with disturbances of the function of consciousness—most of them following traumatic experiences. He had called these cases "epileptoids." He added that it would be interesting, indeed, if Dr. Freud would come to his clinic, and demonstrate to him, on *his* cases, the validity of all that Freud had asserted in his report. Meynert also stated that he could not confirm the cortical origin of hysteria, which Rosenthal had claimed as possible.

Next to take the floor was Bamberger who confessed that, in spite of his great admiration for Charcot and his interest in the subject, he could find nothing new in Freud's presentation, for everything that he had said had been well known in Vienna for a long time. He found Charcot's classification of grande and petite hystérie unconvincing because some cases of grave hysteria did not produce seizures. As an illustration he mentioned the case of a girl who from the age of two had suffered from a paralysis of the legs, marked contractures of the extremities, and bladder paralysis, yet while no one would doubt the gravity of her hysteria, it did not belong to Charcot's hysterical type. The existence of male hysteria, he continued, was also well known. The traumatic etiology might be new, but it was not valid. "Railway spine" was hardly a hysteria, he said, although its symptoms did show some similarity to it.

Leidesdorf, the last discussant, said that he had seen many cases where severe spinal disturbances developed after railway accidents, as, for instance, progressive paralysis. He did not want to exclude the possibility of hysteria sometimes following a trauma, yet he had seen too many cases, particularly of young men, where trauma produced temporary insomnia, instability, and other such symptoms that had no connection whatsoever with hysteria.

Then Latschenberger was given the floor for his paper "On the Presence of Bile in Tissues and Fluids During Grave Illnesses of Animals." A brief but sharp controversy between Bamberger and Latschenberger concluded the meeting, which was just one of the hundreds of routine weekly discussions of the Physicians' Society.

Freud in his *Autobiography* summarized this discussion as "I met with a bad reception," which was not an exaggeration. Not only Rosenthal, a neurologist held in little esteem by his contemporaries, but also Bamberger, Meynert and Leidesdorf—leaders of the Medical School—had kept their objections on a remarkably low level. The point raised by Freud had not been how frequently male hysteria occurred, but rather that the existence of even rare cases in males invalidated the then-current conception of hysteria as a disturbance of, or caused by, the uterus. Bamberger even mistook the meaning of Charcot's establishment of types. The severity of a case and the degree of

257

its approximation to a type (i.e., whether certain spectacular and characteristic symptoms such as fits, were present or not) were points of view that should not have been confused. In the introduction to his paper, Freud had warned against just such mistakes. The various remarks on "railway spine" were obviously far from the point of Charcot's theory. Meynert realized and admitted that only a thorough investigation of his epileptoids could determine whether or not they belonged to Charcot's hysteria, but he phrased this insight in the form of a facetious or even scornful invitation to Freud.

What motivated their hasty, non-scientific judgments? What emotions could have interfered with reason? It is true that quite generally the leaders of the Physicians' Society were not much inclined to listen to newcomers, whom they only wanted as their audience. This attitude had irked the younger members of the Society for years, and led eventually to the founding of the Medical Club, where young research men felt protected against the impolite, not to say rude, ways of Bamberger and his like. Yet the unanimous rejection on October 15 was directed not so much against Freud personally—the young privat-dozent who dared to instruct the wise men—but against a traitor to the Vienna Medical School. After all, Freud had been a student of Bamberger, Leidesdorf and Meynert. He had been a close research associate of Meynert for two years (1883–1885). He had been sent to Charcot by the University on University funds, but instead of bringing back the reassuring and expected news that Paris had nothing to teach Vienna in neurology, he had returned as an apostle of Charcot, the foreigner, praising his merits, which implicitly were the shortcomings of the Vienna School.

The word "traitor" has no place in the sphere of objective science, where observation and experiment lead to unanimous acceptance of proven facts—*Sine ira ac studio*. But, as is well known, the emotions and irrational demands of the men who create science play their tricks. Freud had, in fact, discovered someone in Paris whom he could admire more than Meynert; and on his return he started to find fault with Meynert's teachings in brain anatomy. In August 1886 Freud's paper on the *nervus acusticus* appeared, the findings of which he was to use in an argument against Meynert in 1891. Further, in 1886 he gave a lecture on Aphasia at the Physiology Club, in which the theory expounded contradicted some of Meynert's basic tenets. Against this background, Meynert's aggressive attitude in the October meeting of the Physicians' Society can be understood as the beginning of that hatred which a few years later caused him to attack Freud in print, almost to the point of calling him a renegade from the Vienna School of scientific medicine.

Freud's report on his visit to the Salpêtriére was certainly not the act of a diplomat. His attitude was entirely independent; he did not show the traditional modesty of a young man who knows that anything he has to say is not really interesting, and who considers it his natural duty to applaud his medical elders. How far he was aware of the implications of giving such a speech to such an audience, we do not know. We may be certain that if a friend had advised him of the need for caution, he would have rejected the advice. Freud never could tolerate compromise in matters of scientific truth, nor in the frank expression of his feelings for or against individuals. On this occasion both his scientific and his personal integrity were at stake. His then still strong, naïve respect for authority and his hero worship would not permit him to doubt seriously that only great men attain positions of power, or that these great men, when judging scientific propositions, had any other motivation than pure searching for truth. That such naïveté can be a sophisticated way of denying deep-rooted suspicions against all men in power—this discovery was still far away. It was, however, a grave mistake to introduce the peripheral and controversial issue of the railway accidents, a topic that had probably interested Freud for personal reasons, of which at that time he was not consciously aware.

The leaders of the medical school failed the test not only in the discussion on October fifteenth. Freud had found cases of male hysteria in several departments of the General Hospital, but the chiefs of these divisions were disinclined to help him and science against Bamberger, Meynert, Leidesdorf and the compact majority. He was refused permission to present these cases before the Society. "At length, outside the hospital, I came upon a case of classical hysterical hemianesthesia in a man." This term "at length"—which Freud uses in his *Autobiography*—leads us to suspect that he had to search and wait for a long time, but the phrase is in fact only a measure of his indignation and impatience. In fact, only one week after his appearance before the Society, Freud had diagnosed as hysteria the complaints of a twenty-nine year old engraver, August P. The case was sent to him by Dr. von Beregszazcy, a young privat-dozent and practitioner of laryngology. On October 23 the opthalmologist Königstein began—in Freud's office—a thorough examination of P's eyes (hemianopsia) and on November 24, only five weeks after Meynert's challenge, Freud presented "A Case of Male Hysteria" to the Physicians' Society.

This time Bamberger was not in the chair; in his place was the physiologist Sigmund Exner, a jovial and polite little man with an extensive goiter. The meeting was one of those which did not center around one main paper, and since a large number of short communications and case presentations had been scheduled, Exner asked all speakers to keep strictly to their allotted ten minutes. Exner knew Freud well from their days in Brücke's Physiology Institute. Not a practicing physician, he was no party to the question: "Is Charcot a greater clinician than the masters in Vienna?" and therefore may have provided a friendly atmosphere for Freud.

Freud presented the case of August P.—the young engraver—a very convincing example of hemianesthesia and hemianopsia of a high degree and who showed many of Charcot's "hysterical stigmata" in an extreme form of development including the hysterogenic regions. Freud had found that his symptoms were direct responses to a dramatic trauma and related the following data.

His present illness dates back about three years. At that time he quarreled with his disreputable brother, who had refused to repay him a loan; the brother threatened to stab him, and went after him with a knife. This sent the patient into indescribable fears; he perceived a roaring in his head and felt as if it were about to split, rushed home without being able to remember how he had arrived there, and collapsed unconscious on his doorstep. . . . For two hours afterward he underwent the most violent convulsions, during which he talked about the scene with his brother. When he awoke he felt very limp. In the following six weeks he suffered severe aches and pressures on the left side of his head. The feeling in the left half of his body seemed altered to him, and when he went back to work, soon thereafter, his eyes tired easily. Thus, with some variations his condition remained for three years.

Seven weeks ago, a new disturbing incident led to its aggravation. A woman accused the patient of theft; he experienced violent palpitations of the heart, and for about fourteen days was so depressed that he thought of suicide. At the same time a more pronounced tremor in the left arm and leg; the entire left half of his body felt, he thought, as if it had been struck by a blow; his eyes tired easily and frequently everything looked grey. His sleep was often disturbed by fearful apparitions and dreams, in which he seemed to fall from a great height. Pain manifested itself in the left part of the neck, the left part of the groin, the lower back, and in other areas; the stomach seemed frequently "as if bloated," and he was compelled to discontinue working.

The patient furthermore suffers from violent pains in the left knee and the sole of the left foot; when he walks for long periods he experiences a strange sensation in the throat, as if his tongue were immobilized; frequently he has ringing in his ears. . . . His memory about events of his illness is diminished. The convulsions have recurred six to nine times within the last three years. However, most of them were very mild; only one night attack, last August, was combined with stronger "trembling."

Freud demonstrated these symptoms in the brilliant manner of Charcot; expertly, precisely and yet with more consideration toward the patient than was usual in medical case presentations.

The skin on the left side of the head, however, reacts quite differently than one would expect; it is completely insensitive to stimuli of any kind. I can prick, pinch, roll the ear lobe between my fingers, without the patient feeling anything. In other words, a high degree of anaesthesia exists here which does not affect the skin alone, but also the mucous membranes, as I shall demonstrate on the lips and tongue of the patient. If I insert a small, rolled-up piece of paper into the left auditory canal and then through the left nostril, no reaction whatsoever results. I repeat the attempt on the right side, and can observe a normal sensitivity. . . .

The same kind of diverted attention applies to the left leg. Today the patient walked briskly beside me for a good hour on the streets, without looking at his feet: I could notice only that he flung out his left leg slightly, placed it somewhat to the outside, and frequently dragged his left foot on the ground. But when I ask him to walk, his eyes follow all movements of the anaesthetic leg, which are slow and uncertain and tire him easily. Finally, his gait is completely uncertain when his eyes are shut; then he pushes himself forward, both feet feeling the ground, as we would do in the dark if we were unfamiliar with a place. It is also very difficult for him to remain standing on his left leg; if he shuts his eyes in this posture he falls down immediately.

261

Königstein concluded the presentation with a report on his very careful examination of the patient's vision, demonstrating the existence of those hysterical eye symptoms, especially the hemianopsia that Charcot had described, and which "we in Vienna have up to now overlooked or underestimated in our cases."

The contemporary reports of the meeting in the medical journals do not mention a discussion of Freud's paper. Probably none took place. When Freud says in his *Autobiography* "This time I was applauded," that is undoubtedly what happened, and nothing more. No doubt: this round was won by Freud.

"A Case of Male Hysteria" appeared, together with Königstein's report, in the *Wiener Medizinische Wochenschrift* on December 4 and 11, 1886, under the optimistic serial title "Contributions to the Clinic of Hysteria, No. 1." But Freud did not continue this series.

In fact, with the advent of 1887 began the meager four years of Freud's published works. "I did little scientific work and published scarcely anything. I was occupied with establishing myself in my new profession and with assuring my own material existence, including that of a rapidly increasing family." Besides the translation of Bernheim's book on hypnotism, the introductory essay to it, a few articles in a medical dictionary and four book reviews, only two short scientific contributions appeared in the years 1887–1890; one on "Fear of Cocaine"; one on "A Case of Hemianopsia." But that he continued intensive research is shown by the sudden burst of productivity in 1891. During this silent period he had worked steadily in the fields of brain anatomy, infantile cerebral palsies, hypnotism and the neuroses. However, he delayed the publication of his findings for years.

The reason for this shyness and unwillingness or inhibition is not known to us and we do not intend to draw definite conclusions before the facts can be more fully presented. Certainly one factor at work in these barren years was the conflict with Meynert; another was the disappointment with cocaine. (These two subjects will be dealt with in future papers.) A third factor clearly seems to have been the reaction of the leading medical men to his reports before the Vienna Physicians' Society. Freud wrote that in spite of the applause on November 24, "no further interest was taken in me. The impression that the high authorities had rejected my innovations remained unshaken, and with my hysteria in men . . . I found myself forced into the opposition."

This, of course, had not altered Freud's conviction that he—and Charcot—were right; but it radically diminished his admiration for those great men who, confronted with demonstrated new facts, did not feel moved to revise their old theories. Paraphrasing an expression that Freud used years later, one might say that in such men "the voice of the intellect is too low" to deserve the respect and the authority which they claim. He recognized this in bitter and angry disappointment. Still less able at that time to hide his contempt than in later years, unwilling to lie and act hypocritically then, as ever, and yet reluctant and afraid to fight his unmasked heroes in an open arena, he was in no mood to permit them to judge either his really important thoughts and experiences, or even those that were only on the level of the average contemporary scientific paper.

In his *Autobiography* Freud's report on how he was "forced into the opposition" is followed by the remark: "I withdrew from academic life and ceased to attend the learned societies. It is a whole generation since I visited the Physicians' Society."

The emotions of those days, still reverberating forty years later in the writer of the *Autobiography*, might give the cursory reader the impression that, hurt by the lack of response, he had ceased to attend the meetings of the Physicians' Society immediately, or soon after his second paper had been presented there. As a matter of fact, he did not act on his impulsive judgment for over a year. From the reports of the Physicians' Society meetings, as published in the medical journals, we know that on May 13, 1887, and again on October 21, 1887, he had participated in discussions of the Society. In February 1888 he wrote to Fliess: "Yesterday we had a prime scandal in the Physicians' Society. They wanted to force us into subscribing to a new weekly, which is to represent the purified, exact and Christian point of view of a few *Hofraete* (Privy Counsellors), who have long ago unlearned how to work. Naturally they will push it through: I feel very much like resigning." At the end of the eighties, anti-Semitic attitudes gradually influenced academic policies more openly and had, as Freud's remark in his letter proves, intensified his attitude to the point of outright contempt.

We do not know when Freud definitely ceased to attend meetings of the Physicians' Society. The expression that he used in 1926, "not attended for a generation" might very well not be a metaphor, but date the last of his sporadic appearances in the year 1896.°

° In the Psychiatric Society, in the Medical Club, and "in learned societies" other than the Physicians' Society, Freud participated as discussant and as lecturer until about 1909. His classes at the University—as privat-dozent until 1902 and with the title "aus-

However, the immediate walkout that the *Autobiography* seems to indicate was certainly his desire at that time. It had not taken more than a few minutes for him to evaluate the expostulations of Bamberger, Leidesdorf and Meynert. Then he understood that he did not belong to their group; that he no longer wished to belong to it; that, in fact, he ought to separate himself completely from his former teachers. But not until two years later—after several more test cases, especially after Meynert's fight against him and his defense of hypnotism—was Freud ready to express his clear feeling in equally clear words: "Most people find it difficult to accept that a scientist, who in some fields of neuropathology has gained much experience and shown acute understanding [Meynert], should be denied acclaim as an authority in other problems of whatever kind. And certainly the respect for greatness, especially intellectual greatness, belongs to the best qualities of human nature. But it should take second place to the respect for facts. One need not be ashamed to admit it when one sets aside reliance on authority in favor of one's own judgment, gained by study of the facts." Freud's rejection by the leaders of the Vienna Medical School turned into a powerful stimulus in his effort to attain complete intellectual independence. In the beginning, however, it contributed toward making the first year of his economic independence the "darkest and least successful year of my life."

Bibliography

Bernfeld, Suzanne C.: Freud and Archaeology. *Amer. Imago* 8:107–128, 1951.

Charcot, J. M.: *Neue Vorlesungen über die Krankheiten des Nervensystems, insobesondere über Hysterie.* Trans. by Sigmund Freud. Leipzig und Wien, Toeplitz & Deuticke, 1886. The publisher's advertisements appeared in the medical journals from Oct. 1886 on. The advance publication of part of a chapter appeared in *Wien. med. Wchnschr.* 36: 711ff., May 15, 1886, under the title, "Ueber Einen Fall von hysterischer Coxalgie."

Personal communication from Miss Anna Freud, London.

Freud-Bernays, Anna: My Brother, Sigmund Freud. *Am. Mercury* 51: 341, 1940.

Freud, Sigmund: *An Autobiographical Study.* Trans. James Strachey. London, Hogarth, 1936. Pp. 25, 26, 30.

—:*Aus den Anfängen der Psychoanalyse,* M. Bonaparte, Anna Freud, Ernst Kris, eds. London, Imago Publ. Co., 1950. Pp. 63, 64.

—: Beitrag. zur Casuistik der Hysterie. *Wien. med. Wchnschr.* 36: 1633–1638, 1886, and Königstein, L.: Untersuchung des Sehorgans. *Ibid.* 36: 1674–1676, 1886.

—: Bemerkungen über Cocainsucht und Cocainfurcht. *Wien. med. Wchnschr.* 37: 929–932, 1887.

ser ordentlicher Professor" from then on—he continued regularly up to 1917 when he read his Introductory Lectures in Psychoanalysis.

—: Hypnotism and Suggestion. Trans. James Strachey. *Collected Papers*, V. 5. London, Hogarth, 1950. Pp. 11–24.

—: The Interpretation of Dreams. *The Basic Writings of Sigmund Freud*. A. A. Brill, ed. New York, Modern Library, 1938. P. 446.

—: Reviews of : Averbeck, "Die Akute Neurasthenie," in *Wien. med. Wchnschr.* 37: 138, 1887; S. Weir Mitchell, "Die Behandlung gewisser Formen von Neurasthenie und Hysterie," *ibid.* p. 138; H. Obersteiner, "Anleitung beim Studium des Baues der nervösen Centralorgane," *ibid.* pp. 1642–1644; Forel, "Der Hypnotismus," *ibid.* 39: 1097–1100 and 1892–1896.

—: Review of Forel's "Der Hypnotismus," *Wien. med. Wchnschr.* 39: 1098, 1889.

—: Über den Ursprung des Nervus Acusticus. *Monatsschr. f. Ohrenheilkunde* 20: 245–251, 1886; 20: 277–282, 1886.

—: Ueber Hemianopsie im frühesten Kindesalter. *Wien. med. Wchnschr.* 38: 1081–1086; 1116–1121, 1888.

—: *Zur Auffassung der Aphasien. Wien, Verlag Deuticke, 1891.*

–, and O. *Rie: Klinische Studie über die halbseitige Cerebrallähmung der Kinder. Beitrage zur Kinderheilkunde*, V. 3, 1891.

Meynert, Theodor: *Wien. klin. Wchnschr.* 2: 501, 1889.

Some Memories of Sigmund Freud

(1952)

BRUNO GOETZ

Bruno Goetz, a Swiss poet and author, studied at the University of Vienna around 1905 and met Freud for consultations. It is a delightful interview and shows Freud's humaneness and warmth. The following exercepts were selected and translated by the editor from "Erinnerungen as Sigmund Freud," Neue Schweizer Rundschau 20 (May 1952): 3–11.

It was in my first seminar at the University of Vienna, where I attended lectures in Psychology and Indology, [that] I got in close contact with my professor of psychology. At that time I wrote my first poems. At the same time I suffered from eye trouble and severe headaches. None of the medicine prescribed helped and I often had to spend days in a half-dark room since I could not bear daylight. My professor, who knew that the medicine did not have any effect, suggested that I see Professor Freud. He would be glad to introduce me.

I had never heard of Freud but I learned he had written a remarkable book on dream interpretation. I got the book at the library and was shocked beyond words. I felt that this approach to dreams disturbed the image one had of one's dreams. Especially as an artist I could not see how this would help me. I decided not to go. My professor, however, told me he had spoken to Freud, who expected to see me the next afternoon, and added laughing, "Don't be afraid. He won't hurt. He just wants to help you, and in the meantime I have given him a few of your poems." With mixed feelings I arrived the next day at Freud's apartment. I had been in serious pain since early morning. I doubted very much his art of healing, but as it turned out, I had a unique experience.

Freud approached me, shook my hand, asked me to sit down, and looked me over. I looked into his warm and expressful eyes, and felt as if a hand had touched my head—the pain had disappeared. Then I thought, this is like Indian witchcraft, but I really did not care what it was, since immediately I felt I could trust him. Freud smiled and said: "Tell me a little bit about yourself. I have some of your poems here. Very beautiful—but disguised. You hide yourself behind words, instead of showing yourself. But do not be distressed. There is no need for you to fear yourself . . . In your poems the theme of the sea is very prominent. Is that symbolic? Or is the sea really a part of your experience and life? Where do you come from?"

All of a sudden I opened up and told him my whole life without any resistance. Moreover, I told him things I had never told anybody. What would have been the use to hide them from him? He knew these things already, I felt.

He listened for almost an hour without interrupting me. Often he laughed softly. Finally he said:

"Now let us sum it up. Your father was a ship captain, and later a teacher in navigation at the Rigaer Seamans School, and you spent your youth with sailors. But where do the tension and rigidity originate in your poems?"

"That was quite a struggle for me," I answered. "I was afraid that I would completely lose myself."

"Aha," he said, and after a while, "your father was not very severe with you?"

"No," I answered. "He was my best friend. We understood each other very well. The only things I never told him about were unlucky love affairs with a young girl and with an older woman, and of my falling in love with sailors, whom I would have liked to kiss. He never reproached me. Nor did he ever reproach me for not being married . . . and then later when I was in my bed . . . But you understand, don't you? . . ."

"Certainly," Freud grumbled. "And the matter with the sailors has never upset you?"

"Never," I said. "I was terribly in love. And when one is in love, everything is fine. Or not?"

"With you for sure!" he said, and laughed. "You took care of it yourself and in a sense educated yourself. You are not rigid as a result and you do not look rigid. . . . Enviable, and you have a marvellous conscience. That you owe to your father. And your mother?"

"I could not get along with her. She was very puritanical. But that has never disturbed me."

Again Freud laughed heartily.

"What about your story of your father with Poseidon?" he asked suddenly. "Tell me about it again. I would like to hear more about it."

"At that time I was about twelve years old. My father came to my room and put *Götterlehre* by Moritz on my table. Perhaps he wondered why (under the influence of my mother) I read so much of the Bible. 'Read something of this, my boy,' he said, and pointed to the Moritz. 'It contains stories similar to the Bible's. But perhaps more beautiful. Do you know that we sailors have a different faith. Poseidon and so on . . .' He never asked me about the book, which he so discretely recommended to me. But it had a lasting influence on my life and thinking."

"Poseidon and so on . . . Marvellous, marvellous," Freud said. "Yes, the sea. . . . Now my student Goetz, I will not analyze you. You can become most happy with your complexes. As far as your eyesight is concerned, I shall write you a prescription." He sat down at his desk and wrote. In the meantime, he asked me: "They told me you have hardly any money and live in poverty. Is that correct?"

I told him my father received a very small salary as a teacher, I had four younger brothers and sisters, and I survived by tutoring and selling newspaper articles.

"Yes," he said. "Severity against onesself sometimes might be good, but one should not go too far. When did you last have a steak?"

"I think about four weeks ago."

"That is what I thought," he said and rose from his desk. "Here is your prescription." And he added some more advice, but then he almost became somewhat shy. "I hope you don't mind, but I am an established doctor and you are a young student. Please accept this envelope and allow me to play your father this time. A small fee for the joy you have brought me with your poems and the story of your youth. Let us see each other again. I am quite occupied, but I can always find a half hour or so for you. Auf Wiedersehn!"

Imagine! When I arrived in my room and opened the envelope, I found 200 Kronen. I was so moved I broke out in tears.

Freud and Boas: Secular Rabbis?

(1954)

STANLEY EDGAR HYMAN

Hyman taught at Bennington College and is well known for his literary writings. This selection first appeared in Commentary 17 (1954): 264–67.

We are too enlightened these days to admit that we want a picture or a poem (or even a novel) to tell us a story, but non-fiction remains an enclave where the reader is still Caliph. The biographer in particular is greeted with a brusque "None of your fancy art or style, now, don't bother placing the subject or discussing his ideas, just tell me what sort of man he was. Was he like me?"

Here are recent biographies [*The Life and Work of Sigmund Freud: Volume I*, by Ernest Jones (Basic Books, 427 pp.) and *Franz Boas*, by Melville J. Herskovits (Scribner's, 131 pp.)] of two men who have substantially reshaped our world, and the degree to which they are personal is exactly defined by their subtitles: the Freud, "The Formative Years and the Great Discoveries," about half; the Boas, "The Science of Man in the Making," not at all. Ernest Jones, the dean of living Freudian analysts, has written what appears from this first volume to be one of the great biographies, a perfect blend of devotion and objectivity, with a dash of suppressed hostility to give it tartness. Jones is the only person outside the family who has seen Freud's love letters, which he uses richly but with basic good taste; he knows how the historic case of "Miss Anna O" came out because Breuer told Freud and Freud told him (she worked up a false pregnancy by Breuer, causing treatment to be abruptly terminated, and ended as a social worker); he is not beyond a few sly psychoanalytic interpretations of his own.

Melville Herskovits, a student of Boas who has become one of the foremost American anthropologists, gives us a brief study that, within the impersonal confines of Scribner's Twentieth Century Library series, is a model of intelligent popularization. We learn such personal reactions as Boas's reservations about Ruth Benedict's *Patterns of Culture* and his resolute failure to appreciate Freud (whom he had known at Clark University on Freud's only trip to America), but these are handled as scientific evaluations rather than private biases. Even where later American anthropology has repudiated Boas (on his classification of American Indian languages, for example) we are given this, not in such terms as "error" and "repudiation," but as the inevitable progress of scientific knowledge. Herskovits omits any mention of Boas's entanglement with the "left" in the last decade of his life.

The overwhelming first impression we get from *The Life and Work of Sigmund Freud* is of familiarity, of knowing the story so well. Here is the boy growing up in a middle-class Jewish family with a fable of descent from famous scholars and a legendary family history going back to the destruction of the Temple. He was his mother's first-born and darling, his father's spoiled "scholar" and pride, the pet of his teachers. We know that he will be a little radical as a young man but will settle down, and that he will become a good husband and a loving and indulgent father, a passionate card-player, a great talker among his cronies. He is ambivalent about his Jewishness like a hundred semi-intellectuals we know: he dislikes Christianity without any corresponding Jewish faith, his friends are almost entirely Jewish, he is fascinated by Jewish ritual but mocks it all as superstition, he toys with conversion but is never serious, he has a burning ambition for success and fame and a corresponding contempt for ambitionless *goyim*, he is incredulous that any Gentile author (in this case George Eliot) could write about Jews and know those things "we speak of only among ourselves," he suffers from "*schnorrer* fantasies" (Freud's own term) about inheriting undeserved wealth, he identifies himself with Jewish heroism in history and legend ("I have often felt as if I had inherited all the passion of our ancestors when they defended their Temple"). We can be sure that this fellow will end up in B'nai B'rith, and he does. If we had been told that this Doctor Freud made a good living as a general practitioner, provided a first-class education for his children, and was never heard of outside the neighborhood, we would not have been surprised.

Jones has spared us few of Freud's failings and weaknesses. We see him twice nervously destroying all his papers, learn of his horror of blood and his curious resentment of music (entering a restaurant that

270

had a band, he would cover his ears). His lifelong ambition (ungratified) was to have enough money to buy his wife a gold snake bangle. The story of Freud's misguided propagation of the use of cocaine (he thought it harmless) furnishes an incredible comic chapter (his later psychoanalytic discoveries could be discounted in Vienna as the latest nonsense from crazy Dr. Freud, the cocaine-pusher). Full use is made of the correspondence with Wilhelm Fliess, which has not yet appeared in English. Fliess was a smalltime German physician full of crazy theories about the periodicity of life; for half a dozen years just before the turn of the century Freud had toward Fliess what Jones calls a "really passionate relationship of dependence." So sentimental was Freud about this that he arranged for International Psychoanalytic Congresses many years afterwards to be held in one town after another where he had spent time with Fliess. Freud had migraine attacks and what he called "neurasthenia" for most of his life, he was childishly superstitious, and for at least the decade of the 1890's his psychological ailments were serious enough for Jones to describe them as "a very considerable psychoneurosis" and "anxiety hysteria."

What is remarkable about this good Jewish bourgeois with his card games and his B'nai B'rith, this ambitious and erratic doctor with a horror of blood, what distinguishes him from the hundreds we know just like him, is the strength that came out of his weaknesses. If Freud foolishly identified himself with the Maccabees, he nevertheless showed himself fearless in every encounter with the anti-Semites. The card-playing somehow left him enough time to master Latin and Greek, French and English, Italian and Spanish, besides Hebrew, Yiddish, and German. Of a thoroughly pugnacious and dogmatic bent, he resolutely avoided controversy (even eliminating discussion of the papers delivered at psychoanalytic congresses). If his methods were naturally intuitive, he nevertheless made himself an expert technician, and did his own scientific drawings. For the man who opened up the Great Cloaca, he was personally reserved and rather puritanical, and in his own life quite prudish about sexual matters.

With all his psychic ailments, Freud met the severe physical pain of the jaw cancer that ended his life with absolute stoicism; "Most uncalled-for" was the one complaint Jones heard him utter in three decades of close association. Out of the absurd Fliess relationship came unsparing self-awareness ("There is some piece of unruly homosexual feeling at the root of the matter," Freud told Jones) and the first self-analysis in history, beginning in 1897 and continuing for half an hour a

day all of Freud's life, which produced not only "the serene and benign Freud" of later years but a therapeutic method of general application. Most of the great discoveries came out of Freud's suffering and
failures: he deduced the Oedipus Complex from his own feelings;
wrote *The Interpretation of Dreams* as a reaction to "the most poign-
ant loss in a man's life," his father's death; developed analytic techniques from difficulties with his patients; and inaugurated free association out of his humility about interrupting a patient and breaking her
flow of thought.

Franz Boas is more of a problem for us. He appears in the first
paragraph of Herskovits's book as an unidentified "young physicist-ge-
ographer" on shipboard, and he remains similarly remote throughout
the book. Boas must have been rather a cold fish. He was a Jew by ancestry, but his culture and loyalties were German, and he seems to
have put his faith entirely in assimilation. The rise of Hitler apparently
reminded Boas forcibly (as it did others similarly assimilated) of his
Jewish identity: "as one of Jewish origin," Herskovits writes with more
delicacy than grammar, "his many relatives in Germany were among
the proscribed." Long before that, however, Boas had revealed one
curious race prejudice, according to one of his most famous students
(Herskovits nowhere mentions it), the belief that only Jews have a capacity for languages, and this prejudice seems to have confined his favorite students, who became the leaders of American anthropology, almost entirely to Jews.

A few personal characteristics appear in the book, most of them
unattractive: a prudishness at least equal to Freud's (one of the theses
Boas chose to defend for his degree was that "modern operetta is rep-
rehensible from the standpoint of art and morality"); an extreme quarrelsomeness and a ferocious addiction to polemic; a general crustiness
in all personal relations except those with devoted students, where he
was fatherly, and with primitive peoples in the field, where he was
genuinely humble. Like Freud, Boas seems to have been remarkably
stoical about his facial cancer, and Goldenweiser reports visiting Boas
in the hospital after an operation and finding him practicing Kwakiutl
phonetics with the half of his mouth he was able to move.

Franz Boas gives no sense of Boas's discoveries and contributions
as rooted in any personal needs or weakness, but the correlations are
not hard to work out. The famous 1910 study of the changes in bodily
form of the children of immigrants, showing how they became physi-

272

cally assimilated to the dominant population, was the work of a German Jewish immigrant who believed in assimilation and had children. As the founder of comparative linguistics, the originator of the concept of the "culture area" (although the term seems to belong to his student Clark Wissler), our most influential voice for cultural pluralism with its vision of "different ultimate and coexisting types of civilization" living in peace and mutual appreciation, one of the first students of acculturation, a lifelong warrior against any form of racism, Boas is clearly the exiled Jew writ large, but this is easy to overlook in the cold tonality of statistical method, anthropometry, and experimental verification.

Boas himself deliberately obscured it every chance he got, as when he explained his delight in Indian myths and tales, which he collected and translated with rare sensitivity, as a desire for "the best linguistic data," or "objective material which will stand the scrutiny of painstaking investigation." The pattern is one of extreme repression, and only on rare occasions, as in the public letter he wrote in 1924 protesting the suppression of the potlatch among the Kwakiutl as a step that would demoralize them culturally, did he put on record the passionate appreciation of the lifeways of primitive peoples that underlay his neutral concern with "cultural dynamics" and his statistical interest in "acculturation." Yet this passion shines through all his work I have read, and it makes *The Social Organization and the Secret Societies of the Kwakiutl Indians* one of the imaginative triumphs of our century.

Actually, of course, it is an illusion that biography "gives us the person"; to learn that, we have only to read two biographies of the same man. The subject patterns himself one way in his work, the biographer patterns him another way in writing about him, we pattern him in our own fashion at every stage of the process. For many of us, the shape the lives of both Freud and Boas took is one it would be hard to deduce from either biography—that of the *secular rabbi*, the figure of moral authority filling the gap left in our private culture by the retreat of the religious leader. Being nasty to his bride about her family, Freud wrote, "They would have preferred you to marry an old Rabbi or Schochet," but Freud himself became more than that, really, before his death. He became a great wonder-working rabbi after the ancient fashion, perhaps the Vienna Gaon himself. Most of this transformation occurs after 1900, when the sacred texts and commentaries appeared, and is not covered in this first volume of the Jones biogra-

273

phy, but we can see the pattern taking shape: the followers beginning to gather around, addressing him simply as *"Herr* Professor"; the religious concern with the physical spot (the table in the northeast corner of the terrace of the Bellevue restaurant) where the Master analyzed his first dream; the early splits and schisms that mark rebellious disciples going off to found rival centers of learning, or, as in the case of Breuer, the supplanted and rejected older leader. And if Freud is the great Gaon of Vienna, Boas is surely the Tsaddik of Morningside Heights, the "Papa Franz" who used to strike his students, leading his Talmudic disputations on one topic a year at the graduate seminars, preserving in perpetuity the roles of master and disciple (for someone who apparently chafed under this, Herskovits describes the problem with great tact and fairness: "It is difficult to know whether he ever fully granted, in his unconscious reactions, that an associate who had once been a student no longer held this relationship to him").

Milton Himmelfarb wrote in last August's COMMENTARY: "In classical Jewish tradition a rabbi's authority is personal, in proportion to his reputation for learning and piety. Maimonides and Elijah Gaon of Vilna were not appointed to their authority; it grew out of a general recognition of their moral and intellectual eminence." In our day, this is precisely the process that has produced the figure of the secular rabbi. It is a characteristically Jewish process—we think of Freud and Boas, Einstein, even Marx—but not exclusively so: Emerson, Dewey, Burke, have all been American secular rabbis in this sense, expounding varieties of scripture to rapt disciples. In any earlier culture, these would be the tribe's Holy Men, its priests and saints; we may be the first civilization to have divorced wisdom from piety. And what is it that turns an ambitious young Austrian doctor or an arrogant young German geographer into this saintly figure, transforms all his flaws and weaknesses into blessings, makes him the repository for all the tribal wisdom and, ultimately, so *unlike* the rest of us? On this point, neither biographer has much to enlighten us. Perhaps, as Ernest Jones says with unconscious humor, "The answer to this question we must leave to the psychoanalysts."

Freud's Early Travels

(1954)

ERNEST JONES

Ernest Jones (1879–1958) deserves a monument in the history of the psychoanalytic movement. Often one feels that his role as the great compromiser has been underestimated. Not only did he play a part in the formation of the psychoanalytic movement in its early years, but he was left as the only survivor of Freud's early circle, and in the last years of his life completed a monumental biography of Freud. He came to know Freud in the very early years of psychoanalysis and then practically never left his side. Although his own practice was in London, he kept in constant touch with Freud.

This selection was originally delivered as a paper at the 18th International Psycho-Analytical Congress in London on 27 July 1953, and was published in The International Journal of Psychoanlysis *35 (1954): 81–84.*

The theme I have chosen for this paper has more than one source of interest. In the years between the ages of 20 and 40 Freud did far more travelling and sightseeing than was customary among young doctors in his position, especially at that time. Moreover, he enjoyed such experiences with an extraordinary gusto. Freud's capacity for keen enjoyment and also his sense of beauty were, contrary to some ideas that have been expressed of him, very highly developed. This enjoyment was partly visual and partly intellectual. He was always exhilarated by a lovely landscape or town, by beautiful architecture, and to a lesser extent painting. His keen powers of observation, and the minute attention he would devote to such objects, is well illustrated in his well-known studies of Leonardo and Michel Angelo's Moses. They also illustrate the intellectual interest that accompanied the pleasure in observing. This interest was always directed, like most of his interests, towards the past, which was one reason why Italy with its classical remains attracted him so powerfully. We shall presently see, however, that all these enjoyments had a deeper and more personal significance than their external sources in the world of reality.

Freud had a divided attitude, one common enough, towards the differing attractions of the South and North of Europe, one corresponding to the contrast between the pleasure and the reality principles respectively. On the one hand there were the undeniable virtues of the North. In his twenties England was the land of his dreams, which he first visited when he was 19. It was its tolerance, with its sense of fair play and justice, that drew him towards it, and perhaps above all the fact that Jews led a freer life there than elsewhere. His half-brother Emmanuel, whom he loved throughout his life, had gone to live there just when his father had dragged the young boy Freud to the poverty and persecutions of Vienna, a fact he never ceased to resent. Then in his early thirties his admiration turned to Berlin, where his great friend Fliess lived and flourished. He was impressed by the energy, hard work, and stern sense of duty that characterized Berlin in those days, and which contrasted with the casualness and corruption of Vienna.

The South, on the other hand, had a magic that far transcended these more homely virtues. Its softness and beauty, its warm sun and azure skies, above all its visible remains of man's early stages in development: to Freud as to so many others all this made an irresistible appeal. It represented pleasure, happiness, and all the opportunities for phantasy and far-reaching interest that stirred the very depths. We may date the first evocation of its appeal to the months Freud spent at Trieste at the age of 20 when a travelling grant enabled him to make his first researches there, a study on the structure of the male eel. So even the South was not associated with pure pleasure only; this could be combined with intellectual interests, as indeed it was with Freud throughout. Later on he would dash back to Trieste or Abbazia for one or two days only, the warm sun of the blue Adriatic more than compensating for the discomforts of the long journey from Vienna.

Freud seldom went far from Vienna until his visit to England when he was 19. Then came those to Trieste, a week spent near Hamburg to see his betrothed, and a short trip to Hungary escorting a sick friend. That brings us to 1883, when he was 27 years old. In that summer Breuer invited him to accompany him for a couple of days on a visit he was paying to his family in a house outside Gmunden which he had rented for the holidays. Freud was familiar with the Semmering district near Vienna but this was his first experience of real Alpine scenery. In his letters he always gave descriptions of the places he visited, and I propose to quote two of them, those of Gmunden and Brussels, omitting the tender personal passages with which they are interspersed.

I will now quote some extracts from a letter of 23 July 1883.

At the railway station Breuer greeted a couple whose curious story he related to me. The woman was 36 years old and the man 26. He had wooed her for ten years. When she finally yielded to his pleas she was so ashamed because of the difference in their ages that the wedding had to take place secretly. Breuer asked me to explain this curious relationship, and I replied that an immature man is often attracted by a mature woman and that such marriages are usually successful. You must be wondering where I get such wisdom from. The journey was very pleasant. I had seen nothing of the district served by the Western Railway and he did not tire of explaining it all to me. The Wiener Wald to St. Pölten is quite charming. Then we went along the valley of the Danube, where the most beautiful sight was the monastery of Melk; it is similar to that of Klosterneuburg, but is larger and more nobly built. On a hill nearby we saw the Maria Taferl church and we agreed that, like so many others, the site must have been one of ancient heathen sacrifices which has simply changed its name. We crossed several tributaries of the Danube which had previously only been names to me, and then the Alpine chain came into view, including the Traunstein which is visible from everywhere in Upper Austria. Towards evening he got sleepy and I took out the book he had given me for the journey, the *Tentation de St. Antoine* by Flaubert. I didn't read much and the full impression of this remarkable book, a very intense one, came only on the following day. I will tell you about it in my next letter. We went on chatting about all possible topics. To travel with a man whose mind is so alive, a man of such keen judgment, wise knowledge and freely flowing thoughts, was a pleasure that was disturbed only by the consciousness of my own inferiority. We got to Gmunden at half past nine, but the station is half an hour away, so all we could see was a sheet of water and two dark masses of rocks.

The next two letters were occupied with other topics, but three days later he continued with his account. He accompanied it with a sketch and a couple of photographs.

After our evening meal we went for a stroll about eleven o'clock to the Seeschloss, a massive building, now unoccupied, on an island in the lake, but joined to the land by a bridge that you can see on one of your pictures. The wash of the waves sounded wonderful; it was quite dark and the full moon could not break through the clouds. I went back to my room, opened the window and went on reading my wild book. At five in the morning I woke out of a deep sleep and scarcely knew what to do. The others would not get up before eight or nine; it was a lovely morning, so I went forth to discover Gmunden. The delight of the first moments in a strange place is overpowering. I observed that we lived at a distance from the town; I took a good look from my window and absorbed the details of the fine view. There was the dark green lake extending so far that one could not see the end of it. Looking across it one sees two mountains. The first one slopes gently, with a few villas at its foot. It is the Grünberg, so-called because of the clothing of verdure that matches the green of the lake. And near it, dominating the whole landscape, is the mighty Traunstein, of a lighter colour because of the absence of vegetation, that rises perpendicularly from the lake to a height of 5,000 feet. That is really the end of the Alps, for on the other side the Gmunden bowl is formed by a couple of hills belonging to the Danube chain. It is hard to believe that the Traunstein is five times as high as the Grünberg; it looks as if it were only slightly topping it. Besides the Traunstein there is a series of mountain peaks with a contour as I have sketched it for you; popular phantasy sees a human profile in it, the classical profile of a sleeping Grecian woman. Beyond there are more and more high mountains towards Aussee. Below our villa I found on my voyage of discovery another one, belonging to the Archduchess Elizabeth, the mother-in-law of the King of Spain. Then I descended to the town, curious to know what was this "Esplanade" of which I had heard. It turned out to be a long avenue along the side of the lake, shady and with charming views on the lake, into which various little pavilions, cafés and bandstands are built out. Parallel with it is the main street from which the side streets climb up the steep hill. At the end of the Esplanade are two or three squares, one with a kursaal and garden, another with the Town Hall. Then suddenly one passes through an archway into a narrow street with high houses, and down the middle of it runs a stream of bubbling clear water coming from the lake which roars over foaming waterfalls above and below the sluices.

Well, I had discovered the town. I then went back, but at half past six the others were still fast asleep, so I finished my wild book.

278

At the end I was quite dizzy and so deeply stirred that throughout the day I felt its presence most burdensome. I was already excited by the splendid panorama and now on top of it all came this book which in the most condensed fashion and with unsurpassable vividness flings in one's face the whole dross of the world, for it calls up not only the great problems of knowledge (*Erkenntnis*), but the real enigmas of life, all the conflicts of feelings and impulses, and it confirms the awareness of our perplexity in the mysteriousness that reigns everywhere. These questions, it is true, are always there, and one should always be thinking of them. What one does, however, is to confine oneself to a narrow aim every hour and every day and one gets used to the idea that to concern oneself with these enigmas is the task of a special hour, in the belief that they exist only in those special hours. Then they suddenly assail one in the morning and rob one of one's composure and one's spirits.

Freud disliked being shown places and often disdained the use of guidebooks. What gave him pleasure was to discover things for himself, a general characteristic of his independent and inquisitive mind.

Two years after Gmunden he broke his journey from Hamburg to Paris twice, spending a few hours at Cologne and Brussels. He sent his betrothed descriptions of both places, as he always did on his travels. This is his account of Brussels.

Brussels was wonderfully beautiful, an enormous town with splendid buildings. To judge from their names the people are mostly Flemish and the majority understand a little German. In three and a half hours, without a guide, I discovered the main sights of the town. First of all the rich Exchange and Town Hall; with the latter the Viennese one is not to be compared. One remarks that the town has a history which Vienna lacks. Many statues which *really* belonged to olden times; inscriptions and images around the houses. I walked through the whole town, passing from the Boulevard du Nord to the Boul. du Sud, and deviating wherever there might be something beautiful. The proper discoveries I made only when I came upon a steep hill where there was a building so massive and with such magnificent columns as one imagines an Assyrian Royal Palace to have had, or as one finds in the Doré illustrations. I really took it for the Royal Palace, especially since a crown-like cupola rose above it. But there was no guard, no life there, and the

279

building was evidently not finished; over the portal there was a lion bearing the Ten Commandments. It was the Palace of Justice, and from the edge of the hill one had the grandest view of the town lying below. . . . Going farther up the hill I soon came to the Rue Royale, and then one find followed another; the monument to Egmont and Horn was the finest. Opposite an old church there is an oval place surrounded by a railing of iron-work that had the loveliest flowers of iron separated by columns with representations of all the social classes. In the enclosure was a garden, a small pond, and at the broad end stand the two heroes, one of them with his arm embracing the other and pointing to a particular spot; I think that is where they were beheaded. A little farther on I came across a man in a crusader's garb high up on a steed and bearing a flag; when I looked closer it turned out to be Godfrey of Bouillon, the first King of Jerusalem after the First Crusade. I was very pleased to be in such good company, but in the meantime had got very hungry. So I took *déjeuner* in the nearest café, which cost me two francs; it had to last till I got to Paris the next day. After it I discovered the Congress columns and a number of palaces, each of which I took in turn to be the royal one. An advertisement of a farm to let in Waterloo made a peculiar impression.

After this three and a half hours' peregrination he dashed back to the station to catch his overnight train for Paris.

Freud was 40 before he caught a sight of the promised land of Italy, the picture of which had for years filled his thoughts. He spent a wonderful week in Venice with his brother, and in the following years carried out extensive tours in Italy. It was six more years before he dared approach much nearer to Rome, which was for long under a special taboo, than Trasimen, the spot where his beloved hero Hannibal had made his inexplicable and fatal halt. But it would take me all my time merely to enumerate the list of other towns that Freud explored in these years. His wife, being occupied with the children, accompanied him only once or twice, so he wrote or sent her a telegram every day of his tour, and these letters have all been preserved.

There were two striking features in these journeys. One was the restless energy with which they were pursued. Freud was determined to see all he possibly could in the time at his disposal and he would simply gut town after town, often in a few hours for each. His sister-in-law, who accompanied him on one or two of the tours, said that his ideal was to sleep in a different place every night, and sometimes he really did so for a week or two on end. But in spite of the rush his remarkable memory served him so well that years afterwards he could recall where he had seen this or that artistic object or classical relic.

The other feature was the quite exceptional enjoyment Freud experienced on these tours. All the anxieties and moods of depression from which he suffered considerably in those years, as we know from the constant complaints to his friend Fliess, quite vanished when on holiday, and the letters he wrote then are full of an almost boyish gusto and the keenest appreciation of all he was seeing. Freud was pretty well destitute of worldly ambitions, but one is not surprised to learn that the one reason why he would have liked to be affluent would be so that he could visit Italy as often and for as long as he liked.

Yet despite all this love of travelling, Freud several times in his letters mentions his suffering from what he called a bad 'travelling phobia.' Whatever the condition was it certainly did not correspond with the word phobia as he and everyone else was to use it later, since the most prominent feature of a true phobia is its function of inhibiting some activity, and never for a moment did Freud hesitate to carry out any journey he had a chance of. What troubled him was his susceptibility to attacks of acute anxiety at the moment of embarking on the journey. There were even in later years some traces remaining from this old trouble; he always wanted to be in very good time when catching a train, and by good time he could mean half an hour beforehand.

It is plain, therefore, that the enjoyment of travelling must have been in part derived from some deep source, one that at a certain level was forbidden. It is easy to guess in general terms what it symbolized, but I do not find any interest in doing so. I may, however, mention a few considerations that seem pertinent in this connexion.

Anxiety or excitement at embarking on a journey followed by the exaltation of delight when it has been successfully accomplished may be either because of the importance of reaching a given goal or because of the wish to escape from something unpleasant. In Freud's case there are good reasons for thinking that both of these factors were operative. That the beauty of Italy has in addition to its inherent charm and interest a pronouncedly feminine connotation is familiar knowledge. I remember Freud nodding a warm approval when I quoted to him Browning's lines:

> Oh woman—country, wooed not wed,
> Loved all the more by earth's male lands,
> Laid to their hearts instead!

Then Freud always had, especially in the years we are considering, a strong dislike for Vienna. There were moments where it was so intense as to become a physical loathing. Even the beloved Steffel of the songs was to him 'that abominable steeple of St. Stephen's.' In one letter to Fliess he wrote: 'I hate Vienna almost personally, and in contrast to the giant Antaeus I gather fresh strength as soon as I remove my foot from the soil of my *urbs patriae* (*vom vaterstädtischen Boden*).' Antaeus, it will be remembered, gained strength every time he made contact with his Mother Earth, whereas Freud gained strength from making a corresponding renunciation. He had, it is true, very good reasons for disliking the air of Vienna. There was the prevailing anti-semitism, the narrow and restrictive atmosphere of its professional circles and the hostility with which his new ideas had been greeted. But over and above these there was the ineffaceable memory of the terribly hard years of his childhood and youth, with its poverty, privation and hardship. And after all, it was his father who was responsible for plunging him into those distressing circumstances, after tearing him away from his happy early childhood in the Moravian countryside.

It is not my intention to draw any general conclusions from the material I have brought before you, but I thought that any information or reflections concerning the life of the great pioneer to whom we all owe so much should be of some interest.

Fragments of an Analysis
(1954)

JOSEPH WORTIS

Joseph Wortis is a psychiatrist in New York City. He had a short didactic analysis in 1934 and wrote of his experiences in Fragments of an Analysis with Freud *(New York, Simon & Schuster, 1954). The following excerpts were selected by the editor.*

October 10, 1934

I lay on the couch, Freud behind me, his dog sitting quietly on his haunches at the foot of the bed . . . a large dog . . . a big chow I thought it was . . . I didn't notice exactly. Freud began by saying that I was about to speak of my relations to Ellis, which were important. This was not literally true—we broke off on another subject, but I told in some detail how I grew interested in Ellis, what I thought of him, and how encouraging and helpful he had been. I then went on to give some history of my earlier relationship to my wife, and some more about myself. Freud seemed interested in Ellis, asked occasional questions about him: was he a doctor? when did I first actually meet him? etc. When I spoke of my adolescent friendship with my wife, described my uncertainty about leaving her when I first came to study in Europe, and the resulting confusion, Freud commented, "In jeder Beziehung liegt eine Abhängigkeit, selbst mit einem Hund. (There is an element of dependence in every relationship, even with a dog)."

Speaking of Ellis's manner and his friendliness in discussion, I said he never went to great lengths to defend his own views. "Er ist nicht rechthaberisch (he is not self-righteous)," said Freud. I said Ellis was inclined to think that both sides in a controversy were usually right, in part.

"In a controversy," said Freud, "I would say that both sides are usually wrong." But I did more of the talking this time on a theme that interested me and was not unpleasant. Freud said little. He seemed to be a bit hard of hearing, but did not admit it. On the contrary, he continually criticized me for not talking clearly and loudly enough.

"You're always mumbling," he said with some petulance, and he gave a mumbling imitation, "like the Americans do. I believe it is an expression of the general American laxity in social intercourse, and it is sometimes used as *Widerstand*."

I said I didn't think that applied to my case; it wasn't easy to change years of habit on notice, but I would do my best.

I said to Freud that it was impossible, I thought, to let my thoughts flow freely, since I was undoubtedly influenced by Freud's presence, and what he brought to mind: sex and neuroses. He made no comment but said I was just to go on. It seemed obvious to me that one's thoughts were bound to be different in different situations, and that the mere presence of a psychoanalyst tended to elicit certain thoughts or memories.

I remarked how glad I was to see my first Leonardo in the National Gallery at London.

"A Leonardo in the National Gallery?" asked Freud skeptically.

"Yes," I said, " 'The Virgin of the Rocks.' It may only be a copy of the one in the Louvre . . . or the Louvre may have the copy . . . It is hard to say and experts disagree."

I mentioned a note Ellis wrote, in which he spoke of his liking for the composer Dukas. "Who?" asked Freud.

"Dukas," I repeated, and told Freud something about him.

"I don't know," said Freud, "Ich bin kein grosser Kenner der Musik (I'm no great connoisseur of music)."

I stopped at 7 p.m. and rose to leave, saying, "Goodbye, Herr Professor," but Freud did not respond, perhaps, I thought again, because he was a little hard of hearing.

October 15, 1934

This was another uneventful hour. Freud moved into his city home (IX Berggasse 19) over the weekend, and I went there for the first time today: a simple Viennese residence on the first floor of an ordinary house, in an ordinary part of Vienna. There was a butcher-shop downstairs. The entrance was dilapidated, like most entrances in Vienna during that period. Upstairs there was a glass plate on the door with "Prof. Dr. Freud 3-4" on it. I was admitted to a cozy, simple but somewhat cluttered waiting room whose walls were covered with pictures, diplomas, and honorary degrees from many lands. Among the pictures was an excellent one of Havelock Ellis in his prime, sitting back at his

284

desk, with folded arms and clear eyes. There was an inscription on it: "With sincere regards and admiration." Among the books was the Goldberg biography of Ellis, likewise inscribed from Ellis to "Professor Freud." Among the pictures were several group photos taken at Clark University in 1909 with Stanley Hall, Freud, and Jung in the foreground. There was an assortment of other miscellaneous books in all languages (including Chinese) and on all subjects, many of them inscribed in flattering terms to Freud: Woodworth's book, *Contemporary Schools of Psychology*, H.D.'s poems, Calverton's book on sex, Malinowski in German, *Das Geschlechtsleben in Japan*, *Mein Weltbild* by Einstein, *The Old School* collection of essays, as well as the hand-press Joseph Ishill volume on Ellis with a simple inscription from the printer. None of the books looked as if they were much read.

Freud was again mild, earnest and friendly when I came in. "These are our new quarters," he said.

October 17, 1934

Yesterday's hour was pleasant and informal. Freud's dog, the handsome chow, was in the hall when I came in, and the maid told me it was the Professor's great favorite. "When the dog doesn't eat, the Herr Professor is unhappy." The dog and I were both admitted at the same time.

I spoke a little of politics this time, for it occupied my mind, and Freud seemed interested, though noncommittal. Regarding Communism, I said, it sometimes seemed that if you were not for it, you were against it. "Precisely," he said.

I then said that his criticism of me yesterday ought to disqualify me as a scientist, but I didn't take it too seriously.

"I simply said you had a certain undesirable tendency (*Neigung*)," said Freud.

"In any case," I said, "since you said Ellis had the same defect, I feel I am at least in good company."

"That's right—*Eben*," said Freud.

I resumed the account of my early childhood. Freud asked particularly precise questions about early sexual experiences. I led up to my first social experience with a girl, when at the age of fourteen I took her to the theater.

"That," I said, "was my first . . ."

"*Abenteuer*," suggested Freud, and the hour thus ended with my first adventure.

285

November 12, 1934

I was unfortunately (and really unavoidably) late again. "That means *Widerstand*," said Freud, and I was at pains to explain that it was really unavoidable. Freud was, I think, not altogether convinced.

I remarked that parts of the last letter from Ellis saddened me, for he spoke of his failing energies. "When one is old," said Freud, "what can one expect?"

"It is a sad world," I said, "everything is topsy-turvy and rotten; all that Ellis stands for is forgotten, and war may come now any minute. What has a young man to look forward to? What chance has he to feel he can do useful work against the background of this huge rottenness —this *Scheusslichkeit*?"

"I am sorry I can say nothing against that," said Freud, "for I share your opinion. People like Ellis have little power now."

I spoke of various things in my past—my feelings about being a Jew, my views on anti-Semitism, and my not infrequent thoughts about death. "That is quite common in young people," said Freud. With reference to the Jewish question, he agreed that Jews were forced into closer relations to each other by pressure from the outside.

"In England, France, and Italy especially," he said, "where the Jews are freely recognized, they are all strongly patriotic."

I had occasion to mention an article Ellis once wrote against anti-Semitism, in which Freud's name was mentioned with high praise, and Freud again seemed pleased. I spoke of my great liking for England. "I can understand that," said Freud. "I have always been a strong Anglophile." He said his son was now in London. I had heard of him through Ellis. I said it was only in England that one could find so many high-minded people in so small a space, and Freud agreed. We came to speak again of the frequency of homosexuality in England, and Freud again said he felt it was particularly common there—and in Germany too. Ellis had denied this. Freud said it was particularly pronounced among the leaders of English thought . . . among writers and the like. I did not know if he was right. He said it was merely his impression.

I told Freud of Professor Pötzl's lecture last night on "Brain and Mind (*Gehirn und Seele*)," an ambitious subject, and Freud was interested to hear what Pötzl said. He was pleased to hear that his name was prominently mentioned. "Pötzl, you know, was a pupil of mine," he said, "but he has since gone his own way."

There was not much more to say. Freud told me to speak of anything. "Just let your mind drift," he said in English. "You don't have to speak of things that happen now," he added. "Anything will do, past or present, since it is all of one piece, and our purpose is to see the structure of your mind, like an anatomist."

I spoke of various little things, such as peculiarities I thought I had. I said for example that I sometimes absent-mindedly scratched my head or cleaned my nails.

"You ought to break yourself of the habit," said Freud. Of my dreams, I could remember nothing, though I thought I must have had some. But I had followed Freud's advice and made no effort to remember. At the end of the hour, Freud rose quietly as usual, and I followed.

December 20, 1934

Today Freud was in a very good mood indeed. I commenced by saying that I dreamed I was on a skiing trip with my wife.

"Are you planning to go skiing for the holidays?" asked Freud, and wanted to know when and where we planned to go. I told of my dream, said there was a peak in the distance, where the snow gave way and slipped, and I interpreted the entire dream as showing a contrast between danger and peace: danger in the distance and peace with my wife or, perhaps fancifully, annoyance with the analysis but inner peace and love anyway. That seemed to be the only way in which I could combine both elements. Freud accepted that interpretation, on the basis of my associations, and I went on to say that corresponded with my feelings toward him: he wasn't treating me particularly nicely, I felt, but it was perhaps my fault, and in any case, I ought not to judge him by whatever his personal behavior was like, and moreover his personal behavior was probably very different with other people. I think Freud rather approved of this attitude. Freud then made it clear to me that he was not interested in criticizing me, or changing me, or passing judgment on me. He wanted to teach me and remove impediments which stood in the way of instruction.

"I do the best I can, but I always half expect you will throw me out; in fact I don't know why you keep teaching me if you find me so unteachable. Are you afraid of insulting me, or do you do it out of regard for Ellis?"

"That is one reason," said Freud, "and what is more, I don't like to give up something I have started. But you must learn to absorb things and not argue back. You must change that habit."

287

"I thought that to understand, is to pardon—*tout comprendre est tout pardonner*," I replied.

"This isn't a question of pardoning," he said. "It is just a question of getting on. Anyway, I am not so sure that maxim is correct. My son once undertook to criticize a German aristocrat for being rude to a lady. 'Sir,' the nobleman said, 'do you realize that I am Count von Bismarck?' 'That is an explanation,' my son said to him, 'but no excuse.' "

"What am I to do then?" I asked, "Not tell you what I feel?"

"Accept things that are told you, consider them, and digest them. That is the only way to learn. It is a question of *le prendre ou le laisser* —take it or leave it. The trouble with a *Lehranalyse*—a didactic analysis—is that it is difficult to give convincing demonstrations, because there are no symptoms to guide you."

"Why am I such a difficult subject?"

"I told you once before, it is your narcissism, your unwillingness to accept facts that are unpleasant."

"That doesn't sound convincing," I said, "because I have up to now heard nothing about myself which was intolerably unpleasant." So we talked on, and I finally said I would be very glad to give up my narcissistic conceit.

"That would be altogether desirable (*erfreulich*)," said Freud.

January 21, 1935

"An acquaintance of mine," I said, "a rich American woman, is now in her fifth year of analysis."

"She must be rich to afford it," said Freud.

"The question is, how far do analysts yield to the temptation to keep their patients overlong."

"It is a question of medical ethics," said Freud. "Abuses are possible in analysis as in other branches of medicine."

"Except," I said, "for the special weapon of the positive transference. At any rate, it raises the whole question of the importance of money to patients in analysis."

"Now that we have free clinics and the psychoanalytic institutes, the question no longer arises. Anybody can now be analyzed; they may have to wait a little, but everybody has the privilege. Besides, every analyst has a number of free patients. Here in Vienna, for example, every analyst undertakes to treat two free patients. When one considers that an active analyst can at best treat seven or eight patients at a time, then you must appreciate that it means a considerable sacrifice."

I spoke of the place of psychoanalysis in socialized medicine, but Freud did not like the notion. "It is not suited to state supervision and has found no place in the social insurance schemes here; the present system seems best, and there is no occasion to worry about it. Psychoanalysis is not a field where one grows rich easily."

Freud spoke of the special nature of psychoanalytic practice. "One soon learns to be attentive to hours of narrative without a strain," he said. "It is only original thought which is tiring. When you simply play a passive part, it is no different from sitting in a railway carriage and watching the landscape roll by; one soon learns what is significant and worth remembering, and it is always interesting."

I asked Freud whether he found writing difficult. "No," he answered, "because I have usually not written until a thing was ripe and I felt a real compulsion to express myself. When I have had to write to order on the other hand—introductions and the like—it has always been hard."

The only dream I could remember was concerned with a medical school for women, and with libraries, both suggesting an interest in certain women doctors I knew, especially in F.

How I Made the Bust of Freud

(1955)

OSCAR NEMON

Oscar Nemon (1909—), a sculptor, was born in Yugoslavia. He portrayed Freud in 1936 at the request of a number of Freud's pupils on the occasion of his eightieth birthday. This selection appeared as "Comment j'ai fait le buste de Freud" in Psyche 10 (Paris 1955): 483. Translated by the editor. The bust is at the New York Psychoanalytic Institute (see frontispiece).

The pupils of Freud decided to give him a portrait bust on the occasion of his eightieth birthday and they bestowed on me the honor of executing it. Freud posed for twelve sessions. At the beginning he was in a rather bad mood and wondered if this present from his pupils was at all necessary.

But slowly he took an interest in my work and asked me all kinds of questions about it. The psychology of art was one of his great preoccupations. I do not know whether he learned a great deal about sculpture, but he taught me the most interesting things about the psychology of art. Those sessions with Freud are to be counted among the most beautiful memories of my life.

Memories of My Visits
with Freud
(1955)

MARYSE CHOISY

Maryse Choisy (1903—) is a well-known French psychoanalyst and for years editor of Psyche. She knew Freud in the thirties when she went to him for analysis. This selection contains excerpts from an article "Qu'est-ce qu'ils en feront? Souvenirs de mes visites a Freud" published in Psyche 10 (Paris 1955): 471–76. They were selected and translated by the editor.

Never did my heart beat for a lover as it did the day I walked up the Berggasse. Was that Vienna street really a steep climb? Or did it only appear so to me because I was at last going to see my God (at that time), who by some miracle had become accessible?

I had just left my teens without regret. You know that absurd moment when one is ready to swallow up the world, when one is a daredevil in order to hide that one is very timid, when one is disarming because one is disarmed, when one puts on a high-and-mighty manner just to deny that one is vulnerable, when naïveté bears the mask of skepticism. Being twenty-two is a horrible disease of which only time cures you.

I forget the face of the person who opened the door. I don't remember how I found myself in that bourgeois waiting room, with the conventional furniture, the conventional red plush armchairs, the conventional diplomas of honorary membership framed under conventional glass hanging on conventional walls, and the etching of a nude woman, which might seem less conventional but was more so, perhaps, since I recognized one of the many French prints supposed to give conventional folk quite conventional shivers of vice. It took me ages to catch my breath.

As soon as the door of the large consulting room yawned, however, a ray of beauty entered my eyes. There was a long gallery filled with pagan terra cottas and bronzes. The inquisitive young student I was then remained spellbound by all these goddesses and satyrs. Neither at

Paris nor at Cambridge had I ever met a Herr Professor who possessed such works of art—not even that fascinating mask of Dante. Above the psychoanalytic couch was a photograph which Charcot had dedicated to Freud.

Only much later did I actually grasp the symbolism of Freud's home. Wasn't psychoanalysis, after all, a mixture of oldfashioned notions of the decadent nineteen-hundreds and the open window freedom? Didn't psychoanalysis harmoniously incarnate an infinite line of ancestors and an infinite line of scions in the finite substance of a living man? Wasn't Freud the last of the mechanists with a foot on the threshold of the cosmic force? His tragedy was to waver on the threshold, just as I was now myself wavering before stepping into the Holy of Holies.

Silly details worried me. In one of Freud's essays I had read that I must shut the door behind me. To neglect to do so meant some unconscious scorn of the master. But the master very courteously let me in first. There was no door for me to shut. Nothing happened as I dreamt it would. I felt lost. I felt stupid. No word slipped from my tongue.

Fifteen hundred kilometers I had traveled—fifteen hundred kilometers to reach the Berggasse, lie down and say nothing! He waits. It's the custom. Our first relation is a total silence. It is not true to pretend that analysis is an action in words. It is silence, which bears the weight of all memories without evoking any particular one; silence, which measures all possibilities without broaching any of them; silence, which binds analyst and analysand like two accomplices; silence, which fills the room with weird voices. Silence is Freud's greatest invention on the threshold of the unknown world.

No, nothing happens as it should. I had imagined Freud as a tall imposing hero. What? Is this Freud—this old, bearded, bespectacled little fellow? Would I have noticed him in a crowd? He looks as if he had a bulldog's character and was full of fads.

Yes, it *is* Freud, that finely domed forehead, that noble forehead which seems to have no end. His dark, brilliant eyes penetrate beyond your mortal flesh. From them a force rains down on me like some sacred dew. A radiance which it is impossible to resist without giving the lie to that something in me beating my deep rhythm. His glance rested on all kinds of layers, levels, backgrounds, subtleties.

Freud's delicacy fascinated me as much as his hidden strength. The pattern of his thin lips, his ascetic chin, his small gestures—all these at once revealed the fine nuances of his approach to people, his understanding, broken in like a horse to the sufferings and lies of motherhood.

"Well, what do you think of me?" he asked. (His strident and rough voice startled me.)

I didn't know then that this was a classical remark of a psychoanalyst who wants to fathom transference. How did he guess that I was trying to take the measurements of genius? He was stealing my thoughts. He was breaking into my heart. I felt as *ungemutlich* as a child who still believes in witches. Yes, his tone was rude. Irony ran between the words. Or did I project that irony? But Freud *was* rude. Yes, that rude, bitter, misanthropic, utterly pessimistic outlook was Freud's business. It had nothing to do with my personal style.

Why then so much kindness in his eyes? Was his caustic manner a defense mechanism? Of course he was a good fighter. He had to be. Could he otherwise have foisted his libido theory on his puritan colleagues? If only I could somehow creep behind the superficial armor, then that kindness, that immense generosity would pass easily from heart to heart. For instance (who knows this fact?), he had asked his publisher to pay the money due him to his pupils, so they might get their own theses printed.

Suddenly, with that flair of a young animal who has already weighed the stamina of friend or foe, I realized that the man sitting there in his professorlike armchair was the type we call in France *bourru bienfaisant* (rough diamond). I always got on well with the *bourrus bienfaisants*. Their strengths were familiar to me, also the weak spots in their armor. We immediately made contact.

With his rough voice he grumbled something like, "You have a lot of diplomas for a girl of your age." Was he going to insinuate penis envy, next? He didn't. Perhaps I forgot to mention that his eyes were exceptionally kind that day.

Suddenly, I remembered that the seventeen-year-old Freud, after hearing Goethe's *Ode to Nature*, chose medicine instead of law. What had interested him, after all, was the unveiling of Isis rather than the healing of the sick. I admired his literary style even more, perhaps, than his scientific discoveries. I still think there is something wrong with ideas that are clumsily expressed. The only honor that Germany ever bestowed on Freud had nothing to do with his clinical work. He received the Goethe Prize for literature. Finally, I recalled that he had confessed, "In France the interest in psychoanalysis originated in the literary circles." So I made a joke about my diplomas as if they were mere dust, and to dust would return. I explained blushingly (maidens without penis envy *had* to blush) that I had published a book of verse, a novel and a *manifeste suridealiste*. In that case didn't I somehow deserve to be analyzed by him?

He smiled gently. Would I please bring him my writing? "What a poet imagines is more important than his dreams," he said. My previous analyst had never showed the slightest interest in my literary work. He had no time to read fiction. Freud had.

Then I expressed enthusiastic admiration for the universality of his culture. It was very wide indeed. He had neglected only one aspect—music. For a Viennese this was surprising. There must have been extremely strong motives for rejecting this important part of his culture. We shall see further on that it is associated with his relationship to his mother.

In this first interview Freud made the famous remark that I often quote: "What will they do with my theory after my death? Will it still resemble my basic thoughts?"

I have often met with this kind of concern among great writers or artists, but never among scientists. It has the free, prophetic sound of a genius who breaks down the academic conventions. "What will *they* do later with me?" A feeling of melancholy comes over me when I recall this conversation. When the genius dies, the bureaucrat becomes king.

My analysis started out with spirit, enthusiasm, and speed. It went *too well*. It was interrupted in the third session. I told of a dream which seemed quite incomprehensible. I might just as well tell it here. I do not run the slightest risk of disclosing personal secrets, for I do not know any living psychoanalyst who would be able to interpret that dream as Freud did, especially with the poor associations I had.

It all happened in the big somewhat old-fashioned kitchen of our family castle near St. Jean de Luz. I was a pretty Siamese cat with a very long pedigree. Since I was the youngest kitten, despite my ancestry I had to wait for my food until all the alley cats without any pedigrees had finished their plates on the flag-stone. I felt humiliated and hungry. Then I began to scratch everybody. I woke up with a start and remained anxious for awhile.

Associations. It was the castle where I was born and raised. I was not allowed in the kitchen. Good little girls weren't in those days. I sometimes slipped unnoticed into the kitchen because it was forbidden fruit. This was a plot between the cook and me. I once stole some pudding and got indigestion.

I always had Siamese cats. I love them. I have one now.

Freud pondered for a few minutes over my dream, then uttered without warning, "Such and such an event happened in your family when you were still in the cradle."

The reader will forgive me if I don't give Freud's exact words. This is an analysis of Freud, not of me. Many a good family has a skeleton in the closet. Closets are quite useful for that purpose. Still it was a shock. I did not believe Freud. I even became indignant.

"What you say is quite impossible. I would have known it. Such things are simply not done in *my* family. It's against their principles."

Though I could not see him behind me, I knew he was smiling. He just gave me the following advice, "Well, you'd better ask them."

I jumped on the first plane back to Paris. I ran to my aunt's house. I spoke to her the moment I got there. Believe it or not, Freud's extravagant story of an event which I had never suspected (at least consciously) turned out to be true.

There was something uncanny about this dream interpretation. I did not return to Vienna. Freud now symbolized for me the magical father, the medicine man. He saw through me. I felt as transparent as glass. I was scared. I was so scared that I would go to great lengths to avoid analysts. It took me eight years to overcome my panic.

Freud had overestimated me. He believed he could tell me anything. In spite of my independent airs there was still a truth I could not face at twenty-two. Freud did then what he later warned all his pupils to avoid: he interpreted too early, when the analysand was still unable to accept what he was. This Freud called *wild psychoanalysis*. Today an analysand who terminates the analysis prematurely is classed among our failures. After all, the famous case of Dora is also a failure. Of course to develop a technique, distinguished guinea pigs are necessary. Only a genius is able to build up a magnificent success out of two failures, and to obtain a plus from two minuses. Bureaucrats never fail. They never discover anything either. After the inventor comes the inventory.

The Human Image
of Sigmund Freud
(1956)

ERNST BLUM

Ernst Blum, Swiss psychoanalyst, entered analysis with Freud in 1922. The following selections are excerpts from an article about his experiences with Freud. It appeared first in Schweizerische Zeitschrift für Psychologie und ihre Anwendungen 15 (1956): 141–47. *Selected and translated by the editor.*

In the Freud I experienced through my analysis there was no intolerance. The term "who is not for me is against me" was not his. Above all, Freud was a good man. Those who did not observe his goodness were totally ignorant of his personality. And Freud was an enthusiastic and inspiring man. During my analysis Freud had arranged that I could stay at the beautiful home of his friend Professor Pribram. Once at a small party I was introduced to a charming and vivacious old lady who asked me to send Freud her regards. With obvious delight Freud told me that this lady was the cause of his discovery of psychoanalysis. She was his first patient, who refused to be hypnotized!

Thirteen years later in 1935 I met Freud for the last time. Regardless of his physical ailment he was still erect and full of life. I was astounded that he still knew everything about me: the plans I had discussed with him in 1922 and things he had heard about me from others. He insisted that I tell him everything about my first years in Berne and my difficulties in introducing psychoanalysis. Then he asked me suddenly, "And why didn't you write to me?" I told him that when I arrived for my analytic hours at Berggasse 19 I was always struck by the number of letters deposited every day on the mantelpiece and that I decided then and there I would not write in order to save him the trouble of having to answer me. Freud objected and said: "You did me an injustice. Perhaps I would have enjoyed your letters!" With these words we said goodbye. The times and circumstances prevented me from making up for this injustice.

Reflections on Freud's
One Hundredth Birthday
(1956)

FELIX DEUTSCH

Felix Deutsch (1884–1964), husband of Helene Deutsch, wrote extensively on the relationship between psychoanalysis and internal medicine. He was considered one of the foremost experts in psychosomatic medicine. He and his wife were very close to Freud for about thirty years. This selection was originally delivered as an address at the Annual Meeting of the American Psychosomatic Society, 24 March 1956, in Boston. It was published in Psychosomatic Medicine 18 (1956): 279–83.

With mixed feelings, I have accepted the invitation of our president, Dr. Stanley Cobb, to address you today on the occasion of Freud's one hundredth birthday, and to talk about some of my personal recollections of him.

I have been asked several times to speak on one of his birthdays, first on his seventieth birthday in 1926, again in 1931 on his seventy-fifth birthday, and in 1949, on the tenth anniversary of his death. Then I wrote by invitation an obituary dealing with Freud's illness, which I withdrew from publication for personal reasons. The manuscript is now deposited in the Library of Congress.

However, since Ernest Jones has published his two volumes of Freud's biography, and since the third volume will surely deal with Freud's later years until his death, it is permissible to select some of the contents of this paper and to reveal a few events of the years 1923–24, the first years of his fatal sickness and how he took it. This may throw some light upon his heroic stature. It seems to me that the American Psychosomatic Society is the appropriate place to deal with it in retrospect.

The American Psychosomatic Society is—as it was pointed out recently in an editorial of the society's journal—"an eclectic forum where internists, medical specialists, physiologists, neurologists, psychiatrists, psychoanalysts, psychologists, anthropologists, sociologists, and others can pool their knowledge and perhaps cooperate in the study of certain problems which confront them commonly."

I am speaking today as a member who takes part in more than one of these specialties. I hope that all of you will be interested in what I pose as a problem: "How much and when shall a patient be told about his condition, about the nature of his illness and the threat to his life he has to face?" Recently, the whole public of this country were witnessing this problem to a certain degree, when they had occasion to identify and sympathize with the President who fell sick with a coronary thrombosis. He as well as the public reacted first with the attitude that he is now done for good. There is evidence that the President had already some premonitory symptoms during the war years. And there is much evidence that a man who can come to terms with his job, and stays working at it, has a better life expectancy than a man who at the first signs of such an illness retires into permanent convalescence. The psychological hazard of that means accepting defeat.

I have touched upon the question of how much should a patient know about his sickness? This problem did not give us so many headaches 35 years ago as it does now. At that time, psychosomatic medicine was beginning only slowly and gradually to penetrate into medical circles, and was not a very popular concept. Nevertheless, within the psychoanalytic group the mind-body problem had been brought up for discussion by Ferenczi, Groddeck, and myself in Europe, and by Jeliffe in this country. Thus the thinking of both the doctors and the patients had just started to be influenced thereby.

Since a number of analysts close to Freud at that time were seeking my advice, it was often difficult for me to put on a blank face, so to speak, when I wondered whether I should be as frank as I would have liked in touching upon psychogenic implications of a disease. Today the psychosomatic concept is taken for granted as a matter of course.

The story I am going to tell now is not intended to be an analytical investigation of Freud as a person, nor an interpretation of his reactions to his illness. He disliked nothing more than to be used as the object of analytical guesswork. What is permissible, however, is to bring a few highlights of his own reactions to this illness. The recounting of events marked by worry and final relief will—I hope—show how Freud mastered the disease, cancer of the mouth, once he recognized it as a reality threatening his existence.

Just before leaving Freud late one evening in April 1923 (he was then 67 years old), after a conversation about private matters, he surprised me by asking me to have a look at something unpleasant in his mouth, and he said warningly, "Be prepared to see something you will not like." At the very first glance, I had no doubt that it was an advanced cancer. To gain time I took a second look and decided to call it a bad case of leukoplakia, due to excessive smoking, which requires a biopsy and removal of the diseased mucous membrane by operation. Freud agreed to follow this advice. He then told me that he had had the condition for a long time, but that it had become worse lately, and that he had that same afternoon consulted a dermatologist who also diagnosed it as leukoplakia. The specialist, Freud thought, looked rather concerned, but without expressing any urgency recommended an ambulatory operation. What was most painful to Freud was this man's advice to stop smoking. This admonition discouraged him and he hoped for the indulgence of the physician. Freud, who was an incessant smoker, had often remarked, "Smoking has rendered me such invaluable service during my life, that I can only be thankful. Without it I could not have worked as hard or as long as I did."

Then we talked about the choice of a surgeon. He speculated on how he might avoid being operated on by one who was the most outstanding surgeon in this field, but a friend of his. He said he knew the ambivalent attitude of this man and that no one should ask a friend for an operation on oneself. He went no further into the matter.

Next day I communicated with the dermatologist and found out that Freud had postponed his appointment. When I called Freud for an explanation, he asked whether I considered his condition that serious, and then promised not to delay the consultation any longer. A few days later he told me that the ambulatory operation was arranged for the next morning at the hospital department of this very friend whom he had not considered for the surgery. I wondered why he acquiesced against his better judgment, but I never asked him and he never told me. Later he was to regret the choice very deeply.

We drove to the hospital together, with the understanding that he would be at his home immediately after the operation. But he lost more blood than it was foreseen and as an emergency he had to rest on a cot in a tiny room on a ward of the hospital, since no other room was available, with another patient who, by tragicomic coincidence, I might say, was an imbecile dwarf. It was this very man, however, who, when Freud suddenly suffered a profuse hemorrhage, alarmed a nurse and stayed with him until the doctor was summoned. He may have

299

saved Freud's life. This incident led to his remaining in the hospital for two more days.

After convalescing, local radium therapy was started. It was not too helpful. At this time the question arose whether it was now timely to tell Freud the diagnosis. But there was still the prospect that a second, more successful operation might make it unnecessary to spell out the nature of the process. In retrospect, since Freud lived sixteen very productive years thereafter, I believe it paid not to have told him the diagnosis "cancer" that fateful night, before he could see the "term" in another light.

Freud, however, did not share this opinion when we talked about it in later years. From the beginning of the radium therapy onward, as he wrote four months later, he had not had one hour free of discomfort. With each treatment, the swelling of the radiated area of the mouth produced a kind of toxic depression and general malaise. He comforted himself that this distress was due to the treatment, because otherwise it would have been almost unbearable.

From a summer resort he wrote to me that he felt at a loss as to what was going on in him. His distrust turned against the surgeon who had predicted these reactions about which there was nothing to do, yet had asked him to report biweekly. He asserted that his "dear neoplasm" had really not troubled him before, and that he could not have any fondness for an overprotective kind of therapy which made one feel so miserable. But again: Was that the time to tell him what it meant to be doomed? I had doubts for two reasons: first, his most beloved grandchild, a six-year-old boy, had meanwhile died of meningitis. Freud had hoped for the child's recovery almost to the end, and he took this loss very much to heart. His mourning was intense. Second, Freud had always shown an enormous capacity to surmount physical suffering. Once, at a scientific meeting at his house, he stated that while stomach trouble, like nausea or vomiting, always made him feel particularly miserable, heart trouble did not disturb him when he had it.

In the late 90's he once had extra systoles from acute nicotine poisoning. This had been serious enough to make him give up smoking for a year and a half. Eventually the cardiac symptoms receded, immediately after his friend Fliess had treated what Fliess called the "Genitalpunkte" in the nose. Even after Freud's more serious heart attack in 1912, during the Psychoanalytic Meeting in Munich, when the final open break with Jung occurred, he got over it without concern. Again in February, 1926, during a short walk, he had a typical attack of angina pectoris, but he felt no anxiety over it, as he wrote me, and did not consult anyone. When it happened again some days later, under similar circumstances, he went to the office of an old friend, a professor of cardiology, on whose doorstep the attack recurred, and who insisted on hospitalization. From then on he was never permitted to walk as before; to this interdiction he submitted readily. It was different with this growth in his mouth which, further, imposed many food restrictions and frequently made eating very unpleasant indeed.

During the period of the radium treatment and the toxic depression at his summer resort, he wrote "no ideas—not one line," and added apocryphally that from his "indifference to most trifles such as science" he would guess that "the mourning process must carry on in darkness." At the same time he expressed a wish to visit Rome again where he had not been for ten years. I was fearful of this under the circumstances, and in view of the true situation proposed that I come down to see him in his summer resort in Italy and talk the matter over (it was in August 1923). Surprisingly enough, he agreed and said he would not make definite plans for this adventurous trip before seeing me, but that he hoped for my blessing. He stated, "Now it is this organ, now another giving way." He was very doubtful whether to attribute all of his difficulties to the radium treatment. Fortunately he had some comfort, for in spite of all that, he was still the excellent sleeper he had always been.

We did not talk about the trip to Rome immediately after I arrived. In view of the fact that a second very drastic operation was unavoidable and that not much could be lost by waiting a couple of weeks, I made up my mind that he should not be deprived of a last opportunity to see Rome once more. Besides, to let him go would unquestionably be encouraging to him; I gave my permission.

Then he told me that all of the men in the "ring of seven" were coming for a collective visit within two days: Abraham, Eitingon, Ferenczi, Jones, Rank, and Sachs. I welcomed this, eager to have their views, even though it meant letting them in on the truth. It was the last time they were to be at Freud's home as a group. All agreed with my proposition that Freud should be allowed to make the journey to Rome, with a promise not to be away for more than two weeks, and with the understanding that another surgeon be consulted upon his re-

301

turn. He felt forever grateful afterwards for having been helped to terminate the doctor-patient relationship with his friend, with whom he had allowed himself to become involved.

In the fall (October 1923) two successive radical operations were performed. The recovery, though very painful, proceeded extremely satisfactorily, although a biopsy of the healthy looking part of the mucous membrane bordering the extirpated one still showed cancer cells. The hope that Freud could be spared a further operation in the future was shattered.

It was scarcely possible by this time that he should not have become aware of the character of his disease. His steady improvement under the continuous, clever care of the surgeon for whom he had the greatest respect and fondness, apparently led him to see the sickness in another light—especially in view of the fact that he was able to pick up his work again at the beginning of the new year, though handicapped by impaired hearing and speaking faculties. These infirmities prevented him from ever again attending scientific meetings of the Psychoanalytic Society, with the one exception of the meeting in memory of Abraham.

A new attitude toward his disease became apparent in his tolerance of the discomfort and the daily aftercare of the mouth. As his strength and accustomed ways of life returned, and with his adjustment to the enormous defects produced by the operation, his former attitude toward cancer as a hopeless disease became incompatible with his evident recovery in every other respect. Much later, in a correspondence referring to the past events in connection with his disease, he mentioned how full of reproach he had been because the right diagnosis had been withheld from him at the time of his first operation, and that he had felt deceived. As he wrote, "I could always adapt myself to any kind of reality, even endure an uncertainty due to a reality —but being left alone with my subjective insecurity, without the fulcrum or pillar of the *ananke*, the inexorable, unavoidable necessity, I had to fall prey to the miserable cowardice of a human being and had to become an unworthy spectacle for others." This is the way he saw the matter in retrospect.

Freud was always a fighter. About his own work he thought very modestly indeed. Once he wrote, "I am no more than a scientific investigator who by a remarkable concurrence of circumstances have succeeded in making a discovery of particular importance. My own merit in this success is limited to the unfolding of otherwise not fre-

302

quently practiced characteristics, such as independent thought and love of truth." For that he fought relentlessly. He could not countenance weakness in himself any more than in others. He would admit no surrender. Uncertainty as to whether he must ward off a wish for disintegration or must face the external danger of cancer was intolerable for him. At the outset he looked upon cancer as an enemy against which resistance was in vain. Of this he was not afraid—he did not lack the courage to die. He only insisted on his right to determine his own destiny. But when he found that he had overestimated his adversary, he took a determined stand. His stoic resistance to the painful experiences of the disease enabled him to endure the suffering for 16 years. He never complained about his misfortune to me; in these years he simply treated the neoplasm as an uninvited, unwelcome intruder whom one should not mind more than necessary.

Thirty-four years have gone by since then. Time and again I have had occasion to meditate over this event and the question of the individual's right to determine his own destiny. I was often reminded of the words of the philosopher Lynkeus, whom Freud revered, and who wrote in his book *The Duty to Live and the Right to Die*: "Nobody else can ever feel how preciously I am willing to evaluate my life, [but] it is better to make greater than lesser sacrifices, if one is convinced of their indispensability. I know only one aim, which is security for myself and for my neighbors."; and "The knowledge of always being free to determine when or whether to give up one's life inspires me with the feeling of a new power and gives me a composure comparable to the consciousness of the soldier on the battlefield, who, if it comes to the worst, trusts in a fortress behind him to which he can retreat." Freud would never permit himself to retreat. His life could not be measured with common measures.

As I said, 34 years have gone by and I have often ruminated about the meaning of death from an inexorably destructive disease like cancer. At that time this word almost meant an inevitable doom.

Every medical man has been confronted at one time or another with a patient's question: "Have I got cancer?" The answer to this question cannot be settled by the biopsy alone. It has to be weighed from the point of view of the circumstances under which the question is asked; that is, on the prevailing emotional condition of the patient. Whether the physician answers according to the facts or not, is not merely a matter of truth or falsehood. Those who expose the patient at once to the plain fact may be ignoring the mental climate behind the

303

question, taking it only at face value. Certain patients who insist on their right to know "the full truth" often betray by their insistence a concern about a condition which, though it is called "cancer," means for him a decaying, devouring growth with a far different, more ominous meaning than the word itself necessarily conveys. I thought Freud had been insufficiently prepared in the beginning to face a reality as he saw it, and therefore I acted as I did.

A few aphoristic afterthoughts before I close. Every person has his own way of coming to terms with his innate fear of disintegration, of his self-destructive instincts; accordingly he wants to know whether this fear is perhaps about to become a material one. Moreover, any person bears within him fantasies of the infantile past in which he wished and feared their fulfillment, being afraid because these fantasies contain also the threat of destruction and death. Those fears of the past give the term "cancer" the meaning of a pitiless, destroying enemy, in the face of whom one may feel doomed. Other conflict-bringing thoughts inseparable from those mentioned above are such ideas as the right, the duty, the courage, the fear to live.

Being born into this world, having received life—although not having asked for it, nor having been able to refuse it—instills into us the idea of a wholeness and the need of keeping it intact, and consequently the urge, the inner command to live. This idea leads to the instinctual drive for preservation of this wholeness and to the resistive power against self-destruction, because life is continually threatened by the danger of disintegration and decay, which in fact takes place partly all the time.

The instinct of self-preservation is intimately connected with this perpetual threat against the wholeness. The wish to live is abandoned when the danger of disintegration can no longer be met. Therefore the courage to live depends on how much a person can rely on and trust his means of overcoming and warding off the inner danger of the self-destructive, life-undermining tendencies. The courage to live collapses when confidence in one's wholeness is threatened on too many fronts at the same time, from within and from without, and, if still weakened from former threats, one cannot resist when a new one breaks in.

Uncertainty about a reality danger from without feeds on the unconscious. But certainty, forced untimely on a sick person, drives the unconscious deeper underground. Only timely instilled certainty starves the unconscious and strengthens the ego to face reality.

Here ends my story of Freud's illness. He could endure the tortures after the first assault was over more bravely than anyone I have known, since he did not have to fear the dangers from within. He knew enough about his own unconscious and was not afraid to meet it. His one hundredth birthday reminds us that if he had not been able to go through his self-analysis we should never have had what he has taught us.

Analysand of Freud
(1956)

HILDA DOOLITTLE

Hilda Doolittle, better known as H.D., was a renowned poet in the 1930s and 1940s. She was analyzed by Freud in the middle-late thirties and was one of his few patients who related their analytic experiences with him. The following passages were selected from Tribute to Freud *by H.D. (New York, Pantheon, 1956).*

It was Vienna, 1933–1934. I had a room in the Hotel Regina, Freiheitsplatz. I had a small calendar on my table. I counted the days and marked them off, calculating the weeks. My sessions were limited, time went so quickly. As I stopped to leave my key at the desk, the hall porter said, "Some day, will you remember me to the Professor?" I said I would if the opportunity arose. He said, "—and ah, the Frau Professor! There is a wonderful lady." I said I had not met the Frau Professor but had heard that she was the perfect wife for him and there couldn't be—could there?—a greater possible compliment. The porter said, "You know Berggasse? After the—well, later when the Professor is no longer with us, they will name it Freudgasse." I went down Berggasse, turned in the familiar entrance; Berggasse 19, Wien IX, it was. There were wide stone steps and a balustrade. Sometimes I met someone else coming up.

The stone staircase was curved. There were two doors on the landing. The one to the right was the Professor's professional door; the one to the left, the Freud family door. Apparently, the two apartments had been arranged so that there should be as little confusion as possible between family and patients or students; there was the Professor who belonged to us, there was the Professor who belonged to the family; it was a large family with ramifications, in-laws, distant relatives, family friends. There were other apartments above but I did not very often pass anyone on the stairs, except the analysand whose hour preceded mine.

My hours or sessions had been arranged for me, four days a week from five to six; one day, from twelve to one. At least, that was the arrangement for the second series of sessions which, I have noted, began the end of October 1934. I left a number of books and letters in Switzerland when I left there, actually after the war had begun; among them was my 1933 Vienna diary. I am under the impression that the Professor had arranged the second series to accord with the first, as I had often said to him that near-evening hour was almost my favorite of the whole day. Anyhow, I had five weeks then. The last session was December 1, 1934. The first series began in March 1933, and lasted somewhat longer, between three and four months.

The Professor was 77. His birthday in May was significant. The consulting room in the strange house contained some of his treasures and his famous desk. The room looked the same, except for the desk. Instead of the semi-circle of priceless little *objets d'art*, there was a carefully arranged series of vases; each contained a spray of orchids or a single flower. I had nothing for the Professor. I said, "I am sorry, I haven't brought you anything because I couldn't find what I wanted." I said, "Anyway, I wanted to give you something different." My remark might have seemed a shade careless, a shade arrogant. It might have seemed either of these things, or both. I do not know how the Professor translated it. He waved me to the couch, satisfied or unsatisfied with my apparently casual regard for his birthday.

I had not found what I wanted so I did not give him anything. In one of our talks in the old room at Berggasse, we had gone off on one of our journeys. Sometimes, the Professor knew actually my terrain, sometimes it was implicit in a statue or a picture, like that old fashioned steel engraving of the Temple at Karnak that hung above the couch. I had visited that particular temple, he had not. But this time it was Italy; we were together in Rome. The years went forward, then backward. The shuttle of the years ran a thread that wove my pattern into the Professor's. "Ah, the Spanish Steps," said the Professor. "It was those branches of almond," I said. "Of all the flowers and the flower baskets, I remember those best." "But," said the Professor, "the gardenias! In Rome, even I could afford to wear a gardenia." It was not that he conjured up the past and invoked the future. It was a present that was in the past or a past that was in the future.

Even I could search Vienna for a single gardenia or a cluster of gardenias. But I could not find them. Another year, I wrote from London, asking a friend in Vienna—an English student there—to make a special effort to find a cluster of gardenias for the Professor's birthday. She wrote back, "I looked everywhere for the gardenias. But the florists told me that Professor Freud liked orchids for his birthday; they thought you would like to know. I sent the orchids for you."

I did not argue with the Professor. In fact, as I say, I did not have the answer. If he expected me to rouse to some protestation of affection, he did not then succeed in doing so—the root or the current ran too deep. One day he said, *"Today we have tunnelled very deep."* One day he said, "I struck oil. It was I who struck oil. But the contents of the oil wells have only just been sampled. There is oil enough, material enough for research and exploitation, to last 50 years, to last 100 years —or longer." He said, "My discoveries are not primarily a heal-all. My discoveries are a basis for a very grave philosophy. There are very few who understand this, *there are few who are capable of understanding this.*" One day he said to me, "You discovered for yourself what I discovered for the race." To all that I will hope to return later. At the moment, I am lying on the couch. I have just readjusted the rug that had slipped to the floor. I have tucked my hands under the rug. I am wondering if the Professor caught me looking at my wrist watch. I am really somewhat shattered. But there is no answering flare-back.

Then it was quiet and the hotel lobby seemed strangely empty. Even the hall porter disappeared from behind his desk. Maybe, this was the following Monday; in any case, I was due at Berggasse for my usual session. The little maid Paula peered through a crack in the door, hesitated, then furtively ushered me in. She did not wear her pretty cap and apron. Evidently, she was not expecting me. "But—but no one has come today; no one has gone out." All right, would she explain to the Professor in case he did not want to see me. She opened the waiting room door. I waited as usual in the room, with the round table, the odds and ends of old papers and magazines. There were the usual framed photographs; among them Dr. Havelock Ellis and Dr. Hanns Sachs greeted me from the wall. There was the honorary diploma that had been presented to the Professor in his early days by the small New England university. There was also a bizarre print or engraving of some nightmare horror, a "Buried Alive" or some such thing, done in Düreresque symbolic detail. There were long lace curtains at the window, like a "room in Vienna" in a play or film.

The Professor opened the inner door after a short interval. Then I sat on the couch. The Professor said, "But why did you come? No one has come here today, no one. What is it like outside? Why did you come out?"

I said, "It's very quiet. There doesn't seem to be anyone about in the streets. The hotel seems quiet, too. But otherwise, it's much the same as usual." He said, "Why did you come?" It seemed a puzzle to him; he did not seem to understand what had brought me. What did he expect me to say? I don't think I said it. My being there surely expressed it? *I am here because no one else has come.* As if again, symbolically, I must be different. Where was the Flying Dutchman? Or the American lady doctor whom I had not seen? There were only four of us at that time, I believe, rather special people. It is true that Mrs. Burlingham, Miss Anna Freud's devoted friend and the Professor's disciple or pupil, had an apartment further up the stairs. I had gone up there to tea one day before my session here. The Professor was not really alone. The envoys of the Princess, too, I had been informed, were waiting on the door-steps of various legations, and they would inform her of any actual threat to the Professor's personal safety. But, in a sense, I was the only one who had come in from the outside; Little Paula substantiated that when she peered so fearfully through the crack in the front door. Again, I was different. I had made a unique gesture, although actually I felt my coming was the merest courtesy. This was our usual time of meeting, our session, our "hour" together. I did not know what the Professor was thinking. "I am an old man—*you do not think it worth while to love me.*" Or if he remembered having said that, this surely was the answer to it.

He is at home here. He is part and parcel of these treasures. I have come a long way, I have brought nothing with me. He has his family, the tradition of an unbroken family, reaching back through this old heart of the Roman Empire, further into the Holy Land.

> Ah, Psyche, from the regions which
> Are Holy Land!

He is the infinitely old symbol, weighing the soul Psyche in the Balance. Does the Soul, passing the portals of life, entering the House of Eternity, greet the Keeper of the Door? It seems so. I should have thought the Door-Keeper, at home beyond the threshold, might have greeted the shivering soul. Not so, the Professor. But waiting and

309

finding that I would not or could not speak, he uttered. What he said —and I thought a little sadly—was, "You are the only person who has ever come into this room and looked at things in the room before looking at me."

But worse was to come. A little lion-like creature came padding toward me—a lioness, as it happened. She had emerged from the inner sanctum or manifested from under or behind the couch; anyhow, she continued her course across the carpet. Embarrassed, shy, overwhelmed, I bend down to greet this creature. But the Professor says, "Do not touch her—she snaps—she is very difficult with strangers." *Strangers?* Is the Soul crossing the threshold, a stranger to the Door-Keeper? It appears so. But, though no accredited dog-lover, I like dogs and they oddly and sometimes unexpectedly "take" to me. If this is an exception, I am ready to take the risk. Unintimidated but distressed by the Professor's somewhat forbidding manner, I not only continue my gesture toward the little chow, but crouch on the floor so that she can snap better if she wants to. Yofi—her name is Yofi—snuggles her nose into my hand, and nuzzles her head, in a delicate sympathy, against my shoulder.

May 1936

My Sincere Thanks for your Kind
Remembrances on the Observance
of my Eightieth Birthday
Your Freud

Will you forgive me this barbaric reaction to such loving expressions [of friendship]? I am sure Yofi is very proud of being mentioned by you. Believe it or not, early on the 6th she came into my bedroom to show me her affection in her own fashion, something she has never done before or after. How does a little animal know when a birthday comes around?

[24 May 1936]
XIX Strasserg 47
Wien IX, Berggasse 19

Dear H.D.

All your white cattle safely arrived lived and adorned the room up to yesterday.

310

I had imagined I had become insensitive to praise and blame. Reading your kind lines and getting aware of how I enjoyed them I first thought I had been mistaken about my firmness. Yet on second thoughts I concluded I was not. What you gave me was not praise [but] affection and I need not be ashamed of my satisfaction.

Life at my age is not easy, but spring is beautiful, and so is love.

Yours affectionately,
Freud

My Uncle Sigmund
(1956)

HARRY FREUD

Harry Freud was Freud's nephew, the son of his brother Alexander. Richard Dyck of the New York German newspaper Aufbau *interviewed Harry on his impressions of his uncle (11 May 1956). The following excerpts were translated by the editor.*

I was always very close to my uncle Sigmund. I visited him many times in Vienna and later in London. My father Alexander was his only brother. There was a difference of about ten years between them. My father died in 1943 in Toronto.

Question: What about Sigmund Freud as a father?

Uncle Sigmund was always very friendly with his children. However, he was somewhat formal and reserved with them, as he was with other relatives. He very seldom kissed them. Even when he kissed his mother on his weekly visits, one felt he did this out of duty. In the education of his children he certainly was not very strict and he left them completely free in deciding what career to pursue. The only thing he insisted on in his children was a sense of order.

Question: What was his attitude towards money? Was he thrifty?

No, he certainly was not thrifty. As a matter of fact, he really did not care about money. He left only 20,000 pounds when he died. Certainly not much for a man of his status. He earned a great deal of money during his life, but he spent much on his hobbies, such as travel and other pleasures. What he could get with the money was more important for him than the money itself. Also, since 1923, the year of his first operation, he spent an enormous amount of money on doctors.

Question: Could you tell me a little bit more about Freud's habits?

First of all my uncle was an avid reader. He read everything. He read novels, biographies, philosophy and history, and . . . detective stories, which he had in common with other great minds. He never forgot what he read. He had a photographic memory. He never left anything unfinished. When he died there were no unfinished manuscripts among his papers. He loved his collection of archeological antiques, of course, and spent a great deal of money on it. Also, many friends gave him new items for his collection. One of his hobbies was letter writing, which he loved very much. He did not use typewriters or dictaphones, which he despised, but wrote every letter by hand. He also did not like the telephone and refused to use it.

He despised music and considered it solely as an intrusion! For that matter the whole Freud family was very unmusical. He never went to a concert and hardly to the theater. But he loved to play cards, especially Tarock and Mah-Jongg. And he loved to smoke cigars. In his healthy days he smoked about twenty cigars a day. Even in the last days of his life he refused to quit smoking. When I was seventeen years old he offered me a cigarette; when I refused he said, "My boy, smoking is one of the most wonderful delights in this world." The last time I saw my uncle was on 12 August 1939 in London. When I left I told him I would return for Christmas, whereupon he smiled sadly and said, "You won't see me here when you return."

A Letter by Sigmund Freud with Recollections of His Adolescence

(1956)

MARTIN GROTJAHN

Martin Grotjahn, a psychoanalyst in California, is well known for his interest in the history of the psychoanalytic movement. With Franz Alexander and Samuel Eisenstein he edited Psychoanalytic Pioneers *(New York, Basic Books, 1966), a major contribution to the history of the psychoanalytic movement. Dr. Grotjahn delivered this paper at the Annual Meeting of the American Psychoanalytic Association, Chicago, 27 April 1956. It was printed in the* Journal of the American Psychoanalytic Association *4 (1956): 644–52.*

The letter by Sigmund Freud reported here requires a short explanation of the history of its writing. Without such orientation the meaning and the beauty of Freud's words may not be fully appreciated.

Heinrich Braun, about whom Freud writes in this letter, was born on 23 November 1854, which makes him one and a half years older than Freud. He came from a family of independent, liberal-thinking engineers, all of them pioneers in the development of European railroad systems.

Heinrich was financially independent and studied economy and political science. He edited several scientific and political journals and became an outstanding expert and leader in the theory of social economy and its political application. In the year 1903 he became a member of the German parliament.

The other name mentioned by Freud in his letter refers to Victor Adler, a physician, psychiatrist, and political leader in Vienna. Victor Adler and Heinrich Braun had the same political philosophy.

Heinrich Braun died on 8 February 1927 in Berlin. His widow— the writer Julie Braun-Vogelstein—had already published several books about some important members of the Braun family. After the death of Heinrich, she started to collect material as preparation for a book about her late husband. As a part of the research, she wrote a let-

314

ter to Sigmund Freud asking him what he remembered about his former friend. Sigmund Freud, by then seventy-one years of age and still living in Vienna, Berggasse 19, wrote the following account of his associations and recollections. He answered in long hand. The letter is dated Vienna, 30 October 1927.°

PROF. DR. FREUD

30.X.27

WIEN IX., BERGGASSE 19

Hochgeehrte Frau

Es bedarf keiner Fürsprache mich zur Erfüllung Ihres Wunsches zu bestimmen. Ich fürchte nur ich kann Ihnen nicht so viel bieten als Sie erwarten. Unsere Beziehung, so stark während der Gymnasialjahre, ist schon während der Universitätszeit verronnen. In den letzten 50 (!) Jahren habe ich kaum etwas von ihm gewusst. In dieser ganzen langen Lebenszeit traf ich ihn einige Male zufällig auf der Strasse in Wien, einmal mag er mich in meinem Haus besucht haben. Ein andermal erhielt ich einen Brief von ihm, in dem er mir die analytische Behandlung eines seiner Söhne antrug der ihm Schwierigkeiten machte. Es muss im ersten Jahrzehnt der Psychoanalyse gewesen sein. Ich lehnte ab, denn ich war auf die Beeinflussung Jugendlicher nicht eingerichtet und meinte—mit Recht—dass persönliche Beziehungen für die analytische Situation nicht günstig sind.

Ich besitze also keine Briefe von ihm. Die letzte eindrucksvolle Begegnung die wir hatten mag 1883 (?) oder 84 (?) stattgefunden haben. Er kam damals nach Wien und lud mich zu einem Mittagessen bei seinem Schwager Victor Adler ein. Ich weiss noch, dass er damals Vegetarianer war, und dass ich den kleinen Fritz zu sehen bekam der 1-2 Jahre alt war. (Mir fällt es als merkwürdig auf, dass es in denselben Räumen war, die ich jetzt seit 36 Jahren bewohne.)

Ich weiss dass ich Heinrich Braun's Bekanntschaft im ersten Gymnasialjahr, am Tage der ersten "Zensur" machte und dass wir bald unzertrennliche Freunde waren. Ich brachte alle von der Schule freigelassenen Tagesstunden mit ihm, meist bei ihm zu, besonders solange seine Familie noch nicht in Wien war und er mit seinem nächsten Bruder Adolf und einem Hofmeister wohnte. Dieser Bruder suchte unseren Verkehr zu stören, wir selbst vertrugen uns aber ausgezeichnet. Ich erinnere mich kaum an Streitigkeiten

° This letter is published with the approval of Sigmund Freud Copyrights Ltd.

zwischen uns oder an Zeiten, in denen wir miteinander "böse" waren, wie es in diesen jungen Freundschaften so oft vorkommt. Was wir all diese Tage taten und worüber wir sprachen das ist jetzt nach so vielen Jahren schwer vorzustellen. Ich glaube, er bestärkte mich in der Abneigung gegen die Schule und was in ihr gelehrt wurde, weckte eine Menge von revolutionären Regungen in mir und wir bestärkten uns gegenseitig in der Überschätzung unserer Kritik und besseren Einsicht. Er lenkte mein Interesse auf Bücher wie Buckle's Geschichte der Civilisation und ein ähnliches Werk von Lecky, die er sehr bewunderte. Ich bewunderte ihn, sein energisches Auftreten, sein unabhängiges Urteil, verglich ihn im Stillen mit einem jungen Löwen und war der sicheren Überzeugung, dass er einmal eine führende Stellung in der Welt ausfüllen werde. Ein Lerner war er nicht, aber ich nahm es ihm obwohl ich bald Primus wurde und es blieb nicht übel; ich verstand in der dumpfen Ahnung jener Jahre, dass er etwas besass was wertvoller war als alle Schulerfolge, was ich seither als die "Persönlichkeit" benennen gelernt habe.

Weder die Ziele noch die Wege unseres Strebens waren uns sehr klar. Ich bin seither zur Vermutung gekommen dass seine Ziele wesentlich negative waren. Aber es stand fest ich würde mit ihm arbeiten und seine "Partei" nie verlassen. Unter seinem Einfluss war ich auch damals entschlossen an der Universität Jus zu studieren.

Eine erste Unterbrechung erfuhr unser Verhältnis als er—ich glaube es war in der Septima, der vorletzten Klasse, die Schule leider nicht freiwillig verliess. Im ersten Jahre der Universität war er wieder da. Aber ich war Mediziner geworden, er Jurist. Er machte bald die Bekanntschaft von Victor Adler, der dann sein Schwager wurde. Unsere Wege trennten sich langsam, er hatte immer mehr Beziehungen zu Menschen gehabt als ich, immer leichter neue angeknüpft. Der Umgang mit mir, war ihm wahrscheinlich längst nicht mehr Bedürfnis. So kam es, dass ich ihn in den späteren Studentenjahren ganz aus den Augen verlor. Ich weiss nicht einmal, ob er sein Doktorat in Wien machte. Ich glaube es nicht. Eines Tages, im Jahre 81 oder 82 begegnete ich ihm nach langer Entfremdung auf der Strasse. Es verstand sich noch von selbst, dass wir sofort wieder intim sprachen. Er zeigte mir das Bild des Mädchens, mit dem er sich verlobt hatte, und ich gestand, dass ich in derselben Lage war. Vielleicht war es damals, dass er mich zum Mittag bei Adler einlud. Und dann gab es lange keine Gemeinsamkeit mehr und überhaupt nicht wieder eine richtige Beziehung zwischen uns.

In vorzüglicher Hochachtung

Ihr

(gez.) FREUD

PROF. DR. FREUD

30 October 1927

WIEN IX, BERGGASSE *19*

Hochgeehrte Frau:

No special introduction is required to make me fulfill your wish. I only fear that I cannot offer you as much as you expect. Our relationship, so strong during the years of the gymnasium, had already dissolved during the time at the university.

During the last 50 (!) years I have known hardly anything about him. During all these years of a long lifetime I met him several times accidentally on the streets of Vienna, once he may have visited me at my home. On another occasion I received a letter from him in which he asked me to treat analytically one of his sons who had caused him trouble. It must have been during the first decade of psychoanalysis. I refused because I was not equipped to guide adolescents and thought—rightfully—that personal relations are not favorable to the analytic situation.

I possess no letters from him. The last impressive meeting which we had may have taken place in 1883 (?) or 1884 (?). He came to Vienna then and invited me for lunch at his brother-in-law's, Victor Adler. I still remember that he was a vegetarian then and that I had a chance to see the little Fritz who must have been one or two years of age. (I think it is remarkable that this happened in the same rooms in which I have been living for thirty-six years.)

I know that I made the acquaintance of Heinrich Braun during the first year at the gymnasium on the day when we got our first "report card" and that we were soon inseparable friends. All the hours of the day which were left after school I spent with him, mostly at his home, especially as long as his family was not yet in Vienna and he lived with his next oldest brother Adolf and a private tutor. This brother tried to interfere with our relationship. We ourselves, however, got along marvelously. I hardly remember any quarrels between us or times during which we were "mad" at each

317

other, which happens so frequently during such young friendships. What we did all those days and what we talked about is difficult to imagine after so many years. I believe he reinforced my aversion to school and to what was taught there; he awakened a multitude of revolutionary trends in me and we reinforced each other in the overestimation of our criticism and of our superior knowledge. He turned my interest to books like Buckle's *History of Civilization* and to a similar work by Lecky, which he admired greatly. I admired him: his self-confident poise; his independent judgment; I compared him secretly with a young lion and I was firmly convinced that sometime in the future he would assume a leading position in the world. A scholar he was not, but I did not mind that, though I myself soon became *primus* and remained it; in the vague feeling of those years I understood that he possessed something which was more valuable than all success in school and which I have since learned to call "personality."

Neither the goals nor the means of our ambitions were very clear to us. Since then I have come to the assumption that his aims were essentially negative ones. But one thing was certain: that I would work with him and that I would never desert his "party." Under his influence I was also determined at that time to study law at the university.

Our relationship experienced its first interruption—I think it was during the septima, the next to the last grade—when he left school, unfortunately not voluntarily. During the first year at the university he was there again. But I had become a student of medicine and he a student of law. Soon he made the acquaintance of Victor Adler, who later became his brother-in-law. Our ways separated slowly: he always had more relationships to people than I had and it was always easier for him to establish new ones. Contact with me had probably ceased to be a need to him long before. So it happened that I completely lost sight of him during the later years of study. I don't even know whether he took his doctor's degree in Vienna. I do not believe so. One day, perhaps in the year '81 or '82, I met him on the street, long after we had become strangers. As a matter of course we again immediately talked quite intimately. He showed me the picture of the girl whom he was engaged to marry; and I confessed that I was in the same situation. Perhaps it was then that he invited me to lunch at Adler's. And then there was nothing in common between us any more and no real relationship was ever established again.

In vorzüglicher Hochachtung

Ihr

(Signed) FREUD

One of the remarkable features of this letter is the style of almost free association in which it is written. Freud associated to the request for information and his mind at first turned to recollections of recent events before he reached far back to the beginning of his friendship with Heinrich Braun. Then he proceeded in chronological sequence. Once he interrupted his freely flowing associations with a reflection about the strange fact that he, Freud, later lived for more than forty years in the same home in which he met Victor Adler. Freud put this thought in parentheses. After some hesitation, so it seems, comes the report about what Freud calls the "youthful friendship" with this firebrand of a person, who was not a "scholar" but a "personality."

All the typical features of a boyhood friendship, with their deep feeling, their loyalties, their declaration of undying faith are implied in this recollection. It is remarkable to see how Freud attempts to combine the pride of being *primus,* the first one in his class, with his admiration for the Promethean young man who was asked to leave school. In German-Austrian tradition such advice amounted to a deep shame and disaster for the whole family.

Perhaps it is amusing to note how tactfully Freud mentions the fact that Heinrich Braun was thrown out of school. It seems that he was not quite sure whether he should mention it, and how Heinrich's widow would react to it. He is much less apologetic for his harsh judgment of Heinrich Braun's "essentially negative aims" in his political philosophy.

There is a slip of the pen or memory in Freud's letter when he calls the brother of Heinrich who interferes with the friendship by the awful name *Adolf*; his true name was Anton. Perhaps Freud did not like "Adolf."

Mrs. Suzanne A. Bernfeld of San Francisco gave the following commentary to the letter by Freud to Mrs. Julie Braun-Vogelstein.

In this extraordinary letter in which Freud talks about the last meeting he had with Heinrich Braun, he makes the following remark: "(I think it is remarkable that this happened in the same rooms in which I have now been living for thirty-six years.)"

Whenever Freud casually remarks that a coincidence is noteworthy, this is sufficient to arouse the curiosity of any biographically minded psychoanalyst. I think this remark refers to the psychological determinants that had led to the selection of his home.

Until 1891 the Freuds had lived in a four-room apartment near the Schottenring. This apartment was situated in the best part of Vienna. Several of their children were born there. One was on the way, I believe, when the family decided to move.

The move was carefully planned by both Professor and Mrs. Freud. They made lists of their most important requirements. They spent a considerable time in planning their new home. They decided that the most necessary features were the number of rooms, the location and accessibility for patients, and the availability of appropriate schools for their children.

At this time Freud still used a rented carriage with horses to make calls on his patients. One afternoon, after he had finished his calls, he dismissed the carriage and went for a walk. After enjoying the many gardens that he passed, he found himself in front of a house that had a sign, "For Rent." He suddenly experienced a great attraction to this house. He walked in, looked at the apartment that was opened to him, found that it fulfilled all his requirements and immediately signed the lease. This house was Berggasse 19. He went home, told his wife that he had found the ideal place for them and took her that same evening to look at it. Mrs. Freud immediately realized that the house was located in a very poor neighborhood—the Porzellangasse and the Tandelmarkt were near and no physician of repute had his offices located there. They would need two apartments in order to accommodate children and practice. The staircase was steep, dark, and of bare stone. With characteristic intuition Mrs. Freud realized that Freud had to have this house and that no other house would do. So she said that she liked it and that she thought they would be able to manage. They did manage to live in this gloomy and impractical house for forty-seven years.

What could lead so careful and thoughtful a man as Freud to such an impulsive and inconsiderate act and what could keep him for so many years in this house from which he finally had to be driven by the National Socialist storm troopers? The key is to be found in the luncheon to which he refers in this letter. Victor Adler, the founder of the Austrian Socialist Movement, was four years older than Freud and a psychiatrist who at that time outranked Freud in Meynert's laboratory. Freud spent a few happy hours with his host and hostess and with their little son, of whom he used to say, "The future assassin of the War Minister of Austria was then a blond, curly-headed, pretty little boy."

After Freud had left the hospitable Adlers, he found himself in a melancholy mood. Never, he must have thought, would he be able to achieve what Adler had achieved; never would he be able to marry his fiancée; never would he have a son; never would he be a respected member of the community. All his hopes and with them all the hopes of Martha seemed doomed. The simple Adler household must have appeared far beyond his reach at that time, when one considers that almost ten years later when he was already married and had a son of his own, he still unconsciously responded to the vision of fulfillment with the hunger of a struggling young student.

How important this visit to the Adler house must have been for Freud is still further indicated by the confusion about the dates in the letter. When he first mentions the visit, he puts the date at 1883 or 1884. At the end of the letter he says: "One day, perhaps in the year '81 or '82, I met him [Heinrich Braun] on the street, long after we had become strangers. As a matter of course we again immediately talked quite intimately. He showed me the picture of the girl whom he was engaged to marry; and I confessed that I was in the same situation. Perhaps it was then that he invited me to lunch at Adler's."

The atypical use of the word "confess," which is even more unusual in German, betrays the stress this meeting evoked in him and emphasizes the almost insurmountable obstacles that seemed to be lying in the way of his own marriage. Here he was confronted by a friend who was engaged and whose attractive sister had already established a family, and by an older colleague who had achieved everything for which he was still longing. We can infer how he felt upon seeing this little boy when we remember that thirteen years later he was to write to Fliess: ". . . I want to tell you how glad I was to hear your family news. . . . You have a son and with him the prospect of other children; I did not want to admit either to you or to myself what you would have missed when the hope for him was still distant."

Mrs. Freud's understanding of her husband was justified. Despite all the limitations of this house they lived in it happily and successfully. Fifteen years after they had moved into Berggasse, Freud discov ered for himself the impulse which had compelled him to choose this house, and this unassuming building that had had a private history for Freud achieved in time a new historical significance as the world center for psychoanalysis.

The Living Image of Freud

(1956)

FREDERICK J. HACKER

Frederick J. Hacker is a psychoanalyst in Beverly Hills, California. He has a long-standing interest in Freud and the history of psychoanalysis, and recently co-founded the Freud Society. This selection first appeared in the Bulletin of the Menninger Clinic 20 *(1956): 103–11.*

Some apology and explanation may be in order when a relatively young psychoanalyst expresses his homage to Freud's birthday not by a contribution demonstrating the fruitfulness of Freud's discoveries, but by explicit remarks about the master himself, his person and his work.

At first glance, it might appear as if we knew a great deal about Freud: some of us remember him personally; his early collaborators and pupils have published their memoirs; painstaking research continuously unearths new letters and information about little-noticed incidents of his daily life; Freud's part of the correspondence with his only friend Fliess is declared, with suspiciously precipitous haste and enthusiasm, as the valid substitute for his personal analysis; and, after the recent detailed and admirable biography by Ernest Jones, the consensus of psychoanalytic opinion seems to indicate that all legitimate curiosity about the man Freud has been satisfied—all the more so since he himself did not at all encourage any further inquiries concerning his personality and his life.

In some of the most brilliant essays of world literature (about Dostoevski and Leonardo da Vinci), Freud showed how much can be gained in understanding of artistic and scientific creation by intimate knowledge of its author. However, in his own case, he frequently expressed the wish to recede completely behind his work. He did not want to be considered beyond the carefully edited statements he reluctantly made about himself. The creator of the most "indiscreet" science, which insists on the absolute, complete, and full disclosure of everything as its immutable therapeutic and research principle, was himself uncompromisingly discreet. He defended his right of personal privacy with more than conventional insistence and even reproached one of his favorite pupils for being not an inaccurate but an unauthorized biographer, as if the interest in greatness could ever be controlled by special permission.

Freud's name is so much identified with psychoanalysis, not only as its founder, but as its most creative and productive contributor, that many inner conflicts have to be faced by any psychoanalyst when talking about Freud in any but the usual ways. Most psychoanalytic papers begin with a Freud quotation, often end with another one, and the bulk of their content is either a confirmation, modification, or at times a tentative reformulation of a Freud thesis. The master's picture hangs on the walls of our consultation rooms; our libraries are full of books by him and about him; our working day consists largely in the constant application of his theories to our therapeutic task; and as he has taught us never to stop asking "why" and "how," we hourly agree with him, wrestle with him, debate with him. We are socially singled out, admired, feared, or derided because of our special intimate relation to his science; we are his spokesmen, his crusading knights, his representatives. For us, psychoanalysis is not only our science but also our daily occupation, our livelihood, our pride, or our personal conflict. Psychoanalysis determines our way of life, and our critics tell us that it has become our substitute for life, our escape, our religion, our racket, our obsession, our grand rationalization, and our prison.

Innumerable ties connect us with the founder of our science, who was also the organizer and head of our professional organizations; all kinds of subtle, intimate, secret relations exist between the venerable and awesome Freud figure and the group (or horde) of his sons and grandsons. Sincere admiration for his genius combines with "objective" appreciation of his contributions and respect for his honesty and integrity to enforce observance of Freud's taboo against undue curiosity about his inner life. But as this veil of respect covers up our often ambivalent emotions, it also removes the man Freud from our gaze and makes his person as remote on his one-hundredth birthday as his theories retain their burning actuality.

Of course, nothing could be more vulgar than the crude, debunking approach that confuses pseudo-intimacy with knowledge. Nothing is less revealing than to call a great man disturbed, neurotic, or contradictory. Nothing is cheaper than the glib satisfaction of showing that Freud, too, had his foibles, his prejudices, his irrationalities, and his symptoms. Yet, has not the theory and practice of psychoanalysis made us detectives by reflex, so to speak; does not the presence of a taboo alert us by unconscious habit to look into its motivations? Freud has convincingly demonstrated that the very presence of a taboo constitutes an unconscious challenge to the searching intellect. Hence, I cannot think of any more timely task than to try to rediscover Freud, or some aspects of him, for ourselves as a personal, living, present experience before he has completely ossified into the remote monument of "the great man." His familiar picture as the sage of Vienna, sitting seriously and in somewhat Olympian fashion behind his desk, peering at us with searching and critical eyes, hides as much as it reveals of the phenomenon Freud, that largely transformed and created today's world. The authoritarian liberal, the discreet discoverer of the curative value of indiscretion, the sober scientist with a passion for dreams, art and the obscure origins, the dissector of faith with a burning faith in humanity—Freud, this epitome of modern man, was not at all like the Freud legend.

His external life seems indeed so devoid of any striking and dramatic experiences as to discourage even the most persistent seeker of the human-interest story. Even the strained efforts of generations of critics have not been able to throw the slightest shadow on his integrity and his sober fairness or his personal conduct, which complied with all the demands of the same conventional morality that he had discovered to be repressive, rigid, and even dishonest. Surely this is neither coincidence nor an overlooked detail, but significant for the inner law of this puzzling personality. The man who, with the bold daring of a revolutionary genius, questioned all the comfortable assumptions of bourgeois life and found them wanting, behaved in his personal sphere as if he were just another fairly successful practicing physician of his day. He was constantly dissatisfied, complained and grumbled, but never rebelled. In strict compliance with the specific moral code that he had discredited, he was a model paterfamilias of a respectable household, inconspicuously living an average existence in an atmosphere which he presumably hated and despised.

He came to Vienna as a four-year-old boy and remained there for 76 years, although his complaints about this city never ceased. He felt uncomfortable among the feudal trimmings of Viennese social and academic life and stifled by its reluctance to move ahead. In many letters he expressed his admiration for the much more active and progressive Berlin and his utter dislike of static Vienna, which did not appreciate him and rejected all of his efforts by ridicule or, even worse, by a stubborn refusal to take cognizance of his existence. Early in his life he recognized his better opportunities for a lucrative practice elsewhere —a consideration not unimportant to Freud, who could never permit himself to forget that he had been a poor Jewish immigrant and had to defend himself against a basically hostile environment. Even his formulation of the reality principle betrays the scarcity-economics of his own poverty in youth and his fear of poverty in later years.

He also knew that he was the best living example of the prophet's lot in his own country. At a time when his fame had spread around the entire world, he was still regarded in Vienna with disgust, treated as a nobody or with slightly ridiculing condescension. On his seventieth birthday no representative of the University congratulated him, and the Nobel prize-winning professor of psychiatry recommended him, with heavy-handed irony, for a Nobel prize in literature, thereby relegating his discoveries to the realm of fiction.

Yet for 46 years he inhabited the same modest apartment in a shabby district of Vienna, a few steps away from the University which had so bitterly wounded him by deliberate neglect as much as by its malicious reluctance to grant him the coveted professor title, which he finally had to obtain by engaging in hateful, political wire-pulling. Even when, in 1938, Hitler's army forcibly occupied Austria, he still refused to leave Vienna and almost missed the last opportunity to escape his barbaric opponents, who recognized and hated him as one of their prime enemies, before he, the great psychologist, finally awoke to the realization of his mortal danger.

What strange attraction this town, in which he remained a life-long outsider, must have had for him! Freud did not belong—at first because he could not and then because he would not belong. For many decades he stood alone and lonely, his longing for recognition breaking through in frequent bitter remarks, until his remarkable "nerve of failure" turned rejection into the self-chosen fate of splendid isolation.

Indeed, no greater contrast is thinkable than the one between the non-joiner Freud and the gregarious Vienna of his day. Of course, Vienna was never like its Hollywood image—a city of eternal leisure, erupting into incessant singing, dancing and carousing; nor did it consist exclusively of coffee-house-visiting, waltzing party-goers, and gallant aristocrats or their bourgeois imitators. But Vienna did have a world-famous opera (which Freud's wife loved to frequent, although she regularly missed the first act of every performance in order to be present at the family's evening meal). Vienna loved its music in all forms and its many excellent theaters. Composers, writers, poets, actors and actresses, the masters and servants of the beautiful illusion— they were the invariable conversational topics of the intellectual bourgeoisie, to which Freud would have belonged if he had belonged to any social group. Freud admitted that music meant little to him but, curiously enough, he also managed to keep himself almost completely aloof from any direct contact with contemporary literature. He preferred to use "safe" literary references from the classics Goethe and Schiller, from C. F. Meyer and Shakespeare, while avoiding any personal meeting or closeness with his writing contemporaries, although among them were such kindred souls as Beer-Hoffman, Altenberg, Wassermann, Hofmannsthal, Karl Kraus, and even Schnitzler, the doctor-colleague who lived only a few blocks away and whose main themes are poetic variations on Freudian ideas. It seems as if Freud almost insisted on his isolation, from which he suffered so bitterly that he considered himself lacking in a basic quality of lovability; after his famous initial rebuff by the medical fraternity, he did not want to bother or to be bothered, particularly not by representatives of the Vienna Medical School, which then stood at the peak of its fame as the world's most renowned center of medical science. More and more, he remained aloof, without many connections and without any intimate friends, alone with his family, his patients and his pupils, an isolated rock in the turbulent sea of the imperial city around him.

The mood of much-praised and much-maligned Vienna was utterly sophisticated and utterly conservative, tolerant from an abundance of skeptical knowledge, completely persuaded only by the one conviction that nobody or nothing deserved to be taken seriously. Vienna was charming and charmed, cautious and mistrustful of any new idea or of any fundamental change that might upset the precarious balance of the slowly and elegantly decaying empire that concealed behind its façade of splendor the signs of inevitable dissolution. The Viennese were cultured, gentle, well mannered, witty, gay, ironical, constantly ready for any compromise that would preserve the *status quo,* or at least its appearance. The favorite Austrian way of making decisions was to delay them interminably, if they could not be avoided altogether. Not only were sleeping dogs left to lie, they were lulled to sleep by the many sweet diversions of existence. Nothing was "either-or"; every-thing, "a little bit of this and that." Being and appearing, reality and fancy imperceptibly merged into each other to produce the durable Viennese mixture of lightheaded muddling-through, of elastic inflexi-bility and gay melancholy.

Freud was the embittered and enthusiastic antagonist of this at-mosphere that denied conflicts by ridicule, in order never to have to come to grips with them. He hated the half-hearted and tentative, noncommital acceptance of half-solutions and continuous escapes which offered themselves with seductive reasonableness as the best possible way out. He wanted a way *into* problems. He mercilessly dragged them to the surface and exposed them, with the fanaticism of the incorruptible truth-searcher, to the penetrating Klieg-light of ob-jectivity. He insisted stubbornly on calling things by their right names.

There was never any lack of clarity in Freud. His masterly eco-nomic prose reports soberly, without ingratiating phrases of hopeful-ness or consolation, what he saw and heard, what he concluded, and what he foresaw as possibility. Surrounded by sloppiness, this proudly upheld Viennese vice, he stressed clinical exactitude as the main scien-tific virtue. He refused to accept the irresponsible relief of the quick aphorism as the coin with which to honor the sacred obligation to the pursuit of truth. Against an all-pervading immobilism, he had the courage to develop an all-comprehensive system of human function-ing. He is the only twentieth century thinker with the sweep of the great system-builders, without their naïveté or their dogmatism. In a world of conciliatory delay, he knew no compromise. He disdained to change even a word of what he believed to be true for the sake of bet-ter effect. He would rather antagonize friend and foe than make the slightest concession, although he was, at the same time, ever ready to revise or discard important parts of his theory when new observations gave him new ideas. With little humor and no pathos, he pursued the first things up to the last consequence until the ultimate limits of rec-ognition were reached, a radical indeed in his undeviating determina-tion to penetrate to the very origins, to the individual and collective sources and beginnings.

The Socratic insight into the inevitable limitations of the intellect stood at the start of Freud's scientific career. He realized that com-plete knowledge was as unachievable as the three other great impossi-bilities: he said that one could neither govern, nor educate, nor heal. But he did not rest until he knew more about human beings than anybody before him. He did not stop until he had found the seemingly obscure answers to why people permit others to guide them, why people want to learn and how they can be taught, and what can relieve man of the terrible afflictions that the secret alliance between his drives and the frustrating forces of the world has brought down upon him. He did not relent in his inquiries until the last symptom had been explained and the very last refuge of self-deception exposed, and thus he found, in the innermost recesses of the individual's unconscious, the universals of human existence.

Why, then, did Freud remain tied to Vienna, which stood for everything he hated and despised? He suffered a whole life long, not only spiritually but personally, from its snobbish social structure that excluded him, from its oppressive Catholicism that inhibited and disgusted him, and from its false surface optimism that buried every serious problem. It would be too easy to explain Freud's ambivalence—his hatred of Vienna and his inability to break away from it—by stating that it provided him with material for observation; nor could it have been merely habit or economic factors that tied him to his home. Only a Freud could give the real explanation for this peculiar phenomenon, and it is indeed regrettable, though quite characteristic of him, that he did not let us have the most exciting of all adventure-stories of the mind, the greatest of all psychological documents—namely, a complete report of Freud's psychoanalysis by Freud himself; for, despite his uneventful life, he was probably the most complex and intracately fascinating of personalities, reflecting within himself the division and tragedy of modern man. Other great persons display many curious facets, but in few of them—except in the closely related Nietzsche and Thomas Mann—do so many trends appear in ever-new shades and nuances on different levels. Rarely has one person combined such strange interconnections and interrelations between seemingly contradictory elements which yet somehow belong together, and never before dared a man explore all of these inner possibilities to their last consequence in the clear light of rational consciousness until they yielded their secrets—in everybody else except himself.

The tenacious love-hate relationship to Vienna serves as only one of many possible illustrations of the strangely interlocked complexity of Freud's being. Even now, it is almost impossible to decide whether he was the rationalist enlightener, the positivist natural scientist, or the extoller of the night side of life, awed and bewitched by the mystical forces within man. Thomas Mann has asked legitimately, in truly

Freudian spirit, whether Freud's interest in the depths does not betray a close affinity to them. Could the wish to know and to cure be partly a rationalization for the desire to search and remain in the depths? For the unconscious, the secret innermost part of every one and all of us, is not a research object like any other. The first mine-digger of the most intimate must indeed be an adventurer of a very special sort. Did he descend to these depths only to come up with his treasure, and did not every new find send him back to the chthonic abysses of the most sacred taboos? Innumerable passages in his works reveal him as the sober scientist who believes only what he can see and demonstrate. We know of his inimitably masterful clinical dissections, his reluctance and refusal to speculate beyond the well established. We hear him convincingly argue against philosophy; and yet, with his ingenious instinct-theory, with his discoveries of the conservatism of drives, and his grandiose dualistic biopsychological concept, he created, in brilliant speculative strokes, one of the greatest philosophies of all times. And is it conceivably coincidental that he gave his scientific discoveries names from Greek mythology, or that, in the cautious style of the modest observer, he developed the most extravagant theories of past and present, which implicitly also contain his prognosis for the future?

What is his message to mankind? Is it the word of optimistic progress, that the voice of reason, small as it may be, will ultimately triumph; or does he condemn us to an essentially futile struggle, in which every cultural advance necessitates ever more patient instinct-renunciation, thus making the period between birth and the inevitable triumph of the death instinct increasingly more painful? Freud quotations could easily support either view. Critics optionally describe him as "naïve positivist," who ignored the transcendental side of man, or as "unscientific idealist," who succumbed to a speculative bias in theories that are unproved and unprovable. He has been called a typical child of the nineteenth century for his biologizing tendencies, and the promoter of a new pseudo-religion and cult for his insistence on a coherent system. He is designated a mystic for his belief in the possibility that early phylogenetic events are reflected in the individual's unconscious, and a shallow materialist unable to comprehend man except as a conglomeration of various mechanisms.

Freud annihilated the narcissistic pride of man when he showed that he was not even master in his own inner household; he destroyed the soothing illusion of some religious beliefs and the deception of the fairy tale that we are born good and become bad only as we are exposed to a bad world. He was a determined revolutionary because he penetrated the taboos of the various hidden forms of sexuality with the intention to liberate by recognizing, and he succeeded. Implicitly and explicitly, he became a critic of the prevailing forms of sexual and social control and showed their repressive, neurosis-producing character. Yet to many he appears as a reactionary, incapable of conceiving fundamental changes in human nature, an old-fashioned bourgeois who perpetuated the social system which moulded him, a willing instrument or unwitting dupe of those who wanted to continue man's exploitation of man. Can it be that the cosmopolitan Freud was so provincially narrow as to believe in the universality of certain conflicts produced by passing sociological constellations? How can the same man stress the significance of history, of the time category, for mental life, thereby discovering the exciting dynamics of mental functioning, and yet insist on the basic immutability of the instinctual organization and the psychic apparatus? Was the individual for Freud the last developmental product of evolution or just a temporary historical manifestation of the ever-constant, supra-individual forces of Eros and Thanatos? Did he seek the cure of society through the individual and was an increase in universal happiness his goal, or did he forget about society in his concern for the sick individual?

It is one of Freud's most original contributions that his phylogenetic and ontogenetic concept of the individual is at all times explicit sociology. Even the earliest conflict situations he describes as occurring between the child and the persons in his environment. The social category thus is not later superimposed but exists as crucial from the very beginning. But equally strong is Freud's biological emphasis, the insistence that the crucial conflict situations are inevitable projection products of a growing biological structure. Was Freud's real concern with the complexities of the sick, whom he wanted to cure by understanding, or with the problems of the so-called healthy in society? Were his sympathies with the Id, that he wanted to liberate; or with the Superego, that he wanted to reduce so that it could control better; or with the Ego, that he wanted to extend and strengthen, while reminding us constantly how fragile, temporary and incomplete this victory must necessarily be?

What is the *real* Freud? And where can we find him—in his clinical papers, in *Beyond the Pleasure Principle*, in his *Moses and Monotheism?*

All these very real Freuds together do not lend themselves easily to

331

the justification of orthodoxy or the administration of a dogmatic creed in his name. But the temptation to forget the obligation of his heritage —to ruthlessly question, examine and re-examine everything around ourselves and within ourselves—is all the stronger the more successful and respectable psychoanalysis becomes. To remain faithful to this main psychoanalytical duty was relatively easy when a small, cohesive group of scientific outcasts had to fight the whole world in order to be heard and to be believed. This fight has been won. The most cursory glance around the contemporary scene will confirm the modern miracle that psychoanalysis, possibly just because of Freud's refusal to compromise, has conquered on all fronts. Psychoanalytic terms have become household words; psychoanalytic concepts are the conversational topics of educated and uneducated alike; all forms of psychotherapy live off psychoanalytic insights; the theater, poetry, the novel, all bear the indelible imprint of psychoanalytic insight; psychoanalysis has decisively influenced all modern sciences—medicine, biology, psychology, sociology, anthropology, education, philosophy, theology, even physics. The Freudians have become a powerful, large organization, its members widely respected and with income and prestige close to the top of the professional hierarchy.

With this growing recognition by the formerly hostile or indifferent world, serious new problems have arisen that should give us thoughtful pause when self-gratulation, naturally enough, enters into the mood of Freud's birthday celebration. For to quote him, to teach his insights, to apply his message and extol his genius is not enough if we are to avoid a repetition of Dostoevski's famous Grand Inquisitor scene, when the faithful pupils chase away the returning master (after considering the idea of executing him) so that he will not prevent them, by new deeds, from practicing his teachings and ruling in his name.

Freud has taught us that recognition alone is not sufficient. The manifold mechanisms of the mind, the ingenious tricks and schemes of the unconscious, the narcissistic deceptions, cleverly concealed scotomata and skillful projections permit the pursuit of truth (not absolute truth but man's best truth) only at the price of eternal vigilance and never-relaxing radical search. The living image of Freud must not be obscured behind the venerable mask of the Viennese professor. For he who treated the smallest symptom of the sick and the largest manifestation of social life in the same unmistakable style, with his unheard-of combination of objective detachment and violent phantasy, was very different from the current cliché picture of him. The stereotype of the inaccessible and unreachable genius should not stifle continuing controversy with him and about him.

Because Freud lived, the forces of individual and collective repression will never triumph again as completely or as unrecognized as before. Mankind may consciously or unconsciously attempt to forget as hard as it may; the vision of the central significance of sexuality, which propels and reflects the truly human development from biological to mature love, and the recognition that the complex laws of man's inner bondage are also his only means of liberation will never be totally erased from consciousness. The edifice of psychoanalysis mirrors the image of the founder by the unity of startling complexity and utter simplicity. All the subtleties and amazing ramifications of psychoanalysis, the most self-reflective, most skeptical, most sophisticated theory of human motivation are based on Freud's surprisingly simple and humane approach: he listened without interruption and recorded without distortion. In the despised waste products of the mind—in dreams, slips and phantasies—he found the truth; in suffering man, he found man himself and the essence of his humanity.

Freud's Mother and Father

(1956)

JUDITH BERNAYS HELLER

Judith Bernays Heller wrote this selection for Commentary 21 (1956): 418–21. *It was preceded by the following comment:*

> Sigmund Freud, born a hundred years ago on May 6, was the first to demonstrate the all-important influence of parents on the psychic life of people. It is entirely appropriate therefore that we should mark the occasion with a niece's memoir of Freud's parents that shows them–especially his mother–in a light rather different from that in which he (and his biographers) have let us see them. Judith Bernays Heller is the daughter of Freud's sister Anna, who married Ely Bernays, who was himself the brother of Freud's wife Martha. Mrs. Heller was born in Vienna but has lived most of her life in this country. Educated at Barnard College, she taught for some years in the public schools of New York City. Her Austrian-born husband, Dr. Victor Heller, was a research economist with the federal government until his death.

Before embarking upon an account of my impressions of Sigmund Freud's parents, who were my own maternal grandfather and grandmother, it might be well to give some account of myself.

My life from the age of six on has swung back and forth between the Old World and the New. It started when my father and mother left me and my younger sister Lucy behind in our native city of Vienna, while they, accompanied by our younger brother Edward, emigrated to the United States. There, Father hoped to find better conditions in which to establish himself. My sister was left with our aunt and uncle, and I in the care of our maternal grandparents, the father and mother of Sigmund Freud, my mother's brother.

We were sent for a year later, and traveled to the United States under the protection of one of Mother's sisters, Aunt Paula. Mother received regular news of her brothers and sisters. She would describe Vienna to us with a kind of nostalgia that endowed it with glamor. As a matter of fact, the first money that I ever earned—teaching in the New York public schools for several years—I spent on a trip to Europe. But even before that, Mother had taken all five of us children abroad to visit our grandparents on both sides—the Freuds and the Bernayses, and we had come to know our cousins, the children of Sigmund Freud and of my mother's sisters.

During my first journey on my own, I spent weeks in the Freud home. Then the First World War separated us for four long years. When I returned to Vienna in 1921, it was like coming back to a second home. Again I stayed with the Freuds, and was proud to be permitted to translate three of my uncle's papers into English; these were published in 1924 by the Hogarth Press in London, as part of the International Psychoanalytical Library. Then, when I married an Austrian economist, Dr. Victor Heller, Vienna became my home once more, which did not displease me.

Subsequently, I journeyed back to the United States several times to see my family and to renew my American citizenship, which I prized. And in 1938, with Hitler's annexation of Austria, I returned to this country for good, accompanied by my husband.

Sigmund Freud himself, as well as others, spoke about his father— in the *Interpretation of Dreams,* in his letters to Fliess, and in his autobiographical writings. It was my privilege as a child to be quite close for a time to this patriarchal figure, whose room I shared during the year that I remained in Vienna while my parents were establishing themselves in New York.

That was in 1892–93, when Sigmund Freud was living with his wife and four children in a modest apartment not far from my grandparents, with whom three grown daughters and their youngest son, just starting out with a newspaper, were still staying.

I cannot say who really supported this establishment. I do know that my grandfather was no longer working, but divided his time between reading the Talmud (in the original) at home, sitting in a coffee house, and walking in the parks. Occasionally, he took me with him, when the others were too busy to occupy themselves with me. Tall and broad, with a long beard, he was very kind and gentle, and humorous in the bargain—much more so than my grandmother, whom I really feared, though I admired her stateliness and the nice clothes she wore when she went out with her friends.

It seems to me, as I look back now, that Freud's father lived somewhat aloof from the others in his family, reading a great deal—German and Hebrew (not Yiddish)—and seeing his own friends away from

335

home. He would come home for meals, but took no real part in the general talk of the others. It was not a pious household, but I do remember one Seder at which I, as the youngest at the table, had to make the responses to the reading of the song about the sacrifice of the kid; I was greatly impressed by the way my grandfather recited the ritual, and the fact that he knew it by heart amazed me. I liked, too, to hear the stories he would tell about my mother, who, as eldest daughter, seemed to have been his pet; he held her up to me as an example to follow.

But what I think struck me most about my maternal grandfather was how, in the midst of this rather emotional household, with its three young women who sometimes did not get on well with one another, and their mother, who was usually troubled and anxious—probably with financial worries—he remained quiet and imperturbable, not indifferent, but not disturbed, never out of temper and never raising his voice. My grandmother, on the other hand, had a volatile temperament, would scold the maid as well as her daughters, and rush about the house.

It was not a very spacious apartment. As I have said, I had to share my grandfather's bedroom; the three daughters, grown young women, shared one room with my grandmother, and the young son had a dark little room facing the court; while the maid, as was customary in Vienna at that time, slept on a folding cot that was opened up at night in the kitchen, I believe, while it stood in the hall under a cover in the daytime. I do not remember whether there was a bathroom in the place, but I know that I was usually washed by being stood in a basin and sponged down. The whole place was simpler and less comfortable in every way than my parents' home had been and, of course, it was not home, in spite of the kindness of my three young aunts and grandfather. I greatly envied my sister, who had been left in the Sigmund Freud household, where there were three boys and a girl to play with. When I was brought there so that we might play together once in a while, I hated to go back to my grandparents', where there were only grown-ups, among them my somewhat shrill and domineering grandmother.

I cannot remember any special incident that might account for the prejudice that I had and continued to have all my life against my grandmother. She was a fine-looking woman, efficient, and capable in the household, lively and sociable, much visited by friends, and loved

and honored by her children until her death at ninety-five. Was it because I already felt as a child that she preferred the male members of
her brood to the female ones? I did not get to know her really until
many, many years later, when I returned to Austria as a young girl and
spent the summer with one of my married aunts in Ischl, the resort
where my grandmother kept house with the single unmarried daughter who had been designated by the family to stay and look after her.
She was still handsome and upstanding then, with a fine head of gray
hair that was combed *à la Pompadour* every morning by a hairdresser.

She had many friends and acquaintances and spent the afternoons
playing cards with them at the coffee and tea "stations," as they were
called, in the woods and villages around Ischl, then the summer residence of the Austrian emperor. My aunt, who did not play cards,
would be forced to go with her, whether she liked it or not, and when
I was around I would trot along, too, very unwillingly, for although I
did not mind the walk, I hated just to sit around and watch the elderly
ladies at their tarock or poker. I think my prejudice against cards was
founded there and then.

My grandmother did not like us to go off by ourselves; at the time I
thought that she was a most selfish old lady and altogether disap-
proved of her. And she no less of me. She could not take pride in a
young girl who did not care to promenade in her best dress up and
down the Esplanade while the band was playing; who preferred, instead, to spend her mornings in rough clothes, climbing round the
rocks on the mountain paths, or sitting on hidden benches with her
nose buried in some book that was surely not suitable for her. But she
made no effort to discipline or change me; after all, was I not going
back to New York in the fall, where such behavior might be proper?
There was no mistaking her lack of interest in all that concerned me.

My grandmother's delight in card-playing persisted throughout her
life. In her nineties, when she had grown feeble and was no longer
able to go out, her partners would come to the house for a game. She
would play dominoes with her young grandsons and even a great-
grandson, and be very angry if they did not play with concentration,
or if they "let her win," as she said, out of deference to her age. She
kept her interest in making a good appearance on appropriate occasions until almost the last year of her life. When there was a special invitation, as for instance to the celebration of my uncle Sigmund's seventieth birthday in 1926 (when she was already ninety), she insisted

that she be bought a new dress and hat to go to the *Jause* (coffee party) at his house. She had to be carried down the stairs from her own home and up the stairs to the Freuds', but she did not mind that so long as she could be present to be honored and feted as the mother of her "golden son," as she called her Sigmund.

She was charming and smiling when strangers were about, but I, at least, always felt that with familiars she was a tyrant, and a selfish one. Quite definitely, she had a strong personality and knew what she wanted, and the best evidence of that is the way she held her two sons and five daughters together, in spite of all the divergences and differences in their interests and their temperaments. And she had a sense of humor, being able to laugh at, and at times even ridicule, herself. I remember her saying to me, when I was supposed to choose some present for myself from her cabinet, where she kept a few treasured antiques: "After all, the best antique in my house is myself, and me you cannot take." She was eighty-four at the time.

Among her other good qualities was the fact that she was not a complainer. You did not hear her bewail the privations and difficulties of the First World War; she did not groan about the weaknesses attendant on old age. Even when she broke her arm at eighty-five and had to give up her beloved crocheting and knitting, she did not waste time pitying herself, but praised the doctor, her children who had nursed her so patiently, and the friends who had come to help her pass the time.

Some of the more intimate of her son Sigmund's student-patients made a point of paying their respects to her regularly, and she would tell them stories about her "golden son," as well as about her "darling Alexander," and her faithful and devoted daughters—more particularly, the next to the youngest of them, Dolfi, who had been chosen by her brothers to take care of their mother.

Whenever Dolfi went out my grandmother would stand at the window watching for her return, and not be content or easy until she saw her. There was a story in the family that when Dolfi was young she had had a chance to marry and found a family of her own, but had been dissuaded by her brothers, who preferred to have her there looking after their mother. As it was, when Grandmother at last died this poor aunt of mine, then not far from seventy herself, was completely broken and left without any real interest or purpose in life. Only later, when two of her widowed sisters came to live with her, one a refugee from Nazi Berlin, did her spirits pick up again.

338

I think that one of the circumstances that helped reinforce my impression of my grandmother's selfishness was the fact that she so successfully used her increasing deafness in order to avoid hearing what she did not want to hear—principally the report of any event that might require her to bestow an extra measure of sympathy or consolation upon some member of the family. She was over seventy by the time I noticed this, but still hale and hearty enough to stand up to such obligations had she wanted to. Thus, when a young granddaughter died tragically at the age of twenty-three, and she heard grief-stricken whispers all around her, she manifested no desire to learn their cause, nor was she expressly told of it. When the bereaved mother came to see her she never asked about the girl, nor did she inquire afterwards about her, though this granddaughter had visited her frequently in the past. Ten years later, however, she began to talk again about "poor Cecily," revealing that she had been fully aware all along of what had happened. . . .

My grandmother's sitting room on Sunday mornings was the weekly meeting place for her busy sons, her daughters and daughters-in-law, her grandchildren and their children. Even when convalescing from operations and illness, Professor Freud would always find time of a Sunday morning to pay his mother a visit and give her the pleasure of petting and making a fuss over him. When he could not come, her younger son, Alexander, with his son would be there to listen to all her troubles, and to those of his unmarried sister, too, and he would comfort them with promises of finding remedies. Though both brothers shared equally in the financial support of the female members of the family, one might say that Sigmund, the elder, was more the moral support, while Alexander, the younger, was more the practical one. Both were looked up to as the strong and successful males of the family.

When my grandmother was younger, there had been family reunions at Uncle Sigmund's house one evening a week, but these were discontinued when she began to find it more difficult to climb the stairs. Aunt Martha often accompanied Uncle Sigmund on his Sunday morning visits, and when she did not, she and her sister, Minna Bernays, who was now living permanently with them, made a point of coming to see my grandmother some time during the week. Relations between Aunt Martha and my grandmother were unmarred as long as I can remember.

My grandmother died in the fall of 1930, after several weeks of great weakness, of no particular ailment aside from old age and a worn-out body. Up to the last four months, she had continued to make her will felt and had insisted that, instead of spending the summer in Vienna, she be taken to her beloved Ischl in the mountains as before. Everybody was against it: her sons, the doctor, her daughters. But she had her way. She had to be carried to the train on a stretcher, looked after in her sleeping-car compartment by her doctor, and taken to her country apartment in an ambulance. But once there, she rallied for a while and sat on her balcony, enjoying both the view of the mountains and the consciousness that she was Ischl's oldest summer guest. Towards the end of summer, however, she grew weaker, and two weeks after her return to Vienna she fell into a coma and died peacefully.

With her going, the strong and vivid bond that held the family together was broken.

Personal Memories of Freud
(1956)

RENÉ LAFORGUE

René Laforgue, one of France's outstanding psychoanalysts, knew Freud for many years. This selection was first presented by Laforgue as a lecture at the Lindauer Psychothera- piewoche in May 1954. It then appeared in French in Action Pensée, *Geneva, 1956. It was translated from the French by Dr. Richard McConchie.*

Here is how the treatment of my first paranoiac took place. It gave me the opportunity to discover what real humanity could be hidden be- hind the symptomatic façade. This case was followed by many similar ones, habitually advised against by Freud, but he let me do as I pleased under the circumstances. It was through these treatments that I truly learned the meaning of the neurotic defense mechanisms of the self and of their action in certain social situations. Freud's tolerance and perspicacity were also demonstrated, contrasting with his preoc- cupation to establish clear, precise, and at times too rigid rules about psychoanalytic treatment.

One often mentions the contradictory aspects of his personality in speaking of the good and the bad Freud, but it is important to distin- guish one from the other. He himself was not unaware of his need to have in each friend an enemy; he does not, however, tell us whether he is treating the enemy as a friend or vice versa. He was aware of his own ambivalence about men and their problems. On the other hand, Freud does not seem to have realized to what extent this ambivalence was conditioned by his own religious superego. I happened to become acquainted with his negative aspect without however being overly im- pressed by it. I had always considered it as a façade behind which the other aspect was hidden, for he had in him treasures of loyalty, of ab- negation, and of a spirit of sacrifice for which he did not ask recogni- tion. All those who find themselves in the situation of pioneers, work- ing for the development of a science, will understand the price.

One day one of Freud's collaborators told about the story of Schwind's painting of St. Hieronymus. It took place at Freud's house at the close of a lecture by one of his pupils on the Ego. After having given his opinion on the discourse, Freud spoke about Schwind's painting which showed the saint selling his soul to the devil to get the materials necessary for the construction of a cathedral. Freud asked his listeners who, in their opinion, represented the saint and who the devil. Naturally, everyone replied that Freud was the saint. "You don't know then that I am the devil?" he exclaimed. "During my lifetime I have had to play the role of the devil in order that others might construct cathedrals with the materials I have brought." Even if this anecdote is not authentic—and there is no reason to doubt the veracity of the person who told it—it corresponds to reality. It is Freud, the atheist, to whom we are beholden for our knowledge of the role of faith and myth in the development of the ego, on both the individual and collective planes.

Here is another anecdote showing how lonely was Freud's struggle to impose his truth. Mme Freud was a practical woman, marvelously skillful in creating an atmosphere of peace and *joie de vivre*. Moreover, she was an excellent housewife, a rather rare phenomenon in a milieu such as hers. She and her daughter Anna never hesitated to do things themselves and were not afraid to peel potatoes or to plant vegetables in the garden. She never cultivated that sickly pallor fashionable with so many female intellectuals, nor did she appear to comprehend much about her husband's work. During one of my trips to Vienna she asked my advice about a problem, a tic which troubled a little boy of her acquaintance. I told her of my astonishment at her addressing herself to me and not to her husband. She replied with her customary frankness, "Do you really think one can employ psychoanalysis with children? I must admit that if I did not realize how seriously my husband takes his treatments, I should think that psychoanalysis is a form of pornography!"

The science elaborated by Freud has now moved beyond its purely medical framework. We are familiar with the knowledge it has permitted us to acquire in the domains of criminology, the social sciences, and history—art, civilizations, languages. Moreover, one realizes that knowledge of individual conflicts permits us to understand collective conflicts. Studying the mechanisms of paranoia, for example, shows us in miniature what one can observe on a larger scale in the revolutions which shake the earth. One cannot but admire the astonishing energy with which Freud cleared his path, braving the incomprehension and the mockery of the world; and that until he wavered under the load which he had assumed. His success is explained by the necessity which men of a disturbed epoch must accept in order to master, by help of the intellect, the sense of guilt dormant in the unconscious and by the need to illuminate the depths from which a new humanity may emerge. Psychoanalysis has permitted us to understand that the individual ego is part of a collective ego and that the life of the one can be affected by the sacrifice or even the death of the other. Freud foresaw all that. How many times did he give one of his pupils Faust's answer to Wagner: "You will not be able to acquire it if you do not feel it, if it does not come from the soul and joyously force its way into the heart of the listener."

Who could reproach Freud for having become bitter beneath the weight of the general incomprehension he met, often greater among his fervent enthusiasts than among his adversaries? And let us not forget the painful illness which struck him in his sixtieth year, making it difficult for him to speak.

I remember particularly his 80th birthday, for which I had had a certain number of medals made by the sculptor Nemon. When I showed Freud the medal, he was satisfied with it, adding that he felt as precious as a quintuplet. (The Dionne quintuplets were much spoken of then.) But our celebrity, feted at the University and in all Vienna, took but little part in these solemnities. A colleague gave a learned but interminable panegyric of the master. No one yet dared admit to himself the tragedy which was imminent and how events would strike those whose lives appeared secure forever. We believed in the supremacy of reason and the modern spirit, failing to recognize the forces ready to rise into a fratricidal war of nations and peoples. Yet Freud's teaching itself should have enlightened us in time.

As early as 1932, in *Angoisse et Civilisation*, a small book on the libido, I tried to show how the tendencies of peoples can provoke catastrophes, under the thrust of certain conflicts conditioned by collective feelings of guilt and a need for self-punishment. This warning of what was going to happen was published in vain, as is always the case. Precisely those who ran the greatest risk of being harmed by the circumstances I described responded to it with sharp criticism, categorizing me as an arrogant ambassador of the "Great Nation," for it was impossible for them to consider the situation from a point of view other than personal or national. I came to Vienna in 1937 to advise Freud, among others, to leave his country. He responded almost with contempt: "The Nazis? I am not afraid of them. Help me rather to combat my true enemy." Astonished, I asked him just which enemy was in question, and I heard him reply: "Religion, the Roman Catholic Church." I have already said that Freud as an old man had slipped into ideology. Nine years earlier, he himself had warned me of what could be expected from him. However, his response was a trial to me.

In spite of all we know, we wish the ego of an individual to remain identical throughout its existence. Personal and emotional ties attach themselves to the image we have made of a person, all the more because we venerate him. Our education has created the habit of not questioning what significant people affirm. We believe in the teaching of our masters, in the precision of schedule, in the predictions of the weather reports, or the effectiveness of a remedy or a mineral water for which we have seen advertisements. We also almost automatically believe in the value of our cultural principles, in the persuasive force of reason; nothing, up to the present, has prepared us for the fact that this faith is not based on unshakable foundations.

So in 1937 Freud still believed in his safety and found it beneath his dignity to think that public events could suddenly deprive him of the very bases of the life he had so painfully constructed. In attempting to get me to adopt an anti-religious position, he was following a very old tradition, as if this were the most important or even the only problem of the hour. The moment had come for me to break officially with this narrowly anti-clerical tradition, so out of place under the circumstances; the more so because the position taken by Freud would evoke a reaction opposite to what he anticipated. He considered religious practices equivalent to obsessional neuroses. He did not perceive the enormous difference between a ritual freely practiced out of religious conviction, and the behavior of the obsessional neurotic who has no choice, since he is unable to free himself of the constraint of his obsessional ideas. In denying man the possibility of abreacting conflicts with his super-ego by means of religious practices, Freud risked condemning him to neutralize, by symptoms varying in gravity, guilt remaining unexpressed. Freud thus transformed a position, irrational perhaps but normal for the time, into an obsessional symptom. He thus ran the risk of encouraging the neurosis and, in the domain of affect, deepening individual and social regression in the name of the very psychoanalysis through which he desired to liberate individuals from their conflicts.

344

I hesitated at first to reply to Freud, paralyzed by my pity for this courageous and unhappy old man. I tried to show him that the fanaticism of religious neurotic fantasies could just as easily be found among atheists; the pathological element not necessarily being conditioned by belief in God. I added that, in my humble opinion, belief in God could not constitute the criterion of neurosis; this appeared in the manner in which the believer handled his faith or the atheist his lack of faith. I did not hide from Freud that I considered his position erroneous, owing to his lack of comprehension of the believer who needs his faith, for whom the church is a symbol of the eternal woman, the mother. Freud himself seemed to react against this position with especial violence. (There are in fact very good reasons for thinking that Freud was quite ambivalent in this respect.) Thereupon, he replied to me with that rather brutal frankness which characterized him: "I cannot follow you in this area, nor moreover in your reasoning in *Relativité de la Realité*." I had just submitted this paper which he dismissed as being "philosophical."

In this paper I tried to introduce in psychology the notions Einstein had introduced into mathematics and physics. From my point of view the intellect is no longer an absolute given, but is conditioned, in part, by affectivity, since the ego is formed by contact with a known context. Certainly, these considerations do not spare ideas on the omnipotence of the ego and of reason. The individual loses his absolute character and, reduced to his constituent elements, becomes a product of energy. Consequently, he is no more than the resonance of innumerable waves of energy, with their interferences. The age-old play of these waves in the unconscious and the conscious would condition the embodiment of individuals in the animal, vegetable, and perhaps mineral realm.

We know how much the modern chemist and physicist regret their former harmonious notion of knowledge, nothing of which remains when one places oneself on the plane of an atomic scientist or of the undulatory mechanism of the great French physicist De Broglie. It is not surprising, therefore, that Freud violently rejected my ideas, telling me: "There is a whole world for other people's theories; my reviews remain open to you, but our paths are separating." I date my divergence from Freud to this precise moment, although divergence is an improper term, for it is really only a matter of the development of the science which we owe to him in great part, a science which must

345

necessarily evolve beyond individuals and their personal reactions on the affective plane.

All this may seem somewhat regrettable, but it is not in the nature of life that we must vanquish the past which has served us as support? In any event, the concepts which Freud leaves us lose nothing of their value. By discovering Plato's Eros in the libido he had opened the way to a new tradition of the spirit. By showing us that the individual's ego is formed by means of successive identifications, Freud showed us the route to be followed. Once again, one can speak of the symbolic aspects of the mind, of metamorphoses of the soul, in an age when materialism seems to have seized all of human thought for all time. Moreover, it is unfortunately only too true that this great precursor believed it necessary to contest with certain of his pupils, and not the least important among them, their right to psychoanalytic thought. Even today the more orthodox disciples of Freud all but forbid mentioning the names of Jung or Maeder in scientific articles. One might well note that the Old Master fostered a narrow dogmatism in his immediate pupils, after having himself returned to materialism. He, who had so well seized the multiple possibilities of the unconscious, began to struggle for a unique faith, that of a science alone capable, according to him, of aiding in the evolution of humanity.

For my part, I have always energetically opposed all sectarianism, and I refuse to share the belief cultivated by certain psychoanalysts that they possess the sole knowledge capable of freeing men from their complexes. I do not hesitate to recognize, for example, that it is to Jung, and his work on schizophrenia, that I owe my first contacts with the problems arising when psychoanalysis is applied to psychiatry. I am far from entire agreement with his many speculations and impressions, yet that does not prevent me from recognizing him as one of those precursors who admits us to knowledge of these forces which the rationalist treats so contemptuously. About Maeder, one can state that few men work as honestly and seriously in this area of ours. His last book, *Le Medecin, Agent Psychotherapeutique*, is rich in these truths with which every real psychoanalyst should familiarize himself.

My position led me to resign from the Paris Psychoanalytic Society; I have fully spelled out my reasons for this in the following letter. After pointing out that I was the pioneer of psychoanalysis in France, founder of the Paris Psychoanalytic Society, initiator of the course in psychoanalysis at Ste Anne, founder and director of the *Revue Fran-*

çaise de Psychanalyse which I presented in 1939 to the Société Française de Psychanalyse as a gift, I continued:

> I recall the alarm I raised at the 1950 Congress of Psychiatry when, at the plenary session at the Sorbonne, I felt it necessary to denounce those who pretended to cure an obsession by substituting the obsession of psychoanalysis or the obsession of nothing more than money. Today I need my liberty, not to protest or to wash our dirty linen in public, but in order to support those young psychoanalysts who, breaking with a policy of usurpation practiced in the guise of psychoanalysis, desire to defend psychoanalysis as a science, and because of this need to be protected against malevolence and lies.

> At all times men have been found who make a career of medicine by exploiting human misery if necessary. At all times, also, the pioneers in the science have clashed with those who conformed to the establishment and, by defending their place, defended their security or their privileges. Sincere psychoanalysts today cannot escape the need to combat conformists and the orthodox. Freud has courageously given the example by breaking with the conformity of the officials of his time. But today conformism has changed sides. Unfortunately for us, it is to be found, paradoxically enough, among psychoanalysts, who replace those whom Freud once denounced as barbarians or enemies of the science when it was a matter of stigmatizing their behavior when they substituted defamation for the arms permitted in scientific discussions.

This letter reached the Paris Psychoanalytic Society on October 22, 1953, and it replied curtly, accepting my resignation. For me, this ends a chapter in French psychoanalysis. A new movement was born almost at the same time: the French Psychoanalytic Society, through which we hope to defend the cause of psychoanalysis in France in a more acceptable spirit.

Such conflicts and such ruptures are inevitable. It is in the nature of life and thought that one-sided attitudes and exaggerations be corrected by opposing, and at times extreme, reactions. It is impossible to consider an ideology recognizing only mechanisms transforming men into robots and reducing the mind-body duality to a monism of matter as uniquely or scientifically valid. Our thought, our European culture, was born of different sources. We are familiar with the ethical and religious treasure of the Greco-Roman tradition, and with the Semitic

347

tradition of the Bible, to which one must add the influences of the Orient, Mesopotamia, Egypt, and Arabia.

We have in large part inherited from the Jews the monotheism which has formed our ethic. But there is a great difference between monotheism as it developed in Europe, and the monism which corresponds to the Semitic tradition. Studying the evolution of these two conceptions helps us to understand their influence and their effects on our modern, scientific manner of thinking. But it would take too long to go into detail on this question. Observing the Arab super-ego, formed by the life of the desert nomad, made it possible for me to distinguish between these two patterns of thought and to understand them better.

My reflections permit me to grasp why psychoanalysis, at a given moment, became a sort of mythology for Freud, or if one wishes, a religion to which it is forbidden to give its true name. Only by understanding the myth which is at the base of this unconscious religion can one explain Freud's rank prejudice about the religious problem, as well as the fanaticism of some of his disciples.

Still, I should like to show the significance of the fact that the cure, theoretically at least, should take place only between the patient and his analyst, and why Freud advises "not to alloy the pure gold of analysis with the impure metal of psychotherapy." One of his fundamental rules is the passive and neutral attitude of the analyst, seated behind the patient without being seen by him, and permitted to appear only impersonally in the process of abreaction and of association. Does it not seem that the analyst is to behave vis-à-vis his analysand as a god whose face one must not see and of whom it is forbidden to make a graven image? It is possible that this tendency corresponds to a very ancient ideology, like that which developed among the Semites of the desert. It is not an accident, in my opinion, that Freud believes that science alone can bring about a successful cure, without the personal example of the psychoanalyst intervening in his dealings with the patient. Belief in the omnipotence of the intellect and of the will, excluding personal contact, is also a product of the desert mind. Averroes, the famed Arab philosopher, taught that the intellect is immortal, but that the soul is mortal. The god of the desert, immaterial, without carnal envelope, is as the sands of the desert, eternal, intangible, merciless. In a strict sense, it can be symbolized by a stone as, for example, the stone of the Kaaba in Mecca or the Tables of the Law of Sinai.

There is certainly a profound reason for the fact that in Europe, north of a certain meridian, it is the water of baptism which puts man in contact with his God, whereas south of this meridian, it is circumcision which establishes the contact. In the north, the European family is represented by the couple, and a certain equality exists between the partners. Human exchange is possible to the extent that one belongs to the other, not as an object of merchandize or an instrument, but as a person. In the south, the family tends more toward a tribe, in which the patriarch considers the wife as an object. These differences are to be noted also in the language, in the notions of time and of space, as well as in art.

North of this meridian, the plastic arts are animated by representations of men, animals, and plants. South, this expression of life vanishes before symmetrical ornament and geometrical line, the sole symbols of affective need of the Semites. Language in the north is based on associations linked with each other by affectivity; language in the south is still constructed from the base of the same primitive roots, changing meaning according to their vocalization.

All these causes naturally have a considerable effect on the structure of the human personality and on men's perception of reality. In *Super-Ego Individuel et Collectif* I tried to characterize this structure, but today I can give only a few indications of the influence it can have on the manner of thinking, on the organization of the emotions, and on life in society. In the north man is conceived in the image of the Trinity, but in the south he is identified with that of the Unique God, with a totalitarian law accepting nothing alongside it which might go beyond it and levelling all as the wind of the desert.

It is from the contact of these opposing mentalities, however, that at times gushes the spark of genius, thanks precisely to the frictions and to the struggles to which it gives birth. I believe that we are indebted for too many discoveries to Freud's brilliant specialization, to his intellect born of the age-old earth of the Jewish tradition, for us to reproach him for being unable to surmount the problem completely. It is for us to recognize the characteristics and limits of this intellect, and to diverge from it when necessary. It is not always an easy task to defend the work of Freud against his own intransigeance which leads him away from his true goal. If, in the beginning, it was useful for the acquisition of our knowledge, psychoanalysis now has the right to free itself from Freud's intransigeance in order to put itself into the service of men.

Freud and the Sculptor

(1956)

HEINRICH MENG

Heinrich Meng, well-known Swiss psychoanalyst, met Freud first in 1918, when as a young physician he went to Vienna to explore the possibilities of psychoanalysis. Freud recommended he study analysis with one of his outstanding pupils, Paul Federn. In later years Meng became active at the Institute for Psychoanalysis at Frankfurt and taught there with Erich Fromm, Frieda Fromm-Reichmann, Karl Landauer, and Foulkes. This selection was first published in Schweizerische Zeitschrift für Psychologie und ihre Anwendungen *15 (1956): 149–51. It was translated and adapted by the editor.*

I

Sigmund Freud always objected to being photographed. Many photographers, painters, and sculptors sought the honor of portraying him, but few succeeded.

Shortly before Freud's 75th birthday in 1931 Dr. Paul Federn, a pupil and very good friend, introduced the young sculptor P. Olem Nemon to him. After some sketches Nemon created three busts, in wood, stone, and bronze. Freud chose the wood one for himself, the second one went to his brother, and the third to Dr. Heinrich Meng in Basel. At the same time Nemon made sketches for a life size statue, which was completed later and was given anonymously to the New York Psychoanalytic Institute.

On the pedestal there are two lines in Greek with an interesting history. In May 1906 on the occasion of his fiftieth birthday, Freud's pupils and colleagues honored him at a banquet and presented him with a medallion. Freud's profile was on one side; on the other, Oedipus and the Sphinx were framed by two lines of Greek poetry from the final chorus of Sophocles' *Oedipus Rex*. Freud was deeply moved. He then recalled that as a young man with much ambition and many ideas he had gone through the Hall of Fame of the University of Vienna and daydreamed how one day he would be famous and his statue would be

350

placed in this hall. In his reverie he had envisioned on his statue the very lines that now appeared on the medallion.

Today one finds these same lines on the statue placed in the auditorium of the New York Psychoanalytic Institute. No honor could have been more meaningful to him "who knew the famous riddles and was a man most masterful."

II

I talked several times to Nemon about his work with Freud. In the beginning Freud was distant and reserved toward him. For days he did not speak. The first time he spoke he said, "I am sure that you know your profession is the oldest in the world." Nemon was surprised—and then Freud added, "Did not God create man from clay?"

Nemon did not allow Freud to look at his work before it was finished, but when the bust was almost finished he showed it to Freud's housekeeper, who said, "The Professor looks too angry." When Nemon told Freud, he answered, "But I am angry. I am angry with humanity." When the statue was finished, Freud looked at it and remarked, "I am glad you put in enough anger."

Nemon asked Freud what he felt about the fact that the surrealists considered him the inspirer of surrealism. "It is wonderful," he answered. "The surrealists send me daily their newspaper with a wonderful dedication on the first page. I read it every day—but when I am finished with it—I have to admit—I do not find anything in the paper I really understand."

In another talk with Nemon about Freud's modesty we discussed a letter Freud wrote shortly before his death to the editor of *Time and Tide*. The editors had asked him for a contribution to a special number on the persecutions of the Jews. Freud wrote:

I came to Vienna as a child of four years from a small town in Moravia. After 78 years, including more than half a century of strenuous work, I have to leave my home, see the scientific society I founded dissolved, our institutions destroyed, our printing press (Verlag) taken over by the invaders, the books I published confiscated and reduced to pulp, my children ousted from their professions. Don't you think the columns of your special number might rather be reserved for the utterances of non-Jewish people less personally involved than myself?

351

In this connection I find comfort in an old French saying:

Le bruit est pour le fat
La plainte pour le sot
L'honnête homme trompe
S'en va et ne dit mot

Sigmund Freud

A Character Trait of Freud's
(1956)

JOAN RIVIERE

Joan Riviere belonged to that remarkable generation of British female analysts, including Sylvia Payne and Melanie Klein, who made significant contributions to the theory and practice of psychoanalysis. Joan Riviere met Freud in 1920 and started her analysis with him in 1922. She subsequently practiced analysis in London and also translated some of Freud's works. This selection was delivered as a short lecture in May 1956 in London and was published in Psychoanalysis and Contemporary Thought *(London, Hogarth Press, 1958), edited by John Sutherland.*

Always one of the most interesting things to me about Freud was his writing; I met him first in his writings before I knew him. You get an impression of the man from them, quite apart from the impression their content makes on you. As is well known, his style and presentation are very different from that of most scientific writers. (Actually, Freud's writings do vary and are of more than one description, but I am speaking now of the style which predominates and characterises the main volume of his work.) Its general character is not only direct and plain-spoken—simple statements without padding—but in particular it conveys vividly an awareness of his readers or hearers, as if he were speaking directly to them, and were concerned to put forward his views in a form intelligible to *them.* The structure of his argument is not built up in a vacuum, as it were; it has a direct reference to the reader; he is addressing you. There is a personal quality, a personal relation, implicit in his style.

When I came to know Freud himself, however, I found that he did not appear especially interested in impressing himself on people or in seeking to convince others of his views. We know that he needed the support of an outside recognition and the acceptance of his work; he hoped for it, but in everyday life he appeared to take no direct steps to obtain it. There seemed to be a paradox here: on the one hand he had no strong impulse to influence others, to teach or convince them—not

353

even in fact a marked interest in curing them, as he has told us; the aim of impressing himself on people seemed to be lacking or minimal in him. Yet he had developed this special capacity for presenting his conclusions as if he were bent on enabling the reader to take them in —so much so that it colours his whole style and gives the presentation a simplicity and lucidity (often when the content is obscure) that is peculiar to him and most rare in such work.

I wondered about this paradox and why he had this relation to his readers—as if they and *their* thoughts were an essential factor in the process of formulating his views.

He once said something to me which had little meaning for me at the time but which later threw light on this problem for me. I suppose I had mentioned some analytic explanation that had occurred to me. He said: "Write it, write it, put it down in black and white; that's the way to deal with it; you get it out of your system." I didn't feel that this prescription meant much to me, and it fell by the way. It must obviously have been true for him, however, and I remembered it. In later years, as I acquired more knowledge and understanding of him and his work, and especially under the stimulus of his biography, I came more and more to realise the underlying importance in him of the creative side of his work—his work must have meant to him a structure he was building and creating. He almost says so once or twice. This idea then linked up in my mind with his former remark to me: "Get it out, produce it, make something of it—*outside you*, that is; give it an existence independently of you."

He clearly did not consciously or explicitly think of his work as creative; as we all do, he thought of it as scientific, as discovery or acquisition of facts and knowledge, which indeed it is. But when we look at the vast fabric he raised, it is evident that even his unique capacity to recognise facts would in itself not have produced the great body of knowledge he left us. It was a deeper impulse in him—a capacity to construct and create something, a living body, to build up outside himself a body of knowledge that comprehends the single facts of which it is formed and yet transcends them, thus becoming an independent whole in itself—it was this that played such a notable part in his work. There was a marriage in him of the seeker after existing truth and the creator giving the world a new living truth—the scientist and the artist in one. The outcome represents a fusion of external reality and internal phantasy, in which each contributes to fulfilling the aims of the other as well as its own. And the extremely high degree of satisfaction

354

that results when this fulfillment is achieved betokens, I believe, the essence of that quality we call greatness.

As I see it, then, the act of writing his ideas, of conveying them, putting them over into the minds of others, represented a process of building up those ideas into a whole outside himself and inside the minds of others. His concern was not primarily to obtain their acceptance; primarily he was engaged on an act of creation in which his hearers and readers were his medium, his vehicle in the process, as well as both the source and the abode of his creation. When the new living body was born, it had been shaped and framed and housed in other minds outside his. This for me explains the paradox that in ordinary life Freud had no great interest in directly influencing another person, but that what he was interested to do, consciously or not, was to work out and construct the edifice of his thought into an intelligible whole by means of their co-operation and their thought. And for this he had to make his direct personal appeal to them in plain and simple terms.

I said in simple terms. Freud's simplicity was a familiar characteristic to those who knew him, yet it is something very hard to convey. One tends to think of this great man who produced this immense volume of work in his lifetime, and who was occupied with such totally new, unheard-of, and sometimes obscure ideas, as a completely sophisticated being, surveying the world and the objects of his study from a detached distance. It is quite untrue; behind the dignity and reserve of a serious, much-occupied professional man, he was a most unsophisticated person and sometimes quite naïve. Ernest Jones has quoted evidences of it in the biography. He was not a man of the world, though he was in no way retiring or withdrawn, and he was not a judge of men. He habitually reacted with simple spontaneous naturalness to whatever he met, on the assumption that whatever he perceived was valid in itself. Nothing else concerned him at the moment. He established an instantaneous, direct relation to his perception, which automatically excluded cut-and-dried assumptions, or *arrière-pensées*. Second thoughts and suspended judgment only came much later. The impulse to reject and dismiss at first sight was singularly lacking in him. In using the word naïveté of him, in spite of its usual rather disparaging connotation, I have done so because it alone, I feel, conveys the strength of this immediate acceptance of whatever he met with as valid. It was this quality which enabled him to by-pass the scepticism of an ordinary physician about the patients' Oedipus phantasies and to perceive the element of reality in them; just as it was this capacity that had led to the brilliant results of his study of dreams. One could say that his simple direct personal response to whatever he perceived as valid in itself was the unique characteristic of his genius; other faculties of his others have also had, perhaps no one else had this as he had it.

And so by these means and in this way he gradually discovered the unconscious. First he thought of it as a storehouse of memories; then he discovered its character as the mental side of the instincts we are born with, those dynamic forces in us which issue in all our emotions, actions and behaviour, thoughts and feelings, and activate them. He saw the unconscious as the connecting-link—the clearinghouse, as it were—between these biological forces of instinct and the conscious life of adult men and women. He bent his energies to building up for us in his writings a picture of this world which is unknown to us and yet is so powerful in determining our lives. Only if we can recognise it can we make better use of it; for we do not know of it, and we protect ourselves from doing so largely by thinking of it as in other people's minds! I think in analysis it is as necessary to keep in mind how strong the *not* seeing and *not* knowing is in us as to learn all we can about what is unconscious in the mind.

What I am speaking of now springs from another of Freud's sayings to me. In my analysis he one day made some interpretation, and I responded to it by an objection. He then said: "It is *un-con-scious.*" I was overwhelmed then by the realisation that I knew nothing about it—I knew nothing about it. In that instant he had created in me his discovery of the powerful unconscious in our minds that we know nothing of, and that yet is impelling and directing us. I have never forgotten this reminder from him of what unconscious means.

Sigmund Freud
(1956)

RAYMOND DE SAUSSURE

Raymond de Saussure, probably one of Switzerland's most notable psychoanalysts, lives in Geneva. He was analyzed by Freud in the early twenties. This selection was first published in Schweizerische Zeitschrift für Psychologie und ihre Anwendungen 15 (1956): *136–39. That issue was devoted to recollections by Swiss pupils of Freud. The article was especially translated for this volume by Dr. Richard McConchie.*

I was still in my adolescence and not yet at the University when, with older classmates, at times I used to slip into the lectures Theodore Flournoy, Professeur de Psychologie, was giving at the "Faculte des Sciences de Geneve." With the clarity that was so natural to him he presented the theories of psychoanalysis and the dynamic point of view of Freudian conceptions. How interesting to us were these ideas, which shed a completely new and dazzling light on our adolescescent crises! This was shortly before the First World War but Flournoy had been interested in psychoanalysis for many years. As early as 1900 he published accounts of Freud's methods in *Archives de Psychologie.*

From this contact I became interested in dynamic psychology, a revolutionary doctrine (one must remember just how rigid social structure actually was before 1914) well suited for the seduction of youth. The orientation of my career was decided. Moreover, I had two friends, unfortunately both deceased, who followed along on the same path: Henri Flournoy and Charles Odier. We constituted a group that facilitated the exchange of ideas. Thus was born the psychoanalytic movement in French Switzerland which has continued to develop and has been fertilized by constant contacts with German Switzerland and France.

But let us return to Freud the person. In 1920, at the International Congress of Psychoanalysis at The Hague, I saw him for the first time. I was struck by that grave countenance where intellect seemed constantly at work. His wrinkled forehead, penetrating and thoughtful, concealed a brain on the look-out everywhere not only to surprise facts that could be integrated into his theories, but also to coordinate and systematize everything that impressed him. It was interesting to see him react to communications which brought new ideas. He took possession of them and isolated them from the context in which they had been presented in order to incorporate them immediately into the framework of his personal conceptions.

He took as active a part in the organization of the psychoanalytic movement as in scientific communications. Unquestionably a certain need to dominate played a role, but the desire not to waste time with badly informed or badly analyzed doctors, who continually raised objections a hundred times rejected, was the principal reason for the organization of the working cadres in different countries. By 1920 Freud had already experienced the departure of some of his pupils, including Adler, Stekel, and Jung, and wanted strongly to maintain the unity of his doctrine throughout the world.

At each stage of his work his fertile mind immediately apprehended the consequences of his ideas; at times this made him impatient with speakers too persuaded that they were right. His courtesy did not fail, although he could drop a cutting remark which would put his adversary in his place.

Absorbed in his work this man, who still had so many things to say and who measured the value of time exactly, had a great kindness for serious young people who were willing to work in his context. I remember his great hope at our first meetings at The Hague that, through the Swiss, perhaps French medical circles would become interested in psychoanalysis.

It must be said that in this period psychoanalysis was still more discussed than accepted. Although it had made many startling advances in the Germanies and had forced psychiatrists to pay attention to it, on the other hand, England had only a small group of researchers, gathered around Jones.

In America, Putnam, Jeliffe, Brill, and Oberndorf had scored some success, but the "Institutes" had not yet been created. The group assembled around Freud was spirited, certainly, but small in comparison with the army of psychiatrists and psychologists who were multiplying their criticisms.

The congress at The Hague represented a triumph for Freud. He had lost the collaboration of Jung in 1914. The war had prevented international exchanges. What would be found in the aftermath of that holocaust? Many physicians, old and young, came to the congress. Great cordiality reigned; the Dutch welcome was one of overflowing hospitality; and Freud, full of hope, was also full of energy.

In Vienna, a few months later, I was stretched out on the master's couch. I no longer saw the features which had so profoundly struck me in Holland. Contact was established only by means of his voice and the odor of the cigars he ceaselessly smoked. But one was also won over by the atmosphere of his office, a rather dark room, which opened onto a courtyard. Light came not from the windows but from the brilliance of that lucid, discerning mind.

Freud was not a good psychoanalytic technician. Since he had not been analyzed himself, he tended to commit two kinds of errors. First, he had practiced suggestion too long not to have been materially affected by it. When he was persuaded of the truth of something, he had considerable difficulty in waiting until this verity became clear to his patient. Freud wanted to convince him immediately. Because of that, he talked too much.

Second, one rapidly sensed what special theoretical question preoccupied him, for often during the analytic hour he developed at length new points of view he was clarifying in his own mind. This was a gain for the discipline, but not always for the patient's treatment.

After 1920 I did not see Freud again except briefly at certain congresses and a bit longer during a trip he made to Berlin in 1930. He maintained a very keen interest in his pupils, encouraging them in their work. He stimulated them by his questions and gave them the opportunity to collaborate in the reviews he directed.

During the 1920s and 1930s Freud's theories spread; criticism lowered its tone, and this triumph certainly brought him some serenity. Unfortunately, the pain, all too constant, had also altered his face and marked certain wrinkles more deeply. With the years he took on the grandeur of a sage of antiquity. No longer needing to fight, he could calmly contemplate the immense work he was leaving behind and the army of researchers he had inspired.

Freud's work will not be ephemeral; it will be discussed for centuries. If at times Freud was discouraged by the incessant struggles he had to carry on and by the base calumnies of which he was the object, in the last years of his existence he could say to himself: "My life was worth the trouble of having lived it."

My First Three Visits with Freud in Vienna

(1957)

LUDWIG BINSWANGER

The relationship between Freud and Binswanger was unique in that their differences never affected their friendship. A Swiss psychiatrist and the father of existential psychoanalysis, Binswanger met Freud in 1907 and remained close to him until the day of his death. Although Binswanger certainly deviated from the principles of orthodox psychoanalysis, Freud never lost respect for him and his work, as is illustrated in the words of Freud to him, "Quite unlike so many others you have not allowed the fact of your intellectual development, moving away more and more from my influence, to disturb our personal relationship, and you do not know how agreeable I find such decent behavior–even though you praise my indifference, which is merely a concomitant of old age." The Vienna Academic Society for Medical Psychology invited Binswanger to address it for Freud's eightieth birthday. Binswanger wrote Freud informing him of this request of the society and that he had reread the whole correspondence between them. "How much suffering and joy–there was more suffering than joy–we shared. . . . In any case you were with me in spirit in the three most grievous times of my life–my illness and the deaths of my two sons–and stood by me as few men did. These are things one can never repay in one's lifetime."

The following selection is from Sigmund Freud: Reminiscences of a Friendship *(New York, Grune & Stratton, 1957).*

In the spring of 1906 I passed my state medical examination, and in June of the same year I joined the Burgholzli Mental Hospital in Zurich as a volunteer physician. Prior to this, while I was serving in the clinic, my admiration had been aroused by Eugen Bleuler, who was already doing preliminary work on his "Gruppe der Schizophrenien," which revolutionized the theory of dementia praecox. Bleuler greatly stimulated my "hereditary" love for psychiatry; I can still see him as he was then, scribbling notes at every opportunity on little slips of paper that he drew from his waistcoat pocket. Karl Abraham, my predecessor in the male section of the hospital, was rather reserved by nature, but he too was an influence on his younger colleagues because of his great intelligence and his subtle, often somewhat ironical personality. But it was C. G. Jung, then chief physician of the hospital, under whom I planned to write my doctor's thesis, who turned out to be the greatest inspiration of those days. He kept his students spellbound by his temperament and the wealth of his ideas. In 1906, in collaboration with Riklin, he published the first volume of his "Diagnostische Assoziationsstudien" and had completed an epoch-making work on the psychology of dementia praecox. Jung suggested as a subject for my thesis "The Psycho-Galvanic Reflex Phenomenon in the Association Test," a subject that proved not only to be more and more fascinating the deeper I went into it, but one that brought me into particularly close contact with Jung. Indeed, he was constantly helping me by giving me the benefit of his advice and his knowledge, and even by letting me use him as a subject in experiments.

But the chief reason I must call my year at Burghölzli by far the most inspiring year of my psychiatric apprenticeship is that this mental hospital, even as early as 1906, was at the center of an intellectual movement that had begun in Vienna. This movement bore the name of psychoanalysis, and its origins could be traced to one man: Sigmund Freud. No great amount of imagination is needed to understand how joyfully and gratefully I answered yes when Jung one day surprised me by asking whether I would accompany him and his wife on their (first) visit to Freud in Vienna. Our trip took place at the end of February 1907, if I remember correctly. Herr and Frau Professor Jung stayed in Vienna only about a week, but to my great delight I was able to stay for another week.

The day after our arrival Freud questioned Jung and me about our dreams. I do not recall Jung's dream, but I do recall Freud's interpretation of it, namely, that Jung wished to dethrone him and take his place. I myself dreamed of the entrance to his house at No. 19, Berggasse, which was then being remodeled, and of the old chandelier swathed in a shabby covering to protect it from the plastering. Freud's interpretation of this dream, which I found rather unconvincing—he recalled it thirty years later when my wife and I visited him on the occasion of his eightieth birthday—was that it indicated a wish to marry his oldest daughter but, at the same time, contained the repudiation of this wish, since it actually said that—I remember Freud's words— "You won't marry into a house with such a shabby chandelier."

The easy-going, friendly atmosphere that marked our visit from the first day on can easily be seen in these interpretations. Freud's dislike of all formality and ceremony, his personal charm, simplicity, natural openness, and kindness, and not least his humor, left no room for constraint. And yet one could not for a moment deny the impression of greatness and dignity that emanated from him. To me it was a pleasure, albeit somewhat skeptical, to see the enthusiasm and confidence with which Freud responded to Jung, in whom he immediately saw his scientific "son and heir." I was present at several conversations between the two, which, needless to say, revolved solely around psychoanalytic problems. Freud's family also received us—and me alone after the departure of the Jungs—with the greatest friendliness. I can still remember a Sunday walk with the whole family on the Cobenzl; both Madame Freud and her sister, Fraulein Mina Bernays, were amiability and kindness personified. The children were very well behaved at the table, even though here too a completely unconstrained atmosphere prevailed.

Freud impressed me most strongly during the evenings when I saw him in his study or consulting room. He was then fifty and I twenty-five. What enchanted me was not merely the time Freud devoted to me (he did the same with many others) after a day of hard work, in his quiet, dimly lit study, which even then contained important works of ancient and Oriental art, but even more the indefatigable, detailed, and most instructive and stimulating manner in which he answered my eager questions. Freud sat behind his desk, smoking a cigar, his hand resting on the arm of his chair or on the desk; occasionally he would pick up an art object and gaze at it, then keenly yet benevolently scrutinize his visitor, never asserting his superiority and always citing case histories rather than going into theoretical explanations. Sharp and accurate in his choice of words, sparing in gesture, natural and open in his facial expressions, never raising his well-modulated voice—this is Freud as I remember him to this day. His manner of speaking was conditioned by his unswerving and passionate devotion to the matter under discussion, to the scientific subject and its various implications. At the same time his visitor was repeatedly reminded that the entire edifice of psychoanalytic theory—the tracing of the tangled pathways of the dream, the theories of neuroses, of paranoia, of infantile sexuality, and so on—had been erected only through many years of solitary and self-effacing investigation and intellectual labor against the resistance of a scientific world that was not merely obtuse but actively hostile and animated by a fanatical will to destroy the new ideas. Freud often referred to his scientific Calvary. On one occasion he told me that the ten years of complete isolation and constant attacks had weighted heavily upon him. Only once—I suppose because of his disappointment, repeatedly mentioned in his writings, at the untenability of his theory of the infantile sexual trauma as the indispensable "cause" of hysteria—did he become doubtful of the course his investigations were following, he said, but he weathered this "crisis" like the others. I remember distinctly what a deep impression these confidences made upon me and how central they became to my understanding of Freud's personality and development. For what Dilthey says of man in general, namely, "What man is, we learn only from his history," applies also to individuals, and is particularly true of Freud.

Even though I had no complete knowledge at the time of the extent to which Freud and his theories had been rejected, and of the forms this rejection had assumed (and was to assume time and again), I had depressing and thoroughly eloquent proof at it when I went to see Breuer to convey to him my father's greetings. I do not recall Breuer's exact words, but I do remember the vivid gestures and facial expressions with which he responded to my naive question of what his position was regarding Freud since the "Studies." His look of downright pity and superiority, as well as the wave of his hand, a dismissal in the full sense of the word, left not the slightest doubt that in his opinion Freud had gone scientifically astray to such an extent that he could no longer be taken seriously, and hence it was better not to talk about him.

I had a distressing experience of an entirely different kind when Freud, after a meeting with not more than six or seven of his followers in his home, took me aside afterward and said, "Well, now you have seen the gang." Here was another instance, during this first visit, that showed me how alone Freud still felt and yet how keen he could be in his judgments.

My second visit to Freud took place from the 15th to the 26th of February 1910. This time I came with my wife (I had married two years earlier), who was received with particular friendliness by Freud's entire family. After that visit she was an equal partner in our friendship. I made notes on this second visit immediately after my return, which are reproduced here in somewhat abridged form.

On the day of our arrival I attended the seminar that Freud held once a week from 7 to 9 p.m. About thirty persons were present, beginners and advanced students, among them many nonmedical men; not one of them was an academic psychiatrist and, aside from the old

363

guard (Hitschmann, Federn, Sadger, Adler, Stekel, Rank), most of them were young men. Freud suggested a subject for discussion, asking some of the students to report on it at the next meeting. The first item on the current agenda was Shakespeare's "Hamlet," some scenes of which had been analyzed by a student along the lines laid down in the well-known note on "Hamlet" in The Interpretation of Dreams (edition of 1900, pp. 183ff). Another student, in an uncritical and very confused manner, discussed Hamlet's relation to his father according to the above-mentioned approach, pointing out in particular the splitting up of a personality (referred to in The Interpretation of Dreams), instanced in this case by the redirection of Hamlet's father complex toward two persons, the stepfather and Polonius. A younger participant likened the masquerading of one person as another, a dramatic device often resorted to by Shakespeare, to the substitutions of setting in dreams. Freud observed that in the discussion of the present subject the aim was to advance more or less plausible ideas, not to discover well-established facts! At the same time he underscored the value of such analyses as exercises.

Then I attended one of the Wednesday evening meetings, lasting from nine to well past midnight, which corresponded to the meetings of our Swiss Psychoanalytic Society at the time. About fifteen persons, almost all of them physicians, participated. Stekel began the session by delivering a lecture on obsessive idea. First, he produced some examples, with generally plausible interpretations; then he launched into a theoretical discussion of obsessive processes which, however, was so unclear that I can no longer remember it. I know only that I was struck by his strong mania for generalizations, and that everything was traced back to doubt, just as in his book on anxiety hysteria everything is traced back to anxiety. He thought he could go beyond Freud's views on the phenomenon of doubt. While it was clear from Freud's latest work that in the last analysis he himself traced doubt back to the ambivalence of love and hate—a theory supported by detailed and objective arguments—Stekel insisted that other forms of doubt had to be taken into consideration, e.g., the hesitation between religious faith and "unfaith." Such conflicts, Stekel maintained, always reflect a primary doubt which, by means of displacement, produces the brooding mania and all those doubts that characterize obsessional neurosis, whose content is so incomprehensible to us. Everything that Freud had so painstakingly clarified was thus once again confused. So far as I can remember, Stekel failed to substantiate his views. He had spoken in the same breath about the opposition between faith and "unfaith," intellect and affectivity, and consciousness and the unconscious! Noteworthy, however, was Stekel's statement, which he illustrated by a good example, that obsessive impulses are always traceable to a displaced parental prohibition or commandment. After the lecture each participant in the seminar had to express his opinion on it; the order was determined by drawing lots. Sadger, who spoke first, approved the part of the lecture dealing with case histories, but sharply condemned the theoretical part. There then followed a long and entirely fruitless discussion on the question whether the primary element in obsessional neurosis was doubt or anxiety. I was struck by the lack of psychiatric training in the majority of the participants, even though there were very few beginners present; they had not even mastered the terminology.

The high point of the evening was Freud's criticism of Stekel's lecture. He shared Sadger's opinion, though he expressed himself in milder terms. He pointed out to Stekel the danger of his deductions; he himself could hardly accept the fact, he said, that his own conclusions about obsessional neurosis, which had required years of preliminary study, could be enlarged upon after only a few weeks. Otherwise, Freud said, Stekel was a most talented "detector of the unconscious," from whom all of us could learn. (He often told me this personally, although he did not think much of Stekel's theoretical capacities.) He also pointed out an error in Stekel's interpretations, which arose as a result of an arbitrary disregard for the conscious content of the symptom (confusion between gas tap and gas meter). Here, too, Freud emphasized the fact that neurotic symptoms must not be judged, as they had been heretofore, on the basis of their conscious façade, but rather on the basis of their unconscious background. Stekel had changed the content—the conscious façade of the symptom—by transforming the gas tap into a gas meter. Naturally, the interpretation could not be correct under such circumstances. I took note of a very wise and significant saying of Freud's, which is unfortunately often disregarded: "None of us has acquired the habit of thinking simultaneously of the ego and conscious processes on the one hand, and the processes of the unconscious and of the sexual instinct on the other." The demand for such simultaneous thinking showed me, to my surprise, that Freud had a genuinely philosophical vein, even though he was not aware of it.

What he himself referred to as "philosophical" always applied to that which the philosophical layman calls by that name, i.e., pure speculation about ultimate things.

Freud then discussed Stekel's thesis that every doubt was a doubt of the ego, and that every anxiety was fear of death. He rejected both ideas as unwarranted generalizations and sought to restore order in Stekel's confused ideas. According to Freud, the actually pathological obsessive doubt always relates to reality and thus is always a reality doubt, as when someone compulsively wonders whether he has really turned off the gas. The reality doubt is opposed to the anticipatory doubt. (Stekel's example: "How can I raise the money for the goods I bought?")

I attached great value to Freud's opinion, for it showed me how critical he was and how he was able to bring clarity into confusion with a few words, and, more generally, how he strove to maintain order and scientific discipline among his own followers.

As for the rest, I was favorably impressed by the fact that conflicting opinions were voiced freely, and that no one pulled his punches— Freud himself, for all the respect shown him, was often contradicted. Stekel energetically defended himself against the latter's criticisms, pointing out that many ideas that originally had been rejected by their circle were later recognized as valid by Freud himself. Stekel received most support from Adler.

Later I attended another seminar at which Freud took the floor because he had forgotten to give assignments at the previous meeting. He discussed Rank's The Myth of the Birth of the Hero. In a strikingly masterful manner he brought out the book's essential ideas, which concern the nuclear complex of neurosis. My notes of this meeting conclude with the remark, "Freud is deeply convinced of the need for and the usefulness of further psychoanalytic investigations of myths."

I had several conversations with Freud; my notes give highlights of some of them, but above all, those in which he expressed his views on the unconscious. On one occasion I referred to the statement he had made during a Wednesday meeting that "the unconscious is metaphysic, we simply posit it as real," meaning, of course, that we acted as if the unconscious were something real, like the conscious. Being a true scientist, Freud said nothing about the nature of the unconscious, precisely because we know nothing certain about it; rather, we merely deduce it from the conscious. He thought that just as Kant postulated the thing in itself behind the phenomenal world, so he himself postulated the unconscious being the conscious that is accessible to our experience, but that can never be directly experienced. (With reference to this comparison, which is philosophically untenable, cf. Haberlin, cited below.) On another occasion he said that the unconscious is a more primitive form of psychic organization than the conscious, and that, like Lipps, he looked upon the unconscious as the psychic par excellence.

I found it interesting that Freud felt little need of philosophy. "He is and remains," I wrote at the time, "the conscientious natural scientist who does not go beyond what experience gives him." To have this confirmed was the most important result of my second visit to Vienna, when I noted, "Needless to say, just as in the case of physics and chemistry, there is no way here of avoiding certain prejudices, presuppositions, and more or less speculative hypotheses; I shall mention only the assumption that everything in psychic life is just as exactly determined as it is in nature."

The labeling of the unconscious as metaphysic seemed to me misleading, especially because the unconscious was supposed to be the psychic par excellence. Freud agreed with me, and it was soon clear that the proper term was not "metapsychic"—which seemed to me a superfluous term—but "metaconscious."

I was interested in Freud's ideas on fetishism, which he now treated psychoanalytically, just as he did the neuroses. This was particularly important to me because I had never been really able to accept his view, stated in the third of his Three Essays on the Theory of Sexuality, that fetishism held a unique position in relation to the neuroses. He gave me some instructive examples, stressing the great part played by osphresophilia in the genesis of fetishism, and explained clothes fetishism, among other things, by the scopophilic instinct and the pleasure experienced in gazing at the naked body. As a result of repression, value is attached precisely to that which covers the body, or clothes.

On my third visit to Freud in Vienna, the last one before the First World War (between my second and third trips, Freud visited me at Kreuzlingen around Eastertime in 1912, of which I shall deal later, in connection with our correspondence), I was accompanied by my friend Paul Haberlin. The visit occurred in April 1913, and I stayed several days which, at Freud's wish, were grouped around a Sunday. In our correspondence I find a letter from him (March 27, 1913) referring to this visit in which he expressed his delight at the impending arrival of the "sympathetic ensemble," adding, "People should see each

367

other from time to time. Letters are no substitute. To return my Whitsun visit is an excellent idea of yours." I have only a few recollections of this third visit, but Paul Haberlin has put his memories of it at my disposal, for which I am most grateful to him. He says that he remembers these few essentials from his conversations with Freud:

1. I objected to Freud's derivation of the phenomenon of conscience ("censorship") from the instinct, arguing that an agency that attributed no determining authority to the instinctual demand as such could not for its part have an instinctual character. But Freud stuck to his view, which he later sought to strengthen with his concept of narcissism. [In this argument I was entirely on the side of Haberlin.]

2. Freud asked me whether Kant's thing in itself was not identical with the unconscious. I denied this, laughing, and suggested that the two notions were on entirely different levels. [Here again I side with Freud's opponent.]

3. Freud said—but not quite seriously, it seemed to me—that philosophy was one of the most respectable forms of the sublimation of repressed sexuality, nothing more. I countered with the question, "What then is science, and psychoanalytic psychology in particular?" Thereupon, visibly somewhat surprised, he said evasively: "At least psychology has social usefulness."

4. I questioned him as to how it had come about that it was precisely his oldest and perhaps most talented disciples, Jung and Adler, to give examples, who had broken away from him. He replied: "Precisely because they too wanted to be Popes." Finally, I asked why so many psychoanalysts gave the impression of being quacks. He replied: "I always thought that my theory would be seized upon at first by scoundrels and speculators."

When we were leaving Vienna after this visit, Freud said to me, "Follow me as far as you can, and for the rest, let us remain good friends."

Some Notes on Freud's Personality
(1957)

HEINRICH RACKER

Racker delivered this paper first as a lecture at the Argentine Psychoanalytic Association in June 1956. It was published in Samiksa *11 (1957): 147–56.*

When we come into touch with a scientific or artistic work we feel how, through it, little by little, the personality of the man who created it begins to acquire life. Through and behind the content in itself, traits of the author's spirit and character arise one after another until they form an image. Thus it was that all of us, as we became progressively acquainted with Freud's writings, also became acquainted with Freud the man. Needless to say, according to our own individual structure, we shall have seen and lived his personality in different ways; we shall have perceived more one aspect or more another. There are, however, some traits that are so outstanding that it is unlikely that any of us will have failed to feel them. Allow me, to begin with, to recall once again some of these well-known traits on this commemorative occasion.

It is, I believe, above all his unconditional and unswerving love of truth, a love that will not be seduced by any personal interest. Freud seeks, finds, and proclaims the truth against everything that opposes it, whether coming from within or without. He never hides the imperfections of his findings and even emphasizes how far his work has remained incomplete. There is in him in this sense, a deep *devotion* to reality. Freud himself refers to this attitude, when he speaks, in all modesty, of his back being used to bowing before the facts. It is also Freud himself who mentions the *patience* that had to assist him in his arduous research work. We well understand that these two virtues, devotion and patience, were present together, for the two are closely connected: *patience* as a readiness to accept things as they are, and in the time they demand, is nothing else, in essence, but an expression of *devotion* to reality, an expression of a silent veneration, in this case, of reality in its spiritual aspect, that is to say, of truth. Equally united to these two qualities by bonds of psychological kinship is *tenacity*, which is active patience or patient activity, capable of contending with many difficulties, a characteristic highly developed in Freud. And there is another virtue as well, also a sister to devotion, that we have all felt in reading his writings: it is Freud's *fidelity*, here again the fidelity to reality, to the facts, which we felt through the *confidence* that arose within us as regards what Freud describes and relates.

Such fidelity is not to be taken for granted in great thinkers. There were those who lacked it or possessed another kind of fidelity. It is stated, for instance, that the great Haeckel, the discoverer of the fundamental biogenetic law could not resist the temptation to "comb" the facts on which his conclusions were based, that is to say, to do a little cheating. And when the disciples of another great thinker, the philosopher Hegel, raised the objection: "but, Professor, your ideas do not agree with reality!", he is said to have replied, "Well,—so much the worse for reality." This too is fidelity of a sort, a fidelity to the principles and *logic of one's own thinking*, as we might also speak of a fidelity of what ought to be (which would be an *ethical* fidelity) or to what might be (which would be an *artistic* fidelity); so that Freud's fidelity had its specific quality, namely, fidelity to what *is*, i.e. *scientific* fidelity par excellence.

Some of you may already be feeling apprehensive lest I should pursue a line of conduct not infrequent on such commemorative occasions, namely to catalogue the finest virtues of the man we are here to honour. That would be hardly faithful to what psychoanalysis has taught us and it is not my intention to do so. But I too wish to be true to the facts and the points I have made are, I believe, facts indeed. I shall have to continue a while along these lines, but more specific traits of Freud's are already beginning to emerge. Moreover, the moment will come for adding some shade to all this light.

To return to what I was saying before. Every true fidelity is a bond of love that has memory of the past, and in Freud this bond referred to the facts, i.e. to what was already done, to the product of the past. It is indeed the knowledge of the *past* and the reawakening of it to new life that constitutes one of the most outstanding features of his vocation. The *individual* and *collective* past, the infancy of *each man* and of *all humanity*, his animal and instinctual history, and the history of primitive and ancient cultures. Starting with his first studies, on the development of nerve cells in the evolutionary scale running from the lower to the higher fish, and ending with his last great work "The Man Moses and the Monotheistic Religion" we are ever and again confronted with Freud the "historian"—taking this word in its widest sense—with the Freud who more than anything wished to know the *genesis of the facts*. To be sure, he assumed, as Darwin did, that in this genesis the egg came before the chicken; but this is truth, albeit only a part of it. And I think mankind owes gratitude to him for this limitation to certain aspects of the truth, this limitation won from himself against a strong leaning to philosophical speculation, which can still be discerned on some occasions, as, for instance, in a certain rejection of philosophy wherein we may perceive his struggle against an attraction. It is also thanks to this voluntary limitation, to this severe scientific discipline that Freud was able to give humanity what he did.

I said above that Freud's vocation was one of awakening a buried past to new life. To this should be added something more. The field to which Freud directed his tireless attention, his ever-renewed scrutiny, and his constant search after the origin was, in fact, the past internal and external. But the road he travelled, and how he travelled it, was in strange opposition to this; for his road was quite a new one and even meant a total break with the past. You all know how the science, and especially the medicine, of the end of the last century regarded the human psyche; even today, 60 years after the birth of psychoanalysis, we meet with no few remnants of this outlook. If we consider that in those days Freud was the only one who thought in another way, against the principles and axioms of his scientific fathers and with no brothers to accompany him, we have some idea of the revolutionary nature of psychoanalysis and we realize how much courage, how much capacity for the renunciation of fathers and history was necessary for creating this new science, and how strong must have been Freud's urge to go his own way and find and produce by himself. It is true that, outside the empirical sciences, in philosophy and in literature, there were some few spirits, such as Schopenhauer and Nietzsche, who had already intuitively sensed something of what was to become scientific and objective psychoanalytic knowledge. But it was more a matter of sporadic penetration into psychological depths, and, besides, Freud knew very little of these philosophers. He did not want to know much about them because, I think, it was so important to him to discover man by himself.

Various psychoanalytic considerations suggest themselves here, in

371

the first place concerning Freud's relationship with his father. We know something more about this to-day, thanks to Freud's correspondence with Fliess and the biography by E. Jones. Never the less, even these data only allow us a measure of conjecture. Freud discovers the boy's ambivalence towards his father through his self-analysis, traversing the conscious level of his mind in which there was almost exclusively admiration and love for his father. I think that his unflagging will to know and create by himself is an expression of his desire to be a father *himself* and his need of confirming his paternity ever and again. The argument, for instance, that Freud gave to explain why he had not acquainted himself with the above-mentioned philosophers or with other thinkers who had anticipated him in one or another of his ideas, was that he wanted to be free from preconceived ideas in his investigations. One must recognize a certain objectivity in this argument, but we cannot help feeling that it was not the only motive. The wish to be unhampered by preconceived ideas is, in one respect, a sound scientific aim, but when one believes it is really attainable or has actually been attained, it becomes an illusion. Illusions spring from wishes, and I think that the above-mentioned argument also served Freud, in point of fact, for the fulfilment of a wish. The wish to have no preconceived ideas is the wish to have no father or, I should say, to be the father oneself. In general terms, the object of the battle for knowledge is always, basically, the mother. "Truth is a female," said Nietzsche, and added: "she loves the warrior." Indeed, since those distant times in which Adam "knew" Eve (as the Bible says, in consequence of which she gave him his no less famous sons), *gnosis* and *genesis* have been one and the same thing. Knowledge is the union of love with the object of investigation and we may accept Freud's warrior courage and his great self-confidence as regards his work was largely based on the experience having been his mother's favourite.

As we have said, in Freud's case this object of knowledge—the mother for whose conquest he fought—was above all, the past i.e. the origin of the facts. E. *Jones,* in posing the question of what childhood circumstances had incited to such a high degree this search for the genesis of things, points out the extraordinarily complex character of Freud's family setting which must have greatly troubled the mind of the young Sigmund. The complexity of the situation lay in the fact that Freud found himself with two stepbrothers, the offspring of his father's former marriage, twenty-odd years older than himself, one of whom already had a son when Freud was born. Freud thus came into the world an uncle, and this nephew, who had the advantage of him in age, was the main companion and rival in his play during early childhood. The younger of Freud's stepbrothers, Philipp, was the same age as Freud's mother. It was upon Philipp that the little Freud seems to have placed the image of his sexual father but this phantasy clashed with the fact that it was another man, his father, who slept with his mother. The early appearance of younger siblings—the first was born before Freud was one year old and died when Freud was one and a half, the second, a sister, was born a year later—the repeated trauma, then, of the mother's pregnancy and the birth of these and other rival siblings must have greatly stimulated the boy Freud's search after the genesis of "things," complicated as they were by the family constellation I have described.

However, the intensity and multiplicity of external stimuli do not explain genius. As Freud himself affirmed, we have not as yet sufficient access to this enigma. What, on the other hand, the data set forth and the brief analytic considerations do indeed show us is how a characteristic—as the urge to uncover the past—may be understood in its roots or else in its instinctive and infantile expressions. In a similar manner we may assume that the death of the first brother-rival, which caused a great deal of unconscious guilt feelings in Freud, served to stimulate to a high degree his desire to make repair through creative action.

Let us now continue with our attempt at building up and defining the image of Freud from the glimpses his work has afforded us. We have seen how Freud felt called upon to explore the history of the facts and we have seen how wide this sphere of interest was for him. Yet we cannot fail to note that there was one main object in his field of investigation, namely, man's *psychological suffering* and *its genesis*.

When Freud describes the path he followed, from his choice of profession to the creation of psychoanalysis, and, in particular, when he tells of the gradual shifting of his interest from neurology to psychopathology, he draws attention to a series of external factors, such as the financial problem, the fact that he could not maintain his growing family on what was to be earned from his very limited neurological consultations. He also stresses his desire to know the nature and causes of pathological phenomena and his aversion to blindly applying unspecific therapeutic methods such as hydro- or electro-therapy or suggestion technique of hypnosis. But these two factors, the financial and the scientific ones, do not suffice to explain this evolution in Freud. His evolution and his work point to one further inclination and one further capacity: the inclination to identify himself with those who suffer in the spirit and the vocation and capacity to understand and aid them. In several of his writings Freud denies in some measure this concern for therapy and it is true that it was not predominant in him. But it is no less true that psychoanalysis could only have been created by someone who tended strongly towards psychological union with others, and perhaps even towards suffering with them, and who through this union desired to be and was able to be an understanding, strong, and kind father, who never condemns and can therefore help, protect and guide. His works and especially his clinical case-histories speak clearly of this power of being the kind father whom one can confide in and trust, in spite of all Freud's attempts at modestly covering up this capacity and these affective motives and in spite of a certain dampening they do indeed undergo on account of another psychological factor in his nature. I refer to Freud's so-called pessimism, a trait that will concern us later.

Freud's capacity for empathy with another's feelings and passions also leads us to another of his capacities: that of empathy with the *thinking* of his fellow men. Although these two capacities are associated by their quality of empathy, we are, as a matter of fact, dealing with two quite different factors of Freud's personality. The former had much of vocation about it (though an unconfessed and dampened vocation) whereas the latter, the intellectual empathy, was merely a gift, one more talent among several but a particularly marked one. One of its most delightful expressions we find in those parts of his writings where he makes the reader or listener speak, for instance, in raising objections to what Freud has just stated. You will remember how frequently these passages recur in the "Introductory Lectures to Psychoanalysis" or in "Lay Analysis," this latter book being almost entirely a dialogue between Freud and an imaginary opponent. This empathy with the other's thinking is the consequence of a bent towards dialectic reasoning, i.e. towards reasoning in thesis and antithesis, towards inner intellectual duality, that is to say, doubt. This inner intellectual struggle renders him familiar with the most diverse intellectual standpoints, just as his own emotional and instinctual struggles opened the way for him to the psychological depths in others. When Freud makes a statement, there stands next to it, with remarkable frequency, an antithesis which, as the case may be, he either expresses as a doubt of his own or projects onto the reader. Hence the "intellectual empathy" which confers upon him, at the same time, such extraordinary intellectual universality, skill and ease. This is, moreover, one of his capacities that, together with his artistic gifts, make the reading of his works a feast for the spirit.

Doubt appears in Freud in yet another form, deeper but graver. Not only as talent, play and art but also as burden, need and sorrow. I refer to a certain *compulsion to doubt* and for this I find support in part in Freud himself who was of the opinion that, in the event of his ever having developed a full neurosis, this would have been an obsessional neurosis, an illness in which, as you know, doubt plays a central part. This compulsion to doubt is expressed in various aspects; in its mildest form in his scepticism and in its extreme form in what some of his adverse critics have called his "pessimism." Against this criticism, E. Jones rightly points out the many expressions of Freud's optimism and accepts the term "pessimism" only insofar as this may mean one's being free from illusion i.e. as realism. But it is plain that this is not what those critics mean and I believe that they did indeed point to something that ready existed in Freud, only that it was greatly moderated by other characterological components of a different and more optimistic nature. Further: thanks to his creative powers, Freud converted this burden, this pessimism, into a stimulus (like a physical resistance may act as a stimulus to our muscles) and it even became a factor that codetermined the *direction* that Freud's investigations took. For I think that it demanded a considerable dose of scepticism and mistrust as regards everything that is usually called "higher" in human nature to discover the unconscious and, in particular, its instinctive part. This mistrust is at the same time a mistrust of higher things in general so that it was not a matter of chance that Freud should have repeatedly taken as the subject of his research ideas about God and religion, i.e. beliefs about something higher than man. To this mistrust and pessimism we owe, then, the deepest insight into the origins of religion and infantile religiosity in the collective and individual history of man. It was a scepticism made fruitful and Freud was, as he himself said, a "gay pessimist."

Yet in certain respects he had something of the lack of faith that characterizes a true pessimist. Take, for instance, to cite but one example, the following words from his book "The Man Moses and the Monotheistic Religion," in which Freud refers to the question of the nature of "higher things": "Perhaps," says he, "man proclaims as *higher* what is *more difficult to achieve,* and his pride in this is no more than his narcissism of having overcome a difficulty." We see then, how Freud, thanks to his great scepticism, obtains a new psychological under-

375

standing: narcissism determines our *evaluations*. But at the same time we feel—or I do at least—a certain absence of faith, a lack of hope for the existence of *objective values*, which even implies a certain despair. Furthermore, if we accept in its full bearing what Freud says, his words imply something like a spiritual suicide. For if there are no objective values, if the "higher" is only the "more difficult" and our striving for it is merely a product of our narcissism, then all the works of culture, science, and art, and among them Freud's own achievements are devoid of objective worth.

It might be said that objective values become at times the terrifying spectre of a conscience smitten by neurotic guilt, where the ego feels safer under the shelter of relativism. For if everything is relative, so is what we unconsciously deem our unforgivable sins and our irreparable, i.e. absolute, misdeeds. In this sense our lack of faith would spring from a fear of punishment and would be a protection against it. Nevertheless, I have the impression that the lack of faith is even more the punishment itself, an unconscious self-punishment. If this is so, then we fear the faith in objective values and we repress it in the same way as the moral masochist fears and represses anything good, since what is bad, i.e. punishment, offers him greater safety. On the other hand as happens with neurotic symptoms, here as well the repressed returns in the defence, for faith returns within scepticism and relativism itself, the faith in something absolute, indubitable, this faith in values, which is a reflection of love itself that lets us know what is good, even if this knowing begins so modestly with the knowledge that *the good* is the mother's milk. I say that faith returns in the scepticism itself for now it is relativism that is taken as objective truth par excellence, as the absolute. That is to say that, in reality, even the relativist and pessimist continues to believe. To return to Freud, we have already mentioned that there acted upon him intense unconscious guilt feelings, increased by the death of his first younger brother, and I think that it was the fear and need of punishment they entailed, that overshadowed his profound faith in objective values and submerged it, in part, in his unconscious. The passing attempt at spiritual suicide I cited above as an example confirms it, for it is murder that is paid with one's own death. In Freud's physical life there was, besides, something similar: some fainting-fits after certain personal triumphs, which Freud himself connects with the death of his little brother. We may say once again that they were passing suicide attempts, here on the bodily plane. And in fact in the physical we find what we supposed, about the spiritual suicide: it is self-punishment and the same time a protection against the punishment, a protection prompted by the motto: "Better a horrible end than an endless horror." But in Freud it was, in both the spiritual and the physical respects, no more than a transitory phase, a partial and secondary component of his psychism. Even in the above-mentioned example, he puts a "perhaps" at the start of his "pessimistic" affirmation. The doubt, the scepticism, induced perhaps by the repressed faith, avails itself of this very scepticism and opens to more optimistic thoughts, "gayer ones" (as he said), access to the faith in objective values, to enthusiasm for truth and beauty, to which his mind heart—thanks to many other qualities of his rich nature—were open to the highest degree.

So we may celebrate the day on which, one hundred years ago, a man was born who not only devoted his life to striving for the victory of truth over falsehood, of love over hatred and of health over sickness, but also found it in him to bring to light a work that was destined to be one of the most precious gifts to humanity that one man alone has ever been able to offer. This gift is the knowledge that has been sought by many since man has existed, the knowledge that frees humankind from the worst enemy of his happiness and of what he feels to be his true destiny. This enemy is anxiety and the whelp of anxiety, hatred, which bar man's path to his innermost self, to his capacity for creation and to his love for his neighbour. Hitherto it has been given to few to enjoy this great gift well. Much remains to be done for all to partake fully. But the great harvest will come, for the seed has been cast and the first fruits have already ripened. Our thanks for what this sowing has yielded us, and has yet to yield us, go out to the great sower—Sigmund Freud.

Freud: My Father

(1958)

MARTIN FREUD

Martin was Freud's oldest son. Before leaving Austria in 1937 he was in charge of Verlag, *the company in Vienna which published all of Freud's works. He settled with his
family in London, where he published* Sigmund Freud: Man and Father *(New York,
Vanguard Press, 1958), from which the following selections were made.*

In 1923 father became aware for the first time of the disease, cancer of
the palate, which was to cause his death sixteen years later, the beginning of a long chain of operations—some severe, others less severe—
and continuous medical supervision. Travelling far from home was
now out of the question; and so the family, so reduced in numbers,
had to make the best of the friendly seasons by moving out each spring
to some villa in the outer suburbs of Vienna and remaining there until
the autumn.

I recall three of these villas as being particularly charming. Built on
the hills bordering the Wienerwald before the war by wealthy people,
some of whom had now become the Viennese new poor, people who
were glad of some increase in their reduced incomes, these homes
were most comfortable if a little old-fashioned. They each had large
and beautiful gardens. The last villa father and mother took in Grinzing had a garden, large enough to be called a park, in which one
could get lost, and it had a fine orchard which offered delicious early
apricots. Where the park ended, vineyards began and stretched for
many miles.

From this Grinzing villa one had a magnificent view over Vienna.
The steep road leading from the city to the hills passed the house.
Mother loved this particular view and liked to sit in one of the bow
windows watching people approaching like black ants in the distance
and gradually assuming human form as they drew near. She was always aware of my approach even while I still remained hardly bigger

378

than a black ant. I suggested during one of my frequent visits that she must have been guessing, that without binoculars she could hardly identify me. Her reply was characteristic of her methodical and observant mind. "When," she explained, "these little ants reach a point where the road becomes notably steep, they slow down. If one, an exception, marches on as if there were no difference in the road's grading, I know it's you."

The parks and gardens of the villas were the delight of the family dogs. It is no criticism of the British way of life to suggest that a British family dog appears to be the most important member of the family. Nor would I, myself, dare to offer criticism at this time when, in my own small Highgate household, a Welsh corgi's appetite or loss of appetite, his amiable moods or signs of displeasure, and even what appear to be his fancies, control the lives of the inhabitants. My family, and father emphatically so, had unconsciously become dog-lovers. Yet neither father nor mother had kept dogs in their youth. In mother's case, Jewish practice, which tended to regard the dog as an unclean animal, made keeping one as a family friend unthinkable. In father's case, it was a matter of poverty: he never permitted himself to be affected by religious considerations.

It was Marie Bonaparte (the maiden name and nom de plume of the Princess George of Greece) who showed father what a delightful friend and companion a dog can be.

During the period of the summers spent in the outskirts of Vienna, father kept Chows, and my sister Anna favoured an Alsatian.

Jofi was father's favourite and never left him, not even when he treated patients. Then she would lie motionless near his desk, that desk adorned with its Greek and Egyptian antique statuettes, while he concentrated on the treatment of patients. He always claimed, and we must accept his word since there were never witnesses during analytical treatment, that he never had to look at his watch to decide when the hour's treatment should end. When Jofi got up and yawned, he knew the hour was up: she was never late in announcing the end of a session, although father did admit that she was capable of an error of perhaps a minute, at the expense of the patient. The two young red Chows which appear in the photograph with father on the balcony of one of the villas died of the disease which at this time destroyed nearly every second puppy in Austria. No expense was spared and everything possible was done to save his pets. Their loss caused much grief.

Anna's Alsatian, Wolf—a name that fitted perfectly—was highly intelligent. Anna used to take him for a walk early every morning in the Prater, having no difficulty whatever with him since he was well trained and obedient; but one morning, a squad of soldiers exercising near by fired a blank salvo into the air which so frightened Wolf that, much to Anna's distress, he disappeared like a streak of lightning. Certain that he would sooner or later return to his mistress, to whom he was completely devoted, Anna searched in every direction as she called him; but at last, seriously distressed since there was no sign of him, she was forced to return home. Here she was cheerfully welcomed by Wolf. He had taken a taxi home.

According to the taxi-driver, Wolf had jumped into his cab and courteously resisted all efforts to remove him while, at the same time, raising his nose sufficiently high to permit the taximan to read his name and address on the medallion hanging from his collar. Wolf must have thought the man rather stupid in not immediately understanding what he meant. The address, "Professor Freud, Berggasse 19," was plainly written.

There was already some concern at the flat through Anna's unusually late return and, while Wolf was welcome, the family feared something unfortunate might have happened to his mistress. However, Wolf's fare had to be paid.

"Herr Professor," said the taximan, "for this passenger I have not switched on the taxi-meter."

He was not disappointed with the fare father gave him.

Our dogs had the freedom of the flat and met everybody who came, being quite selective, even judicious, in the receptions they offered. The whole family, including Paula, our faithful maid, showed considerable respect for this canine sensibility. When the dogs condescended to be stroked, the visitor enjoyed the best possible introduction. If Jofi, for instance, sniffed somewhat haughtily around the legs of a caller and then stalked off with a touch of ostentation, there was at once a strong suspicion that there was something wrong with that caller's character. Contemplating Jofi's selective qualities at this distance of years, I feel bound to admit that her judgment was most reliable.

From the moment my father became internationally famous, he was continuously photographed until the end of his life and the result distributed throughout the world. For these posed photographs he used what his children called his *Photographier Gesicht,* his photographing face, rather a stern, serious face which did not for a moment reflect his kindly and friendly nature, not severe and reserved, as the world must regard him if they judge him by posed photographs. Sigmund Freud was a very nice grandfather and his true nature is always shown when he is photographed with a grandchild or two.

It might be imagined that life at Berggasse 19, presided over by an old professor and his old wife, the former suffering from an incurable disease, would be dull and even sad; but this was not so. When father was free from actual pain, it was gay and cheerful. It remains associated in my mind with smiles and happy faces. Family jokes were welcome, but one practical joke I attempted tended to misfire and still makes me feel uncomfortable when I think of it.

A man in Sigmund Freud's position is bombarded by much correspondence, and it was often heavy work to sort father's mail, which was sometimes addressed to the press and sometimes to Berggasse 19. The cranks and other queer correspondents generally chose the press, and I would carry their letters as well as the more important communications with me on my twice-daily calls on father to discuss business. Father dealt with everything speedily and efficiently. For some weeks there had arrived most regularly letters from a German whose notepaper boldly proclaimed him to be an "Astrologer and Psychoanalyst." The letters asked for a meeting to discuss matters of mutual scientific interest, and their phraseology clearly proclaimed a crank. Father's verdict before destroying each of this man's letters was, "No reply!"

Nevertheless the letters from the "Astrologer and Psychoanalyst" continued to arrive and to grow so much in urgency that I felt bound to advise father to send some kind of reply, signed by me as his secretary, regretting firmly that a meeting could not be arranged. But father was adamant: there should be no reply.

The "Astrologer and Psychoanalyst" became something of a joke but, as it turned out, not quite so much of a joke as I had imagined when I got our printers to design a visiting card boldly printed with the gentleman's name, address, and profession. A theatrical hairdresser having turned me into a grizzly old gentleman with abundant grey hair and a long beard, I placed horn-rimmed spectacles on my nose and walked to Berggasse 19, no passer-by taking the slightest notice of me and thus allowing me to know that my disguise was perfect. Paula was in the plot and admitted me and, although we had not confided in the dogs, they accepted me without question and nearly ruined the joke forthwith by their normal display of friendliness.

381

Paula went before me with the card, and I arrived in time to hear father shout, "By all means keep that man out!"

"Herr Professor," I began in a voice well disguised by my thick beard, "between scientists there are certain rules of behaviour, even if they differ in their theories——"

This was as far as I got. As father leant back in his chair, giving the "Astrologer and Psychoanalyst" so furious a glare that I must have paled under my disguise, Anna, whom it is very difficult to deceive and who was probably helped by the friendly behaviour of the dogs, cried, "It is Martin, Papa!" and the tension eased in general laughter. Nevertheless, I must admit that when I had removed my disguise, I endured an anticlimax that was not pleasant. Father's furious glare, although not really meant for me, had shocked and shaken me.

One of my jobs at this time was to look after father's income tax. Knowing that he would insist on accurate figures being given, I always made a full and true return, showing a sum which in Britain or the United States would not have been considered extraordinary in view of Sigmund Freud's eminence, but in Austria at this time, where most professional people were poor, the figures appeared staggering. On one occasion when I carried the returns to the income-tax inspector, a middle-aged gentleman with a face so German that he could easily have posed as an extra in a *Nibelungen* film, I was astonished to hear him remark after studying the figures, "With such a return, the old gentleman would not have enough money to live on." He thereupon replaced my total with one of his own calculation, reducing the former by two-thirds, the corrections being made neatly with a perfectly sharpened pencil.

What Ernest Jones in his biography of my father calls "the emergence from isolation" did not make a welcome change to us. I think we preferred father's isolation. Father was not only generous with his money, he was also generous with his time, although, in all conscience, he had not much of the latter to give. He worked ten hours a day on practising analysis, apart from his writing and correspondence.

The children's contacts with the learned men who came to see him to discuss his theories were naturally of the slightest. Such visitors were usually asked to stay for a meal and nearly always, we saw, they had little interest in the food they were offered and perhaps less in mother and us children. However, they always worked hard to maintain a polite conversation with their hostess and her children, most often about the theatre or sport, the weather not being a useful stand-by as it is in England on these occasions. Nevertheless, it could be seen quite easily that all they wanted was to get this social occasion over and done with and to retreat with father to his study to hear more about psychoanalysis. Jung was an exception. He never made the slightest attempt to make polite conversation with mother or us children but pursued the debate which had been interrupted by the call to dinner. Jung on these occasions did all the talking and father with unconcealed delight did all the listening. There was little we could understand, but I know I found, as did father, his way of outlining a case most fascinating. I can recall today the case of a man who, after being shy and inhibited during the first two-thirds of his life, developed in late middle age a forceful and dominating personality, and the story of another man, a schizophrenic, whose drawing showed an amazing vitality and excellence.

Neither cases had in themselves much importance. Discussed by Jung, they became clear pictures.

Those of my readers who have studied modern psychology have learned much about Jung—probably as much as about Freud—but to others his name may mean nothing. Jung held a leading position in Switzerland's most famous psychiatric clinic and he was a scientist of high reputation. I think his most outstanding characteristics were his vitality, his liveliness, his ability to project his personality and to control those who listened to him.

Jung had a commanding presence. He was very tall and broad-shouldered, holding himself more like a soldier than a man of science and medicine. His head was purely Teutonic with a strong chin, a small moustache, blue eyes, and thin close-cropped hair. I met Jung only once. When, later in life, I moved much in psychoanalytical circles, he had already left the Freud-adherents; I cannot flatter myself that he ever noticed me.

Sister Mathilde told me that one day when she was shopping in Vienna with Jung and his family, soldiers lining the street were ordered to attention. The Emperor was about to pass. With a quick "Excuse me, please!" Jung ran to join the crowd as enthusiastic as any boy.

One of the very few psychoanalysts who showed interest in his host's children at the Berggasse was Dr. Sandor Ferenczy of Budapest. He was high in father's favour. A lively, witty and most affectionate man, he found not the slightest difficulty in winning my devoted friendship, a friendship not affected by the fact that I knew he was assuming the role of a mentor in a worthy desire to help me on my way through adolescence to manhood.

I never met Dr. Adler, so often associated with my father's name by biographers and those who write about psychoanalysis.

We were aware of the Wednesday night meetings in the waiting-room of the Berggasse flat, where great minds, led by father, strove to bring to the surface knowledge long suspected but still fugitive and still unrecorded with that precision science demands. We heard people arriving, but we seldom saw them. The inevitable curiosity of a boy allowed me to inspect the arrangements in the waiting-room before the guests arrived. Near each chair on the table there was always an ashtray from father's collection, some of them of Chinese jade. I saw the necessity for this multiplicity of ashtrays one night when, on returning from a dance, I looked into the waiting-room from which the guests had only just withdrawn. The room was still thick with smoke and it seemed to me a wonder that human beings had been able to live in it for hours, let alone to speak in it without choking. I could never understand how father could endure it, let alone enjoy it: which he did. It is possible that to some of his guests the smoke-charged atmosphere was an ordeal, but it is certain they thought the price low in exchange for the high privilege of a close personal contact with a great teacher.

It was very seldom that I met Dr. Fliess, father's best friend for sixteen years, and I cannot recall any personal details about him. His portrait, even after the ending of this great friendship, always remained in father's study in a place of honour. Another friendship, that with Dr. Breuer, had ended long before my years of consciousness; but relations with Dr. Breuer's family remained most cordial and I still have a few pictures showing a mixed bag of Freud children and the grandchildren of Josef Breuer playing in summer holiday mood in Altaussee. By a strange coincidence a grandson of Josef Breuer and a grandson of Sigmund Freud (my son, in fact), both British officers in No. 1 Special Force, parachute-jumped from the same aeroplane into enemy territory during the last months of the war, and both survived.

Freud's Aesthetics
(1958)

LUDWIG MARCUSE

The German Kultur-Philosoph Ludwig Marcuse is well known for his writings about Freud. This selection first appeared in German in PMLA (June 1957). It was then published in The Journal of Aesthetics & Art Criticism 17 (September 1958) no. 1, in a translation by Ludwig Marcuse and Herbert M. Schueller of Wayne State University.

Freud, the philosopher, was at odds with philosophers. He treated religion with disdain, as did the *philosophes* of the eighteenth century, but more subtly, for he wielded the weapons of a psychology which they had not known. With the arts, however, he was at peace. One might almost say that he lived in longing admiration of them.[1]

He rejected the philosophers because he felt that the fundamental concepts of their systems were not pure in origin; he opposed the theologians even more strongly because they enjoyed greater popularity. The fact that metaphysicians and religious dogmatists purported to proclaim "scientific" truths particularly aroused Freud's resentment. Since the artists had never had this ambition, he was able to enjoy their creations without being disturbed. Since they were not subject to scientific reason, they did not conflict with it. To him, artistic works were, in this sense, "harmless," because they had nothing to do with reality and consciously created only lovely illusions.[2]

But, in relegating the accomplishments of art to a sphere beyond reality, Freud failed to realize how strongly they have influenced man's picture of reality. For, by the magical alchemy of art, they have transformed metaphysical and religious dogmas into the "stuff that dreams are made on," and thereby have made individuals and groups more poignantly aware of these dogmas than they would otherwise have been. It was, for example, the artists who raised Platonic as well as Christian concepts to tremendous importance. But Freud, when he talked thus of art, was probably thinking only of those conscious so-

385

journs into fantasy which both the artists and public recognize as purely fictional.

Of course, we must admit that no artist—not even Richard Wagner—has ever yet tried to make his realm of make-believe appear as literal truth. That is why artists have never been thought of as dictators, as philosophers and theologians have been. They have always seemed less authoritative because, even in the time of Homer and Dante, the element of make-believe was visibly mixed with their creations. So it came about that Freud, who saw Reason as the great hope of all men, did not see any danger in the arts, as he did in the teachings of the priests and the speculative thinkers. For art does not pretend to be guided by reason, whereas these other realms of thought do so pretend.

However, Freud had more to say in favor of art than merely to approve its "harmlessness." He praised it as an indispensable benefit, although he by no means concurred with the idealistic philosophy of art; every Platonism, every cult of "pure form," was foreign to his nature, and he had no use for that idealism which, according to Kuno Fischer, values art for art's sake and claims that art has a purpose only in and of itself and does not fulfill any other purpose in life.[3] Freud, rather, sought to find in man's aesthetic expression—as he did in every other important expression—the life-purpose which had brought it into being. He found this purpose in what he called "fantasy-satisfaction."[4] According to Freud, the realm of fantasy gives us our only glimpses of a better world than the actual one. Man's desires (particularly his erotic and self-seeking ones—also noted by Balzac in his *Comédie Humaine*), which are not able to achieve their aims in the harsher medium of reality, reach a modest fulfillment here. One is reminded of the familiar concept of *catharsis* when Freud finds the accomplishment of artistic creation in what he calls the freeing of instincts. The artist, then, *frees* himself by giving shape and form to the instincts and desires which drive him, just as, one might say, the patient does in analysis.

But what sort of artist does Freud describe? He says of this artist that he tones down what is objectionable in his wishes; that he conceals the personal origin of these wishes; and that, through adherence to the laws of aesthetics, he offers fascinating rewards to others. In this respect, Freud was describing, for example, his contemporary, Conrad Ferdinand Meyer, whom he very much admired. And clearly, Freud's portrait of the artist was influenced by the mild and gentle climate of

German art at the end of the nineteenth century. Had he grown to manhood after 1914, he would have seen that the "make-believe" reality of art is capable of using much that is unaltered, unconcealed, and not at all mild or gentle. And if he had thought of Aeschylus and Shakespeare, he would have had to ask himself whether they really toned down the passions and made them gentle; or whether Goethe concealed the personal origin of his wishes; or whether Beethoven and Wagner abided by these rules of aesthetics. This concept of art as the transformation of the passions into beautiful make-believe certainly cannot be ascribed to art in general, for it is not valid for all times or for all artists. Freud's picture of art as a mild reflection is thus primarily an indication of his personal point of view.

There is a tendency which, secretly or openly, dedicates itself to the undertaking which Freud sees as artistic activity; it is called escape. But this word has connotations which imply moralistic condemnation. It suggests that certain works of art are escape, but that there is an art which is nondecadent and which, as people imagine, inspires human beings in their thoughts of the beyond, or, as all activists think (among whom the Marxists are one group among many), becomes a weapon in a good fight. It is chiefly this activistic aesthetics in vogue during recent decades which has seen to it that Freud's theory of the function of art has not been discussed outside professional circles.

If one frees himself from the fashionable "sociological" approach to art, he quickly recognizes that political art is an escape like every other kind; but it is both more disguised and more superficial. People live in ivory towers of madness, or in those ivory towers of illusions which effect a release from the difficulties of life. Political art can be a substitute for revolution, as an examination of the aesthetic works of Richard Wagner will reveal. And the aesthetic activists undervalue the activity of escape, so-called; for this activity is so strong that it breaks through into the realm of fantasy and imagination because reality bars it from its very doors.

Freud's escapist theory of art, however, is not reactionary, but moved by humane considerations. He starts with the recognition that reality is hard for everyone to bear all of the time; that one needs occasional vacations; that art, as a source of pleasure and as a comfort in life, helps him who creates it and him who enjoys it (XIV, 439). If, thereupon, one were to ask him whether church dogmas and the teachings of the philosophers were not also sources of pleasure and comfort in life, he would reply that only art has no bad consequences, that although men have crucified in the name of Aristotle and Thomas Aquinas, they have never done so in the name of Michelangelo.

According to Freud, the great accomplishment of art—its ability to present a world free of danger or trouble and to cast a semblance of reality over "that which never was on land or sea"—points to its prehistoric origin. One of the most fruitful questions, he believed, that can be raised about myths, religion, philosophy, art, and science is: What human need brought them into being? For we can assume that the urgency which called these creations into existence for the first time, calls them forth again and again. But Freud did not forget that the complex richness, which we call by the generic name of art, most assuredly had more than one single source. In contrast to the Freud legend, Freud was no scientific "monotheist," attributing everything to one single all-powerful cause or source.[5] In *Totem and Taboo* he says one need not be concerned that psychoanalysis will be able to trace everything as complicated as religion back to a single source. In Freud's works one can find at least three sources, and nowhere does he say that these are all that there are, as many a Freudian and probably every Marxist does. We must bear this in mind when we admire his superb deductions, as for example, that of the genealogy of fantasy.

He saw the first vigorous source of art in an escape into a reality created by fantasy. He thus outlined the escape which must historically have been the first: "The first poet invented reality because of the longing in his heart." He posed as a hero; and "only the man who had killed his father was a hero" (XIII, 152). This is not the place to mention the comprehensive theory according to which the root of all expressions of culture is patricide.[6] In any case, the birth of art was the first example of the realization of an ideal given direction by the germinating power of psychic impulse—but of realization through representation. The first poet was a person who accomplished this process for the first time; he imagined himself a hero and deceived himself with his conceit. The "invention" of reality mentioned in the above quotation from Freud is the invention of an actor—a middle ground between the identification of the hero with the heroic actor and with the comic actor. Here is an important starting-point for research in history, anthropology, and animal-psychology.[7] But one should not use the word "poet" for the creator most gifted in fantasy because with this word the critical difference is wiped out. Only the powerful aestheticism of the young Nietzsche and of Richard Wagner, who tried to bring reality under the laws of art and who tried to turn back the flight away from reality by way of the acquisition of reality through fantasy—only an offensive in art as aggressive as theirs has the right to identify poet and creator.

One of the difficulties of the Freudian aesthetic is that a very different kind of play is pointed out as the source of art. Freud states that "the opposite of play is not seriousness, but—reality" (VIII, 214). He shows that one can discover the pre-historical root of artistic play in the playing of children: in the creation of an unreal world, but a world sketched from reality. As always, here too he looks for the hidden sources in situations which can be checked and which, it is true, are more clear and more easily understood than are contemporary, everyday conditions. That which binds together children, primitives, the sick, and genius (Freud's favorite avenues to the soul) is this: The original impulses are not yet hidden, or not so completely hidden, by conventional habits. Thus in the play of children Freud discovers that the dangerous, painful situations found in reality are repeated freely, are therefore brought under the influence of the persons doing the playing, and are therefore also deprived of power. The origin of tragedy, puzzled over in all periods by the aestheticians, which offers the most painful impressions to the spectator (and to his pleasure), is given new meaning in his theory (XIII, 15). Indeed, it may be added further that this origin of artistic play has no correlatives at the present time. But Freud correctly calls attention to the fact that art certainly did not begin as *l'art pour l'art* (IX, 111).

According to Freud, art arose as a substitute for instinct-satisfaction, "protecting" men during their painful transition from the pleasure principle to the reality principle.[8] The most varied types took refuge in the general realm of fantasy: the paranoid, the neurotic, the dreamer, the pious, the speculative, as well as the artistic. The artist's place, however, is a realm between what Freud called "wish-denying reality" and the "wish-fulfilling world of fantasy"—in other words, between the bitterness of daily existence and the even more bitter realm of delusion. The psychotic is imprisoned in a world of delusions; the neurotic attempts, too often unsuccessfully, to derive satisfactions from actions, ideas, and emotions in a sort of make-believe world which can make life very hard for him; the artist has, if one may so express it, all of the advantages and none of the disadvantages of illusion, because he can travel freely on the road from fantasy to reality. If the psychotic could also recognize make-believe as make-believe, Freud might have said, he would not be deluded and would no longer be a psychotic. To Freud, then, the artist is evidently a man who is better able than anyone else to get along with his troubles, and who is thus not at all a "genius" akin to the "madman," as the old platitude has it. For such a hackneyed expression, Freud had no use.

The Romanticists had the same concept of the artist, seeing him as freer, more released, more a human being than the rest of mankind. Freud presented him as a sort of uncensored, particularly healthy and sound variety of humanity, the kind of person described in a passage in Heine's *Thoughts and Ideas*, which Freud particularly liked: "I am a man of the most peaceful cast of mind. My wishes consist of a modest little hut, a thatched roof, a good bed, good food; milk and butter, very fresh; flowers at the window, a few good trees in front of the door; and, if God would really want to make me completely happy, then he will let me have the pleasure of having some six or seven of my enemies dangling from these trees. With a heart full of emotion, I will forgive them for all of their iniquities—but not before they have been hanged."

There is, of course, a third source of art. The fundamental category of art has again and again been called "beauty," which is a parallel to "truth" and "goodness." A detailed exposition of the history of this word would show that it is identical with the suggestive, the fascinating, the effective, the enlightening, and the elevating; the concept of the beautiful because of what floats up, alongside, and within it, is without a definite contour. Thus it can probably be said that "beautiful" in its specific meaning is primarily a category of seeing. Whence does this beauty come?

Freud says that "the science of aesthetics examines the conditions under which beauty is perceived; but it cannot shed any light about the nature of beauty or its origin" (XIV, 411). This is not consistent with the entire field of aesthetics, though it agrees with the aesthetics of strict classifications. For example, Goethe and Schiller as aestheticians have been very resourceful about the "nature and origin" of the beautiful. In his "Maxims and Reflections on Art" Goethe insists that "the arts do not imitate exactly what one sees with his eyes, but look back toward the reasonable from which nature stems and according to which it acts." [9] This "reasonable" is the beautiful. Schiller gives the same thing a Kantian version: "The beautiful is not a concept of experience, but rather an imperative of it." [10] The imperative reads thus: Set the basic idea of any given object into relief!

Freud's hostility toward every kind of metaphysics of reason caused a separation between his deduction of the beautiful and such metaphysical theories and similar speculation. A social psychology vaguely based on biology would always like to make any kind of descent or source intelligible. In a short note Freud traces the beautiful back to sexual attraction (V, 55). The beautiful is "the premium of seduction" (XIV, 90). It is self-evident that such *aperçus* are nothing but indications of a direction in research which had not yet been taken. But before one goes in this direction, one must ask himself the question: From what does visual-sexual attraction derive? Does one not presuppose "pleasure in the observing of beauty of form"?

Freud's three historical sources for art (that of the first "poet," that of mastery through repetition in play, and now also that of the connection of beauty with sexual attraction) have something in common: They originate in an impulse of a need. In this derivation of beauty, Otto Rank saw too high an estimate of the "Id" and too low an opinion of the "I," of the bearer of the creative process. Lionel Trilling goes even further: He sees here not only an error, but a disparagement of art. He says that "Freud speaks of art with what we must indeed call contempt" (p. 51).[11] But Freud never had "contempt" for a cultural phenomenon when he explained it as "the satisfaction of impulses." There are evident vestiges of theological-idealistic judgments when a person differentiates between fine and coarse origins and when he then meets the "coarse" ones with contempt. Freud did not show disdain for art, but he was indifferent to those of its elements which seemed the farthest removed from the vital ones.

Freud was not at all interested in what he called "aesthetics"—he might better have called it "formal aesthetics"—as it was practiced, for example, by the Swiss art historian, Wölfflin, and today by the American "New Criticism." According to Freud, the psychoanalyst works with the different layers of the life of the soul, whereas the aesthetician is concerned, for the most part, only with certain senses which have been inhibited and dulled.[12] This, of course, is not a fair judgment. The great works on aesthetics—from the *Poetics* to the third book of *The World as Will and Imagination*, Richard Wagner's *The Art of the Future*, and Busoni's *Plan for a New Aesthetics of Music*—have attempted to do the same thing that Freud did, namely, to find the source of creative art by determining its effect upon both the creator and the public. Freud, therefore, should have been able to accept the word *aesthetics* without hesitation, since he himself practiced it—in his reflections upon artists and works of art, his study of

Jensen's short novel *Gradiva*, his investigation of "The Uncanny," and his biographical sketches of Leonardo, Goethe, and Dostoevski.

It is no accident that he attempted to solve aesthetic problems by primarily biographical means. But one must "purify" the word "biographical" of many of its associations. To whom is the poem directed? In what actual sorrow was this line of verse created? What kind of reading is the source of the subject? Biographical questions like these are nothing but matters of jest when the answer is sought for its own sake. In this connection Freud can say that "the relations between the life of the poet and his creations" have been interpreted in too simple a fashion (VII, 221). It is this too simple a conception which has made gossips of biographers. For Freud biography is not private life; he does not recognize, as is customarily done, a lack of connection between a life and a work; for him the work is a real utterance of the life which is not merely an accidental prerequisite to divine existence.

In the essay, "A Childhood Recollection of Leonardo da Vinci," he outlines clearly "the ability of psychoanalysis to play a part in biography" (VIII, 208): "Our aim remains the knowledge of the coherence between outward expressions and the reactions of the individual or his way of reacting to impulses" (VII, 209–210). What can such knowledge mean for the illumination of a work, and where do the limits of this method of study lie? The answer reads thus: "If psychoanalysis cannot explain the fact of Leonardo's artistic character [and therefore one may add: no theory of art has explained "the fact of the artistic character" of any single artist], then it will make understandable his expression and his limitations. Thus it would seem as if only a man with the childhood experiences of Leonardo could have painted the *Mona Lisa* and *St. Anne and Two Others*, could make use of that sad fortune in his work, and therefore could be seized by unheard-of rapture as an investigator of nature" (VIII, 210). Leonardo's life is not narrated, but it is interpreted in terms of the situation which Freud thinks is decisive in every life: the early relation to father and mother. From the accident of Leonardo's illegitimate birth and its difficult results, from the overfondness of his mother who "by kissing excited him to an early sexual maturity" (VIII, 204), Freud derives real and plain facts of this life as well as outstanding characteristics of his art (by coordinating evidences from his life and works): not only Leonardo's (platonic) homosexuality, his passion for science at the expense of art, the smile of Mona Lisa, but also a petty tendency found in the pedantic notation of expenditures in his journal.

In a sceptical attitude typical of him he anticipates the objection that he wrote "a psychoanalytical work of fiction": he "certainly does not over-rate the certainty of these results" (XIV, 549–550), he writes.[13] But every hypothesis is a "work of fiction" before it is generally accepted. Freud's biographical explanation of the elements of form (for example, of the structure of St. Anne) is not conclusive, but it is very plausible and methodologically more fruitful than a description by the formalists which never is able to reach beyond and above this plane.

But in thus practicing his own brand of "aesthetics," Freud cannot be called—as he is by many who are hostile to theory as such and to "Freudian" theories in particular—a cold rationalist lacking respect for artistic inspiration.[14] Artists, in particular—and some "appreciators" as well—despise as "crass sophistry" all meditations on art which attempt to bring creative processes to consciousness. However, it should be remembered that a number of the greatest musicians, artists, and poets have also tried to understand and explain the creative process. And though Freud did not accept the assumption that creative artists are endowed with "divine inspiration," although he did subject artists and works of art to his theory, he was ever conscious of the complexity of the artist and his art. One might more justly accuse him of being too cautious, too sceptical rather than too rationalistic. Tirelessly, almost anxiously, he pointed out his own limitations.[15] At the beginning of the work on Dostoevski, he said that unfortunately, analysis must put up its arms when faced with the problem of understanding the poet. He held that psychoanalysis cannot "explain" artistic talent, in that it cannot trace such talent back to primeval instincts of the soul.[16]

Any sort of rationalistic over-simplification of art was foreign to his nature. He could not, in a manner characteristic of the Enlightenment—which found its most extreme expression in Kant's philosophy of music—interpret it as an illustration of theoretical and moral concepts. Unlike Kant, who applied the categories of science to art, Freud, it might be said, applied the categories of art to science. There are, for example, very dramatic elements in his arrangement of his basic concepts. The so-called rationalist Freud spoke emphatically of the much-abused priority of conscious activity which, whenever it plays a part, is permitted to cover up all other activity. This overemphasis on conscious activity conceals the fact—which is not often revealed—that even scientists make their new discoveries as the result of

393

a flash of insight rather than conscious thought. The talk about Freud as rationalist is almost as empty as is the talk about the enemy of reason who sees life only as impulse.

As a psychologist, Freud was particularly interested in those works in which he found anticipations of his own views. Thus he was drawn to Sophocles, Shakespeare, and Goethe more than to any composer or other creative artist; his work is replete with quotations from all literature. He admired in the poets what he called their sensitivity to the hidden soul-stirrings in others; he admired also "their courage in allowing their own unconscious to be audible" (VIII, 66). In a quite melancholy manner, he compared their brilliant contributions with his own gray science, which seemed to him clumsier, less like the work of genius. In recalling a lovely verse of Goethe, he had to sigh because the poet, it appeared to him, had brought forth effortlessly what the psychologist could attain only through torturing uncertainty and endless fumbling. What would Freud have said if he had known the early *Journals* of Stendhal, who at the age of nineteen and with a minimum of experiences in life, made new discoveries every day, even if with a powerful passion for the dark ways of the soul. These poets who did not search into and analyze the soul but who penetrated it gave meaning, he thought, to this science.[17] And yet, he declared, because he had worked systematically, by slow and prosaic steps, that his findings were therefore more reliable than those of the poets in their flights of genius.

It may be, however, that Freud, in so differentiating "art" and "science," was doing an injustice not only to many other thinkers, but also to the great psychologist Freud. Perhaps, in drawing the boundaries between poet and thinker in too schematic a way, he undervalued the creative elements in his own work and that of other thinkers. He once said of Leonardo that at a certain epoch of his life, he had put his scientific findings at the service of his art. It can also be said of Freud that in all the epochs of his life, he placed his artistic visions at the service of his science.

Speculative aesthetics had created hierarchies in art. The *philosophes* had set literature on the throne; the Hegelian Hebbel especially the drama; the romanticist Schopenhauer, music. As Freud was bound to no particular metaphysics with which an art theory would have had to be reconciled, he did not feel impelled to "rank" the arts. But he did have his personal preferences, namely, literature and sculpture and, to a lesser extent, painting.

However, it must be admitted that his "appreciation" and enjoyment of art was somewhat limited. In his introduction to his study of *Michelangelo's Moses,* he admitted that in order to "grasp" a work of art, he had to try to understand the reasons for its effect on him. For him, then, the enjoyment of art was possible only after he understood why he had been moved by it. More simply, one might say that *originally* he was not moved at all and had to intellectualize his impressions before enjoyment became possible. In his admission, he goes on to say that he had often noticed that he was more attracted by the contents of a work of art than by its formal and technical qualities, upon which, as is well known, the artist primarily lays value. The artist does not, for any kind of professional whim, rely on the value of professional ingenuity; what Freud contrasts as professional and technical to the content is the art in the art-work.

So perhaps Freud merely deceived himself when he said that *only* in relation to music was he almost incapable of enjoyment. However, his general incapacity was brought out particularly clearly by music, because in general it lacks—if one excepts the occasional tone painting or tone poem—what Freud calls *content.* The other arts, for the most part, contain elements which represent something real—shapes, colors, objects, and creatures, and ideas as well. Music alone does not possess these elements. But Freud's equation of the pleasure in *understanding* a work of art with *enjoyment* of art simply shows how little he knew of this specific enjoyment.

It is possible that he himself recognized his unreceptivity, even though he was inclined to limit it to music. He tried to explain it by saying that a rationalistic or perhaps analytical predisposition in him objected to his being moved, without knowing why he was moved and what it was that was moving him. Could it not therefore be said, more cautiously, that the original effects (perhaps even in music) showed themselves only when he had succeeded in incorporating them into a conceptual system? But when they did appear, would they not *then* be independent of "understanding"? And surely if he had experienced an effect at all, he would undoubtedly have expressed it somewhere in the body of his work, in which are found many statements about artists and works of art. If one looks over what Freud wrote about Leonardo and Michelangelo, about Shakespeare, Goethe, Dostoevski, and Heine, he repeatedly comes across the conclusion found in the last sentence of Freud's introduction to the book *Edgar A. Poe* by Marie Bonaparte:

"There is a special charm in studying the psychic lives of human beings in the distinguished individual" (XIV, 276).

The role played in his work by music is small indeed, but this is not true of a specific type of the art. He makes it "understandable" to himself just exactly as he does the *Mona Lisa* or *Poetry and Truth*. "Melodies which reach one directly," as he says in the *Introductory Lectures on Psychoanalysis*, reveal themselves "as conditioned by and attached to a train of thought which has a right to engage a person without one's knowing anything about the activity itself. It can easily be shown what the relation of a melody is to its text or to its source" (XI, 106). When Freud mentioned operas, he mentioned only their texts: *Tristan and Isolde* or *The Tales of Hoffmann* or *Helen the Beautiful*. A spiritual relative of Kant of the Enlightenment, who very grudgingly gave a nod to music as an art when it was not attached to words, Freud nevertheless is an exception to the "truly musical people" with whom he had "by chance no experience" (XI, 106). By chance? Did he have experience with artists in general? And is such an experience necessary if one has observed art itself?

One could demur by saying that Freud's work reveals strong artistic leanings: the rich fantasy which gave rise to his useful and his useless theories; the dramatic vein for conflicts from which all of his conceptual dualisms originate, conflicts which he finally saw all together as the world of two primary impulses rebounding from one another; the plain style which (thank God) is not only plain, but which also has the imprint of a high degree of literary mastery. Lessing was his model. But probably an artist is naturally susceptible to art; the faculty for perceiving art might rather as a gift be dependent on his education; for which reason, because pedagogues know little about this connection, there are probably more people who claim to be artists than there are those who are really susceptible to art. Preconceived opinion says that one can enjoy Homer without more ado even if one has to study the *Phaedrus*. Did Freud learn how to see and how to hear? What is known of the history of his education allows one to suppose that, from the beginning almost, he was brought up with abstractions.

Although he insisted that works of art had exerted a strong influence on him, "particularly poetry and sculpture, less often painting," it must be admitted that this receptivity to the creative arts is scarcely discernible. He occasionally made casual and not too informative reference to Giotto and Botticelli, and was apparently also

familiar with a few paintings of his contemporaries Schwind, Kaulbach, and Boecklin, such as neighbors, landscapes, and mythological
figures. A grateful female patient gave him "The Isle of the Dead" as a
"farewell-present"; [18] he compared the "mixture of persons in a
dream" with "centaurs and animals from fables found in Boecklin's
pictures" (XI, 175). A piece from Schwind's cycle *Melusine* called
"Surprise at the Bath" formed one of his dreams (II, 662); he made use
of a reproduction of Schwind's picture *The Dream of the Captive* in his
lectures to show his hearers "how accurately the painter had grasped
the source of a dream out of a dominating situation" (XI, 134). And he
quotes (almost as a poetical expression) Kaulbach's *The Battle of the
Huns* in order to show, by way of the battle which is taking place in
high regions in this work, that even the way between impulses does
not stop or come to an end by way of a "hasty sublimation or identification" (XIII, 267). Sometimes pictures appear as particles of his
world of ideas, but more frequently as witnesses of it. But, above all
the others, he used certain paintings of Leonardo as star witnesses for
his theory. He once wrote to Fliess that Leonardo, who is not known
to have had any love dealings, was perhaps the most famous left-
handed person in the world. And then he asked whether Fliess could
"make any use of him." [19] This expression "make any use of" gives us a
deep insight into Freud's relation to artists and their works. Although
he had said that we pay homage to the artist in learning from him,
Freud's own homage to the artist consisted mainly in making use of
him in the service of psychoanalysis.

There are exceptions. He had a strong liking for certain Egyptian
sculptures—Hellenic portraits of the Alexandrian period, which were
being dug up at that time and which he collected. And one piece of
sculpture in particular apparently moved him strongly—Michelangelo's *Moses*, to which he devoted a superb study. In one of the passages
of this study the very reserved Freud makes a rare disclosure of his
feelings. He relates that the marble statue in the Romanesque Church
of S. Pietro in Vincoli had compelled him to hold himself erect before
the contemptuous, wrathful glance of the hero, and that he had sometimes cautiously stolen out of the semi-darkness of the interior, as if he
himself belonged to the motley crew upon which the eye of Moses is
directed—the mob that is not able to hold fast to any conviction, that
is not ready to wait or to trust, and that bursts into jubilation when it
has once more received the illusion of the idol's image. Here, at any
rate, he succumbed not to a thought, but to a face.

And probably it is characteristic that here where he is visibly engaged with persons, he does not think of a "use" (*Brauchen*)—of service to his theory; he attempts nothing but the illumination of the situation in which Moses is placed. Indeed, it seems as if the tack he takes is followed in the customary pursuits of scholarship. He introduces his studies with an allusion to *Hamlet*; and he refuses to "base" the "magic" of this piece "on the impression of thoughts and the polish of speech alone." But why? His answer for *Hamlet* and for many other works was always the hidden relationship of the work with the most decisive and secret impulses of human beings—with the early "constellation" made up of the artist, his father, his mother, his brothers and sisters. He pursues this aim by pursuing situations as does an ingenious detective; he finds out the situation in which this particular Moses finds himself: Out of the relation between hand and beard he clarifies that aspect which Michelangelo wanted to treat. The essay does not run into dogma. In a certain measure, it has no aim; the single aim is insight into the plan of the sculptor. Clearly, Freud was so much affected by this work that it did not occur to him to show it as an example or "case." His "analysis" remained an exception among his interpretations of works of art.

Summarizing, we may say that Freud had looked deeply into the origin and the important function of the arts, and yet that he did not have any strong bond or relation to them. He was an artist himself rather than one of those who are privileged to enjoy art. A person could express it thus: At least he was an artist in that he enjoyed art. He used Leonardo and Goethe and their works in veneration, but only as a confirmation of his ideas and insight. He also used his own ideas and insights to interpret a picture by Schwind, *Hamlet*, a passage from *Dichtung und Wahrheit*, and *The Brothers Karamazoff*. He was a great interpreter of man and of the works of man—in the realm of art as elsewhere.

He himself recognized the limits of his method. He did not use it as a yardstick for aesthetic judgments. He did not praise and reject, as did Marx and his school. In fact, Freudians are very critical of Freud, because he did not proceed to the deduction of an aesthetic scale of values. In his restraint in the face of what he called "the mystery of art," they see defeatism on the part of psychology. But perhaps he approached this "mystery" as closely as it is possible for psychoanalysis to do—for example, in the longest of his aesthetic treatises *Delusion and Dreams*, on Jensen's *Gradiva*.

Short Digression: Freud and the German Poets

As has been mentioned, Freud discovered the same new world which contemporary poets and artists, some independently and some under his influence, were portraying.[20] He anticipated the Neo-romanticists, the Futurists and Cubists, the Dadaists and Expressionists. Similarly, the thirty-year-old Schopenhauer described the music which the then six-year-old Richard Wagner was to create thirty years later, to the chagrin of the philosophical aesthetician.[21]

For Schopenhauer, in spite of his attention to *new* means of musical expression, was nevertheless devoted to Rossini. Freud, as well, had little concern for contemporary art, to which he was related in spirit, and much enthusiasm for the classic German authors, with whom he had little in common, with the possible exception of Lessing, whom Freud acknowledged, a few years before his death, as his conscious, chosen model. And actually, his style does bear some resemblance to that of his great forebear—in the simple language, which upon occasion becomes striking and rich, with pungent, epigrammatic sentences summarizing an entire theory in a few brilliant lines. Both of them wrote the poetical prose of men who, though reserved, were great enthusiasts. Moreover, there was in both of them a tolerance born of scepticism and a realistic humanitarianism.

Thomas Mann wrote that if Freud had been more familiar with literature, he would not have felt himself so isolated. But Freud knew world literature quite well and valued the agreement between himself and the greatest masters. His work is well larded with quotations from the literature of every land. Quoting can be a great many things, from intellectual snobbery to the art of decking out one's own thoughts in the more attractive expressions of someone else. Freud quoted for still another reason: Once, in lecturing to his students, he said that he thought they would consider it a welcome relief if he were to offer them something poetic, after the essentially "dry fantastic" of science, and then proceeded to read aloud the famous dialogue between Goethe's Suleika and Hatem. And he often alluded to the brilliant remarks of the poets, such as Jean Paul's "The wit is the disguised priest, who performs the marriage ceremony for every couple."

But, above all, Freud wanted to have his ideas confirmed. In *Oedipus Rex*, in *Hamlet*, in *The Brothers Karamazoff*, he found the Oedipus complex formulated in classic fashion, even though without the theoretical consciousness that he himself had just developed. His finest,

399

most frequent witness was Goethe. Freud owned the most complete collection of Goethe's works, the Sophien edition, and it is reported that often, in the midst of a conversation, he would jump up to see what "Old Goethe," as he was wont to call him, had to say on the subject. It was his reading of Goethe's short, incomparably fine paper, "Nature," that had pushed the vacillating young candidate for college examinations into the study of the natural sciences. Freud occasionally dreamed of Goethe, and recognized that Goethe had become a father-symbol for good Germans.

Educated Germans of the last 150 years have grown up with Goethe as an intimate member of the family. Many can recall Goethe's love affairs more vividly than their own, and they refer to sentences from Goethe on every possible occasion. Again and again, Freud was being reminded of a quotation from *Faust*. In some connection or other, a mocking speech of Mephistopheles occurs to him—a verse, as he puts it, that no German will ever forget, though with Freud it was not a matter of not forgetting, but rather a sort of compulsion to re-member; he was continually compelled to recall, for example, the Spirits' Chorus from *Faust*, which bemoans the fact that the world has been destroyed—only, according to Freud, to be rebuilt by the para-noid; or Faust's desire for Gretchen's garter, as an illustration of fetish-ism as a part of normal sex life; and when he wrote on "Character and Anal Eroticism," naturally the famous quotation from *Goetz von Ber-lichingen* occurred to him at once.

"And here, too, a poet may have something to say," Freud said somewhere, and usually when he said "poet," he almost always meant Goethe. It was Goethe who provided the motto for his book, *The Psy-chopathology of Everyday Life*. And at the head of the chapter of "Se-cession Movements" Freud inserted something that does not seem very "tame" from Goethe's collection of *Tame Verses*:

> Make it short!
> On the Day of Judgment, it's just a fart!

Sometimes a Goethe quotation forced its way in irrelevantly and sometimes even inappropriately. Goethe was compulsively dragged in even when Freud had to add that maybe the poet was not quite in the right. All of Freud's associations, sooner or later, seemed to end up with Goethe.

Goethe's biographical data were so ever-present to Freud that they constantly appeared as elucidations. For example, he wrote to Dr.

Fliess that a certain mechanism is the same as that in hysterical fantasy, illustrating his point by an allusion to the important role which *Werther* played in Goethe's life. And when he was investigating the "Misuse of Names," he thought of Goethe's sensitivity to Herder's misuse of his name as one who stems from the gods, from the Goths, or from excrement. And Freud's study on Goethe, "A Childhood Memory out of *Dichtung und Wahrheit*," was devoted to a biographical episode. From Goethe's only revealed childhood memory—of an episode which occurred when he was six years old—Freud unearthed, with the help of his method, the secret of the Goethean inner harmony. Goethe had revealed that, as a child, he used to throw his little toy cups and saucers out of the window, and finally—spurred on by the applause of the three Ochsenstein brothers who lived across the street—a great part of the household dishes. Freud, with help from his patients who recalled similar incidents from their early childhood, was able to explain a great deal more than this one episode. He showed that throwing away things symbolized a wish that the new-born baby in the house should disappear. For little Goethe, this wish was fulfilled. The newborn brother died soon thereafter, and he did not have to share his mother's love with him. Freud felt that here lay the secret of Goethe's never-troubled attachment to life. For, as he said, if you have been the unchallenged favorite of your mother, then for all your life you retain that feeling of being a conqueror, that confidence in success which not infrequently draws success after it.

In criticism, we might perhaps add that the special interpretation of throwing things away may be correct, without justifying the more extensive explanation. Even if the scene portrayed by Goethe had occurred for the psychological reason provided by Freud, can the events and actions of this period provide the basis for the poet's whole wide world and later life? In answer to this doubt, one might reply that the great oak does not resemble the acorn. But is the oak really the acorn? Is it not only the beginning out of which, later on, something is made by the sun, moon, stars, and earth? Perhaps we might say that nothing looks less Goethean than this particular sketch of Goethe.

But Freud was not alone in confusing intimacy with Goethe's life with the Goethean manner. In 1930, Freud received the Frankfurt Goethe Prize. The poet, Alfons Paquet, Secretary of the Board of Trustees, wrote to Freud that by virtue of his research methods and his Mephistophelian tendency ruthlessly to tear away all veils, he was the inseparable companion of Faustian insatiability and awe in the

401

face of the creative-pictorial powers slumbering in the unconscious. However, we must point out that the "powers slumbering in the unconscious" are precisely the opposite of creative-pictorial powers, which do not come into existence until those unconscious instincts have been sublimated. Paquet's error, however, might have arisen from his acquaintance with Freud's *The Discomforts of Civilization,* wherein Mephisto's

> For everything that comes into being
> Deserves to be destroyed.

is identified with the *destructive instinct,* forgetting that Goethe saw in Mephistopheles a portion of that power which always wills the Bad and always creates the Good, while Freud arrived at that Empedocletian dualism which ultimately conceived of the opposite elements, construction and destruction, eros and the death instinct, as having *equal value* for life. Also, without any doubt, Freud interpreted Goethe as Freud: At the end of his address on "Goethe's Relation to Psychoanalysis," which his daughter read for him at Frankfurt, he indicated that Goethe was great not only in *professing* knowledge but also in cautiously *concealing* it. And this statement was not made *only* because Freud was called upon to "say something" befitting a ceremonial occasion; rather, Freud's failure to recognize the boundaries between Goethe and himself was one of the few illusions of this very illusion-less scientist. For the differences are obvious. Freud might, for example, have done well to consider Goethe's

> He who has science and art also has religion;
> He who possesses neither of these two, let him try to get religion.

Did Freud in this instance really believe—as Goethe did—that science and art were similar to religion in their life-values, or that these different fields could replace each other? But although Freud opposed religion mainly because of his enthusiasm for science and admitted art mainly because it did not do any harm to science, he never seemed to notice the chasm that separated Goethe from him in this respect. He lived, as he put it, in traditional awe of one of our great poets and wise men.

It is also notable that, for all his extensive use of Goethe's maxims, not one really indicates that Goethe was Freudian in sympathies or point of view, and vice versa. On the other hand, when he quoted Hebbel and Fontane—as he did on rare occasions—the quoted passages do seem to contain Freudian key words. He dissected Hebbel's *Judith,* which might very well have been influenced by Freud, in his article on "The Taboo of Virginity," quoting Hebbel's warning, "Thou shalt not touch the sleep of the world." And his own horror, which imprinted Hebbel's expression indelibly in his mind, indicates the secret anxiety which probably fundamentally compelled his urgent proclamation of "Reason." For Freud emphatically had "touched the sleep of the world," and hastened to strengthen the prison warden, Reason, in order to keep the world which arose in revolt under control.

Freud also quoted Fontane's central idea, expressed in his novel, *Effie Briest*—"it cannot be done without supporting structures"—not only once but twice, and that in two different decades; and with all the differences between the conservative German and the liberal Austrian, it seems as if no contemporary German writer resembled Freud more closely than the author of *Stechlin.*

For all those who have grown up in the German tradition, Schiller and Goethe are inseparable, so that Freud did not *choose* Schiller any more than he had *chosen* Goethe, but rather, had Schiller "thrust upon him," as it were. If one reads the reports of the celebrations on the occasion of the one-hundredth anniversary of the birth of Schiller in 1859—when Freud was three years old—one can understand why Freud, as a matter of course, instinctively thought of Schiller too in his official role of "the great poet and thinker"; as a variation, he sometimes termed him "our great poet-philosopher," or sometimes—as with Goethe—he designated Schiller simply as "the Poet."

Of the two German classical writers, Goethe was probably considered the greater god; Schiller, the more popular. Something of this attitude is evident in Freud. He uses Goethe more frequently, for there was no Schillerian *Faust.* But only with reference to Schiller do parodies from *Die Fliegenden Blaetter* occur to him, and in reading Freud, one cannot avoid such expressions as "to quote Schiller," "to exclaim in the words of Schiller's diver." It must be admitted, though, that the Viennese liberal did not quote Schiller on those occasions when he was providing the flag-waving *Reichsgermans* with patriotic slogans, for Freud was, after all, a liberal Austrian living under Lord Mayor Lueger. But Schiller—though very rarely *the man as such*—finds his way into Freud's life and his dreams. In Schiller's biography, there is no Sesenheim and no Madame von Stein. And primarily it was probably these more or less fictional love adventures in Goethe's biography which transfigured Goethe's whole life and made it beloved of the people. Freud indicates the intimate effect of Goethe's life upon him when he says that Goethe seemed to become more and more like his father from decade to decade. Schiller's life, on the other hand, never became public property; *it* never entered Freud's mind. Nor did he mention Schiller's prose, which was left to the private preserve of specialists and literary connoisseurs. His plays alone, especially *Wallenstein,* seem to have created Freud's picture of Schiller. The characters and the lines of the plays provide colorful commentaries on Freud's themes: Schiller, in his plays, speaks of hunger and love as the dynamic forces of man's universe; of identification with one's superior; of plays on words with given names; of slips of the tongue, of unconscious death wishes—and of many other Freudian themes. But it is not a coincidence that Freud dedicated two of his important pieces of work, not to Schiller, but to Goethe. One of these expresses his admiration for the poet as the child of fortune, and the other was intended to *bind* Goethe and Freud to one another and to indicate their *bonds.* There is not a single passage to show that he tried very much to gain Schiller's blessing.

Other German authors—classicists, romanticists, naturalists, younger contemporaries—are mentioned only now and then, and supplied with non-committal attributes such as "one of our best poets," as in the case of Anzengruber. Boerne and Heine he was very familiar with. He even visited their graves in the Père Lachaise cemetery in Paris. Boerne was the first author to whom he had become close. When he was fourteen, he had received a volume of his works, the only book which he kept from his childhood period. Boerne's sketch, "The Art of Getting to be an Original Author in Three Days," closes with the following sentence:

Take a few sheets of paper and, for three successive days, jot down, without cheating or hypocrisy, everything that comes into your head. Write down what you think of yourselves, of your wives, of the War with the Turks, of Goethe, of Fonk's criminal trial, of the Last Judgment, of your superiors—and at the end of the three days you will be quite beside yourselves in admiration of the new, unheard-of thoughts you have had. This is the art of becoming an original writer in three days.

When this passage, which anticipated his teachings about free associations, was called to the attention of Freud, Boerne's old admirer, he commented as follows: "It seems to us . . . that it is not out of the

404

question that what has just been pointed out to me has uncovered a piece of that hidden amnesia which, in so many cases, is assumed to be back of any decidedly original idea."

To the highly educated German of the nineteenth century, Heine was not considered a classicist of the rank of Goethe and Schiller. It is worthy of note that Freud, too, never introduced him with such ceremonious, majestic titles as he did the two from Weimar. And yet there must have been much more to connect him with Heine than can be proved by documentary evidence—such things, for instance, as hatred of German-Austrian reaction; freedom from religious dogmatism; the pleasure principle. Freud never speaks of this. It is scarcely likely that he was delighted, as was many a contemporary, by Heine's sentimental aspects. What then could it have been? The poet appears in the work of the psychologist almost exclusively as material for the analysis of "The Technique of Wit." And it is to be noted that Freud shows a comfortable enthusiasm when he examines a not-so-very-funny kind of joke, such as "famillionaire," and a verse in quite poor taste, such as:

> Until at last, all the buttons
> On the trousers of my patience, snapped.

For, quite aside from the fact that Freud was one of the most dynamic forces of the twentieth century, he also made his obeisance abundantly to the most musty, plush-furniture Victorian tradition. Just as Heine became important to him for the theme of "Wit," so E. T. A. Hoffmann did, for the theme of "The Uncanny."

Of all the artists, Freud mainly invoked the poets as witnesses, and he showed scarcely any real enthusiasm for any singer or musician. To none of them did he have the relation of Kierkegaard to Mozart, or of Nietzsche to Wagner. He wrote mainly about works of literature, but not because he was moved by them; and it is significant that his most extensive study in the literary field was devoted to the tale *Gradiva*, which he himself spoke of as not very valuable in and of itself.

It is also surprising that he seldom mentions the contemporary author Arthur Schnitzler, who in many of his characters strikingly portrayed Freud's gentle resignation. In 1888, Dr. Schnitzler had defended him in the cocaine affair. In appreciation, Dr. Freud wrote to Schnitzler, his colleague in science and literature, calling him "a poet who, to be sure, is also a physician." And in some of his letters of 1906, 1912, and 1933, Freud stated his consciousness of the very extensive agreement between Schnitzler and himself. But seldom does Freud, in

405

his works, give this contemporary poet-psychologist, who was so near to his world, a hearing, relying, rather, upon traditional writers—basically far from his own thinking—to provide quotations. Freud wrote to Schnitzler that he had "avoided" him—and here one questions whether he consciously "avoided" only the man himself, and not his work as well, from a sort of fear, perhaps, of his own alter ego. But was it not actually a different sort of fear? A dedication to the alter ego reads: "With becoming modesty." Was this not, perhaps, more than just a generous gesture? Freud's reserve before the poets *of his day,* who were related to him, may have been rooted in a hero-worship of the artist which is characteristic of many scientists. Even Kant held that only an artist, never a scholar, can be a genius.

Also striking in this connection is the absence from Freud's works of any important statement concerning Thomas Mann, who, in 1929, wrote his first article on Freud. In 1935, Freud expressed his thanks that "one of the leading spokesmen of the German people" had accorded him a place in modern intellectual history. And in the same year, he wrote, in a letter of congratulation on the occasion of Mann's sixtieth birthday, that he was one of his "oldest" readers and admirers. Freud, almost 80 years old, emphasized the word "oldest" by putting it in quotation marks—indicating, perhaps, that as a reader of Thomas Mann, he was still very young. And one notes, the "admirer," in his very short letter, does not say what it is that he admires. In short, then, one may say that Freud was not very close to any of the writers of his own time.

Perhaps, however, one is justified in pointing out two authors who were nearer to his heart than both the often-quoted classical authors and the seldom-quoted Schnitzler and Zweig and Mann—namely, Nestroy and Conrad Ferdinand Meyer. For Nestroy he seems to have had a sort of family-attachment, an attachment full of sentiment and comfortable feelings. The sharp-witted satirist of the old Austria, as he called him, seems to have represented the *Austrian* element in this anti-Viennese. Nestroy's "Nur Immer Halb So," as Freud probably recognized, gave explicit expression to a very significant characteristic of Freud's own picture of man. Freud's allusions to "our Nestroy" on the surface sound no different from those to "our Goethe," and yet, if one reads carefully, he notes that a heartier, more intimate "our" is used for Nestroy.

Freud praised, analyzed, and criticized the other author to whom he was particularly close, Conrad Ferdinand Meyer, who appeared to attract Freud a great deal, perhaps because of his poet's melancholy, which was not alien to Freud's own. Also, Meyer's working-out of what Freud called ideal types, such as the King, the Saint, the Monk—the presentation of historical figures as the embodiment of ideas—corresponded to Freud's own attitude toward art. And the Boecklinesque quality of Conrad Ferdinand Meyer, the "brocade," as Keller called it —the pompous and at the same time aristocratically gentle rarity, the metaphorically muted, the romantically elevated, the passionate without any false pathos—all of this corresponded very closely to Freud's nature.

The great trends in Freud's work have their parallels in very different contemporary art tendencies—one might say, rather, in the most revolutionary art creations of the period. How much here was really contemporaneousness, how far direct influences took place in either direction, has heretofore scarcely been examined—and yet all influences are vehemently denied by the artists, who have always, not surprisingly, objected to being seized hold of by analysis. Besides, here again, one discovers the age-old battle for supremacy between the philosopher and the artist, which began with Plato's belittling of the poets and did not end even with the attack of the Hegelian Hebbel on Hegel, the tyrannical proclaimer of the primacy of philosophy. In our own time, a very militant thinker has written that there is no such thing as Understanding *and* Poetry, but only Poetry *or* Understanding —or, in other words, *distortion* or *reality*. So we find that the poets, subjected to this kind of distinction, are very suspicious of philosophical treatment, and in Freud's biography, one reads of at least two cases in which poets declined to be made sponsors of anything psychoanalytical: The publication *Imago* was named after a short novel by Spitteler, at the suggestion of one of Freud's disciples; and Freud himself, in his book on dreams, quoted the author of *Imago* very approvingly, but was constrained to add that this great man did not wish to have anything to do with psychoanalysis and the interpretation of dreams. Just as little accord did Freud find in Wilhelm Jensen, a very prolific writer who, although neglected today, was at one time compared with Raabe. Freud subjected his story *Gradiva* to a very extensive examination, which brought Jensen's name to posterity. But when Freud expressed his desire to meet the author, Jensen emphatically refused, just as hundreds since have rejected analysis as hostile to art.

But all this is only a small chapter in the age-old battle between philosophy and the arts for primacy—something which Freud never strove to attain.

Notes

1. Freud did not write an aesthetic. I am attempting here to construct one out of his works. In very many places, and especially in a series of essays, there are fragments devoted to the interpretation of art-works and of happenings in the lives of the artists; there are also analyses of aesthetic categories. Here is a list of these works listed in chronological order: *Wit and its Relation to the Unconscious; Delusion and Dreams in Jensen's "Gradiva"; The Poet and Make-Believe; The Family-History of the Neurotic; A Childhood Recollection of Leonardo da Vinci; Fairy-Tale Materials in Dreams; The Motive of Caste-Illusions; The Moses of Michelangelo; A Childhood Recollection from "Dichtung und Wahrheit"; The Uncanny; Supplement to a Work on the Moses of Michelangelo; Humor; Dostoevsky and Patricide; The Goethe-Prize, 1930; To Romain Rolland; Thomas Mann on His Sixtieth Birthday; Letter to Romain Rolland; Foreword to "Edgar Poe, étude psychoanalytique" by Marie Bonaparte.*

Some of his first students have tried to clarify aesthetic questions more than anything else: namely, Otto Rank, Hanns Sachs, and Theodor Reik. And the result is that analytic literature about questions related to scientific studies of art has grown from year to year. One may say that the outline which Freud drew has been filled in with valuable materials, chiefly anthropological, but that it has not been enlarged itself.

2. Freud, *Gesammelte Werke* (London, 1950), XV, 173: From now on I shall indicate only volume and page of this edition. It could easily be shown that Freud knew that the naïveté (*Harmlosigkeit*) of art has its limits—that works of art can influence our lives decisively. Thus, after reading the novel *Joseph and his Brothers*, he wrote a "Draft of a Letter to Thomas Mann" (29 November 1936), which has remained a fragment. In it he began to prove that the Joseph story had profoundly influenced the life of Napoleon, whose oldest brother was named Joseph, whose first wife was Josephine, and whose "prototype in myth" decided his march to Egypt (printed in *Internationale Zeitschrift für Psychoanalyse und Imago* [1941], numbers 3–4). Hence one must modify with a certain precision Freud's description of art as "harmless" and as "illusion."

3. Kuno Fischer, *Über den Witz* (Leipzig, 1889), p. 18. Freud cites this passage (IV, 103). Indeed, he tries to understand Fischer in such a way that they both seem to entertain the same view. But he ruins his own undertaking immediately with the statement: "I doubt that we are capable of attempting anything in which our intention is of no concern." This could equally well have been written against Kant's *Critique of Judgment*.

4. In his book *Dynamische Tiefenpsychologie* (Bern-Stuttgart: Haupt, 1953), Felix Mayer calls Freud's derivation of fantasy a "strange opinion." For example, this kind of an opinion is very clearly revealed in the following sentence (XI, 389): "Creation in the psychic realm of fantasy has a complete counterpart in creations like forest preserves where the demand of agriculture, of commerce, and of industry threaten to change the face of the earth to such an extent that it can hardly be recognized. The natural park preserves the old conditions which were usually sacrificed for reasons of expediency. Everything in it may grow luxuriously, just as it wishes, the useless as well as the harmful. The realm of the psychic is also such a preserve of withdrawal from the principle of reality." Here Mayer begins: Instead of Freud's "fantasy," he prefers to use the metaphor of the "poacher . . . who brings nothing home from the hunt. In the first place he has killed nothing, and then he has no home where he can hide the plunder he so eagerly anticipated" (p. 106). This image is an unhappy contrast with Freud's distinguished, precise illustration. Once for all, it should be said that "poachers" often

bring home a good deal and licensed hunters nothing at all. But, then, Mayer's "poacher" does not need a home to hide plunder in; in any case, he does not bring anything home. Paying no attention to the insufficiency of his metaphor, Mayer says nothing more than that he does not find a theological-idealistic metaphysic.

5. Lionel Trilling, *The Liberal Imagination* (New York, 1953), p. 54. In his essay "Freud and Literature" he says that "Freud's assumption of the almost exclusively hedonistic nature and purpose of art bars him from the perception [and in the following he quotes Jacques Barzun] that the work of art leads us back to the outer reality by taking account of it." Here also Trilling probably overlooks the fact that Freud again and again emphasizes only the particular achievement of the analytical method for the understanding of the art-work.

6. Ernst Kris ("Probleme der Ästhetik," *Internationale Zeitschrift für Psychoanalyse und Imago* [1940], 1, 153–154) says that "We possess no scientific method to verify the accuracy of this fantasy." One should call such a conjecture, not fantasy, but rather a hypothesis. Hypotheses of this kind are verified in all sciences only because more and more material can then fit into the scheme. Moreover, Géza Roheim in a very learned article, "The Psychoanalytical Meaning of the Idea of Culture" (*Internationale Zeitschrift für Psychoanalyse und Imago* [1941], 1) reaches the following conclusion: "Myth informs us of the spectacles of our forefathers, not of crude reality." This is a wholesome warning against the over-evaluation of the "historical" elements in early poetry.

7. Géza Roheim (*loc. cit.*): "New researches in the area of animal psychology have shown that when there is an uncertainty that the urgent tensions of life will be satisfied, a disturbance in the behavior of the animal results; and the result is the prototype of a neurosis or a psychosis." He cites material from which it appears that in hordes of baboons one can observe not only real battles, but simulated ones also; this latter cannot be called anything other than myth-creation by animals.

8. Lionel Trilling, *op. cit.* In his excellent essay, "Art and Neurosis," Trilling defends the thesis that artists are just people who, better than people who are not artists, can get along with their neuroses. But his judgment of Freud's psychology of the artist is problematical: "Indeed, it is possible to say of Freud that he ultimately did more for our understanding of art than any other writer since Aristotle; and this being so, it can only be surprising that in his early work he should have made the error of treating the artist as a neurotic who escapes from reality by means of 'substitute gratifications' " (p. 160). While the first half of the sentence over-rates Freud as an aesthetician, the second is unfair to him. Trilling gives not a single item of support for the fact that Freud identifies the neurotic and the artist. But there are many examples proving that Freud was entirely of the opinion espoused by Trilling, according to whom an artistic work is a kind of convalescence. Trilling's theory is not the contrary of Freud's, but instead agrees with it.

For the rest, the German poet and physician Gottfried Benn, in a speech he recently made in Germany, said (and we are quoting from the translation, "Artists and Old Age" printed in the *Partisan Review* [1955]): "Regarded from one point of view art is, after all, a phenomenon of liberation and relaxation, a cathartic phenomenon, and such phenomena are closely associated with the physical organism itself."

9. *Jubiläums-Ausgabe*, XXXV, 317.

10. F. Jonas, *Schiller-Briefe* (Leipzig, 1892–96), XLIV.

11. In his essay, "Freud and Literature," (*op. cit.*, p. 47) Trilling points out that Tieck and Schopenhauer had alluded to the sexual origin of art. This is not true of Schopenhauer; on the contrary, Trilling should have pointed to the aesthetic writings of Richard Wagner and Nietzsche. Because the will-to-live and sexuality are almost identical and because in his system art represents the opposite essence, aside from philosophy and aestheticism, one cannot from Schopenhauer's writings establish a coherence between sexuality and art—beyond that of a coherence of opposites.

409

Like Thomas Mann in the more important, but less well known of his two works on Freud ("The Place of Freud in History"), Trilling also points out Freud's connections with the German Romanticists. But he misunderstands Thomas Mann when he says that "He gives us a Freud who is committed to the 'night-side' of life" (p. 49). The opposite is true: In this essay, which appeared in 1929, when the Nazi myth was predominant, Freud is represented as one who brought light into darkness, not as one who worshipped it. With the best of political intentions, Thomas Mann went too far in those days; he under-rated Freud's ambivalent attitude to "It" (*"Es"*).

12. His deliberate effort to put aesthetics at a distance is expressed in phrases like, "I know little about aesthetics" (VI, 104).

13. Occasionally he went so far in his scepticism that in the speech of thanks which he wrote upon receiving the Goethe-prize from the city of Frankfurt (1930), he asserted that "Even the best and most complete [biography] can not help us better to understand the work and its effect." But can Freud put in question what he himself has accomplished, for example with respect to a picture like that of da Vinci's *St. Anne?*

14. A reproach usually brought against psychoanalytical aesthetics is that at times it is a "rationalism touching on the cynical." This is the attitude of Walter Muschg in his inaugural lecture given at the University of Zürich and called *Psychoanalysis and the Scientific Study of Literature* (Berlin, 1930). There he says that "The greatest distance separating the psychoanalyst from the literary historian [lies in a] disrepect for the integrally created personality." The inaccuracy of this judgment lies in the word "disrespect." For the rest of it, one needs only open any kind of literary history to see that at the beginning of every attempt at scientific understanding of a work or artist there is a decomposition of an "integrally created personality." This is even true of the biographies of the George school, in which the dismemberment is disguised with pious words. "He unloosened that which had been formed," says Muschg about the psychoanalyst, as if every scientist did not unloosen "that which had been formed." "The exception, even that of genius, is made relative everywhere": but Freud hated the word "genius" (*Genie*), even when people applied it to him, as a symbol of a taboo for the researcher. Muschg recommends, by contrast, an "awe before the form-giving ability of genius." But "awe" is not exactly a quality of a scholar, who always tries to penetrate a mystery. "Awe" before an individual as "the counterpart of the psychoanalytic destruction of personality" is the attitude of priests as compared with that of investigators. When Muschg points with aversion to "the integral parts of the art-work that is torn to pieces," one may ask how an art-work is to be scientifically examined without its being torn apart. Muschg's attitude of celebration towards literature was suitably expressed in that solemn book, *Tragische Literaturgeschichte*. The distasteful side of the solemnity revealed here can be found in his aspersions, as unsolemn as they are unscientific, against, for example, Heinrich Heine and Thomas Mann. (This science of literature had its origin chiefly in the works of C. G. Jung. His essay, "On the Relations of Analytical Psychology to the Poetic Work of Art," appeared in the volume, *Psychic Problems of the Present* [*Seelenprobleme der Gegenwart*], Zürich, 1931.)

15. Frederick J. Hacker, "On Artistic Production," writes (in the collection *Explorations in Psychoanalysis*, ed. Robert Lindner [New York, 1953]): "In short, our science has clarified everything concerning art but art itself" (p. 129). This sharp antithesis is not just to Freud. Because he always pointed out the limits of his methods, Freud in challenging this criticism is unnecessarily modest. Moreover, Gregory Zilboorg says that "science cannot solve the problem of beauty or goodness scientifically" (*Sigmund Freud: His Exploration of the Mind of Man* [New York, 1951], p. 81).

16. Compare also VII, 209; VIII, 417: XIV, 401.

17. Plato in the *Republic*: "Poets reveal great and wise matters which they cannot understand."

18. Freud, *Aus den Anfängen der Psychoanalyse: Briefe an Wilhelm Fliess* (London, 1950), p. 343.

410

19. *Ibid.,* p. 286.

20. In his essay, "The Psychoanalyst Looks at Contemporary Art" (which appeared in the collection *Explorations,* see note 16), Franz Alexander begins thus: "Products of art can be looked upon from two different points of view: the aesthetic and the psychologic." Freud would not have accepted this distinction. For him there were only two sciences: psychology and natural science. The aim of all of his aesthetic efforts was psychological interpretation.

21. Gregory Zilboorg (*loc. cit.*) cites a letter by Thomas Mann to Frederick J. Hoffman (27 January 1944): "One could be influenced in this sphere without any direct contact with [Freud's] work, because for a long time the air had been filled with the thoughts and results of the psychoanalytic school" (Frederick J. Hoffman, *Freudianism and the Literary Mind* [Baton Rouge, 1945]). While Zilboorg points out that Proust never mentions the name of Freud, Bernard de Voto ("Freud's Influence on Literature," *SRL,* 7 October, 1939) insists that Freud influenced Proust; he would not have written what he did "without the instruments that Freud fitted to their [Proust's and Joyce's] hands." But how can this be demonstrated?

411

Freud and Schnitzler— (Doppelgänger)
(1959)

HERBERT I. KUPPER and

HILDA S. ROLLMAN-BRANCH

The number of fascinating and intriguing relationships in Freud's life seem endless. One is described and analyzed in this article. Schnitzler was a famous Viennese playwright who knew Freud well over many years. Freud called him his Doppelgänger. This selection appeared in the Journal of the American Psychoanalytic Association 7 (1959): 109–26. *We should like to express our thanks to Henry Schnitzler, Associate Professor of Theater Arts at UCLA, for making available portions of his father's autobiography and diaries. We wish to acknowledge the assistance of the late Dr. Ernest Jones for his corrections and additional information about Schnitzler. The letter quoted is one of ten letters from Freud to Schnitzler written between 1906 to 1931.*

In 1922 when Freud was sixty-six years old, he wrote a letter to Arthur Schnitzler on the occasion of the latter's sixtieth birthday:

14 May 1922

My dear Doctor:

Now you too, have arrived at the 60th birthday while I, six years older, have moved up closer to the terminus of life and may soon expect to see the end of the fifth act of this rather unintelligible and not always amusing comedy.

If I had kept even a small residue of belief in the "omnipotence of thoughts," I would not be amiss in now wishing you many happy returns for the proper number of years. I leave these foolish doings to the vast multitude of contemporaries who will remember you on the 15th of May.

I shall make you a confession, though, which you will kindly, in consideration of me, keep to yourself and not share with either friend or stranger. I have been struggling with the question of why I have never, in all these years, made any effort to meet you and to talk with you (not considering, at that point, whether you on your part would have wanted such acquaintance).

The answer to this question contains what appears to me as too intimate a confession. I think I have avoided you out of a kind of fear of finding my own double [*Doppelgänger Scheu*]. Not that I otherwise tend to identify easily with others or that I should wish to ignore the difference in talent which separates me from you; it is rather that when I read one of your beautiful works I seem to encounter again and again, behind the poetic fiction, the presumptions, interests, and conclusions so well known to me from my own thoughts. Your determinism as well as skepticism—what is generally called pessimism—your ability to be deeply moved by the truths of the unconscious, by the instinctual nature of man, and to analyze the accepted cultural-conventional "verities," the recurrence of your thoughts to the polarity of love and death—all of this had for me an uncanny familiarity. (In a little book of 1920 [*Beyond the Pleasure Principle*] I have tried to present Eros and the Death Instinct as the basic forces whose interplay dominates all the riddles of life.) I have thus gained the impression that you have learned through intuition—though actually as a result of sensitive introspection—everything that I have had to unearth by laborious work on other persons. I even believe that basically you are yourself an explorer of psychological depths, as honestly unbiased and courageous a one as ever was; and if you were not that, then your artistic skill, the beauty of your style and your imaginativeness would have had free play and would have made you into a writer of far more popular appeal.

I, of course, tend to prefer to be the researcher. But forgive me that I strayed into analysis, that is all I know. Except that I know that analysis is no way to become popular. With heartfelt devotion.

Freud

Freud's designation of Schnitzler as his *Doppelgänger* implied an uncanny similarity which is most difficult to convey in English. There is a quality of *déjà vu* and a feeling as if he had encountered his spectral double. It is as though a person were confronted in reality by the ghostly, ectoplasmic regurgitation of characters and events of the imagination.

The idea of losing one's identity and seeing it again in someone else is often described in German literature (Hoffmann, Chamisso). Otto Rank[11] in his monograph, *Der Doppelgänger*, wrote at some length about the meanings and origins of the term.

413

Freud himself touched on the characteristics of the *Doppelgänger* in his paper on "The Uncanny." [5] The double is insurance against destruction of the ego, an energetic denial of the power of death, in fact the "immortal" soul may have been the first double of the body. Still, a folk superstition holds that to see one's double presages one's death.

The *Doppelgänger* is another person who embraces the whole of one's emotional potentialities. He represents the personification of one's own dormant possibilities. He stands for the life one could have, but did not live. When Freud wrote Schnitzler that he had "a kind of fear of finding my own double," he once again revealed the remarkable insight which has made him famous. For with the biography of Freud, recently published, and access to the unpublished autobiography and diaries of Schnitzler up to 1903, a surprising number of similarities have become apparent in the early lives, education, and work of these two men.

Their analogous assumptions, ideas, interests, and conclusions will be investigated from the standpoint of similarities in their biographies. Schnitzler's dramatic form and Freud's concept of psychic conflict will be discussed to show points in common. Why Schnitzler abandoned medicine for literature and Freud abandoned medicine for a new psychology will be discussed in terms of their similar childhood experiences. The paper will conclude with a summary of those values which they share.

I

Schnitzler, like Freud, was an eldest child, and was followed by two brothers and one sister. He was born in Vienna, of middle-class Jews, who, at the time of the "liberal ideal," were being assimilated into the higher echelons of the Hapsburg Empire. His father was an ear, nose, and throat specialist who founded an independent clinic and who was a professor at the University of Vienna Medical School. Both Arthur and his younger brother Julius became physicians.

When Arthur Schnitzler was fourteen months old his next youngest sibling died. It will be recalled that Freud was nineteen months old when he lost his baby brother, an event to which he ascribed a residual of guilt for the remainder of his life. Both Freud and Schnitzler were cared for by Catholic nursemaids whose ideas of salvation and resurrection were vividly recalled by both men and may have influenced their later ideas of love and death. The ugly but comforting maid stayed with Freud until he was two and one half years old. Jones[9] mentions her awesome qualities and the suggestion of Freud's that he may have been bathed in water tinged with her menstrual flow. Schnitzler retained his nursemaid for a longer time. A memory at a lake in which he experienced the "horror of nature" may allude to some frightening experience similar to Freud's fear of the female genital.

Schnitzler's oedipal struggle extended over both professional fields. He regarded his father as a superficial, friendly man without a deep knowledge of people; a man more interested in being the throat specialist for famous singers than in his patients as individuals. One gathered that Schnitzler was in considerable awe of his father as a physician and felt hopeless ever to equal him. While accepting this defeat eventually, he continued his rivalry with his "literary" father who wrote many medical articles and amateurish poetry. His themes often embraced problems in the field of medicine.

After a disturbed adolescence which included sleepwalking, fears of death, etc., Schnitzler entered medical school under bitter protest. He never ceased to be intrigued and repulsed by these years. Some of his remarks were self-explanatory. "Internal medicine inspired me more than surgical disciplines. Against the latter I felt revulsion and my hypochondriacal tendency found itself in almost pathological contradiction. . . . My interest in mental and nervous disease was the only one existent in me, because this interest stemmed not so much from medical, as from poetic and belletristic roots."

In the 1880's he had to serve his military term, as did Freud, and here he first became acutely aware of anti-Semitism and the peculiar honor code of student fraternities and army officers. In the army, he also began to engage in numberless sexual affairs. Some of these were group love affairs. He once plotted with his cronies to seduce the wife of a mutual friend. The latent homosexuality seemed quite obvious. He later epitomized his feelings about women as follows: "The smile of remembrance never dies completely on the lips of women. They are more vengeful but also more grateful than men, sometimes taking revenge for the caresses and sacrifices they receive and even decades later are still grateful for the disappointments and insults they had to suffer."

Schnitzler's professional career after the army was at first an attempt to work in his father's noted ear, nose, and throat clinic. After a time, he became interested in neurology and joined Meynert's Clinic.

In view of Freud's difficulty with Maynert, who was the leading specialist of his day, it was interesting to note Schnitzler's opinion of him. "He was not very understanding and a rather cold man. He tried to convince patients with delusions that they could not possibly have them."

Thereafter Schnitzler went to Bernheim in Nancy, in order to study hypnosis for which the French schools were noted. After his return in 1887, he became an editor of the *Internationale klinische Rundschau*. He wrote articles upon hypnotism, telepathy, neurasthenia, and psychotherapy. He also was given the task of reviewing Freud's translation of Charcot's "work." He wrote a most favorable review.

He regularly attended his father's clinics to perform hypnotism upon the hysterical deafnesses and aphonias of the day. He recalled that the public demonstrations of his role with these patients and the exposure of sexual material became known as "performances" so that he could no longer *perform publicly*. Perhaps it helped the creativity of his "private" exhibitions when he stopped serious medical practice. But not until his success with the *Anatol* plays in 1892 did he give up neurologic practice except as an avocation.

He employed a good deal of his psychiatric training and knowledge in his plays. In *Paracelsus*, for example, written in 1897, the theme was that of the husband who boasted of his faithful wife's devotion. Paracelsus, the famous physician, had formerly wooed the wife but had been rejected and had wandered as a healer all through Europe. Stung by the husband's boasting and insults, Paracelsus hypnotized the wife who, under hypnosis, revealed that she loved Paracelsus and would have slept with him any time during her marriage. This unfaithfulness in thought astounded her husband who implored Paracelsus to tell him whether his real wife was the faithful or the hypnotized one. Paracelsus replied that the husband had witnessed an unreal play. "Dream life and wakeful life, truth and fiction flow into one another. . . . Certainty is nowhere to be found. We know nothing of others, nothing of ourselves. (We are always play acting.) One should not forget that human relations have their 'sicknesses.' If recovery follows one should not mutter obsolete words, such as 'immorality or crime.' "

Schnitzler's insight into depth psychology was now recognized by Freud who wrote of *Paracelsus* in 1898: "It is astonishing that such a writer knows of these things." [9,p.146] But *Paracelsus* was followed by other plays exploring hidden conflicts. In *Reigen*—more widely known as *La Ronde*—Schnitzler scored the roundelay of sexuality which he compared to the universal dance of death. The barrenness of the instinctual need for sexual satisfaction without love was portrayed against the moral pretenses of his time. And in *Leutnant Gustl*, published in 1901, Schnitzler used the "stream of consciousness" technique—the internal monologue resembling free association—to reveal the hero's hidden conflicts.

Schnitzler's use of psychoanalytic concepts in his works seems to exhibit the same progressions as Freud's scientific investigations. His early works—*Anatol* and *Paracelsus*—use hypnosis as a comic and plot device to penetrate the realms of the unconscious. Later plays—*Shepherd's Flute, Intermezzo, Comedy of Seduction*—stress unconscious motivation of behavior not unlike the emphasis in *Studies in Hysteria*. These were followed by concepts of "resistance," transference and depression. (In the case history of Dora, Freud [3] called Schnitzler his "poetical witness.")

Repression, for example, is one of the key concepts in *The Call of Life*. A young girl who has been caring for a hopelessly invalid father suffers from anxiety and depression. Her father's physician through judicious use of interpretations makes her aware of her latent death wishes toward her father. Torn by ambivalent feelings, she poisons her father. Thereafter, she reacts to her grief by impulsive love affairs, until, at the end of the play, war breaks out and she becomes a heroic nurse who saves sick, wounded men, i.e., the return of her dead father. Schnitzler thus clearly depicts a variety of mechanisms such as repression, return of the repressed, and "acting out" at a time when Freud was formulating these same concepts.

It is difficult to discover in these themes just where Schnitzler's intuitive feelings may have been molded by Freud's writing. It is certain that Schnitzler read Freud. In 1900, he mentions in his diary a dream "exactly like one in Freud's *Dream Interpretation*." Reik, Wittels, and von Winterstein explained analysis to Schnitzler and argued with him about his interpretations, even of his own work. Reik, who in 1913 wrote a book entitled *Arthur Schnitzler as Psychologist*,[12] stated in a personal communication that Freud's direct influence became obvious in Schnitzler's story "Beata and Her Son" (1912). Schnitzler denied this. However, an examination of the story reveals the oedipal theme, whether or not he was influenced by Freud.

The autobiographical character of Schnitzler's writings—their frequent melancholic and speculative fancies—was made very clear in

417

1907 when he published *The Road to the Open* (*Der Weg ins Freie*). He labored for five years on this novel, and his diaries contain admissions that the work is largely autobiographical. Significantly, he started to write it on the day his son was born. This novel introduces a condensation of many heroes of preceding works. The hero's father has just died, his musical career is floundering, and his father's choice of the law for his career has failed to satisfy him. The hero, George, is a dilettante in the likeness of Anatol, the aesthetic epicurean. He is a composer who has neither the patience nor will power to write music. This passive, unheroic drifter falls in love with a poor girl. However, her presence is never enough, he always longs for an absent or unattainable woman.

The heroine, Anna, becomes pregnant and he still remains indecisive about marrying her. To avoid disgrace, they go to Italy; and on her return to Vienna she gives birth to a stillborn son. Guilty because he has had another affair on which he blames the baby's death, he leaves her.

As the story unfolds, another hero, Henry, a further prototype of Schnitzler, advises the dilettante hero and makes sage comments upon their love affair. Henry is a man who curses his gift of understanding because he feels that understanding does not affect his emotions or actions. He feels that George, the dilettante, is free and can toss the love affair from his conscience. Henry, however, has had an affair with an actress and is almost driven insane with guilt and remorse when she commits suicide because of him. He feels that depth of insight and his compulsion to know does not lead him to clarity but rather to a knowledge of his helplessness. "It does not simplify our lives but rather renders us aware of the infinite, uncontrollable threads that determine our acts."

"A person afflicted with insight can never take refuge in a religion or an established 'cause' which uncritical people may. Everyday he must discover anew the world and himself. In every person and relation, in every thought and deed, there is a unique element which requires a new interpretation."

In such an unstable world, fiction becomes like truth and vice versa. A murder may prove an act of kindness, and a kindly deed lead to murder.

Schnitzler's diary revealed that his only genuine love was for Marie Reinhardt which began when Schnitzler was thirty-five, just a few years before the book was begun. Marie was intelligent, affectionate, and devoted. The history of her actual pregnancy and stillbirth was described in *The Road to the Open*. Unlike his many other mistresses, she was not on the stage, but Schnitzler became alarmed when she began taking singing and acting lessons. He was as afraid of her gaining independence as he was of losing his by marrying. While he was still hesitating, she died within a few days of an infectious disease.

The Road to the Open was his most philosophic and mature book. It was written following the loss of the only woman he had genuinely loved in his life. It accompanied his marriage several years later and the birth of his only son—named Henry. The characters are all enmeshed in their fates. Henry tells George it is better not to know anything, but to live irresponsibly. Yet at the end, each hero goes off to a cause, as if real strength can come only with freedom from internal restraints.

II

Freud, too, freed himself from his internal restraints. The facts of his crucial years between 1890 and 1900 have become generally known from Jones's biography.[9] The key fact, Freud's self-analysis, can be compared to Schnitzler's "abreaction" via his book *The Road to the Open*.

Freud's medical contemporaries in a parallel fashion referred to his theories as "a scientific fairy tale," but Freud insisted on the scientific basis of his case histories: "I have been brought up with strict science and cannot help it if my case histories sound like novels."[3] Although Jones believes that Freud had the "technical literary qualities" for creative writing, Freud never moved in that direction; creative writing would have remained a picture of the truth, not the literal truth itself. And the literal truth was Freud's goal.

Discussion

1

What is the unique quality of psychological conflict which makes it the core of psychoanalysis and of much of Schnitzler's work?

The chief substance which unites literary works of art and the concept of unconscious conflict is the dramatic and tragic conception in each. Psychological conflict is in itself a kind of tragedy. It is unknown

419

to its sufferer and if it comes to light, it is often too late to avert the consequences. Imaginative literature has always dealt with inner conflicts. Even when the protagonists deal with external conflicts which are conscious and observable, these may often be mere representations of deeper forces raging within. Characters in literature are unaware of these deeper forces, as are neurotic patients whose first discomfort is felt as anxiety, but who attribute their difficulties to fate.

These strata of unawareness, relative or complete, make each person an inner battlefield. Schnitzler intuitively showed how these conflicts led to various tragedies. His works were replete with an uncanny and remarkable knowledge of these subjects. But like most creative people, he seemed to have little insight into his own problems.

Freud struggled against immense odds to convey a deepened insight into inner conflicts, including his own. Although his tragic case histories were dramatic and followed no preconceived methodology, as a scientific observer, he described psychical mechanisms as he uncovered them, and then attempted to evolve general formulations from these. To do this, he had to overcome his own resistances and later those of his patients and students whom he asked to enter into this process of uncovering.

In contrast to psychoanalysis, literature invites one to participate in an emotional conflict. Whereas analysis has the task of making the patient aware of the painful conflict, literature may invite a transient awareness but one from which we can always detach ourselves.

Analytic science has the further task of translating individually observed conflicts into general laws. Thus literature and analysis have independent goals and, although to some extent they may assimilate something from each other, their aims are essentially different.

Schnitzler and Freud reintroduced in their concepts of psychic conflict the key idea that character is fate. (In a brilliant article Hyman[8] described it as follows: "Its moral ingredients were 'hybris,' the protagonist swollen with pride, 'peripetia' a terrifying change in fortunes, and an awaiting of the fateful outcome, that 'small moment' when all is in doubt.") Greek tragedy contained a protagonist filled with pride, a fateful change of external fortunes, and a desperate awaiting of the fateful outcome which was inevitable. The emphasis was upon the external events which buffeted about all human fortunes. Drama and tragedy as it became influenced by Judaic-Christian religion had very few tragic conflicts which followed a long and inevitable course of disaster. The only sins became disobeying God or worshiping rival gods, and in so far as the stories were literature, they were less tragic. Jesus in His reincarnation and His atonement made all private atonement unnecessary. In this sense, great insight into human motivation and great literature were basically heretic. For heroes like Captain Ahab, Hamlet, and King Lear were imperfect men driven by unconscious motivations which finally proved their downfall.

Schnitzler in his drama and Freud in his dramatic case histories emphasized the role of internalized conflicts which were once called fate. The unconsciousness of these conflicts and their force were considered part of human character. Both men in their respective fields minutely dissected the origins, the inevitability, and the individual fight against these drives which could often overcome the so-called "fate" of the individual.

Freud, in his work, was essentially gloomy, stoic, and *tragic*. Man was imperfect and in fact from the moment of his birth he was a dying animal. The first protoplasm "had death within easy reach," Freud observed in *Beyond the Pleasure Principle*.[6] For Freud the aim of human existence was to reclaim ego from id, and this limited victory could be gained only by self-knowledge. Man's animal nature was to be controlled and channeled, and cure did not lie in cutting out the animal part, but in facing and living with it. All of Schnitzler's later, more mature themes shared this basic feeling.

2

What were some of the explanations for the "uncanniness" of the ideas of these men? Freud's letter, mentioned earlier, praised Schnitzler for his ability to analyze the "accepted cultural, conventional so-called verities." Not only Schnitzler, but Freud, too, had the ability to analyze the hypocrisy of his time! What was the source of this ability? The cultural sources certainly included the cosmopolitan center in which both men lived. Vienna reacted sharply to the increasing industrialization of society, and socialism had an early and firm foundation there. Moreover, it was fashionable, especially among the enlightened, to strive for sexual freedom, one focus of which was the rebellion of women. The moral law of the times was a hypocrisy which on the one hand permitted the most lawless instincts full play in private life, yet did everything to repress public manifestations.

Freud and Schnitzler were members of a minority group and, having been themselves sharply discriminated against, were the first to perceive the hypocritical repressions of their corrupt society. What better proponents to point up hyprocrisy than two heretic Jews in an allegedly moral, Hapsburg Catholic environment? The constant awareness of being different, the projection of so many base instincts upon their people, must have had the effect of making them fight in the age-old manner of the Jew, namely, through the written and spoken word.

3

A search into similarities of deeper psychological significance is necessary to understand Freud's comparison, in the quoted letter: "Your determinism as well as skepticism—what is generally called pessimism—your ability to be deeply moved by the truths of the unconscious, by the instinctual nature of man, the recurrence of your thoughts to the polarity of love and death . . ."

Both were first-born sons of young mothers and their early oral satisfactions were too quickly disrupted by a second pregnancy and the birth and death of male siblings during the first one and a half years of life. Other siblings followed immediately.

In his paper on "Screen Memories," [2] Freud mentioned what proved to be his own famous memory.[1] This occurred in a green meadow where he, with another boy and girl, were gathering dandelions. Then the boys tore the flowers from the girl who had the most beautiful bouquet. The crying girl was consoled with a piece of savory black bread cut with a long knife by a nursemaid who was standing with another woman in front of a house. The boys also received a piece of the delicious-tasting bread. A comparable screen memory of Schnitzler's from ages two to three was revived during his adolescence. It concerned a lawn interspersed with flower beds in a park called "Paradise Gardens." Chairs and tables stood in front of the building. A child in a dress was playing in front of the nursemaid and a red parasol was a striking picture in the scene.

Both of these screen memories seem to concern sexual play and curiosity about a little girl. The repeated pregnancies of their mothers necessitated nursemaids and this, combined with the loss of the younger sibling, may provide an early basis for their attitude toward women and toward death.

As to the "polarity of love and death," unresolved conflicts with women in their early lives can be generally accepted as being rather marked. The screen memories may be said to concern a common childhood fear of the female genital to which they seemed to react by identification with their mothers and a drawing closer to their fathers. Schnitzler's highly ambivalent attitude toward women need hardly be amplified. Schnitzler's plays were filled with his mixed feelings toward them, and Freud in his writings expressed equal bewilderment. Both showed a comparable ambivalence toward women in their private lives. Both over-idealized certain men and to both women were essentially perplexing.

But what about the whimsical idea of their being doubles? Perhaps the most speculative fantasy might be that Freud seemed in constant hope and fear of meeting his double. One might possibly explain his friendship with and even awe of Jung and Fliess in some part on these terms. They were imaginative people who relieved his anxiety and emotions on this score, but could they, like Schnitzler, have also been his "doubles"? In further speculation, did they contain the element of the uncanny? Were they feared younger siblings who had died? Did they revive childhood hopes and fears that "mother had wanted my brother to live and me to die"? Were they "reincarnations" which caused him to live within a short distance of Schnitzler whom he mentions in his early works and yet made no effort to meet or even to write him a note? Freud often expressed great admiration for poets, but as in the case of Dostoyevsky and Schnitzler whom he held in awe, he could rarely hide a feeling of personal antipathy. At best, his ambivalence might support an idea of an alter ego whom he feared he might meet —who was similar in some ways and like a mirror image, different from what we expect to see.

4

After demonstrating the similarities, it remains to demonstrate the contrasts in this pair of *Doppelgänger*. In Freud, the passion to know, scientifically, conflicted with the wish to dramatize and to project in the manner of the artist. Like Leonardo da Vinci with whom he identified, he struggled hard to reach a decision, and he chose science. Jones thought this choice was determined by an early sexual curiosity aimed at the stark, naked truth of childbirth, and an ego structure developed in a family life of strict reality.

In the letter, Freud approximated his work to Schnitzler's by calling him an "explorer of psychological depths" and implied an uncanny similarity in their understanding of human behavior. But the kind of "knowing" practiced by the analyst is considerably different from the "knowing" exhibited by the artist. The artist simply does not "know" in the sense of the scientist. He may reconstruct and project his unconscious fantasies, but he has only a slight glimmering of what these fantasies are, what their roots were, and why they were expressed in such a manner. As a matter of fact, it would seem as if the creative artist tries not to know what is going on by projecting his fantasies upon a work of art! Often his fantasies and reality cannot be reconciled with one another!

The only control an artist has is in the aesthetic aim of his reconstructed fantasies. He may write a novel or a play and the form of art is the limitation upon his thinking. Schnitzler, judging by his personal life, may be said to have "lived out" his fantasies by projecting them onto a series of characters representing himself and having these characters do many of the things he did or wished he could do. In this way we may say that he unwittingly "remembered" his own forbidden urges by visualizing and dramatizing them, but without ever realizing that they were part of himself!

While the poet does *not* "know," he is by far the better dramatizer of *hidden urges* and desires. One can respond without inhibition to a play and then isolate its meaning from one's self upon leaving the theater. By the same mechanism, the artist is *responsible* only for artistic validity but not the scientific validity of his themes.

"I believe," wrote Schnitzler, "that there are 'particular persons' who know about themselves even when they only have a vague idea; who make their decisions freely even when they think they have been carried away by accidental happenings and moods; and who are always on the right path, even when they accuse themselves of errors and oversights." But Freud put all the emphasis, especially in his work on dreams, on really knowing. Vague intuition was not enough. A scientific formulation was generally attempted, and speculations kept to a minimum. (In "The Relation of the Poet in Daydreaming," Freud [4] attempted an explanation of the psychological novel which includes Schnitzler's works. "It has struck me in many so-called *psychological* novels that only *one* person—once again the *hero*—is described from *within;* the author dwells in *his* soul and looks upon other people *from outside.* The psychological novel in general probably owes its peculiarities to the tendencies of modern writers to split up their ego by self-observation into many component egos and, in this way, to personify the conflicting trends in their own mental life in *many heroes.*")

5

Why did one choose literature and the other science? Schnitzler's diaries are fairly revealing. His earliest years were spent in the company of children of wealthy families or with the offspring of theater folk. He was taken to a stage performance of Offenbach's *Orpheus* at the age of five. At about this age a governess seemed to have played a decisive part in his daydreams and fantasies. Her suitors visited constantly and her fiancé was a lieutenant in the army. He recalled listening to their romantic conversations and vividly recollected words and phrases which he fancied. Indeed, he claimed that the cornerstone of his plays was laid down by a childhood incident.

He was taken to Gounod's *Faust* and two singers, while hiding in the bushes onstage, waved to the Schnitzler box. He recollected they were patients of his father and he was quite flattered and moved by this intimacy. For the first time he became aware of the make-believe of the theater. "This occasion may have been the cornerstone upon which I built the leitmotif of my plays; namely, merging seriousness and play, life and comedy, truth and lie, which again have moved me and interested me beyond all theater and performance, yes, beyond all art."

One could speculate upon the reasons for his having become stagestruck. This may have become an acceptable condensation of his daydreams. There were elements of love for his governess, the fact that the theater was a field where his father did not excel, but where he might more easily compete with the "professor." The gist seemed to be the relief he felt when he said, "I realized that there was such a thing as 'fictional truth.'" This offered an outlet for fantasy, exhibitionism, and other key daydreams.

Freud's manner of handling his early fantasies was entirely different. The motive of his boyhood fantasies had elements in common with Schnitzler. There were military ones where each identified with Napoleon and other soldiers. But gradually Freud gave up conscious romantic and lyric fantasies and ruthlessly checked all ruminations. An interest in science, a retreat from a wish for power over men occurred in his adolescence. Ernest Jones[9] has speculated that the control of Freud's early aggressive fantasies was characterized by the search for intellectual rather than political or military power. Freud checked all erotic fantasies and went to great lengths to disguise his childhood and adolescent sexual fantasies in his article on "Screen Memories" (1899).

6

After the war of 1918, Schnitzler was regarded as a historical rather than a contemporary figure. He was criticized for his alleged indifference to economic and cultural problems. How could one keep writing about men and women with their individual and "petty" problems when vast economic problems reared their head throughout Central Europe?

Schnitzler acknowledged the importance of bread and butter problems but calmly said that the eternal problems still lay underneath. When he was charged with never offering a solution to these problems, he stated that these problems would no longer be eternal if they could be solved! When it was suggested that his range was narrow and his subjects unimportant, he pleaded guilty. But he stated that he really did not know any themes which were more important than the call of life, the dance of death, the lure of love.

Freud, with his strict view of psychological determinism, soon began to have his revolutionary truth denied as soon as it affected culture. (Revisionists like Horney, Fromm, Thompson saw man as needing only a "good" environment and a changed social structure. The latter would alter the former. Man can be made "perfect" and the world is tractable and alterable. A Freudian is a synonym for the "orthodox" analyst.) When society but not the individual is at fault, archaic parts of the personality are deprived of their vigor. There has been a retreat from the insights of Schnitzler and Freud which are necessarily tragic. Freud and Schnitzler showed us that life is often nasty, brutish and short. If we are serious, our reaction to the bitter truth is not to evade it or lose hope but to set out to trace our conflicts as best we can with the aid of self-knowledge. Without self-knowledge we live as meanly as ants.

Summary

1. A letter from Freud to Arthur Schnitzler in 1922 revealed a curious confession that he regarded the playwright as his *Doppelgänger*. This was so because Freud had encountered in Schnitzler's poetic fiction the same presumptions, interest, and conclusions. "Your skepticism, your ability to be moved by the truth of the unconscious, by the instinctual nature of man, to analyze the accepted cultural-conventional 'verities,' the recurrence of your thoughts to the polarity of love and death . . . had for me an uncanny familiarity."

2. The autobiography and diaries of Schnitzler up to 1903 reveal fascinating similarities to Freud's background and partially account for their similiar interests and their final divergence from medicine to interests in literature and the discovery of a new science.

3. Both were the eldest children in large families. Each lost a sibling before he reached two, and this fact, according to Freud, accounted for his "residual guilt." The key screen memories and the vicissitudes of their early life with their governesses were compared. Their early erotic and aggressive fantasies were examined for indications of their choice of a life's work.

Both became physicians and turned to neurology and then to the French school of psychiatry. Freud originated a new science with a dramatic, dynamic and tragic view of psychic conflict. Schnitzler made famous a narrative form of stream of consciousness and a heightened awareness of psychic conflict which was startling for the times because it revealed the concepts of unconscious motivation, free association and determinism as well as repression and other concepts which were simultaneously formulated by Freud.

4. Schnitzler's dramatic and tragic conflicts were similar to the concept of psychic conflict as visualized by Freud.

5. The permanent validity of these concepts concludes the paper.

Bibliography

1. Bernfield, S. An unknown autobiographical fragment by Freud. *Am. Imago*, 4:3–19, 1946.
2. Freud, S. Screen memories (1899). *Collected Papers*, 5:47–69. London: Hogarth Press, 1950.
3. Freud, S. Fragment of an analysis of a case of hysteria (1905). *Collected Papers*, 3:13–146. London: Hogarth Press, 1925.
4. Freud, S. Relation of the Poet to Daydreaming (1908). *Collected Papers*, 4:173–183. London: Hogarth Press, 1925.
5. Freud, S. The "Uncanny" (1919). *Collected Papers*, 4:368–407. London: Hogarth Press, 1925.
6. Freud, S. *Beyond the Pleasure Principle* (1920). London: Hogarth Press, 1922.
7. Friedman, L. J. From *Gradiva* to the death instinct. (Unpublished.)
8. Hyman, S. E. Freud and the climate of tragedy. *Partisan Review*, Spring, 1956.
9. Jones, E. *The Life and Work of Sigmund Freud*, Vol. I. New York: Basic Books, 1953.
10. Liptzin, S. *Arthur Schnitzler*. New York: Prentice-Hall, 1932.
11. Rank, O. Der Doppelgänger. Imago, 3:97–164, 1914.
12. Reik, T. *Arthur Schnitzler als Psycholog*. Minden: J. C. C. Bruns, 1913.
13. Wittels, F. *Sigmund Freud*. New York: Dodd, Mead, 1924.
14. Zilboorg, G. *Sigmund Freud*. New York: Scribners, 1951.

A Note on Freud's Neighbor

(1959)

JEROME M. SCHNECK

Schneck, Clinical Associate Professor of Psychiatry, State University of New York, College of Medicine, New York, is a well known expert in hypnotherapy. This selection was published in The American Journal of Psychotherapy 13 (1959):139–41.

During a recent visit (1958) to Berggasse 19, the writer and his wife unexpectedly encountered an elderly woman who had been a neighbor of the Freud family at this address in Vienna for thirty-one years. The commemorative plaque on the building reads:

> IN DIESEM HAUS LEBTE UND WIRKTE
> PROFESSOR SIGMUND FREUD
> IN DEN JAHREN 1891–1938
> DER SCHÖPFER UND BEGRÜNDER
> DER PSYCHOANALYSE
> GESTIFTET VON DER 6. JAHRES
> VERSAMMLUNG DER WORLD
> FEDERATION FOR MENTAL HEALTH
> IM AUGUST 1953

The English translation of the inscription in Jones' biography differs slightly from the actual wording on the tablet as reproduced here.

The neighbor had moved into the building in 1907 so that her period of residence has spanned fifty-one years. At present, the several apartments house many families. There are stores at the street level, one of which, for example, deals with linoleum and plastics. The courtyard remains, and in it still stands the little statue of a girl about which Jones has commented in connection with another visitor's impression. It had been implied that the view of this statue might have had psychologic significance for Freud in connection with certain aspects of the development of psychoanalytic thought. Jones was not impressed. The statue, incidentally, appeared to have little artistic appeal or merit, aside from differing opinions about its possible importance for Freud.

Our elderly informant was evidently an octogenarian. She happened to be passing by when we were making inquiries, offered to help, and discovered we were interested in the location of Freud's quarters. She was alone, dressed completely in black except for a white grosgrain ribbon around her neck and a circular gold brooch on her dress. Slight, and of medium height, she was alert, friendly yet shy, and pleasantly matter-of-fact in offering information. She showed us the entrances to the apartments Freud had occupied for his home and office. Three families occupy them now. The interiors were said to have been considerably transformed from Freud's day so that they would no longer be recognizable.

This woman told of her contact with Freud's wife, whom she described as quite friendly, communicative, and occupied essentially with the routine concerns of caring for an active family and busy household. It was a daily, pleasant, neighborly relationship. She had less contact with the children but was aware of many of their activities, and asked about what had happened to them since the family had moved. She had a tendency to comment, in recall, about the physical appearance of each individual, including Freud's sister-in-law whom she saw frequently and to whom she made reference as having been involved in the educational rearing of the children. Her contact with Anna Freud may have been casual. She referred to her as having been a teacher, knew in a general way that Anna Freud had become interested in psychoanalysis and had then become more intimately connected with the work of her father, although she had not studied medicine.

This neighbor also mentioned that she recalled having taken a grandson of Freud to her apartment in order to show him a Christmas tree which he had been longing to see, having not as yet had the opportunity. She had been particularly impressed by the expression in this child's eyes, described as beautiful and bright, evidently considering it an unusual attribute in him.

Her few comments about Freud were of interest. She would encounter him from time to time when he was leaving or returning to his home. He rarely spoke with any of his neighbors and her contact with him was the opposite of the neighborly intimacy with his wife. There

429

might be a brief greeting or a nod but these would have been unusual because the major recollection was one of no greeting at all. He might walk with his head bowed, or in any case, he would simply ignore her. She ascribed this to what she inferred was his intense preoccupation and absorption with his professional interests and intellectual concerns. The degree of detachment was impressive.

Our informant stated that the neighbors knew of course that Freud was a physician and a "specialist." Exactly what his work consisted of was not, she said, a matter of general interest to these people at that time. She too had not known then the precise nature or significance of his work. Now she was aware of his reputation but made no special reference to it.

This neighbor had not been questioned before in this way, at least not to a considerable extent. She was not familiar with Ernest Jones and his name did not register with her as a physician and psychoanalyst colleague and friend of Freud. She did not know about the recently published biography. It is conceivable that more extensive contact with her might elicit much information of interest on this or other levels. Her shyness and reserve, however, might preclude this form of interchange. The spontaneity that unfolded gradually as a result of a chance and informal encounter might be impaired and lead to some distortion. These points are mentioned for whatever value they may serve.

Letter to Freud
(1965)

MARIE BONAPARTE

Marie Bonaparte (1882–1962) was one of Freud's favorite pupils, analysands and friends. Great-grand-daughter of Lucien, Napoleon I's brother, and married to Prince George of Greece, she became a founder of the French Psychoanalytic Society. She entered analysis with Freud in 1925 after her father Prince Roland had died and kept a diary of their relationship. Unfortunately, neither this diary nor her vast correspondence with Freud is available to the historian of psychoanalysis. The narrowmindedness of her literary heirs in this respect is astounding. Since I felt that she should be represented in this volume, I reprint parts of a letter she wrote to Freud concerning the Fliess correspondence, which she rescued in Berlin and kept intact against Freud's wishes. The letter was published in Drives, Affects, Behavior *(edited by Max Schur), New York, International Universities Press, 1965.*

January 7, 1937

Mr. Stahl has just delivered to me the first part of the Fliess papers: scientific essays scattered through your letters, which he has collected separately. The rest, the letters themselves, of which there are about 200 to 250, are still in Germany, and he will ask someone to bring them to Paris in a few weeks.

The letters and manuscripts have been offered to me on condition that I not sell them, either directly or indirectly, to the Freud family, for fear that this material, which is so important for the history of psychoanalysis, will be destroyed. This would not be a decisive reason for me not to discuss the matter with you. But you will not be surprised, as you know my ideas and feelings on the subject, that I *personally* have an immense aversion to any destruction of your letters and manuscripts.

Perhaps you yourself . . . do not perceive your full greatness. You belong to the history of human thought, like Plato, shall we say, or Goethe. What a loss it would have been for us, their poor posterity, if

Goethe's conversations with Eckermann had been destroyed, or the *Dialogues* of Plato. . . .

In your letters there could be nothing . . . if I know you, that could lower your stature. And you yourself . . . have written a beautiful paper opposing the idealization at any cost of great men, mankind's great father figures. Furthermore, if I predict correctly, some of the history of psychoanalysis, that unique new science which is your creation, and which is more important than even Plato's theory of ideas, would be lost if all of the material were destroyed because of a few personal remarks contained in these letters.

My idea was the following: to acquire the letters and thereby prevent them from being published by just anyone, and to keep them for years, e.g., in some government library—say Geneva, where one needs to be less afraid of the dangers of wars and revolutions—with the proviso that they not be looked at for 80 or 100 years after your death. Who could be hurt then, even among your family, by what they contain?

Moreover, I don't know what they contain. I shall not read any of your letters, if you so desire. I looked at just one of them today, which went along with one of the essays; there was nothing compromising in it.

Do you really recall what they contained after so many years? You have even forgotten whether you destroyed or hid the letters from Fliess—the rupture of your friendship must have been that painful.

. . . Besides, I do not yet have the letters. I shall receive them only in a few weeks.

If you would like, I can stop off in Vienna for a day or two on my way to Greece at the beginning of March, to discuss this matter with you.

I . . . revere you, and have therefore written to you in this way.

Marie

P.S. I want to acquire the letters by myself. We will talk about it more freely!

Sigmund Freud and the Art
of Letter Writing

(1967)

MARTIN GROTJAHN

Martin Grotjahn is a distinguished psychoanalyst and Freud scholar. This selection was published in the Journal of the American Medical Association *200 (3 April 1967): 13–18.*

The study of Freud's letters is a rewarding experience. The sensitive reader feels the pleasure of a personal contact with Sigmund Freud, almost like a personal visit. His letters show, at different times, a young man's passion for life, the maturity of a scientist and discoverer, and finally the wisdom of an aged man who had suffered from life's tragedy which, nevertheless, he accepted with the strength of Moses or Job. The letters give a diary-like account of his life and work—and speak intimately to the reader who has the gift of empathy.

Always he had a simple, direct, personal response to what he experienced. He trusted his perception, he was a true witness of his time and felt a great urgency to write it all down. Once he told Joan Riviere during her analysis, after she had mentioned some thoughts which occurred to her: "Write it, put it down in black and white; that's the way to deal with it; you get it out of your system." He actually said, "Get it out, produce it, make something of it outside you; give it an existence independently of you." For Freud, writing was an act of creation, and letter writing was a special form of his wish to live, to see, to experience, to tell about it, and to master it.

Freud wrote his letters as he did his books, and his books often sound like letters. He wrote with the ring of truth and with classical simplicity and frequently with pictorial images, eg, when he described himself in his isolation as a freshly painted wall, which everybody anxiously avoids touching. He disliked corrections, and once when two corrections were needed on one page he was sure it was time to diagnose senility. He considered it, however, his privilege to change the direction of his thoughts in midstream. Such sentences appear awkward and give the translator a new problem to deal with.

The volume of his correspondence is enormous. There are perhaps 2,500 family letters and 900 love letters to his fiancée, later his wife (who answered with 600 letters). He wrote more than 2,000 letters to Ferenczi and almost 500 to Abraham.

The secret and unstated motive for this writing passion may be found in the assumption that every letter was more or less related to his self-analysis, either a preparation, or a part, or finally a postscript. It started with his letters to his beloved Martha, later his wife, and continued in the correspondence to his "analyst by correspondence," Wilhelm Fliess, and also in many letters to friends and foes alike.

All letters directed to Freud he answered in his characteristic German handwriting. A typewriter which found its way into the Freud household rather late was used rarely. All letters were registered in a big, long, legal-sized ledger, kept by Freud himself, not by any secretary. Paper was naturally always used on both sides. Every free minute between patients was used for letter writing. In the evening when the work was over, more letters would be written.

According to graphologists, Freud's handwriting is outstanding, quite expressive, upsetting and disquieting for the reader. It is clear, genuine, moving, vivid, and at the same time disciplined. It is close and uniform, but ambivalent, not a "typical" handwriting for a scientist or philosopher. It shows an astonishing resemblance to that of Johann Sebastian Bach. The handwriting is a peculiar combination of tension and pride of achievement, indicating constant conflicting emotions in a man with an enormous vitality and a fighting nature. Freud's reaction to graphological interpretation was disbelief and skepticism.

The deciphering of Freud's handwriting is often a challenging task, and he had his own difficulties in reading other people's handwriting. Frequently in Freud's letters we find complaints that he had been irritated trying to decipher letters received (for instance, from Ludwig Binswanger). On such occasions daughter Anna, herself blessed with a calligraphic handwriting, had to serve as reader and interpreter.

Self-Analysis by Correspondence

With His Wife and Family.—Many of Freud's letters to his bride, Martha Bernays, were published by Ernest Jones,[1] and they show clearly that this long engagement, recorded in hundreds of letters, was part of Freud's self-analysis or at least a preparation for it. He described sensitively, and in detail, the events of his life, his reflections, reactions, and opinions, often stated with great emotion. He described the early days in Vienna, the periods of working and waiting, of poverty and misery, long talks with friends in the hospital and in the coffeehouses. He spoke about his love, his hopes, his disappointments, his faith in himself, and his doubts in his future. All of this was told to the girl he loved but whom he rarely saw.

Adventures in Dresden, Berlin, Hamburg, and Paris are told, repeated, and worked through. Books are discussed and reading recommendations are given. Life, love, and death, the "curse of trying to be a genius," of being haunted by his demon, and all the problems of existence, as seen by a young man growing up, leaving school, having his first great encounter with the world outside of Vienna, are recorded here, externalized, examined, and finally mastered. His life and the lives of his friends become vivid when he describes them to his fiancée. In spite of his enormous work load Freud never felt that he worked enough. He chided himself at being lazy, and often wished to renounce the exhausting pursuit of destiny and distinction. He longed in vain for mediocrity and for liberation from his demon. It is difficult to see how Freud would have been able to master later the difficulties of his self-analysis without going through this preparatory phase of letter writing to Martha.

There are also many other letters to the family. They show Freud as a husband and father, but always as a man ready to experience life as it happens, to mature and to grow. Many of these family letters, masterpieces of literature, show his humanity and his deep love for his children. Some, to his daughters, are the most moving human documents in this correspondence. They show Freud in his shy tenderness and love, his patience, his understanding, and his compassion.

During World War I, he revealed the worry of a father for his sons in the army, combined with confidence that they will be able to take care of themselves (which they did). The occasional self-analytic mood of his family letters breaks through even in his old age, when he finally had to leave Austria for England; to his son Ernst he interpreted himself in Biblical terms, "I like to compare myself with the Old Jacob whose children also took him in his old age to Egypt. I hope that not another Exodus will follow as before. It is time that Ahasver came to rest."

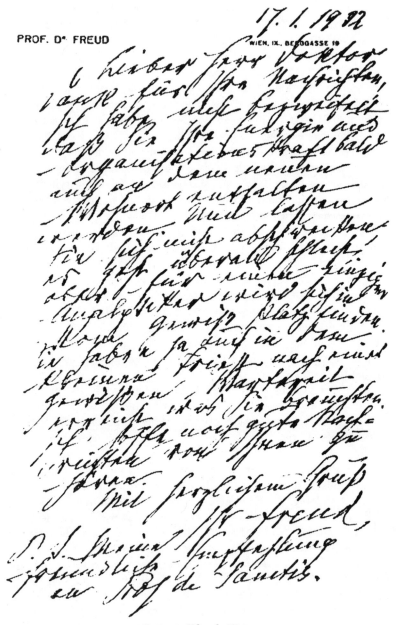

PROF. D.ᵣ FREUD

17. 1. 1932

WIEN, IX., BERGGASSE 19

Letter to Edoardo Weiss.

With Wilhelm Fliess.—Almost 15 years after his death, Freud's letters to his friend and "analyst by correspondence," Wilhelm Fliess, were published.[2] They show Freud in the titanic dual task of analyzing himself and of proving through his findings the general human validity of psychoanalysis. Already the history of these letters is in itself an adventure story: Marie Bonaparte, Princess of Greece and Denmark, friend, patient, and pupil of Sigmund Freud, saved the letters from being burned by the Nazis and brought them to Vienna, where she kept them from Freud himself, who was determined to have them back in order to destroy them. During the war the documents were hidden in Paris and finally arrived safely in England.

Fliess, a physician in Berlin, specialized in diseases of the nose and throat; he had an intense interest in the cycle of woman, and later devised a complicated and untenable system of periodicity common to all life. During the years of this correspondence (1887–1902). Freud moved from neurology to psychoanalysis; he wrote *The Study of Hysteria* with Joseph Breuer, then *The Interpretation of Dreams,* and finally *The Psychopathology of Everyday Life.* Freud made his first Italian journey; ended his friendship with Breuer; the new analytic friendship with Wilhelm Fliess grew, deepened, was analyzed, and finally died.

In these letters we see Sigmund Freud as he saw himself and as he began to recognize the existence and dynamics of his unconscious. We see him happy and unhappy, anxious and in despair. We see him at work and on vacation, worrying about his patients in Vienna and wishing to have a chance to analyze the Czar of Russia in order to get enough money to live free of worries and support his research. We see him struggling to stop smoking and starting again with the next cigar before the letter is finished. We see him collecting mushrooms with his children, walking and talking with his friends, and endlessly searching the depth of his own unconscious. He records and analyzes his dreams, his slips, and the neurotic symptoms which are phobic in nature. We see a man possessed by a passion—or "demon." He found the answers to the riddle of the sphinx in his own unconscious, with methods he developed tentatively and testingly and used first of all on himself.

The letters are written during the heroic times of psychoanalysis, a period of scientific and personal isolation ending about 1910. The inner connection between the great discovery of the unconscious and Freud's self-analysis is strikingly real. After the death of his father, Jacob (23 Oct. 1896), Freud found within himself his "most important patient," and wrote to his friend in Berlin about it. He remembered and felt again the infatuation with his own mother and the hostility toward his father. He almost broke under the impossible task of analyzing himself, and of doing so alone. Never before and never again was such struggle revealed in such detail and with such results of scientific discovery.

Many letters illustrate the style of almost free association. One of the most convincing examples is a letter dated 30 Oct. 1927. The widow of Heinrich Braun, who was writing a biography about her late husband, had asked him for recollections. Braun had been an intimate friend during Freud's boyhood and youth. At first Freud's mind turned to recollections of recent events, then he reached far back to the beginning of his friendship with Braun, and then he proceeded in chronological sequence. Later he interrupted his freely flowing associations with a reflection about the strange fact that he later lived for more than 45 years in the same home in which he met Victor Adler. After some hesitation, so it seems, came the report about what Freud called the "youthful friendship" with Braun, firebrand of a person, who was not a "scholar" but a "personality."

All the typical features of boyhood friendships, with their deep feeling, their loyalties, their declaration of undying faith, are implied in this recollection. It is remarkable to see how Freud attempted to combine the pride of being "Primus," the first one in his class, with his admiration for Braun, the Promethean young man who was asked to leave school.

With Georg Groddeck.—A special place in Freud's "analytic correspondence" must be reserved for the little-known letters to Georg Groddeck, who called himself proudly a "wild analyst." He was an exhibitionistic masochist who lived a very different life from that of the Victorian professor in Vienna. He wrote his first discouragingly long letter to Freud in May 1917, and continued the correspondence through many years, not quite to the time of his death in 1934. Only a selection of the letters has been published.[3,4] Freud recognized the contributions of Groddeck to metapsychology and accepted from him the term "Id" (Groddeck's "It"). We also know that for a while there was a triangular correspondence between Groddeck, who wrote to Freud, who forwarded the letters to Sandor Ferenczi, who returned the letter with a commentary to Groddeck, and with whom there later developed a deep and lasting "therapeutic friendship."

With ease and joy, yet with great inner strength, Groddeck trespassed the borderline between conscious and unconscious, always to return with new insights. What Freud had done with painful and scientific work in his own analysis, Groddeck did in wild artistic back-and-forth journeys into his own unconscious. Freud may have felt that part of his own projected unconscious lived and walked in Groddeck, as a kind of strange brother. Freud defended and loved him, tried to control and help him, and finally had to leave him alone.

Groddeck's first book appeared soon after World War I, under the title of *Der Seelensucher,* a term taken from Goethe and meaning approximately "a man in eternal search for his soul." The book amused Freud, who sponsored it, but it scandalized many of the early analysts. It seems that Freud enjoyed a man who for once felt free in communication with the unconscious—and with death.

Dialogues and Monologues with Psychoanalytic Pioneers

The enormous correspondence between Freud and the pioneers of psychoanalysis passes through all phases of Freud's life. He wrote as a teacher, analyst, physician, colleague, occasionally as a friend or stern monitor; rarely as an enemy. He was consultant, therapist, scientist, and thinker, always puritanical for himself but liberal and tolerant and preaching freedom to others. He often wrote like an emperor leading his pioneers into uncharted lands, organizing the provinces, commanding, reassuring, helping, advising, always thinking of the way psychoanalysis would stand up to the judgment of time.

Karl Abraham, the First German Psychoanalyst.—The long-awaited correspondence between Sigmund Freud and Karl Abraham has been published now, and recently reviewed.[5] One can safely say that a great dialogue has been added to the world's literature with the publication of these letters.

Oskar Pfister, Man of Faith.—In 30 years of correspondence with Parson Oskar Pfister, Freud wrote 134 letters, from which 100 were chosen for publication,[6] together with 30 of the Pfister letters. Anna Freud mentions in her introduction that the parson was a strange figure in the house of her father, who had turned so far away from any church or temple. Pfister differed from other visiting analysts in his warmth, his enthusiasm, and his interest in the life of the Freud family.

Even when the difference in stature, style, and depth of the two correspondents became obvious, both men stand their ground well. Freud envied the therapeutic position of the parson, who could guide his patients' transference from the therapist towards God. Oskar Pfister was quick to answer, "The Protestant Reformation is nothing but psychoanalysis of Catholic sexual repression," whereupon Freud called Pfister and himself "sexual Protestants." Again and again, Freud admonished Pfister not to shy away from sexuality; he declared that all censorship is bad and cuts deeply into the body of psychoanalysis.

In his correspondence Freud continued his self-analysis. For example (10 May 1909), he confessed that he had analyzed his "father complex" and had corrected his compulsion to do better financially than his father. He finally claimed victory of a certain "money anxiety" and gave credit to Oskar Pfister. Significantly enough, Freud warned against philosophy and religion; all fundamentals should be left in the semi-darkness in which they look so good.

The Jewish-Christian question is discussed in detail. In October 1918, Pfister wrote:

> In the first place you are not a Jew, which my endless admiration for Amos, Isaiah, Jeremiah, with the men who composed Job and the Prophets makes me greatly regret; and in the second place you are not so godless, since whoever lives for the truth lives in God and whoever strives for the freeing of love "dwelleth in God." If you would fuse your own contribution with the great world harmony, like the synthesis of notes in a Beethoven symphony into a musical whole, I could say of you, "There never was a better Christian."

Both men discussed matters of religion with ease because, as Pfister explained, "The danger is not great that you will apply for baptism or that I will come hopping down from my pulpit."

After publication of *The Future of an Illusion* (1927), Freud wrote that he had great understanding of the words: "Your sins are forgiven you. Arise and walk." He wondered what would happen if the patient were to ask, "How do you know that my sins are forgiven?" Freud could not simply answer, "I am the Son of God. I forgive you." He would have to say, "I, Professor Sigmund Freud, forgive you your sins," which, he admitted, would not work very well.

This letter (25 Nov. 1928) concludes with a remarkable paragraph:

> I do not know whether you have guessed the secret bond between "Lay Analysis" and "Illusion." In the first one, I want to protect analysis against physicians; in the other one, against priests. I

would like to hand it over to a profession which does not yet exist, a group of worldly physicians of the soul, who do not need to be physicians and who should not be allowed to be priests.

Ludwig Binswanger, Existential Philosopher.—The reading of this dialogue[7] is not easy. The German original is complicated by peculiarities of the existential philosophic style in which Binswanger writes. It is also not easy to accept that Ludwig Binswanger was struggling all his life with the ambivalence of a son toward a father figure. The correspondence starts with a recollection of the first three visits that Binswanger and Jung made to Freud, who was 51, while Binswanger was 25 and Jung was 32. The two Swiss physicians represented "the professors," the accepted ones, the gentiles, the potential protectors, and Freud was anxious to have some such men among his friends and seemed to be self-conscious when he introduced them to the Vienna group of friends.

As Binswanger remembers it, Freud asked both of his visitors, whom he met for the first time, about their dreams, and he was not reluctant to give deep-going interpretations without much regard for resistance. Freud tried to avoid unnecessary involvement in Binswanger's philosophy. With some resignation Freud finally said: "Follow me as far as you can and for the rest let us remain good friends." With this motto they remained in good relationship through a lifetime. Freud had trouble reading Binswanger's handwriting, especially once when he was tempted to send the letter back unread until his daughter showed him that the message contained the tragic fact that Binswanger's son had died.

Without any disguise Freud tried hard to engage Binswanger as a negotiator with Jung, whom he did not want to give up since he considered Switzerland as almost the heart of the psychoanalytic empire, a word used by Freud himself. When the break with Jung was inevitable, Freud was bitter and remarked to Binswanger, "This is your fault."

Edoardo Weiss, Pioneer in Italy.—The 30 years of correspondence between Sigmund Freud and Edoardo Weiss started in October 1908.[8,9] When the two men met, Freud was past 50 and Weiss was then a young medical student. These letters have a unique character; they give us a chance to study Freud as a psychoanalytic consultant, therapist and supervisor, as the editor of a journal, as the author who arranges the translation of his works in a most generous way, and also

441

as a man in charge of the psychoanalytic movement, advising his tough
and most faithful pioneer in Italy.

Freud made frankly moral judgment between worthwhile people
and some not so worthwhile (28 May 1922). In the privacy of his correspondence he was using sharp words, including the word "scoundrel"
(22 May 1922), and he was skeptical about the therapeutic efficiency
of analysis in such cases. The letters are also full of advice and opinions
given from Freud's immense clinical experience; for instance, when he
said: "The patient who talks too much about his analysis prepares the
betrayal or hostile exposure of analysis" (11 June 1922). He explained
with great kindness and patience, which characterizes all of these letters to his young colleague, that the doctor in question is perhaps too
young in order to invite the necessary father transference. At all times
Freud is careful not to be overwhelming with his advice. Whatever he
said was said "without obligation" to the recipient of the letter (9 Feb.
1934).

Again and again Freud sounded a warning against excessive therapeutic ambition. This does not necessarily indicate Freud's therapeutic
pessimism, but it seems to represent the general early European attitude of skepticism and guarded expectancy towards psychoanalysis (or
any kind of therapeutic approach) as a method of treating mental sickness or of changing the personality. The original attitude of using psychoanalysis as a method of study shines through the words of Freud.

Most striking in all these letters on psychoanalytic therapy is the
superb, simple, direct, convincing reconstruction of psychodynamics.
For the recipient of these letters they must have amounted to a training in psychodynamic reasoning. The letters also show one other feature which in previous literature about Freud's correspondence has
perhaps been taken for granted and not been emphasized enough—
Freud's far-reaching training and experience in straightforward psychiatry (4 April 1921; 7 Jan. 1923; and others).

Theodor Reik.—Freud continued his friendship with Theodor Reik
for 30 years[10] and recognized the young man as not only a gifted analyst but also an excellent and skillful writer who could express himself
well and communicate the message of psychoanalysis to the world.
Freud also knew the difficulties of his young friend.

Freud gave warnings against Reik's masochistic trends, guilt feelings, and "too much repentance." At another time there was the remarkable sentence: "I wish you a sclerotic conscience. . . ." At a
later time Freud would not accept any more of Theodor Reik's com-

442

plaints about his miserable poverty, for which Freud originally had considerable empathy. He did not quite see why a man in a dependent situation has to marry; he later indicated that he did not want to hear any more of "your jokes of starvation."

Freud's last letter was written on 3 July 1938. In it he asked, after Theodor Reik immigrated to America: "Could you not have stayed in Holland longer?" And then comes the sentence summarizing his attitude: "When I think of you, sympathy and annoyance fight within me."

Otto Rank, a Tragically Disappointing Student.—Freud had great warmth and affection for Rank, whom he called his son.[11] As with Theodor Reik, Freud made all kinds of sacrifices for Rank: promoting him, giving him interviews, arranging for work, taking him into the inner circle, and finally losing him shortly after Freud himself got desperately sick. He was careful and cautious with any kind of critique: "I do not like to judge the product of my close friends and colleagues because I have the fear that my criticism will hamper their independence and because I myself am so slow to take on anything new and to work away in my own province" (10 July 1922).

Postcard greeting with typical signature.

In the same letter Freud gave surprising advice about the character of scientific meetings. Referring to a manuscript that Rank wanted to present, Freud said: "I believe it is not suitable for presentation before the Congress. Little new, and that very clear, is the stipulation for an effective Congress lecture."

The best of mutual intimacy and trust which usually prevailed between Freud and Rank is revealed in a remarkable exchange of analytic letters in which Rank analyzed a dream of Freud (26 Nov. 1922); it shows that Freud could utilize his relations to a friend in his ever continued self-analysis: "It is a long time since you have tried to inter-

443

pret one of my dreams in such a powerful analytical way. Since then much has changed. You have grown enormously and you know so much more about me and the result too is different."

Sandor Ferenczi, Pioneer of Pioneers.—The correspondence between Freud and Sandor Ferenczi is veiled in secrecy. The number of letters has been variously estimated between several hundred and two thousand. Ernest Jones decided not to publish any of this correspondence in his Freud biography.

Ernst Freud, president of the Sigmund Freud Archives, published a few letters which allow us to guess the relationship between Freud and his most original, intuitive, and creative but sometimes erratic pupil and friend. Already in 1910 this friendship was well established, but Freud apologized for perhaps not living up to Ferenczi's exaggerated expectations: "You were disappointed because you probably expected to swim in constant intellectual stimulation, whereas I hate nothing more than striking up attitudes and out of contrariness frequently let myself go" (2 Oct. 1910).[3]

There are a few letters which give deep insight into Freud's personality. In one, he wrote about the death of his mother, with the words, "At the same time a feeling of liberation, or release, which I think I also understand. I was not free to die as long as she was alive, and now I am. The values of life will somehow have changed noticeably in the deeper layers" (16 Sept. 1930).[3] There are also reports about the self-analysis, some hints about "that murderous firebrand and ever-active devil in me (who has now become visible) . . . bury him so deeply even from myself that I could regard myself as a peace loving man of science" (22 Feb. 1915).

The final evaluation of the letters and of the friendship between these two great men has to wait until the publication of all the material which is known to rest in the Freud Archives.

Other Letters

Psychoanalysis is in the first place a method of clinical investigation of the unconscious. It is furthermore a body of knowledge, a structured system of theories, concepts, and terms, a tool for the treatment of the sick, and an instrument for the training of the therapist. In addition, psychoanalysis is also a well-constructed and formally developed organization which now embraces the Western world.

To the governors of all the psychoanalytic provinces, Freud had written many letters.[12]

The correspondence between Freud and Ernest Jones, his most faithful biographer, has not been published, except for a few specimens. The correspondence seems to have suffered from two things. The first one was not the language barrier but rather Jones' resistance against Freud's gothic handwriting. In regard to this, Freud once remarked (20 Nov. 1926):

> You will be surprised when I reveal the reasons that hamper my correspondence with you. It is a classic example of the petty restrictions to which our nature is subject. I find it really very difficult to write German in Latin characters as I am doing today. All fluency —on a higher level it is called inspiration—leaves me at once. But you have often told me that you cannot read Gothic script, which leaves me with but two means of communication, both of which impair the sense of intimacy: either to dictate the letter to Anna on the typewriter, or to use my clumsy English.

There is a second reason why these two good friends remained at a certain distance: "It is not in my nature to give expression to my feelings of affection, with the result that I often appear indifferent but my family knows better" (1 Jan. 1929).

To Max Eitington he wrote, "You were the first emissary to reach the lonely man" (7 Jan. 1913). Eitington was a quiet and unobtrusive man who must have been very close and very dear to Freud. Frequently Freud has to thank him, at first in Berlin and later in Israel, for favors given. Eitington quotes Freud as saying that the secret of therapy is to cure through love, and that with greatest personal effort one could perhaps overcome more difficulties in treatment but one would "lose his skin by doing so."

If the space for this essay were unlimited, we could deal with letters to psychiatrists who got lost to psychoanalysis: C. J. Jung, W. Silberer, Wilhelm Stekel; or to the "professors," Josef Breuer, Eugen Bleuler, and Wagner-Jauregg; or the great women in Freud's life, Lou Andreas-Salome, Marie Bonaparte, Yvette Guilbert, "H.D.," (besides family letters to wife, daughter, and sister-in-law). Then there is the flood of letters to friends and foes, to men of fame, and finally miscellaneous and "open" letters. And vast numbers of unpublished letters are known to exist as cherished documents hidden in private collections.

The Ending

But perhaps it is fitting to conclude, not with a letter from Sigmund Freud, but with one from the great silent lady who was always standing closely behind him. Here is a quotation from a letter written by his wife Martha on 7 Nov. 1939, thanking Ludwig Binswanger for his condolences on the death of her husband:

How good, dear Dr., that you knew him when he was still in the prime of his life, for in the end he suffered terribly, so that even those who would most liked to keep him forever had to wish for his release! And yet how terribly difficult it is to have to do without him. To continue to live without so much kindness and wisdom beside one! It is small comfort for me to know that in the fifty-three years of our married life not one angry word fell between us, and that I always sought as much as possible to remove from his path the misery of everyday life. Now my life has lost all content and meaning.

Bibliography

1. Jones, E.: *The Life and Work of Sigmund Freud,* New York: Basic Books, Inc., 1961.
2. Freud, S.: *The Origins of Psychoanalysis: Letters to Wilhelm Fliess, Drafts and Notes: 1887–1902,* M. Bonaparte, A. Freud, and E. Kris (eds.), New York: Basic Books, Inc., 1954.
3. Freud, E. (ed.): *The Letters of Sigmund Freud,* T. Stern and J. Stern (trans.), New York: McGraw-Hill Book Co., 1964.
4. Grossman, C. M., and Grossman, S.: *The Wild Analyst: The Life and Work of Georg Groddeck,* New York: George Braziller, 1965.
5. Grotjahn, M.: Letters of Sigmund Freud, *JAMA* 196:193–194 (April 11) 1966.
6. Meng, H., and Freud, E. L. (eds.): *Psychoanalysis and Faith: The Letters of Sigmund Freud and Oskar Pfister,* E. Mosbacher (trans.), New York: Basic Books, Inc., 1963.
7. Binswanger, L.: *Sigmund Freud: Reminiscences of a Friendship,* N. Guterman (trans.), New York: Grune & Stratton, Inc., 1957.
8. Grotjahn, M. (ed.): Freud as a Psychoanalytic Consultant: From Some Unknown Letters to Edoardo Weiss, *Psychoanal Forum* 1:132–137 (No. 1) 1966.
9. Grotjahn, M. (ed.): Sigmund Freud as a Consultant and Therapist: From Sigmund Freud's Letters to Edoardo Weiss, *Psychoanal Forum* 1:223–231 (No. 2) 1966.
10. Reik, T.: *The Search Within: The Inner Experiences of a Psychoanalyst,* New York: Farrar, Straus, and Cudahy, 1956, pt. 6, pp. 629–657.
11. Taft, J.: *Otto Rank: A Biographical Study Based on Notebooks, Letters, Collected Writings, Therapeutic Achievements and Personal Associations,* New York: Julian Press, Inc., 1958.
12. Alexander, F.; Eisenstein, S.; and Grotjahn, M.: *Psychoanalytic Pioneers,* New York: Basic Books, Inc., 1966.

Reich on Freud

(1967)

WILHELM REICH

Wilhelm Reich (1897–1957) knew Freud very well in the 1920s and 1930s in Vienna. His early work on character analysis placed him among the great pioneers of psychoanalysis. His relationship to Freud deserves a better presentation of his opinions than the present selection. Unfortunately, however, as with so many of the early pioneers, he did not leave an organized account of his relationship with Freud. The interview with Kurt Eissler, representing the Sigmund Freud Archives, was recorded on 18 and 19 October 1952. Over the protests of the Sigmund Freud Archives, it was published in Reich Speaks of Freud, *edited by Mary Higgins and Chester M. Raphael (New York, Farrar, Straus & Giroux, 1967). This is a short excerpt.*

DR. EISSLER
You perhaps remember still some personal anecdotes or personal experiences?

DR. REICH
You mean about Freud?

DR. EISSLER
Little things, yes, habits he had—

DR. REICH
Well, I never paid too much attention to these things. I know that he didn't like it when Rie's daughter cut her hair short. She came home with a Bubikopf. He disliked it intensely. That's gossip. Shall we go into that?

DR. EISSLER
I think gossip—for the historian, gossip is extremely important.

DR. REICH
Do I have to take part in that? Well, there was a question whether Anna Freud had a love life. That was a very much discussed thing. Many analysts in Vienna thought she lived in abstinence. And it was

447

regretted. I, personally, felt somehow that it wasn't good for the development of the education of children. Problems of genitality arise in education and if one of its leaders lives that way it is important. This is what everybody felt. I know nothing about her. I wouldn't like to utter any opinions about it. Is that clear enough?

DR. EISSLER

Yes.

DR. REICH

Other anecdotes? I don't know. Once, as a young physician, he came home drunk at night, or something of that kind, was brought home drunk. Such things— But he did not discuss that. Oh, yes. He used to analyze his children. If the child had wet himself, he would ask, "Why did you do it?"

He was not sarcastic, but he used a biting wit to whip people. Snap! He was very sharp. He never did it with me. Never! With me, he was oh, mad, mad, later—in the late thirties. [In 1952, when Reich was rereading Freud's letters to him, he commented that, for the first time, he felt a certain fear on the part of Freud toward him.]—Oh, Silberer. You know that Silberer committed suicide?

DR. EISSLER

Yes.

DR. REICH

After meeting Freud. Tausk, I think, went this way, too. Freud liked Helene Deutsch very much.

DR. EISSLER

Yes?

DR. REICH

He liked pretty women. For instance, Princess Bonaparte was quite pretty at that time, and Deutsch was a very pretty woman. . . .

Freud and H.D.
(1969)

NORMAN N. HOLLAND

Norman N. Holland, a literary critic and professor, Department of English, State University of New York, Buffalo, is well known for his work in the field of psychoanalysis and literature. This selection is from The International Journal of Psycho-analysis 50 (1969).

Behind the initials which, like a signet, she used to identify all her work, was the woman Hilda Doolittle. She was a well-known poet, and her hours with Freud, she tells us, were "four days a week from five to six; one day, from twelve to one" (Aldington 1956). She saw him altogether about a hundred hours, on the couch, and she wrote a book about it, a book I find read by few students of psychoanalysis, though it is, so far as I know, the only extended account by a sympathetic analysand of an analysis (or something like an analysis) with Freud himself. Jones (1953–7), for example, does not even mention Hilda Doolittle.

H.D.'s *Tribute to Freud* is short (168 pages), elliptical, a rather cryptic series of more or less free associations. Rife with mystical and mythological references, the book conceals as it reveals, although, inevitably, the poetess exposes enough of her own psyche to enable one to make connections between her life-style and her poetic style (Holland 1969). The book was written in London in autumn 1944, based on a diary she had kept in Vienna in 1933 (but left in Switzerland during World War II and so not consulted during the writing of the book in 1944). It is composed as a series of memories in free association so that details about Freud come in as they mingle with the visions and themes of H.D.'s own life. Yet, with a little persistence and reading between the lines, the reminiscences can be unscrambled to give a clear and, I believe, unique picture of Freud's style as a therapist.

The story of H.D. and Freud begins in 1915, the year she lost her first child through a miscarriage. Daughter of a distinguished astronomer "who seldom even at table focused upon anything nearer, literally, than the moon" (Williams 1951) and a mother who seems to have been equally abstracted, she was the one girl among five brothers, one of whom, the one just older than she, was not only her mother's admitted favorite, but an important identification-figure for H.D. herself. In 1915 she was 29, her poetry just coming to be recognized. Two years earlier, she had married her fellow-poet Richard Aldington, but he had left to fight in France when the war broke out. "From shock and repercussions of war news broken to me in a rather brutal fashion," she lost her first child. Her autobiographical novels *Palimpsest* (1926) and *Bid Me to Live* (1960) imply that sometime during this period Aldington took a mistress, perhaps during the pregnancy itself; at any rate, their marriage broke up in 1919 (although, interestingly, she does not mention this in *Tribute to Freud*).

In 1918 her favorite brother was killed in action in France. Her father died a year later from the stroke he suffered at the news. At the end of 1919 she was sick with double pneumonia and awaiting the birth of her second child, determined that this child would live. Perdita (so her mother named her) did live, but H.D. herself went into a "nervous breakdown" (Swann 1962), perhaps a post-partum depression—she does not describe it in *Tribute to Freud*. She was rescued by the poetess Bryher (pen-name of the wealthy Winifred Ellerman) who took her off to Greece to recover. While there she had an hallucination or mystical vision of extraordinary intensity. As she describes it in the memoir, it was not frightening to her, though she felt it as occult and so described it to Freud. He, however, singled this vision out as "the most dangerous or the only actually dangerous 'symptom' " (Aldington 1956: 60. Hereafter, I shall refer to *Tribute to Freud* simply by page number.) Her literary executor, Professor Norman Holmes Pearson, has informed me that she originally entitled the memoir *Writing on the Wall*.

H.D.'s close relationship with Bryher continued even after the latter's marriage to Robert McAlmon, who told "of long train trips about the continent with the two women quarreling in the compartment driving him nearly insane." Their friend William Carlos Williams spoke of the two women as McAlmon's "family." Clearly, the McAlmons were incompatible, but apparently H.D. too had some part in the marriage's final "disastrous outcome" (Williams 1951). Although Freud had read her novel *Palimpsest* before meeting H.D. and its autobiographical sections at least raise that issue, he did not (in H.D.'s account, at any rate) single out anything relating to homosexuality as part of her psychic life. She was, from all accounts, passionately heterosexual. The loss of self-object boundaries in the mystical vision would have seemed of more moment to him, anyway.

It is not clear what motivated H.D. herself to psychoanalysis—this symptom or her wish.

> to free myself of repetitive thoughts and experiences—my own and those of many of my contemporaries . . . to take stock of my very modest possessions of mind and body . . . to dig down and dig out, root out my personal weeds, strengthen my purpose, reaffirm my beliefs, canalize my energies . . . to sort out, relive and reassemble the singular series of events and dreams that belonged in historical time, to the 1914–1919 period (17, 138).

This last, she tells us, she did not finish. "The war closed on us, before I had time." Later on she did describe herself as doing in this period "studies in . . . psychological investigation" (Swann 1962).

However they came about, she began

> some fascinating, preliminary talks with Dr Hanns Sachs in Berlin and wanted to go on with the work, but he was leaving for America. Dr Sachs asked me if I would consider working with the Professor if he would take me?

She would, he did, and she began work with Freud on 5 March 1933 (138, 176).

Freud conducted the analysis in English (as he had often done for English and American patients after World War I). H.D. speaks of her own German as "sketchy," while Freud "was speaking English without a perceptible trace of accent." Her hours with Freud were "four days a week from five to six; one day, from twelve to one." She worked with him for "between three and four months," at least until "late in June or early July 1933." More precisely, Sir John Ellerman, Bryher's father, died on 16 July, and H.D. seems to have left Vienna then, to be with her friend, not planning to return (175). She did return, however, at the end of October 1934. Austria's relations with Germany were deteriorating rapidly—Dollfuss was assassinated that summer—but what brought H.D. back was the news that one of the Professor's other patients, Dr. J. J. van der Leeuw, nicknamed "the Flying Dutchman" because he flew his own plane, had died when he crashed over Tanganyika. "You have come to take his place," Freud bluntly interpreted. This second period of work with Freud was shorter: it lasted five weeks, from the end of October 1934 to 1 December 1934. She saw Freud twice more, in London, once in November 1938, once in the summer of 1939. "He sat quiet, a little wistful it seemed, withdrawn." She was in Switzerland when she heard the news of his death.

H.D. was above all a poet of the thingness of things. All her writings show a remarkable ability (and defensive need) to recreate the touch and feel of various objects; she is much less able to recreate people. She is, for instance, the only memoirist of Freud I have read who did not find his eyes his most striking feature.

> His eyes, set deep and slightly asymmetrical under the domed forehead (with those furrows cut by a master chisel), were unrevealing. His eyes did not speak to me. I cannot even say that they were sad eyes.

H.D.'s special talent for describing things has a serendipitous result in *Tribute to Freud:* a description of Freud's office even more detailed than Ernest Jones's.

Like other psychoanalytic visitors to Freud, she was staying at the Hotel Regina. She would walk down the Berggasse to the familiar entrance at 19. There were occasions when swastikas were chalked along the pavement leading to his door; at least once there were rifles stacked at the street corners. She would proceed up the wide stone steps with their balustrade to the landing. Two doors opened off it: the one to the left led to the Freud apartment, the one to the right to the Professor's office. Though there were other apartments above the Freuds', she did not often meet anyone on the stairs except the previous analysand. She would hang her hat and coat on pegs in the hall "that somehow suggest school or college, [as the] pretty little Viennese maid Paula" [Fichtl], in cap and apron, opened the waiting-room door. There was a round table in the room with "odds and ends of old papers and magazines." On the wall were a number of framed photographs—H.D. could recognize Havelock Ellis and Hanns Sachs—and the framed honorary degree from Clark University, also a richly detailed and symbolic Düreresque print of some horror—perhaps a "Buried Alive." There were long lace curtains at the window (1–2, 88–91, 145).

The other door from the waiting-room opened into Freud's consulting room. (The reader may wish to compare H.D.'s description with the Engelmann photographs of Freud's consulting room and study which appear in Ernest Jones's biography.) Against the wall opposite the waiting room door was the famous couch, an old-fashioned horsehair sofa, slippery, with a hard head-piece at the back and a rug on the foot which H.D. would pull over her during the hour and carefully fold on leaving, wondering as she did so how it was that she always found it folded. Did Paula do it? Or the preceding analysand?

Above the couch hung an old-fashioned steel engraving of the Temple at Karnak. At the foot of the couch—H.D., being tall, could almost touch it with her toes—was an old-fashioned porcelain Nürnberg stove giving off a "pleasantly perceptible glow." At her head, in the three-sided enclosure formed by the head of the couch, the wall adjacent to the couch, and the wall at right angles to it, sat Freud, facing the waiting room door. To his right was a wall and against it, so that it projected out in front of him, a cabinet and desk holding a semicircle of Greek and Egyptian figurines. On the same wall, beyond the desk and cabinet and at right angles to the entrance door was the exit door—it led out into a little laboratory-like pantry room and from thence to the hall (10, 23–27, 31).

From H.D.'s "reclining yet propped-up, somewhat Madame Récamier-like position on the couch," she saw, at her feet, the porcelain stove, then to the right of it another cabinet holding "exquisite Greek tear-jars and iridescent glass bowls and vases that gleamed in the dusk." To the right of this cabinet were the large double doors leading into Freud's study. It was lined with books, though there were not many books in the consulting room. The double doors were very wide, taking up most of the wall facing the foot of the couch, and the study appeared dark or as "broken light and shadow" depending on the time of day. The study had a window as did the consulting room, both facing out on a "courtyard, I believe. I am not sure of this." In fact, they give out onto a garden, the same onto which the waiting room window opened (Jones, 2:381). There was a desk in the study and on it, the famous semi-circle of figures of the Egyptian and Greek gods, among them the ivory carving of Vishnu given Freud by his Indian students. A cabinet held, among other objects, a handful of rings (27, 31, 101).

Returning through the double doors to the consulting room and lying down again, H.D. would see from the couch still another cabinet of curiosities and antiquities to the right of the double doors, filling up the remainder of that wall. On top of this case were busts—one was of Sophocles, but the other bearded men she did not recognize, Eurip-

453

ides perhaps, perhaps also Socrates. On the next wall, the one facing the length of the couch, was a window, next to the cabinet right of the double doors. After the window, this wall held still another case, this one containing pottery images and flat Greek bowls. Next to this cabinet was the door to the waiting room (31, 33).

H.D. saw Freud, not only in the Berggasse, but at the big house in Döbling that the family rented for the summer months of 1933. For her, at least, it was not the same: "One did not have quite the same sense of authenticity or *reality* as in the Professor's own home." Certainly, she says little about it except to mention a "large, unfamiliar drawing-room."

H.D.'s description of Freud's office holds some historical or biographical interest. Of much more interest, of course, is the twenty-four or so week period when she was in treatment with Freud, particularly in view of Freud's use of what a therapist of today would call "parameters." It is not exactly clear, however, just what the nature of the therapeutic relationship was. Obviously, five months is a short time for an analysis, though not impossibly short for Freud, and it is clear from H.D.'s account that "deep" material was reached, including the issue of penis envy which, Freud suggests, may possibly be regarded as a sign that the analysis has hit bed-rock (1937). Jones (1957), in his review of *Tribute to Freud*, is unequivocal: "She was analysed by Freud for some months in the years 1933–4."

Several statements, though, suggest that Freud's relation to H.D. was as didactic as it was therapeutic. Sachs originally suggested that she work with Freud "as analysand or student," and she herself felt that

> to be accepted by him as analysand or student, seemed to crown all my other personal contacts and relationships. . . . The Professor had said in the beginning that he classed me in the same category as the Flying Dutchman—we were students. . . . Seekers or 'students' . . . he calls us. . . . One day he said to me, 'You discovered for yourself what I discovered for the race.'

As early as 1924 Freud had written to the Committee, "I scarcely take any patients, only pupils," and he clearly regarded this teaching as central to his work, for as late as 1938 in London, he was contemplating taking on as a candidate the poet Edward James (Jones, 3:61, 235). It seems most likely, then, in 1933 that Freud undertook the treatment of H.D. in order to make a poet and student of the classics familiar with psychoanalytic ideas, perhaps too, to satisfy his own persistent curiosity about creative artists, and perhaps even as a training analysis—at least as he pessimistically described it in "Analysis Terminable and Interminable" (1937):

> For practical reasons this analysis can only be short and incomplete. . . . It has accomplished its purpose if it gives the learner a firm conviction of the existence of the unconscious, if it enables him, when repressed material emerges, to perceive in himself things which would otherwise be incredible to him, and if it shows him a first sample of the technique which has proved to be the only effective one in analytic work.

Certainly H.D. seems to have achieved these three ends.

"There were only four of us at that time, I believe, rather special people." She listed herself, the Flying Dutchman, and an "American lady-doctor whom I had not seen," and perhaps meant to include also "Mrs. [Dorothy] Burlingham, Miss Anna Freud's devoted friend, and the Professor's disciple or pupil." Van der Leeuw

> was an eminent scholar. He had come officially to study with the Professor with the idea of the application of the principles of psychoanalysis to general education, with the greater practical aim of international cooperation and understanding.

Some of Freud's statements fit a therapeutic situation as well as an educational one. For example, "He himself—at least to me personally —deplored the tendency to *fix* ideas too firmly to set symbols, or to weld them inexorably" (141), and this was a problem for H.D., both emotional and intellectual. Freud avoided technical terms and jargon. When, on one occasion, H.D. asked him whether the word was pronounced "ambi-*valence* or am-*bi*-valence," Freud replied

> in his curiously casual ironical manner, 'Do you know, I myself have always wondered. I often wish that I could find someone to explain these matters to me' (132–3).

If, however, the analysis was thought of by both parties as more educational than therapeutic, a number of its special features become more understandable. For example, Freud insisted on one thing from H.D.,

> 'Please, never—I mean, never at any time, in any circum-

455

stances, endeavour to defend me, if and when you hear abusive remarks said about me and my work' (130–1).

That sounds as though H.D. were being inducted into the movement.
Indeed, she often felt treated as an intellectual equal:

> 'Of course, you understand' is the offhand way in which he
> offers me, from time to time, some rare discovery, some priceless
> finding, or 'Perhaps you may feel differently' as if my feelings, my
> discoveries, were on a par with his own (130).

This sense of a teacher-student relation of companionship and inquiry
seems to underlie her intriguing characterization of psychoanalysis as
like the Socratic method but with one important difference:

> The question must be propounded by the protagonist himself . . .
> he himself must find the question before it could be answered
> (127–8).

Both these comments sound as though Freud made many more interventions in H.D.'s free associations than most analysts of today
would, at least in the analysis of a neurotic. In 1924 he had written to
the Committee, rejecting (for himself, at least) Rank's shortened therapeutic analyses:

> Personally, I shall continue to make 'classical' analyses, since, in the
> first place, I scarcely take any patients, only pupils for whom it is
> important that they live through as many as possible of their inner
> processes.

His phrasing "live through," plus the biographical accounts of Jones,
Reik and others, make me think that the picture H.D. gives—of Freud
as an unusually "active" therapist—probably applies generally.

It is possible, though, that he was so active only with H.D. For
example, he may have thought activity was necessary to establish a
transference with this shy, withdrawn woman of 47. On the first day
she entered his consulting room, he waited for her to speak. She, however, silently took an inventory of the contents of the room. Finally,

> waiting and finding that I would not or could not speak, he uttered.
> What he said—and I thought a little sadly—was, 'You are the only
> person who has ever come into this room and looked at the things
> in the room before looking at me' (148).

456

"Worse," wrote H.D., "was to come." Jo-fi was present at this first interview and H.D., originally awestruck but now somewhat hostile at what she took to be an accusation, chose to try to befriend "the Professor" by patting the chow. Thinking "love me, love my dog," thinking to prove Freud wrong (for he warned her that Jo-fi was difficult with strangers), she succeeded in getting a nuzzle from the dog and proving to her own satisfaction that the Professor was not always right. "Undoubtedly, the Professor took an important clue from the first reaction of a new analysand or patient."

In line with this opening episode, Dr. Heinz Lichtenstein has suggested to me that Freud may have decided that H.D. was closer to psychosis then neurosis and so may have adopted a more active therapeutic strategy than was his practice in the classical analysis of a psychoneurosis. He did find "megalomania" in the mystical vision and so labelled it to H.D. Certainly, this "narcissistic neurosis" would fit her over-concern with her own body and her schizoid tendency to reinterpret the real world in terms of symbolic structures (415). If so, H.D.'s account of her analysis would be a valuable supplement to Freud's study of the "psychotic-on-paper" Schreber. Freud might have taken her on in order to see how a psychotic could use artistic creativity to adapt. I do not feel, however, there is any more indication in H.D.'s memoir that she was psychotic than that she was neurotic. As of 1933 she was a highly successful poet and mother who had survived a brutal series of losses. Her circumstances suggest a strong, even if beleaguered, ego.

The severity of H.D.'s disorder bears on what interpretation we are to give to the glimpses she gives of Freud at work, of his analytic technique. Everything she says suggests an analytic relationship with much more confrontation, more give-and-take, than a classical analysis of a neurotic of today or even a didactic analysis of today. For example, the position of Freud's chair permitted him to break into the analysand's field of vision. H.D. gives us a patient's-eye view:

He will say nothing at all or he will lean forward and talk about something that is apparently unrelated to the progression or unfolding of our actual dream-content or thought association. He will shoot out an arm, sometimes somewhat alarmingly, to stress a point. Or he will, always making an 'occasion' of it, get up and say, 'Ah—now—we must celebrate *this*,' and proceed to the elaborate ritual—selecting, lighting [his cigar]—until finally he seats himself again (32).

Freud evidently spoke freely in the analytic situation: on one occasion, speaking of immortality, he ran over the names of his grandchildren and their parents. On another they talked of gardenias and the Spanish Steps. To ease tension, when H.D. entered, he would use small talk,

> some kindly old-world courtesy, some question: What had I been reading? Did I find the books I wanted in the library his wife's sister had recommended? . . . Had I heard again from Bryher, from my daughter?

Once, he gave her a branch of an orange tree from a box of oranges his son had sent (136). H.D. responded, as one would expect, with associations to the Golden Bough—it is one of the more delicate appreciations in *Tribute to Freud* that H.D. ends the book with her own grateful (and oedipal) associations to Goethe's lyric *Kennst du das Land, wo die Zitronen blühn?*

Not only did H.D. have this much contact with Freud's family, she had tea with Mrs. Burlingham, "the professor's disciple or pupil, [who] had an apartment, further up the stairs" (92). The arranging of hours was evidently handled in a similarly informal way; H.D. recalls her meeting with "the Flying Dutchman":

> We had spoken once in the house at Döbling, outside Vienna. The Professor waved him across the large, unfamiliar drawing-room. Dr. van der Leeuw bowed, he addressed me in polite distinguished German, would the *gnädige Frau* object to altering her hour for one day, tomorrow? I answered him in English, I would not mind at all.

We have already seen Freud's insistence on "one thing" from H.D., that she not try to defend him against abuse. He was equally direct when,

> The other day the Professor . . . reproached me for jerking out my arm and looking at my watch. He had said, 'I keep an eye on the time—I will tell you when the session is over. You need not keep looking at the time, as if you were in a hurry to get away' (24).

Still more startling, however, was the time when Freud seemed to lose his temper (19–26):

> I did not know what enraged him suddenly. I veered round off the couch, my feet on the floor. I do not know exactly what I had said.

I veer round, uncanonically seated stark upright with my feet on the floor. The Professor himself is uncanonical enough; he is beating with his hand, with his fist, on the head-piece of the old-fashioned horsehair sofa.

Consciously, I was not aware of having said anything that might account for the Professor's outburst. And even as I veered around, facing him, my mind was detached enough to wonder if this was some idea of *his* for speeding up the analytic content or redirecting the flow of associated images. The Professor said, "The trouble is—I am an old man—*you do not think it worth your while to love me.*"

The impact of his words was too dreadful—I simply felt nothing at all. I said nothing. What did he expect me to say? Exactly it was as if the Supreme Being had hammered with his fist on the back of the couch where I had been lying. Why, anyway, did he do that? . . . Maybe, anyway, it was just a trick, something to shock me, to break something in myself of which I was partially aware. . . .

He was a terribly frightening old man, too old and too detached, too wise and too famous altogether, to beat that way with his fist, like a child hammering a porridge-spoon on the table.

I did not argue with the Professor. In fact, as I say, I did not have the answer. If he expected to rouse me to some protestation of affection, he did not then succeed in doing so—the root or the current ran too deep.

At the moment, I am lying on the couch. I have just readjusted the rug that had slipped to the floor. I have tucked my hands under the rug. I am wondering if the Professor caught me looking at my wristwatch. I am really somewhat shattered. But there is no answering flare-back.

Given modern notions about countertransference and the management thereof, I find it difficult to make any comment on this episode—except to share H.D.'s bafflement.

Considerably less baffling, but less uncanonical, are Freud's walks with his analysand into the study (33). She wondered, as, I suppose, any patient would,

if the Professor's excursions with me into the other room were by way of distraction, actual social occasions, or part of his plan. Did he want to find out how I would react to certain ideas embodied in these little statues, or how deeply I felt the dynamic *idea* still im-

459

plicit in spite of the fact that ages or aeons of time had flown over many of them? Or did he mean simply that he wanted to share his treasures with me, those tangible shapes before us that yet suggested the intangible and vastly more fascinating treasures of his own mind?

On the occasion she is describing, he led her into the study and showed her a statue of Vishnu (though H.D. was not sure), given him by his Indian students. *En passant* he added, "On the whole, I think my Indian students have reacted in the least satisfactory way to my teaching" (103). But it was not this statue which interested him at the moment. "*This* is my favourite," he said, holding out to H.D. a little bronze Pallas Athené. "She is perfect," he said, "*only she has lost her spear.*"

The italics are H.D.'s, for Freud was using the statue to make an interpretation. It is part of H.D.'s style in the book to conceal—or, more accurately, not to reveal—her most intimate insights, but to present a series of free associations which will tell to the initiated what she herself is unwilling to say right out. After the spearless Pallas Athené, her thoughts run to: Nike A-pteros, the Wingless Victory; Freud's ability in speech to make words take on another dimension; his ability to make a sentence a standard "fluttering aloft on a pole, to lead an army"; Athené, born from her father, God, without a mother; Freud, as Jew, assessing the worth of the figure; the pound of flesh become a pound of spirit to be weighed and measured and not found wanting. One gets a glimmering of what went into H.D.'s own quest for the hardness and solidity of things.

Though his way of making interpretations through statues may seem odd today, the actual interpretations he made seem familiar enough. For example, when H.D. returned for the second series of interviews, effusively sympathetic over the loss of van der Leeuw, Freud simply said, "You have come to take his place." Similarly, "The Professor had said in the very beginning that I had come to Vienna hoping to find my mother." Again, after H.D. had reported some "dingy" episodes in her life, he dismissed the confession, "Why did you think you had to tell me? . . . But you felt you wanted to tell your mother." It is quite fascinating to watch through the memoir Freud take on the transference roles successively of mother, brother, and father. As for the crucial visions, "The Professor translated [them] as a desire for union with my mother" (65).

Not unlike most patients, H.D. found these "explanations" "too illuminating or too depressing." Freud would say, "Today we have tunnelled very deep" (25) or, more commonly, in a metaphor which fascinated H.D. with its commerciality, that he had "struck oil" (25, 114, 125–6).

H.D. herself, in the course of the analysis (or whatever you wish to call it), developed an ability to interpret her own actions. For example, she remarks on her failure to bring him flowers on his birthday, "I had not found what I wanted so I did not give him anything," repeating the sentence to bring out its ambiguities, as Freud himself might have done. "I am here because no one else has come," she said to herself when she came on the day the rifles were stacked at the street corners and no other patients showed up; it was her answer to his earlier accusation that she did not love him. When the transference was at its strongest, she wished she could, like Alcestis, give her remaining years to Freud. Projecting herself into his mind to fantasy the origins of psychoanalysis in terms of the inmates of the Salpêtrière, she ended her reverie with the statement, *"If her husband went away again would her symptoms return?"* Once more, her italics suggest that she herself is making an interpretation both of Freud's role in the transference and her own fears of approaching termination.

In short, H.D.'s little book gives us a picture of a patient who made considerable headway in a rather short time. More interestingly, it gives us a unique and valuable picture of Freud at work: direct, even blunt, resorting to frequent confrontations and interventions; informal to the point of casualness, yet incredibly deft; drawing heavily on his own rich historical and aesthetic experience. It is possible that Freud's active therapeutic style was in response to a potential psychosis. It seems more likely to me, though, that with both van der Leeuw and H.D., Freud was essaying a kind of "general education" in psychoanalysis. He was using a short-term analysis, modelled on a teacher-student relationship, to give the analysand a real experience of psychoanalysis and so enable him to use Freud's concepts in other fields. As such, his procedure corresponds to some recent proposals for a similar kind of "general education" that would both further applied psychoanalysis by providing more appropriate training and also bring psychoanalysis more into the intellectual mainstream of the universities. H.D.'s experience suggests how successful and effective such a general education could be—at least in the hands of the master analyst. Her charming and subtle book is indeed a "tribute to Freud."

Bibliography

Aldington, H. D. (1926). *Palimpsest*. Paris: Contact Editions.
Aldington, H. D. (1956). *Tribute to Freud*. New York: Pantheon Books.
Aldington, H. D. (1960). *Bid Me to Live (A Madrigal)*. New York: Grove Press.
Freud, S. (1915). The unconscious. *S.E.* **14**.
Freud, S. (1916–17). Introductory lectures on psychoanalysis: III. *S.E.* **16**.
Freud, S. (1937). Analysis terminable and Interminable. *S.E.* **23**.
Holland, N. N. (1969). H.D. and the 'Blameless Physician'. *Contemp. Lit.* **10**.
Jones, E. (1953–7). *The Life and Work of Sigmund Freud*, vols. 1–3. New York: Basic Books.
Jones, E. (1957). Review of *Tribute to Freud*. *Int. J. Psycho-Anal.* **38**, 126.
Swann, T. B. (1962). *The Classical World of H.D.* Lincoln, Nebraska: University of Nebraska Press.
Williams, W. C. (1951). *Autobiography*. New York: New Directions Books.

H.D. and the
"Blameless Physician"

(1969)

NORMAN N. HOLLAND

This selection was published in Contemporary Literature 10 *(Autumn 1969): 474–506.*

The Greeks, a certain scholar has told me, considered that myths
are the activities of the Dæmons, and that the Dæmons shape our
characters and our lives. I have often had the fancy that there is
some one Myth for every man, which, if we but knew it, would
make us understand all he did and thought.

—Yeats

Yeats was writing about Shakespeare,[1] and Hilda Doolittle, fine poet
though she was, is nevertheless no Shakespeare. She is, however,
unique among poets in that she has left us an astonishingly detailed account of her "myth" as it emerged in her psychoanalysis with Freud
himself.[2] She gives us, thus, an unparalleled opportunity to explore the
continuum between a personal myth or life-style and the expression of
that style in literature.

"All [she] did and thought"—a large order! Space requires that we
settle for a generalized description, leaving it to others to derive H.
D.'s style in detail from particular poems. We can begin with a phrase
Horace Gregory quotes from H. D. herself, that her concern was "a
wish to make real to myself what is most real"[3] or, again in H. D.'s
words, to "re-dedicate our gifts/to spiritual realism."[4] The tension in
a phrase like "spiritual realism" or the paradox of a "most real" which
must be made real illustrates the polarities or oxymora from which her
poetry builds: hot-cold; fertile-salt; blunt-pointed; dark-bright; soft-
hard; fire-as-passion-fire-as-destruction; new-old; passion-reason, and
so on and so on.

The most basic of these polarities, however, is the tension between
the small, precise, and named and the huge, abstract, and blank. Most

463

obviously, this tension shows in her formal style: short, unrhymed lines; brief, two-line stanzaic structures set in poems often placeless, timeless, structureless. But this polarity applies to her imagery, too. A flower is seldom a flower with H. D.: it is a rose or a violet or a lily or a gentian or a plum blossom. Naming and precision give power, strength, and reality. Trees, types of rock, buildings, colors—all are set out with the exactitude Pound admired. The body is seen in defined body-parts, while it is difficult for H. D. to show us a whole person—or personality. Men are hard and armored, while women who yield to men dissolve into flowers, rocks, or water:

> but how reconcile
>
> the magnetic, steel-clad Achilles
> with the flowering pomegranate? [5]

Yet despite this pattern—or because of it—one often, in her dramatic monologues, cannot tell whether the speaker is male or female.[6]

H. D.'s strength lies in her rendition of detail: her weakness is in structuring those details into a poetic, characterological, or, still more acutely, fictional whole. Poems, fiction, even essays like *Tribute to Freud* or *By Avon River* become a series of isolated images or events linked by free associations, often through mythological themes. At the very sentence level, her boundaries tend to be ill-defined. A sentence modifier from one sentence will seem to apply to the next. Lists (of which H. D. uses many) will be oddly broken between sentences. The word to which a pronoun or adjective refers may be one or two sentences back; the reference itself may be twinned or multiple. Often, for structure, she will resort to a series of parallel structures to be summed into a totality. Sometimes she will use negations—a series of *not*'s or *nor*'s to strip off the extraneous and come to the final, finely rendered residue as a climax.

Doubtless no small part of H. D.'s propensity for myth is a quest for similar organizing structures. If one can see present people, events, and feelings as projections or continuations of a simpler, more structured mythic past, they become more manageable and, for H. D. at least, somehow more real. She uses for living people the image of a palimpsest or a series of old photographic negatives on top of one another; the sign one sees on the surface implies a deeper reality underneath.[7] She seeks to turn herself, her very body, into an hieroglyph or emblem[8]—as in the use of her initials for a seal or sign. Her poetry, like the myths she emulates, manifests that which is spiritual, abstract, and timeless by the hard, the real, the objective, the exact.

We can use as first statements of the "H. D. myth" Professor Swann's generalizations: he speaks of "escape into the hard impersonality of nature" and her "merging with the hard, changeless integrity of the natural world." [9] Joseph N. Riddel, in an adjoining essay, points out, "H. D.'s images of the real invariably accentuate the manifest 'shape' of subjectivity, of inwardness objectified and hence rendered in the universal shape of art." The world of the early poems, he shows,

> is a world of stark, pristine beauty, occasionally threatened by the softness of decay or the oppressiveness of a suffocating heat; a world of willed objectivity which hardly conceals the inwardness that reminds the self of its imminent nothingness. The objectivity of H. D.'s world is a kind of ultimate subjectivity.

Now, can we reach from those critical *aperçus* to the personality of the poet?

Psychoanalysis, even with no information at all about the poet, would guess that the wish to set oneself in a timeless union with a past stems from an oral wish to fuse with the nurturing mother. We would expect—and we find—a great deal of oral imagery in H. D.'s writings. Psychoanalysis would also suggest that, in a woman, the wish to make her own body or another's into hard, exact, and real parts derives from a wish to replace something that was lost—penis, mother, father, love —something. But we have much more than mere surmise or hypothesis about her personality with which to work.

The story of H. D. and Freud begins in 1915, the year H. D. lost her first child through a miscarriage. Daughter of a distinguished astronomer, "who seldom even at table focused upon anything nearer, literally, than the moon," [10] and a mother who seems to have been equally abstracted, she was one girl among five brothers, one of whom, the one just older than she, was not only her mother's favorite child, but an important identification-figure for H. D. herself. In 1915 she was twenty-nine, her poetry just coming to be recognized. Two years earlier she had married her fellow-poet, Richard Aldington, but he had left to fight in France when the war broke out. "From shock and repercussions of war news broken to me in a rather brutal fashion," she lost her first child. Sometime during this period, perhaps during the pregnancy, her autobiographical novels seem to say,[11] Aldington took a mistress, and their marriage broke up in 1919 (though, interestingly, she does not mention this in *Tribute to Freud*). In 1918, her favorite brother was killed in action in France; her father died a year later from the stroke he suffered at the news. At the end of 1919, she was sick with double pneumonia and awaiting the birth of her second child, determined that this child would live.

Perdita (so her mother named her) did live, but H. D. herself had a "nervous breakdown," [12] perhaps a postpartum depression—she does not describe it in *Tribute to Freud*. She was rescued by the wealthy Winifred Ellerman (pen name, Bryher) who took her to Greece to get well. There, she had an hallucination or mystical vision of extraordinary intensity. As she describes it in the memoir, it was not frightening to her, though she felt it as occult and so described it to Freud. He, however, singled this vision out as "the most dangerous or the only actually dangerous 'symptom' " (*Tribute to Freud:* 60).

H. D.'s relationship with Bryher continued even after the latter's shaky marriage to Robert McAlmon, who told "of long train trips about the continent with the two women quarreling in the compartment driving him nearly insane." W. C. Williams said H. D. had some part in the marriage's final "disastrous outcome" and the McAlmons' separation and divorce,[13] and (Norman Holmes Pearson tells me) McAlmon "broke with [him] on this." Pearson describes H. D. as "passionately heterosexual," and Freud, in H. D.'s account, did not single out anything relating to homosexuality as part of her psychic life, although he had read *Palimpsest* before meeting H. D., and the autobiographical sections of this novel at least raise the issue. Given Freud's theories, the loss of self-object boundaries in the mystical vision would have seemed of more moment to him, anyway.

It is not clear what motivated H. D. herself to seek therapy—this symptom or her wish "to free myself of repetitive thoughts and experiences—my own and those of many of my contemporaries," to "take stock of my very modest possessions of mind and body" (*Tribute to Freud:* 17), "to dig down and dig out, root out my personal weeds, strengthen my purpose, reaffirm my beliefs, canalize my energies," "to sort out, relive and reassemble the singular series of events and dreams that belonged in historical time, to the 1914–1919 period" (138). This last, she tells us, she did not finish: "The war closed on us, before I had time." In later life, she described herself to Professor Swann as doing, in this period, "studies in . . . psychological investigation." [14] However, it came about, she began "some fascinating, preliminary talks with Dr. Hanns Sachs in Berlin and wanted to go on with the work, but he was leaving for America. Dr. Sachs asked me if I would consider working with the Professor if he would take me?" (138)

She would, he did, and she began work with Freud on 5 March 1933. Freud conducted the analysis in English (as he had often done for English and American patients). H. D. characterizes her own German as "sketchy," while Freud "was speaking English without a perceptible trace of accent." Her hours with Freud were "four days a week from five to six; one day, from twelve to one" (2). She saw him altogether about a hundred hours—on the couch. Beginning in March, they worked for "between three and four months," at least until "late in June, or early July, 1933" (4). Apparently Sir John Ellerman, Bryher's father, died on 16 July, and H. D. seems to have left Vienna then, not planning to return (175).[15]

She did return, however, at the end of October 1934. Austria's relations with Germany were deteriorating rapidly—Dollfuss was assassinated that summer—but what brought H. D. back was the news that one of the Professor's other patients, Dr. J. J. van der Leeuw, had died when his plane crashed in Tanganyika. Her second period of work with Freud was shorter: it lasted five weeks, from the end of October 1934 to 1 December 1934. "The war closed on us." H. D. kept a diary in Vienna in 1933, but it was not available to her when she wrote *Tribute to Freud* in 1944.

It is not entirely clear just what the nature of the relationship between H. D. and Freud was. Obviously, five months is a short time for an analysis, though not impossibly short for Freud, and it is clear from H. D.'s account that "deep" material was reached. Ernest Jones, in his otherwise uninformative review, says quite directly, "She was analyzed by Freud for some months in the years 1933–34." [16]

There are, however, many indications that Freud's relation to H. D. was as much didactic as therapeutic. "The Professor had said in the beginning that he classed me in the same category as [van der Leeuw] —we were students." "There were only four of us at that time, I believe, rather special people." She listed herself, van der Leeuw, and an "American lady-doctor whom I had not seen," and perhaps meant also to include "Mrs. [Dorothy] Burlingham, Miss Anna Freud's devoted friend, and the Professor's disciple or pupil" (92). Van der Leeuw "was an eminent scholar. He had come officially to study with the Professor with the idea of the application of the principles of psychoanalysis to general education" (4–5). "Seekers or 'students' . . . he calls us" (28).

467

"One day he said to me, 'You discovered for yourself what I discovered for the race' " (25). All this sounds as though Freud undertook the analysis of H. D. and the others like her in order to give a group of intellectually special people a "feel" for psychoanalytic ideas and method.

"The beautiful tone of his voice had a way of taking an English phrase or sentence out of its context (out of the associated context, you might say, of the whole language)" so that the word took on special overtones and new life (104–105). The analysis seems to have proceeded much more by this kind of exploration of connotation and association than by ideas about symbols or theory. "He himself—at least to me personally—deplored the tendency to *fix* ideas too firmly to set symbols, or to weld them inexorably" (141), and apparently this caution was especially necessary with H. D. Nevertheless, H. D. often felt treated as an intellectual equal: " 'Of course, you understand' is the offhand way in which he offers me, from time to time, some rare discovery, some priceless finding, or 'perhaps you may feel differently' as if my feelings, my discoveries, were on a par with his own" (130).

H. D. wrote *Tribute to Freud* almost like a psychoanalysis itself, as a series of free associations, letting her thoughts lead her where they would. The associations are not entirely free, however; she omits so as to protect her privacy. H. D. says almost nothing about her contemporary life and very little about her adult life at all. She is completely silent on matters of adult sexuality (although it is clear that she and Freud worked with infantile sexual material). Instead, she produces a whole series of mythological associations. Most of the time she relies without explanation on connotations and verbal echoes in her own and, particularly, in Freud's phrasings. Only once does she make a straightforward interpretation. We, her readers, are left to make the connections ourselves, though the connections are there to be made, at least for her developmental years.

Because she wrote in a series of free associations, the book became a seamless web: to pick up any one point is to involve oneself in all. Perhaps the best way to give the material sequence is to follow out Freud's changing roles. One would expect H. D. (or any other analysand) in the transference situation of psychoanalysis to transfer or project onto the analyst her positive and negative feelings toward the key figures of her childhood—her mother, her father, and, in H. D.'s case, the brother who was so singularly important to her. In seeking, then, the common source in childhood of H. D.'s life-style and her literary style, we can use Freud himself, as he is assigned various roles in the transference, for our Ariadne thread.

We can enter the labyrinth with H. D. herself, for "undoubtedly," she noted, "the Professor took an important clue from the first reaction of a new analysand or patient." When first she entered his consulting-room, Freud stood waiting for the tall, shy woman of forty-seven to speak. H. D., however, silently took an inventory of the contents of the room, Freud's collection of Greek and Egyptian antiquities. Finally, "waiting and finding that I would not or could not speak, he uttered. What he said—and I thought a little sadly—was, 'You are the only person who has ever come into this room and looked at the things in the room before looking at me'" (148). The Professor might have taken a clue to H. D.'s tendency to approach someone she desired through an intermediary, particularly a mythological object or symbol.

The first such intermediary in the book is "the Flying Dutchman," J. J. van der Leeuw, so nicknamed because he flew his own plane. "His soul fitted his body," wrote H. D., and she surely had not forgotten when she wrote, much later in the book, of her own soul, "Its body did not fit it very well" (161). H. D.'s only contact with van der Leeuw was that, one day, "We had exchanged 'hours'" (9), and perhaps her quotation marks suggest that she recognized the pun on *ours*. When H. D. heard that he had crashed his plane and died in Tanganyika, she rushed back to Vienna to express her sorrow and sympathy for Freud. "'You have come,'" he bluntly interpreted, "'to take his place'" (6). Indeed, she speaks of van der Leeuw as her "brother-in-arms" (129) and Mercury (7).

Her brother was in arms when he was killed in France in 1918, and H. D. herself links soldier and airman when she has her mystical vision at Corfu (66) or when she numbers her brother among the "poised, disciplined and valiant young winged Mercuries" who fell from the air during the war (153). Freud's remark "that the analysand who preceded me [van der Leeuw] was 'actually considerably taller'" than H. D. leads her directly to a statement and a memory, "My brother is considerably taller" (28).

Though she does not even give us his name, this older brother was obviously a key figure in H. D.'s childhood, for he "is admittedly his mother's favourite" (42). H. D. loved and admired him, too,[17] but she also envied him: "I was not, they said, pretty and I was not, it was very easy to see, quaint and quick and clever like my brother. My brother? Am I my brother's keeper?" (153). And perhaps she did feel like Cain, even when she most treasured and preserved her slain brother's memory (as in the "undisciplined thoughts" of this passage)—or when they were children together.

Yet that very brother seemed to be the intermediary through whom she could reach her distant mother: "The trouble is, she knows so many people and they come and interrupt. And besides that, she likes my brother better. If I stay with my brother, become part almost of my brother, perhaps I can get nearer to *her*" (49).[18]

Thus, her brother becomes the first of the many mythological lover-heroes in H. D.'s quests: Perseus, Hermes, the Flying Dutchman, the Professor (s)—in Norman Holmes Pearson's apt phrase, "the one searched for (who himself searches)." They are mythological twins, like Little-Brother, Little-Sister in Grimm, the twin brother-sister of the Nile, or Castor and Pollux (but, as she writes this, H. D. corrects the gender, adding Helen and Clytaemnestra). "One is sometimes the shadow of the other; often one is lost and the one seeks the other" (41).

H. D. herself tells us that what she sought in her brother was to get closer to her mother. A memory of him, however, suggests another *motif* (35–39). He had taken one of the "sacred objects" from his father's desk, a magnifying glass, and was showing his sister how he could focus the sunlight to burn a piece of paper. His father sternly told him to stop, pointing out his double crime, that he had done something like play with matches and that he had taken something from the study table. Possibly, to become one with her brother meant to acquire the special powers that men seemed to have, the power to bring fire from heaven like Prometheus (36), to understand the mysterious symbols her astronomer-father used or her brother's larger vocabulary, to be "quaint and clever" instead of "not very advanced," perhaps most important, to have arrived first, to be older, to be not a foreigner or "a little stranger" (37). All these things might be possible with a boy's body instead of a girl's. As she puts it in an enigmatic comment, left to stand by itself after a story about her brother and discoveries under a log, "There were things under things, as well as things inside things" (29).

H. D. suggests still another goal she sought in her brother, another memory, the wish that she could be a mother: perhaps her brother could be her doll's father, perhaps her own father could be. She would be the virgin mother, "building a dream and the dream is symbolized by the . . . doll in her arms" (56). To Freud, in the transference, she brought all these fantasies and investments of her brother, just as she brought the dreams concretized as the doll.

Freud is Saint Michael, who will slay the dragon of her fears (165), but Michael was also regent of the planet Mercury—"in Renaissance paintings, we are not surprised to see Saint Michael wearing the winged sandals and sometimes even the winged helmet of the classic messenger of the Gods" (161). Thus there are associations: "Thoth, Hermes, Mercury, and last Michael, Captain or Centurion of the hosts of heaven" (165).

When she compares Freud to the Centurion of heaven, she cannot have forgotten that ten pages earlier, she had said that, in his refusal to accept her notions of immortality, his slamming the door on visions of the future, he was standing "like the Roman Centurion before the gate at Pompeii, who did not move from his station before the gateway since he had received no orders to do so, and who stood for later generations to wonder at, embalmed in hardened lava, preserved in the very fire and ashes that had destroyed him" (155). She goes on to quote Freud, "At least, they have not burnt me at the stake." Earlier, she had been grateful that the Professor had not lived until World War II. "He was a handful of ashes" "before the blast and bombing and fires had devastated this city" (143). The wish is kindly meant, but underneath, it shows the same ambivalence as toward that other Mercury, her brother.

Freud, like Prometheus, like her brother, had stolen fire from heaven, from the sun (114). He, too, was not only the victim, but the cause of explosions: "Many of his words did, in a sense, explode . . . opening up mines of hidden treasures" (113). More gently, after an especially striking insight, he would say, "Ah—now—we must celebrate *this*"; he would rise, select, light, and then, "from the niche [where he sat rose] the smoke of burnt incense, the smouldering of his mellow, fragrant cigar" (32).

She identified Freud with Asklepios, the "blameless physician," son of the sun god Apollo (75). "He was the son of the sun, Phoebos Apollo, and music and medicine were alike sacred to this source of light" (152–53). "And here was the master-musician, he, too, a son of Apollo, who would harmonize the whole human spirit" (160). She identifies herself as a fellow-servant of Apollo, the Priestess or Pythoness of Delphi; thus she suggests that Freud is her peer and brother.

471

But by punning on "son" and "sun," she makes Apollo himself, the father, the "son." It is well to remember her father was another "Professor."

In short, Freud has come to stand for the whole ambiguous network of wishes and relationships associated with the oedipal wishes of a little girl: that she could become a mother with her brother as father; that she could, by marrying her father, become her brother's mother; that she could, by marrying her brother, become her father's mother. She seems to recognize these ambiguities when she calls Freud "the Old Man of the Sea," Proteus, the shapeshifter (147), or compares him to two-faced Janus, who leads her to Thoth, Hermes, Mercury, and finally the Flying Dutchman (152). But Janus is also Captain January, a beloved old lighthouse keeper who takes in a shipwrecked child. Freud becomes in the transference not only her brother but also her father. This dual relationship with Freud matches H. D.'s extended identification of herself with Mignon, the boy-girl, from *Wilhelm Meister*, who is both sister but also would-be sexual object to the hero (161–69).

Even so, in the strangely labile world of a psychoanalysis, Freud can become H. D.'s father, but so can H. D. She herself makes the connection: her father, being an astronomer, often slept on a couch in his study during the day, and she was not to disturb him. "But now it is I who am lying on the couch in the room lined with books" (27). Her father had in his study a "white owl under a bell-jar" (26, 49); she has the Professor, sitting "there quietly, like an old owl in a tree" (32). (And, one should remember, the owl is an emblem for Athené with whom H. D. identified herself.) At the top of the astronomical tables he made up, her father would write something which was neither a letter nor a number: "he will sketch in a hieroglyph; it may stand for one of the Houses or Signs of the Zodiac, or it may be a planet simply: Jupiter or Mars or Venus" (36).[19] Dreams (53), visions (70), and all the shapes, lines, and graphs she speaks of are "the *hieroglyph of the unconscious*" (140; H. D.'s italics). As for herself, "Niké, Victory seemed to be the clue, seemed to be my own special sign or part of my hieroglyph" (83). Similarly, in *Helen in Egypt* Helen's body becomes the hieroglyph: "She herself is the writing." [20] If one is a writing, one is looked at—by Freud, by the aloof father, perhaps even by the distant mother.

Later H. D. will identify herself with Freud by seeing *him* as victorious, but at the moment we are concerned with Freud's becoming, in the transference, H. D.'s father. Obviously, the bearded seventy-seven-year-old physician more easily suggested a father-figure than a gallant, winged Mercury, particularly when he listed off his grandchildren as his claim to immortality (93–94). On at least one occasion, H. D. felt with Freud "like a child, summoned to my father's study or my mother's sewing-room or told by a teacher to wait in after school" (130). The time Freud seemed to lose his temper, "it was as if the Supreme Being had hammered with his fist on the back of the couch" (22), but it was also (in the fluid world of transferences) "like a child hammering a porridge-spoon on the table" (23).

Freud reminded H. D. of her father, however, in more specific ways than as an authority-figure. For one thing, he seemed able to persist. Her father had died at the shock of learning of her brother's death, while "the Professor had had shock upon shock. But he had not died" (45). Another line of association leads to what men have and what doctors do: "my father possessed sacred symbols . . . he, like the Professor, had old, old sacred objects on his study table" (36). In his study, her father had a photograph of Rembrandt's *Anatomy Lesson*, and her father identified his forebears with the Puritans—"Their hats were like the hats the doctors wore" (50), and indeed he rather liked to identify himself with doctors. Further, "a doctor has a bag with strange things in it, steel and knives and scissors" (38). Doctors know secrets. Her father "entrusts" her with his paper-knife to cut the pages of some of his journals. "The half-naked man on the table was dead so it did not hurt him when the doctors sliced his arm with a knife or a pair of scissors" (50). She sees psychoanalysis as a special form of Socratic method and Socratic method in turn as fencing (127). Freud, in the transference, has acquired both phallic power and the power to cut.

She speaks of the Tree of Knowledge: "His [Freud's] were the great giant roots of that tree, but mine, with hair-like almost invisible feelers . . . the invisible intuitive rootlet . . . the smallest possible subsoil rootlet" (149) could also solve mysteries. One of the difficulties, Freud noted about this time, in the analysis of a woman is "that her strongest motive in coming for treatment was the hope that, after all, she might still obtain a male organ, the lack of which was so painful to her." [21] We should bear in mind this belief (that the analyst—the doctor—will restore what has been, in fantasy, cut off) in considering Freud's interpretive "gifts" to H. D.

One day he led her from the couch into his study to show her one of his Greek figurines: " *'This* is my favourite,' he said," and he held out a little bronze Pallas Athené. " 'She is perfect,' he said, *'only she has lost her spear'* " (104; H. D.'s italics). H. D. remembered that Athené's winged form was Niké, so that this was a Niké without wings, Niké A-pteros, as, for example, H. D. had seen her in Athens (made so that Victory would never fly away to another city). She meditates on "She is perfect." ". . . The little bronze statue was a perfect symbol, made in man's image (in woman's, as it happened), to be venerated as a projection of abstract thought, Pallas Athené . . . sprung full-armed from the head of her father, our-father, Zeus . . ." (105–106).

Maybe it wasn't a spear she had been holding—"It might have been a rod or staff" (135). H. D. had been remembering Aaron's rod which turned into a living reptile; Moses, Adam and Eve; the Tree of Life cursed so that it would bring forth only thistles, related to a vision of hers in adolescence of a thistle and a serpent inscribed on a stone. Seal, symbol, serpent, signet, Sigmund—all these *s*'s remind her of the question marks that surrounded her mystical vision on Corfu (133–134). The serpent makes her think of Asklepios, the serpent being the sign of healing and wisdom and rebirth (97). There was a serpent crouched at the feet of Athené (135).

"It might have been a rod or staff," and she goes on to remember the occasion when the Professor gave her a little branch from a box of oranges his son had sent. In effect, Freud was giving her symbolically what Freud felt every woman patient wanted. She herself could associate to that golden bough another gift or compliment Freud gave her: "There are very few who understand this [that "my discoveries are a basis for a very grave philosophy"], *there are very few who are capable of understanding this*" (25; H. D.'s italics). Freud was, in effect, giving H. D. back the understanding that leads to victory, the masculine power represented in sacred objects, the ability to live in her wingless self, all of which, at some level of her being, H. D. felt, her real father had taken away. Or, perhaps, her mother had never given her.

From psychoanalytic theory, one would expect the father to inherit the conflicts and feelings associated with the mother. Indeed, H. D. is quite explicit about this: "*If* one could stay near her always, there would be no break in consciousness—but half a loaf is better than no bread and there are things, not altogether negligible, to be said for *him*" (49). Thus, on the occasion when her brother took the magnifying glass, "Our father came down the steps. This picture could be found in an old collection of Bible illustrations . . ." (30). We are hearing a verbal echo of what H. D. and Freud called "the dream of the Princess." A mysterious, beautiful Egyptian lady is coming down a flight of steps. "I, the dreamer, wait at the foot of the steps. . . . There, in the water beside me, is a shallow basket or ark or box or boat" (54) containing a baby which, of course, the Princess must find, protect, and shelter. This is, obviously, the Doré illustration, *Moses in the Bulrushes*, and H. D. is perhaps the baby or perhaps the child Miriam half concealed in the rushes. "Do I wish myself, in the deepest unconscious or subconscious layers of my being, to be the founder of a new religion?" These religious wishes were her one point of difference with Freud: "About the greater transcendental issues, we never argued. But there was an argument implicit in our very bones" (16). It was in this context that she cast him as the burnt centurion.

"We touched lightly on some of the more abstruse transcendental problems, it is true, but we related them to the familiar family-complex" (18). "A Queen or Princess," she notes, "is obvious mother-symbol . . ." (57), but equally obviously her need for a religious level of being (and, clearly, psychoanalysis provided one outlet for her need to have faith in something) does not simply come down to her wish to become a "Princess" or "prophetess." Participation in another level of being makes her a mother in a far more powerful sense. She can restore her own lost ones, for "The dead were living in so far as they lived in memory or were recalled in dream" (18).

Further, we can look at the wish for an eternal order from the point of view not of the child wishing to become the mother, but of the child wishing to be mothered. That other level of reality implies a being who is always there. The analyst never dies or goes away: ". . . I looked at the things in his room before I looked at him; for I knew the things in his room were symbols of Eternity and contained him then, as Eternity contains him now" (154). When Freud one day spoke as though his only immortality lay in his grandchildren, "I was deeply distressed," "It worried me . . ." (63). ". . . I felt a sudden gap, a severance, a chasm or a schism in consciousness . . ." (93). She is echoing something she had said earlier about her mother, "*If* one could stay near her always, there would be no break in consciousness . . ." (49). It is striking, I think, that she does not complain of her mother's coldness, but of the many people who "come and interrupt" their relationship.

In short, H. D. has shown, in the transference, how her mystical and religious wishes hark back to the early mother-child relationship.

The timeless world of myth becomes, for her, a way of avoiding gaps, breaks, interruptions. In earliest infancy, the child does not perceive itself as a being separate from its mother. Only as it must wait, expect, trust in that nurturing other to come and minister to its needs does it begin to recognize that that other is a separate being; that therefore it is itself a separate being. In other words, our very sense of identity is predicated upon our ability to trust in a nurturing other. If too much hate and frustration are mobilized by that other (as in "interruptions"), that sense of "basic trust" and with it, identity, will be impaired. In later life, Erikson has shown, political ideologies, personal love, or religious faith can serve the maternal function, gratifying "the simple and fervent wish for a hallucinatory sense of unity with a maternal matrix." [22]

Thus Freud interpreted H. D.'s mystical vision on Corfu "as a desire for union with [your] mother" (65). In the transference, he becomes that mother: "Why did you think you had to tell me? . . . But you felt you wanted to tell your mother" (44). Indeed, H. D.'s whole faith in Freud and psychoanalysis should be so interpreted: "The Professor had said in the very beginning that I had come to Vienna hoping to find my mother" (23).

It is not surprising, then, that H. D. uses images of fluids to describe the psychoanalytic process. She had entered analysis because she felt she was, like other intellectuals, "drifting," that she was "a narrow birchbark canoe" being swept into the "cataract" of war (17). Her friends provided only "a deluge of brilliant talk," but no "safe harbour" (162). Thus she sees herself as "a ship-wrecked child" turning to old Captain January (152). "The flow of associated images," the "fountainhead of highest truth," "the current [that] ran too deep"—H. D.'s images of fluids suggest, beautifully, the way something which is experienced passively, as an overpowering and terrifying deluge or flood, can, in the microcosm of the analytic relationship, be accepted and mastered. "He would stand guardian, he would turn the whole stream of consciousness back into useful, into *irrigation* channels" (156).

Other images of fluids show the feeling of "oceanic" unity that is related to that first unity with the mother. Freud she identifies as naming and discovering "a great stream or ocean underground" that, "overflowing," produces inspiration, madness, or creative idea. This ocean transcends all barriers of time and space (107–8). Thus, for any patient, "his particular stream, his personal life, could run clear of obstruction into the great river of humanity, hence to the sea of super-human perfection" (128); and again the issue of gender colors H. D.'s visions of immortality and fusion. H. D. had indeed "come to Vienna hoping to find [her] mother," even as she had found her on Corfu.

She began to see pictures outlined in light on the wall of her hotel room 66). The first was a head-and-shoulders silhouette of a soldier or airman with a visored cap. The second "was the conventional outline of a goblet or cup, actually suggesting the mystic chalice, but it was the familiar goblet shape we all know, with round base and glass-stem." The third is another mythological adaptation of a familiar object: the stand for a small spirit-lamp metamorphosed into the tripod on which the prophetess at Delphi sat. H. D. sees the tripod as the triad of religion, art, and medicine. These figures—hieroglyphs, she calls them—appear like "formal patterns" stamped on playing cards, but it is very much part of H. D.'s psychic patterns that she cannot tell whether she is projecting the images or whether "they are projected from outside."

Around the base of the tripod appears a swarm of tiny people, like insects. "They were people, they were annoying—I did not hate people, I did not especially resent any one person" (71–72). H. D. seems to accept Freud's interpretation of the vision "as a suppressed desire for forbidden 'signs and wonders,' breaking bounds, a suppressed desire to be a Prophetess, to be important anyway, megalomania they call it." (76),[23] and perhaps this megalomanic fantasy is why the people appear as a swarm of "small midges." At any rate, the people disappear, and the pictures begin to move upward.

Two dots of light appear and trace lines toward each other until they meet and become one line. She is stiff, says H. D., as though she were looking at the Gorgon head. The dots form another line, then another, then a series. H. D. feels as though she is drowning: "I must be born again or break utterly" (80). The lines become a Jacob's ladder linking heaven and earth.

The last figure forms: "There she is, I call her she; I call her Niké, Victory," around her a pattern of half-S's—question marks. "She is a common-or-garden angel" (82), three-dimensional, floating up the ladder, "free and with wings." "Niké, Victory seemed to be the clue, seemed to be my own especial sign or part of my hieroglyph." "I thought, 'Helios, the sun . . .' And I shut off, 'cut out' before the final picture, before (you might say) the explosion took place." H. D. let go, then, from complete exhaustion, but Bryher saw "the last concluding symbol." "She said, it was a circle like the sun-disc and a figure within the disc; a man, she thought, was reaching out to draw the image of a woman (my Niké?) into the sun beside him."

Obviously this vision has an almost unbelievable richness of symbol, association, and theme. It consolidates a whole mass of charged materials for H. D. No wonder she felt completely exhausted; no wonder Freud singled out this vision "as the most dangerous or the only actually dangerous 'symptom' " (60). Indeed, she originally entitled the memoir "Writing on the Wall," but went along with Norman Holmes Pearson's suggestion of a change.

As one would expect, the final vision is the least defended against or disguised, the first vision the most so. To the last picture, H. D. associates memories of her father and mother (61). Clearly, then, the most obvious interpretation of the man in the sun-disc is her Apollo-father, and to be the chosen woman of the father would indeed involve an "explosion." H. D. herself, however, suggests another interpretation and association: "The shrine of Helios (Hellas, Helen) had been really the main objective of my journey" (73). "I was physically in Greece, in Hellas (Helen). I had come home to the glory that was Greece" (65), and she identifies the phrase as from "Edgar Allan Poe's much-quoted *Helen*, and my mother's name was Helen."

Such associations take us back to early, oral wishes for a timeless at-oneness with the mother; now H. D. is victorious in her quest. There is, however, still another pattern of fusion: the vision is not only H. D.'s; it is also Bryher's, a further blurring of the boundaries between self and nurturing other. Dots come together to form a Jacob's ladder linking heaven to earth: the dots themselves merge; the ladder from earth to the realm of the gods suggests a child's wish to merge into the world of the parents.

To this part of the vision, however, H. D. associates staring at the Gorgon's head. There are few universal symbols in psychoanalysis, and Freud was quite right to caution H. D. against one-to-one symbolic decodings. But Medusa's head is a virtual universal: it represents the child's trauma at the sight of the female genitals accompanied by the horrifying fear that castration is indeed performed.[24] Here H. D. identifies herself with Perseus, guided by "Athené (or was it Hermes, Mercury?)," and the Gorgon head is not only "an enemy to be dealt with, "the ugly Head or Source of evil," but also "he was himself to manipulate his weapon, this ugly severed head of the enemy of Wisdom and Beauty" (78). She seems to be saying the vision—the sight itself—is

478

the combination of male weapon and ugly, female hostility. In one of her poems she describes lovemaking as two weapons one of which will "break" the other.[25]

Still working backwards through H. D.'s images, we come to the tripod, a homely, familiar object. It is the "base" for the spirit-lamp, but it is also what the Pythoness of Delphi sat on. It may also represent what H. D. sat on; certainly her description of it stresses the emptiness of its circles. Yet it is this stand that is associated with her megalomania—again, we seem to be coming to the theme of overcompensating for what she feels is the inferior quality of her feminine body. What the prophetess sits on is at once "homely" and "all the more an object to be venerated."

The "soldier or airman" H. D. identifies as "dead brother? lost friend?" In any case, he seems to represent that hard, weaponed masculinity that H. D. longed for. Between this masculine figure and the tripod is the chalice, another "familiar" object transformed. H. D. associates it with the "mystic chalice," hence with a quest of some kind. Like the tripod, it is empty, and its place in the sequence suggests a relation between oral needs and the quest for a lost masculinity or masculine figure.

To sum up, in the mystical vision H. D. does two things: she concretizes the abstract; she mythologizes the commonplace. The vision on Corfu brings us to the heart of the H. D. myth. It was implicit in her first meeting with Freud: to approach the outer object of an inner desire through an intermediary. We can now explicate those terms. The intermediary is perfect, timeless, symbolic (that is, mythological, hieroglyphic), combining past and future, male and female, with "no interruptions." The outer object tends to be hard, real, everyday, prosaic, even brutal; the inner desire, vague, soft, empty, abstract, and spiritual. We can make at least a preliminary statement of the H. D. myth: *when I concretize the spiritual or mythologize the everyday, I create a perfect, timeless hieroglyph-world which I can be and be in.* Or, very briefly, *I want to close the gap with signs.*

Consider, in the H. D. myth, the theme of fusion with a timeless, uninterrupted region of immortality (related originally, I should think, to H. D.'s mother, but often imaged as a masculine figure, like Helios-Helen in the sun-disc). For example, H. D. repeatedly insists that the core of Freud's achievement was a fusion: "He had brought the past into the present with his *the childhood of the individual is the child-*

479

hood of the race—or is it the other way round?—the childhood of the race is the childhood of the individual" (16). H. D. could see her living in England as an attempt at fusion:

> The sea grows narrower, the gap in consciousness sometimes seems negligible; nevertheless there is a duality, the English-speaking peoples are related, brothers, twins even, but they are not one. So in me, 2 distinct racial or biological or psychological entities tend to grow nearer or to blend, even, as time heals old breaks in consciousness. (47)

The two entities blending resemble the dots in the vision or her comment on Shakespeare: "Pied? Dappled, two-coloured, part-coloured, two-souled. Where was the advantage in that, *O master-mistress of my passion?"* [26] The concern with gaps and breaks in consciousness reminds one not only of her thoughts about her bodily gap but the deeper wish, "*If* one could stay near her always, there would be no break in consciousness" (49). Thus her quest for timelessness and immortality stems from a deeper wish to avoid the interruptions that marred her relation with her mother.

"One can never get near enough, or if one gets near, it is because one has measles or scarlet fever" (49). In other words, one can get close to this mother only if one accepts sickness, passivity, and bodily deficiency, and this H. D. did not do. "She likes my brother better. If I stay with my brother, become part almost of my brother, perhaps I can get nearer to *her*" (49).

Fusion with a man meant both fusion with and escape from the mother:

> Hermes, Hermes
> the great sea foamed,
> gnashed its teeth about me;
> but you have waited,
> where sea-grass tangles with
> shore-grass.[27]

Fusion with a man insures against deficiency: thus H. D. found it easy to project into and identify with Freud. But fusion with a man makes the man into a mother. Hence H. D. associates the Berggasse, Freud's street, with Athens, which she has already associated with her mother and her childhood home. In still a third variant, fusion with a male means that H. D. can assume the mother-role herself, as when she wishes to give, like Alcestis, her own life to Freud, or, in her last words about Freud: "O, let's go away together, pleads the soul," then retreating to "the simple affirmation . . . of uttermost veneration." Like any classicist, she knew the etymology of that word:

> . . . O holiest one,
> Venus whose name is kin
>
> to venerate
> venerator.[28]

Her poems reveal, too, the terrible anger and bitterness behind such veneration (the first love-hate for the mother) as in this painful poem based on the feminine and masculine words for "bitter":

> Now polish the crucible
> and in the bowl distill
>
> a word most bitter, *marah*,
> a word bitterer still, *mar*,
>
> sea, brine, breaker, seducer,
> giver of life, giver of tears;
>
> now polish the crucible
> and set the jet of flame
>
> under, till *marah-mar*
> are melted, fuse and join
>
> and change and alter,
> mer, mere, mère, mater, Maia, Mary,
>
> Star of the Sea,
> Mother.[29]

The astronomer-father, that distant mother, the deserting lover, here equated in the two forms of the oral word "bitter"—how H. D. must have longed for closeness, yet feared it as destruction!

The opposite of fusion in the H. D. myth is the sense of being a foreigner, left out, someone who exists, as it were, in the third person. "It was a girl between two boys; but, ironically, it was wispy and mousey, while the boys were glowing and gold" (161–162). She is painful on the subject of the two's in her family—"There were 2 of everybody (except myself)" (46). In her memories (mother with brother on the curbstone; father with brother and the magnifying glass), in her dreams (the Princess and the baby), or in her visions (the serpent and the thistle; Helios and the Niké-angel), H. D. finds herself in triangular situations, watching the other two—the triumphant climax of the Corfu vision is to end this isolation and fuse with Helios and Bryher. Similarly, she lives an exile in England or Switzerland as though acting out over and over again her own separateness. By coming for her hour on a day when rifles were stacked on the street-corners and no other patients appeared, she acted out once again her sense of her difference. "*I am here because no one else has come.* As if again, symbolically, I must be different" (92).

To compromise between total fusion and total alienation, H. D. likes to establish the boundaries and edges of things. For example, she gives a highly detailed cartography of Freud's consulting-room and study, wall by wall and door by door. Her vision came in units or steps like the cards in fortune-telling, and she can even see her dreams and visions as "steps in the so-far superficially catalogued or built-up mechanism of supernormal, abnormal (or subnormal) states of mind" (61). The word "steps" itself reminds her of the steps the Princess was descending or the Jacob's ladder in the Corfu vision.

This over-concern for boundaries and discrete units perhaps explains H. D.'s choppy stanza forms and her difficulties with the boundaries of sentences. Certainly it explains her insistence on treating symbols as having fixed meanings and the dream as "a universal language," despite Freud's cautions to the contrary. I suspect that this is the point at which the analysis could go no further: the wish or need to convert the insubstantial into something both substantial and immortal. This had become too basic a defensive strategy in H. D.'s character to be changed in a few months; this "was an argument implicit in our very bones" (16). This one defense or adaptation met both sides of the H. D. myth: the wish to fuse with something (father, brother, mother); the related wish to close the gap and restore what was missing (interrupted mother, dead brother, dead father, lost masculinity, missing penis).

Early in the book, H. D. tells of her difficulty in finding a birthday gift for Freud. "I had not found what I wanted so I did not give him anything" (10). The ambiguity of her phrasing suggests that the analysis itself was, for her, a search for a missing object and an attempt almost concretely to remake it. "We had come together in order to substantiate something. I did not know what" (16). Freud she saw "weighing the soul, Psyche, in the Balance" (147). Looking at the "perfect" little statue of Athené, she thought of Freud as a Jewish dealer in antiquities: "this pound of flesh was a *pound of spirit* between us, something tangible, to be weighed and measured, to be weighed in the balance and—pray God—not to be found wanting!" (106)

In the analysis, she felt, "thoughts were things, to be collected, collated, analysed, shelved or resolved. Fragmentary ideas . . . were sometimes skilfully pieced together" (18) like the jars and bowls and vases Freud's office displayed. Her special "memories, visions, dreams, reveries . . . are real. They are as real in their dimension of length, breadth, thickness, as any of the bronze or marble or pottery or clay objects that fill the cases around the walls" (51). Such a wish for solidity carries inevitably with it a fear: "There are dreams or sequences of dreams that follow a line . . . like a crack on a bowl that shows the bowl or vase may at any moment fall in pieces" (140).

H. D. makes a more familiar analogy to unconscious materials: Freud unlocks "vaults and caves" in his "unearthing buried treasures" (114). "The so-called findings of the unconscious mind revealed by the dream-content" can include "priceless treasures, gems and jewels" (133). As symbol, treasure might refer to a prized person or object (in H. D.'s case, all those missing things). Treasure might also refer to feces,[30] implicit in H. D.'s statement "that what he offered as treasure, this revelation that he seemed to value, was poor stuff, trash indeed, ideas that a ragpicker would pass over in disdain" (114).

In general, H. D. looks askance at soft substances like rags. When, for example, Freud refers to an insight as "striking oil," H. D. converts his discovery into finding "the carved symbol of an idea or a deathless dream" (141). Again, "striking oil," H. D. stresses "the outer rock or shale, the accumulation of hundreds or thousands of years" (125). Oil itself she makes a "concrete definite image." " 'I struck oil' suggests business enterprise. We visualize stark uprights and skeleton-like steel cages, like unfinished Eiffel Towers." Then, having concretized and phallicized the oil, H. D. attributes to others the anal fantasy that psychoanalysis is "some mechanical construction set up in an arid desert, to trap the unwary, and if there is 'oil' to be inferred, the 'oil' goes to someone else; there are astute doctors who 'squeeze you dry' with their exorbitant fees for prolonged and expensive treatments."

Down in that cloacal region where the Professor has "tunnelled" are "the chasms or gulfs where the ancient dragon lives" (168). On the one hand, Freud is the Saint Michael or Hercules who will slay "the Dragon . . . the Hydra-headed monster . . . the ancient brood of the Dragon [that] lives in the caves" (165). On the other hand, H. D. herself had left friendly surroundings "and come to a strange city, to beard him, himself, the dragon, in his very den. . . . Vienna? Venice? My mother had come here on her honeymoon" (22). H. D. admits that the analysis was interrupted before she dealt with her personal war-shock. She had to calm as best she could "my own personal little Dragon of war-terror" and order him "back to his subterranean cavern":

> There he growled and bit on his chains and was only loosed finally, when the full apocryphal terror of fire and brimstone, of whirlwind and flood and tempest, of the Biblical Day of Judgement and the Last Trump, became no longer abstractions, terrors too dreadful to be thought of, but things that were happening every day, every night, and at one time, at every hour of the day and night, to myself and my friends. (142–43)

In this (to use the clinical term) "world-destruction fantasy," we get a glimpse of that overpowering rage and fear somewhere in H. D.'s development, associated with fire as a destroyer, with the subterranean caves of her body, with terrors in the night, with the abstract and inner becoming concrete, and, I would guess, most deeply with the resentment the little girl must have felt toward the mother who rejected her and preferred her brother. Clearly, all these feelings were brought up again by the two wars; equally clearly, H. D. did not finally deal with them in the analysis. Yet it is well to remember that she did her most distinguished creative work during the two wars: a graphic illustration of the theory that artistic creativity stems from the wish to reconstitute what has been lost in aggressive fantasy. Consider this poem she wrote about the same time as *Tribute to Freud*: one should remember that she called Freud both dragon and Hermes-Thoth:

> Hermes took his attribute
> of Leader-of-the-dead from Thoth
>
> and the T-cross becomes caduceus;
> the old-church makes its invocation
>
> to Saint Michael and Our Lady
> at the death-bed; Hermes Trismegistus

spears, with Saint Michael,
the darkness of ignorance,

casts the Old Dragon
into the abyss.[31]

A dragon breathes destructive fire. A dragon also has wings, and we have already seen how wings were associated in H. D.'s mind with the phallic powers of a Flying Dutchman, Mercury, or her brother. Thus she could speak of "the black wing of man's growing power of destruction" (124). Certainly one of Freud's great achievements in the analysis was to get his patient to accept herself as wingless. Wings, she found, symbolized flight as well as power: "my mind . . . escaped the bars of that ladder, no longer climbing or caged but free and with wings" (82). And she came to recognize that wings and flight were not power, really, but just the opposite: "Perhaps my trip to Greece, that spring, might have been interpreted as a flight from reality. Perhaps my experiences there [among them, the vision] might be translated as another flight—from a flight" (65). "We must forgo a flight from reality" (128); the Flying Dutchman "flew too high and flew too quickly." She recognized her own quest for an absolute as flying too high and flying too quickly (128–29). Flying killed van der Leeuw, and Freud singled out H. D.'s "writing-on-the-wall as the most dangerous or the only actually dangerous 'symptom' " (60), "a suppressed desire for . . . breaking bounds . . . megalomania" (76), in which people appeared as midges—as they would from an airplane.

Quite the opposite of these unbounded flights is the more adaptive, more discrete way H. D. saw her life, in terms of Holmes's "Chambered Nautilus." The shell was linked in her mind to her preoccupation with immortality, "the personal soul's existence in some form or other, after it has shed the outworn or outgrown body" (64). "Build thee more stately mansions, O my soul," and she felt she had, in coming to the Professor. Her work with him seemed to "justify all the spiral-like meanderings of my mind and body. I had come home, in fact" (64). At that critical moment when Freud gave her the orange branch, among its many symbolic values an acceptance of her as a total person, she found herself thinking of a Goethe lyric which she had sung in school. The words echoed in "the curled involuted or convoluted shell skull, and inside the skull, the curled, intricate, hermitlike mollusc, the brain-matter itself" (137). The image sums up many of H. D.'s attitudes toward herself: the hard protective shell; within it, the soft, vul-

485

nerable self; within the self, the still more precious work of art, made hard, so that "thoughts are things." And it was for hardness she longed, even in sounds and smells as in the early poem, "Sheltered Garden":

> O for some sharp swish of a branch—
> there is no scent of resin
> in this place,
> no taste of bark, of coarse weeds,
> aromatic, astringent—
> only border on border of scented pinks.[32]

Imagism, clearly, served her defensive needs.

Softness implies fusion, as in her extended image of Freud unravelling the threads of her unconscious mind (109) or her statement: "The years went forward, then backward. The shuttle of the years ran a thread that wove my pattern into the Professor's" (11). In speaking of something sordid in her life, she "painfully unravelled a dingy, carelessly woven strip of tapestry" (44). By contrast, when Freud spoke, it was

> as if he had dipped the grey web of conventionally woven thought and with it, conventionally *spoken* thought, into a vat of his own brewing—or held a strip of that thought, ripped from the monotonous faded and outworn texture of the language itself, into the bubbling cauldron of his own mind in order to draw it forth dyed blue or scarlet, a new colour to the old grey mesh, a scrap of thought, even a cast-off rag, that would become hereafter a pennant, a standard, a *sign* again, to indicate a direction or, fluttering aloft on a pole, to lead an army. (105)

H. D. seeks to turn something soft like cloth into something with masculine, warlike hardness and force.

By contrast, "we all know that almost invisible thread-line on the cherished glass butter-dish that predicts it will 'come apart in me 'ands' sooner or later—sooner, more likely" (140). Breaking is her image for dying in "Adonis," while birth is becoming hard:

> Each of us like you
> has died once,
> each of us like you
> has passed through drift of wood-leaves,

cracked and bent
and tortured and unbent
in the winter frost,
then burnt into gold points,
lighted afresh,
crisp amber, scales of gold-leaf,
gold turned and re-welded
in the sun-heat. . . .[33]

It would be easy to see H. D.'s longing to create, then fuse with
hard objects as purely defensive or pathological: the attempt to recreate a lost masculinity or a "hard," ungiving mother. But it is perfectly clear that this symptom or character-trait had adaptive virtues
as well. To it, we owe H. D.'s interest in and ability to bring out her
unconscious life in enduring artistic forms.

But we fight for life,
we fight, they say, for breath,

so what good are your scribblings?
this—we take them with us

beyond death; Mercury, Hermes, Thoth
invented the script, letters, palette;

the indicated flute or lyre-notes
on papyrus or parchment

are magic, indelibly stamped
on the atmosphere somewhere,

forever; remember, O Sword,
you are the younger brother, the latter-born

your Triumph, however exultant,
must one day be over,

*in the beginning
was the Word.*[34]

In her Corfu vision, she paused between images "as if a painter had
stepped back from a canvas the better to regard the composition of
the picture, or a musician had paused at the music-stand" (69). "This
writing-on-the-wall is merely an extension of the artist's mind, a *picture* or an illustrated poem" (76). "Dreams are as varied as are the

books we read, the pictures we look at or the people we meet" (52). "The books and the people merge in this world of fantasy and imagination" (139).

To create a work of art was to immortalize an inner wish, to create, as well, an immortal person ministering to an immortal self.

> grape, knife, cup, wheat
>
> are symbols in eternity,
> and every concrete object
>
> has abstract value, is timeless
> in the dream parallel
>
> whose relative sigil has not changed
> since Nineveh and Babel.[35]

Sigil, signet, *signum*—she talks about these words in *Tribute to Freud*. "And as I write that last word, there flashes into my mind the associated *in hoc signum* or rather, it must be *in hoc signo* and *vinces*" (100). We are reminded of the "megalomania" Freud found in the "dangerous symptom" of the Corfu vision. "Signet," too, has its associations, among them "the royal signature, usually only the initials of the sovereign's name. (I have used my initials H. D. consistently as my writing signet or sign-manual, though it is only, at this very moment . . . that I realize that my writing signature has anything remotely suggesting sovereignty or the royal manner.)"

I feel sadness for a woman who had to become a royal and mythic sign to make up for all those missing things. But I honor the poet. She did indeed close up the gap with signs and, in doing so, left to us a body of poems for which we can be grateful.

She also left behind this unique document, *Tribute to Freud*, from which we have been able to infer the H. D. myth as it evolved through the successive psychosexual stages of her own development and as it revealed itself through Freud's taking on a succession of roles in the transference: brother, father, oedipal mother, and, most important, the cosmic, oral mother of earliest infancy. To repeat, the H. D. myth, as expressed in the memoir, involves an attempt *to close up the gap between inner and outer, spiritual and physical, male and female, by perfect, timeless signs which she can be and be in.* Such a myth is not just an abstraction but develops in stages dynamically, toward an adult life-style that permeates "all [she] did and thought."

As for so many lyric poets, the psychosexual mode that dominates H. D.'s psyche is the earliest: the oral. At her very center, H. D. wishes and fears to fuse with, be devoured by, close the gap between herself and—her mother, felt as a timeless, uninterrupted, unbroken mystical level of experience. The wish (and fear) develops in two directions: she transforms the imperfections and frustrations of the real world into more perfect poetic signs; she concretizes inchoate, inner longing into hard, tangible, reachable realities—again, usually mythological. In classical myth and other poetic signs, H. D. found the compromise: perfections she could have. She becomes the poet of hard, cold things or, alternatively, bristly pine trees and hedgehogs. The strategy is a cosmic one and gives rise to imagery of oceans, floods, her sustaining use of mythology and her destructive fantasies of fiery world-destruction.

The first, oral, psychosexual stage colors its successors: anal, phallic, oedipal. H. D.'s writings have very little of the anal mode in them. What there is seems focused on the transformation of soft, dirty, oily, or raglike objects into hard, firm works of art. Soft materials might be forced out of her by another, might belong to that other (a version of the earlier fusion), while hard objects are her own creation. The phallic mode has more importance: H. D.'s wish to create a hard, phallic object so as to replace a lost masculinity. To yield in a feminine way is to melt, dissolve, flow away, or be transformed. It is at this phallic level that she wishes instead to fuse with the winged and weaponed Mercuries—ultimately, her brother (and, back of him, father, then mother). The oedipal level of H. D.'s development seems to have the usual triangles, but primitivized by her pervasive oral fantasies. Thus she sees both mother- and father-figures as mythically or religiously or magically powerful. The usual wish to *have* the father becomes, for her, a wish to be her father with all his phallic potency and castrating power. Behind this oedipal wish is the oral one: if she can fuse with brother or father, she can have and be mother—still conceived as the cosmic supplier the infant longs for.

Such developmental phases one can identify in any human being. When we see them in a creative writer, though, our curiosity is piqued. We tend to ask, as the Cardinal asked of Ariosto, "Where did you find so many stories, Lodovico?" It is not too difficult to see the connections between H. D.'s developmental stages and such literary insights as Professor Riddel's:

The threatened flower of self, caught between the great maternal ocean and the hard, firm, enduring shore (the fragile flower and the stalwart tree) compose the essential landmarks of H. D.'s condition. They are the components of her recurrent myth—her *cogito*—in its purest form.

Inwardness is projected as transient and insubstantial—soft and decaying like a fragile flower . . . or as the decaying fragments of a heat-oppressed space.

The poet affirms her identity not by solving the mystery but by reifying it.

But how can one locate in the stages of H. D.'s development the wellsprings of her creativity? What, for example, is the relation between her creative writing and her mental health or illness?

To close the gap with signs. H. D.'s myth could have taken a psychotic or pre-psychotic form. Apparently it did, if we credit Freud's singling out of "megalomania" in the Corfu vision. The terrible losses of the 1914–1919 period fitted into the pattern of her childhood deprivation; psychotic mechanisms were mobilized to "close the gap." As for neurosis, H. D. makes it clear that part of her wish to close the gap took neurotic forms—anxieties about her body: penis envy, her height, her femininity. Whether there was character disorder—perversion, sociopathy, schizoid tendencies—her silence about her adult life makes it impossible to say. If, however, we apply Freud's basic criteria of normal functioning—*lieben und arbeiten;* to love and to work—it is clear that H. D. was a productive poet and a sufficient mother. She was functioning in large part as a healthy adult.

In short, H. D.'s account of her analysis with Freud makes it clear that creativity does not stem from mental illness; neither is it a simple alternative. Rather, the key variable is *style*. Both illness ("megalomania," to take the gravest case) and creative activity (imagistically rendered myths) will have the same style.[36] Put another way, both will act out the same underlying myth. The megalomanic vision will distort reality, the Imagist mythographer will create an artifact, both "to close the gap with signs." [37]

"Where did you find so many stories, Lodovico?" What turned H. D. to poetry? The strong forces in H. D.'s myth must have happened to many women: a style of mothering that created "gaps," the distant father, the envied brothers. But not every woman who experienced such a childhood became a poet. What was critical in H. D.'s life? In other words, plenty of children experienced the "gaps"; what made H.

D. take "signs" as a way of dealing with "gaps"? She was born in Beth-
lehem, Pennsylvania. She lived on Church Street. At an early age, she
experienced the special rituals and language of her mother's religion,
the Moravian Brotherhood. Her brothers used words she could not understand. Her father would look at stars, numbers, hieroglyphs, but
not at her. One gets, I think, a feel for, glimmerings of, the factors in
H. D.'s early environment that made "signs" (religious, alphabetic,
hieroglyphic, numerical, mythic) the most economical way to close the
gap.

Only a full biography could make firm connections, but a preliminary formulation seems to emerge.[38] Healthy infancy involves a series
of needs, longings, fears, and frustrations. Those in the early mother-
child relation seem to have most to do with literary creativity. However, these earliest stresses are much the same for most people. They
vary but not enough to say why one person becomes a writer and another not. Highly variable, however, are the possibilities the environment offers for dealing with these "gaps." (And, of course, heredity
also imposes limitations on these possibilities.)

> Under the name of "the principle of multiple function" Waelder
> has described a phenomenon of cardinal importance in ego psychol-
> ogy. This principle expresses the tendency of the organism toward
> inertia, that is, the tendency to achieve a maximum of effect with a
> minimum of effort. Among various possible actions that one is
> chosen which best lends itself to the simultaneous satisfaction of de-
> mands from several sources. An action fulfilling a demand of the ex-
> ternal world may at the same time result in instinctual gratification
> and in satisfying the superego. The mode of reconciling various
> tasks to one another is characteristic for a given personality. Thus
> the ego's habitual modes of adjustment to the external world, the
> id, and the superego, and the characteristic types of combining
> these modes with one another, constitute character.[39]

"Signs" evidently achieved for H. D. a maximum of effect with a minimum of effort and hence became part of both her character and her
poetry, her life-style and her literary style, or, in Yeats's term, her
myth. In another environment, storytelling, role-playing, verbal games
like rhyme, or coined languages—any of these might have proved
more economical and so made for a different kind of writer. Creative
writing, like any other act "in character," satisfies a combination of
pleasure-giving and defensive needs.

491

What is striking, though, is that these determinants toward writing and toward a certain style of writing are not buried in the obscurity of infancy (at least not for H. D.). They are there for the biographer to see—provided he knows what to look for. H. D., by revealing herself in the memoir of Freud, enables us to formulate an H. D. myth. (For other writers, one would hypothesize such a myth from the writings alone—as Yeats did for Shakespeare. But H. D.'s work with Freud gives her "myth" a special validity.) Once formulated, the myth tells us which of the external biographical factors would be likely to combine with her inner needs to give rise to H. D.'s special poetic character.

In short, H. D.'s generous revelation of herself in *Tribute to Freud* gives us more than insight into H. D. It leads to a general method of psychobiography that, without her, we would not have. We can be grateful to her not only for her poems, but for her willingness to lend us the insights she achieved with the "blameless physician." Every biographer must be in her debt, and *Tribute to Freud* is a tribute to H. D. as well.

Notes

1. W. B. Yeats, "At Stratford-on-Avon," *Ideas of Good and Evil* (London 1903): 161–62.

2. *Tribute to Freud* (New York 1956). Hereafter, I shall refer to this book simply by page numbers in parentheses in the text—and only for the more important references lest the text become too cluttered. I owe a particular debt of gratitude to Norman Holmes Pearson of Yale University, H. D.'s literary executor, who has been more than generous both with his comments and his knowledge of those works of H. D.'s which are still unpublished or underwent important revisions (as did *Tribute to Freud*).

3. Horace Gregory, Introduction to *Helen in Egypt* (New York 1961): ix.

4. *The Walls Do Not Fall* (London 1944): 40.

5. *Helen in Egypt*: 188.

6. Thomas B. Swann, *The Classical World of H. D.* (Lincoln, Neb., 1962), on which I have drawn very generally and extensively.

7. *Palimpsest* (Paris 1926): 218.

8. *Helen in Egypt*: 23, 271, et al.

9. *Swann*: 62, 36.

10. *The Autobiography of William Carlos Williams* (New York 1951): 67.

11. *Palimpsest* and *Bid Me to Live (A Madrigal)* (New York 1960).

12. *Swann*: 19.

13. Williams, *Autobiography*: 190, 219.

14. *Swann*: 20.

15. See also Bryher [Winifred Ellerman], *The Heart to Artemis: A Writer's Memoirs* (New York 1962): 263–64.

16. *International Journal of Psycho-Analysis* 37 (1957): 126. There may be a question of terminology here, since Freud could write, "I analyzed Mahler for an afternoon

in the year 1912." Theodor Reik, *The Haunting Melody: Psychoanalytic Experiences in Life and Music* (New York 1953), letter of 4 Jan. 1935. Jones does not mention either H. D. or van der Leeuw in his biography of Freud.

17. Her positive feelings for her brother show, beautifully, in the figure of André in that charming and highly revealing children's book, *The Hedgehog* (London 1936).

Although the book was written in 1925, the figure of Dr. Berne Blum markedly foreshadows Freud. H. D. may have had such a strong positive transference in 1933, because Freud fit into a matrix of preexisting fantasies and expectations.

The central fantasy works out H. D.'s recurring adaptive pattern: replacing something needed and missing by a magical word (the meaning of which this little heroine does not know). What is an *hérisson?* "Little girls shouldn't ask" (64) but André had one. Why should she ask the moon for things André can get (76–77)? The *hérisson* is something someone gives you, "big as a mountain," associated with the fur of her mother's coat, with having babies, with frightening snakes away.

18. Swann recognizes the importance of this and other passages from the memoir in his short but extraordinarily perceptive account of H. D.'s life in *The Classical World*.

19. Later, to Swann, H. D. noted, "Perhaps, as my father and half brother were astronomers the *names*, Venus, Mercury, and so on, were subconsciously potent." Swann: 10.

20. *Helen in Egypt*: 23, 260, 271.

21. "Analysis Terminable and Interminable" (1937), *Standard Ed. of the Complete Psychological Works of Sigmund Freud* 23 (London 1953–66): 252.

22. This classical explanation of the sense of "oceanic" unity occurs in the opening chapter of *Civilization and its Discontents* (1930), *Standard Ed.* 21: 64–73. Freud had earlier identified "Obsessive Actions and Religious Practices" (1907), *ibid.* 9: 115–27. It remained for Erikson to provide a more comprehensive view of the relation of religion to childhood, combining Freud's early and later positions. Erik Erikson, *Young Man Luther* (New York 1958): 263–66; quotation: 264.

23. In "Toward the Piraeus," H. D. takes the role of the "Pythoness" for whom words of prophecy substitute for words of love. *Collected Poems* (New York 1940): 260–61.

24. Among the many psychoanalysts and analytical psychologists who have come to this conclusion are: Freud, "Medusa's Head" (1940 [1922]), *Standard Ed.* 18: 273–74; "The Infantile Genital Organization" (1923), *ibid.*, 19: 144; Sandor Ferenczi, "On the Symbolism of the Head of Medusa" (1923), in *Further Contributions to the Theory and Technique of Psycho-Analysis* (London 1926): 360; Otto Fenichel, "The Scoptophilic Instinct and Identification" (1935), *Collected Papers of Otto Fenichel, First Series* (New York 1953): 389–91; Erich Neumann, *The Great Mother: An Analysis of the Archetype* (New York 1955): 166–70, plates 70, 80, 100; Erik Erikson, "The Nature of Clinical Evidence," in *Insight and Responsibility* (New York 1964): 70.

25. "Toward the Piraeus," *Collected Poems*: 263–64.

26. *By Avon River* (New York 1949): 35.

27. "Hermes of the Ways," *Collected Poems*: 57.

28. *Tribute to the Angels* (New York 1945): 17.

29. *Ibid.*: 14–15.

30. *Introductory Lectures on Psycho-Analysis* (1915–16), *Standard Ed.* 15: 156; *The Interpretation of Dreams* (1900–01), *ibid.* 5: 403.

31. *Tribute to the Angels*: 33–34.

32. *Collected Poems*: 25.

33. *Ibid.*: 68.

34. *The Walls Do Not Fall* (London 1944): 18.

35. *Ibid.*: 23.

36. On the use of "style" as a variable, see my "The Art of Scientific Biography," *Kenyon Review* 30 (1968): 702–7.

37. In these conclusions, I am most grateful to my colleagues in the Group for Applied Psychoanalysis (Buffalo): Warren Bennis, C. L. Barber, Marvin Feldman, Edgar Z. Friedenberg, Joseph Masling, Marvin Opler, and R. Robert Rogers, who have made many helpful suggestions.

I am particularly grateful to Heinz Lichtenstein for emphasizing the importance of the word "megalomania" in the diagnosis of H. D. and its relation to schizophrenic verbal structures as set out by Freud in "The Unconscious" (1915), *Standard Ed.* 14: 196–204.

Joseph N. Riddel has been more than kind in giving me during the writing of this essay his insights (in his own essay on H. D.) from a philosophical point of view.

Andrew J. Silver of Brandeis University has made what I think are a series of very astute interpretations of the role of H. D.'s relation to her father in her poetic vocation. That is, in her wish to fuse with him and get him (it) back, astronomy undoubtedly took on special significance. For example, the dots in her vision may have been stars, as the signs, signets, and myths she lived in were constellations. To use symbolism (like her father and brother) may have meant to take their tools, to be masculine—thus, for her, symbols *must* have a fixed, rigid meaning. Her interest in puns might be an attempt to "telescope" words—indeed, her father's being such a distant man engaged with such distant things may have over-determined all attempts to close distances. Flying, which interested her in Mercury and the Flying Dutchman, may have been "reaching for the stars." In general, to "close the gap with signs," to establish the boundaries and edges of things (like connecting stars with lines to form constellations) or, still more generally, to concretize the abstract may have meant at the deepest level of her being: to touch my father.

I have not included Mr. Silver's insights in the text because they are, ultimately, inferences, and I wished to limit the body of this paper to what was demonstrably "there" in the memoir. Nevertheless, they seem right to me.

38. For a still more preliminary formulation of this idea, see my *Dynamics of Literary Response* (New York 1968), "Style and the Man" (ch. 8): 237–42.

39. Otto Fenichel, *The Psychoanalytic Theory of Neurosis* (New York 1945): 467. The article he refers to is Robert Waelder's classic, "The Principle of Multiple Function," *Psychoanalytic Quarterly* 5 (1936): 45–62.

Freud's Case-Load

(1970)

BENJAMIN BRODY

Benjamin Brody is with the William Alanson White Institute in New York. This paper is one of the first serious attempts to study Freud's practice. It first appeared in Psychotherapy 7 *(Spring 1970): 8–12.*

Probably more than most other sciences, psychoanalysis is the creation of a single man. The clinical experience, social ideology, and perhaps even personal idiosyncrasies of Sigmund Freud are still the cornerstones of analytical practice and theory some sixty years after his initial observations. Regardless of the fervor of their orthodoxy or the exact nature of their heresies, it seems clear that most analysts are still following, sifting over, or rejecting some phase of Freud's work.

Under these circumstances, a careful examination of the cultural, psychological, and clinical bases of Freud's thinking seems imperative for an evaluation of the validity and limitations of his conclusions. Thus, Fromm and Horney, reconsidering Freud's biological orientation, concluded that it is theoretically cumbersome and therapeutically superfluous in the light of the newer knowledge of culture and Freud's milieu. In a more personal vein, through a critical study of his writings, David Riesman (1950a and b) examined the influence of Freud's attitudes to work, play, authority, and liberty. There is a growing realization that Freud himself, as a human being with personal and clinical assets and limitations, must be considered in any evaluation of psychoanalysis.

Through an analysis of his clinical writings, this study will estimate the nature of Freud's clinical experience in terms of the characteristics of the population of patients with which he dealt.

Method

The writings alone probably give only a small and highly selected sample of Freud's total case load. However, until his files and clinical notes become available for analysis—if they exist—his published works remain the best approximation. In spite of their lack of completeness, they possess a unique value; it seems reasonable to assume that they represent those cases which stimulated Freud sufficiently to motivate him to a full report or passing reference and, accordingly, formed the important raw material for both his own conclusions and the studies of his disciples.

The case-reports themselves range from full clinical histories containing a relatively complete anamnesis, some record of the therapeutic process, and a theoretical discussion to the barest mention of a patient in connection with a single point. However, even in the most detailed account it is frequently difficult to ascertain the kind of vital statistic in which we are interested, perhaps because of the need for professional discretion as well as a certain literary predilection that frequently obscures the presence of factual life-history material. Thus, in the famous Wolf-Man (Freud 1918) case, some rather involved calculation is necessary to establish that the patient was about twenty-three years old when he first came for treatment. Freud frequently conducted armchair analyses of literary and historical characters he had never seen or of incidents and personalities outside the confines of his consulting room, utilized case-material offered by colleagues or from his personal life and nonclinical observations, and, on at least one occasion, constructed an ideal-type case (Freud 1896) for illustrative purposes. To further complicate the data, a favorite case is frequently utilized in several different papers; references to the Wolf-Man case, for example, appear in at least four different sources.

To obviate these difficulties, only patients whom Freud personally treated are considered in this study. In all instances, the criterion of inclusion is categorical evidence that Freud himself actually saw the patient in clinical contact. Insofar as identification is possible, a case is cited only once at the date of its earliest publication.

Obviously, a full clinical report of several hundred pages resulting in important theoretical and therapeutic considerations demands quite different treatment than a passing reference of a few lines. Not only is the former more important from a historical point of view, but our confidence in the reliability and completeness of the data is proportionately greater. Accordingly, the case material is divided into major and minor categories and treated separately. The major category is composed of those cases that are at least several pages in length, include some statement of the patient's life circumstances, and serve as the vehicle for a theoretical discussion; the minor cases are simply the remaining ones. This definition of the major case, it should be noted, has some claim to operational validity; with only a few additions, it includes all the case presentations in Freud's two clinical volumes: the *Studies in Hysteria* and Volume III of the *Collected Papers*.

Both major and minor cases were analyzed in terms of sex, age, marital state, diagnosis and social class. Especially in his fuller presentations, Freud himself provides fairly accurate information on the first four of these variables though, as we have noted, it is frequently incomplete and occasionally requires reconstruction from the available evidence. Within these limitations, we can be certain that whatever information does exist is valid. As Freud (1915) says: "I have altered the *milieu* . . . in order to preserve the incognito of those concerned, but . . . I have altered nothing else. I consider it an undesirable practice, however excellent the motive may be, to alter any detail in the presentation of a case. One can never tell which aspect . . . may be picked out by a reader of independent judgment, and one runs the risk of giving the latter a false impression."

The situation is somewhat different in relation to social class. Though clearly realizing the fact of social stratification, Freud rarely explicitly identified his patients as belonging to one or another status hierarchy; indeed, it is probable that such a task was beyond the state of sociological knowledge during most of his working life-time. However, W. Lloyd Warner and associates (1949) at the University of Chicago evolved a group of indices which are closely associated with actual levels of social participation. By a systematic, empirical evaluation of such information as occupation, source of income, education, religion, and ethnic origin, a statistically valid estimate of social status can be computed. Although complete calculation of the index is rarely possible with our data, Warner's scales can be utilized toward a reasonably accurate estimation of social class. Thus, we can be certain that the Wolf-Man was of at least middle class status because of the references to his family estates, nurse and English governess. Similarly, Dora's (Freud 1905) extensive education and her father's position as "a large manufacturer in very comfortable circumstances" place her in the middle class group. Warner's three primary class divisions have been consolidated into two groups; our "upper" class is equivalent to his upper and middle classes, and our "lower" class is identical with his lower class. Because of the incompleteness of our data, any attempt at precise class placement is avoided by this technique and the effect

TABLE 1

Major Cases

No.	Period	Date	Name	Sex	Age	Marital State	Social Class	Diagnosis
1	I 1889–1900²	1893	—	Female	20–30	Married	Upper	Hysteria
2		1893	Lucie R.	Female	Young Lady	Single	Upper	Hysteria
3		1895	Emmy Von N.	Female	About 40	Married	Upper	Hysterical Delirium
4		1895	Katherina	Female	About 18	Single	Upper	Hysteria
5		1895	Elizabeth R.	Female	24	Single	Upper	Hysteria
6		1899	—	Male	38	—	Upper	Phobia
7	II 1901–1912²	1905	Dora	Female	18	Single	Upper	Hysteria
8¹		1909	Hans¹	Male	5	Single	Upper	Phobia
9		1909	"Rat-Man"	Male	Youngish Man	Single	Upper	Obsessional Neurosis
10	III 1913–1924²	1915	—	Female	30	Single	Upper	Paranoia
11		1918	"Wolf-Man"	Male	23(c.)	Married³	Upper	Post Obsessional Neurotic Condition
12		1920	—	Female	18	Single	Upper	Homosexuality

[1] Freud actually saw this patient personally only once.
[2] Periods of psychoanalytical development according to Thompson (1950).
[3] Information from R. Brunswick (1928).

498

of changes in class identification from Freud's time to our own is minimized.

Results

With the exception of a few obituaries, prefaces, and minor papers, Freud's complete works were analyzed as cited in Strachey's (1946) bibliography of Freud's writings in English translation. A total of 114 papers were searched for major and minor cases and all of Freud's twenty-two books were examined in terms of the major category alone. Table 1 summarizes the results for the twelve major cases and Table 2 for the 133 minor cases.

It is interesting to note that about half of both the major and minor cases were published from 1889 to 1900, a period that is equivalent to the first stage of psychoanalytical development according to Thompson (1950), and that ended with Freud's growing involvement in the intricacies of instinct psychology. As Thompson says: "This was a time of great discovery gleaned from clinical observation . . . the period of Freud's greatest creativeness. No theories he later developed can compare with the brilliance of the early discoveries." The sharp decrement in the number of case presentations after 1900 is thus closely associated with the development of the libido theory. It seems clear that Freud's interest in people and their relationships diminished around 1900 in favor of constitutional factors. To quote Thompson once more: "He came to minimize what actually happens between people, failed to take into consideration . . . that it is the dynamic interaction between people which provides the locus of functional mental illness." In the 1920s, during the period of pessimism about the efficacy of psychoanalytical therapy and the first experiments with therapeutic technique, Freud published no major cases and comparatively few minor cases.

Sex

Tables 1 and 2 reveal that women composed about two-thirds of Freud's published cases. Though such a preponderance is understandable because of the limited outlets and opportunities available to women during most of Freud's time, it is noteworthy for the light it casts on his own cultural ideology. In spite of the composition of his case-load, Freud, like many contemporary classical analysts, confessed comparative difficulty in formulating the psychology of women. As

499

TABLE 2
Minor Cases

	Sex			Marital State			Age					Diagnosis						Social Class			Total
	Male	Female	No data	Single	Married	No data	Children: Under 12	Adolescents: 12-20	Young Adults: 21-30	Adults 30+	No data	Primary Dx: Obsessional Neurosis	Primary Dx: Anxiety Neurosis	Primary Dx: Hysteria	Unclassified Neurosis	Primary Dx: Psychosis	No data	Upper Class	Lower Class	No data	
Period I[2] 1889–1900	14	34	22[1]	9	19	42[1]	1	4	9	34	22[1]	21	13	31	2	2	1[1]	9	0	61[1]	70
Period II[2] 1901–1912	4	9	0	0	3	10	0	1	0	10	2	5	1	0	0	1	6	3	0	10	13
Period III[2] 1913–1924	15	21	4	0	8	32	0	3	10	23	4	5	2	2	4	7	20	10	0	30	40
Period IV[2] 1925–1938	8	2	0	0	2	8	0	1	3	6	0	1	0	1	4	0	4	4	0	6	10
Total	41	66	26	9	32	92	1	9	22	73	28	32	16	34	10	10	31	26	0	107	133

[1] Does not include a reference (Freud, 1898) to "over 200 patients" but with no other information given.
[2] Periods of psychoanalytical development according to Thompson (1950).

late as 1924, for example, in discussing the psycho-sexual development of girls, he (1924) says: "Here our material—for some reason we do not understand—becomes far more shadowy and incomplete." Similarly, Hendrick (1941) writes: "The psychology of the female has proved to be no simple problem for Freud and other analysts. She has remained an enigma. . . . Few doubted that she existed; no one seemed able to prove with certainty how she got that way." "Incomplete" as Freud's formulation of female psychology may be, critics such as Horney and Thompson have felt that Freud's formulation of female psychology reflected Victorian attitudes and, in effect, discriminated against women. From our data, on the basis of a clinical practice largely devoted to women, Freud derived a male psychology. The limitations of Freud's culture affected and perhaps outweighed the influence of his clinical experience.

Diagnosis

Freud diagnosed half of his twelve major cases as hysteria, two as obsessional neurosis and phobia, and one each as homosexuality and paranoia. In general, these proportions are maintained in the minor group; about 65 percent have as their primary diagnosis hysteria and obsessional neurosis, 15 percent anxiety neurosis, and the remainder are divided equally between unclassified neurotic conditions and psychoses. Freud's limited and, from our tables, relatively late experience with psychotic patients may be reflected in his belief that they are incapable of transference and hence not amenable to analytical therapy. His extensive experience with hysteria and obsessions may have resulted in the belief, still held by many analysts according to Thompson, that "only hysteria, obsessions and phobias are suitable cases for analysis." Although it is difficult to be certain of the exact causal relationships, the inference is strong that a limitation of Freud's clinical experience has been elevated to the dignity of a therapeutic principle.

Age

Nine of Freud's major cases were between eighteen and twenty years of age, only two were older than thirty, and only one was a child. These trends are maintained by the minor cases as well. Only one patient is under twelve, nine are between twelve and twenty, and only two are over forty-five. About 90 percent of the total patient group is between twenty and forty-four. Freud's cases, then, were derived almost exclusively from the adult and young adult groups; he had very few adolescents and practically no children as patients. One wonders to what extent his limited experience with older patients is responsible for the dictum that psychoanalysis is not indicated with older people.

Social Class

The data on the social class affiliations of the major cases is definitive. Every one of these patients is a member of the upper class as we have defined it. As a matter of fact, it is our impression that probably only a minority are as low in status as middle class by Warner's more detailed divisions. Freud provides less data permitting class identification for the minor cases than with any of our other variables indicating, perhaps, a relatively limited realization of the importance of social affiliation. In any case, the data is consistent here as well; all twenty-six minor cases are upper class. It is clear that Freud's patients were drawn exclusively from the upper and middle class. Wassermann (1958; Ansbacher 1959), working in Poland, has corroborated these findings to a remarkable extent in spite of the incomplete nature of his data and a somewhat impressionistic technique of arriving at class affiliation. The insistence of the cultural school of analysis that Freud's conclusions were derived from a limited social group is confirmed.

In all probability, this is true of present-day American analysis as well. The extensive occupational data on patients treated at the Institute for Psychoanalysis in Chicago (*Ten Year Report*, 1942) and Kubie's (1950) statistics on the scale of analytical fees makes it highly unlikely that more than a few lower class patients have been analyzed. Crowley (1950) has called attention to the comparatively small numbers of lower class patients even in the Low Cost Psychoanalytical Service of the William Alanson White Institute where financial inability presumably represents no objection. Brody (1949) and Grey (1949) in the Middle West and afterwards Hollingshead and Redlich (1958) in New England found a similar situation in psychiatric clinics and hospitals where the treatment is not strictly psychoanalytic but psychoanalytically oriented. Is it possible that something in the ideology and technique of analysis makes it difficult for lower class people to use successfully? The class origins of both analytical patients and practitioners seem to make this a likely hypothesis.

Marital State

Seven of the ten adult major cases were single in contrast to only 22 percent of the minor ones. The significance of this difference, however, should not be overestimated because of the small number of cases in the major category. In the minor group, however, about 85 percent of the female patients were married while about 55 percent of the males were. Though the evidence is not clear, it seems probable that a majority of Freud's patients were married.

Bibliography

Ansbacher, H. L. The significance of the socio-economic status of the patients of Freud and of Adler. *Amer. J. Psychotherapy*, 1959, **13**, 378–383.

Brody, B. Relationships between Slavic ethnicity and psychological characteristics of psychiatric patients. Ph.D. thesis, U. of Chicago, 1949.

Brunswick, R. M. A supplement to Freud's History of an infantile neurosis. *Int. J. Psycho-Anal.*, 1928, **9**, 439–476.

Crowley, R. M. A low-cost psychoanalytical service: first year. *Psychiat. Quart.*, 1950, **24**, 462–482.

Freud, S. The aetiology of hysteria; 1896. In *Collected papers*, Volume I. London: Hogarth Press, 1924. Pp. 183–219.

Freud, S. Sexuality in the aetiology of the neuroses; 1898. In *Collected papers*, Volume I. London: Hogarth Press, 1924. Pp. 220–248.

Freud, S. Fragment of an analysis of a case of hysteria; 1905. In *Collected papers*, Volume III. London: Hogarth Press, 1924. Pp. 13–148.

Freud, S. A case of paranoia running counter to the psycho-analytical theory of the disease; 1915. In *Collected papers*, Volume II. London: Hogarth Press, 1924. Pp. 150–161.

Freud, S. From the history of an infantile neurosis; 1918. In *Collected papers*, Volume III. London: Hogarth Press. Pp. 473–605.

Freud, S. The passing of the Oedipus-complex; 1924. In *Collected papers*, Volume II. London: Hogarth Press, 1924. Pp. 269–276.

Grey, A. Relationships between social class and psychological characteristics of psychiatric patients. Ph.D. thesis, U. of Chicago, 1949.

Hendrick, I. *Facts and theories of psychoanalysis.* New York: Knopf, 1941.

Hollingshead, A.,& Redlich, F. *Social class and mental illness.* New York, Wiley, 1958.

Kubie, L. S. A pilot study of psychoanalytical practice in the United States. *Psychiatry*, 1950, **13**, 227–246.

Riesman, D. The themes of work and play in the structure of Freud's thought. *Psychiatry*, 1950, **13**, 1–16 (a).

Riesman, D. Authority and liberty in the structure of Freud's thought. *Psychiatry*, 1950, **13**, 167–187 (b).

Strachey, J. Bibliography: list of English translation of Freud's works. *Psychoanalyt. Quart.*, 1946, **15**, 207–225.

Thompson, C. *Psychoanalysis: evolution and development.* New York: Hermitage House, 1950.

Warner, W. L. *Social class in America.* Chicago: Science Research Associates, 1949.

Wassermann, I. Letter to the editor. *Amer. J. Psychother.*, 1958, **12**, 623–627.

Ten Year Report. Institute for psychoanalysis, Chicago, 1942.

Sigmund Freud and
Thomas Mann
(1970)

HERBERT LEHMANN

Thomas Mann and Sigmund Freud greatly admired one another's work. As far as I know the following article is the first attempt to analyze their relationship. It was published in The Psychoanalytic Quarterly 37 (1970): 198–214.

In the chronicle of Freud's encounters with contemporary men of literature an important chapter will have to be devoted to Thomas Mann. When I scanned the potential material for that particular chapter, my attention was caught by Freud's confession of an act of forgetting which occurred in reaction to Mann at the height of their relationship. What might have remained for me a catalogue of letters, meetings, and respectful utterances became a chance of discovering what feelings these two men might have had toward each other.

Freud refers to the parapraxis in the last paragraph of a remarkable letter. He wrote it in November of 1936, six months after Mann read to him his famous address, Freud and the Future, on the occasion of Freud's eightieth birthday and after Mann had sent him his newly published volume in the Joseph series, Joseph in Egypt. Freud writes:

> The effect of this story [Joseph in Egypt] combined with the idea of the 'lived *vita*' in your lecture and the mythological prototype has started within me a trend of thought. . . . I keep wondering if there isn't a figure in history for whom the life of Joseph was a mythical prototype, allowing us to detect the phantasy of Joseph as the secret daemonic motor behind the scenes of his complex life. I am thinking of Napoleon I.[3,p.432]

Freud then goes on to develop the thesis that the name of Napoleon's eldest brother, Joseph, 'was fateful for him.' On this supposition, Freud constructs a compellingly plausible interpretation of the Emperor's destiny. It explains Napoleon's relationship to Josephine, his

504

expedition to Egypt, his taking care of his brothers by making them kings and princes. It was when 'he forsook his myth' and repudiated Josephine that his decline began. His eventual 'being cast into the pit' repeats another chapter in the Joseph legend.

The letter deserves to be considered as an unusual example of the application of psychoanalysis to the art of biography. It is also of special interest to the Freud biographer, because of the parapraxis referred to in its final paragraph:

> My daughter reminds me that I have already divulged to you this interpretation of the daemonic man after you read your essay here. She is right, of course, I had forgotten, and the idea revived after reading your book. And now I hesitate whether to hold onto these lines or send them to you after all with many apologies.[3,p.434]

Freud did, of course, send the letter, and Thomas Mann's reply to this extraordinary letter has become available recently with the German publication of Thomas Mann's letters:

> How vividly your letter once again evoked the afternoon with you, one which belongs among the most beautiful memories of my life, and on the occasion of which I was permitted to present my anniversary speech to you, in private this time. Your daughter is quite right: immediately after the conclusion of the reading, you developed for me and the guests the remarkable, indeed fascinating thoughts about Napoleon and the unconscious fixations in his life which you set down in this memorable letter. Thus they were not new for me any more, but they retain their quality of surprise and their striking probability, compared to which the question of their erstwhile reality is of secondary importance to me. In any case, this letter is an exciting example of your ingenious flair in matters of unconscious psychic functioning and the effects emanating from the depths, and I consider myself fortunate to be able to call myself its recipient.[21] (Author's translation.)

Thomas Mann placed great importance on this meeting with Freud. In his address[19] he refers to the occasion as 'this hour of formal encounter between creative literature and the psychoanalytic' and states that 'the solemn significance of this hour lies, at least in my eyes and as a matter of personal feeling, in that on this evening is taking place the first official meeting between the two spheres, in the acknowledgment and demonstration of their relationship.' It seems extraordinary that Freud should have forgotten his contribution to such an occasion. He too is on record that this tribute by the greatest contemporary figure in German literature pleased him. He wrote to Arnold Zweig on May 31, 1936: "Thomas Mann's visit, the address he presented to me, and the public lecture he delivered for the celebration, were gratifying and impressive events." [3,p.430]

A partial interpretation of this parapraxis is provided indirectly by Freud himself. It was only the year before that Freud caught himself in a parapraxis when he prepared to send a birthday gift (a ring) to a friend. The episode is reported in a brief paper, The Subtleties of a Faulty Action, and it involved a curious parallel with the event under discussion in that Freud forgot that he had made the same offering once before. Moreover, Freud's daughter played the identical role: "But you gave her a stone like that for a ring once before. *That's* probably the repetition you want to avoid. One doesn't like always to be making the same present." Freud writes he was convinced by this and went a little further with his analysis to arrive at the realization, "I wanted not to give the stone away at all. I liked it very much myself. . . . A consoling thought soon occurred to me: regrets of this kind only enhance the value of a gift. What sort of gift would it be if one were not a little bit sorry to part with it?" [7,p.234]

I think Freud's interpretation of Napoleon can be regarded as a gift to Thomas Mann. The following sentence from the preamble would corroborate this. He calls the letter 'a talk with you as though you were sitting opposite me here in my study, but without wishing to provoke a polite reply, let alone a detailed appreciation.' [3,p.432] Mann's[21] reply, 'I consider myself fortunate to be able to call myself its [the letter's] recipient,' shows that he too responded to it as a gift, as something of value. Having forgotten that he presented it to Mann already is an act of undoing, a taking back of the gift. Then as in the episode with the ring he is embarrassed. "I hesitate whether to hold onto these lines or send them to you after all with many apologies."

We are justified in drawing the conclusion that something in Freud worked against parting with this ingenious interpretation of Napoleon, but we are in the dark about what might have contributed to the conflict. Jones in his Freud biography mentions two facts which could have a significant bearing on the complete interpretation of this parapraxis. First, Freud had already communicated his interpretion of Napoleon's 'Joseph Complex' to Arnold Zweig in a letter written in November, 1934, two years before. Second, Jones claims that it was he

who suggested to Freud more than twenty years before the importance of Joseph in Napoleon's life. He says he 'spent two years in collecting material for a book to be called Napoleon's Orient Complex,
and had talked over its contents several times with Freud.'[11,p.191] Jones
adds without reproach that Freud passed on some of these ideas to
Ludwig Jekels who then wrote an excellent essay on Napoleon, but
states that his own book never got written because 'the cream was
gone, the war and other interests supervened.' Thus it is possible that
Freud had some unconscious conflict about using this material again.
In this essay, however, our main interest revolves around the possibility of ambivalence on Freud's part toward Mann, and how this might
have contributed to the parapraxis. Our next task, therefore, is to see
what can be discovered about the relationship between the two men.

We find out that although Buddenbrooks[13] and The Interpretation
of Dreams[4] first appeared within the same year (1901), it was not until
the 1920's that the two men began to take official notice of each other.
Hoffman[10] who was also interested in the beginnings of this relationship and seems to have had a correspondence about it with Mann
writes: "Just when Mann first encountered the theories and practices
of psychoanalysis in general is not certain; it is not unreasonable to assume, however, that he was well aware of the discussions and writings
of a variety of psychologists sometime before he offered his first public
tribute to Freud." In an unpublished letter to Hoffman in January
1944, Mann says: "One could be influenced in this sphere without any
direct contact with his [Freud's] work, because for a long time the air
had been filled with the thoughts and results of the psychoanalytic
school." Mann's first reading of the major works of Freud began in
1925, after the publication of The Magic Mountain[15] in which Mann
presents his first understanding of psychoanalysis through the character of Dr. Krokowski. Irony and caricature contributed much to the
painting of this portrait of the psychoanalyst.

Mann's ambivalence toward Freud and psychoanalysis at that particular time is well illustrated by two references in the psychoanalytic
literature. The first [22] is the report of an interview in an Italian newspaper in 1925 in which Mann discussed the influence of the sciences
on modern literature.

> As far as I am concerned, at least one of my works, the short novel,
> Death in Venice, originated under the immediate influence of
> Freud. Without Freud I would never have thought of dealing with

this erotic motive, or I would certainly have treated it differently. If it is permissible to express it in military language, I would say that Sigmund Freud's thesis represents a kind of general offensive against the Unconscious with the objective of its conquest. As an artist I have to confess, however, that I am not at all satisfied with Freudian ideas; rather, I feel disquieted and reduced by them. The artist is being X-rayed by Freud's ideas to the point of violation of the secret of his creative act.

Death in Venice was published in 1912.

The second reference appears in the *Almanach der Psychoanalyse* in 1926. It is a brief article by Mann entitled My Relation to Psychoanalysis.[16] He calls this relationship 'unsimple.' Mann says one can see in psychoanalysis something great, admirable, a bold discovery, a profound advance of insight, a surprising even sensational increase of the knowledge of man. One can find on the other hand that it can—improperly introduced to people—grow into an instrument for malicious enlightenment, for an uncivilized mania for disclosure and discreditation. Its concern is insight, melancholic insight, especially where art and artist are concerned at whom it is aimed in particular. Mann says this was nothing new to him when he first encountered it. He had experienced it essentially with Nietzsche, especially in his Wagner critique, and it had become, in the form of irony, an element of his intellectual make-up and production. This is a circumstance to which he undoubtedly owes the fact that psychoanalytic scholars have shown a predilection for critical attention to his writings. Mann quotes a passage from Death in Venice which he calls 'strongly anti-analytic' but which he says has been interpreted as a characteristic example of 'repression.' Somewhat crisply he states that indeed what may lend the artist-neurotic the impudence to do what is *his*, despite all analytic uncovering, will have to be marked not only as repression but—more aptly, even if more unscientifically—as 'letting a thing be.' With this somewhat angry reproach out of the way, Mann begins to concede— perhaps begrudgingly—the usefulness of psychoanalysis and the incontrovertible fact that it can no longer be eliminated. He says that his preceding remarks mean in no way simply hostility, because insight, in principle unproductive, may yet, as the phenomenon of Nietzsche demonstrates, have much to do with art, and the artist can be on excellent terms with it. It also means nothing less than the delusion that the world can never again get around the discoveries of Freud and his group by closing its eyes. The world cannot get around them at all and neither will art. Psychoanalysis plays into the fiction of our whole sphere of culture, has colored it, and will possibly influence it to an increasing degree. Mann mentions that psychoanalysis plays a role in the just published novel, The Magic Mountain. "Dr. Krokowski, as its agent is named in the novel, is admittedly a little comical. But perhaps his funniness is only an indemnification for the deeper concessions which the author makes to psychoanalysis in the core of his works."

In 1925 Mann arrived at an important turn in his development. His intense preoccupation with disease and death as artistic concepts approaches some resolution in The Magic Mountain and gives way to a fascination with the mythological-psychological in the Joseph series.[18]

It is in this development of the foremost figure in contemporary German literature that the influence of Freud and psychoanalysis plays an important part. A psychoanalytic discussion of Mann's personal neurotic conflicts and how they are reflected in his short novel, Death in Venice, has been published by Kohut.[12] Brennan[1] in his comments on The Magic Mountain writes: "At some time during the composition of the work, Mann had experience with psychoanalytic treatment. The novel itself can be conceived as self-administered analysis, in which the author brings to the surface of consciousness the roots of the disease and death concepts, objectifying in a work of art what had for long years weighed on his mind. In short, The Magic Mountain can be regarded as a dissolving of Mann's own personal bond to disease and death. In dislodging an incubus, Mann produced his greatest work."

This is the only reference to a personal experience with therapy that I have been able to locate in the literature about Thomas Mann. Its veracity has to be accepted since in the acknowledgments in Brennan's book he writes: "Thomas Mann himself graciously read the manuscript and supplemented his kind words with a welcome to his home."

The result of Mann's more serious study of Freud's works, after the completion of The Magic Mountain, is his essay, Freud's Position in the History of Modern Thought.[17] It begins by informing us that Totem and Taboo made the strongest impression on Mann because, 'for the reader who is interested in the riddles of Man, it opens up immense perspectives of the psychic past, the primeval, moral, social, mythic-religious prehistory of mankind.' While acknowledging the valid application of the clinical viewpoint, he extols the essay as 'artistically the greatest of Freud's works' and calls it 'a piece of world literature.' The main body of Mann's essay, however, is devoted to a long, scholarly discussion of the German Romantic movement in its philosophical and political implications. Mann thinks that Freud as 'explorer in depth and psychologist of the instinct joins the ranks of the 19th and 20th century writers who, as historians, philosophers, social critics, or archeologists emphasize the dark side of nature and the soul as the really life-determining and life-creating force.' This emphasis stands 'in contrast to rationalism, intellectualism, classicism, in a word, the credo of the 18th and perhaps also the 19th century.' In the last few pages Mann returns to a discussion of Freud, psychoanalysis, and its relationship to the romantic movement, to point out that Freud's research interest in the affective processes does not degenerate into the glorification of them at the expense of the intellectual sphere. Freud serves the revolutionary future victory of reason and the intellect. He serves the enlightenment. He quotes Freud: "We may emphasize over and over again that the human intellect is powerless in comparison to human instinctual life and be correct in this. But there is something special about this weakness. The voice of intellect is soft but it does not rest until it has obtained a hearing." Alluding to the political exploitation of romanticism in Germany, Mann adds that it would be difficult to make reactionary use of a doctrine in which the primacy of reason is tersely called 'the psychological ideal.'

Mann devotes some space to the fact that Freud was not familiar with the great romantic literature like Novalis or Nietzsche, 'where Freud's insights are lightningly anticipated everywhere.' He finds the phenomenon of influence to be mysterious. "It is often of such indirect, atmospheric and intellectual nature which can only be described inadequately with words." He speaks of an 'unconscious tradition.' He illustrates what he means by quoting from The Magic Mountain and comparing it with a passage from Beyond the Pleasure Principle, yet, 'when I wrote my novel, The Magic Mountain into which psychoanalysis enters, I did not know more of Freud than the most general ideas; I had not seriously read any of his writings.' He uses a similar comparison of passages from Freud and Novalis to illustrate Freud's 'most remarkable relations' to German romanticism. Freud's libido theory, 'to say it briefly, is romanticism divested of mysticism and converted into natural science.' This essay was sufficiently important to Freud to elicit from him in 1929 the first letter to Thomas Mann, and the gift of his latest book. Unfortunately this interesting letter is not available, but something of its content can be learned from Thomas Mann's reply dated January, 1930.[21]

Verehrter Herr Professor,

In the confusion of a correspondence which, thanks to the herd instincts of our world, has taken on catastrophic dimensions, I can thank you only most inadequately for the extraordinary gift of your book—this work whose inner greatness so far exceeds its external size. I have read it without interruption, touched by a sense of truth, in which the older I become, the more I recognize the source of all genius. Accept my thanks on this occasion also for your magnificent letter of November. Since I received it there have been all kinds of adventures, but they were not able to detract in the least from the significance of that event for me. Your correction of certain conjectures in my article concerning your insight into the nonmedical importance of your discoveries, is of the greatest interest to me, and it shows me that I would have done better had I sought out contact with you before the composition of the work. On the other hand one writes, I believe, freer and better, as long as the personality with whom he is concerned has not yet achieved social reality, but remains in the realm of myth.

Not without emotion I read what you tell me of the years of your loneliness and isolation. It is funny to say it, but I can to some extent gauge what you experienced from what I have come to hear now, today, after this victory of your teachings, on account of my essay, from all kinds of German piety and complex-conservatism. It was not well meaning, but alas, I have little reason to be proud of it. I have come ashamedly late—slow in nature, which I am in general. Everything has to become very ripe in me before I can communicate it.

You love writers? Probably mainly as objects of your research, for which, with boring exceptions, we are all born—I especially, I would say, if it did not sound conceited. A conversation with you about this subject and related matters would be good. I have been requested to come to Vienna this month in order to attend the Halsmann trial in the Obersten Gerichtshof, and I am tempted. If I agree (and it's true I've had a little too much travel) may I call on you then?

With respectful greetings, yours,

Thomas Mann (Author's translation.)

511

The only direct comment we have by Freud on Mann's essay is contained in a letter to Lou Andreas-Salomé, 28 July 1929. "Thomas Mann's essay is no doubt quite an honour. He gives me the impression of having just completed an essay on romanticism when he was asked to write about me, and so he applied a veneer, as the cabinetmaker says, of psychoanalysis to the front and the back of this essay: the bulk of it is of a different wood. Nevertheless, whenever Mann says something it is pretty sound." [3,p.390] While these words express respect for Mann's intellect and scholarship, they also convey a certain pique at the secondary place ascribed to psychoanalysis in relation to philosophy.

When did the first face-to-face meeting of the two men take place? Jones reports that Mann's first visit with Freud did not take place until 17 March 1932. He writes that 'Freud at once got on intimate terms with him [Mann]: "What he had to say was very understanding: it gave the impression of a background." His [Freud's] wife and her sister, who were enthusiastic readers of Mann, were still more delighted. Mann's association with the Hanse Towns was an additional link.[11,p.170] The *Neue Freie Presse* reported Mann as saying: "I was very pleased to talk again to the great investigator and to find him intellectually as lively as ever. To my question whether he is satisfied with the triumph of his life's work and feels happy, Professor Freud answered he had to suffer too bitterly for this good fortune. I made the claim to Sigmund Freud that the seed which he planted years ago had grown by today to a tree whose shadow covered the whole world—a fact which surely must fill him with satisfaction, which he finally admitted." [23] This newspaper article would indicate that Mann had talked with Freud before, but no record of an earlier visit can be found. It may have taken place in 1930 when Mann had asked for permission to call on Freud.

The next reference to the personal relationship is a letter of Freud to Mann in honor of the latter's sixtieth birthday, in June 1935. In this letter Freud calls himself one of Mann's 'oldest' readers and admirers. He ends the letter: 'in the name of countless numbers of your contemporaries I wish to express the confidence that you will never do or say anything—an author's words, after all, are deeds—that is cowardly or base, and that even at a time which blurs judgment you will choose the right way and show it to others.' [3,p.423] Freud tells Arnold Zweig (2 May 1935) that he composed this letter at the suggestion of the *Fischer*

Verlag and into it 'slipped a warning which I trust will not go unnoticed.' [3,p.425]

At this point Thomas Mann was already in political exile from Germany, yet it sounds as if Freud expresses here a measure of distrust. This is not astonishing when one considers that many liberal intellectuals in Europe shared this distrust of Mann's political positions. It originated in the days of World War I when Mann expressed himself quite enthusiastically in support of Imperial Germany's cause. His views and his at times passionate anti-Western and anti-liberal feelings are recorded in Mann's essays of this period, Reflections of a Nonpolitical Man, 1918. It is of interest that because of these ideas a serious rift developed between Thomas Mann and his older brother Heinrich, an eminent German novelist himself and always unequivocally aligned with the large group of European pacifist writers. The two brothers did not speak to each other for years, but carried on a bitter literary polemic. When Thomas Mann, after the German defeat, came out in support of the Weimar Republic he was accused in many quarters of political opportunism. Many readers of The Magic Mountain still thought they found support for their suspicions in the book. They were dismayed at its resolution with the hero returning from Switzerland to Germany to fight in the war. They believed that the debates between Settembrini and Naphtha represented the respective ideologies of the two Mann brothers. Some even thought that the choice of the half-Polish, half-Jewish sounding name of Krokowski for the psychoanalyst in the book was a subtle manifestation of anti-Semitism.

Did Freud feel this? As one examines the communications between Freud and Mann, one is forced to conclude that their friendship did not extend beyond the limits of respect, formality, and a certain self-consciousness. This becomes particularly apparent in a comparison with the exchange of letters between Freud and Arnold Zweig, another major literary figure. Those letters exude warmth and intimacy.

This brings us to the high point of the relationship between Freud and Mann: Freud's eightieth birthday in 1936, when Mann came to Vienna to honor Freud with his important essay, Freud and the Future.[19] Mann discusses the relationship of creative literature and psychoanalysis and reiterates much of what he said already in his first Freud essay in 1929 and to which Freud reacted so wryly. The emphasis is given to Freud's precursors. "Sigmund Freud took the path alone without knowing that reinforcement and encouragement lay to his

hand in literature. . . . Freud did not know Nietzsche . . . Novalis
. . . Kierkegaard . . . Schopenhauer. . . . Probably it must be so."
Does Mann sound incredulous?

Freud had stated explicitly in his autobiographical study that he
'carefully avoided any contact with philosophy proper.' "This avoid-
ance has been greatly facilitated by constitutional incapacity. . . .
The large extent to which psycho-analysis coincides with the philosophy of Schopenhauer . . . is not to be traced to my acquaintance with
his teaching. I read Schopenhauer very late in my life. Nietzsche, another philosopher whose guesses and intuitions often agree in the most
astonishing way with the laborious findings of psycho-analysis, was for
a long time avoided by me on that very account; I was less concerned
with the question of priority than with keeping my mind unembar-
rassed." [6,p.59]

It must be in response to this paragraph that Mann in his essay
goes on to 'indulge on this festive occasion in a little polemic against
Freud himself. He does not esteem philosophy very highly,' whereas
Mann believes 'that in actual fact philosophy ranks before and above
the natural sciences . . . one might strain the point and say that science has never made a discovery without being authorized and encouraged thereto by philosophy.'

It is also worth mentioning that this 'little polemic' is inserted into
a paragraph in which C. G. Jung, 'an able but somewhat ungrateful
scion of the Freudian school,' is given considerable appreciation. "Nobody has focused so sharply as he [Jung], the Schopenhauer-Freud
perception that 'the giver of all given conditions resides in ourselves.' "

If Freud reacted to this polemic we have no record of it. I am
tempted to suggest that a second memory failure found in Freud's letter may betray the presence of a reaction. When describing the family
constellation of Napoleon, Freud writes: "In a Corsican family the
privilege of the eldest is guarded with particularly sacred awe. (I think
Alphonse Daudet once described this in a novel. In *Le Nabob?* Or am
I mistaken? Was it in some other book? In Balzac?)." [3,p.432] Freud is in
fact partially mistaken. The Nabob is not Corsican himself, but by
using dishonest means furthers his social ambitions in Paris by getting
himself elected deputy from Corsica. But Freud is right and demonstrates his fantastic memory in that Daudet[2] does mention the right of
primogeniture in this context and in the same sentence tells that the
Nabob's oldest brother was sent to Paris and 'had started with four or

five marshal batons in his trunk'—a figure of speech generally associated with Napoleon.

That Freud should have thought of Daudet at the beginning of this communication to Mann cannot be without significance. Not only is Daudet one of the first, if not the first prominent literary man with whom Freud had a personal encounter during his stay in Paris, but a parapraxis involving the novel *Le Nabob* played a part in Freud's life before and was subjected by him to a careful analysis published in The Psychopathology of Everyday Life. I suspect that the association to that particular piece of self-analysis is the reason for Daudet's appearance and the uncertainty about the correctness of the quotation in this particular letter to Mann. Freud states: "In Paris . . . I frequently walked about the streets, lonely and full of longings, greatly in need of a helper and protector, until the great Charcot took me into his circle. Later I more than once met the author of *Le Nabob* in Charcot's house. . . . But the irritating part of it is that there is scarcely any group of ideas to which I feel so antagonistic as that of being someone's protégé. . . . I have always felt an unusually strong urge 'to be the strong man myself.' " [5,p.149]

I think Mann's implied assertion that Freud made his discoveries by being authorized and encouraged thereto by Schopenhauer and Nietzsche touched on precisely this group of ideas to which he feels so antagonistic. Perhaps this contributed to Freud's unconscious conflict about making Mann a present of his brilliant interpretation of Napoleon.

But much of what Mann says in his essay must have had great interest and appeal for Freud, particularly when Mann speaks about his own work, especially his mythological novel, Joseph and His Brothers. Like Mann, Freud himself was then engaged in writing a work about a mythical figure from the Old Testament and we have some evidence that he drew comparisons between himself and Thomas Mann. When he first mentioned his Moses work to Arnold Zweig in September of 1934 he said 'my essay received the title: The Man Moses, a Historical Novel.' [3,p.421] Two months later, however, he wrote to Eitingon: "I am not good at historical romances. Let us leave them to Thomas Mann." [11,p.194] The difference in form between Mann's Joseph and Freud's Moses is undoubtedly characteristic of a difference between the two men.

Mann is generous in acknowledging his debt to Freud and psychoanalysis as he discusses the development of his understanding of myth and 'lived *vita*—life as succession, as a moving in other's steps, as identification.'

> The typical is actually the mythical and one may as well say 'lived myth' as 'lived life'. . . . It is plain to me that when as a novelist I took the step in my subject matter from the bourgeois and individual [Buddenbrooks, Magic Mountain] to the mythical and typical [Joseph] my personal connection with the analytic field passed into its acute stage. The mythical interest is as native to psychoanalysis as the psychological interest is to all creative writing. Its penetration into the childhood of the individual soul is at the same time a penetration into the childhood of mankind, into the primitive and mythical. . . . The myth is the foundation of life; it is the timeless schema, the pious formula into which life flows when it reproduces its traits out of the unconscious. . . . Certainly when a writer has acquired the habit of regarding life as mythical and typical there comes a curious heightening of his artist temper, a new refreshment to his perceiving and shaping powers. . . . What is gained is an insight into the higher truth depicted in the actual . . . a knowledge of the schema in which and according to which the supposed individual lives, unaware, in his naïve belief in himself as unique in space and time, of the extent to which his life is but formula and repetition and his path marked out for him by those who trod it before him. His character is a mythical role which the actor just emerged from the depths to the light plays in the illusion that it is his own and unique, that he, as it were, has invented it all himself.[19]

The reader who is interested in the unconscious communications cannot help wondering whether this thought is not behind Mann's insistence to link Freud to the romantic philosophers and whether Freud's unconscious reaction manifested itself in the parapraxis.

The final portion of Mann's essay is an expression of the author's appreciation of psychoanalysis and the conviction that its teachings will lead to a wiser and freer humanity in the future. Freud then reciprocates generously with his demonstration of the applicability of Mann's thesis of the 'lived myth' to the life of Napoleon.

With this intellectual exchange on Freud's eightieth birthday the Mann-Freud relationship reached its zenith. Mann visited Freud once more in January of 1937 and in February of the same year joined vain efforts with Romain Rolland to win a Nobel prize for Freud. The last recorded communication is a congratulatory telegram from Mann on the occasion of Freud's birthday in 1939, a few months before his death. It is noteworthy that in 1943 Mann chose to write a novella entitled *Das Gesetz*.[20] This is the story of Moses, the subject of Freud's last book, Moses and Monotheism,[9] which put forward his controversial theory that Moses was an Egyptian. Moses and Monotheism was one of the important source books in Mann's research. Perhaps it is characteristic of Mann's relationship to Freud and psychoanalysis that he made his Moses half Egyptian and half Jewish.

Bibliography

1. Brennan, Joseph Gerard: *Thomas Mann's World*. New York: Russell & Russell, Inc., 1962.
2. Daudet, Alphonse: *The Nabob*. Boston: Little, Brown & Co., 1898.
3. Freud, Ernst L., Editor: *Letters of Sigmund Freud*. New York: Basic Books, Inc., 1960.
4. Freud: *The Interpretation of Dreams* (1900, 1901). Standard Edition, IV, V.
5. —: *The Psychopathology of Everyday Life* (1901). Standard Edition, VI.
6. —: *An Autobiographical Study* (1925 [1924]). Standard Edition, XX.
7. —: *The Subtleties of a Faulty Action* (1935). Standard Edition, XXII.
8. —: *A Disturbance of Memory on the Acropolis* (1936). Standard Edition, XXII.
9. —: Moses and Monotheism (1939 [1934–1938]). Standard Edition, XXIII.
10. Hoffman, Frederick J.: *Freudianism and the Literary Mind*. Baton Rouge: Louisiana State University Press, 1945.
11. Jones, Ernest: *The Life and Work of Sigmund Freud, Vol. III*. New York: Basic Books, Inc., 1957.
12. Kohut, Heinz: 'Death in Venice' by Thomas Mann. PSYCHOANALYTIC QUARTERLY, XXVI, 1957, pp. 206–228.
13. Mann, Thomas: *Buddenbrooks*. New York: Alfred A. Knopf, 1924.
14. —: *Stories of Three Decades*. New York: Alfred A. Knopf, 1936.
15. —: *The Magic Mountain*. (1924) New York: Alfred A. Knopf, 1965.
16. —: *Mein Verhältnis zur Psychoanalyse*. In: *Almanach der Psychoanalyse*. Vienna: Internationaler Psychoanalytischer Verlag, 1926.
17. —: *Die Stellung Freuds in der Modernen Geistesgeschichte*. Psa. Bewegung, I, 1929, pp. 3–32.
18. —: *Joseph and His Brothers*. New York: Alfred A. Knopf, 1963.
19. —: *Essays*. New York: Vintage Books, Inc., 1957.
20. —: *Das Gesetz*. Stockholm: Bermann-Fischer Verlag, 1944.
21. —: *Briefe, 1889–1936*. Frankfort am/Main: S. Fischer Verlag, 1962.
22. *Thomas Mann und die Psychoanalyse*. Int. Ztschr. f. Psa., XI, 1925, p. 247.
23. *Thomas Mann bei Sigmund Freud*. Psa. Bewegung, IV, 1932, p. 278.

An Impression of Freud

(1970)

EDOARDO WEISS

Edoardo Weiss got to know Freud in 1908 when he was still a young medical student. He was a forerunner of psychoanalysis in Italy and came to America in 1939. Recently he published his impressions of Freud, together with the letters he received. This selection is from his Sigmund Freud as a Consultant *(New York, Intercontinental Medical Book Corporation, 1970): 21–22.*

Thinking of Freud, I recall some personal characteristics and mannerisms; for example, those he showed when he lectured at the psychiatric clinic of the University of Vienna. These lectures were attended mostly by members of the Psychoanalytical Society, and he showed great appreciation of those few students who enrolled in his elective courses. He spoke slowly, pronouncing each word clearly. From time to time he looked at a ring he wore, with a green stone, slowly spreading and closing the fingers of his right hand. When he talked with someone before or after the lecture, he usually had a pencil in his hand. He would put the end of the pencil on his desk, slide his thumb and index finger along it, then reverse it and repeat the gesture. I interpreted this mannerism as evidence of Freud's desire to be precise and complete in what he said.

In recounting the impressions I formed of Freud during my years of contact and correspondence with him, I must emphasize that he was kind, gracious, and sensitive. He was never petty. My first impression that he was a great man became a firm belief, strengthened continually as our relationship grew.

Index

Hendrik M. Ruitenbeek is a psychoanalyst in private practice, and a training analyst and faculty member of the American Institute for Psychotherapy and Psychoanalysis in New York City. He is the author of some twenty-six books in the fields of psychoanalysis and sociology.

Charles H. Elam prepared the manuscript for publication. Richard Kinney designed the book. The typeface for the text is CRT Laurel based on Linotype Caledonia designed by W. A. Dwiggins about 1938; and the display faces include Columna, designed by Max Caflisch about 1955 and Garamont based on designs by Aldus Manutius in the sixteenth century.

The text is printed on Nashoba paper and the book is bound in Columbia Mills' Riverside Chambray cloth over binders boards. Manufactured in the United States of America.